INDIAN WRITINGS ON EDUCATION
1979-86

CONCEPTS IN COMMUNICATION INFORMATICS & LIBRARIANSHIP (CICIL)

For a list of titles in this series, see pp. 735-36 at the end of the book.

Concepts in Communication
Informatics & Librarianship-28

General Editor: **S.P. AGRAWAL**

INDIAN WRITINGS ON EDUCATION 1979 to 1986

An Indicator to Indian Educational Journals Grouped by 2465 Subject Descriptors

(IN TWO PARTS)

S.P. AGRAWAL

in collaboration with
J.C. AGGARWAL

CONCEPT PUBLISHING COMPANY, NEW DELHI 110059

Indian Writings on Education Part I

ISBN 81-7022-381-4

First Published 1992

Published and Printed by
Ashok Kumar Mittal
Concept Publishing Company
A/15-16, Commercial Block, Mohan Garden
NEW DELHI 110059 (India)

Lasertypeset by
Microtech Advance Printing Systems (Pvt.) Ltd.
H-13, Bali Nagar,
NEW DELHI 110015

GENERAL EDITOR'S INTRODUCTION

Like the political scene, the educational system seems prone to be in a state of flux.

Once in a while somebody feels that it is time 'To grasp this sorry scheme of things entire . . . and then . . . Remould it nearer to the heart's desire.'

But then after the dreamland design is complete, someone blows the whistle and points out that the king has no clothes.

This is because the field of education is so vast and the matters that need attention are so many, that any amount of financial jugglery is unable to take care of them.

However, those interested in education keep mulling over various aspects of the subject and express their views through print as also other communication media.

The present CICIL publication going over the period, 1979-1986, provides a key to items grouped in 2465 subject descriptors from 31 educational journals in English published in India.

While the acronyms, abbreviations and signs in entries are easy to follow, for the benefit of a novice, an explanatory note is given on a succeeding page.

S.P. AGRAWAL

CONTENTS

SUBJECT DESCRIPTORS*

---

* Note: *Italics* indicate Cross References.
——— Indicates references under the relevant Descriptor.

: Nutrition : India : Tamil Nadu
: *Vocabulary*
: *Writing*
Children, Abnormal and Backward
Children, Backward
Children, Books and Reading for
Children, Deaf
Children, First-born : India : Rajasthan
Children, Indian : UK : Education
Children, Isolated
Children Books
Children Illustrated Books
Children Literature
———
: Curricula
: Indian
Children Stories
China (People's Republic)
Choice : Psychological Aspects
Choice of Books
Choice of Non-Book Materials
Choice of Profession
Church Colleges : India : Kerala
Citizenship Education : India
Civic Education
Civil Engineering : Study and Teaching
Civilisation and Science
Classification of School Children
Classroom Management
Clinical Psychology
Clubs
Co-education
Cognition
———
: Child Psychological Aspects
Collagen Diseases
College Admissions
College Autonomy
College and School Periodicals
College Community Centres
College Faculty
College Libraries
College Life
College Periodicals
College Personnel : Management
College Students
———
: India
: India : Bihar
: India : Rajasthan
: India : Tamil Nadu
: India : Uttar Pradesh
: Psychology
: Social and Economic Status
: *Socio-Economic Status*
College Teachers
———
: Africa
: Attitudes
: India
: India : Andhra Pradesh
: India : Bihar
: India : Chandigarh
: India : Tamil Nadu
: India : Uttar Pradesh
: Nigeria
: Recruiting
: Salaries, Pensions, etc.
: Training
College Teaching
College Unions
Colleges
Colour and Form Recongnition Test
Commercial Education
Commercial Schools
Communalism
Communication
Communication Arts
Communication in Agriculture
: India : Andhra Pradesh
: India : Bihar
: India : Himachal Pradesh
: India : Karnataka
: India : Madhya Pradesh
: India : Punjab
: India : Tamil Nadu
: India : West Bengal
Communication in Education
Community and Schools
———
: India
Community and Teachers
Community Colleges
Community Development
———
: Asia
: India
: India : Gujarat
: India : Maharashtra
Community Life
Comparative Education
Competitive Examinations
Comprehension
Compulsory School Attendance
Computer in Education
Computers

JOURNALS SCANNED

1. Asian Journal of Psychology and Education (Tri-A)
   Agra Psychological Research Cell
   Tiwari Kothi, Belanganj, Agra, Uttar Pradesh 282004

2. Bharatiya Shiksha Shodh Patrika, (Bi-A)
   Indian Institute of Educational Research
   Saraswati Kunj, Nirala Nagar, Lucknow, Uttar Pradesh 262001

3. Bulletin of Non-Formal Education (Q)
   National Council of Educational Research and Training
   NIE Campus, Sri Aurobindo Marg, New Delhi 110016

4. EPA Quarterly Bulletin (Q)
   Educational Planning and Administration Bulletin
   National Institute of Educational Planning and Administration
   17B Sri Aurobindo Marg, New Delhi 110016

5. Education and Psychology Review (Q)
   Faculty of Education and Psychology
   Maharaja Sayajirao University of Baroda, Fatehganj
   Baroda, Gujarat 390001

6. Education Quarterly (Q)
   Ministry of Human Resource Development
   Department of Education, Government of India
   Room No. 503, C Wing, Shastri Bhavan, New Delhi 110 001

7. Educational Review (M)
   41, Sankuwar Street, Triplicane Madras, Tamil Nadu 600 005

8. Experiments in Education (M)
   SITU Council of Educational Research
   No. 3, 1, Trust Link Street, Mandavelipakkam
   Madras, Tamil Nadu 600 028

9. Indian Education (M)
   (V.P. Raghavachari), 2-1-408/3 University Road
   Nallakunta Hyderabad, Andhra Pradesh 500 044

10. Indian Educational Review (H Y)
    National Council of Educational Research and Training
    NIE Campus, Sri Aurobindo Marg, New Delhi 110 002

11. Indian Journal of Adult Education (M)
    Indian Adult Education Association
    17-B, Indraprastha Estate, New Delhi 110 002

12. Indian Institute of Education Bulletin (A)
    28/2 Kothrud, Karve Road
    Pune, Maharashtra 411029

13. Indian Journal of Extension Education (Q)
    Indian Society of Extension Education
    Division of Agricultural Extension, IARI, New Delhi 110 012

14. Journal of Education and Psychology (Q)
    M.B. Patel College of Education
    Sardar Patel University, Vallabh Vidyanagar, Gujurat 388 120

15. Journal of Educational Research and Extension (Q)
    Sri Ramakrishna Mission Vidyalaya
    College of Education, Coimbatore, Tamil Nadu

16. Journal of Higher Education (Tri-A)
    University Grants Commission
    35, Ferozeshah Road, New Delhi 110 001

17. Journal of Indian Education (Bi-M)
    National Council of Educational Resrarch and Training
    NIE Campus, Sri Aurobindo Marg, New Delhi 110 016

18. Journal of the Institute of Educational Research (Tri-A)
    59, Usman Road
    Madras, Tamil Nadu 600 017

19. National Journal of Education (H Y)
    Faculty of Education
    Banaras Hindu University, Kamachha
    Varanasi, Uttar Pradesh 221 010

20. New Frontiers in Education (Q)
    C-6, Community Centre
    Safdarjung Development Area, Delhi 110 016

21. Our Education (M)
    Asutosh Building
    University of Calcutta, Calcutta, West Bengal 700 073

22. Perspectives in Education (Q)
    Society for Educational Research and Development
    46, Harinagar, Gatri Road, Baroda, Gujarat 390 007

23. Prasar (Q)
    Department of Adult Education
    University of Jaipur, Jaipur, Rajasthan 302 004

24. Primary Teacher (Q)
    National Council of Educational Research and Training
    NIE, Campus, Sri Aurobindo Marg, New Delhi 110 016

25. Progress of Education (M)
    1786, Sadashiv Peth
    Pune, Maharashtra 411 030

26. Quest in Education (Q)
    Indian Council of Basic Education
    Gandhi Shikshan Bhavan, Juhu, Bombay, Maharastra 400 049

27. Rajasthan Board Journal of Education (Q)
    Evaluation and Academic Programmes
    Board of Secondary Education, Government of Rajasthan
    Ajmer, Rajasthan 305 001

28. Research Bulletin (Q)
    Maharashtra State Council of Educational
    Research and Training
    Pune, Maharashtra 411 030

29. Student Action (M)
    A I S F, 417, Asaf Ali Road, New Delhi 110 002

30. Teacher Today Naya Shikshak (Q)
    Directorate of Primary and Secondary Education
    Government of Rajasthan, Bikaner, Rajasthan 334 001

31. University News (W)
    Association of Indian Universities
    16, Kotla Marg, New Delhi 110 002

GEOGRAPHICAL COVERAGE

- Afghanistan
- Africa
- Asia
- Australia
- Bangladesh
- Belgium
- Botswana
- Brazil
- Bulgaria
- Canada
- China (People's Republic)
- Cuba
- Czechoslovakia
- Europe
- Europe : West
- France
- Germany : East
- Germany : West
- Ghana
- Great Britain
- India :
  - Andaman and Nicobar Islands
  - Andhra Pradesh
  - Arunachal Pradesh
  - Assam
  - Bihar
  - Chandigarh
  - Delhi
  - Eastern
  - Goa
  - Gujarat
  - Haryana
  - Himachal Pradesh
  - Jammu and Kashmir
  - Karnataka
  - Kerala
  - Madhya Pradesh
  - Maharashtra
  - Meghalaya
  - Mizoram
  - Nagaland
  - Northeastern
  - Orissa
  - Pondicherry
  - Punjab
  - Rajasthan
  - Sikkim
  - Tamil Nadu
  - Uttar Pradesh
  - West Bengal
- Indonesia
- Iran
- Iraq
- Israel
- Jamaica
- Japan
- Kenya
- Korea
- Latin America
- Malaysia
- Nepal
- Netherlands
- Nigeria
- Norway
- Norway
- Pakistan
- Philippines
- Poland
- Rumania
- Russia
- Saudi Arabia
- Scotland
- Sri Lanka
- Sweden
- Switzerland
- Tanzania
- United States
- Vietnam
- Yugoslavia

ABBREVIATIONS ACRONYMS AND SIGNS

Abbreviations

A	:	Annual
appen	:	Appendix
Bi-A	:	Bi-Annual
Bi-M	:	Bi-Manual
D	:	Daily
Ed	:	Edited/Editor
F	:	Fortnightly
ftns	:	Footnotes
HY	:	Half Yearly
illus	:	Illustrations
M	:	Monthly
P	:	Pages
Q	:	Quarterly
refs	:	References/Bibliography
repr	:	Reproduced
Rev	:	Review
tabs	:	Tables
Tr	:	Translated/Translator
Tri-A	:	Tri Annual
W	:	Weekly

Acronyms

AIAEC	:	All India Adult Education Conference
AIEC	:	All India Educational Conference
AIFEA	:	All India Federation of Educational Association
AISF	:	All India Student Federation
AIU	:	Association of Indian Universities
BDO's	:	Block Development Officers
IAEA	:	Indian Adult Education Association
ICAR	:	Indian Council of Agricultural Research
ICSSR	:	Indian Council of Agricultural Research
IRDP	:	Integrated Rural Development Programme
M.Ed	:	Master of Education
NAEP	:	National Adult Education Programme
NASSDOC	:	National Social Science Documentation Centre
NCERT	:	National Social Science Documentation Centre
NCTE	:	National Council for Teacher Education
SFDA	:	Small Farmers Development Agency

SFI	:	Student Federation of India
SSDC	:	NASSDOC
TRYSEM	:	Training of Rural Youth for Self Employment
UGC	:	University Grants Commission (India)
UNESCO	:	United Nations Educational, Scientific and Cultural Organisation
UPSC	:	Union Public Service Commission
VLW's	:	Village Level Workers

Signs

+	:	Continued on later pages in the same issue
=	:	Equals to

CLASSIFIED INDEX

Ability

Ability of estimation by approximation : A study. S. Parmajit and A. Suryaprakash Rao *New Frontiers in Education* 13(4) Oc-De 1983 p 69-72

Developing superior ability. Kshanika Bose *Education Quarterly* 32(3) Jl 1980 p 18-21

See also

Leadership
Learning Ability
Mathematical Ability
Mental Tests
Spelling Ability

Ability : Testing

Ability of estimation by approximation. A. Suryaprakash Rao *Experiments in Education* 12 (4) Je 1984 p 71-74

Interest of boys with superior scholastic ability. Perin H. Mehta *Indian Educational Rev* 19 (2) Ap 1984 p 1-8

An investigation of sex differences in general intellectual ability in rural and urban children. R.L. Worison and A.G. Linford *J Education and Psychology* 37(1) Ap 1979 p 10-18

Relationship between difficulty level and internal consistency of item. Biranchi N. Puhan *Education Quarterly* 32 (3) Ap 1980 p 21-22

See also

Creative Ability : Testing
Mathematical Ability : Testing
Mental Tests
Motor Ability : Testing
Teachers : Rating of

Ability Grouping in Education

Abilities and subject specialisation. J.K. Pillai and J. Gabriel *J Higher Education* 9(1) Mon 1983 p 108-14

A socio-econometric study of peer grouping patterns among primary school pupils of Kerala. P. Kelu *Experiments in Education* 12(12) Fe 1985 p 209-15 refs tabs

Ability Tests

See

Ability : Testing

Abnormal Children

See

Exceptional Children
Handicapped Children

Absence from School

See

School Attendance

Academic Achievement

Academic achievement among children of working and non-working mothers in relation to socio-economic status and mothers' attitude towards education. Sharanjit Kaur and Sudesh Gakkar *Quest in Education* 18(3) Jl 1981 p 228-34 refs

Academic achievement and family size : An anomaly. S.P. Suri *J Education and Psychology* 42(3) Oc 1984 p 123-27 refs

Academic achievement and its relation to general mental ability academic adjustment and neuroticism. M.S. Ameerjan *et al J Education and Psychology* 36(3) Oc 1978 p 107-12

Academic achievement in relation to achievement motive affiliation motive on power motive Pritty Gandhi *EPA Bulletin* 6(1) Ap 1983 p 29-35

Academic achievement of primary school children. Sharmistha Chakrabarti *Progress of Education* 60(9) Ap 1986 p 209-15 tabs

Academic achievement of rural and urban students of agriculture : An analysis. M.S. Ameerjan *Asian J of Psychology and Education* 6(1) Ja 1980 p 17-22 refs tabs

Academic achievement of the pupils of class X in the background of their previously attended school.Yashomati Patel *J Education and Psychology* 36(1) Oc 1978 154-59

Academic achievement of the scheduled castes and tribal students : An analysis M.S. Ameerjan and M.S. Thimmappa *J Education and Psychology* 44(1) Ap 1986 p 29-35 ref

Academic attainment and prolonged deprivation in relataion to some personal variables. V.P. Sharma and Mahesh Bhargava *J Education and Psychology* 37(4) Ja 1980 p 247-54 refs

Academic difficulties of college youth : A case study of the scheduled castes. G.R. Sudame and A.P. Thiagarajan *Indian Education* 12 (5-6) Ag-Se 1982 p 23-29

Academic motivation and academic achievement. K. Jagannath *Experiments in Education* 14(12) Fe 1986 p 207-10 ref

Academic performance as a function of prolonged deprivation. Mahesh Bhargava and Madhu Marwah *Indian Educational Rev* 17 (3) Jl 1982 p 114-122 refs tabs

Academic promise and fulfilment. R.N. Nagpal. New Delhi, New Soc Pub 1981. 139p. Rs.48 *Book Rev J Higher Education* 8(3) Spr 1983 p 403-04

Achievement motive in low and high achievers : A comparative study. P.N. Rai *Indian Educational Rev* 15(3) Jl 1980 p 117-23 refs

Achievement of regular and correspondence students : A comparative study. Laxmi Shankar and Santosh K. Panda *Progress of Education* 56(1) My 1982 p 236-40 refs

Adjustment and scholastic achievement of low and high achievers : A comparative study. P.N. Rai *Quest in Education* 16(2) Ap 1979 p 106-13

An analysis of relationships between creativity and academic achievement of eleventh graders, R.P. Goyal *Educational Review* 90 (5-6) My-Je 1984 p 84-87 refs tabs

Anxiety and academic achievement. P.K. Ganguli *Asian J of Psychology and Education* 7(2) Jl 1981 p 39-43

Anxiety and academic achievement. P.K. Ganguli *J of Educational Research and Extension* 19(4) Ap 1983 p 233-48 refs

Anxiety in relation to academic achievement of high school students. Zakia

A. Siddiqi and Shamim Akhtar *Indian Educational Rev* 18(4) Oc 1983 p 106-10

Appraising pupil achievement. Marlow Ediger *Experiments in Education* 9(7) Se 1981 p127-29

Classification and comparison of different approaches to identify over and under achievers. Tehal Kohli *J Education and Psychology* 38(1) Ap 1980 p 22-27 ref

Cognitive, non-cognitive factors of personality as a predictions of academic achievement of high and low creative grade students. S.K. Jindal *J Education and Psychology* 42(3) Oc 1984 p 147-53

A comparative study of academic achievement of active and regular participants in co-curricular activities and that of non participants. Ram Chander *J of Educational Research and Extension* 16(3) Ja 1980 p 135-41 refs

A comparative study of academic achievement of the scheduled caste and tribe students of agriculture. M.S. Ameerjan *J Education and Psychclogy* 37(2) Jl 1979 p 121-29 refs tabs

A comparative study of personality characteristics of over- achievers and under-achievers. P.L. Gupta *Progress of Education* 57(3) Oc 1982 p 53-57 refs

A comparative study of personality needs and academic achievement of scheduled and non-scheduled caste graduate and post-graduate students. L.P. Gupta *Quest in Education* 17(1) Ja p 44-51 ref

A comparative study of the learning abilities academic achievement and disposition towards school of the primary school children from progressive and less progressive schools. K. Mayari and S.V. Reddy *J Educational Research and Extension* 19(3) Ja 1983 p 180-86

Computational ability as a determinant of achievement in tenth grade algebra. C.P. Singh Chauhan *Indian Educational Rev* 16(1) Ja 1981 p 43-47

A comparison of academic achievement of Santal and non-Santal undergraduate students of Santal Parganas district of Bihar. Lal Bahadur Singh *J Educational Research and Extension* 16(3) Ja 1980 p168-73 refs tabs

Construction of an achievement test in physics. V.T. Deshpande and V.K. Gautam *Progress of Education* 55(6) Ja 1981 p 165-66 ref

Contribution of intelligence, adjustment, dependency and classroom trust to academic achievement. M.M. Shah and R. Kishan *J Institute of Educational Research* 6(1) Ja 1982 p 13-16

A correlational study of school examination mark, intelligence and achievement scores. R.P. Pandey and R.A. Singh *Asian J of Psychology and Education* 3(3) Nv 1878 p 6-8 refs tabs

Correlating among I.Q. age academic achievement and patental income of high school research students. R.S. Yadav *J Institute of Educational Research* 10(3) Se 1986 p 12-17

Creativity and academic achievement among secondary school children. C.B. Asha *Asian J Psychology and Education* 6(1) Ja 1980 p 1-4 refs

Creativity intelligence and academic achievement : Their relationships and difference with reference to sex and academic subjects. Gurpal Singh

Jarial *J Education and Psychology* 39(2) Jl 1981 p 91-96 refs

Creativity, intelligence and achievement. Krishna Kumari Gupta *Educational Rev* 85(11) Nv 1979 p 208-11

Difference of locus of control and educational achievement among children across : SES and sub-cultures. Chintamani Mishra *Indian Educational Rev* 19(1) Ja 1984 p18-26

Discrepancy between high school examination : Scores and the scores predicted on the basis of intelligence, scientific interest, clerical interest, educational adjustment and family status. R.K. Joshi and Niti Srivastava *Indian Educational Rev* 18(2) Ap 1983 p 100-06 refs tabs

Dogmatism and academic achievement. Harikesh Singh *J Educational Research and Extension* 19(3) Ja 1983 p 138-44

The effect of anxiety and aspiration on academic achievement of adolescents boys and girls. Govind Tiwari *et al Asian J Psychology and Education* 6(1) Ja 1980 p 35-38 refs

Effect of intelligence, adjustment, achievement. M.M. Shah and R. Kishan *J Education and Psychology* 39(4) Ja 1982 p 241-47 refs

Effect of personality, intelligence and their interaction on achievement through instructional strategy. D.M. Sansanwal and Anuradha Joshi *Indian Education* 10(5) Ag 1980 p 23-26

Effect of schooling, on learning abilities and academic achievement of primary school children. K. Mayuli *Asian J Psychology and Education* 11 (3) 1983 p 32-37 refs tabs

Effect of schooling, on learning abilities and academic achievement of primary school children. S. Moses and K. Mayuli *Indian Educational Rev* 19(1) Ja 1984 p 12-25

Effect of socio-economic status and academic achievement on risk taking behaviour of student teachers. R.C. Hooda and H.R. Paul *J Institute of Educational Research* 10(2) My 1986 p 1-3 refs

Effect of socio-economic status on the academic achievement of XI grade students. Lal Singh *J Education and Psychology* 42(4) Ja1985 p 223-28 refs

The effect of the medium of instruction on the achievement of the students. B.A. Parikh *J Educational Research and Extension* 17(3) Ja 1981 p 137-41 refs

The effects of ecological differences on subject preferences, academic aspiration and achievement among primary school pupils. E.E. Ezewu and C.C. Ahadi *Progress of Education* 60(5) De 1985 p 98-102 refs tabs

Enhancing academic achievement : Role of some personality factor. Radha R. Sharma. New Delhi, Concept Pub. 1985. 151p. Rs.70 *Book Rev, Education Quarterly* 38(2) Sum 1986 p 42-44

Evaluation and achievement. Marlow Ediger *New Frontiers in Education* 12(4) Oc-De 1982 p 25-31

An experimental study of contribution of learning objective to achievement scores through lecture and guided discovery methods. R.S. Yadav *Asian J Psychology and Education* 14(1-4) 1984 p 1-14 refs

An experimental study of the effect of dependency and adjustment on the achievement of students studying through programmed learning material using different response modes. D.N. Sansanwal *et al Indian Educational*

Rev 17(4) Oc 1982 p 140-46 refs tabs

Factorial analysis of achievement of high school students. S.P. Gupta *National J Education* 3(1) Se 1980 p 50-54 refs tab

Factors affecting academic achievement of school children. A.Q. Siddiqui *et al J Education and Psychology* 41(3) Oc 1983 p 126-32 refs tabs

Family background, intellectual ability and academic achievement. Govind Tiware *et al Asian J Psychology and Education* 7(2) Jl 1981 p 12-15

Figural creativity and concrete operational logic as correlates of school achievement in IV, V and VI grade children. Sudesh Gakhar and Jagdip Kaur *J Education and Psychology* 40(3) Oc 1982 p 162-68

Impact of non-detention on scholastic achievement and school stage. Ramesh Chandra Sharma *EPA Bulletin* 6(1) Ap 1983 p 23-28

The impact of pupil control ideology, teachers locus of control and quality of school life on academic achievement of pupils. K.A. Gandhi *Experiments in Education* 10(10) De 1982 p 184-89 refs tabs

The impact of socio-economic conditions on achievement. M. Ganapathy and M. Raghuram Singh *Experiments in Education* 9(8) Oc 1981 p 144-47 refs

Impact of socio-economic status (Rural) on academic achievement. K. Jagannadhan *J Institute of Educational Research* 9(3) Se 1985 p 27-31 refs tabs

Impact of some personality variables on academic achievement : A replication study. Bhasker Patel and Gita Bhaumik *J Education and Psychology* 40(4) Je 1983 p 207-13 refs

The impact of study habits of intellectually backward pupils upon their academic achievement. D.M. Patel *Quest in Education* 18(4) Oc 1981 p 335-43 refs

The impact of study habits of intellectually backward pupils upon their academic achievement. *Progress of Education* 18(4) Oc 1981 p 33-37 refs

The influence of levels of achievement amongst students. Zaibun Y. Jesdanwalla *New Frontiers in Education* 11(2) Ap-Je 1981 p 73-80

An inquiry into the relation of creativity to academic achievement of the intellectually gifted. R.J. Joshi *J Educational Research and Extension* 18(3) Ja 1982 p 142-48 refs

Intelligence and socio-economic factors as predictors of academic achievement. Agamoni Lahiri *Our Educations* 6 Jl 1985-86 p 43-48 refs tabs

Intelligence, socio-economic status and family size as correlates of achievement. H. Sam Sananda Raj and Rita Krishnan *J Institute of Educational Research* 4(3) Se 1980 p 1-6 refs tabs

Interests of boys with superior scholastic ability. Perin H. Mehta *Indian Educational Rev* 19(2) Ap 1884 p 1-8

An investigation into the causes of backwardness in children in higher secondary schools of Pilibhit city. C.B. Misra *J Education and Psychology* 37(3) Oc 1979 p 187-92 refs

Locus of control among high and low achievers at different levels of socio-economic status. N.R. Sharma *J Institute of Educational Research* 9(1) Ja 1985 p 1-4

Parental deprivation in relations to academic achievement of denotified tribes. M.A. Khan *Indian Educational Rev* 14(4) Oc 1979 p 95-98

Parental influences on academic achievement of students. Esogwa C. Osuala *Asian J Psychology and Education* 7(1) Ja 1981 p 1-7

Parental influences on academic achievement of students. Esogwa C. Osuala *Indian Education* 10(6) Se 1980 p 4-9

Personal and situational variables and academic achievement. K. Jagannadhan *J Institute of Educational Research* 9(1) Ja 1985 p 10-12 refs

Problems of academic over and under achievers in different curricula. P.C. Saxena *National J Education* 3(2) Mr 1981 p 57-71 refs tabs

Promotion of creativity and achievement by discovery method. Vandana Prasad *Indian Iducational Rev* 14(4) Oc 1979 p 86-94

Pupil achievement in successive school examinations. Ucharan Deka *Asian J Psychology and Education* 7(3) 1981 p 33-42 refs figs tabs

Relationship between academic achievement, extraversion and neuroticism. Tarlok Singh *J Education and Psychology* 40(4) Ja 1983 p 202-06 refs

Relationship between anxiety and academic achievement. Ratna Mookerjee *et al J Institute of Educational Research* Ja 1982 p 10-12 refs tabs

Relationship between personality factors and academic achievement of students. Arvinda Chandra and Raj Kala Kundu *J Education and Psychology* 39(1) Ap 1981 p 35-41 tabs

Relationship between personality factors and academic achievement of students. Arvinda Chandra and Raj Kala Kundu *J Educational Research and Extension* 18(1) Jl 1981 p 1-7 refs tabs

Relationship between self concept and academic achievement. B. Jeyakanthan *Experiments in Education* 7(3) My 1979 p 42-48 refs

Relationship between socio-economic status and academic achievement. V. Rajasekaran *Experiments in Education* 6(1) Mr 1978 p 233-36 refs tabs

Relationship between sociometric index N-ach and rated pupil characteristics. Namita Panda *J Educational Research and Extension* 19(4) 1983 p 224-32 refs tabs

Relationship of disciplined and indisciplined behaviour with academic achievement of adolescent students. Zakia A. Siddiqi and R. Fatima Bilgrami *J Education and Psychology* 42(3) Oc 1984 p 119-22

Relationship of study habits of home science undergraduate students with academic achievement and residence. Suman Bhatnagar and Sadhana Bordia *Progress of Education* 58(6) Ja 1984 p 143-45

Role of achievement anxiety, alienation and value discrepancy in academic achievement of scheduled caste students. Renu Sood *J Higher Education* 6(1-3) 1980-81 p 117-22 refs tabs

A schematic model of the departments of academic achievement. M.S. Ameerjan *J Education and Psychology* 39(2) Jl 1981 p 111-16

Scholastic achievement as a function of aspiration religion and socio-economic status. Asudulla Khan *et al J Education and Psychology* 39(4) Ja 1982 p 218-23 refs

Scholastic achievements and vocational interests as correlated to prolonged deprivation. V. P. Sharma and P.R. Kasthuria *J Education and Psychology* 41(1-2) Ap-Jl 1983 p 69-76

School achievement of BC and non-BC pupils in the context of reading ability and reading speed. D.N. Patel *Progress of Education* 58(11) Je 1984 p 258-62 refs tabs

School achievement of pupils belonging to different levels of socio-economic status. Rita Krishnan *Asian J Psychology and Education* 9(3) 1982 p 11-17

School adjustment and its relation to academic achievement of socially disadvantaged children. B.N. Sujatha *J Education and Psychology* 43(3-4) Oc 1985-Ja 1986 p 197-205 refs tabs

School grade, sex and academic achivement differences in Peer rating. Sujata Acharya *et al J Education and Psychology* 42(4) Ja 1985 p 214-18

Security-insecurity, adjustment, socio-economic status and family structure as the predictions of academic achievement at intermediate students. S.K. Jindal and Netranand Padhan *Indian Educational Rev* 18(4) Oc 1983 p 58-65

Selected social norms of the home science students. A. Chandra and Aparna H. Khaund *J Higher Education* 8(3) Spr 1983 p 356-63 refs tabs

Self concept and achievement. Vasantha Ramkumar *J Higher Education* 1(1) Mon 1975 p 124-26

Self-concept and adjustment as factors in academic achievement. Radha Rani Sharma *Indian Educational Rev* 18(2) Ap 1983 p 46-59

The self-concept and scholastic achievement of the socially disadvantage. S. Ushasree *J Institute of Educational Research* 10(1) Ja 1986 p 17-20

Self-esteem and academic achievement : A study on ninth grade students. Immanuel Thomas and H. Som Sonanda Raj *J Institute of Educational Research* 6(3) Se 1982 p 24-28 refs tabs

Self-esteem and children's academic achievement : cross cultural study. G.C. Blawal and N.B. Biswas *Experiments in Education* 12(12) Fe 1985 p 220-22

Sex-wise and age-wise difference in some educationally significant variables : Institutional stress academic stress need for academic achievement, school climate and academic achievement. Abha Rany Bisht *National J Education* 6(2) My 1984 p 32-39 refs

Socio-economic status "urban" and academic achievement. K. Jagannadhan *J Education and Psychology* 44(3-4) Jl-De 1986 p 128-34

A study in prediction of academic achievement through personality tests. G.N. Prakash Shrivastava and S.S. Srivastava *J Institute of Educational Research* 4(3) Se 1980 p 20-27 tabs

A study into the effect of impulsiveness and controlledness over the academic achievement. M. Shree Ram Murthy *Indian Educational Rev* 15(3) Jl 1980 p 103-16 appdc refs

A study of academic achievement in relation to motivation and self-concept. R. Shanmuga Sundaram *J Educational Research and Extension* 18(2) Oc 1981 p 40-48 refs tabs

A study of academic achievement interests and psychological integration of orthopaedically handicapped adolescents. R.N. Syag and R.C. Hooda *J Institute of Educational Research* 6(1) Ja 1982 p 1-5 refs tabs

A study of academic performance in relation to teacher-pupil relations. K.A. Gandhi *Progress of Education* 56(5) De 1981 p 110-13 refs tabs

A study of achievement of students of different socio-economic status. M. Venkatiah *J Institute of Educational Research* 4(3) Se 1980 p 42-45

A study of graduate teachers adjustment and its relationship with students academic achievemment. Surender Wadhwa *J Education and Psychology* 36(3) Oc 1978 p 118-22 refs

A study of language development scholastic achievement and tribal students. K.R. Sharma *Research Bulletin* 14(1-2) Mr-Je 1984 p 3-21 refs

Study of personality of academic achievement of children. Jitendra Mohan *et al J Education and Psychology* 39(3) Oc 1981 p 163-68 refs

A study of reading achievement in relation to sex attitude and anxiety. I.A. Vora *J Education and Psychology* 36(1-2) Ap-Je 1978 p 41-53 refs

A study of security and insecurity in respect to the academic achievement. Umesh Agrawal and R.M. Saraswar *J Educational Research and Extension* 18(4) Ap 1982 p 247-53 refs tabs

A study of relationship between adjustment level of aspiration and achievement. B.B. Pandey *J Institute of Educational Research* 10(3) Se 1986 p 18-20 refs

A study of self-concept, intelligence and achievement of IX grade students. P.M. Buch *et al J Educational Research and Extension* 16(2) Oc1979 p 94-99 refs tabs

A study of self-concept of adolescents and its relationship to scholastic achievement and adjustment. Pramod Kumar Goswami *Indian Educational Rev* 15(1) Ja 1980 p 95-98

A study of social acceptance, class room behaviour and academic achievement. B.K. Tripathi *Teacher Education* 13(8-9) Jl-Oc 1979 p 85-88

A study of socio-economic status of the first year college students of M.S. University, Baroda in relation to the academic achievement. M.M. Shah *Experiments in Education* 11(3) My 1983 p 44-47

A study of some background factors underlying scholastic performance. B.M. Contractor *J Education and Psychology* 41(4) Ja 1984 p 215-19 refs

A study of some intellectual correlates of scholastic attainment of VII class children. S. Subramanyam *J Education and Psychology* 44(3-4) Jl-De 1986 p 112-17

A study of the effect of family climate on students academic achievement. Beena Shah and Bashy Sharma *Progress of Education* 59(5) De 1984 p 103-06 tabs

A study of the relationship between study habits and scholastic achievement of students of secondary schools. M.P. Pande and Geethadevi G. Patil *J Educational Research and Extension* 20(3) Ja 1984 p 197-202

A study of the relationship between teaching efficiency attitude towards teaching profession and academic achievement of the trainees (E.T.C.) Y.K. Gupta *et al Educational Rev* 91(11) Nv 1985 p 196-97 refs

To investigate the relationship between achievement motivation and academic achievement of socially deprived students. Beena Thadani *Rajasthan Board J Education* 20(3) Jl-Se 1984 p 13-16

Towards an achieving classroom. N.K. Jangira *Rajasthan Board J Education* 19(4) Oc-De 1983 p 30-37

Verbal and non-verbal intelligence as correlates of achievement in mother tongue and foreign language. Harnek S. Karile *Educational Rev* 9(8) Ap

1985 p 130-33 refs

Youth problems, adjustment and scholastic performance : A comparative study. J.S. Jha and D.K. Saxena *J Educational Research Extension* 18(2) Oc 1981 p 49-54 refs tabs

See also

Achievement Motivation

Motivation in Education

Academic Achievement and Personality

See

Personality and Academic Achievement

Academic Adjustment

See

Student Adjustment

Academic Dishonesty

See

Cheating in Examinations

Academic Dissertations

See

Dissertations : Academic

Academic Freedom

See

University Autonomy

Academic Motivation

See

Motivation in Education

Acceptance : Social

See

Social Acceptance

Accommodation : Psychological Aspects

See

Adjustment : Psychological Aspects

Achievement : Academic

See

Academic Achievement

Achievement Motivation

Academic achievement in relation to achievement motive, affiliation motive and power motive. Prithy Gandhi *EPA Quarterly Bulletin* 6(1) Ap 1983 p 29-35

Academic motivation among high school students in relation to academic achievement and sex. Kulwinder Singh *J Education and Psychology* 43(3-4) Oc 1985-Ja 1986 p 164-68

Achievement motivation and aspirations of tribal adolescents : A comparative study. A.B. Phatak and R.R. Singh *Rajasthan Board J Education* 19(1) Ja-Mr 1983 p 6-11

Achievement motivation and anxiety among school students. Surya K. Srivastava *J Institute of Educational Research* 10(3) Se 1986 p 9-11 refs tabs

Achievement motivation and job satisfaction in primary school teachers. S.K. Srivastava and Solan Gupta *J Education and Psychology* 43(3-4) Oc

1985-Ja 1986 p 193-96 refs

Achievement motivation and self-concept in the settings. Neelu Srivastava *Asian J Psychology and Education* 4(1) Ja 1979 p 5-9

Achievement motivation of college students and its relations to socio-economic factors. Z.M. Quraishi and J.B. Patel *J Education and Psychology* 41(1-2) Ap-Jl 1983 p 55-58

Achievement motivation of the most and the least confident students. Kusum Gupta *Educational Rev* 92(3) Mr 1986 p 55-58 refs tabs

Anxiety and achievement : A Research study of high and low-achievers. C.R. Jindal and S.K. Panda *Indian Educational Rev* 17(4) Oc 1982 p 118-24 refs

Contextual effects on achievement motivation among lecturers. Puspa Singh *et al J Education and Psychology* 43(1) Ap 1985 p 50-53 refs

Discrepency between aptitude and achievement in relation to achievement motivation. *J Education and Psychology* 37(3) Oc 1979 p 198-202 refs

Effect of academic motivation on cognitive and affective behaviours. S.N. Sharma *Indian Education Rev* 16(2) Ap 1981 p 108-12 refs

The effect of performance attribution on attitude to study, achievement motivation and tendency to cheat in examination. H. Johnson Nenty *Progress of Education* 59(10-11) My-Je 1985 p. 224-34

Effect of achievement motivation on learning outcomes following programmed instructional material. B.D. Verma *Indian Educational Rev* 20(3) Je 1985 p 37-46

Intelligence, anxiety extraversion, and achievement motivation as a function of sex-difference in Santal. L.B. Singh *et al J Institute of Educational Research* 7(3) Se 1983 p 26-31

Intelligence, motivational tendencies of scheduled caste and non-scheduled caste secondary students. S.K. Yadav *J Education and Psychology* 37(2) Jl 1979 p 83-89 refs tabs

Mothers'attitude towards acquiring need achievement in children. Narayan Deb Bhattacharjee and Manjaree Sengupta *Our Education* 6 Jl 1985-1986 p 13-20 refs tabs

Motivating achievement in rural children. A. Agrawal *Quest in Education* 17(1) Ja 1980 p 52-58 refs

Nature of origin need achievement or achievement motivation. Digvijai Singh and B.N. Mehta *Teacher Education* 15(16-17) Jl-Oc 1981 p 64-68 refs

Relationship between teacher attitude and pupil achievement. J.C. Goyal *J Educational Research and Extension* 20(3) Ja 1984 p 158-66

Sex differences in achievement motivation. B.S. Raizada and Beena Thadani *Rajathan Board J Education* 20(1-2) Ja-Je 1984 p 38-42

Study habits as a function of need achievements (n.Ach). Jyoti Christian *Asian J Psychology and Education* 11(1) 1983 p 6-12

A study of achievement motivation among graduate, post-graduate, and Ph.D. students. Swarn Pratap and Surya Kumar Srivastava *J Education and Psychology* 41(1-2) Ap-Jl 1983 p 88-91

A study of achievement motivation and its related variables. J.A. Christian *Indian J Psychology Education* 4(1) Ja 1979 p 48-56 refs

A study of achievement motivation in relation to sex, intelligence and

and Ashwani Kumar Sharma *J Institute of Educational Research* 6(2) My 1982 p 1-5 refs

Factors structure of projective outputs. Bishwa B. Chatterjee and Basant Kumar Das *Asian J Psychology and Education* 3(2) Jl 1978 p 19-34 refs

Social and emotional adjustment patterns of adolescent boys and girls at various levels of socio-economic status and general intelligence. B.K. Mattoo *Indian Educational Rev* 15(1) Ja 1980 p 110-14 refs

Status in marital adjustments : Adjusted and maladjusted couples compared. Ramanath Kundu and Atna Ghosh *J Education and Psychology* 38(3) Oc 1980 p 194-202 refs tabs

See also

Conflict : Psychological Aspects

Student Adjustment

Adjustment : Students

See

Student Adjustment

Admission to College

See

Universities and Colleges : Admission

Adolescence

A peep into the remedies of adolescents : High school and college level. H.K. Mehta *Progress of Education* 55(1) Ag 1980 p 2-5

See also

Youth

Adolescence : Psychology

See

Adolescent Psychology

Adolescent Boys : India : Uttar Pradesh

Influene of socio-economec status on the nature of the problems of adolescent boys. H.S. Sharma *J Educational Research and Extension* 18(4) Ap 1982 p 230-35

Adolescent Girls

Family problems in other areas and delinquent tendencies. Madhu Gupta and Prabha Gupta *J Education and Psychology* 37(1) Ap 1979 p 67-72 refs

Adolescent Psychology

Adjustment differences among the high intelligent and low intelligent adolescent students. Umesh Chandra Agrawal and Y.K. Gupta *J Institute of Educational Research* 8(2) My 1984 p 12-15

Adolescents with educational and family adjustment problems. Surabhi Bora *J Indian Education* 12(2) Jl 1986 p 39-41

Changing pattern of inter-personal relationship in adolescent boys and girls. Ramanath Kundu and Chandidas Biswas *Indian Educational Rev* 15(1) Ja 1980 p 46-52 refs

Developing an ascendance-submission reaction scale for Hindi-speaking adolescent population. Vibha Datta *Indian Educational Rev* 17(4) Oc 1982 p 31-39 refs

Home adjustment patterns of adolescent boys and girls and various levels of socio-economic status and general intelligence. B.K.Mattoo *J Education and Psychology* 40(3) Oc 1982 p 136-42

An investigation into the attitude of later adolescent of the KAVAL towns of U.P. towards family and marriage. S.M. Mosavi *Teacher Education* 13(8-9) Jl-Oc 1979 p 39-44 appdc refs tabs

The perception of adolescent problems by the parents. S.S. Mathur and Parmender Vasudeva *J Education and Psychology* 36(3) Oc 1978 p 99-106

Personality adjustment problem of adolescents studying in the school with different socio-economic status. Ashok K.Kalla *Experiments in Education* 12(10) De 1984 p 169-74 refs tabs

Personality characteristics of authoritarian adolescents. *J Education and Psychology* 40(4) Ja 1983 p 225-28 refs

Personality structure of Indian female teenagers. S.P. Gupta *J Educational Research and Extension* 18(1) Jl 1981 p 12-15 refs

Problems of pre-adolescence. G.S. Dhatiwal and Gursharan Kaur *Progress of Education* 55(3) Oc 1980 p 62-66

Socio-psychological makeup of Tharu and Boksa adolescents. Ram Swarup Verma *Bharatiya Shiksha Sholdh Patrika* 4(2) Jl-De 1985 p 27-33

A study of adjustment and insecurity feeling among the adolescents of two types of family. G.B. Shah and S. Guha *J Education and Psychology* 43(1) Ap 1985 p 54-58 refs

A study of some determinants of personality characteristics of preadolescent children Manjaree Sengupta and G.B. Kapat *Our education* 1 Jl 1980 p 2-8 refs tabs

Study of specific global measures of self-concept and adjustment among adolescent. Ajay M. Misra and others *J Institute of Educational Research* 9(3) Se 1985 p 4-7 refs tabs

Value system in the personality of urban and rural adolescents. R.S. Gaur *J Indian Education* 5(6) Mr 1980 p 11-13 refs

Adoption of Improved Farm Practices

Comparative analysis of adoption behaviour of beneficiaries of farm development programmes. Y.C. Sanoria and D.K. Sharma *Indian J Extension Education* 19(1-2) Mr-Je 1983 p 64- 86

Factors affecting the knowledge of adopter and non-adopter small farmers. D. Somasundasam and S.N. Singh *Indian J Extension Education* Ja-Je 1978 p 30-34 refs

A new look at adopter categories and an alternative proposal for target grouping of farming community. Shankarish Chamala *et al Indian J Extension Education* 16(1-2) Je 1980 p 1-18 refs

Selected characteristics of farmers in relation to their adoption of farm mechanisation. Ranjit Singh *Indian J Extension Education* 19(3-4) Se-De 1983 p 11-17 refs tabs

Stimulating effect of mass media as perceived by adopters disconfidants and rejectors. C. Satapathi *et al Prasar* 7(3-4) Oc 1980 Ja 1981 p 16-17

Adoption of Improved Farm Practices : India : Andhra Pradesh

Agro-social status and adoption of farm innovation in two villages. Gummadi Apparao *Indian J Extension Education* 19(3-4) Se-De 1983 p 62-65 refs

Construction of attitude scales, attitude towards improved agricultural practices : Attitude towards adult literacy. N. Vankataiah *Indian J Adult*

Education 40(2) Fe 1979 p 27-40 appdx

Adoption of Improved Farm Practices : India : Bihar

Adoption behaviour of leaders and their followers. N.K. Roy *et al Indian J Extension Education* 20(3-4) Se-De 1984 p 19-26 refs tabs

An analysis of motivational dispositions of farm entrepreneurs. S.P. Mishra and B.P. Sinha *Indian J Extension Education* 19(1-2) Mr-Je 1983 p 46-50 refs tabs

Impact of lab to land programme in increasing, adoption, productivity and income of farmers in Norty Bihar. R.N. Mishra and P.N. Jha *Indian J Extension Education* 21(1-2) Ja-Je 1985 p 77 -79 tabs

Socio-economic and human resources of farm entrepreneurs : A relation and analysis. S.P. Mishra and B.P. Sinha *Indian J Extension Education* 16(1-2) Je 1980 p 25-33 refs tabs

Adoption of Improved Farm Practices : India : Delhi

A study on interplay of belief values and attitudes of farming couples on rational and adoption behaviour under different innovation situation. T.R. Singh and S.N. Singh *Indian J Extension Education* 18(1-2) Je 1982 p 73-82 refs tabs

Utilisation and credibility of the sources of information of various stages of adoption of farm innovations. P.K. Ramchandran *et al Indian J Extension Education* 15(3-4) De 1979 p 46- 51 refs tabs

Adoption of Improved Farm Practices : India : Karnataka

Adoption of new technologies in dry land sorgum crop production. L.B. Kunnal *et al Indian J Extension Education* 20(3-4) Se-De 1984 p 60-62

An experimental study of one-sided and two-sided presentation of messages with advance organisers. B.S. Siddaramaiah and K.A. Jalihal *Indian J Extension Education* 18(1-2) Je 1982 p 45-50 refs

Profile of block demonstration participant farmers : Dharwad study. G.R. Desai and M.K.S. Rao *Indian J Adult Education* 40(6) Je 1979 p 35-38 refs tabs

Psychology of adult needs and adoption of innovations in the changing rural scene. M.G. Kelkar *Indian J Adult Education* 40(6) Je 1979 p 19-24

Adoption of Improved Farm Practices : India : Madhya Pradesh

Comparative analysis of adoption behaviour of beneficiaries of farm development programme. Y.C. Sanoria and D.K. Sharma *Indian J Extension Education* 19(1-2) Mr-Je 1983 p 84-86

Constaints in adoption of wheat technology by the tribal farmers of Madhya Pradesh. S.K. Waghmare and V.K. Pandit *Indian J Extension Education* 18(1-2) Je 1982 p 95-98

Adoption of Improved Farm Practices : India : Maharashtra

Source credibility pattern among small and big farmers. R.R. Chole and W.D. Rahudkar *Indian J Extension Education* 14(1-2) Ja-Je 1978 p 50-53

Adoption of Improved Farm Practices : India : Orissa

Constraints in adoption H.Y. rice technology in coastal Orissa A. Tripathi *et al Indian J Extension Education* 18(1-2) Je 1982 p 51-58 refs tabs

Some entrepreneurial characteristics in adoption of an improved farm technology. B. Sethy *et al Indian J Extension Education* 20(1-2) Je 1984 p 29-37 refs tabs

Adoption of Improved Farm Practices : India : Punjab

Information needs of the small and marginal farmers of Punjab State. G.S. Saini *Indian J Extension Education* 17(3-4) Se-De 1981 p 101-02

Need of coordination between small, marginal farmers and agricultural labourers agencies and other concerned departments in Punjab. C.S. Arneja and Surjeet Singh Gill *Indian J Extension Education* 15(1-2) Je 1979 p 63-66

Role perception of farm youth leaders in diffusion and adoption of agricultural technology in Punjab. S.S. Pawar *et al Indian J Extension Education* 20(1-2) Je 1984 p 58-61 tab

Selected characteristics of farmers in relation to their adoption of farm mechanisation. Ranjit Singh *Indian J Extension Education* 19(3-4) Se-De 1983 p 11-13 refs tab

Adoption of Improved Farm Practices : India : Rajasthan

Constraints analysis in adoption of fertilizers and plant protection measures in Bajra cultivation. Madan Singh and P.N. Mathur *Indian J Extension Education* 20(3-4) Se-D 1984 p 53-54

Adoption of Improved Farm Practices : India : Sikkim

Adoption of the high yielding varieties of maize by the farmers of Sikkim. H.S.P. Sinha *Indian J Extension Education* 16(1-2) Je 1980 p 46-50 tabs

Adoption of Improved Farm Practices : India : Tamil Nadu

Differential perception of farm practice : Attributes by progressive and non-progressive farmers. B. Asul Raj and A. John Knight *Indian J Extension Education* 14(1-2) Ja-Je 1978 p 64-65

Factors affecting the knowledge of adopter and non-adopter small farmers. D. Somasundaram and S.N. Singh *Indian J Extension Education* 14(1-2) Ja-Je 1978 p 30-34

Role of fertilizer dealers in the transfer of new farm technology. V.A. Amalraj and M.S. Prasad *Indian J Extension Education* 20(3-4) Se-De 1984 p 69-70

Some psychological correlates of adoption of improved rice technology by small farmers of South Arcot district. S.Veerasamy and Tej Bahadur *Indian J Extension Education* 15(3-4) De 1979 p 87-89 tabs

Adoption of Improved Farm Practices : India : Uttar Pradesh

Adoption behaviour of small farmers. S.R. Shukla *Indian J Extension Education* 16(1-2) Je 1980 p 55-58 tabs

Literacy and adoption of improved agricultural practices, Deoria study. R. Shankar *Indian J Adult Education* 40(3) Mr 1979 p 31-38 refs

Adoption of Improved Farm Practices : India : West Bengal

Impact of national demonstration on knowledge attitude and adoption levels of farmers in West Bengal. S. Pathak *et al Indian J Extension Education* 15(1-2) Je 1979 p 49-54 refs tabs

A multiple regression analysis of factors related with attitude of farmers. S. Pathak *Indian J Extension Education* 17(3-4) Se 1981 p 73-80 refs tabs

Multivariate regression analysis of adoption behaviour of jute farmers. S. Pathak and A.K. Mojumder *Indian J Extension Education* 14(3-4) Jl-De 1978 p 45-50

Adoption of Improved Farm Practices : Iraq

Farmers information sources at different stages of innovation decision

process. Zaki M. Mohammad and Ranjit Singh *Indian J Extension Education* 14(1-2) Ja-Je 1978 p 79-82 refs

Adoption of Improved Farm Practices : Nigeria

Communication channels and its impact on knowledge of the farmers of the South Western Nigeria. A.U. Patel *Indian J Extension Education* 14(3-4) Jl -De 1978 p 1-7

Adult : Education

See

Adult Education

Adult Dropouts

See

Adult Education Dropouts

Adult Education

Active learning in the context of adult education. Nicholas Nickandrov *Teacher Today* 22(3) Ja-Mr 1980 p 1-5

Adult and continuing education. Peter Jervis, London, Croom-Helm. 317p. $15.95 *Book Rev, Education Quarterly* 36(2) Ap 1984 p 75-76

Adult as a learner : Pedagogical Perspective M. Sree Ramamurthy *Quest in Education* 18(2) Ap 1981 p 117-29 refs

Adult business education : A challenge. K.C.S. Jain *Indian J Adult Education* 43(5) My 1982 p 21-24 refs

Adult education : A challenge to teachers. Karuna Shankar Misra *Education Quarterly* 30(3) Oc 1978 p 11-12

Adult education and communal harmony : Role and relevance. Inder Prabha Sharma *Indian J Adult Education* 45(10) Oc 1984 p 48+

Adult education and inequality. Malcolm S. Adiseshiah Prasar 9(1-4) Ap 1982-Ja 1983 p 33-46 refs

Adult education and political systems. W.E. Styler Nottinggham, Univ of Nottinggham. 227p. $12.95 *Book Rev, Indian J Adult Education* 47(1) Ja 1986 p 30-32

Adult education and the urban poor. Malcolm S. Adiseshiah *Indian J Adult Education* 41(8) Ag 1980 p 13-18+

Adult education and urban poor. Malcolm S. Adiseshiah *Teacher Today* 24(3) Ja-Mr 1982 p 1-13 refs

Adult education : How far real : How far commercial. B.C. Tewari *Teacher Today* 27(2) Oc-De 1984 p 17-20

Adult education in other countries. Paul J. Mhaiki *Indian J Adult Education* 41(6-7) Ja-Jl 1980 p 37-39

Adult education, international aid and poverty. *Teacher Today* 24(3) Ja-Mr 1982 p 85-90

Adult education : Need to expand dimension. V.S. Mathur *Education Quarterly* 32(3) Jl 1980 p 30-32

Adult education : Some more vital dimensions. V.S. Mathur *Teacher Today* 25(2) Oc-De 1982 p 8-13

Adult education : Principles, practice and prospects. C.L. Kundu. New Delhi, Sterling. 1984 107p. *Book Rev, Progress of Education* 69(5) De 1985 p 121-22; *Teacher Today* 27(2) Oc-De 1984 p 95-96

Adult learners, adult education and the community. Stephen Brookfield. Stratford, Open Univ Press. 1983 229p. *Book Rev, Education Quarterly*

37(2) Sum 1985 p 73-75

After literacy, teaching : Paradoxes of post literacy work. Bernard Dumont *J Indian Education* 5(6) Mr 1980 p 32-42

Adult literacy work through national service scheme. Saroj Bala *Experiment in Education* 12(12) Fe 1985 p 222-24

Androgogy versus pedagogy in adult business education programme. Esogwa C. Osuala *Teacher Today* 24(3) Ja-Mr 1982 p 14-19 ref

Approaches to and methods of teaching the adults. Avinash Grewal *Education Quarterly* 32(1) Ja 1980 p 5-7

Awareness in adult education programme : Meaning and scope. S.R. Mohsini *Indian J Adult Education* 44(11) Nv 1983 p 3-7

Characteristics of an effective instructor : A study. P. Adinarayan Reddy *Indian J Adult Education* 46(2) Fe 1985 p 27-29

Comparative adult education. B. Mukhopadhayay *Educational Rev* 85(3) Mr 1979 p 53-55

Continuing and non-formal education. M.N. Palsane *J Higher Education* 4(3) S pr 1979 p 343-48

Continuing education. R. Bala Thripura Sundari *Education Quarterly* 32(4) Oc 1980 p 5-7

Continuing education : Search for identity. A.G. Bhalwanker *Progress of Education* 60(2) Se 1985 p 44-46

A cross-cultural comparison of J.R. Kidd's contribution to adult education. N.J. Cochrane *Indian J Adult Education* 46(3) Mr 1985 p 3-13 refs

Developments in non-formal education. Sushma Bhagia *Rajasthan Board J Education* 21(3-4) Jl-De 1985 p 16-26

Different methods of literacy teaching. Rajkumari Chandrasekaran *Experiments in Education* 7(5) Jl 1979 p 92+

Dimensions of language learning by adults. B.B. Chatterjee *Indian J Adult Education* 40(5) Mr 1979 p 23-27 refs

Discussion. B.S. Mohanty; M.G. Mane and R. Jayagopal *Indian J Adult Education* 44(11) Nv 1983 p 10-21

Education for human needs. C. Bonanni. New Delhi, Indian Adult Education Assn (Series No. 139).1982, 170p. Rs. 15 *Book Rev, Indian J Adult Education* 44(4) Ap 1983 p 39-40

Education for neoliterates. Narmad. H. Trivedi *Progress of Education* 54(1) Ag 1979 p 21-22

Educational technology in adult continuing education. Motilal Sharma *National J Education* 2(1) Se 1979 p 50-56 refs

Emerging perspective on adult education. K. Sivadasan Pillai *Indian Education* 13(10-11) Ja-Fe 1984 p 23

Environmental education for adult education functionaries. D.V. Sharma *Indian J Adult Education* 41(3) Mr 1980 p 3-5

Factors affecting the retention of literacy among neo-literates : A study in adult education. M.G. Mali. Kolhapur, Asha Prakashan. 1979, 200 p. Rs. 30 *Book Rev, Teacher Education* 14(10-11) Ja-Ap 1980 p 77

A few facts and safeguards about learning. Chaman Lal Narang *Progress of Education* 53(7) Fe 1979 p 133-37 refs ft-n

Formal-non-formal and informal education : A classification. Mohuttigue U. Sedere *New Frontiers in Education* 11(1) Ja-Mr 1981 p 73-78 refs

Games and simulations in adult education. V. Mohankumar *Educational Rev* 91(10) Oc 1985 177-79

Guidelines in the preparation of an adult education primer. B.H. Krishnamurthy and C. Naik *Indian J Adult Education* 41(1-2) Ja-Fe 1980 p 3-7

Highlights of the international council of adult education. Malcolm S. Adiseshiah *Indian J Adult Education* 40(8) Ag 1979 p.6

Inaugural address. Thiru C. Aranganayagam *Indian J Adult Education* 41(6-7) Je-Jl 1980 p. 14-16

International Council of Adult Education. Malcolm S. Adiseshiah *Indian J Adult Education* 41(6-7) Je-Jl 1980 p 31

Ivan Illich : De-schooling society and non-formal education. Biswanath Roy *Bulletin of Non-formal Education* 3(1) Je 1985 p 11-15

Languages issues in adult education. Om Shrivastava *Indian J Adult Education* 41(6-7) Je-Jl 1980 p 33-36

Learner's interest in adult education. H.L. Bachhotia *J Indian Education* 12(1) My 1986 p 41-43

Lets look at our assumptions. Beryl Levinger and Tom Drahman *Indian J Adult Education* 41(12) De 1980 p 20-22

Life long education : A conceptual analysis. M.L. Dutt *Experiments in Education* 41(12) De 1980 p 20-22

Life long education : A conceptual analysis. M.L. Dutt *Progress of Education* 57(3) Oc 1982 p 58-59 refs tabs

Life-long education : A way of life. Jagannath Mohanty *Indian Education* 11(4) Jl 1981 p 19-21

Lifelong education as the master concept for educational policies. Mulk Raj Chilana *Education Quarterly* 31(1) Ap 1979 p 8-10 ft-n

Lifelong learning : Some problems and the wayout. D.D. Tewari *Teacher Education* 14(10-11) Ja-Ap 1980 p 69-74

Linking formal and non-formal and education. Milla Mclachlan *et al Bulletin of Non-formal Education* 1(2) 19 Se 1983 p 4-20

Management of non-formal and adult education. J.S. Rajput *Indian Education* 11(1-2) Ap-My 1981 p 59-63

Mass movement for adult literacy : Formidable tasks. Ramlal Parikh *Indian J Adult Education* 47(5) My 1986 p 6-8

Myths and realities of literacy efforts. Manzoor Ahmed *Indian J Adult Education* 41(8) Ag 1980 p 3-6

Non-formal adult education cadres — what, when and how? Malcolm S. Adiseshiah *Indian J Adult Education* 41(6-7) Je-Jl 1980 p 10-13 +

Non-formal adult education : Perspectives of research. P.K. Sahoo *Education Quarterly* 31(3-4) Oc 1979-Ja 1980 p 6-8

Non-formal and alternative structures in education. *Indian J Adult Education* 39(9) Se 1978 p 2-15 ft-n

Non-formal approach in education. Sunil Behari Mohanty *Progress of Education* 55(5) De 1980 p 3-6

Non-formal education : An alternative to formal system. R.P. Singh and Neerja Shukla. New Delhi, Bahri Pub. 1979 90p. Rs.36. *Book Rev, Bulletin of Non-formal Education* 1(1) 1 Je 1983 p 32-33; *Education Quarterly* 32(4) Oc 1980 p 48-49

Non-formal education an integral part of formal education. B.P. Lulla *Progress of Education* 55(1) Ag 1980 p 24-26

Non-formal education and social transformation. Sarla Rajput *Progress of Education* 54(1) Ag 1979 p 2-6 +

Non-formal education as an alternative to universalisation of primary education; editorial. *J Education and Psychology* 44(2-3) Jl-De 1986 p 75-76

Non-formal education : Concept, definition and scope. R.P. Singh *Education Quarterly* 31(3-4) Oc 1979-Ja 1980 p 1-5

Non-formal education : Concept, nature and scope. K.G. Rastogi *Bulletin of Non-formal Education* 1(3) De 1983 p 15-33

Non-formal education in search of a direction. R.S. Sharma *Bulletin of Non-formal Education* 2(2) Oc 1984 p 20-26 refs

Non-formal education : Selected issues. Milla Mclachlan *et al Bulletin of Non-formal Education* 1(1) 1 Je 1983 p 5-20

Oral component in literacy. D.P. Pattanayak *Indian J Adult Education* 40(12) De 1979 p 1-6

Problems in adult education. M.N. Ravindranatha *Experiments in Education* 11(1) Mr 1983 p 5-11

Professional obsolescence and the role of continuing education. P.N. Chaudry and K.G. Agarwal *Indian Education Rev* 15(1) Ja 1980 p 10-26 refs

Programme planning for new immigrants and refugees. Anthony B. Chan *Indian J Adult Education* 44(3) Mr 1983 p 13-20; 44(4) Ap 1983 p 15-22 refs

Presidential address. G.R. Damodharan *Indian J Adult Education* 41(6-7) Je-Jl 1980 p 17

Psychology of adult learning. Asha Mohan *Indian J Adult Education* 45(10) Oc 1984 p 26-30

The psychology of adult learning. M.K. Dutt. *Teacher Today* 25(2) Oc-De 1982 p 72-76 refs

Qualities of an effective adult education organisers from supervisors point of view. P. Adinarayana Reddy and T. Kumaraswamy *Experiments in Education* 12(1) Mr 1984 p 10-15 tabs

Rating scale of motivation for adult learners. Mercy Abraham and K.C. Prasanna *Indian J Adult Education* 47(1) Ja 1986 p 23-29 appdx refs tabs

Role of adult education in active aging, K.L. Zakir *Indian J Adult Education* 45(10) Oc 1984 p 23-25

Role of books in adult education. Asoke Sen *Education Quarterly* 32(4) Oc 1980 p 1-3

Role of non-formal education in the context of universalisation of elementary education. Pravina K.Tripathy *Progress of Education* 60(5) De 1985 p 107-10 refs

Seeking an adequate approach for relating the education of adults with their work. Jorge Qarthein *Indian J Adult Education* 39(9) Se 1978 p 23-27

Sign-posts for a learning society. Kamalini H.Bhan Bali. Nashik, Gokhale Education Society. 146p. Rs.36 *Book Rev, Indian J Adult Education* 46(3) Mr 1985 p 25-27

Significance of non-formal education. S.C. Dube *Indian J Adult Education*

41(4) Ap 1980 p 11-12

Social aspects of non-formal education. Sureshchandra Shukla *Bulletin of Non-formal Education* 2(2) Oc 1984 p 1-19 refs

Structural change and transformation. M.K. Bacchus *Indian J Adult Education* 40(8) Je 1979 p 1-8 refs

Text-book teaching and adult education. B. Mallikarjun *Indian J Adult Education* 41(5) My 1980 p 19-21 +

Thoughts on adult education. Asoke Sen *Education Quarterly* 3(2) Jl 1979 p 5-7

Thoughts on adult education. Asoke Sen *Indian J Adult Education* 43(6) Je 1982 p 11-14

Towards a broader concept of adult education. M. Elias *Indian J Adult Education* 42(1-2) Ja-Fe 1981 p 21-24

Towards a successful adult education programme. H.S. Srivastava *Education Quarterly* 30(3) Oc 1978 p 4-7

Towards learner-centred : Life-oriented education. K. Chellappan *Education Quarterly* 38(1) Spr 1986 p 13-15

Trends and alternate models in adult education. J.K. Pillai *New Frontiers in Education* 13(3) Jl-Se 1983 p 68-71

Understanding adults for teaching. Onkar Singh Dewal *J Indian Education* 6(2) Jl 1980 p 25-29

The unsolved problem. T.R. Nagappa *Indian J Adult Education* 39(11-12) Nv-De 1978 p 35-40

Yet another experiment with adult education. K.Sivadasan Pillai *Indian Education* 12(8-9) Nv-De 1982 p 13-14

See also

Adult Education and State
Educational Broadcasting in Adult Education
Illiteracy
Indian Adult Education Association
Radio in Education
Social Education
Television in Adult Education

Adult Education : Asia

Asian South Pacific Bureau of Adult Education (ASPBAE) region-1 : Summary of recommendations. *Indian J Adult Education* 41(6-7) Je-Jl 1980 p 4-9

Adult Education : Audio-Visual Aids

Adult education and mass media for civic education : A critical approach. B.B. Mohanty *Indian J Adult Education* 46(9) Se 1985 p 10-16 refs

Communication technology for adult education. S. Rehman *Indian J Adult Education* 40(12) De 1979 p 13-18

Educational technology and system design for the production of educational material for adult education programme : A case study. M.M. Chaudhri *J Adult Education* 41(1-2) Ja-Fe 1980 p 25-34

Effectiveness of visual aids : A comparative study. Anupama Shah and Sandhya Gupta *Indian J Adult Education* 47(6) Je 1986 p 21-26 refs

Overhead projector : Its role in adult education. S.A. Ahmad *Indian J Adult Education* 43(7) Jl 1982 p 25-26+

Place of educational technology in non-formal education. S.G. Mathur *Education Quarterly* 31(1) Ap 1979 p 7-8

Preparing teaching learning materials for adult education. Rafat S. Shafi *Indian J Adult Education* 41(5) My 1980 p 15-18

Technology in adult education. A. Kumar *Educational Rev* 86(8) Ag 1980 p 157-58

See also

Audio-Visual Education

Television in Adult Education

Adult Education : Bangladesh

Non-formal education in Bangladesh. *Indian J Adult Education* 40(6) Je 1979 p 9-17 tabs

Adult Education : Canada

Adult education in Canada : The changing scenario. D.Verma *Indian J Adult Education* 40(5) My 1979 p 7-12 refs

Programme planning for new immigrants and refugees. Anthony B. Chan *Indian J Adult Education* 44(3) Mr 1983 p 13-20 refs

Adult Education : China (People's Republic)

A China plant and an Indian cane : Adult learning programme in India and China. J.R. Kidd *Indian J Adult Education* 40(1) Ja 1979 p 9-36 appdx

Adult Education : Conferences

A report on the commonwealth conference on non-formal education for development. *Indian J Adult Education* 40(2) Fe 1979 p 5-21

The right to learn : Declaration of the fourth UNESCO interational conference of adult education. Paris, 19-29 March 1985. *Teacher Today* 27(4) Ap-Je 1985 p 99-100

See also

All India Adult Education Conference

Indian Adult Education Association

Adult Education : Cuba

The political economy of adult education in Cuba. Jorge Werthein *Perspectives in Education* 1(3) Jl 1985 p 135-56 refs

Adult Education : Curricula

Developing curriculum for adult learners. T. Kumaraswamy *Educational Rev* 89(3) Mr 1983 p 51-54 refs

Implementation of nutrition education in the adult education curriculum. Meera Varma *Prasar* 5(3-4) Oc 1977-Ja 1978 p 35-40

Material preparation and curriculum development — A note for consideration. Ginny Shrivastava *Prasar* 5(3-4) Oc 1977-Ja 1978 p 24-27

Adult Education : Developing Countries

Non-formal education for the third world. Inder Prabha Sharma *Bulletin of Non-formal Education* 2(3) Ja 1985 p 18-25

Adult Education : Economic Aspects

Economics of non-formal education. Shribatra L. Jena *Indian Educational Rev* 17(4) Oc 1982 p 40-47 refs

Adult Education : Evaluation

Assessment and evaluation in adult reading. S. Jaleel Saheb *Indian J Adult Education* 40(9) Je 1979 p 39-41

Evaluation in adult education. Jagannath Mohanty *Indian J Adult Education*

47(6) Je 1986 p 27-30 refs

Evaluation in non-formal education. J.S. Grewal and V.P. Gupta *Education Quarterly* 34(2) Ap 1982 p 29-30

An evaluation of the adult education progrmme in Goa during the period, 1978-82.

M.R. Nimbalker *EPA Quarterly Bulletin* 8(3-4) Oc 1985-Ja 1986 p 45-54

Evaluation techniques in adult education. D. Janardhana Reddy *Indian J Adult Education* 46(4) Ap 1985 p 14-18

Problems in evaluating adult literacy programmes. C. Rajyalakshmi *Indian J Adult Education* 41(6-7) Je-Jl 1980 p 25-29

Utilisation of feedback from evaluation studies of adult education programme. R.S. Mathur *Indian J Adult Education* 45(3) Mr 1984 p 17-22

Adult Education : Finance

Expenditure on education with special reference to adult education. N. Venkataiah and P. Adinarayana Reddy *Educational Rev* 89(5-6) My-Je 1983 p 81-84 tabs

Adult Education : Great Britain

Adult education programmes in Britain. Jagannath Mohanty *Indian J Adult Education* 41(1-2) Ja-Fe 1980 p 35-39

Non-formal education in Britain. K. Sivadan Pillai. Trivandrum, Kalaniketan. 124p. Rs.50 *Book Rev, Indian J Adult Education* 46(4) Ap 1985 p 26-28

Adult Education : India

Acknowledgement of the award. S.C. Dutta *Indian J Adult Education* 47(2-3) Fe-Mr 1986 p 43-47

Adult and continuing education : The Indian scene. Savita Markanda *Indian J Adult Education* 46(2) Fe 1985 p 21-26+

Adult and non-fromal education : A few observations. Satyen Maitra. Calcutta, BSSL. Rs.10 *Book Rev, Indian J Adult Education* 40(10) Oc 1983 p 32

Adult education - A reminiscence. Jeevan Nayak *Indian J Adult Education* 43(1) Ja 1982 p 3-5 +

Adult education : An article of faith. Vinod Patel *Progress of Education* 55(7) Fe 1981 p 172-76 refs

Adult education and schooling of slum children. Jacob Alkara *Indian J Adult Education* 41(1) Ag 1980 p 7-12 tabs

Adult education : Continuing education and national development. G.S Dongre *Teacher Today* 22(3) Ja-Mr 1980 p 23-26

Adult education development and the NAEP. Malcolm S.Adiseshiah *Indian J Adult Education* 40(10-11) Oc-Nv 1979 p 15-19

Adult education in India. !nder Prabha Sharma. New Delhi, NBO. 1985, 160 p. Rs. 90 *Book Rev, Education Quarterly* 38(1) Spr 1986 p 42

Adult education in India. N.A. Ansari. New Delhi, S. Chand. 168 p. Rs.65 *Book Rev, Indian J Adult Education* 46(1) Ja 1985 p 31-32

Adult education in India. P.P. Satyanarayana Rao *Educational Rev* 91(5-6) My-Je 1985 p 84-85 refs

Adult education in India : Retrospect and prospect. V.S. Mathur *Education Quarterly* 30(3) Oc 1978 p 8-10

Adult education in India : Some aspects. M.A. Ansari *Teacher Education* 14(10-11) Ja-Ap 1980 p 60-64

Adult education — Its impact upon democracy. M. Vijayabharathy and D.R. Portia *Education Rev* 90(3) Mr 1984 p 53-55

Adult education : Its importance and problems. Hans Raj *Educational Rev* 85(7) Jl 1979 p 133-35

Adult education : Problems and techniques. Gurpal Singh Jarial *Experiments in Education* 7(10) De 1979 p 173-76

Adult education programme : Some apprehensions. R.S. Tiwari *Indian J Adult Education* 39(10) Oc 1978 p 14-18

Adult education : Retrospect and prospect. R.N. Patil *Progress of Education* 54(4-5) Nv-De 1979 p 74-77

Adult learning : A psycho-social analysis in the Indian context. R. Jayagopal. Madras, Univ. of Madras. 82p. Rs.40 *Book Rev, Indian J Adult Education* 47(5) My 1986 p 29

Adult/non-formal education programmes in India — Legislative, conceptual and evaluative analysis. K. Sivadasan Pillai *Indian J Adult Education* 41(5) My 1980 p 7-10

Aspects of adult education. Rajkumari Chandrasekhar. Madras, New Era Pub.1982,viii,151p. Rs.60 *Book Rev, Education Quarterly* 35(1) Ja 1983 p 47-48

Attacking adult illiteracy in India : Problems and strategies. R.P.Singhal *EPA Bulletin* 6(3-4) Oc 1983-Ja 1984 p 1-14 refs tabs

A China plant and an Indian cane : Adult learning programmes in India and China. J.R. Kidd *Indian J Adult Education* 40(1) Ja 1979 p 9-36 appdx

Continuing education in schools : Plan and prospect. P. Behera *Education Quarterly* 38(2) Sum 1986 p 13-15

Development of adult education. G. Srinivasa Charyulu *Educational Rev* 86(1) Ja 1980 p.14-16

The dynamics of instruction in adult education : A perspective and plan. D. Subba Rao and B.S. Vasudeva Rao *Educational Rev* 88(8) Ag p 133-34

Education of the socially disadvantaged through non-formal education, an intergrated part of formal education. B.P. Lulla *Indian Education* 10(1-2) Ap-My 1980 p 44-47

Effective participation of voluntary agencies in the national programme for eradication of illiteracy. Kamala Rana *Prasar* 5(3-4) Oc 1977-Ja 1978 p 11-19

Field-work in adult education. Hans Raj Gugnani *Indian J Adult Education* 41(6-7) Je-Jl 1980 p 19-24

General secretary's report, 1977-78. S.C. Dutta *Indian J Adult Education* 39(11-12) Nv-De 1978 p 9-12

Group discussion reports. *Indian J Adult Education* 47(2-3) Fe-Mr 1986 p 13-23

Group dicsussion reports. T.A. Koshy *Indian J Adult Education* 44(1-2) Je-Se 1983 p 25-28

Guidelines for adult education programme : A blue print for action at the micro-level. Rajkumari Chandrasekaran *Education Quarterly* 30(3) Oc 1978 p 13-14

Mass movement for adult education. *Indian J Adult Education* 47(2-3) Fe-Mr 1986 p 8-12

A mass movement for functional literacy. P.K. Patnaik *Indian J Adult*

Education 47(2-3) Fe-Mr 1986 p 24-41 +

NCERT's experience of non-formal education programme. *Bulletin of Non-formal Education* 1(3) De 1983 p 3-14

Nehru literacy award,1985 : Citation. *Indian J Adult Education* 47(2-3) Fe-Mr 1986 p 42-43

Non-formal adult education for tribes. R.N. Venkataiah and B.V. Subba Reddy *Educational Rev* 86(6) Je 1980 p 111-14

Non-formal education : A perspective, Inder Pandit *Indian J Adult Education* 41(12) De p 13-19 refs

Non-formal education : An alternative to formal system. R.P. Singh and N. Shukla. New Delhi, Bahri Pub. 1979, 90p. Rs. 35 *Book Rev, National J Education* 3(1) Se 1980 p 76

Non-formal education. K.G. Rustogi *Experiments in Education* 9(2) Ap 1981 p 33-36; 9(3) My 1981 p 39-43 refs

Non-formal education. K.G. Rustogi *J Indian Education* 6(3) Se 1980 p 34-39

Non-formal education : To earn more and live better. T.S. Avinashilingam *Indian J Adult Education* 39(11-12) Nv-De 1978 p 13-15

Objective and modes of non-formal education. K.G. Rustogi *Teacher Today* 22(3) Ja-Mr 1980 p 42-48

People's participation in rural development : The rationale and significance. Jaya Gajanayake *Indian J Adult Education* 45(3) Mr 1984 p 13-16+

A possible model for non-formal education. Neerja Shukla *Education Quarterly* 31(1) Ap 1979 p 4-6

Preparing 'readers' for tribal adult learners — Some viable topics. M. Kundu *Indian J Adult Education* 42(9) Se 1981 p 21-24 refs

Putting the clock book. B.G. Varghese *Teacher Education* 14(12-13) Jl-Oc 1980 p 23-26

Reconstruction and adult education. Narmad H. Trivedi *Educational Rev* 87(5) My 1981 p 81-83

Reply by A.R. Deshpande on receiving the Nehru Literacy Award for 1977. *Indian J Adult Education* 39(11-12) Nv-De 1978 p 16-22

Renewing the adult education movement. Ramlal Parikh *Indian J Adult Education* 45(4) Ap 1984 p 3-4

A report of the seminar on the role of voluntary agencies in the national adult education programme. S.N. Maitra *Indian J Adult Education* 40(1) Ja 1979 p 37-43

Resource development for adult literacy. V.D. Singh *J Indian Education* 5(2) Jl 1979 p 13-17

"Role of adult education in promoting and effective functioning of rural institutions and organistions". *Indian J Adult Education* 42(11) Nv 1981 p 22-25

Role of adult education in promoting people's organisations of the rural poor. *Indian J Adult Education* 42(11) Nv 1981 p 27

Role of teachers organisations in non-formal education programme. K.G. Rustogi *Primary Teacher* 9(4) Oc 1984 p 1-4

Seventh plan and adult education. Inder Prabha Sharma *Education Quarterly* 38(2) Sum 1986 p 16-18

Social reconstruction through adult education. Narmad H. Trivedi *Progress of Education* 55(7) Fe 1981 p 177-78+

Some critical considerations in adult education. S.C. Bhatia, ed. Delhi, Univ. of Delhi. 1980, 64p. *Book Rev, Education Quarterly* 33(4) Oc 1981 p 35-36

Strategies for adult and non-formal education programme. S.B. Mohanty *Indian Education* 39(11-12) Mr-De 1978 p 23-26

Under one roof. Banbehari Mukopadhyay *Indian J Adult Education* 10(4) Jl 1980 p 11-14

Understanding adults. Onkar Singh Dewal *Indian J Adult Education* 41(8) Ag 1980 p 19-22+

Working paper : *Indian J Adult Education* 44(1-2) Ja-Fe 1983 p 19-24

Working paper. Towards a dynamic adult education programme. *Indian J Adult Education* 41(11) Nv 1980 p 9-14

Zakir Husain Memorial Lecture : Role of continuing education. Madhuri R. Shah *Indian J Adult Education* 42(12) De 1981 p 19-33

See also

National Adult Education Programme : India

Adult Education : India : Andhra Pradesh

Non-formal education in the context of universalisation of primary eduction in Andhra Pradesh. P Adinarayana *Bulletin of Non-formal Education* 1(1) 1 Je 1983 p 21-29

Personality characteristics affecting participation in AEP : A study. G. Lokanandha Reddy *Indian J Adult Education* 47(8) Ag 1986 p 11-14 refs

Learning choices of adults. N.Venkataiah and P. Adinarayana Reddy *Experiments in Education* 9(5) Jl 1981 p 85-87 refs

Promoting family planning through non-formal education. K.S. Chalam *Indian J Adult Education* 42(1-2) Ja-Fe 1981 p 25-29

Adult Education : India : Bihar

Adult education for tribal population. Binod Sinha *Indian J Adult Education* 43(6) Je 1982 p 7-10

Adult Education in Bihar : An Appraisal. Prashant K. Ganguli *et al Indian J Adult Education* 46(2) Fe 1985 p 14-20

Role of AEP in development : Some observation from Bihar. K.N. Pathak *Indian J Adult Education* 46(4) Ap 1985 p 19-22

Adult Education : India : Chandigarh

Adult education programme in Chandigarh : An empirical study. Inder Prabha Sharma and Sushil Kumar Patel *Indian J Adult Education* 47(5) My 1986 p 24-28

A study of performane of the entrants of adult education centres of Chandigarh in relation to their intelligence and socio-economic status. Harish Sharma and Madhu Mati *Quest in Education* 19(1) Ja 1982 p 58-63+

Adult Education : India : Delhi

Behaviour pattern of educators : A study. M. Seth *et al Indian J Adult Education* 44(3) Mr 1983 p 24-30+

Group interaction among adult women participating in the functional literacy programme in Delhi. M. Seth *et al Indian J Extension Education* 19(1-2)

Mr-Je 1983 p 62-68

Impact of functional literacy programme in rural areas near Delhi. V. Chaturvedi and Braham Prakash *Indian J Adult Education* 44(3) Mr 1983 p 31-35 refs tabs

Promoting adult literacy through mobile teacher. Anita Deghe *Indian J Adult Education* 41(10) Oc 1980 p 5-14 tabs

Adult Education : India : Goa

Adult education in Goa : Retrospect and prospects. M.R. Nimbalkar *Indian J Adult Education* 47(1) Ja 1986 p 17-22 tab

Adult Education : India : Gujarat

Adult education in a slum of Baroda city. P.K. Sahoo and T.N. Dwivedi *Indian J Adult Education* 40(8) Ag 1979 p 35-41 refs

Adult education in Gujarat : An evaluation study. K.R. Shah *Indian J Adult Education* 44(11) Nv 1983 p 22-27+

Adult Education : India : Haryana

Adult education for socio-economic development in Haryana. Vijay Kumar Gupta *Indian J Adult Education* 41(9) Se 1980 p 26-28 refs

Adult Education : India : History

Adult education in India : A historical review. B.S. Vasudeva *Educational Rev* 42(8) Ag 1986 p 130-34 refs

Adult Education : India : Karnataka

Evaluation of adult literacy materials in Kannada. H.S. Ananthanarayana *Indian J Adult Education* 40(8) Ag 1979 p 7-15 refs

Adult Education : India : Kerala

Adult education in Kerala : Some innovative experiments. K.S. Pillai *Indian J Adult Education* 45(3) Mr 1984 p 7-12

Adult Education : India : Madhya Pradesh

Non-formal education in Madhya Pradesh. P.N. Rusia *Bulletin of Non-formal Education* 1(2) 19 Se 1983 p 21-30

Adult Education : India : Maharashtra

Role of school and coaching class in formal education : A comparative perspective. Gullistan J. Kerawalla and Naaz S. Dhakam *Progress of Education* 61(1) Ag 1986 p 5-12 refs

Adult Education : India : Mizoram

Non-formal education programmes in Mizoram : Retrospect and prospects. M.A. Sudhir Kumar and Lalrinkimi *Indian J Adult Education* 44(11) Nv 1983 p 28-33 tabs

Adult Education : India : Orissa

Non-formal education : A new challenge. Shiv K. Gupta *Teacher Today* 21(2) Oc-De 1978 p 1-7 refs

Non-formal education for universalisation of education : A study in Orissa state. Sunil Behari Mohanty *Primary Teacher* 11(4) Oc 1986 p 17-22 tabs

Adult Education : India : Orissa : History

Adult education in Orissa before independence. Sura Prasad Pati *Educational Rev* 92(12) De 1986 p 209-11 refs

Adult Education : India : Punjab

Discrimination learning among illiterate rural adults as function of their intelligence. Rajinder Singh Mann *Progress of Education* 55(7) Fe 1981 p 189-91+

Adult Education : India : Rajasthan

Adult education in Rajasthan. F.S. Das *Indian J Adult Education* 40(7) Jl 1979 p 28-30

A critical look at a micro-level adult education project. Om Shrivastava *Indian J Adult Education* 44(3) Mr 1983 p 21-23

Non-formal education in Rajasthan. S.E. Robinson *Bulletin of Non-formal Education* 1(4) Mr 1984 p 27-36

Non-formal education programme in Udaipur district. Pushpa Gupta and Alpana Kavita *Progress of Education* 60(9) Ap 1986 p 205-08 refs

Organisational stucture of adult education programme in Rajasthan. R.C. Mehta *Prasar* 5(3-4) Oc 1977-Ja 1978 p 5-10

Adult Education : India : Tamil Nadu

Adult education in Tamil Nadu : The sixth five year plan : An outline. R. Gomez *Experiments in Education* 10(3) My 1982 p 43-50 refs tabs

The hidden dreams : The neo-literates aspects. L.S. Saraswathi and D.J. Ravindran *Indian J Adult Education* 41(12) De 1980 p 23-27

Leadership training through non-formal education : The RUHSA experience. Victor Kolipilla *New Frontiers in Education* 13(1) Ja-Mr 1983 p 31-36

A profile of the clientele in the NFE centres for 6-14 years in Tamil Nadu. L.S. Saraswathi *Experiments in Education* 6(6) Ag 1978 p 106-08; 6(7) Se 1978 p 111-16

A profile of the clientele, in the NFE centres for 6-14 years in Tamil Nadu. L.S. Saraswathi *Indian J Adult Education* 40(9) Se 1979 p 22-30

State resource centre for non-formal education in Tamil Nadu. R. Rajan *Educational Rev* 90(2) Fe 1984 p 25-27 refs

Adult Education : India : Uttar Pradesh

Adult education : Problems and solutions. P.K. Dongre and Digvijaya Singh *Indian Education* 10(6) Se 1980 p 10-13

Universalisation of elementary education : Non-formal education progrmme and the instructor. A study on Uttar Pradesh. R.D. Yadav *Bulletin of Non-formal Education* 3(1) Je 1985 p 1-10 refs

Adult Education : Kenya

Non-formal education for school drop-outs. T. Mulusa *Indian J Adult Education* 41(1-2) Ja-Fe 1980 p 41-47

Adult Education : Motivation

Dynamics of motivation for adult learners. M.P. Uniyal and Beena Shah *Indian J Adult Education* 44(10) Oc 1983 p 3-5 + refs figs

Impact of motivational aspects of attendance in adult education centres : A case discussion. Gomathi Mani *Indian J Adult Education* 43(5) My 1982 p 25-28 tabs

Motivation in non-formal education : Tanzania experience. E.P.R. Mbaklle *Indian J Adult Education* 40(7) Jl 1979 p 9-18

Adult Education : Nigeria

Development of adult education in Nigeria. Thomas O. Fasokan *Indian J Adult Education* 42(1-2) Ja-Fe 1981 p 13-19 refs tabs

Mass literacy campaigns in Nigeria, 1940-1960. Michael Omolewa *Indian J Adult Education* 41(9) Se 1980 p 15-23

Adult Education : Norway

Adult education in Norway. *Indian J Adult Education* 46(1) Ja 1985 p 12-18

Adult Education : Research

Mode of priority of researches in adult education. M.V. Sudhakara Reddy *Experiments in Education* 10(1) Mr 1982 p 14-15

Research in adult education. M.V Sudhakara Reddy *Educational Rev* 87(9) Se 1981 p 174

Adult Education : Research : India

Role of universities in training research and evaluation of adult education. Amrit Kaur *Indian J Adult Education* 40(5) My 1979 p 13-22 refs

Adult Education : Sri Lanka

Promotion and co-ordination of non-formal education in Sri Lanka.W.M.K. Wijetunga *Indian J Adult Education* 39(11-12) Nv-De 1978 p 50-52

Adult Education : Study and Teaching

Expectations of teaching in individuals of lower socio-economic class. M. Sree Ramamurthy *Indian J Adult Education* 39(11-12) Nv-De 1978 p 27-34 tabs

Adult Education : Sweden

Study circles in Sweden : A participants viewpoint. John Benseman *Indian J Adult Education* 41(10) Oc 1980 p 15-19 refs tabs

Adult Education : Teacher Training

Adult education and teacher education. Sunil Behari Mohanty *Educational Rev* 87(5) My 1981 p 94-95 refs

Emerging needs and preparation on non-formal education teachers for rural areas. S.P. Ahluwalia and Ashok K. Kala *Educational Rev* 91(1) Ja 1985 p 7-10

An evaluative study of the training for adult education functionaries of Maharashtra. Anuradha Sahasrabudhe *Progress of Education* 60(10-11) My-Je 1986 p 239-48

Frustrations and suggestions of an adult education trainer. V. Mohan Kumar *Indian J Adult Education* 46(3) Mr 1985 p 13-18

Life-long education and teacher preparation. Lal Pratap Singh *Teacher Today* 22(3) Ja-Mr 1980 p 29-33

Methods and contents in teacher preparation for adult education. Nandita Sharma *Teacher Education* 16(18-19) Ja-Ap 1982 p 48-52 refs

Orientation of teachers for non-formal education centres. H.L. Sharma *Primary Teacher* 11(3) Jl 1986 p 26-28

Pre-service training programme for continuing education instructors in Thailand M. Khajapeer *Indian J Adult Education* 40(9) Se 1979 p 11-16

Preparation of adult education teachers : Methods and contents. Nandita Sharma *Indian J Adult Education* 43(5) My 1982 p 18-20 +

Role of universities in training, research and evaluation of adult education. Amrit Kaur *Indian J Adult Education* 40(5) My 1979 p 13-22 refs

Search for a skilled friend, philosopher and guide. Kamla Vashishtha *Teacher Today* 24(4) Ap-Je 1982 p 44-49 refs

Tapping resources to train adult education fuctionaries. S. Rangasamy *Indian J Adult Education* 46(1) Ja 1985 p 28-30

Training field functionaries : Teachers and supervisors. K. Sivadasan Pillai *Experiments in Education* 9(2) Ap 1981 p 31-33

Training for cadres for adult education : An outline. S.C. Dutta *Indian J Adult Education* 41(12) De 1980 p 5-8

Training kit for instructors. Rafat S. Shafi *Indian J Adult Education* 41(9) Se 1980 p 11-14

Training needs of adult educators in the Norwegian situation. Hallgjerd Brattset *Indian J Adult Education* 46(1) Ja 1985 p 10-20

Training of adult education functionaries. *Indian J Adult Education* 41(3) Mr 1980 p 20-21

The training of adult education manpower at home and abroad : The Eastern African scene. Y.D.M. Bwatua *Perspectives in Education* 1(2) Ap 1985 p 99-109 tabs

Training of adult literacy instrucators : Some observations. S.A. Ologe *Indian J Adult Education* 47(8) Ag 1986 p 22-30 refs

Training of teachers for adult education. V.S. Mathur *Teacher Today* 21(2) Oc-De 1978 p 8-11

Adult Education : Thailand

Adult education in Thailand. Kishore Sant *Indian J Adult Education* 40(4) Ap 1979 p 17-26 refs

Adult education in Vietnam and Thailand : A study-visit report. S.K. Chowdhry and P.K. Shukla *Indian J Adult Education* 44(10) Oc 1983 p 19-23

Adult Education : United States

Planning university adult education programmes for the 1980s : Prospects and problems. Donald K. Smith *Indian J Adult Education* 40(3) Mr 1979 p 15-29

Adult Education : Vietnam

Adult education in Vietnam and Thailand : A study visit report. S.K. Chowdhry and P.K. Shukla *Indian J Adult Education* 44(10) Oc 1983 p 19-23

Adult Education, Rural

Motivating adult learners in rural areas : An analytical study. Hemlata Prasad *Indian J Adult Education* 46(2) Mr 1985 p 19-24

Non-formal education for the rural child. Inder Prabha Sharma *Kurukshetra* 33(6) Mr 1985 p 8-10

Adult Education, Rural : India

Dynamics of rural learning system. V. Reddy *Indian J Adult Education* 40(7) Jl 1979 p 19-23

Non-formal adult education programme : An aid to rural development. I.P. Aggarwal *Education Quarterly* 31(1) Ap 1979 p 1-3

Non-formal education : A strategy for educating rural masses. R.N. Syag and R.C. Hooda *Progress of Education* 56(3) Oc 1981 p 66-68 refs

Planning adult education programme for peasants. R.R. Shirur *Indian J Adult Education* 40(8) Ag 1979 p 42-44

Role of adult education in promoting and effective functioning of rural institutions and organisations. Malclom S. Adiseshiah *Indian J Adult Education* 42(12) De 1981 p 5-9

Rural adult literacy : An enquiry into the attitudes. G. Haragopal and G. Sudershan *Indian J Adult Education* 39(10) Oc 1978 p 34-42 tabs

Adult Education, Rural : India : Andhra Pradesh

Attitude of teacher-volunteers towards farmers functional literacy programme : Guntur study. M.J. Wilson and B.L. Reddy *Indian J Adult*

Education 40(6) Je 1979 p 29-33 refs

Adult Education, Rural : India : Punjab

A comparative study of awareness across illiterate and literate rural adults. Baghel Singh Sohi *Prasar* 7(3-4) Oc 1980-Ja 1981 p 38-45

Adult Education, Rural : India : Rajasthan

Attitude of tribal and non-tribal farmers towards adult literacy and improved agricultural practices : A study. V.L. Chauhan and G.C. Rai *Indian J Adult Education* 45(3) Mr 1984 p 26-31 refs tabs

Adult education, Rural : Tamil Nadu Attitude of rural adult learners towards adult education. Gomathimani *Indian J Adult Education* 41(5) My 1980 p 11-14

Non-formal education and rural development : A case from rural Tamil Nadu. C.P. Dodge *Indian J Adult Education* 41(10) Oc 1980 p 20-23

Adult Education, Rural : Philippines

In search of alternatives to the schooling model : The case of the NEFRY Project. Blanda R. Sumagao *Bulletin of Non-formal Education* 1(4) Mr 1984 p 1-26 refs

Adult Education and Economic Development

See

Adult Education and National Development

Adult Education and National Development

Adult and continuing education and national development. B.S. Vasudeva Rao and Subba Rao *Educational Rev* 90(1), Ja 1984 p 7-9 refs

Authentic development : The role of adult education. S.R. Mohsini *Indian J Adult Education* 44(1-2) Ja-Fe 1983 p 6-16

Co-ordination between non-formal adult education and development programme. A. Bordia *Indian J Adult Education* 10(1) Ja 1979 p 1-8 refs

Dar-es-Salaam in perspective : The role of adult education in development. Malcolm S. Adiseshiah *Indian J Adult Education* 40(8) Ag 1979 p 1-5

Income generation projects : The link between adult education and the satisfaction of basic needs. Manzoor Ahmed *Indian J Adult Education* 39(10) Oc 1978 p 21-26

Non-formal education and development. H.K. Venkatarangachar and M.N. Ravindranatha *J Indian Education* 8(1) My 1982 p 68-70

Non-formal education and rural development through higher education. M. Deousker *Indian J Adult Education* 44(4) Ap 1983 p 31-38 refs

Non-formal education for development : A critique. D.P. Pattanayak *Indian J Adult Education* 40(2) Fe 1979 p 22-26

Non-formal education for development. Malcolm S. Adiseshiah *Indian J Adult Education* 41(4) Ap 1980 p 3-5

Non-formal education for rural development. Motilal Sharma *Teacher Today* 21(2) Oc-De 1978 p 19-27 refs

Second thoughts on adult education and development. A. Rogers *Indian J Adult Education* 40(7) Jl 1979 p 1-8

Adult Education and State : India

National adult education policy approach : Contradictions in assumptions and implementation. Chandra Kanta Dandiya *Prasar* 5(3-4) Oc 1977-Ja 1978 p 41-47

Adult Education and State : Nigeria
Adult education and the new national policy on education in Nigeria : Problems and prospects. Gidado Tahir *J Indian Education* 12(2) Jl 1986 p 8-14 refs
Adult Education and Universities
College students and adult education. D. Janardhan Reddy *Educational Rev* 87(9) Se 1981 p 175-76
Continuing education and the role of universities. Lakshmi Misra *Indian Education* 9(12) Mr 1980 p 19-22
Mass education involving college students as instruction : A case study. Mirudula Seth *Indian J Adult Education* 47(1) Ja 1986 p 3-7
Non-formal education, extension education programmes of the universities. M.A. Hussain *J Indian Education* 6(6) Mr 1981 p 49-52
Programme planning in university continuing education. Arthur K. Mrimuko *Indian J Adult Education* 41(4) Ap 1980 p 13-16 +
Significance of adult continuing education and extension programmes in universities. N. Venkataiah and P. Adinarayana Reddy *University News* 22(1) Ja 1984 p 17-19
University adult education and national development. Rajkumari Chandrasekaran *Indian J Adult Education* 39(9) Se 1978 p 32-37 refs
University and emerging educational technologies for adult and continuing education. R. Jayagopal *J Higher Education* 4(3) Spr 1979 p 365-71
See also
Continuing Education Centres
Adult Education and Universities : Ghana
Demand on university-based education in Ghana : A review. Kobina Asiedu *Indian J Adult Education* 47(6) Je 1986 p 13-20 refs
Adult Education and Universities : India
Involvement of universities and colleges in the national adult education programme : An appraisal. L.R. Shah *Prasar* 7(1-2) Ap-Jl 1980 p 1-10
National adult education programme : Role of Indian universities. K.C Bastia and G.R. Sudama *Experiments in Education* 8(2) Ap 1980 p 29-32 refs
Role of universities and colleges in the national adult education programme. Ajit Kumar Jain *Prasar* 7(1-2) Ap-Jl 1980 p 27-32
Role of universities in the national adult education programme. L.R. Shah *Indian J Adult Education* 40(7) Jl 1979 p 31-35
Universities involvement in NAFP. Amrit Kaur *Indian J Adult Education* 39(10) Oc 1978 p 43-44
Adult Education Dropouts
Dropping out phenomenon in adult education. A.R. Bisht *Indian Adult Education* 44(5) My 1983 p 25-26
Adult Education of Women
Adult education for women. R.S. Nigam *Educational Rev* 86(3) Mr 1980 p 49
Adult education programme : A study on women's performance. B.S. Vasudeva Rao *Indian J Adult Education* 47(6) Je 1986 p 8-12 tabs
Adult education programmess for illiterate women in the age group 15-35. Amrit Kaur *Indian J Adult Education* 40(12) De 1979 p 19-32
Designing curriculum and technology for women's adult education

programmes. Rajkumari Chandrasekaran *Indian J Adult Education* 41(4) Ap 1980 p 19-24

Develop non-formal structures to educate women. S.C. Dutta *Indian J Adult Education* 46(4) Ap 1985 p 11-13

Develop unconventional measures of education. Mohsina Kidwai *Indian J Adult Education* 45(12) De 1984 p 9-11

Educate women to reduce inequalities. M.G. Mane *Indian J Adult Education* 45(12) De 1984 p 7-8

Eradicating women's illiteracy : A challenge. M.L. Shahare *Indian J Adult Education* 45(12) De 1984 p 32-38

Establishing linkages between women's literacy programmes status, issues and access to family planning. Rami Chhabra *Indian J Adult Education* 41(4) Ap 1980 p 6-9

Evaluation of condensed courses of education for adult women. P. Bhagwat *Indian J Adult Education* 42(10) Oc 1981 p 17-20 refs

Group discussion reports. *Indian J Adult Education* 45(12) De 1984 p 20-27

Needed two revaluations in non-formal education for women and girls. Mina Swaminathan *Education Quarterly* 34(4) Oc 1982 p 5-7

Non-formal education for women. M. Lakshminarayana *EPA Quarterly Bulletin* 8(1-2) Ap-Jl 1985 p 40-44

Programmes of non-formal education for women. S. Jayaweera *Indian J Adult Education* 40(12) De 1979 p 33-45

Recommendations. *Indian J Adult Education* 45(12) De 1984 p 29-31

Adult Education of Women : India

Adult education for women. T.R. Nagappa *Indian J Adult Education* 41(8) Ag 1980 p 23-25 refs

Adult education programme and women. Lakshmi Misra *Educational Rev* 86(2) Mr 1980 p 41-43

Continuing education for women in slums. Ida Singh *Experiments in Education* 9(6) Ag 1981 p 99-102

NAEP and the involvement of educational women. Kamala Rana *Prasar* 7(1-2) Ap-Jl 1980 p 23-47

Adult Education of Women : India : Delhi

Group interaction among adult women participating in the functional literacy programme in Delhi. M. Seth *et al Indian J Extension Education* 19(1-2) Mr-Je 1983 p 62-68 refs tabs

Group interaction among women participants of a functional literacy programme in Delhi : A study. M. Seth *et al Indian J Adult Education* 44(10) Oc 1983 p 24-28 refs tabs

Needs of rural school going girls : Implications for non-formal education. Addila Haque *Indian J Adult Education* 39(10) Oc 1978 p 9-13 tabs

Adult Education Teachers

Experience of adult education teachers : An interview. Mridula Seth *Indian J Adult Education* 43(7) Jl 1982 p 17-20

Investment in adult education instructors. D.V. Sharma *Indian J Adult Education* 41(12) De 1980 p 9-12 +

Adult Education Teachers : India

Profile of the adult educators in India. Chandra Kanta Dandiya *Prasar* 5(1-2) Ap-Jl 1977 p 3-14 tabs

Aesthetics and Aesthetic Education
Aesthetic education : A concept for bahavioural change. Maqbool Ahmad *Teacher Today* 23(1) Jl-Se 1980 p 15-19 refs
Aesthetic education : Historical perspective. G. Ramesh *National J Education* 5(1) Se 1982 p 46-52 refs
See also
Worth

Affiliated Colleges
See
Universities and Colleges

Afghanistan
See also
Illiteracy : Afghanistan

Africa
See also
College Teachers : Africa
Education : Africa
Educational Sociology : Africa

Aggressiveness : Psychologyical Aspects
See
Hostility : Psychological Aspects

Agricultural Administration : India
Management of agriculture and rural development. K.M. Singh *Indian Extension Education* 21(1-2) Ja-Je 1985 p 1-9
Management of agriculture and rural development programme : Problems and prospects. K.P.A Menon *Indian J Extension Education* 21(1-2) Ja-Je 1985 p 10-19
Recommendations of the national seminars on management of agriculture and rural development programme. *Indian J Extension Education* 21(1-2) Ja-Je 1985 p 94-98

Agricultural Administration : India : Tamil Nadu
A study of block level administration for small and marginal farmers agricultural development. J. Vasantakumar and S.H. Singh *Indian J Extension Education* 21(1-2) Ja-Je 1985 p 53-60 tabs

Agricultural Colleges
Role of agricultural universities in training of subject-matter specialists and extension personnel of training. P.N. Jha *Indian J Extension Education* 19(1-2) Mr-Je 1983 p 36-40
See also
Agricultural Education

Agricultural Colleges : India
Role of agricultural universities in training subject-matter specialists and extension personnel of training. P.N. Jha *Indian J Extension Education* 19(1-2) Mr-Je 1983 p 35-40

Agricultural Communication
See
Communication in Agriculture

Agricultural Cooperative Credit Societies : India : Gujarat
Factors associated with farmers attitude towards primary agricultural credit

society in Gujurat. A.O. Kher and P.N. Jha *Indian J Extension Education* 14(1-2) Ja-Je 1973 p 23-29 refs

Agricultural Credit : India : Bihar

An analysis of tribal loanees in repayment of loans. H.S.P. Sinha and R. Ranjan *Indian J Extension Education* 17(3-4) Se-De 1981 p 54-65 refs tabs

Credit orientation of farm entrepreneur. S.P. Mishra and B.P. Sinha *Indian J Extension Education* 17(3-4) Se-De 1981 p 44-53 tabs

Agricultural Credit : India : West Bengal

Who shall repay agricultural loans. G.L. Ray R.K. Samanta. Calcutta, Bokshan. 193p. Rs.40 *Book Rev, Indian J Extension Education* 18(3-4) De 1982 p 74-75

Agricultural Education

Agricultural extension curriculum and change agents : Some New guidelines. C. Prasad *J Higher Education* 5(1) Mon 1979 p 75-88

A critical study of evaluation under different systems of agricultural education. M.P. Gupta *J Higher Education* 5(1) Mon 1979 p 89-96

Factors responsible for the selection of agricultural courses and the career aspirations of secondary school boys. G. Laxmi Narayan and Radha Krishna Menon *Indian J Extension Education* 15(3-4) De 1979 p 33-36 tabs

Role of monitoring and evaluation in making training programme more effective. C.S.S. Rao *Indian J Extension Education* 19(1-2) Mr-Je 1983 p 33-35

Training for agricultural development. C. Prasad *Indian J Extension Education* 19(1-2) Mr-Je 1983 p 12-22 refs

Agricultural Education : Curricula

Developing colleges of basic sciences and humanities in agricultural universities. S.K. Mukherji *J Higher Education* 5(2) Au 1979 p 195-201

Agricultural Education : India

The agricultural university as a multi-functional system. Aqueil Ahmad *J Higher Education* 5(1) Mon 1979 p 57-73

New dimensions for agricultural higher education. R.J. Patel *J Education and Psychology* 36(4) Ja 1979 p 228-33

User instructions in effective use of university library in teaching agricultural education and research. P.P. Deshmukh *University News* 23(22) 8 Je 1985 p 4-7

What constitutes a practical agricultural graduate. V.K. Makhija and Y.P. Singh *Indian J Extension Education* 21(3-4) Jl-De 1985 p 62-67

Agricultural Education : India : Maharashtra

Quality improvement in agricultural university education of Maharashtra. M.C. Varshneya and R.K. Parakale *University News* 23(12) 23 Mr 1985 p 4+

Teacher's time as a resource for students improvement in agricultural university education in Maharashtra. M.B. Shingte and T.R.V. Naidu *Progress of Education* 61(3) Oc 1986 p 62-67 refs

Agricultural Education : India : Pondicherry

Knowledge and attitude of students towards agricultre in secondary school education. G. Laksminarayanan and K. Radhakrishnamenon *Indian J*

Extension Education 18(1-2) Je 1980 p 73-76

Agricultural Education : India : Punjab

Impact of training media. M.P. Gupta *Educational Rev* 17(1) Ja 1982 p 22-27

Agricultural Engineering : Research : India

Agricultural engineering research and the role of agricultural universities in India. S.H. Adhaoo and S.S.Vanjari *J Higher Education* 8(3) Spr 1983 p 381-85 refs

Agricultural Exhibitions : India : Punjab

Communication effectiveness of farmers fair kisan mela. M.P. Gupta *Indian J Extension Education* 17(3-4) Se-De 1981 p 92-95

Agricultural Extension Education

An introduction to extension education. S.V. Supe. New Delhi, Oxf-IBH Pub.1983. viii,166p. Rs.12.50 *Book Rev, Indian J Extension Education* 19(3-4) Se-De 1983 p 98

Agricultural Extension Education : Audio-Visual Aids

Relative effectiveness of lecture, tape recorded lecture and their combinations with selected visuals. N. Nagaraj and H.N. Byra Reddy *Indian J Extension Education* 21(3-4) Jl-De 1985 p 43-52 refs tabs

Agricultural Extension Education : India

Challenges of extension in the eighties. K.N. Singh *Indian J Extension Education* 18(1-2) Je 1982 p 1-9

Evolving new extension and training strategies for rural development. Prayag Mehta *Indian J Extension Education* 19(1-2) Mr-Je 1983 p 1-11 refs

National seminar on training for agricultural and rural development. *Indian J Extension Education* 19(1-2) Mr-Je 1983 p 104-08

Role of agricultural universities in training of subject-matter specialists and extension personnel of training and visit system. P.N. Jha *Indian J Extension Education* 19(1-2) Mr-Je 1983 p 36-40

Role of monitoring and evaluation in making training programme more effective. C.S.S. Rao *Indian J Extension Education* 19(1-2) Mr-Je 1983 p 33-35 refs

Training for agricultural development. C. Prasad. *Indian J Extension Education* 19(1-2) Mr-Je 1983 p 12-22 refs

Training of extension personnel in India : A brief review. N. Perumal *Indian J Extension Education* 19(1-2) Mr-Je 1983 p 23-32

Agricultural Extension Education : India : Haryana

Adequacy of coverage of extension education course contents in relation to the job of agricultural development officers. V.B. Dixit *et al Indian J Extension Education* 21(3-4) Jl -De 1985 p 73-79 tabs

Agricultural Extension Education : India : Maharashtra

Evaluation of foundation course organised by Punjabrao Krishi Vidyapeeth, Akila for village development officers under TCV system. O.P. Ingle *et al Indian J Extension Education* 19(1-2) Mr-Je 1983 p 41-45 refs tabs

Agricultural Extension Education : Research

Research methods in extension education : Techniques of rural research. Sumati Mulay and V.E. Sabarathnam. New Delhi, Manasayan. 1980, xii,

339p. Rs.40 *Book Rev, Indian J Extension Education* 16(3-4) De 1980 p 98

Agricultural Extension Officers

See also

Block Development Officers

Agricultural Extension Officers : India : Karnataka

Job involvement of extension supervisors : A factor analysis. V. Veerabhadraiah and K.A. Jalihal *Indian J Extension Education* 19(3-4) Se-De 1983 p 1-10 refs tabs

Agricultural Extension Officers : India : Punjab

Competencies of the agricultural extension officers regarding selection and use of extension methods. G.S. Sangha and N.S. Sandhu *Indian J Extension Education* 16(3-4) De 1980 p 43-45 refs tabs

Agricultural Extension Work

The challenge of agricultural extensions in the 1980s. A.W. Van Den Ban *Indian J Extension Education* 18(3-4) De 1982 p 1-9

Evaluation of foundation course organised by Punjabrao Krishi Vidyapeeth, Akola for village development officers under T.V. system. O.P. Ingle *et al* *Indian J Extension Education* 19(1-2) My-Je 1983 p 41-45

Linkages among research, extension, farmers and input and credit organisations at various levels. Jagdish C. Sharma *Indian J Extension Education* 18(102) Je 1982 p 16-24 refs

The logic of extension. M.G. Roling *Indian J Extension Education* 15(3-4) De 1979 p 1-8 refs

Recommendations of the national seminar on challenge of extension in the eighties. *Indian J Extension Education* 18(1-2) Je 1982 p 25-33

Role of agricultural universities in training of subject-matter specialists and extension personnel of training. P.N. Jha *Indian J Extension Education* 19(1-2) Mr-Je 1983 p 36-40

A scale to measure extension participation of farmers. B.S. Siddaramaiah and K.A. Jalihal *Indian J Extension Education* 19(3-4) Se-De 1983 p 74-76 tabs

Suspense box : A new visual aid. R.R. Sinha *Indian J Extension Education* 17(3-4) Se-De 1981 p 89-91

See also

Adoption of Improved Farm Practices
Agricultural Education
Agricultural Extension Education
Community Development
Television in Agriculture

Agricultural Extension Work : Administration

Agricultural extension management system in India : Past, present and modalities in future. C.S.S. Rao *Indian J Extension Education* 21(1-2) Ja-Je 1985 p 32-35

Basic management issues in extension. Y.P. Singh and A. Ramesh Babu *Indian J Extension Education* 21(1-2) Ja-Je 1985 p 20-31

Agricultural Extension Work : India

Interpersonal communication patterns of extension system; a path analysis. C.K. Ambastha and K.N. Singh *Indian J Extension Education* 16(3-4) De

1980 p10-15 refs tabs
See also
Small Farmers Development Agency

Agricultural Extension Work : India : Bihar

An analysis of inter system communication patern. C.K. Ambastha and K.N. Singh *Indian J Extension Education* 15(1-2) Je 1979 p 1-8 refs tabs

Interpersonal communication pattern of extension personnel. C.K. Anbastha and K.N. Singh *Indian J Extension Education* 14(3-4) Jl-De 1978 p 8-15 tab

Agricultural Extension Work : India : Madhya Pradesh

Communication patterns of extension personnel : A path analysis. Y.C. Sanoria and K.N. Singh *Indian J Extension Education* 15(1-2) Je 1979 p 19-25 tabs

Impact of intensive agriculture extension and research programme on the farmers knowledge of technology. R.S. Pachori and S.G. Tripathi *Indian J Extension Education* 19(3-4) Se-De 1983 p 72-73

Agricultural Extension Work : India : Maharashtra

Charactertistics of extension personnel of Maharashtra extension system in relation to communication behaviour. N.B. Sehete *Indian J Extension Education* 14(1-2) Ja-Je 1978 p 57-61

A study of mobile farm advisory service. M.G. Bhllegsonkar and A.M. Dakh *Indian J Extension Education* 14(1-2) Ja-Je 1978 p 62-63

Agricultural Extension Work : India : Rajasthan

Differential information gaps under the training and visit extension system. S.N. Panday and P.N. Mathur *Indian J Extension Education* 19(3-4) Se-De 1983 p 18-25 refs

Agricultural Extension Work : India : Tamil Nadu

Communication gap between extension workers and paddy growing small farmers. D. Somasundaram and S.N. Singh *Indian J Extension Education* 14(3-4) Jl-De 1978 p 26-33

Agricultural Extension Work : India : Uttar Pradesh

Channels of communications in rural communities of Uttar Pradesh. G.S Bhatnagar *Indian J Extension Education* 14(3-4) Jl-De 1978 p 34-38

Agricultural Extension Work : India : West Bengal

Differential extension contacts. Pradip Kumar Dey *Indian J Extension Education* 16(3-4) De 1980 p 22-31 refs

Impact of training and visit system of extension on tribal farms in Hoogly district : A case study. A.K. Ray *et al Indian J Extension Education* 18(1-2) Je 1982 p 59-65 refs tab

Agricultural Extension Work : Nigeria

Communication channels and its impact on knowledge of the farmers of the South Western Nigeria. N.U. Patel *Indian J Extension Education* 14(3-4) Jl-De 1978 p 1-7

Agricultural Extension Work : Rumania

Agricultural extension in Romania. Jindra Kulich *Indian J Adult Education* 39(9) Se 1978 p 30-31

Agricultural Extension Workers

Job involvement of extension supervisors : A factor analysis. V. Veenabhadraiah and K.A. Jalhal *India J Extension Education* 19(3-4)

Se-De 1983 p 1-10 refs tabs

Performance appraisal of extension workers. S.V.N. Rao and T.S. Sohal *Indian J Extension Education* 18(3-4) De 1982 p 57-61 refs

See also

Village Level Workers

Agricultural Extension Workers : Education and Training

An evaluation of training programme for extension personnel. M.C. Patel and A.U. Kher *Indian J Extension Education* 32(9) Se 1978 p 42-43

Training of extension personnel in India : A brief review. N. Perumal *Indian J Extension Education* 19(1-2) Mr-Je 1983 p 23-32

Agricultural Extension Workers : India

Job content and context of factors in job satisfaction of Deputy Agricultural Officers. K.R. Menon *et al Indian J Extension Education* 14(1-2) Ja-Je 1978 p 1-5 refs

Agricultural Extension Workers : India : Rajasthan

Attitude of extension workers towards some selected components of T and V programme. M.R. Prajapati and Ashok A. Patel *Indian J Extension Education* 20(3-4) Se-De 1984 p 55-56

Agricultural Extension Workers : India : Tamil Nadu

Job satisfaction and job performance of agricultural extension officers of Tamil Nadu. G. Perumal and G.C. Rai *Indian J Extension Education* 14(1-2) Ja-Je 1978 p 73-75

Agricultural Innovations

See also

Adoption of Improved Farm Practices

Agricultural Innovations : India : Andhra Pradesh

Agro-social status and adoption of farm innovation in two villages. Gummadi Appa Rao *Indian J Extension Education* 19(3-4) Se-De 1983 p 62-65

Caste and formal education in inter-personal diffusion of an innovation in two Indian villages. G. Appa Rao and Everett M. Rogers *Indian J Extension Education* 16(3-4) De 1980 p 1-9 refs

Interpersonal relations in diffusion of an innovation in two Indian villages. G. Appa Rao *et al Indian J Extension Education* 16(1-2) Je 1980 p 19-24 refs

Agricultural Innovations : India : Delhi

Differential perception of the characteristics of innovations of farming couples for high yielding varieties of wheat and family planning practices. T.R. Singh and S.N. Singh *Indian J Extension Education* 16(3-4) De 1980 p 1621 refs

Utilisation and credibility of the sources of information at various stages of adoption of farm innovations. P.K. Ramchandran *et al Indian J Extension Education* 15(3-4) De 1979 p 46-51 refs tabs

Agricultural Innovations : India : Karnataka

Information sources for technology transfer : A study. G.R. Desai and M.K.S. Rao *Indian J Adult Education* 44(10) Oc 1983 p 29-31 refs tab

Agricultural Innovations : India : Madhya Pradesh

Impact of intensive agriculture extension and research programme on the farmers knowledge of technology. R.S. Pachori and S.G. Tripathi *Indian J Extension Education* 19(3-4) Se-De 1983 p 72-73

Agricultural Innovations : India : Rajasthan

Awareness of farm technology among small farmers. A.U. Godewar *et al* *Indian J Adult Education* 43(7) Jl 1982 p 9-12 refs

Agricultural Innovations : India : Tamil Nadu

Some psychological correlates of adoption of improved rice technology by small farmers of South Arcot district. S.Veerasamy and Taj Bahadur *Indian J Extension Education* 15(3-4) De 1979 p 87-89 tabs

Agricultural Innovations : India : Uttar Pradesh

Impact of national demonstration on participant and non-participant farmers. L.V. Hirevenkanagoudar *et al* *Indian J Extension Education* 20(1-2) Je 1984 p 76-78

Agricultural Literature

Differential availability and utilisation of agricultural publications. Haringhata study. P.K. Dey *Indian J Adult Education* 40(7) Jl 1979 p 36-43 refs tabs

Agricultural Mechanisation

See

Farm Mechanisation

Agricultural Research

Agricultural research and primary teacher. Satyapal Bharat Bhushan *Primary Teacher* 4(4) Oc 1979 p 27-28

Agricultural research service scientists : Their value orientation and overall modernity. P.K. Somanla *J Higher Education* 9(1) Mon 1983 p 114-17 ref

Linkages among research, extension, farmers and input credit morganisations at various levels. Jagdish C. Sharma *Indian J Extension Education* 18(1-2) Je 1982 p 16-24 ref

See also

Adoption of Improved Farm Practices

Agricultural Research : India

Perception of work environment by agricultural research service scientists of ICAR institutes. R.K. Samanta *Indian J Extension Education* 21(3-4) Jl-De 1985 p 53-61 refs tabs

Purarank sheet for Q-Sort technique. A. Ramesh Babu and Y.P. Singh *Indian J Extension Education* 20(1-2) Je 1984 p 52-57 tab

Relevance of agricultural research in Indian. S.S. Johl *New Frontiers Education* 14(4) Oc-De 1984 p 18-25

User instructors in effective use of university library in teaching agricultural education and research. P.P. Deshmukh *University News* 23(22) 8 Je 1985 p 4-7

See also

Indian Council of Agricultural Research, New Delhi

Agricultural Research : India : Haryana

See also

Dairy Research : India : Haryana

Agricultural Research : India : Karnataka

Extension role expectation and perception of research workers. C.M. Dudhani and K.A. Jalihal *Indian J Extension Education* 21(3-4) Jl-De 1985 p 68-72

Information input pattern of agricultural researchers at regional research station, Dharwad Karnataka state. Subhashchandra S.Patil and M.B.

Channegowda *Indian J Extension Education* 21(1-2) Ja-Je 1985 p 72-73

Interaction between researchers and farmers in Bangalore district of Karnataka. M.B. Channegowda *Indian J Extension Education* 19(3-4) Se-De 1983 p 66-68 tabs

Agricultural Schools

See

Agricultural Colleges

Agriculture

See also

Dairying

Field Crops

Women in Agriculture

Agriculture : Documentation

See also

Agriculture : Information Services

Agriculture : India

See also

Small Farmers Development Agency

Agriculture : India : Haryana

Role performance of village level workers in agriculture production. R.L. Kherde and B.N. Sahay *Indian J Extension Education* 15(1-2) Je 1979 p 67-69 tab

Agriculture : India : Rajasthan

Role perception and role performance of Sarpancha (Chairman of Gram Panchayts) in Rajasthan. S.I. Intodia and G.S. Shektawat *Indian J Extension Education* 16(1-2) Je 1980 p 64-68 tabs

Agriculture : Information Services

An analysis of inter system communication pattern. C.K. Ambastha and K.N. Singh *Indian J Extension Education* 15(1-2) Je 1979 p 1-8

Communication of information through Rural Youth Club Leaders. G.S Saini and Ch. S. Reddy *Indian J Extension Education* 21(1-2) Ja-Je 1985 p 80-82

Communication pattern of agricultural scientists : A system analysis. Y.C. Sanoria and K.N. Singh *Indian J Extension Education* 14(1-2) Ja-Je 1978 p 17-22 refs

Comparison of the multiple regression and the configurational approaches to predictory correlates of the communication effectiveness village level workers. R. Parshad *Indian J Extension Education* 18(3-4) De 1982 p 16-22 refs

Components of fluency, intelligence and socio-economic status as correlates of the interests in agricultural pursuits. R.L. Bhardwaj *J Education and Psychology* 38(4) Ja 1981 p 227-34 refs

Construction of attitude scales : Attitude towards improved agricultural practices : Attitude towards adult literacy. B.N. Venkataiah *Indian J Adult Education* 40(2) Fe 1979 p 27-40 appdc tabs

The decision-making by farm woman ragarding improved agricultural practices. Rashila Malik *Indian J Extension Education* 15(3-4) De 1979 p 64-69 tabs

Differential information gaps under the training and visit extension system.

S.N. Pandey and P.N. Mathur *Indian J Extension Education* 19(3-4) Se-De 1983 p 18-25 tabs

Differential perception of farm practices : Attitudes by progressive and non-progressive farmers. B. Asul Raj and A. John Knight *Indian J Extension Education* 14(1-2) Ja-Je 1978 p 64-65

Farmers information sources at different stages of innovation decision process. Zaki M. Mohammed and Ranjit Singh *Indian J Extension Education* 14(1-2) Ja-Je 1978 p 78-82 refs

Information needs of the small and marginal farmers of Punjab state. G.S. Saini *Indian J Extension Education* 17(3-4) Se-De 1981 p 101-02

Interpersonal communication pattern in client system : A path analysis. C.K. Ambastha and K.N. Singh *Indian J Extension Education* 14(1-2) Ja-Je 1978 p 9-16 refs

A multiple regression analysis of factors related with attitude of farmers. *Indian J Extension Education* 17(3-4) Se-De 1981 p 73-80 refs

Source credibility pattern among small and big farmers. R.R. Chole and W.D. Rahudkar *Indian J Extension Education* 14(1-2) Ja-Je 1978 p 50-53

Utilisation of household knowledge by farm woman. Neeru Bala and Sumita Roy *Indian J Extension Education* 15(3-4) De 1979 p 22-26 tabs

See also

Adoption of Improved Farm Practices
Agricultural Extension Work
Agricultural Extension Workers
Village Level Workers

Agriculture : Information Services : India : Rajasthan

Communication methods between AEOS, VLW's and farmers in Rajasthan's IAAP districts. Charles T. Ricker *Prasar* 5(1-2) Ap-Jl 1977 p 15-24 refs

Agriculture : Information Services : India : West Bengal

Impact of national demonstration on knowledge, attitude and adoption levels of farmers of West Bengal. S. Pathak *et al Indian J Extension Education* 15(1-2) Je 1979 p 49-54 refs tabs

Agriculture : Periodicals : India

Readership pattern, nature of content and sources of information of farm periodicals in India. P.N. Mathur *et al Indian J Extension Education* 14(1-2) Ja-Je 1978 p 39-44

See also

Unnat Krishi (Periodical)

Agriculture : Research

See

Agricultural Research

Agriculture : Vocational Guidance

See also

Agriculture as a Profession

Agriculture, Folklore of

See

Folklore of Agriculture

Agriculture as a Profession

Problems in professional socialisation as faced by agriculture and veterinary graduates in Assam. K.K. Saharia *J Education and Psychology* 44(2-3)

Jl-Oc 1986 p 135-40

Agriculturists

See also

Agriculture as a Profession

Aging

Life style and aging. Ganesh C. Sharma *Asian J Psychology and Education* 7(1) Ja 1981 p 25-26

Algebra : Study and Teaching

Structure of intellect abilities as predictors of achievement in tenth grade algebra. C.P.S. Chauhan *Indian Education Rev* 19(2) Ap 1984 p 19-27

Alienation : Social Psychological Aspects

Alienation in the school system : A factor analytic model for empirical study. Siba P. Bhattacharya *Our Education* 6 Jl 1986-87 p 21-26 refs tabs

A comparative study of alienation from the school among the first generation learners and *vice versa*. V.K. Rai *Experiments in Education* 11(3) My 1983 p 50-52

Education alternatives, M. Sree Rama Murthy *Experiments in Education* 9(7) Se 1981 p 115-20

Meaning of alienation : Current status. Amita Shukla *Progress of Education* 57(12) Jl 1983 p 269-78 refs

Measurement of alienation : A review of tools. Amita Shukla *J Education Research and Extension* 20(3) Ja 1984 p 203-10

Research on alienation in a few fields : A review. Amita Shukla *Educational Rev* 92(10) Oc 1986 p 171-75 refs

Aligarh Muslim University : Examinations

Comparison of students performance under the semester and non-semester system of education in the Aligarh Muslim University. Zakia A. Siddique and Z. Khatoon *J Higher Education* 3(3) Spr 1978 p 369-79 refs tabs

All India Adult Education Conference

Annual report : 1983-84. J.C. Saxena *Indian J Adult Education* 45(12) De 1984 p 39-47

All India Adult Education Conference, Amritsar, 1979

Declaration and recommendations of 32nd IAEA Conference. *Indian J Adult Education* 40(10-11) Oc-Nv 1979 p 5-8

Group reports. *Indian J Adult Education* 40(10-11) Oc-Nv 1979 p 45-51

Inaugural address (delivered at the 32nd IAEA annual conference). A.J. Kidwai *Indian J Adult Education* 40(10-11) Oc-Nv 1979 p 9-14

32nd annual conference of IAEA (A brief report). J.L. Sachdeva *Indian J Adult Education* 40(10-11) Oc-Nv 1979 p 55-58

Valedictory address. S. Muthu *Indian J Adult Education* 40(10-11) Oc-Nv 1979 p 64-68.

All India Educational Conference, Cuttack, 1978

Presidential address. S.K. Dasgupta *Teacher Education* 14(10-11) Ja-Ap 1980 p 3-7

All India Educational Conference, Jabalpur 1982

The 56th All India Educational Conference : A report. *Educational Rev* 89(2) Fe 1983 p 26-29

56th All India Educational Conference : Presidential address. S.N. Mukherjee *Indian Education* 12(11-12) Fe-Mr 1983 p 31-32

Jabalpur hosts : Fifty-sixth All India Educational Conference. *Indian Education* 12(11-12) Fe-Mr 1983 p 3-7

All India Educational Conference, Kurukshetra, 1980

54th All India educational conference, Kurushetra, Haryana, December, 27 to 31, 1980 : A review. S. Sreedhara Swamy *Indian Education* 10(9-10) De 1980-Ja 1981 p 39-54

54th all India Educational Conference, Kurushetra : Inaugural address 28-12-1980. V.V. John *Indian Education* 10(11) Fe 1981 p 5-10

54th all India Educational Conference, Kurukshetra : Presidential address 28-12-1980. B. Venkat Rami Reddy *Indian Education* 10(11) Fe 1981 p 11-15

Role of teacher organisations in promoting national integration, 30-12-1980 : Presidential address. M. Sreenivasarao *Indian Education* 10(11) Fe 1981 p 16-18

Strengthening the link between AIFEA and its affiliates. V. Sujeevan Rao *Indian Education* 10(7) Oc 1980 p 38-43

Towards a national system of education : Valedictory address, 30-12-1980. V.S. Mathur *Indian Education* 10(11) Fe 1981 p 19-20

All India Educational Conference, Visakhapatnam

57th Conference, Visakhapatnam : Address by Prof. Nirmal Bose. *Indian Education* 13(5-6) Ag-Se 1983 p 5-8

57th conference, Visakhapatnam : Address by Sri Avula Sambasiva Rao *Indian Education* 13(5-6) Ag-Se 1983 p 3-4

57th All India Education Conference, Visakhapatnam : Address by Sri Alwar Das *Indian Education* 13(5-6) Ap-Se 1983 p 9-10

All India Federation of Educational Associations : Conference

See

All India Educational Conference

All India Sane Guruji Kathamala, Pune

Sane Guruji Kathamala : An organisation trying to make children emotionally literate. Yadunath Thatte *Progress of Education* 57(9) Ap 1983 p 200-01+

All India Student Federation

AISF National Council reviewed national and international political situation. *Student Action* 2(12) Jl 1984 p 10-13

AISF's historic victories in Punjab. Tara Singh Sandhu *Student Action* 2(6) Oc 1983 p 7-8

Some important resolutions of AISF National Council. *Student Action* 2(12) Jl 1984 p 3-5

A unite to fight and today's challenges. Pallab Sengupta *Student Action* 2(1) My 1983 p 2-3

American College, Madurai

Four years of autonomy at American College. A.R. Venkitaraman *New Frontiers in Education* 12(2) Ap-Je 1982 p 47-51

Amusements

See

Mathematical Recreations

Andhra Pradesh Open University

Andhra Pradesh Open University : Some reflections. C. Naryan Reddy *University News* 24(42) 8 Nv 1986 p 17-20

Andhra University

UGC study centres : Nature and performance : A case study of Andhra University centres. P. Bhaskara Rao *University News* 23(23) 16 Je 1985 p 5-8

Animal Culture

See also

Animal Husbandry

Poultary

Animal Husbandry

See also

Dairying

Animal Husbandry : India : Bihar

Traditional beliefs of tribal Mundas associated with cattle husbandry. R.M. Srivastava and K.L. Kharde *Indian J Extension Education* 19(3-4) Se-De 1983 p 77-82 refs tabs

Animal Husbandry : India : Madhya Pradesh

Socio-economic factors influencing the adoption and non-adoption of hybrid cattle in Western M.P. K.D. Yadav and N.C. Jain *Indian J Extension Education* 20(1-2) Je 1984 p 71-72

Animal Husbandry : India : Punjab

Multi-rater approaches for performance appraisal of cattle development extension workers. J.S. Sohi and R.L. Kherde *Indian J Extension Education* 21(3-4) Jl-De 1985 p 112-15tabs

Anna University, Madras

Dr. Sanjeevi Rao address convocation of Anna University. *University News* 23(21) 1Je 1985 p 7-9

Annamalai University

Union Education Minister addresses convocation of Annamalai University. K.C. Pant *University News* 23(26) 8 Je 1985 p 6-7

Answers to Questions

See

Questions and Answers

Anxiety

Adjustment, anxiety and conflict. O.P. Verma and S.N. Upadhyay *Asian J Psychology and Education* 7(3) 1981 p 28-32 refs tabs

Anxiety among visually handicapped children. Gerald Soloman *et al* *J Education and Psychology* 38(4) Ja 1981 p 219-26 tabs

Anxiety and academic achievement. P.K. Ganguli *Asian J Psychology and Education* 7(2) Jl 1981 p 39-43

Anxiety and academic achievement. P.K. Ganguli *J Educational Research and Extension* 19(4) Ap 1983 p 233-38 refs

Anxiety and serial verbal learning - A test of the Verkes-Dodson law. S.W. Deshpande and S.D. Kawane *Asian J Psychology and Education* 9(3) 1982 p 18-23

Anxiety and step-size as correlates of performance through programmed instruction. Harish Chandra Sharma and Malvinder Ahuja *J Education and*

Psychology 36(4) Ja 1979 p 173-79

Anxiety in criminals and non-criminals : A comparison. V.B. Misra *J Education and Psychology* 37(3) Oc 1979 p 184-86 refs

Anxiety in relation to academic achievement of high school students. Zakia A. Siddiqi and Shamin Akhtar *Indian Educational Rev* 18(4) Oc 1983 p 106-10

Anxiety, personally types and sex as the determine of the influence of the noise distractibility in reversal and non-reversal shifts. Ramji Srivastava *Asian J Psychology and Education* 4(3) Nv 1979 p 9-13

Anxious attitude of students in relations to some backward variables. M.K. Satyarthi *Asian J Psychology and Education* 4(1) Ja 1979 p 35-38 refs

The effect of anxiety and aspiration on academic achievement of adolescents boys and girls. Govind Tiwari *et al Asian J Psychology and Education* 6(1) Ja 1980 p 35-38 refs

Effect of stress and anxiety on psychomotor performance. Sunil Abrol *Asian J Psychology and Education* 11(1) 1983 p 32-35

Factor structure of psychoticism in relation to hostility, anxiety, neuroticism and ability measures. Satvir Singh and Meena Sehgal *Asian J Psychology and Education* 4(3) Nv 1981 p 18-21 refs

Incidence of anxiety among teachers. Karuna Shankar Misra *Asian J Psychology and Education* 4(1) Ja 1979 p 44-47

Interrelationship among measures of job involvement, job satisfaction and general anxiety. Sagar Sharma and Sadhna Sharma *Asian J Psychology and Education* 3(2) Jl 1978 p 35-39 refs

Locus of control and level of anxiety among college student. G. Rajmohan and A. Kuppan *Asian J Psychology and Education* 6(3) Nv 1980 p 12-16 refs

Locus of control and level of anxiety among college students.

G. Rajmohan *J Educational Resarch and Extension* 17(3) Ja 1981 p 178-84 refs tabs

Problems of girls as a function of maternal employment and anxiety. B.G. Sudha and S. Goetha *J Institute of Educational Research* 6(1) Ja 1982 p 29-37 refs tabs

Relationship between anxiety and academic achievement. Ratna Mookerjee *et al J Institute of Educational Research* 6(1) Ja 1982 p 10-12 refs tabs

Relationship of sex with creativity general anxiety, vocational anxiety and teaching success. G.L. Arora *J Education and Psychology* 36(3) Oc 1978 p 133-39

Some personality correlates along anxiety, extraversion and neuroticism dimensions. Sudhakar Rath *Asian J Psychology and Education* 3(3) Nv 1978 p 46-51 refs tabs

A study in anxiety level of Santal (tribal) and non-Santal (non-tribal) under-graduate students of Santal Parganas. Lal Bahadur Singh *J Institute of Educational Research* 4(1) Ja 1980 p 20-22 refs tabs

A study of anxiety in relation to parental acceptance and Peer acceptance. G. Ansari and Z. Rahman *J Education and Psychology* 39(3) Oc 1981 p 189-96

A study of effects of anxiety and attitude in reading achievement. I.A. Vora *J Education and Psychology* 38(1) Ap 1980 p 36-42 tabs

A study of the effect of anxiety on teacher behaviour. Shashikala Deshpande and Lalitha V. Tirth *Indian Educational Rev* 15(2) Ap 1980 p 1-10 refs

See also

Fear

Applications for Positions

See also

Interviews and Interviewing

Aptitude Tests

See

Ability : Testing

Arithmetical Ability

See

Mathematical Ability

Arithmetics

Triangular numbers. N. Subramanya *Primary Teacher* 6(2) Ap 1981 p 16-17

Arithmetics : Study and Teaching

New challenge in teaching arithmetic. Hem Raj Garg *Primary Teacher* 20(2) Ap 1985 p 31-32

A new technique for teaching arithmetic. Ghanshyam Saran Srivastava *Primary Teacher* 5(4) Oc 1980 p 37-38

Teaching arithmetic to the deaf and dumb. Subhash Chandra Agarwal *Educational Rev* 87(6) Je 1981 p 106-08

Arithmetics : Study and Teaching : Primary

Development of battery of diagonostic tests in arithmetic for the students of standards V, VI and VII in Gujarati medium schools in Greater Bombay. T.M. Patel *Indian Educational Rev* 15(4) Oc 1980 p 81-85

Reading, writing and arithmetic scores as predictors of academic success in primary school children. S. Subramanyam *Experiments in Education* 13(11) Ja 1986 p 195-200

Teaching arithmetic in primary schools. Sachidanand Sharma *Primary Teacher* 8(1) Ja 1983 p 29-30

Understanding counting numbers. Harmesh Lal *Primary Teacher* 9(3) Jl 1984 p 16-19

Army Schools

See

Military Education

Art

See also

Artists

Art : Study and Teaching

Art as unifying principle in education. Ramesh Ghanta *Progress of Education* 61(1) Ag 1986 p 17-19 +

Art education in the new system of education. Jagannath Mohanty *Progress of Education* 60(8) Mr 1986 p 179-82 refs

Art education : The aesthetic relationship between mother and child. Gerhard Winkler *Indian Education* 11(7) Oc 1981 p 5-7

Child and art education. R.K. Chopra *Primary Teacher* 4(2) Ap 1979 p 15-18

Development of skills through art education. Jagannath Mohanty *Primary*

Teacher 10(1) Ja 1985 p 7-9

Trends in art education : A perspective. R.K. Chopra *Primary Teacher* 5(3) Jl 1980 p 27-30

See also

Art schools

Art : Study and Teaching : Primary

Identifying creative potential through arts. R.K. Chopra *Primary Teacher* 10(1) Ja 1985 p 19-24

Art, Indian

A history of fine arts in India and the West. Edith Tomory. New Delhi, Orient Longman. 532p. Rs.40 *Book Rev, New Frontiers in Education* 12(3) Jl-Se 1982 p 79-80

Art, Occidental

A history of fine arts in India and the West. Edith Tomory. New Delhi, Orient Longman. 532p. Rs.40 *Book Rev, New Frontiers in Education* 12(3) Jl-Se 1982 p 79-80

Art Education

See

Art : Study and Teaching

Art Schools

See also

Art : Study and Teaching

Art Schools : Russia

Art schools are accesible to all in the USSR. Lydia Ilyina *Progress of Education* 53(7) Fe 1979 p 138-40

Art Teachers

Art teachers satisfied with their jobs : A study. A. Venkata Rami Reddy and N. Krishna Reddy *J Indian Education* 6(2) Jl 1980 p 59-65 refs

Artists

Studies on creative artists : A survey. M. Sugathan *J Institute of Educational Research* 4(3) Se 1980 p 28-35 refs

Arunachal Pradesh

See also

Education : India : Arunachal Pradesh

Asia

See also

Adult Education : Asia
Community Development : Asia
Education : Asia
Education, Higher : Asia
Educational Planning : Asia
Educational Research : Asia
Moral Education : Asia
Science : Study and Teaching : Primary : Asia
Social Science Research : Asia

Asia : Southeastern

See also

Educational Research; Asia, Southeastern

Audio-Visual Education

Instruction through radio vision : A comparative study. Motilal Sharma and Meena Oberai *Indian Educational Rev* 18(4) Oc 1983 p 37-46

See also

Photography in Education

Radio in Education

Television in Education

Audio-Visual Materials

Factors affecting use of audio-visual aids. R.R. Sinha *Indian J Extension Education* 18(3-4) De 1982 p 62- 64

Aurobindo, Sri

Sri Aurobindo's philosophy of spiritual transformation. Aleta Yori Mastny *J Indian Education* 33(1) My 1985 p 1-8

Aurobindo, Sri : Educational Thought

Sri Aurobindo's philosophy of educator. Ramnath Sharma. Agra, Vinod Pustak Bhandar. 1985, 244p. Rs.30 *Book Rev, Education Quarterly* 37(3) Aut 1985 p 62-63

The integral system of education. Sita Ram Jayaswal *Teacher Education* 13(8-9) Jl-Oc 1979 p 9-15 ref

Australia

See also

Illiteracy : Australia

Authoritarianism

Authoritarianism and some personality traits of school children. C.K. Shah *J Education and Psychology* 40(1-2) Ap-Jl 1982 p 85-89

Authorship : Television

See also

Television Authorship

Autonomy : University

See

University Autonomy

Bachelor of Education

B.Ed. admissions : Non-academic criteria. P.D. Jayal *Educational Rev* 87(5) My 1981 p 90-93 refs tabs

A comparative study of three teaching strategies at B.Ed. level. Jaiprakash Sharma *Experiments in Education* 11(3) My 1983 p 41-44

Development of a question bank for a course on educational evaluation at B.Ed. M.S. Yadav and M.B. Menon *J Higher Education* 3(3) Spr 1978 p 357-67 refs tabs

Internal and external examination marks of B.Ed student : A critical analysis. B.G. Sudha and S.N. Shakuntala *Indian Educational Rev* 20(2) Ap 1985 p 39-50

Management of B.Ed. admission in Uttar Pradesh. P.C. Shukla *Educational Rev* 91(9) Se 1985 p 147- 49

Stability of divisions : A study of B.Eds. T.S. Rao *National J Education* 3(1) Se 1980 p 40-48 tabs

A study of the reactions of teacher trainees towards the evaluation procedure followed at B.Ed. level. B. Bhaskara Rao and G. Sundara Rao

Experiments in Education 12(12) Fe 1985 p 216-19
See also
Master of Education

Bajra
Constraints analysis in adoption of fertilisers and plant protection measures in Bajra cultivation. Madan Singh and P.N. Mathur *Indian J Extension Education* 20(3-4) Se-De 1984 p 53-54

Balwadi Schools : India : Delhi
Job analysis of Balwadi workers of Delhi : A case study. Anita Chandwani *Indian J Extension Education* 5(1-2) Je 1979 p 70-74 tabs

Bangladesh
See also
Adult Education : Bangladesh
Basic Education : Bangladesh
Education : Bangladesh
Education, Primary : Bangladesh
Population : Study and Teaching : Bangladesh
Women, Rural : Employment : Bangladesh

Bangladesh Agricultural University : Students
Students Life at the Bangladesh Agricultural University. A. Rashid Ahmad *et al Indian J Extension Education* 17(3-4) Se-De 1981 p 96-100 tabs

Banks and Banking
See also
Agicultural Credit

Basic Education
Gandhian thoughts on basic education : Relevance and development. M.L. Kaul *J Indian Education* 8(3) Ja 1983 p 11-16 refs
Some basic understandings of socially useful productive work. S.U.P.W. C.B. Patyal *Progress of Education* 53(9) Ap 1979 p 187-90

Basic Education : Bangladesh
Issues and constraints in the introduction of appropriate basic education in Bangladesh. Mohammed Ferdouse Khan *Perspectives in Education* 1(3) Jl 1985 p 157-68

Behaviour Problems : Children
See
Problem Children

Behaviourism : Psychological Aspects
Behaviour problems in schools. S.P. Anand *Quest in Education* 16(4) Oc 1979 p 299-306
Manipulative drive and rearing behaviour. Mithlesh Garg *Asian J Psychology and Education* 3(2) Jl 1978 p 15-18 refs
Scalings of some important class room behaviour attributes of college teachers. Sheela Mangla *J Educational Research and Extension* 20(2) Oc 1983 p 139-52
A study of behavioural rigidity among young adults. Sushil Kumar Goel and Arun K. Sen *J Education and Psychology* 43(1) Ap 1985 p 34-36
See also
Human Behaviour

Belgium
See also
Universities and Colleges : Belgium
Bengali Children : Ability Testing
Adaptation of vividness of visual imagery questionnaire scale for Bengali children. Mihir K. Chatterjee *Indian Educational Rev* 18(2) Ap 1983 p 40-45 refs tabs
Bharatidasan University
Scientific research on educational institutions : Problems and challenges. C.M.R. Rao *University News* 23(27) 16 Jl 1985 p 9-11
Bihar
See also
Adoption of Improved Farm Practices : India : Bihar
Adult Education : India : Bihar
Agricultural Credit : India : Bihar
Agricultural Extension Work : India : Bihar
Animal Husbandry : India : Bihar
College Students : India : Bihar
College Teachers : India : Bihar
Communication in Agriculture : India : Bihar
Education, Secondary : India : Bihar
Education of Children : India : Bihar
Education of Women : India : Bihar
High School Teachers : India : Bihar
Illiteracy : India : Bihar
Rural Leadership : India : Bihar
Schools : India : Bihar
Soil Conservation : India : Bihar
Tribes : India : Bihar
Biological Sciences : Study and Teaching
Efficacy of inductive and deductive approaches in teaching biological sciences. T. Bhima Rao *Indian Education* 10(7) Oc 1980 p 33-37
See as
Biology Study and Teaching
Biological Sciences : Study and Teaching : Aids and Devices
A study of the effectiveness of the use of motion pictures as aids in the teaching of biological sciences as compared to the usual methods. Vishwanath Muddu *Experiments in Education* 8(8) Oc 1980 p 138-41 tabs
Biology : Ability Testing
Discrepancy between high school examination scores and the scores predicted on the basis of intelligence, scientific interests, clerical interests, educational adjustment and family status. R.K. Joshi and Niti Srivastava *Indian Educational Rev* 18(2) Ap 1983 p 100-06
An inverstigation into personality correlates of high and low achievers in bio-sciences. K.C. Vashistha *Progress of Education* 58(5) De 1983 p 118-20 tabs
A study of certain personality variables related to high and low achievers in biology in secondary schools. R. Sukumaran Nair *J Educational Research and Extension* 19(4) Ap 1983 p 207-19 refs tabs

Biology : Study and Teaching

Changes in knowledge and attitude of students attending on environment, oriented sociology courses. Iqbal Aziz Muttagi and Sumirmal Roy *Experiments in Education* 12(6) Ag 1984 p 104-12 refs tab

Effectiveness of field-trips in teaching biological sciences. D. Padmavathy *Educational Rev* 91(10) Oc 1985 p 171-76

Radiovision in biology class : An exploratory study. Motilal Sharma and C.K. Tripathi *Progress of Education* 55(2) Se 1980 p 45-50 refs tabs

A study of some teacher variables and teaching methods associated with learning outcomes in biology. Savitri Masih *Indian Educational Rev* 15(4) Oc 1980 p 71-75

See also

Biological Sciences : Study and Teaching

Biology : Study and Teaching : Higher

Teaching chronobiology in Indian universities. M.K. Chandrashekaran *J Higher Education* 5(3) Spr 1980 p 343-49 refs

Biology Teachers

Influence of anxiety on effectiveness of biology teachers. Karuna Shankar Misra *J Indian Education* 5(1) My 1979 p 50-53

Role expectations, role performance and training needs of biology teachers of secondary schools. Vasantha Ramkumar and Achamma Thomas *J Educational Research and Extension* 16(3) Ja 1980 p 153-61 refs tabs

Biosciences

See

Life Sciences

Birth Control

See

Family Planning

Blind : Education

Educating visually handicapped children. A.R. Bisht and R.S. Pathani *Educational Rev* 92(10) Oc 1986 p 178-79

The predictment of the parents of pre-school blind children. Ramesh P. Saxena *J Indian Education* 6(5) Ja 1981 p 3-7

Sensory training : A basic subject to the personality development of the visually handicapped child. Ramesh P. Saxena *Teacher Today* 23(3) Ja-Mr 1981 p 16-21

Supervision of schools for visually handicapped. R.S. Sharma *Education Quarterly* 36(1) Ja 1984 p 36-45

Blind : Education : India : Andhra Pradesh

Education of the blind in Andhra Pradesh. K. Pandurangam *Indian Education* 11(8-9) Nv-De 1981 p 34-36

Blind : Education : Nigeria

Planning a new school for visually handicapped children in Nigeria. D.G. Shawn *National J Education* 7(1) Se 1984 p 51-56

Block Building : Educational Aspects

Sex stereotyping in block play of preschool children. Margaret Verma *Indian Educational Rev* 15(3) Jl 1980 p 31-37 refs

Block Development Officers

Job satisfaction of developmental personnel : A catalytic force for rural

development. K.M.P. Singh and S. Mulay *Indian J Adult Education* 43(5) My 1982 p 6-12 refs

See also

Agriculture Development Officers

Block Play

See

Block Building : Educational Aspects

Boarding Schools

The residential system. Shantha Rajagopalan *Experiments in Education* 10(8) Oc 1982 p 137-41

Book Groups

See

Group Reading

Books and Reading

A book week in a school. A. Hilda Sales-Pontes *Progress of Education* 55(11) Je 1981 p 295-99

Helping child in reading. M.T. Raja Reddy *Educational Rev* 87(6) Je 1981 p 113-15

The impact of study habits of intellectually backward pupils upon their academic achievement. D.N. Patel *Progress of Eduation* 56(2) Se 1981 p 33-37 tabs

Improving reading through self-selection. Bir Singh *Educational Rev* 87(12) De 1981 p 221-22

See also

Group Reading

Reading

Reading Interests

Supplementary Reading

Books and Reading : Moral and Religious Aspects

See

Literature and Morals

Books and Reading for Children

Developing reading habits among children. R.S. Sharma *Primary Teacher* 4(2) Ap 1979 p 23-26

An inquiry into the efficacy of Cloze procedure as a measure of readability of reading materials and reading abilities of pupils. D.N. Patel *Progress of Education* 55(2) Se 1980 p 36-41

Promotion of reading habits among school children : The role of libraries. K.L. Luthra *J Indian Education* 6(2) Jl 1980 p 66-70

Study habits as a function of need achievements (n.Ach.) Jyoti Christian *Asian J Psychology and Education* 11(1) 1983 p 6-12

What should our children read. Mahendra N. Pandia *Progress of Education* 57(12) Jl 1983 p 266-68

See also

Children's Literature

Book Industries : India

Books : The barometers of cultural well-being. *University News* 24(38) 8 De 1986 p 6-7

Bosco, Don

Don Bosco and the preventive system of education. Mathew Kalathankal *New Frontiers in Education* 11(3) Jl-Se 1981 p 1-25 refs

Botany : Examinations, Questions, etc.

An analysis of questions bank in botany. R.S. Gupta *et al Rajasthan Board J Education* 15(4) Oc-De 1979 p 26-37

Botswana

See also

Education : Botswana

Theatre : Botswana

Brain Drain

Brain drain and drain of brain. S. Sekhar *Experiments in Education* 11(12) Fe 1984 p 214-15

Brazil

See also

Education, Higher : Brazil

Bright Children

See

Gifted Children

Broadcasting, Educational

See

Educational Broadcasting

Buddha, Lord : Educational Thought

Education as perceived by Buddhist society with special emphasis on its aims. B.P. Singh *Educational Rev* 89(10) Oc 1983 p 171-72

Bulgaria

See also

Education : Bulgaria

Business : Study and Teaching

See

Business Education

Buisness, Choice of

See

Vocational Guidance

Business Education

Commerce at the secondary stage in India. P. Raizada *Education Quarterly* 31(3-4) Oc 1979-Ja 1980 p 25-27

Commerce education. M.S. Khan. New Delhi, Sterling. 1982,126p. Rs. 50 *Book Rev, Education Quarterly* 35(3) Jl 1983 p 60-61

Coordination between universities and professional bodies. D.C. Sancheti *University News* 23(26) 8 Jl 1985 p 2-3

Problems faced by departments of commerce. Mangala Mehta *Educational Rev* 90(10) Oc 1984 p 153-54

Vocationalisation of commerce education and the role of university. U.S. Prasad *J Higher Education* 9(2) Aut 1983 p 271-77

Business Education : Curricula

An approach to modernisation of commerce courses. O.R. Krishnaswami *J Higher Education* 2(2) Aut 1976 p 277-79

Commerce curriculum in India : Need for reforms. R. Satya Raju *J Higher*

Education 9(2) Aut 1983 p 277-79

Business Education : India

Changing pattern of business education in India. D.G. Girdhari *J Indian Education* 10(6) Mr 1985 p 39-47

Patterns of commerce education in Indian universities. E.B. Brahmankar *University News* 23(33) 1 Se 1985 p 4-5 +

Business Education : Nigeria

Androgogy versus pedagogy in adult business education programme. Esogwa C. Osuala *Indian Education* 10(9-10) De 1980-Ja 1981 p 23-27

The management of business education in Nigeria. E.C. Osuala *Indian Education* 11(1-2) Ap-My 1981 p 89-91

Butter-fly

Kusiarie : A mysterious butter-fly. V.M. Sharma *Primary Teacher* 4(1) Ja 1979 p 23

Calcutta University : Finance

Financial crisis of the University of Calcutta. K.A. Mukerji *J Higher Education* 1(1) Mon 1975 p 121-24 tab

Campus Disorders

See

Student Unrest

Canada

See also

Adult Education : Canada

Dissertations : Academic : Canada

Education : Canada

Education, Higher : Canada

Social Sciences : Canada

Social Sciences : Study and Teaching : Canada

Caste : India

The caste system and discrimination in historical perspective. S. Bhattacharya and Fleur D'slmeida *New Frontiers in Education* 16(2) Ap-Je 1986 p 25-32 tabs

Cattle : Breeding

See

Cattle Breeding

Cattle : Feeding and Feeds

Adoption of scientific feeding practices by cattle owners of the ICBP, Karnal. Sukhbir Singh and V.K. Dubey *Indian J Extension Education* 14(1-2) Ja-Je 1978 p 70-72

Cattle Breeding : India : Maharashtra

Information sources of the adopters of cross-breeding in cattle in Pune district of Maharashtra. G.K. Sawant and othes *Indian J Extension Education* 15(1-2) Je 1979 p 75-76

Chandigarh

See also

Adult Education : India : Chandigarh

College Teachers : India : Chandigarh

Change, Educational
See
Educational Innovations
Character Education
See
Moral Education
Character Tests
See also
Personality Tests
Cheating in Examinations
Causes of scholastic dishonesty among the examinees. V.K. Rai *Our Education* 5 Jl 1984 p 39-45 ref
Effect of different types of treatment environment on the cheating pattern of school students. S.S. Mathur and Ashok K. Kalia *J Institute of Educational Research* 7(3) Se 1983 p 7-9
The effect of performance attribution on attitude to study, achievement motivation and tendency to cheat in examination. H. Johnson Nenty *Progress of Education* 59(10-11) My-Je 1985 p 224-34
To stop copying : Examinees suggestions. Bir Singh *Educational Rev* 85(3) Mr 1979 p 48-49
Unfair means in examinations. K.L Gandhi *J Indian Education* 8(4) Nv 1982 p 28-32
Unfair means. S.S. Jaswal *Educational Rev* 89(11) Nv 1983 p 192-93
Chemistry : Ability Testing
Construction of an achievement test in chemistry. M.S. Verma *Experiments in Education* 11(2) Ap 1983 p 29-32
Chemistry : Examinations, Questions, etc.
Question bank in chemistry. N.S.Gnanprakasam. *Educational Rev* 90(9) Se 1984 p 125-27
Chemistry : Study and Teaching
A diagonostic test in chemistry. M.S. Verma *Educational Rev* 87(7) Jl 1981 p 131-37 refs
Creative approach and testing of chemistry. Suman Bala Malik *Teacher Today* 31(3) Ja-Mr 1979 p 53-59
An experimental study of programmed instruction method of teaching chemistry in high and low achievers. Arun Kumar Gupta *J Education and Psychology* 37(3) Oc 1979 p 193-97 ref tabs
Low cost equipment for chemistry teaching. K.V. Sanet *New Frontiers in Education* 13(1) Ja-Mr 1982 p 49-52
New educational technology and the teaching of chemistry. R.C. Mehrota *J Higher Education* 1(1) Mon 1975 p 31-42 refs tabs
Chemistry : Study and Teaching : Elementary
What can we contribute to school chemistry curriculum? N.K. Mathur and K.L. Menaria *Teacher Today* 25(2) Oc-De 1982 p 62-65
Chickens
See
Poultry

Child and Parent
See
Parent and Child
Child Care Centres
See
Day Nurseries
Child Development
See
Child Study
Child Psychiatry
See also
Mentally Handicapped Children
Child Psychology
See
Child Study
Child Rearing
See
Children : Management
Child Study

An analysis of the development of self-concepts among children belonging to an orphanage. A. Suria Kanthi *J Educational Research and Extension* 18(3) Ja 1982 p 149-54 refs tabs

Causal thinking in Indian children : A study. K. Bharati and V. Bevli *Indian Educational Rev* 19(2) Ag 1984 p 9-18

The child development curriculum and its relevance to job competencies expected in the field. Amita Verma and Y.S. Saraswathi *J Higher Education* 9(1) Mon 1983 p 119-24

A child with learning difficulties : Importance of play in remedial works. Suresh Majumdar *Indian Educational Rev* 17(3) Jl 1982 p 23-27

Childhood parental loss and subsequent adult depression. R. Singh *et al J Indian Education* 7(2) Jl 1981 p 50-54

Children's attitudes towards mentally retarded peers. Ameela Gupta and Adarsh Sharma *Indian Educational Rev* 18(4) Oc 1983 p 28-36

Children's problems. Banshi Lal Swami *Educational Rev* 84(11) Nv 1978 p 205-06

Cognitive development and the communicative mothers. Subhashini Passi *Progress of Education* 60(6) Jl 1986 p 128-29+

A comparative study of moral judgement in children. Narendra Pratap Singh *Experiments in Education* 12(6) Ag 1984 p 99-103 refs

A comparative study of moral values of the children of working and non-working mothers. Kusum Gupta *Progress of Education* 58(8) Mr 1984 p 193-96 + refs tabs

A comparative study of personal preferences, self-concept and performance of SOS children's village of India and other children of Delhi schools. Jai Prakash *Indian Educational Rev* 18(2) Ap 1983 p 125-33 tabs

Concept development in children. S. Narayan Rao Tripathy. Sri Venkateswara University. 1977. *Book Rev, J Indian Education* 6(2) Jl 1980 p 77-78

Children's curiosity and teaching. Gaya Prasad Sharma *Primary Teacher*

5(3) Jl 1980 p 41-42

Creative development in school children. Dibakar Kunder *Education Quarterly* 37(3) Aut 1985 p 6-7

The deprived and neglected child. T. Dutta *Primary Teacher* 10(4) Oc 1985 p 27-29

Development of personality trait regularity among children. M.K. Kaul *Primary Teacher* 9(4) Oc 1984 p 26-29

A developmental study of some locomotor skills during early childhood. Gharulata H. Badami *J Education and Psychology* 36(4) Ja 1979 p 210-18 refs

Dynamics of children's behaviour. Kuldeep Kumar *Primary Teacher* 10(4) Oc 1985 p 9-12

Energy and child's inquisitiveness. Suman Bala *Primary Teacher* 4(3) Jl 1979 p 15-17

Factor of social deprivation affecting : The primary school children. M. Pushpa *Indian Educational Rev* 16(2) Ap 1981 p 1-14 refs

Isolated children : A new concept. Ramanath Kundu and Basudhara Maite *J Institute of Educational Research* 7(2) Ja 1983 p 16-19

Life and death : Children's concepts. S.S Jayalakshmi *Educational Rev* 87(5) My 1981 p 95-98

Love and respect for the child. Pritam Singh Brar *Educational Rev* 87(10) Oc 1981 p 181-83

Marks of leadership among children. Shamsuddin *Education Quarterly* 32(1) Ja 1980 p 28-29

Mental health problems of school children. V.N. Rao *Educational Rev* 92(12) De 1986 p 201-03

Mentally retarded and normal children : A comparative study. Manju Biswas. New Delhi, Sterling. 1980. 153p. Rs.45 *Book Rev, Education Quarterly* 33(3) Jl 1981 p 47-48

Nature of characteristics of the children enrolled in laboratory nursery school from 1975-1978. M.B. Singh and Sunita Jain *Asian J Psychology and Education* 10(1-4) 1982 p 33-39

Normal development and growth of human personality. S.K. De *Educational Rev* 88(8) Ag 1982 p 124-29

A peep into the child's behaviour. C.V. Narasimhan *Educational Rev* 89(12) De 1983 p 213-15

Personality, age and sex as determinants of reminiscence in children. Jitendra Mohan *et al Asian J Psychology and Education* 7(3) 1981 p 1-7 refs

Profile of Indian child. Alan F. Cass *Asian J Psychology and Education (Special)* 10(1-4) 1982 p 13-16

Relation between physique and intelligence among socio-culturally advantaged and deprived children of class VII. S. Patel and S.K. Mahapatra *J Educational Research and Extension* 19(3) Ja 1983 p 150-54

Research on family as a determinant of child's personality development. G.R. Sharma *J Educational Research and Extension* 17(3) Ja 1981 p 185-90

The secure and insecure children. Rita Sinha *J Indian Education* 8(1) My

1982 p 19-22 refs

Social maturity of children in India. Pramila Sinha *Indian Educational Rev* 18(1) Ja 1983 p 1-11 tabs

Socio-economic status, anthropometric measures and biochemical variables. M.K. Raina and Arunima Vats *Indian Educational Rev* 19(1) Ja 1984 p 52-59

Sociology of psychological weaning. Banshi Lal Swami *Educational Rev* 86(11) Nv 1986 p 207-09

Studies on the social maturity of the Indian child. Sreelakshmi Gururaja *Indian Educational Rev* 16(2) Ap 1981 p 119-24 refs

A study of moral judgement in children. G. Gopaliah *Experiments in Education* 8(11) Ja 1981 p 205-10 refs

A study of the personality characteristics of mentally retarded and normal children. S.P. Ahluvalia and M. Deouskfer *Our Education* 5 Jl 1984 p 51-67 refs

Study of personality of academic achievement of children. Jitendra Mohan *et al J Education and Psychology* 39(3) Oc 1981 p 163-68 refs

Superstitions among school children. Sumitra L. Patel *Educational Rev* 90(5-6) My-Je 1984 p 88-90 tabs

Tactual short term memory of blind and sighted children. V.K. Kool and M. Rana *Asian J Psychology and Education (Special)* 10(1-4) 1982 p 24-32

Teachers' role in pupils mental development : A psychoanalytic approach. K.S. Venkataramu *Educational Rev* 88(9) Se 1982 p 145-47

Training personnel for educating young children. Sunita Kaul and Neena Kapoor *J Indian Education* 12(3) Se 1986 p 53-57 refs

See also

Adolescence
Adolescent Psychology
Children, First-born
Cognition : Child Psychology
Education, Preschool
Education of Children
Emotional Problems of Children
Exceptional Children
Handicapped Children
Mental Tests
Nursery Schools
Parent and Child
Perception : Child Psychology
Problem Children
Reasoning : Child Psychology
Underachievers

Child Welfare

Child's Year and tomorrows world. Asoke Sen *Education Quarterly* 31(3-4) Oc 1979-Ja 1980 p 13-15

See also

Foster Home Care

Child Welfare : India

Law and the national policy for child welfare : Focus on education and

Jl 1984 p 26-32

Children : Law

See also

Juvenile Delinquency

Children : Management

Attitude of women participants towards integrated child development services (ICDS). Suman Bhatnagar and Asha Singhal *Indian J Extension Education* 20(3-4) Se-De 1984 p 67-68 refs

Parenting on dimensions of economic well being culture and education. M.S. Chauhan *et al Asian J Psychology and Education* 6(3) Nv 1980 p 17-22 refs

See also

Discipline of Children

Problem Children

Children : Nutrition

Child health and nutrition. Y.R. Reddi and M. Nagaraj Rao *Indian Education* 9(10-11) Ja-Fe 1980 p 40-42

Profile of nutritional status of children of the marginal farmers and agricultural labourers in Delhi villages. Rekha Bhagat and S. Koshy *Indian J Extension Education* 20(3-4) Se-De 1984 p 43-47 tabs

Some aspects of nutrition education associated with feeding infants and toddlers in rural farm families. S. Koshy and R. Bhagat *Indian J Adult Education* 41(3) Mr 1980 p 15-19

Children : Nutrition : India : Tamil Nadu

Nutritious meal programme of Tamil Nadu. K. Venkatasubramanian *EPA Quarterly Bulletin* 5(3-4) Oc 1982-Ja 1983 p 1-13 refs tabs

Children : Vocabulary

See

Children : Language

Children : Writing

A study of the effectiveness of the programme for improvement of children's hand-writing. J.D. Bhal *Progress of Education* 60(8) Mr 1986 p 174-78 + tabs

Children, Abnormal and Backward

See

Exceptional Children

Handicapped Children

Children, Backward

See

Mentally Handicapped Children

Children, Books and Reading for

See

Books and Reading for Children

Children, Deaf

Adaptation in instructional material : A prime need for hearing impaired children in IED. Premlata Sharma *J Indian Education* 12(2) Jl 1986 p 54-59

Teaching deaf and hard of hearing children. J.T. Jaya Prasad Rao *Progress of Education* 56(12) Jl 1982 p 289-303+ refs

Children, First-born : India : Rajasthan

Personality characteristics of first-born children of Rajasthan. Beena Thadani and B.S. Raizada *Educational Rev* 92(4) Ap 1986 p 75-77 refs tabs

Children, Indian : UK : Education

Indian children in English schools : A study in cultural context. John E. Owen *Educational Rev* 92(8) Ag 1986 p 121-25

Children, Isolated

Isolated children : A psychological study. Ramnath Kundu and Basuchara Maiti *Indian Educational Rev* 20(2) Ap 1985 p 28-38

Children Books

See

Children Literature

Illustrated Books : Children

Children Illustrated Books

See

Illustrated Books : Children

Children Literature

Children books : Some evaluation criteria. Arun Kumar Gupta and Rajni Patha *Education Quarterly* 33(2) Ap 1981 p 24-26

Childrens literature in India. Indira Kulshreshtha *Teacher Today* 24(2) Oc-De 1981 p 10-18 refs

Children literature : Preparation and selection. Indira Kulshrestha *Education Quarterly* 35(4)oc 1983 p 37-40

Evaluation criteria for story books for the age group six to ten years. Ameeta Fozdar and Veena Murthy *Quest in Education* 16(2) Ap 1979 p 142-48

Humanising experiences for young children through literature. Margaret Varma *Primary Teacher* 5(3) Jl 1980 p 5-9

The impact of juvenile literature. Arun Kumar Gupta and Rajni Patra *J Indian Education* 6(6) Mr 1981 p 3-8 refs

Literature for children. Jagannath Mohanty *Primary Teacher* 8(4) Oc 1983 p 14-17 refs

Mental and physical development of a child through children's literature. *Primary Teacher* 6(1) Ja 1981 p 15-18

Unesco citing Venezuelean example, turns the spotlight on children's books. *J Indian Education* 5(4) Mr 1979 p 66-69

Value education through children's literature. Indira Kulshreshtha *Education Quarterly* 38(3) Aut 1986 p 18-27

Want to buy children's books? Indira Kulshreshtha *Teacher Today* 27(4) Ap-Je 1985 p 27-33

Writing of children's literature can shape the life of a child. Rekha Das *Primary Teacher* 5(4) Oc 1980 p 12-14

See also

Books and Reading for Children

Picture-books for Children

Story-telling

Children Literature : Curricula

The literature curriculam. Marlow Ediger *Progress of Education* 58(9) Ap 1984 p 202-07

Children Literature : Indian
Children's literature in India. Indira Kulshrestha *Teacher Today* 24(2) Oc-De 1981 p 10-18 refs
Children Stories
See
Story-telling
China (People's Republic)
See
Adult Education : China (People's Republic)
Education : China (People's Republic)
Education, Elementary : China (People's Republic)
Education, Higher : China (People's Republic)
Education, Primary : China (People's Republic)
Education and State : China (People's Republic)
Moral Education : China (People's Republic)
Television in Education : China (People's Republic)
Choice : Psychological Aspects
See also
Risk Taking : Psychological Aspects
Choice of Books
See
Books and Reading
Choice of Non-Book Materials
See
Selection of Non-Book Materials
Choice of Profession
See
Vocational Guidance
Church Colleges : India : Kerala
Christian colleges in Kerala. *New Frontiers in Education* 12(4) Oc-De 1982 p 73-116
Citizenship Education : India
Moral education and citizenship. Verghese Chandy *Educational Rev* 86(3) Mr 1980 p 59
Civic Education
See
Education, Civic
Civil Engineering : Study and Teaching
See
Engineering : Study and Teaching
Civilisation and Science
See
Science and Civilisation
Classification of School Children
See
Ability Grouping in Education
Classroom Management
Affective dimension of classroom instruction in relation to a few teacher variables. A.S. Raghavakumari *Quest in Education* 17(4) Oc 1980

p 327-37 refs

Affective tone in the primary classroom. J.K. Pillai *Indian Education* 16(3) Jl 1981 p 35-43

Classroom composition : What is the objective? *Primary Teacher* 6(4) Oc 1981 p 29-31

Cognitive behaviour of teachers in the classroom. N.K. Jangira and Madhu Raizada *J Indian Education* 7(3) Se 1979 p 32-37 refs tabs

Dimensions of classroom behaviour. Verghese Chandy *Experiments in Education* 6(2) Ap 1978 p 26-27

Dimensions of classroom behaviour. Verghese Chandy *Experiments in Education* 10(7) Se 1982 p 134+

Dimensions of classroom management. Jyoti Christian *Educational Rev* 89(7) Jl p 105-06

Dimensions of teacher classroom behaviour and their relationship with demographic and professional factors : A review of researches. S.P. Malhotra *Progress of Education* 54(2) Se 1979 p 26-28

Dogmatism and teaching experiences as determinants of pupil control ideology. K.A. Gandhi *J Education and Psychology* 38(3) Oc 1980 p 189-93 refs tabs

Effective classroom management : A teacher guide. London, Collin. 1984 119p. £11.95 *Book Rev, J Indian Education* 10(5) Ja 1985 p 55-57

Effective classroom management : A teachers guide. Robert Uslett and Colin Smith. New York, Nicholas Pub Co. 1984. *Book Rev, Teacher Today* 28(3) Ja-Mr 1986 p 103-04

Efficient classroom management. Pritam Singh Brar *Educational Rev* 88(1) Ja 1982 p 1-3

A factorial study of process variables of teacher classroom behaviour and product variables of pupils reaction. S.P. Malhotra *Quest in Education* 18(1) Ja 1981 p 4-12 refs

Forming good habits. S.L. Makkar *Primary Teacher* 10(2) Ap 1985 p 21-22

An investigation of the relationship between the effective entry characteristics and comments and letter grades on classroom performance. K. Sudha Rao *Indian Educational Rev* 15(2) Ap 1980 p 11-21

Making classroom construction interesting. M.M. Prahallada *Primary Teacher* 10(2) Ap 1985 p 4-5

Measurements of non-verbal communication in the classroom : A review. S.P. Ahluwalia and Rakesh Jain *J Institute of Educational Research* 10(1) Ja 1986 p 25-30 refs

Operate learning classroom applications. Devendra Srivastava *Teacher Education* 14(12-13) Jl-Oc 1980 p 48-56 refs

Problems of overcrowded classes : A pilot study. Usha Rao *Indian Educational Rev* 15(4) Oc 1980 p 107-12

Relationship between teachers classroom verbal behaviour and their attitudes towards teaching. Tahira Khatoon *J Institute of Educational Research* 10(3) Se 1986 p 5-8 refs tabs

Research on classroom climate. L.P. Singh *Indian Educational Rev* 16(3) Jl 1981 p 27-34

Role of classroom management behaviour in teaching effectiveness.

Sushma Sharma *Primary Teacher* 10(1) Ja 1985 p 16-18

Scaling of some important classroom behaviour attributes of college teachers. Sheela Mangla *J Educational Research and Extension* 20(2) Oc 1983 p 139-52

Search for teacher behaviour. Ajit Singh *Teacher Today* 28(3) Ja-Mr 1986 p 1-5 refs

Secondary school teachers attitude towards teaching in relations to their classroom behaviour : A study. Ajit Singh *J Indian Education* 6(6) Mr 1981 p 12-15

Secondary school teachers classroom behaviour in relation to their perceived self : A study. Ajit Singh *J Indian Education* 5(6) Mr 1980 p 20-24 refs tabs

Structural characteristics of classroom questions, pupils responses and pupil response management behaviour of social studies teachers. N.K. Jangira *J Indian Education* 8(2) Jl 1982 p 33-39 refs tabs

A study of correlation between classroom verbal and non-verbal behaviour components. Rakesh Jain *Educational Rev* 90(3) Mr 1984 p 56-58 refs

Teacher adjustment as related to his classroom behaviour. S.P. Malhotra *Asian J Psychology and Education* 9(4) 1982 p 36-41

Teachers perception of their classroom learning climate : A study. J.S. Malik *Progress of Education* 57(8) Mr 1983 p 173-76

Teachers' role as a mender of classroom structure. Jasobanta Roy *Our Education* 5 Jl 1984 p 69-72 refs

Towards a performance based classroom. Lalit Kishana *Primary Teacher* 8(4) Oc 1983 p 23-25

Verbal and non-verbal classroom behaviours as related to teachers first and second order factors of personality. A.R. Bisht *Indian Educational Rev* 20(3) Jl 1985 p 79-90

Clinical Psychology

Clinical psychology and leisure. S.K. Varma *Asian J Psychology and Education (Special Number)* 8 1981 p 1-24 refs tabs

Clubs

See also

Rural Youth Clubs

Youth Clubs

Co-education

Problems of girls in co-educational institutions. Kamala Rai *National J Education* 7(1) Se 1984 p 29-38 refs tabs

Cognition

Cognition development and learning. J.I. Alamina *Progress of Education* 58(9) Ap 1984 p 214-20 refs

Cognitive complexity and approval motivation. N.K.M. Tripathi *J Education and Psychology* 36(1-2) Ap-Je 1978 p 71-77; 37(4) Ja 1980 p 225-30 refs

Reduction of cognitive; affective imbalance : An experiment. S. Bhaskara *Experiments in Education* 6(11) Ja 1979 p 200-01

A study of cognitive tasks in relation to intelligence and school achievement. Harish Sharma and Veena Aggrawal *J Institute of Educational Research* 4(3) Se 1980 p 36-41 refs

See also
Risk-taking : Psychological Aspects
Cognition : Child Psychological Aspects
Cognitive development and the communicative matters. *Experiments in Education* 13(12) Fe 1986 p 215-17
Cognitio-affecto development of high school students : Piagetion perspective. T.S. Sandhu *Indian Educational Rev* 20(3) Jl 1985 p 32-36
Designing classroom instruction through students congnitive styles : A practical approach. Subhash Chandra Agarwal *Quest in Education* 19(1) Ja 1982 p 35-41 refs tabs
Jean Piaget on congnitive development of child. G.N. Prakash Srivastava *Asian J Psychology and Education (Special)* 10(1-4) 1982 p 40-48 refs
Simultaneous and successive cognitive processes. J.P. Dass *et al.* New York. Academic Press, 1979. £17.50 *Book Rev, Indian Educational Rev* 17(4) Oc 1982 p 147-52
Collagen Diseases
See also
Lupus Erythematosus
College Admissions
See
Universities and Colleges : Admission
College Autonomy
See
University Autonomy
College and School Periodicals
Improving school education : The role of magazines. S.R. Deb *J Indian Education* 11(3) Se 1985 p 55-57
School magazine : Problem and remedies. Debasish Paul *J Indian Education* 11(3) Se 1985 p 58-60
Synthesis of a school magazine. G.S. Jolly *J Indian Education* 11(3) Se 1985 p 48-54
What ails our school and college magazine. Adarsh Sharma *J Indian Education* 11(3) Se 1985 p 61-62
College Community Centres
See
Student Unions
College Faculty
See
College Teachers
Universities and Colleges : Faculty
College Libraries
See
Libraries, University and College
College Life
See
College Students
College Periodicals
See
College and School Periodicals

College Personnel : Management

Morale of personnel in agricultural universities. Amar Singh and C. Prasad *Indian Educational Rev* 15(4) Oc 1980 p 91-96

College Students

Contact personality factors of science, agricultural science and agricultural engineering undergraduate students. Usha Kamawat and G.C. Rai *Indian J Extension Education* 19(3-4) Se-De 1983 p 26-31 refs tabs

Faculty leadership styles and intellectual commitment among college students. Chitra Srivastava and Sushila Singhal *J Higher Education* 6(1-3) 1980-81 p 131-36 tabs

The level of activism : A comparative study of male and female college students. J.S. Jha and Vineeta Gel *J Educational Research and Extension* 19(3) Ja 1983 p 162-66

A scale to measure the attitude of college students towards strike. B.S. Siddaramaiah *et al J Education and Psychology* 36(4) Ja 1979 p 200-02

Self concept of high achieving and low achieving students of first year classes of colleges. H.G. Deson and D.A. Uchar *J Educational Research and Extension* 19(3) Ja 1983 p 155-61

Social responsibility in college students. Jyoti Verma *Indian Educational Rev* 18(2) Ap 1983 p 69-74

Student attitudes towards college *vis-a-vis* university. S.B. Kakkar *J Higher Education* 4(2) Aut 1978

A survey on vocational expectations of junior college students. P.L. Nankar *Research Bulletin* 12(3-4) Se-De 1982 p 44-48

See also

Women College Students

College Students : India

War mindedness and aggression amongst Indian university students. Sushila Agarwal *Bharatiya Shiksha Shodh Patrika* 5(2) Jl-De 1986 p 47-52 refs

College Students : India : Bihar

A study in anxiety level of Santal (tribal) and non-Santal (non-tribal) undergraduate students of Santal Pargans. Lal Bahadur Singh *J Institute of Educational Research* 4(1) Ja 1980 p 20-22 refs tabs

College Students : India : Rajasthan

Dominant job values and preferences of undergraduate students. U. Kamawat and G.C. Rai *National J Education* 7(1) Se 1984 p 39-50 refs tabs

College Students : India : Tamil Nadu

Locus of control and level of anxiety among college students. G. Rajmohan *J Educational Research and Extension* 17(3) Ja 1981 p 178-84 refs tabs

College Students : India : Uttar Pradesh

Adjustment problems of non-professional college students. G.R. Sharma *J Higher Education* 4(2) Aut 1978 p 262-66

College Students : Psychology

Neuroticism and extraversion of university student dissidents and non-dissidents. P.S. Wadhwa and C.L. Kundu *Asian J Psychology and Education* 14(1-4) 1984 p 52-56 refs

College Students : Social and Economic Status

See

College Students Socio-Economic Status

College Students : Socio-Economic Status

Background variables of the scheduled castes and tribes college students : A comparative study. M.S. Ameerjan *Indian Educational Rev* 19(2) Ap 1984 p 28-36

College Teachers

College teachers compared with engineers, doctors and lawyers in personality factors. J. Stephen and S. Sethiagirirajan *J Educational Research and Extension* 18(3) Ja 1982 p 187-90 refs tabs

The crisis of professoriate. Phillip G. Altbach *J Higher Education* 5(3) Spr 1980 p 317-30 refs

Integrating education with development in the community : Role of university teachers. M.S. Yadav *et al New Frontiers in Education* 14(2) Ap-Je 1984 p 43-51

Motivational profile or college teachers. J.K. Pillai *Indian Educational Rev* 15(1) Ja 1980 p 115-18

Professional preparation of college teachers. G.M. Patted and G.B. Mends *Quest in Education* 16(2) Ap 1979 p 114-29

Psychological needs of college teachers. Haribhai G. Desai *J Higher Education* 1(2) Aut 1975 p 250-53

Science and non-science college teachers : An analysis of personality traits. N. Muthiah and S. Jaleel Saheb *National J Education* 2(2) Mr 1980 p 1-5 refs

Social, economic and academic awareness and position of colleagiate teachers : A study. U. Lakshminarayana and A. Vizaya Dattatreya Sarma *J Higher Education* 5(3) Spr 1980 p 395-405 tabs

A study into the role diffusion experienced by junior lecturers. Sree Ramamurthy *Quest in Education* 16(4) Oc 1979 p 275-98

A study of scientific attitude of college teachers. S. Jaleel Saheb and S. Sathiyagirirajan *J Higher Education* 4(3) Spr 1979 p 387-92

See also

Universities and Colleges : Faculty

College Teachers : Africa

How much role conflict is there in the job of university lecturer : An international comparison. Christopher Orpen *J Higher Education* 7(3) Spr 1982 p 260-66 refs

College Teachers : Attitudes

Scalings of some important classroom behaviour attributes of college teachers. Sheela Mangla *J Educational Research and Extension* 20(2) Oc 1983 p 139-52

College Teachers : India

Teachers in higher education : A review of their problems and status. R.P. Singh *Education Quarterly* 37(1) Spr 1985 p 4-11

College Teachers : India : Andhra Pradesh

Job satisfaction of college teachers : Venkata Rami Reddy *J Education and Psychology* 38(4) Ja 1981 p 211-18 refs tabs

The image of the personality profile of college teachers. N.Venkataiah

Experiments in Education 11(4) Je 1983 p 66-68

Variations in economic position of college teachers by college management, sex and caste. V.V. Ramana and C.R. Prasad Rao *J Higher Education* 9(2) Aut 1983 p 259-68 refs

College Teachers : India : Bihar

Value orientation among teachers of constituent and affiliated colleges of Bihar. Ashok K. Singh *Educational Rev* 91(5-6) My-Je 1985 p 81-83 refs tabs

College Teachers : India : Chandigarh

Role structure of teachers in relation to modernisation : A study of college teachers in Chandigarh. N.N. Pangotra *National J Education* 5(1) Se 1982 p 5-14 refs

College Teachers : India : Tamil Nadu

Job satisfaction of college teachers relationship with age and experience and sex differences. N. Muthaiah *Experiments in Education* 8(12) Fe 1981 p 218-20 tabs

Need gratification of college teachers. G. Amaladass and S. Sathiyagirirajan *J Educational Research and Extension* 18(4) Ap 1982 p 236-46 refs tabs

Relationship between profession perception and levels of knowledge competence of the college teachers. S. Sathiyagirirajan *J Educational Research and Extension* 18(4) Ap 1982 p 220-23 refs tabs

College Teachers : India : Uttar Pradesh

Job satisfaction and organisational climate among university teachers. S.K. Srivastava *J Higher Education* 9(2) Aut 1983 p 251-54

Value structure of higher education and the university teachers. Sunita Gupta *J Higher Education* 9(2) Aut 1983 p 254-59 refs

College Teachers : Nigeria

How much role conflict is there in the job of university lecturer : An international comparison. Christopher Orpen *J Higher Education* 7(3) Spr 1982 p 260-66 refs

College Teachers : Recruiting

The recruitment and training of university teachers. Armand Hacquaert. Ghent, IAUPL. *Book Rev, Teacher Today* 26(4) Ap-Je 1984 p 91-94 tabs

College Teachers : Salaries, Pensions, etc.

Implications of grades for university teachers. D.G. Samant *J Higher Education* 4(2) Aut 1978 p 271-73

College Teachers : Training

Guidelines in the implementation of faculty improvement programme pertaining to teachers in affiliated colleges. *J Higher Education* 1(2) Aut 1975 p 273-77

A short training programme in question writing for college teachers. D. Raja Ganesan *J Higher Education* 5(2) Aut 1979 p 255-60

College Teaching

College teaching in India : A academic function, a personal relationship or coaching for examinations. J Filella *J Higher Education* 3(3) Spr 1978 p 321-31 refs ft-n tabs

Effective college teaching. N.K. Upasani. Bombay, SNDT Women's Univ. 1980. 100p. *Book Rev, Progress of Education* 55(12) Jl 1981 p 338

Some dilemmas in college teaching. Ruldolf Heredia *New Frontiers in*

Education 16(3) Jl-Se 1986 p 30-33
Tent drain inside universities. Muthyalayya Naidu *Educational Rev* 86(2) Fe 1980 p 31-33

College Unions
See
Student Unions

Colleges
See
Universities and Colleges

Colour and Form Recongnition Test
Colour and colour combination. Kalyan Banerjee *Primary Teacher* 15(3) Jl 1980 p 18-22

Commercial Education
See
Business Education

Commercial Schools
See
Business Education

Communalism
Communalism and the role of the teachers. Brundaban Ch Mishra *Experiments in Education* 12(11) Ja 1985 p 202-06

Communication
Communication : Concepts and skills. K.C. Peter *New Frontiers in Education* 12(1) Ja-Mr 1982 p 54-79 refs
See also
Language Arts
Mass Media

Communication Arts
See
Language Arts

Communication in Agriculture
See also
Agriculture : Information Services

Communication in Agriculture : India : Andhra Pradesh
Communication behaviour of extension personnel with regard to modern rice technology. A. Ramesh Babu and B.P. Sinha *Indian J Extension Education* 21(3-4) Jl-De 1985 p 11-15 tabs

Communication in Agriculture : India : Bihar
Communication pattern of farm scientists. C.K. Ambastha *Indian J Extension Education* 16(1-2) Je 1980 p 34-38 tabs

Communication in Agriculture : India : Himachal Pradesh
The strength of communication dyads and differential adoption in two villages. Gummadi Appa Rao *Indian J Extension Education* 17(3-4) Se-De 1981 p 31-38 refs tabs

Communication in Agriculture : India : Karnataka
Indirect influence of print information under different communication situation on non-participant literate and illiterate farmers. M.B. Channegowda and K.A. Jalihal *Indian J Extension Education* 20(1-2) Je 1984 p 62-65 tabs

Relative effectiveness of combinations of radio, slide show and film show : An experimental evidence. B.S. Siddaramaiah and B. Rajanna *Indian J Extension Education* 20(1-2) Je 1984 p 7-11 refs tabs

Communication in Agriculture : India : Madhya Pradesh

Communication patterns of agricultural scientists : A path analysis. Y.C. Sanoria and K.N. Singh *Indian J Extension Education* 16(1-2) Je 1980 p 39-45 refs tabs

Communicaton in Agriculture : India : Punjab

Effectiveness of some selected modes of communication in imparting knowledge to the members of ladies Charcha Mandals of Ludhiana district. Neelam Bhardwaj and B.S. Hansra *Indian J Extension Education* 19(1-2) Mr-Je 1983 p 99-103 tabs

Communication in Agriculture : India : Tamil Nadu

Communication behaviour of garden land and dry land farmers. K. Vijayaragavan and V.S. Subramanyan *Indian J Extension Education* 16(1-2) Je 1980 p 77-81 tabs

Correlates of interpersonal communication behaviour of farmers in differentially progressive villages. C. Bhaskaran and M.K. Sethu Rao *Indian J Extension Education* 21(3-4) Jl-De 1985 p 16-22 refs tabs

Socio-psychological factors associated with communication behaviour of farmers. K. Vijayaragavan and V.S. Subramanyan *Indian J Extension Education* 17(3-4) Se-De 1981 p 22-30 refs tabs

Communication in Agriculture : India : West Bengal

Channels preference for agricultural messages. Pradip Kumar Dey *Indian J Extension Education* 17(3-4) Se-De 1981 p 17-21 refs tabs

Perceived attributes of messages and communication fidelity. S. Pathak and A.K. Mazumdar *Indian J Extension Education* 21(3-4) Jl-De 1985 p 23-32 refs tabs

Communication in Education

Communication in pedagogy. Gomathi Mani *Experiments in Education* 8(7) Se 1980 p 124-26

Communication media and professional education. K.K. Das *Educational Rev* 86(7) Jl 1980 p 127- 29

Developing communication skills in teachers. Hans Raj Pal *Education Quarterly* 32(3) Jl 1980 p 28-29

Effective communication for positive human relations. Marlow Ediger *Primary Teacher* 10(1) Ja 1985 p 1-6

Mass media in education. R.N. Safaya *Educational Rev* 86(6) Je 1980 p 116-17

Measurement of non-verbal communication in the classroom; a review article. S.P. Ahluwalia and Rakesh Jain *J Institute of Educational Research* 10(1) Ja 1986 p 25-30 refs tabs

Rationalising communication strategy in college classes. V. Subramaniam *J Higher Education* 5(3) Spr 1980 p 335-42

The role of media in education. Arun K. Gupta *Educational Quarterly* 35(1) Ja 1983 p 9-11

Transformation analysis. D.G. Samant and C.V. Bhimasankaran *Progress of Education* 50(3) Oc 1981 p 62-65

See also
Non-verbal Communication

Community and Schools

The community schools. Sunil Behari Mohanty *Educational Rev* 85(2) De 1979 p 238-39 refs

The concept of working with the community. N.N. Prahallada *J Indian Education* 12(4) Nv 1986 p 27-31

Materials and curriculum for community education. R. Rajan *Educational Rev* 92(8) Ag 1986 p 137-38

Community and Schools : India

An investigation into the problems and prospects of school community cooperation for demonstration and improvement of education. J. Mohanty *Experiments in Education* 8(1) Mr 1980 p 16-22 refs tabs

Progressive students in community education : An appraisal. Jayanath Pathy *J Higher Education* 7(3) Spr 1982 p 315-17

Community and Teachers

See
Teacher and Community

Community Colleges

See
Municipal Universities and Colleges

Community Development

Evolving new extension and training strategies for rural development. Praya Mehta *Indian J Extension Education* 19(1-2) Mr-Je 1983 p 1-11 refs

Role of mass media in rural development. R. Srinivasa Rao *Experiments in Education* 6(12) Fe 1979 p 205-06

Rural development : A common sense approach. Eduardo Febbro *University News* 23(24) 8 Se 1985 p 2+

Strategies for rural development. *J Indian Education* 5(2) Jl 1979 p 65-67

Systems approach to community development : An empirical analysis. Ansuya T. Sheth *Indian J Adult Education* 45(4) Ap 1984 p 26-29

Community Development : Asia

Educational rural development in Asia. Udai Pareek. New Delhi, Oxf-IBH. 232p. *Book Rev, New Frontiers in Education* 13(1) Ja-Mr 1983 p 73-74

Community Development : India

Evolving new extension and training for rural development. Prayag Mehta *Indian J Extension Education* 19(1-2) Mr-Je 1983 p 1-11 refs tabs

Management of agriculture and rural development. K.N. Singh *Indian J Extension Education* 21(1-2) Ja-Je 1985 p 1-9

Management of agriculture and rural development programme : Problems and prospects. K.P.A. Menon *Indian J Extension Education* 21(1-2) Ja-Je 1985 p 10-19

Recommendations of the national seminar on management of agriculture and rural development programme. *Indian J Extension Education* 21(1-2) Ja-Je 1985 p 94-98

Women and rural development. M.S. Swaminathan *New Frontiers in Education* 12(3) Jl-Se 1982 p 56-63

See also
Integrated Rurai Development Programme

Community Development : India : Gujarat

Experiments in community development through early childhood intervention experiences of the department of child development. Amita Verma *Quest in Education* 19(1) Ja 1982 p 7-20 refs

Community Development : India : Maharashtra

Rural development in Ralegan Siddhi : A case study G.K. Sawant and H.S. Bhoite *Indian J Extension Education* 21(1-2) Ja-Je 1985 p 61-64

Community Life

See also

Community and School

Comparative Education

Contemporary issues in comparative education. Keith Wetson and Raymond Wilson. Kent, Croom Helm. 227p. £15.95 *Book Rev, Educational Quarterly* 38(3) Aut 1986 p 51

Fourth world congress of comparative education. *J Indian Education* 6(4) Nv 1980 p 54-56

Competitive Examinations

A guide book for competitive examinations. A.R. Ponkshi. Pune, Vidyarthi Griha Pra. 148p. Rs.20 Book Rev, *Progress of Education* 54(10-11) My-Je 1980 p 214+

Comprehension

See also

Listening

Reading comprehension

Compulsory School Attendance

See

Educational Law and Legislation

Computer in Education

Computer assisted instruction. D.K. Sharma and Chandra Garg *J Indian Education* 5(4) Nv 1979 p 17-22 refs tabs

Computers and education. Marlow Ediger *New Frontiers in Education* 13(2) Ap-Je 1983 p 40-44

Computers in education. Lalit Kishore *Indian Education* 13(12) Mr 1984 p 8-9

Computer in the curriculum. Marlow Ediger *Experiments in Education* 11(3) My 1983 p 48-49

Indian educational system : The role of computers. Arun K. Gupta *J Indian Education* 10(5) Ja 1985 p 1-5

Mini calculators and the learner. Marlow Ediger *Experiments in Education* 11(6) Ag 1983 p 103-04

Microcomputers in the classroom. Alan Maddison. London,Hodder. 1982. 189p. £3.95 *Book Rev, Teacher Today* 27(2) Oc-De 1984 p 96-97

Role of computers in education. Asha Jindal *Education Quarterly* 38(2) Sum 1986 p 8-12

The use of computers in education. A.B.L. Srivastava and Satvir Singh *J Indian Education* 8(2) Jl 1982 p 3-11 refs

Computers

Computer for beginners. V.K. Jain. Delhi, Pustak Mahal. 1985, 151p. Rs.20 *Book Rev, J Indian Education* 12(3) Se 1986 p 63-64

Fundamental of computing. Neil A. Sheldon. London, Hutchinson. 128p. *Book Rev, Educational Quarterly* 38(3) Aut 1986 p 46

Concept Formation

See

Concepts

Concepts

Comparison of reception and selection strategies of concept attainment. D.N. Sansanwal *et al J Institute of Educational Research* 10(2) My 1986 p 12-15 refs

Concept development in children. S. Narayan Rao. Tripathi, Sri Venkateswara Univ. 1977. *Book Rev, J Indian Education* 6(2) Jl 1980 p 77-78

Formation of concepts in children. J.P. Gupta *Primary Teacher* 11(2) Ap 1986 p 5-12

Teaching of concepts in early years. K.B. Rath *Primary Teacher* 8(2) Ap 1983 p 22-25

Conduct of Life

See

Honesty

Self-respect

Conference of Education Ministers of States and Union Territories, New Delhi, 1981

Conference of Education Ministers of States and Union territories New Delhi, June 2, 1981 : address by Shri S.B. Chavan *Education Quarterly* 33(4) Oc 1981 p 1-6

Conference of Education Ministers of States and union territories, New Delhi, June2 1981 : address by Smt. Indira Gandhi. *Education Quarterly* 33(4) Oc 1981 p 7-9

Configuration : Psychological Aspects

See

Gestalt Psychology

Conflict : Psychological Aspects

Attitude of creative persons towards conflicting situations. Rita Sinha *J Education and Psychology* 41(1-2) Ap-Jl 1983 p 23-25

Conflict of Generations

Conflict between immigrant mother daughter in United Kingdom. Shamim F. Karim *Asian J Psyhology and Education* 7(2) Jl 1981 p 1-11

See also

Parent and Child

Consciousness

Consciousness : Raising education. Sahdev Kumar *Bharatiya Shiksha Shodh Patrika* 4(2) Jl-Oc 1985 p 21-25 refs

The lotus in the stone : An allegory for explorations in dreams and consciousness. Sahdev Kumar. Delhi, Motilal. 211p. Rs.135 *Book Rev, Bhartiya Shiksha Shodh Patrika* 4(2) Jl-De 1985 p 45-47

See also

Personality

Personality Tests

Ap-Je 1986 p 6-11

Distance education - Problems of coordination, cooperation and functional autonomy. S.K. Gupta *J Higher Education* 7(3) Spr 1982 p 237-42 refs

Distant study systems in science education. S.K. Gupta *EPA Quarterly Bulletin* 8(3-4) Oc 1985-Ja 1986 p 39-44

Effective pupil evaluation in distance learning systems conspectus and considerations. Arun K. Gupta and Renu Arun *University News* 24(42) 8 Nv 1986 p 91-96

Evaluation methodology in distance education system. A practical approach. N.L. Mishra *University News* 24(42) 8 Nv 1986 p 97-103

Genesis and the growth of distance education. K.G. Deshmukh *University News* 24(42) 8 Nv 1986 p 3-6

Instructional media for distance education. Dinesh Kumar Verma *Indian Educational Rev* 20(3) Jl 1985 p 72-78

International perpectives in distance learning - A plea for India. Santosh K. Panda *Education Quarterly* 34(1) Ja 1982 p 7-11 refs tabs

An investigation into teachers reactions to self-instruction multimedia package course. S.G. Shah *Quest in Education* 17(4) Oc 1980 p 360-66 refs

Performance as a function of anxiety and feed back in a self-instruction situations. Harish Chandra Sharma and Malvinder Ahuja *Quest in Education* 18(1) Ja 1981 p 39-45 refs

The philosophy of correspondence education. Harindra M. Singh and Santosh K. Panda *Education Quarterly* 32(4) Oc 1980 p 27-29

Regular colleges and correspondence courses. S. Dandapani *Experiments in Education* 9(5) Jl 1981 p 88-89

Role of mass media in distance education. R.S. Yadav *EPA Quarterly Bulletin* 7(3-4) Oc 1984-My 1985 p 11-12+

A study of reactions of the students of correspondence education : A synopsis. B.N. Biswal *Indian Education* 11(7) Oc 1981 p 27-29

Why distance education? James C. Taylor and Vernon J. White *Indian J Adult Education* 47(8) Ag 1986 p 2-10+

World conference on correspondence education. Bakhshish Singh *J Higher Education* 4(2) Aut 1978 p 267-68

Correspondence Schools and Courses : Administration

Management of distance education. Joginder Kaushal *University News* 24(42) 8 Nv 1986 p 21-24

Organisation and management of distance education : The delivery system. D.P. Verma *University News* 24(42) 8 Nv 1986 p 25-28

Correspondence schools and courses : Aids and Devices

Role of satellites in the promotion of distance education. T.V. Pavate *University News* 24(42) 8 Nv 1986 p 83-84

Role of audio-visual aids in distance education. R. Amutavalli *University News* 24(42) 8 Nv 1986 p 85-90 refs

Correspondence Schools and Courses : Bibliography

Distance education : A bibliography. *University News* 24(42) 8 Nv 1986 p 135-41

Correspondence Schools and Courses : Curricula

Approaches to course development in distance education. N. Jose Chander

University News 24(42) 8 Nv 1986 p 33-36 refs

Correspondence Schools and Courses : Developing Countries

Towards a framework for distance education in developing countries. S.K. Gupta *J Indian Education* 8(2) Jl 1982 p 40-43

Correspondence Schools and Courses : Finance

Finance of distance education and university level. P.K. Sahoo *University News* 24(42) 8 Nv 1986 p 119-20 refs

Financing distance education. J.L. Azad *University News* 24(42) 8 Nv 1986 p 105-10 refs

Correspondence Schools and Courses : India

Accelerating correspondence education in our country. Sant Prakash *Education Quarterly* 32(1) Ja 1980 p 19-20

Conventional and modern media in distance education. Anupama Shah *University News* 24(42) 8 Nv 1986 p 69-72 refs

Counselling in the context of distance education. Gautam Banerjee *University News* 24(42) 8 Nv 1986 p 63-67

The curse of correspondence courses in teacher education. C.S. Subbarao *Quest in Education* 19(3) Jl 1982 p 234-37

Distance education : An overview. Gunvant B. Shah *University News* 24(42) 8 Nv 1986 p 10-12

Distance education backward classes and the new social order. Hem Lata Talesra *University News* 24(42) 8 Nv 1986 p 29-31

Distance education in Indian universities : Some concerns for further development. P.K. Sahoo *Education Quarterly* 37(4) Wint 1985 p 1-10 refs

Distance education systems of the future. D.K. Sharma *University News* 24(42) 8 Nv 1986 p 55-57 refs

Distance learning : A democrative approach to non-formal education. Jagannath Mohanty *Education Quarterly* 37(4) Wint 1985 p 11-14

Educational technology in distance education. Vasant B. Bhat *University News* 24(42) 8 Nv 1986 p 79-82

Media in distance education : Need for an integrated approach. Anil Pathak *University News* 24(42) 8 Nv 1986 p 73-77 refs

Open correspondence institute India. Greville Rumble *Indian Education* 12(1-2) Ap-My 1982 p 36-40

Planning and development of distance education. Ruddar Datt *J Higher Education* 9(3) Spr 1984 p 305-14 tabs

Productivity trends on correspondence education. M.L. Gupta *J Higher Education* 8(3) Spr 1983 p 349-56 tabs

Some thoughts on the concepts and forms of distance education. Malcolm S. Adiseshiah *University News* 24(42) 8 Nv 1986 p 7-9

Status and scope of correspondence education in India. Vinod B. Patel *Progress of Education* 57(7) Fe 1983 p 146-48 + refs

The status of correspondence courses in India. Saraswathi Balasubramaniam *University News* 24(42) 8 Nv 1986 p 13-15

Student support services for distance education. Sneha M. Joshi *University News* 24(42) 8 Nv 1986 p 59-62 refs

Teaching of mathematics in distance education. J.N. Kapur *University News* 24(42) 8 Nv 1986 p 43

Work ethics for distance education. Dawoudbhai A. Ghanchi *University News* 24(42) 8 Nv 1986 p 129-31 +

Correspondence Schools and Courses : India : Andhra Pradesh

Distance education with special reference to Andhra University, Waltair. A.P.S.V.V.S.N.L. Narasimha Raju *Educational Rev* 92(12) De 1986 p 205-09

Correspondence Schools and Courses : India : Maharashtra

Report of the practice teaching programme at Gandhi Shikshan Bhavan, 1979-80. K. Patankar *Quest in Education* 17(2) Ap 1980 p 113-26

Correspondence Schools and Courses : India : Punjab

Reading comprehension of correspondence trainees. Savinder Kaur and Amarjit Singh Dhaliwal *Indian J Extension Education* 20(1-2) Je 1984 p 73-75 tabs

Correspondence Schools and Courses : India : Rajasthan

Achievement and errors in book keeping of regular and correspondence students of Rajasthan : A comparative study. N.C. Dnotia *Indian Educational Rev* 14(4) Oc 1979 p 99-106 tabs

Cotton

Technological gap in adoption of the cotton practices. S.V. Supe *et al Indian J Extension Education* 19(3-4) Se-De 1983 p 69-71

Counselling

Coaching and counselling. M. Raghuramsingh *Experiments in Education* 12(1) Mr 1984 p 3-7

Counselling of the socially disadvantaged child. Vidhu Mohan *Asian J Psychology and Education* 11(2) 1983 p 1-8

Guidance and counselling. Prem Pasricha *New Frontiers in Education* 11(4) Oc-De 1981 p 47-76; 12(1) Ja-Mr 1982 p 1-36

Research on counselor's characteristics : A summary. Gopala Krishna *Quest in Education* 16(4) Oc 1979 p 335-43

See also

Personnel Services in Education

Vocational Guidance

Counsellor-Parent Relationship

See

Parent-Student Counsellor Relationships

Courses of Study

See

Education : Curricula

Cramming

See

Study, Method of

Creation : Literary, Artist, etc.

See also

Creative Ability : Testing

Originality

Creative Ability

Contributions of Wallach and Kogan to creative research. Vadagiri Ganesan *Indian Educational Rev* 14(1) Je 1979 p 131-35

Creative and old age. Sheelendra Chauhan *et al Asian J Psychology and*

Education 11(3) 1983 p 1-4 refs

Creativity : A socio-psychological interpretation. R.J. Singh *National J Education* 7(2) My 1985 p 17-24 tab

Creativity across cultures : The Indian scene. R.J. Singh *Bharatiya Shiksha Shodh Patrika* 4(1) Ja-Je 1985 p 37-50

Creativity as a function of birth order socio-economic status and personality types. Ramji Srivastava *J Education and Psychology* 36(3) Oc 1978 p 113-17

Creativity of adolescent boys and girls in relation to some variables. A. Venkata Rami Reddy and P. Balakrishna Reddy *Indian Educational Rev* 19(1) Ja 1984 p 60-72

Development of creativity : A few methods. Gurpal Singh Jarial *Rajasthan Board J Education* 15(2) Ap-Je 1979 p 35-41

Development of creativity among students. Bhaskara Rao Digumati *Experiments in Education* 11(6) Ag 1983 p 100-03 refs

Developing creativity : The essential human trait. S.B. Malhara *J Indian Education* 10(6) Mr 1985 p 9-14

An experimental investigation of the relationship between creativity and rigidity. P. Anantha Krishnan *J Institute of Educational Research* 4(2) My 1980 p 39-41 refs tabs

Facilitation of creative thinking abilities through transcendent and mediation. D.N. Sansanwal *et al J Indian Education* 6(3) Se 1980 p 9-13 tabs

General awareness and creativity. Gurpal Singh Jarial *Experiments in Education* 7(3) My 1979 p 47-49 refs

Identifying and encouraging children's creativity. Jagannnath Mohanty *Primary Teacher* 11(3) Jl 1986 p 6-8

An investigation into the inter-actional effects of intelligence and grade levels on creativity and its components. Gurpal Singh Jarial and Ashwani Kumar Sharma *J Institute of Educational Research* 4(3) Se 1980 p 15-19 refs tabs

Is creative imagination equivalent to visual and auditory imaginations? N. Hasnain and M.G. Hussain *Asian J Psychology and Education* 6(3) Nv 1980 p 48-52 refs

Promotion of creativity and achievement by discovery method. Vandana Prasad *Indian Educational Rev* 14(4) Oc 1979 p 86-94

Relationship between creative abilities, dimensions creativity and intelligence. Vishwanath Muddu *Experiments in Education* 9(11) Ja 1982 p 189-91 refs tabs

Relationship of sex with creativity, general anxiety, vocational anxiety and teaching success. G.L. Arora *J Education and Psychology* 36(3) Oc 1978 p 133-39

A scientific view of creativity. M. Malla Reddy and Viswanath Muddu *Indian Education* 10(6) Se 1980 p 19-23

Sex differences in creativity among the tribe of Meghalaya. Gitika Dutta *J Institute of Educational Research* 6(2) My 1982 p 23-26 refs tabs

Some aspects of scientific assessment of learning achievement and creativity. J.N. Kapur *Indian Education* 10(4) Jl 1980 p 6-10; 10(5) Ag 1980 p 8-12

Some misconceptions about creativity. Gurpal Singh Jarial *Experiments in*

Education 8(3) My 1980 p 43-46

Structural ideas versus creativity in the curriculam. Marlow Ediger *Experiments in Education* 10(1) Mr 1982 p 12-14 refs

Study of creative abilities of tribal children in relation to their sex and socio-economic status. P. Krishna Kumari *et al J Institute of Educational Research* 10(1) Ja 1986 p 1-4

A study of some personality correlates of intelligence and creative abilities among high school students in Andhra Pradesh. Viswanath Muddu *Indian Education* 10(4) Jl 1980 p 19-23

Teachers role in promotion of creative talent. R.P. Singh *Teacher Education* 18(24-25) Jl-Oc 1983 p 49-52 refs

See also

Creative Thinking : Educational Aspects

Originality

Creative Ability : Child Psychology Aspects

Children and creativity. Pritam Singh Brar *Educational Rev* 88(7) Jl 1982 p 115-18

Creative child : Sikkimese teachers perception. Dinesh Sharma and A.C. Pachaury *J Indian Education* 11(1) My 1985 p 34-41 refs tab

Creativity but isn't there in the classroom. A.C. Pachaury *Progress of Education* 54(12) Jl 1980 p 229-30

Creative pupil perception by the Gujarati teachers. A.C. Pachaury *J Education and Psychology* 43(3-4) Oc 1985-Ja 1986 p 153-57 refs

Development of creative thinking abilities at the primary stage. Satish Kumar Yadav *Primary Teacher* 6(3) Jl 1981 p 11-15

An investigation into the effect of increase in some limits on the performance of children on creativity tasks. Gurpal Singh and Ashwani Kumar Sharma *Experiments in Education* 11(4) Je 1983 p 63-66

The role of sex in creative potential among adolescents. R.P. Singh *Teacher Education* 17(20-21) Jl-Oc 1982 p 46-50 refs tabs

A study of correlation among intelligence, academic achievement and creativity. R.S. Yadav *Progress of Education* 61(3) Oc 1986 p 50-53 tabs

Creative Ability : Research

Creativity research : International perspective. M.K. Raina, ed. New Delhi, NCERT. 1980, 332p. Rs. 20 *Book Rev, Teacher Today* 25(3) Ja-Mr 1983 p 109

Review of researches in creativity and achievement. Hem Chandra Deka *J Educational Research and Extension* 18(3) Ja 1982 p 182-86

Creative Ability : Testing

Creativity and its components as effected by socio-economic status and personality. Ashwani Kumar Sharma *Experiments in Education* 8(7) Se 1980 p 129-32 tab

See also

Prediction of Creative Ability

Creative Activities and Seat Work

See also

Block Building : Educational Aspects

Creative Thinking : Educational Aspects

An analysis of relationships between creativity and academic achievement

of eleventh graders. R.P. Goyal *Educational Rev* 90(5-6) My-Je 1984 p 84-87 refs

Can creativity be fostered in students? Suresh Chandra Mehta *Educational Rev* 89(8) Ag 1983 p 135-38 refs

Contribution of teacher in the development of creativity among students : A review of researches. S.P. Malhotra *Quest in Education* 18(2) Ap 1981 p 158-64

A correlation study of intelligence and various components of creativity. B.C. Mishra *Progress of Education* 60(2) Se 1985 p 36-39 refs tabs

Creative education in primary schools. Bhanwer Lal Nagda *Primary Teacher* 4(4) Oc 1979 p 31-34

Creative thinking abilities of blind school children. Bene Behari Kamila *J Education and Psychology* 41(4) Ja 1984 p 198-203 refs

Creative thinking ability as a function of sex and achievement. Syama Thrimurthy *J Education and Psychology* 44(1) Ap 1986 p 36-40 refs

Creative thinking and culture : A comparative study of tribal and non-tribal high school students of Himachal Pradesh. Kulwinder Singh *Progress of Education* 59(1) Ag 1984 p 11-17 refs tabs

Creativity and academic achievement among secondary school children. C.B. Asha *Asian J Psychology and Education* 6(1) Ja 1980 p 1-4 refs

Creativity and education. R.S. Tanwar *J Indian Education* 5(5) Ja 1980 p 58-64

Creativity and its components as effected by intelligence personality, their interaction. Gurpal Singh and A.K. Sharma *Asian J Psychology and Education* 6(2) Jl 1980 p 26-32

Creativity and mental health. Satish G. Mathur *J Education and Psychology* 39(2) Jl 1981 p 106-10

Creativity and neuroticism : A correlational analysis. Abdul Hamid Zargar *Educational Rev* 89(5-6) My-Je 1983 p 91-93 refs tabs

Creativity as a function of intelligence, socio-economic status and sex among 12th grade school students. N.K. Chadha and Arun K. Sen *J Education and Psychology* 39(1) Ap 1981 p 52-56 refs

Creativity in higher education. *New Frontiers in Education* 15(1) Ja-Mr 1985 p 98-103

Creativity in relation to adjustment. R.P. Singh *Quest in Education* 19(3) Jl 1982 p 227-33 tabs

Creativity in relation to alienation, ego strength and intelligence. D. Pestonjee and S.M. Usmani *J Education and Psychology* 40(1-2) Ap-Jl 1982 p 39-44

Creativity in relation to socio-economic status and academic achievement. Ashwani Kumar Sharma *Experiments in Education* 9(9) Nv 1981 p 153-56 refs

Creativity in students of the types of schools. B.C. Mishra *Experiments in Education* 13(11) Je 1986 p 201-04 refs

Creativity, intelligence and academic achievement : Their relationships and difference with reference to sex and academic subjects. Gurpal Singh Jarial *J Education and Psychology* 39(2) Jl 1981 p 91-96 refs

Creativity, intelligence and achievement. Krishna Kumar Gupte *Educational Rev* 85(11) Nv 1979 p 208-11

Creativity, intelligence and socio-economic status. Arun Kumar Gupta and Suresh K. Sharma *Indian Educational Rev* 17(1) Ja 1982 p 64-70 refs

Degree of neuroticism : Its relation with intelligence and creativity. Motilal Lidhoo and Abdul Hamid Zargar *Indian Educational Rev* 15(4) Oc 1980 p 86-90

Development of creative thinking in the primary school children. S. Kumar and M.J. Ravindranath *Primary Teacher* 4(1) Ja 1979 p 5-9

Education for creativity through simulation. Vasant D. Bhatt and S. Bhaskara *Education Quarterly* 35(3) Jl 1983 p 7-11 refs

Educational technology for creativity education. M.N. Deshmukh *Education Quarterly* 32(2) Ap 1980 p 13-17 refs

Educational technology for creativity education. M.N. Deshmukh *J Indian Education* 5(4) Nv 1979 p 3-11 refs

Effect of birth order upon creative thinking abilities among adolescents. Gurpal Singh Jarial *J Institute of Educational Research* 6(3) Se 1982 p 9-13 refs tabs

The effect of instructional method upon the creativity of students : A review. Gurpal Singh Jarial *Progress of Education* 55(7) Fe 1981 p 179-80 +

Effect of socio-cultural disadvantages on verbal creative thinking ability among school going children. Sultan Ahmad and R.K. Joshi *J Education and Psychology* 37(4) Ja 1980 p 231-38 tabs

Effect of socio-cultural disadvantage on verbal originality, fluency and flexibility of creativity. S. Ahmed and R.K. Joshi *J Institute of Educational Research* 8(2) My 1984 p 16-24 refs

Effects of creative teaching method upon eighth graders. G. Subramania Pillay *J Indian Education* 5(4) Nv 1979 p 12-16 refs

Experimental attitude and creativity : A correlational study. U.S. Chaudhary and V.R. Bindal *Bhartiya Shiksha Shodh Patrika* 1(2) Jl 1982 p 29-32 refs tab

A factor analysis of creative thinking of the standard students. G. Subramania Pillai and R. Palaniyandi *Experiments in Education* 10(6) Ag 1982 p 101-05 tab

A factorial study of the effect of socio-economic status (SES) adjustment and their interaction upon the creativity of high school students. Ashwani Kumar Sharma and Gurpal Singh Jarial *Experiments in Education* 9(9) Nv 1981 p 151-53 refs tabs

Fostering creativity in classrooms. Vibha Premchand *Indian Education* 11(4) Jl 1981 p 26-28

Institutional climate and creativity. Gurpal Singh Jarial and Ashwini Kumar Sharma *Experiments in Education* 8(8) Oc 1980 p 135-38 refs tabs

Instructional strategies for creativity. Kokila S. Thongaswamy *Indian Education* 16(6) Se 1981 p 23-25

Is the first born more creative? Gurpal Singh Jarial *Progress of Education* 54(4) Nv 1981 p 91-94 refs tab

Is the strategy of masterly learning helpful in improving students creative thinking abilities. R.C. Hooda and G.S. Jarial *Rajasthan Board J Education* 19(1) Ja-Mr 1983 p 12-16

Need for qualitative analysis of creative responses. R.S. Tanwar *Progress of Education* 55(7) Fe 1981 p 170-71 refs

Objectives and creativity in the curriculum. Marlow Ediger *Experiments in Education* 9(11) Ja 1982 p 191-94

The prediction of creativity : A study. R.P. Singh *Indian Educational Rev* 17(2) Ap 1982 p 20-26 refs

Relationships between creativity and intelligence of eleventh grade boys. R.P. Goyal *Progress of Education* 58(1) Ag 1983 p 13-16 tabs

The role of sex in the enhancement of creativity among adolescents through a process-oriented training programme : A study. P.C. Katiyar and Gurpal Singh Jarial *Indian Educational Rev* 18(1) Ja 1983 p 40-46 refs tabs

Sex differences in creativity in India : A second look. T.N. Raina *Indian Educational Rev* 17(3) Jl 1982 p 122-28 refs tabs

Should India neglect her creative potential? Karuna Shankar Misra *Quest in Education* 16(3) Jl 1979 p 217-21

Some testable suggestions for the study of creativity in rural children. A.K. Saxena and P. Sharma *J Education and Psychology* 39(3) Oc 1981 p 184-88

Study of creative abilities of tribal children in relation to their sex and socio-economic status. P. Krishna Kumari *et al J Institute of Educational Research* 10(1) Ja 1986 p 1-4

A study of creative thinking ability as a function of intelligence parental behaviour and redication. I.A. Vora *J Education and Psychology* 41(3) Oc 1983 p 146-52

A study of creativity in relation to sex, locality and school subjects. Prakash Chandra Shukla *Indian Educational Rev* 17(2) Ag 1982 p 128-32 refs tabs

A study of creativity in relation to sex, locality and school subjects. Prakash Chandra Shukla *J Eucational Research and Extension* 18(4) Ap 1982 p 255-58 refs tab

A study of creativity in relation to socio-economic status of high school students. R.C. Pandey *et al J Institute of Educational Research* 10(1) Ja 1986 p 9-12 refs

A study of locus of control of high and low creative high school students of different levels of socio-economic status. Lokesh K. Verma *J Education and Psychology* 38(2) Jl 1980 p 99-104 refs

Taxonomy of objectives for creative teaching. M.N. Deshmukh *Quest in Education* 18(3) Jl 1981 p 235-42 refs

Creative Thinking : Educational Aspects : Research

On the conflicting claims about the history of creativity research. R.J. Singh *J Educational Research and Extension* 17(3) Ja 1981 p 129-36 refs

Creativity

See

Creative Ability

Creativity : Educational Aspects

See

Creative Thinking : Educational Aspects

Creches : Day Nurseries

See

Day Nurseries

Crime and Criminals
See
Juvenile Delinquency
Crops
See
Field Crops
Cuba
See
Adult Education : Cuba
Culturally Handicapped Children
See
Socially Handicapped Children
Current Events
The impact of sex and academic discipline on the level knowledge of current affairs. Krishna Sehgal *Progress of Education* 53(12) Jl 1979 p 223-27 +
Curricula : Course of Study
See
Education : Curricula
Curriculum, Choice of
Characterstics of syllabus bond and syllabus free students of class X. Sushil Prakash Guptal *Quest in Education* 19(3) Jl 1982 p 187-93 refs tabs
Co-curricular interests of secondary school students. N.N. Pandey *J Institute of Educational Research* 6(3) Se 1982 p 1-8 refs tabs
Demand patterns for the courses in plus two : A case study. B. Raghuveeran *Experiments in Education* 9(6) Ag 1981 p 95-99 tabs
Interests of learners and the curriculum. Marlow Ediger *Experiments in Education* 9(8) Oc 1981 p 147-48 +
Parental influences over course selection. M. Sree Rama Murthy *Experiments in Education* 7(10) De 1979 p 179-90 + appdc refs tabs
A study of the preference of a school subject. R.R. Sharma *J Institute of Educational Research* 6(3) Se 1982 p 29-32 refs
Curriculum Change
Systems approach to curriculum improvement. M. Malla Reddy and R. Ravishankar *Indian Education* 11(1-2) Ap-My 1981 p 84-88
Curriculum Change : India
Curriculum innovation and implementation : Bridging the gap. J.K. Sood *Education Quarterly* 33(3) Jl 1981 p 17-20 refs
Curriculum Change : India : Andhra Pradesh
Curricular changes at school level in Andhra Pradesh. R. Krishna Rao and R. Papa *Primary Teacher* 8(4) Oc 1983 p 26-29
Curriculum Change : Jamaica
Towards an appropriate strategy for curriculum change in the third world : Experience from Jamaica. Zellynne D. Jenningswray *Perspective in Education* 1(3) Jl 1985 p 175-94 refs tabs
Curriculum Development
See
Curriculum Planning
Curriculum Planning
Administrators and the curriculum. Marlow Ediger *Experiments in Education*

11(9) Nv 1983 p 149-51

Commerce based socially useful and productive works. S.B. Maheswari *Rajasthan Board J Education* 20(4)-21(1) Oc 1984-Mr 1985 p 43-51

The community and the curriculum. Marlow Ediger *Education Rev* 88(10) Oc 1982 p 170-72 refs

Comprehensive evaluation of curricula : A model. Pritam Singh *J Indian Education* 11(1) My 1987 p 52-61

Curriculum development. Haribhai G. Desai *Teacher Today* 21(3) Ja-Mr 1979 p 1-5 refs

Curriculum 11-16 : A review of progress. London, HMSO. 1981, 85p. £2.95 *Book Rev, Education Quarterly* 35(1) Ja 1983 p 87

Curriculum evaluation : Concept and model. K.C.S. Jain *Rajasthan Board J Education* 15(2) Ap-Je 1979 p 13-19

A curriculum of classics. Marlow Ediger *New Frontiers in Education* 16(2) Ap-Je 1986 p 1-24

Evaluating a curriculum : The quantity central approach. Pritam Singh *J Indian Education* 12(1) My 1986 p 9-15

Evaluating the curriculum. Marlow Ediger *Experiments in Education* 12(1) Mr 1984 p 8-9

Evaluation and the curriculum. Marlow Ediger *Experiments in Education* 8(12) Fe 1981 p 224-26 refs

Extension input in curriculum for under graduate. B.N. Biswal *Quest in Education* 18(4) Oc 1981 p 302-06

Goals of curriculum in schools. Chitra Gopalakrishnan *Education Quarterly* 34(3) Jl 1982 p 20-22

Goals of curriculum in schools. Chitra Gopalakrishnan *Indian Education* 11(8-9) Nv-De 1981 p 41-45

Issues in curriculum development. Marlow Ediger *Indian Education* 10(3) Je 1980 p 5-10 refs

Language based SUPW activities. P.L. Verma *Rajasthan Board J Education* 20(4)-21(1) Oc 1984-Mr 1985 p 36-42

Leadership in curriculum development. Marlow Ediger *Experiments in Education* 9(12) Fe 1982 p 215-17 ref

The learner and the curriculum. Marlow Ediger *Experiments in Education* 8(7) Se 1980 p 117-19

Mastery learning and the curriculum. Marlow Ediger *Experiments in Education* 8(3) My 1980 p 47-49 refs

Objectives in the curriculum. Marlow Ediger *Educational Rev* 88(1) Ja 1982 p 8-10 refs

Objectives in the curriculum. Marlow Ediger *Progress of Education* 56(2) Se 1981 p 38-39 refs

Organising co-curricular activities. K. Adinarayana *Educational Rev* 86(9) Se 1980 p 175-77

Organising the curriculum. Marlow Ediger *Experiments in Education* 8(10) De 1980 p 180-85 refs

Organising the curriculum. Marlow Ediger *Experiments in Education* 11(12) Fe 1984 p 207-09

Philosophy and goals in the curriculum. Marlow Ediger *Education Quarterly* 35(1) Ja 1983 p 19-23

Philosophy of education and the reading curriculum. Marlow Ediger *Indian Education* 10(8) Nv 1980 p 8-11

The principal and the curriculum. Marlow Ediger *Progress of Education* 57(7) Fe 1983 p 159-60

A programme of curriculum and methodology for the deprived class. M.K. Pathy *Experiments in Education* 10(1) Mr 1982 p 7-13 refs

A psychological approach on the curriculum. S.P. Anand *J Indian Education* 6(5) Ja 1981 p 17-22

Reorientation of curriculum based on Gandhian values : editorial. *Quest in Education* 16(2) Ap 1979 p 87-96

Restructing of courses at degree level. P.C. Das *Progress of Education* 57(3) Oc 1982 p 60-64 + tabs

Restructing of courses. Raghunath Safaya *Educational Rev* 88(2) Fe 1982 p 37-38

Restructing the academic courses - Its significance and Implications. V. Venkateswara Rao *Progress of Education* 57(6) Ja 1983 p 133-36

Role of chemistry in socially useful productive work and community services. S.C. Bhargava *Rajasthan Board J Education* 20(4)-21(1) Oc 1984-Mr 1985 p 52-55

SUPW and CS as compulsory subject at secondary stage. J.S. Mehta *Rajasthan Board J Education* 20(4)-21(1) Oc 1984-Mr 1985 p 1-7

SUPW and its implimentation. A.K. Dhote *Rajasthan Board J Education* 20(4)-21(1) Oc 1984-Mr 1985 p 30-35

SUPW : Need, concept and objectives. C.K. Misra *Rajasthan Board J Education* 20(4)-21(1) Oc 1984 - Mr 1985 p 8-15

Selecting objectives in the curriculum. Marlow Ediger *Indian Education* 11(4) Jl 1981 p 11-14

Sequence in the curriculum. Marlow Ediger *Experiments in Education* 8(2) Ap 1980 p 27

Social context of the school curriculum : Potential and problems of comparative study. Krishna Kumar *Teacher Today* 22(1) Jl-Se 1979 p 16-19

Social influences on curriculum. G.L. Arora *J Indian Education* 9(1) My 1983 p 38-41

Social sciences : New trends in curriculum. D.N. Gaind *Education Quarterly* 35(3) Jl 1983 p 14-16

Structural ideas versus creativity in the curriculum. Marlow Ediger *Experiments in Education* 10(1) Mr 1982 p 12-14 refs

The teacher and the curriculum. Marlow Ediger *Experiments in Education* 7(9) Nv 1979 p 151-53 refs

Curriculum Planning : India

The administrator and the curriculum. Marlow Ediger *New Frontier in Education* 14(3) Jl-Se 1984 p 24-35

Curriculum development and educational technology. Malla Reddy Mamidi and S. Ravishankar. New Delhi, Sterling. *Book Rev, J Institute of Educational Research* 10(2) My 1986 p 26

Curriculum development for the Indian schools. D.R. Portia. Kakananda, Satyavani Pub. iv, 112p. *Book Rev, J Indian Education* 8(2) Jl 1982 p 93

Curriculum transaction for national intergration. N.K. Jangira *J Indian*

Education 9(1) My 1983 p 45-51

Designing school curriculum for the future. G.L. Arora *Rajasthan Board J Education* 21(3-4) Jl-De 1985

National core curriculum for Indian schools. G.L. Arora *Education Quarterly* 37(2) Sum 1985 p 27-29

National curriculum for primary and secondary education : A framework. *Teacher Today* 28(3) Ja-Mr 1986 p 72-89

Philosophical considerations and committee work in the curriculum. Marlow Ediger *Indian Educational Rev* 15(3) Jl 1980 p 94-96

Philosophical implications in the school curriculum. Marlow Ediger *Progress of Education* 57(2) Se 1982 p 35-38

A Searchlight on community need based curriculum. Vijayakumar Patnekar *Progress of Education* 55(1) Ag 1980 p 6-8

Socially useful productive work : Some thoughts on its implementation in our schools. C.B. Patyal *Asian J Psychology and Education* 6(1) Ja 1980 p 32-34

Socially useful productive work : Some thoughts on its implementation in our schools. C.B. Patyal *Progress of Education* 54(9) Ap 1980 p 186-89

Streamlining curriculum administration. B.P. Lulla *Indian Education* 11(1-2) Ap-My 1981 p 76-80

Syllabuses for inculcation of ethical and social values. *J Educational Research and Extension* 20(1) Jl 1983 p 37-84

Curriculum Planning : Sri Lanka

Curriculum development in Sri Lanka. George Mendis *Rajasthan Board J Education* 16(1-2) Ja-Je 1980 p 72-80

Curriculum Planning : United States

The future of curriculum in America : Facing conflicting expectations. Gary C. Benedict and Robert J. Gerardi *J Education and Psychology* 40(4) Je 1983 p 186-94 refs

Curriculum Research

Research in curriculum. D.R. Darji *J Institute of Educational Research* 4(1) Ja 1980 p 1-7 refs

Czechoslovakia

See

Education : Czechoslovakia

Youth : Czechoslovakia

Dairy Research : India : Haryana

Role of knowledge in adoption of dairy innovations. T.S. Sohal and K.C. Tyagi *Indian J Extension Education* 14(3-4) Jl-De 1978 p 16-25 refs

Dairying

A comparison of techniques for measuring aspiration of dairy farmers. Ram Chand and T.S. Sohal *Indian J Extension Education* 19(1-2) Mr-Je 1983 p 95-98

A study of the technical knowledge of the stockman of the ICDPIs. V.K. Dubey *et al Indian J Extension Education* 15(3-4) De 1979 p 60-63 tabs

Training need of dairy farmers. J.N. Singh *et al Indian J Extension Education* 15(3-4) De 1979 p 77-82 tabs

Dairying : India : Haryana

Antecendents of communication of dairy innovations. K.C. Tyagi and T.S. Sohal *Indian J Extension Education* 17(3-4) Se-De 1981 p 1-6 refs

Antecedents of dairy farmers empathy. K.C. Tyagi and T.S. Sohal *Indian J Extension Education* 19(1-2) Mr-Je 1983 p 51-56

A comparison of techniques for measuring aspiration of dairy farmers. Ram Chand and T.S. Sohal *Indian J Extension Education* 19(1-2) Mr-Je 1983 p 95-98 tabs

Differential dairy farming knowledge and perceived training needs of the trained and untrained farmers. K.D. Kokate and K.C. Tyagi *J Educational Research and Extension* 18(4) Ap 1982 p 201-09 refs tabs

Factors associated with adoption of dairy innovations. K.C. Tyagi and T.S. Sohal *Indian J Extension Education* 20(3-4) Se-De 1984 p 1-8 refs

Dairying : India : Karnataka

Differential adoption of improved dairy practices by small farmers, marginal farmers and agricultural labourers. M.S. Nataraju and M.B. Channegowda *Indian J Extension Education* 20(3-4) Se-De 1984 p 63-66

Impact of dairy development programme of KDDC on small, marginal farmers and agricultural labourers of Bangalore district. L.V. Hirevenkanagoudar *et al* *Indian J Extension Education* 21(1-2) Ja-Je 1985 p 69-71 tabs

Sources of information utilised for adoption of improved dairy management practices by small, marginal farmers and agriculural labourers. M.S. Nataraju and M.B. Channegowda *Indian J Extension Education* 21(3-4) Jl-De 1985 p 99-100 tabs

Dairying : India : Punjab

A study of dairy adoption behaviour of small and marginal farmers in Punjab. J.S. Sohi and R.L. Kherde *Indian J Extension Education* 16(1-2) Je 1980 p 84-86 tabs

Dairying : India : Tamil Nadu

Bottlenecks in modern dairying. R. Balasubramaniam and A. John Knight *Indian J Extension Education* 18(1-2) Je 1982 p 102-05 tabs

Dairying : Research

See

Dairy Research

Dairying : Study and Teaching

Education : An input for dairy industry in India. S.V. Pilkhane *J Higher Education* 8(3) Spr 1983 p 385-90

Day Nurseries : India : Delhi

Promoting adult literacy through mobile creches. Anita Dighe *Indian J Adult Education* 41(10) Oc 1980 p 5-14 tabs

Deaf : Education

Integrated education for children with speech and hearing impairment : A plan of action. K.R.P. Singh *Primary Teacher* 9(1) Ap 1984 p 4-7

To investigate the effectiveness of educational technology in the teaching of mathematics to deaf and dumb children. Subhash Chandra Agrawal *Progress of Education* 54(9) Ap 1980 p 178-81 tabs

Deaf : Education : India

The deaf and their education in India. A.N. Patra *Education Quarterly* 33(1)

Ja 1981 p 1-2

Education of the deaf. S. Sreedhara Swamy *Indian Education* 11(8-9) Nv-De 1981 p 7-11

Death

Education about death. B. Rajaganesan *Experiments in Education* 6(9) Nv 1978 p 151-59 refs

Deccan Education Society

Centanary of Deccan Education Society and Fergusan College. S.V. Kogakar *Progress of Education* 59(6) Ja 1985 p 111-18+

Decision-making in School Management

Decision-making in school administration. Jamnalal Bayti *Progress of Education* 58(6) Ja 1984 p 132-37 +

Decision making in school administration. Jamnalal Bayti *Indian Education*13(8-9) Nv-De 1983 p 23-26

Decision making. N. Muthiah *J Education Planning and Administration* 1(1) Oc 1986 p 67-75

See also

Teacher Participation in Administration

Defective Speech

See

Speech, Disorder of

Defence Mechanisms : Psychological Aspects

Defence mechanisms. Shanta S. Desai *Progress of Education* 53(8) Mr 1979 p 10+

Delhi

See

Adoption of Improved Farm Practices : India : Delhi
Adult Education : India : Delhi
Adult Education of Women : India : Delhi
Agricultural Innovations : India : Delhi
Balwadi Schools : India : Delhi
Cooperative Societies : India : Delhi
Day Nurseries : India : Delhi
Education, Secondary : India : Delhi
Education of Children : India : Delhi
Family Planning : India : Delhi
High School Principals : India : Delhi
High School Teachers : India : Delhi
Municipal Universities and Colleges : India : Delhi
Television Broadcasting : India : Delhi
Television in Agriculture : India : Delhi
Vocational Interests : India : Delhi
Women, Rural : India : Delhi

Delinquency, Juvenile

See

Juvenile Delinquency

Delinquent Girls

Delinquent tendencies in the adolescent girls at different age levels and their effect on verbal learning. Madhu Gupta and Prabha Gupta *Asian J*

Psychology and Education 4(3) Nv 1979 p 6-8
Family problems of adolescent girls as related to problems in other areas and delinquent tendencies. Madhu Gupta and Prabha Gupta *J Education and Psychology* 37(1) Ap 1979 p 67-72 refs

Delinquents
See also
Deliquent Girls
Juvenile Delinquency
Problem Children

Democracy and Education
Education and democracy. G.W. Rama *J Higher Education* 9(1) Mon 1983 p 1-19 refs
Education for democracy. Pritam Singh Brar *Educational Rev* 85(3) Mr 1979 p 43-45
Education for socialism, secularism and democracy. Sahitya Nand Jha. Delhi, Amar Pra. 134p. Rs. 80 *Book Rev, Educational Rev* 91(11) Nv 1985 p 198

Democratic Education
See
Citizenship Education

Demonstration Teaching
See
Teaching Demonstrations

Department Chairmen : Colleges
See
Departmental Chairmen : Universities

Department Chairmen : University
See
Departmental Chairmen : Universities

Departmental Chairmen : Universities
Dimensions of organisational climate : A case study of university departments. Arvinda K. Sinha *Indian Educational Rev* 18(4) Oc 1983 p 1-14

Dependency : Psychological Aspects
Dependency and its antecendents : A review. Venita Kaul *et al Indian Educational Rev* 17(2) Ap 1982 p 35-46 refs

Deprivation : Psychological Aspects
Academic attainment and prolonged deprivation in relation to some personal variables. V.P. Sharma and Mahesh Bhargava *J Education and Psychology* 37(4) Ja 1980 p 247-54 refs
Academic performance as a function of prolonged deprivation. Mahesh Bhargava and Madhu Marwah *Indian Educational Rev* 17(3) Jl 1982 p 114-22 refs tabs
Deprivation and development. Girishwar Mishra *Indian Educational Rev* 18(1) Ja 1983 p 12-32 refs
Effect of parental deprivation on personality adjustment : With special reference to the denotified tribes of U.P. Mohammed Aijaz Khan *Indian Educational Rev* 17(1) Ja 1982 p 99-109
The effect of socio-economic deprivation upon the intelligence of the school

going children. Ramesh C. Dixit and Janki D. Moorjani *J Education and Psychology* 40(4) Ja 1983 p 214-19 refs

Factor of social deprivation affecting the primary school children. M. Pushpa *Indian Educational Rev* 16(2) Ap 1981 p 1-14 refs

Sense of deprivation and intelligence. Usha Upadhyaya *J Institute of Educational Research* 10(3) Se 1986 p 1-4 refs tabs

Developing Countries

See also

Adult Education : Developing Countries
Correspondence Schools and Courses : Developing Countries
Education : Developing Countries
Education, Higher : Developing Countries
Educational Administration : Developing Countries
Educational Innovations : Developing Countries
Educational Planning : Developing Countries
Educational Research : Developing Countries
Educational Sociology : Developing Countries
Science : Study and Teaching : Developing Countries
Teachers : Training : Developing Countries
Unemployment, Educated : Developing Countries
Universities and Colleges : Developing Countries
Youth : Developing Countries

Deviant Behaviour

Personality profile of withdrawing deviance in schools. Saroj Aurora *Indian Educational Rev* 18(2) Jl 1983 p 102-04 refs

Dewey, John

Dewey versus Horns on education. Marlow Ediger *New Frontiers in Education* 13(3) Jl-Se 1983 p 21-23

Diagnostic Psychological Testing

See

Clinical Psychology

Dictation : Educational Method

Is notes dictation bad? I. Satya Sundaram *Educational Rev* 85(4) Ap 1979 p 64-65

Dictionaries

See

Encyclopaedias and Dictioanaries

Discipline : School

See

School Discipline

Discipline of Children

Must we punish children? Sudesh Mukhopadhyay *Primary Teacher* 5(2) Ap 1980 p 15-17

Discovery, Learning of

See

Learning by Discovery

Discrimination

See

Discrimination in Education

Discrimination in Education
Discrimination and inequalities between the sexes and school. Fay E. Saunders *J Indian Education* 5(5) Ja 1980 p 35-42
Dishonesty
See
Honesty
Disorders of Speech
See
Speech, Disorders of
Dissertations : Academic
Evaluations of M.Ed. dissertations : How objective are internal examinations. Haribhai R. Desai *J Education and Psychology* 38(1) Ap 1980 p 17-21 tabs
Journal communication of IARI theses. P.N. Sandhya and Y.P. Singh *Indian J Extension Education* 18(1-2) Ja 1982 p. 34-44 tabs
Raising the efficiency of degree-oriented research. V. Kirillov-Uguyumov and L. Sumarokov *Progress of Education* 56(5) De 1981 p 108-09
Style manual for dissertations theses. H.G. Desai. Rajkot, Saurashtha Univ. 1979,99p. *Book Rev, J Higher Education* 7(3) Spr 1982 p 327-30
Dissertations : Academic : Canada
Trends in social studies education : Theses in Canada, 1971-1977. Harry Dhond *Indian Educational Rev* 16(2) Ap 1981 p 19-28 tabs
Dissertations : Academic : India
Doctoral research in India. Gunvant B. Shah *Teacher Today* 25(3) Ja-Mr 1983 p 1-5
Revamping Indian doctorates. Muthyalayya Naidu *Educational Rev* 87(1) Ja 1981 p 13-14
Distance Education
See
Correspondence Schools and Courses
Divorced Persons
See
Divorcees
Divorcees : Psychological Aspects
A study of certain personality variables of the divorcee and the happily married males. B.A. Purikh *Asian J Psychology and Education* 3(3) Nv 1978 p 35-41 refs tabs
Documentation
National Social Science Documentation Centre. S.P. Agrawal *University News* 24(36) Se 23 1986 p 9-12
Social Science Documentation Centre. S.P. Agarwal *Experiments in Education* 10(7) Se 1982 p 129-34
Social Science Documentation Centre. S.P. Agrawal *Experiments in Education* 11(2) Ap 1983 p 34-36
Social Science Documentation Centre. S.P. Agrawal *Experiments in Education* 11(3) My 1983 p 52-54
Social Science Documentation Centre. S.P. Agrawal *Progress of Education* 57(5) De 1982 p 111-14
Social Science Documentation Centre. S.P. Agrawal *J Educational*

Research and Extension 19(4) Ap 1983 p 239-48

Social Science Documentation Centre. S.P. Agrawal *Indian J Extension Education* 19(1-2) Je 1983 p 109-11

Social Science Documentation Centre, ICSSR : Its activities and services. S.P. Agrawal *J Institute of Educational Research* 8(2) My 1984 p 38-44

University library and documentation services. M.Venkatiah *J Indian Education* 6(1) My 1980 p 19-20

See also

Social Science Documentation Centre

National Social Science Documentation Centre

Domestic Animals

See

Animal Husbandry

Domestic Engineering

See

Sanitation, Household

Dogmatism

Generation gap : A comparative study of parent and children on a measure of authoritarianism. T.N. Raina *Indian Educational Rev* 19(2) Ap 1984 p 37-50

Dockrell, W.B.

Interview with Dr. W.B. Dockrell *Rajasthan Board J Education* 15(3) Jl-Se 1979 p 77-79

Drama : Study and Teaching

See

Drama in Education

Drama in Education

Communicating with adults through drama in mobile creches. M. Swaminathan *Indian J Adult Education* 40(12) De 1979 p 7-12

Learning through dramatics. M.K. Prahallada *Primary Teacher* 9(3) Jl 1984 p 14-15

Teaching reading through dramatisation in primary classes. P.R. Saluja *Primary Teacher* 4(3) Jl 1979 p 22-24

Teaching through dramatisation. Shiv Ratan Thanvi *Primary Teacher* 5(2) Ap 1980 p 25-26

See also

Puppets and Puppet-Plays in Education

Drawing : Instruction

How to draw a cat? K.C. Wagh *Primary Teacher* 4(3) Jl 1979 p 18-27

Lets draw figures from doodling. Swadesh Sharma *Primary Teacher* 5(4) Oc 1980 p 24-30 figs

Drawing : Study and Teaching

See

Drawing : Instruction

Drawing : Techniques

See

Drawing : Instruction

Dreams

The lotus on the stone : An allegory for explorations in dreams and

Ecology

Development of an enviroment and awareness test : A.B. Saxena *et al Indian Educational Rev* 16(3) Jl 1981 p 21-26

See also

Human Ecology

Ecology : Study and Teaching

Education for enviroment the Indian perspective. Sushma Merh *Indian Education* 12(11-12) Fe-Mr 1983 p 16-25

Educo-ecology : A concept for understanding educational milieu. Satya Prakash Singh *J Indian Education* 8(1) My 1982 p 10-14 figs

Environment and education. R.S. Nigam *Educational Rev* 87(6) Je 1981 p 110-13

Environmental education for adult learners. Santosh K. Panda and Nihar R. Swain *Education Quarterly* 38(3) Aut 1986 p 4-7

Environment education : Need for attitudinal change, K.L. Zakir *Indian J Adult Education* 45(3) Mr 1984 p 23-25 +

Environmental approach to education. U.S. Madhyastha *J Indian Education* 8(2) Jl 1982 p 79-83

Environmental education : A total perspective. A.P. Saxena *Education Quarterly* 35(4) Oc 1983 p 29-36

Environmental education and adult education : Need for linkage. S.C. Dutta *Indian J Adult Education* 44(11) Nv 1983 p 8-9+

Environmental education. Bir Singh *Education Quarterly* 34(3) Jl 1982 p 9-11

Environmental education for adult education functionaries. D.V. Sharma *Indian J Adult Education* 41(3) Mr 1980 p 3-5

Environmental education of conceptual framework. Viswanath Muddu *Indian Education* 12(8-9) Nv-De 1982 p 15-17

Environmental education. R.C. Sharma. Delhi, Metropolitan. 1981, 144p. *Book Rev, Indian Educational Rev* 19(1) Ja 1984 p 157-59

Environmental education. Raghuvir Sahay Nigam *Progress of Education* 13(6) Ja 1979 p 111-14

Environmental education : Theory and practice. Daniel Vidart *J Inddian Education* 6(2) Jl 1980 p 35-51 ft-n

Environmental education. V.K. Raina *J Indian Education* 6(2) Jl 1980 p 19-24

Evaluation and environmental studies. A.B. Saxena *Primary Teacher* 6(1) Ja 1981 p 28-34

A framework for environmental education : An overview. R. Diwakaran *New Frontiers in Education* 10(2) Ap-Je 1980 p 14-20 refs

Forest education and environmental awareness. V.P. Gupta *Education Quarterly* 35(2) Ap 1983 p 20-23 refs

From Stockholm to Tbillishi to Jabalpur for environmental education. G. Chaurasia *Indian Education* 12(11-12) Fe-Mr 1983 p 9-12

Linkage of higher education with environment. G. Subramania Pillay *J Higher Education* 4(3) Spr 1979 p 373-80 refs

Need for equatic ecosystem education in the context of environmental science education in the formal school system. A.L.N. Sharma *et al Education Quarterly* 37(3) Aut1985 p 8-12 refs

Promoting attitudes and values through environmental studies. N.M. Bhagia *Teacher Today* 33(2) Oc-De 1980 p 9-21 refs figs

Role of science institute in promoting environmental education. K.D. Pande *Indian Education* 12(11-12) Fe-Mr 1983 p 26-30

Role of teachers in environmental education. S.C. Jain *Indian Education* 12(11-12) Fe-Mr 1983 p 13-15

Ecology : Study and Teaching : Research

Review of researches on environmental education. S. Masiah *Quest in education* 19(3) Jl 1982 p 238-45 refs

Ecology, Human

See

Human Ecology

Economics : Curricula

Hidden curricula in social sciences : An introductory note based on the economics course in Indian universities. M.A. Oommen *New Frontiers in Education* 11(1) Ja-Mr 1981 p 44-65 refs appdc tabs

Economics : Study and Teaching

Case studies in the teaching of economics. M. Raghuramsingh *Experiments in Education* 10(7) Se 1982 p 119-23

Curriculum development in the humanities, economics. *J Higher Education* 1(1) Mon 1975 p 133-37

Teaching economics through case study method : An experiment learning efficiency. T.V. Viswanathan *Experiments in Education* 9(10) De 1981 p 182-86

Teaching of economics through case study method : An experiment. T.V. Viswanathan *J Educational Research and Extension* 18(2) Oc 1981 p 60-64 tabs

Education

Attitude towards education of students parents and teachers. K. Sivasankara Reddy *Experiments in Education* 12(4), Je 1984 p 64-68; 12(6) Ag 1984 p 95-99 refs

Can education strengthen the cohesive bonds of the nation. R.S. Trivedi *J Education and Psychology* 41(3) Oc 1983 p 168-71

A case for education as a discipline. K.J. Srinivasan *Experiments in Education* 11(12) Fe 1984 p 208-09

Concept of man machine system in education. Faruda Khatoon *Indian Education* 13(8-9) Nv-De 1983 p 12-14

Crucial issues in deschooling society. Peter O. Peretti and Emma L. Jones *Education Quarterly* 33(4) Oc 1981 p 19-21 refs

Development of the educand : The role of the teacher. S.O. Makkar *J Indian Education* 12(4) Nv 1986 p 56-58

Dewey versus Horns on education. Marlow Ediger *New Frontiers in Education* 13(3) Jl-Se 1983 p 21-23

Dizzying disorientation. Mali Ram Sharma *Rajasthan Board J Education* 21(3-4) Jl-De 1985 p 1-9

Don Bosco and the preventive system of education. Mathew Kalathunkal *New Frontiers in Education* 11(3) Jl-Se 1981 p 1-25 refs

Education and its purpose. Jeyam Subramaniam *New Frontiers in Education* 14(2) Ap-Je 1984 p 52-54

Education and knowledge. *Educational Rev* 86(2) Fe 1980 p 33-36

Education and scientific temper. Malcolm S. Adiseshiah *New Frontiers in Education* 144(1) Ja-Mr 1984 p 55-58

Education and the survival turning point. Donovan Russell *Experiments in Education* 11(1) Mr 1983 p 3-5

Education and the survival turning point. Donovan Russell *Teacher Education* 13(8-9) Jl-Se 1979 p 5-8

Education as investment in human resource development. Jagannath Mohanty *Indian Education* 11(10) Ja 1982 p 6-15

Education for excellence. S.B. Kalkar *Teacher Today* 27(4) Ap-Je 1985 p 37-41

Education for first generation learners. Sunil Behari Mohanty *Education Quarterly* 36(4) Wint 1984 p 25-30

Education human resources development. M. Pramod Reddy *Indian Education* 11(11-12) Fe-Mr 1982 p 7-11

Education in 1980s. Bir Singh *Education Quarterly* 33(1) Ja 1981 p 3-7

Education in the eighties. *Progress of Education* 55(12) Jl 1981 p 310-14+

Education in 2001 : The emerging scene, a conceptual approach. M. Raghuramsingh *Experiments in Education* 11(7) Se 1983 p 113-20

Education, person and society : A philosophical enquiry. C. Longford. London, Macmillan. 1985. *Book Rev, J Indian Education* 12(4) Nv 1986 p 65-66

Education without schools. Peter Buckman, *ed.* New Delhi, Rupa. 1973. 134p. Rs.10 *Book Rev, Teacher Today* 24(3) Ja-Mr 1982 p 118-20

Educational alternatives. M. Sree Rama Murthy *Experiments in Edcuation* 9(7) Se 1981 p 115-20 refs

Educational expansion and the pedagogical encounter : What can we learn from history. Gevard A. Postiglione *Indian Education* 12(5-6) Ag-Se 1982 p 5-10; 12(7) Oc 1982 p 4-9

Educational facets : Fair and unfair. R.C. Wadhera *J Indian Education* 12(1) My 1986 p 26-30

Educational theory : A logical analysis. C. Seshadri *Perspective in Education* 1(1) Ja 1985 p 21-24 tabs

Educational thought and practice. V.R. Taneja. New Delhi, Sterling. 1984, 351p. Rs.60 *Book Rev, Education Quarterly* 37(1) Spr 1985 p 68-69

Educational values of illiterate and literature adults belong to scheduled and non-scheduled castes. Tarlok Singh *J Educational Research and Extension* 19(3) Ja 1983 p 173-79

Effective education through needs, constraints and teacher motivation. Biswanath Roy *Education Quarterly* 31(1) Ap 1979 p 11-12

Emerging frontiers in education. K. Sivadasan Pillai *Indian Education* 11(4) Jl 1981 p 24-25

Environmental awareness and education systems. D.R. Darji and D.K. Sharma *J Education and Psychology* 40(4) Ja 1983 p 234-38

Exchange of views on education. Indira Gandhi *J Educational Research and Extension* 20(2) Oc 1983 p 85-91

Five models of education : A challenge to education. J. Filella *New Frontiers in Education* 12(4) Oc-De 1982 p 1-13

Formal, non-formal and informal education : A classification. Mohottige U.

Sedere *New Frontiers in Education* 11(1) Ja-Mr 1981 p 73-78 refs

Formal schooling and personal efficacy. Desphane M. De Rebelle. Sterling. 151p. Rs. 45 *Book Rev, Education Quarterly* 31(3-4) Oc 1979-Ja 1980 p 46-47

Formulating Marxist theory of education. W.A. Siddiqui *Progress of Education* 58(1) Ag 1983 p 2-5 refs

Future critical world issues in education : A provisional report of findings. Phillip H. Coombs. Essex, ICED. 1981. 80 p. *Book Rev, Education Quarterly* 34(3) Jl 1982 p 49-51

Future education : Some reflections. M.N. Deshmukh *Asian J Psychology and Education* 3(3) Nv 1978 p 42-45

The future shape of education? Le Thanh Khoi *Education Quarterly* 34(1) Ja 1982 p 17-24

Glimpses of global trends in education. M.R. Paliwal *Teacher Today* 28(3) Ja-Mr 1986 p 38-50

The great train robbery. Ivarn Berg. Penguin Books. 1973 197p. *Book Rev, Teacher Today* 22(3) Ja-Mr 1980 p 97-98

Horizontal and vertical linkages in education. R.P. Singhal *Education Quarterly* 35(2) Ap 1983 p 1-7 fig

Implications of future and the emerging educational personnel profile. S.C. Seth *Teacher Education* 18(22-23) Ja-Ap 1983 p 33-54 refs

In search of panacea for educational ills. Salamatullah *J Indian Education* 8(4) Nv 1982 p 3-8

Interaction between education and productive work. *New Frontiers in Education* 12(4) Oc-De 1982 p 61-72

Meeting the challenge in education. Ramesh Verma *Educational Rev* 92(3) Mr 1986 p 46-49

Mental and physical health through education. S.A. Shafi *Indian Education* 10(7) Oc 1980 p 26-28

Model building in comparative education. Ingrid M.E. Munck. Stockholm, Almqvist. 1979, 199p. *Book Rev, Indian Educational Rev* 15(1) Ja 1980 p 122-24

Multiple class teaching and education of disadvantaged groups. Bangkok, UNESCO. 1982, 98p. *Book Rev, Teacher Today* 26(3) Ja-Mr 1984 p 102-08

New dimensions in education. K. Bhakta Vatsal Rao *Indian Education* 10(4) Jl 1980 p 37-38

New components of education. Raghuvir Sahay Nigam *Educational Rev* 85(2) Fe 1979 p 23-24

A new outlook on education. S.P. Pani and R.N. Pani *J Indian Education* 11(1) My 1985 p 62-70 refs

No education is neutral. A. Etherington *Indian J Adult Education* 40(9) Se 1979 p 1-7

Non-formal approach in education. Sunil Behari Mohanty *Progress of Education* 55(5) De 1980 p 120-21+

Nurturing non-academic talent in the school : A challenge. Ashok K. Hota *J Indian Education* 8(6) Mr 1983 p 35-41 refs

On the development of fellowship and personality in education. Peter Manniche *Indian J Adult Education* 44(8-9) Ag-Se 1983 p 25-28

Participation, learning and change. Paul Fordham. London, Pall Mall. 1980, 223 p. £5 *Book Rev, Indian Educational Rev* 17(1) Ja 1982 p 120-24

Paulo Freire : A revolutionary pedagogue. Narasingha Prasad Sil *Indian Educational Rev* 16(1) Ja 1981 p 25-36 refs

Platonic system of education. D. Bhaskara Rao *Educational Rev* 89(4) Ap 1982 p 68-71

Present trends in education. Torsten Husen *Teacher Education* 17(20-21) Jl-Oc 1982 p 7-22

A programmed text on operant conditioning. Damodar Mohapatra *J Educational Research and Extension* 20(3) Ja 1984 p 107-71

Pursuit of excellence through education : A few issues. Shamsuddin *Primary Teacher* 11(2) Ap 1986 p 1-3

Reflection on new education. Kireet Joshi *New Frontiers in Education* 15(1) Ja-Mr 1985 p 13-50

Restructuring education for a learning society. K. Ramachandrachar *J Indian Education* 11(1) My 1985 p 9-13 refs

The right to education : What kind of management? Daniel Haag. Paris, UNESCO. 1982, 175p. *Book Rev, Indian Educational Rev* 18(4) Oc 1984 p 143-45

Schooling in decline. Gerald Bernbaum, *ed.* London, Macmillan. 1979, 240p. £3.95 *Book Rev, Education Quarterly* 33(1) Ja 1981 p 41-42

A search for alternatives in education. B.G. Tewari *Rajasthan Board J Education* 21(3-4) Jl-De 1985 p 51-62

Self education. Amrit Kaur *Prasar* 5(1-2) Ap-Jl 1977 p 25-35 refs

Some crucial problems in education. S. Vijaya Ratnam *Educational Rev* 86(4) Ap 1980 p 61-63

Stratification in the educational system. Surjeet Singh *J Indian Education* 11(1) My 1985 p 25-33

Stray thoughts on education. S.V. Chari *Educational Rev* 85(5) My 1979 p 94-95

Study service : A practical interaction of formal and non-formal education. D. Fussell and A. Qurrmby *Indian J Adult Education* 40(4) Ap 1979 p 5-10

Symbol systems in the school programme. Suriya Bhimaya *Education Quarterly* 36(4) Wint 1984 p 12-16

Systems approach in education. S.M. Goyal *J Indian Education* 6(3) Se 1980 p 27-30

Theory and principles of education. J.C. Agarwal. New Delhi, Vikas Pub. 381p. Rs.25 *Book Rev, Educational Rev* 87(9) Se 1981 p 177-78

Towards on education for the 21st century. Prem Kirpal *Teacher Today* 28(2) Oc-De 1985 p 50-61

What is wrong with formal education institution; editorial comments. *J Education and Psychology* 40(3) Oc 1982 p 103-06

The world crisis in education : The view from the eighties. Philip H. Coombs. New York, OUP. 1985, 353 p. *Book Rev, Indian J Adult Education* 47(6) Je 1986 p 31-32; *Progress of Education* 61(3-4) Nv-De 1986 p 101-02

See also

Ability Grouping in Education

Adult Education

Agricultural Education

Physical Education and Training
Piaget, Jean
Plato
Private Schools
Professional Education
Radio in Education
Religious Education
Schools
Secularism and Education
Sex Instruction
Socialism and Education
Study, Method of
Teachers
Teaching
Technical Education
Television in Education
Thompson, John N.
Tribal Education
Vacation Schools
University Extension
Vocational Education
Volunteer Workers in Education
Wastage in Education
Youth

See also

Subdivision 'Education' under special people, classes and social groups, e.g., Blind : Education

Subdivision 'Study and Teaching' under special subjects, e.g., Science : Study and Teaching

Education : Africa

Choices in African education. S.R. Gangopadhyay *Teacher Today* 21(2) Oc-De 1978 p 70-75

Education : Aims and Objectives

Aims, objectives and the philosophy of Indian education. R.P. Kathuria *Teacher Today* 24(4) Ap-Je 1982 p 57-64 refs

The aims of education. John Vallomattam *New Frontiers in Education* 10(3) Jl-Se 1980 p 42-46

The aims of education restated. John White. London, Routledge. 1982, 177p. £8.95 *Book Rev, Teacher Today* 26(1) Jl-Se 1983 p 186

The aims of education. Samuel Mathai *New Frontiers in Education* 10(3) Jl-Se 1980 p 35-42

Bloom's taxonomy : Review of researches. Haribhai G. Desai *Indian Educational Rev* 14(1) Ja 1979 p 115-22 refs

Education for human excellence. K.K.S. Rajendran *Educational Rev* 84(11) Nv 1978 p 210-14

Educational aims and philosophy. Ram Shakal Pandey *Educational Rev* 85(1) Ja 1979 p 16-18 refs

Educational objectives and the pupil. Marlow Ediger *Indian Education* 10(6) Se 1980 p 14-18

Objective based evaluation. Jagannath Dash *Educational Rev* 90(5-6) My-Je 1984 p 81-83 refs

Objectives and the pupil. Marlow Ediger *New Frontiers in Education* 13(4) Oc-De 1983 p 7-11

Personalising education : A perspective. V.P. Garg *Teacher Today* 22(2) Oc-De 1979 p 44-45

Pupils'and teachers' perception of the aims of education : A comparative study. Shaheen Saeed *Indian Educational Rev* 17(3) Jl 1982 p 1-9

See also

Education and National Development

Educational Equalisation

Educational Planning

Educational Sociology

Education : Bangladesh

Bangladesh : For democracy and a popular education system. *Student Action* 3(3) Oc 1984 p 7-9

Education : Botswana

Encouraging participation in development : Laedza Batanani Case studies. R. Kidd and M.L. Byram *Indian J Adult Education* 40(8) Ag 1979 p 11-29 refs

Education : Bulgaria

Bulgaria experience in education. *Student Action* 2(9) Mr 1984 p 40+

Education : Canada

Education in Canada. G.B.K. Hooja *University News* 23(22) 8 Je 1985 p 2-3

Education : China (People's Republic)

China's immediate future : Renewed cultural borrowing. R.F. Price *J Higher Education* 8(3) Spr 1983 p 299-310

Education development in the People's Republic of China. *New Frontiers in Education* 13(1) Ja-Mr 1983 p 83-88

Education in China. Wien Jiao *Indian Education* 10(8) Nv 1980 p 20-22

Education in China. Zheng Yanwen *Indian Education* 13(5-6) Ag-Se 1983 p 29+

New patterns in teaching and learning - A look at the People's Republic of China. Mary Kay Hobbs *Indian J Adult Education* 41(4) Ap 1980 p 25-27

Education : Conferences, etc.

See

Under names of individual conferences, e.g., All India Educational Conference

Education : Costs

Educational expenditure : Inflation and economic growth : An empirical analysis. M.M. Ansari *Perspectives in Education* 1(2) Ap 1985 p 111-22 refs tabs

Rates of return occupational patterns of non-professional graduates. P. Neerada Reddy *Indian Education* 10(1-2) Ap-My 1980 p 48-52

A study of private costs of schooling girls at the elementary stage. S.L. Gupta *EPA Bulletin* 6(2) Jl 1983 p 31-40 tabs

Education : Cuba

Socialists development and educational reform in Cuba, 1959-1980. Martin Carnoy *Perspectives in Education* 1(4) Oc 1985 p 237-56 refs

Education : Curricula

College youth, their courses of study and their view of society. M.Z. Khan and D.R. Singh *J Higher Education* 4(1) Mon 1978 p 57-66 refs tabs

Curriculum and creativity. G.L. Arora *J Indian Education* 8(6) Mr 1983 p 49

Curriculum and teaching : Some opposing views. Marlow Ediger *New Frontiers in Education* 14(1) Ja-Mr 1984 p 59-63

Curriculum improvement. Marlow Ediger *Progress of Education* 57(3) Oc 1982 p 65-68

Curriculum theories. T.N. Das *National J Education* 7(1) Se 1984 p 57-60 refs

Discipline and the school curriculum. Marlow Ediger *Experiments in Education* 10(5) Jl 1982 p 93-96 refs

Geometry in the school curriculum. Marlow Ediger *Indian Education* 10(7) Oc 1980 p 7-9

Issues in the writing curriculum. Marlow Ediger *Indian J Adult Education* 42(10) Oc 1981 p 21-24 refs

Leadership in the curriculum. Marlow Ediger *New Frontiers in Education* 11(4) Oc-De 1981 p 28-30

Learning activities and the curriculum. Marlow Ediger *Educational Rev* 87(10) Oc 1981 p 193-95 refs

A model of developing language curriculum of school stage. K.G. Rastogi *Teacher Today* 23(1) Jl-Se 1980 p 36-40 tabs

Modules and modular courses of study. W.A.F. Hopper *New Frontiers in Education* 13(1) Ja 1983 p 53-57 refs

The psychology of learning and the curriculum. Marlow Ediger *Experiments in Education* 7(11) Ja 1980 p 202-04 refs

Reading the curriculum. Marlow Ediger *J Education and Psychology* 43(3-4) Oc 1985-Ja 1986 p 160-62 refs

Reflections on curriculum. G.L. Arora, ed. New Delhi, NCERT. 1984, 98p. Rs.8 *Book Rev, Indian Educational Rev* 20(2) Ap 1985 p 142-43

School curriculum in philosophical perspective. Marlow Ediger *Indian Education* 10(12) Mr 1981 p 13-17

Socially useful productive work : An innovation in school curriculum. Piloo Buch. Baroda, Shweta Pub. 42p. Rs6 *Book Rev, National J Education* 2(1) Se 1979 p 63-64

Subjects for school and college curriculum. R.S. Nigam *Educational Rev* 85(10) Oc 1979 p 181-83

Tasks for schools. M. Sree Rama Murthy *Education Quarterly* 32(4) Oc 1980 p 8-9

Transcendental meditation in school curriculum. Ben Behari Mukhopadhyay *Indian Education* 10(7) Oc 1980 p 21-25

See also

Curriculum Planning

Education : Czechoslovakia

New law on Czechoslavak education. Miluse Vrtilkova *Student Action* 3(2) Se 1984 p 25

Education : Developing Countries

Education for third world countries. Jai Kishan Sharma. Delhi, B.R. Pub. 1986. *Book Rev, J Educational Planning and Administration* 1(1) Oc 1986 p 91-92

Educational leadership for the third world. Proshanta K. Nandi *J Indian Education* 10(6) Mr 1985 p 1-8 refs

Expanding third world educational opportunities. M. Peter McPherson *University News* 24(37) 1 Oc 1986 p 1-4 +

Some inherent problems in the crucial educational issues in developing countries. R.M. Kalra *Education Quarterly* 33(4) Oc 1981 p 15-18

Three channels of education in developing countries : Some needed reforms. J.P. Naik *Indian J Adult Education* 40(5) My 1979 p 1-6

Education : Dictionaries

International dictionary of education. J.B. Thomas *et al.* London, ELBS. 1979, 381p. £1.50 *Book Rev, Education Quarterly* 32(1) Ja 1981 p 51-52

Education : Economic Aspects

Earning and education in OECD countries. George Psacharopoulos. Paris, OECD. 194 p. $5 : £2 F 20 *Book Rev, Indian Educational Rev* 18(1) Ja 1983 p 133-35

The economics of education. G.B.J. Attinson. London, Hodder. 1983, 150p. £5.95 *Book Rev, Perspectives in Education* 2(4) Oc 1986 p 253-56

Economics of education. Narendra Prasad *Indian Education* 11(6) Se 1981 p 33-35

Economy in education. Asoke Sen *Education Quarterly* 32(2) Ap 1980 p 6-7

Education and economics. M.N. Tiku *Educational Rev* 85(9) Se 1979 p 161-65

Education, employment and income inequality : A Marxian perspective. S.K. Patel *Indian Educational Rev* 14(4) Oc 1979 p 13-23 refs

Education is at grand reduction sale. C.L. Joshi *Teacher Today* 27(4) Ap-Je 1985 p 59-61

Expenditure on education as a social investment. M. Ramesh Babu and K.S. Chalam *Educational Rev* 90(12) De 1984 p 193-95

Income pattern and education. B.N. Modi, Ahmedabad, Sonal Pub. 1984. 156p. Rs.121 *Book Rev, Education Quarterly* 37(2) Sum 1985 p 71

Investment in education. V. Rajasekaran *Experiments in Education* 6(5) Jl 1978 p 82-84

See also

Education : Costs

Education : Finance

Wastage in Education

Education : Experimental Method

See also

Educational Innovations

Experimental Education

Open Plan Schools

Education : Finance

Alternatives in financing Indian education. C.B. Padmanabhan *New Frontiers in Education* 13(1) Ja-Mr 1983 p 42-48

Budget formulation for educational planning. V.P. Garg *EPA Quarterly Bull* 7(1-2) Ap-Jl 1984 p 41-50 ref

Financial management in education. C.B. Padmanabhan New Delhi, Select Books. 1984. 236p. Rs.60 *Book Rev, Education Quarterly* 37(2) Sum 1985 p 80-81

Financial management in Indian education : Its functional approach. C.B. Padmanabhan *Indian Educational Rev* 20(4) Oc 1985 p 121-32

Financial resources : Dimensions and dilemmas. S.N. Saraf *University News* 23(19) 16 My 1985 p 2-6 annex

Financial strategy for the development of education in India. K.S. Chalan *EPA Quarterly Bulletin* 8(3-4) Oc 1985-Ja 1986 p 29-38 tabs

Financing of education and equality of opportunity in Indian education. C.B. Padmanabhan *Perspectives in Education* 1(3) Jl 1985 p 167-73 refs

Financing of education in the sixth five-year plan. C.B. Padmanabhan *New Frontiers in Education* 13(2) Ap-Je 1983 p 17-29 tabs

Financing of education in the seventh five-year plan. C.B. Padmanabhan *New Frontiers in Education* 15(2) Ap-Je 1985 p 89-97

Financing of education. R.K. Bhandari *Education Quarterly* 34(1) Ja 1982 p 1-6 tabs

Funding the academic scene the British way. Jack Cross *Progress of Education* 60(10) Ag 1985 p 10-12

An introduction to fund raising. Paula J. Faust, ed. Washington, CASE. 1983, 92p. $16.50 *Book Rev, Progress of Education* 58(11) Je 1984 p 279

Investment in education. R.K. Bhandari *New Frontiers in Education* 14(2) Ap-Je 1984 p 97-111

Principles and techniques of Indian education and finance. C.B. Padmanabhan *New Frontiers in Education* 12(2) Ap-Je 1982 p 36-41

Research needs and priorities in financing of education. J.L. Azad *Quest in Education* 18(4) Oc 1981 p 238-34 refs

Resource allocation on education : An inter-intra-country and intertemporal pattern analysis. G.D. Sharma, New Delhi, Assn of Indian Univ. 1978, 159p. Rs.20 *Book Rev, J Higher Education* 4(3) Spr 1979 p 426-27

Towards rational financial policy for Indian education. C.B. Padmanabhan *Education Quarterly* 37(3) Aut 1985 p 1-5

See also

Education : Costs

Education : Economic Aspects

University Grants Commission

Education : Germany : East

The socialist education system of GDR. V.P. Raghavachari *Indian Education* 11(8-9) Nv-De 1981 p 29-33; 11(10) Ja 1982 p 16-20

Education : Germany : West

A day in German classrooms. Sunil Behari Mohanty *Teacher Today* 23(2) Oc-De 1980 p 44-47

Education : Great Britain

Adopting educational models : India and Britain. Sunil Behari Mohanty *Educational Rev* 87(10) Oc 1981 p 196-98

Britain points the way to multicultural education systems. *Progress of Education* 57(12) Jl 1983 p 282-84

The educationally disadvantaged in the U.S.A. and the U.K. M. Raghuram-

singh *Experiments in Education* 10(5) Jl 1982 p 79-89 refs
The Inner London Education Authority : A record of achievement. John E. Owen *Educational Rev* 91(9) Se 1985 p 141-45
Prominent practices : Baffling dilemmas. M. Raj Chilana *Teacher Today* 21(2) Oc-De 1978 p 76-84

Education : History

Research in history of education : Methodological issues and problems. Surya Nath Singh *National J Education* 5(1) Se 1982 p 33-38 refs

Education : Hungary

Developing education in Hungary. *Student Action* 2(9) Mr 1984 p 36

Education : India

Adapting educational models — India and Britain. Sunil Behari Mohanty *Educational Rev* 87(10) Oc 1981 p 196-98
American influence on Indian education. S.R. Sharma. New Delhi, Raaj Prakashan. 1979. 175p. Rs. 70 *Book Rev, Education Quarterly* 32(2) Ap 1980 p 50-51
Anatomy of the crisis in education. U.L. Kude *University News* 23(11) 16 Mr 1985 p 5+
Bharatiya Rashtriya Shikshan Aayojana. Janarda Nagar. Rajasthan, R.V.L.T.S.M. (Hindi). 1983. 82p. Rs.20 *Book Rev, Progress of Education* 58(6) Ja 1984 p 147
Classroom practices in the past twenty-five years. R.P. Singh *Teacher Today* 26(1) Jl-Se 1983 p 101-06
Crisis in education in India. R.K. Bhandari *New Frontiers in Education* 14(3) Jl-Se 1984 p 74-81
Critique of education for our people. R.P. Tewari. Delhi, South Asian Pub. 210p. Rs. 50 *Book Rev, Education Quarterly* 32(4) Oc 1980 p 44-45
Demands of modernisation and educational process : Two systems. A.L. Srivastava *Teacher Today* 23(1) Jl-Se 1981 p 55-81 refs
Development of education in India : A historical survey of educational documents before and after Independence. A Biswas and S.P. Agrawal, New Delhi, Concept, 1986. xv, 936 p Rs. 700 *Book Review Education Quarterly* 39(2) Sum 1987 p 52-56
Divaswapna. Gijubhai Badheka *Teacher Today* 26(3) Ja-Mr 1984 p 60-83
Education and human resource development, S. Sreedhara Swamy *Progress of Education* 57(11) Je 1983 p 246-49
Education and traditional values in India. Indra Sen *Education Quarterly* 35(1) Ja 1983 p 1-4
Education as an investment in human resources development. G. Haragopal *Indian Education* 11(7) Oc 1981 p 35-38
The education explosion. M.S. Hare *University News* 23(28) 23 Jl 1985 p 9-14
Education for a productive and rewarding life. Atmananda Sharma *J Indian Education* 6(3) Se 1980 p 14-21
Education for all. K. Ramachandra *New Frontiers in Education* 15(3) Jl-Se 1985 p 37-47
Education for all : Dimensions and dilemmas. S.N. Saraf *University News* 23(21) 1 Je 1985 p 2-5
Education for India. Bishnubrata Bhattacharya. Calcutta, Banerjee, Mohit

Kumar. 74p. Rs.8 *Book Rev, Progress of Education* 57(2) Se 1982 p 46

Education in India 1976-78. *New Frontiers in Education* 9(4) Oc-De 1979 p 79-94

Education in modern India : National goals. S.M. Divaker *J Indian Education* 11(1) My 1985 p 20-24

Education in the 21st century. A.D. Khobre *Educational Rev* 90(10) Oc 1984 p 151-52

Education must take into account the various dimensions of the human individual, says E.M. *J Indian Education* 5(4) Nv 1979 p 61-62

Education of the socially disadvantaged through non-formal education, an integral part of formal education. B.P. Lulla *Indian Education* 10(1-2) Ap-My 1980 p 44-47

Education systems : Analysis and reforms. Mohan Prakash. New Delhi, Agricol Pub Acad. 162p. Rs.125 *Book Rev, Education Quarterly* 38(1) Spr 1986 p 41-42

Educational development in rural-urban sectors in India. Sushila Singhal *New Frontiers in Education* 11(1) Ja-Mr 1981 p 19-29 tabs

The Ford Foundation and Indian education : Some issues of motives and power. Neelu Sancheti *New Frontiers in Education* 14(3) Jl-Se 1984 p 1-13 refs

Fundamental questions. Surinder Suri *J Higher Education* 1(1) Mon 1975 p 111-19

Futuristic scenario of educational system : A viewpoint. V.P. Garg *J Indian Education* 5(4) Nv 1979 p 56-60 refs

Hospitalisation of education. C.L. Joshi *Teacher Today* 28(3) Ja-Mr 1986 p 65-68

An illusion about educational growth. R.S. Shukla *Teacher Today* 21(2) Oc-De 1978 p 44-47

Indian education and national culture. R.K. Yadav *National J Education* 3(2) Mr 1981 p 17-23 ref

Indian Education in the emerging society. Jagan Nath Mohanty. New Delhi, Sterling. 1982. 205p. Rs.60 *Book Rev, J Indian Education* 8(2) Jl 1982 p 94

Indian education scene in 1981. S. Sreedhara Swamy *Indian Education* 11(10) Ja 1982 p 42-45; *Progress of Education* 56(8) Mr 1982 p 196-98

Indian education scene, 1982. S. Sreedhara Swamy *Indian Education* 12(10) Ja 1983 p 26-29

Indian educational system : The role of computers. Arun K. Gupta *J Indian Education* 10(5) Ja 1985 p 1-5

Indian educational thought and experiments. *Teacher Today* 22(2) Oc-De 1979 p 1-21

Indian education thought in recent times. Indra Sen *Education Quarterly* 34(2) Ap 1982 p 1-8

Kakatiya vice-chancellor advocates skill-oriented courses emphasises recognition of merit education; an interview. *Indian Education* 10(4) Jl 1980 p 15-18

Modernity of tradition in Indian education : The revival of Indian languages and indigenous systems of education. R.P. Singh *Perspectives in Education* 1(4) Oc 1985 p 231-36 refs

A nation at risk : The imperative of education reform. *New Frontiers in Education* 13(4) Oc-De 1983 p 73-91

Needed change in education. R. Krishna Rao *J Indian education* 6(2) Jl 1980 p 30-34

New education pattern. Goswami Rambalak *Primary Teacher* 5(1) Ja 1980 p 27-30

New education scheme. Raghuvir Sahay Nigam *Educational Rev* 84(12) De 1978 p 221-23

A new educational package. *Teacher Education* 20(30-31) Ja-Ap 1985 p 30-32

A new look for education. Raghunath Safaya *Educational Rev* 91(3) Mr 1985 p 41-43

An overview of India's educational system. Vaman Rao *Indian Education* 10(1-2) Ap-My 1980 p 40-43

Paradoxical experiments and our present day education. Amiya Kumar Basu *Our Education* 6 Jl 1985-1986 p 49-60 refs

Pathology in Indian education. M.N. Ravindranatha *Education Quarterly* 35(3) Jl 1983 p 1-6

Pathology of Indian education. Ramesh Verma *Educational Rev* 86(11) Nv 1980 p 201-03

Patterns of education. D. Sengupta *Education Quarterly* 31(2) Jl 1979 p 1-4

Pivotal issues in Indian education. S.K. Kochhar. New Delhi, Sterling. 344p. Rs.80 *Book Rev, Education Quarterly* 33(3) Jl 1981 p 43-44; *Progress of Education* 55(12) Jl 1981 p 338

Problems in Indian education. V.T. Patel and B.C. Patil. New Delhi, Oxf-IBH. 1982, vii, 168p. Rs. 36 *Book Rev, Indian Educational Rev* 17(4) Oc 1982 p 152-54

Reform entails a predefinition process. Chhaya Dey *Progress of Education* 56(4) Nv 1981 p 85-88

Reforming our educational system : Some perspectives. K.N. Ninan *Progress of Education* 58(11) Je 1984 p 273-75+

Revamping the educational system. *New Frontiers in Education* 16(2) Ap-Je 1986 p 76-81

Revolutionary livable education system. Kranti Chandra Sankarrao Chaudhary *Educational Rev* 87(6) Je 1981 p 115-16

School : A weighted satchel. Anita Kaul *Teacher Education* 14(12-13) Jl-Oc 1980 p 63-67

Selectivity and egalitarianism. Chandran Devanesan *New Frontiers in Education* 10(3) Jl-Se 1980 p 71-77

Shiksha Ke Nutan Ayam (in Hindi). L.K. Oad. Jaipur, Rajasthan Hindi Academi. 1978. 293p. *Book Rev, J Indian Education* 6(1) My 1980 p 77-78

Some needs of Indian education today. J.N. Kapur *Indian Education* 9(12) Mr 1980 p 16-18

Stray thoughts on education in India. Amrik Singh *Indian Education* 12(7) Oc 1982 p 9-14

A study of educational leadership in India. Roy P. Wahle *J Education and Psychology* 44(2-3) Jl-De 1986 p 77-91

Towards new pattern of education in India. P.D. Shukla. New Delhi, Sterling. 1984. *Book Rev, J Indian Education* 10(6) Mr 1985 p 61-62; *J Institute of Educational Research* 4(1) Ja 1985 p 12-34

The Western shadow over Indian education. Prabhakar Singh *J Indian Education* 8(1) My 1982 p 23-31

Whither educational development? Bhavirar Dutt Gururani *Primary Teacher* 5(3) Jl 1980 p 23-26

Why is our education ineffective? A.N. Mishra *Educational Rev* 85(11) Nv 1979 p 213-15

See also

Aurobindo, Sri : Educational Thought
Buddha, Lord : Educational Thought
Gandhi, Indira
Gandhi, Mohandas Karamchand : Educational Thought
Khair, G.S.
Kidd, J.R.
Nanak Dev, Guru : Educational Thought
Narasimharao, P.V.
Premchand, Munshi
Vidyasagar Ishwar Chand : Educational Thought
Zakir Husain : Educational Thought

Education : India : Ancient

Glimplses of education in ancient India. I.V. Chalapati Rao *Indian Education* 11(10) Ja 1982 p 25-32

Impact of ancient Indian philosophical thought and educational theory and practice. G. Srivasudrappa *National J Education* 7(2) My 1985 p 9-16

Education : India : Andaman and Nicobar Islands

Education in the Andaman and Nicobar Islands, 1951-79 : Elementary and secondary levels. Avtar Singh *Education Quarterly* 33(1) Ja 1981 p 26-30

Education : India : Andhra Pradesh

Are the educational standards deteriorating? M. Sree Rama Murthy *Indian Educational Rev* 15(2) Ap 1980 p 36-49 tabs

Educational progress in Andhra Pradesh : A trend report. R. Srinivasa Rao *Education Quarterly* 31(1) Ap 1979 p 21-23 refs

General and technical education in Andhra Pradesh. P. Ramachandra Pillai. Hyderabad, Education Telugu Academy. 1981,viii, 181p. Rs.7.50 *Book Rev, Indian Educational Rev* 17(2) Ap 1982 p 133-35

Radical educational reforms in A.P. *Indian Education* 10(3) Je 1980 p 2-4 +

Education : India : Arunachal Pradesh

Education in Arunachal Pradesh contribution by Vivekanand Kendra. M.K. Sharma *EPA Bull* 7(1-2) Ap-Jl 1984 p 6-14 refs

Education : India : Bibliography

Indian education index (1948-78). S.P. Agrawal, Gen *ed.* New Delhi, Manasayan. 1200p. Rs.450 : $100 *Book Rev, Progress of Educaiton* 56(5) De 1981 p 123

Education : India : Gujarat

A profile on background determinants of education in Panchmahal district. G.B. Shinde *Quest in Education* 17(1) Ja 1980 p 35-43

See also

Continuing Education Centres : India : Gujarat

Education : India : Haryana

Costs of supply of education at micro level : A case study of two education clusters in the district Gurgaon, Haryana. J.B.G. Tilak and G.K. Bhatt *EPA Quarterly Bulletin* 8(3-4) Oc 1985-Ja 1986 p 55-59

Glimpses of education in Haryana. S.S. Kaushall. Delhi, Rakesh Prakashan. 1981. 118p. Rs.15 *Book Rev, J Indian Education* 8(2) Jl 1982 p 94

Education : India : History

Development of education in India : A historical survey of educational documents before and after independence. A. Biswas and S.P. Agrawal. New Delhi, Concept, 1986. xv, 936 p. Rs. 700 *Book Rev, Education Quarterly* 39(2) Sum 1987 p 52-56

Education in an imperial colony. R.P. Singh. New Delhi, National Pub H., 1979, 140p. Rs.50 *Book Rev, Indian Educational Review* 16(1) Ja 1981 p. 125-26; *J Indian Education* 5(6) Mr 1980 p 64

Education in India, 1781-1985. Kuldip Kaur. Chandigarh, Centre for Res in Rural and Industrial Development. 1985. 534p, Rs.280 *Book Rev, Perspective in Education* 2(4) Oc 1986 p 251-53

Education in past-present, future. M.C. Mallikarlunaiah *Educational Rev* 87(10) Oc 1981 p 191

Education under Moslem rule. Shamsuddin *Indian Education* 9(12) Mr 1980 p 27-30

Educational aims in British India. Bhanu Pratap Singh *Educational Rev* 85(10) Oc 1979 p 196-97

Essays in the history of Indian education. Aparna Basu. New Delhi, Concept Pub. 1982, x, 108p. Rs. 60 *Book Rev, Progress of Education* 58(3) Oc 1983 p 71

History of education in middle ages. K.N. Deshpande. and A.I. Mali. Pune, Nutan Prakashan. 1985. 124p. Rs. 17.50 *Book Rev, Progress of Education* 61(3-4) Nv-De 1986 p 100

One teacher, one school, the Adam's reports on indigenous education in 19th century India. Joseph Dibona. New Delhi, Biblia Impex. 1983. 309p. Rs.150 *Book Rev, Education Quarterly* 36(2) Ap 1984 p 70-72; *Indian Educational Rev* 19(2) Ap 1984 p 118-19

"Public" educational system in a colonial context. Suresh Chandra Shukla *Teacher Today* 26(4) Ap-Je 1984 p 41-50 refs

Research in history of education in India. R.P. Singh *Teacher Today* 25(3) Ja-Mr 1983 p 15-23 refs

Education : India : Jammu and Kashmir : History

Education under Dogra rule 1846-1947. Romesh Verma *Educational Rev* 91(5-6) My-Je 1985 p 86-87

Education : India : Kerala

Shift system in Kerala colleges. George Malancherwvill *New Frontiers in Education* 9(4) Oc-De, 1979 p 46-57

Education : India : Madhya Pradesh

Education for the unwilling. Bir Singh *Educational Rev* 86(11) Nv 1980 p 213-14

Education : India : Northeastern

Educational profile of North East India. Kathita Hatibaruah *Educational Rev* 91(2) Fe 1985 p 29-33 refs

Education : India : Punjab

Education in Kenya and the Punjab state of India : A comparative study. T.S. Sodhi *J Indian Education* 12(3) Se 1986 p 44-52 refs

Help books in Punjab schools. S.P. Koura *Educational Rev* 85(1) Ja 1979 p 3-8

Education : India : Rajasthan

Education and assistance : A case study of governmental college. Sawai Madhopur, Rajasthan. Pradeep Kumar Mehta *J Higher Education* 3(3) Spr 1978 p 390-99 tabs refs

Socially useful productive work and community services : Concepted status in Rajasthan. J.S. Mehta *Rajasthan Board J Education* 19(4) Oc-De 1983 p 1-8

Education : India : Tamil Nadu

A profile of the clientele in the NFE centres for 6-14 years in Tamil Nadu. L.S. Saraswathi *Indian J Adult Education* 40(9) Se 1979 p 22-30

Education : India : Uttar Pradesh

Education in the scheme of plan priorities in Uttar Pradesh. Mohammad Muzammil *Education Quarterly* 33(2) Ap 1981 p 16-20

Progress of education in Uttar Pradesh. Mohammed Muzammil *Education Quarterly* 32(4) Oc 1980 p 17-21 tabs

A study of educational leadership in relation to teachers attitudes. P.C. Shukla *EPA Bulletin* 7(1-2) Ap-Jl 1984 p 15-23 refs

Education : India : West Bengal : History

Educational pioneers : Episodes from Calcutta history. Pansy Chaya Ghosh *New Frontiers in Education* 9(4) Oc-De 1979 p 28-36

Education : Israel

Education in Israel. M.I. Kazi *Progress of Education* 58(3) Mr 1984 p 181-82

Education : Japan

Development of school for special education in Japan. S.C. Chaturevedi *National J Education* 7(1) Se 1984 p 19-28 refs

Peace education versus mass media in Japan. Shingo Shibata *Indian Education* 13(8-9) Nv-De 1983 p 19-22

Problems of education and economy in Japan. Kazuko Hashiguchi *Indian Education* 12(10) Ja 1983 p 5-9

Education : Kenya

Education in Kenya and the Punjab state of India : A comparative study. T.S. Sodhi *J Indian Education* 12(3) Se 1986 p 44-52 refs

Education : Nepal

Development of education in Nepal. W.H. Siddiqui *Educational Rev* 85(9) Se 1979 p 166-69 tabs

National development service : A scheme of study service in Nepal. W.H. Siddiqui and Wizarat Husain *Education Quarterly* 32(2) Ap 1980 p 36-38

Education : Nigeria

The new structure of Nigerian educational system. J.P. Gabial; and J.K. Pillai *EPA Quarterly Bulletin* 7(3-4) Oc 1984-Ja 1985 p 8-16 refs

Education : Periodicals

Educational journals in India. Ram Ratan Harsh *Indian Education* 11(3) Je 1981 p 21

Professional journals in education in India : Some issues. R. Govinda and

S.B. Menon *J Indian Education* 11(3) Se 1985 p 13-20

See also

Under titles of individual educational journals, e.g., Indian Educational Review (Periodical)

Education : Personnel Service

See

Personnel Service in Education

Education : Philosophy

Beyond domination : An essay in the political philosophy of education. Patricia White. £11.95 *Book Rev, Education Quarterly* 36(4) Wint 1984 p 54-55

Can education ignore metaphysics, epistemology and ethics. Ram Shakal Pandey *Progress of Education* 53(7) Fe 1979 p 74-76

A case for Indian philosophy of education - Some issues. K.K. Sharma *et al* *Progress of Education* 57(4) Nv 1982 p 122-25 refs

In search of a philosophy of education. K.L. Shrimali *National J Education* 5(1) Se 1982 p 1-4

Indianisation of education and philosophy : A critique. W.A. Siddiqui *J Indian Education* 8(5) Ja 1983 p 3-10

A introduction to philosophy of education. Robin Barrow and Ronald Woods. London, Mathuen. 1982, 207p. £4.75 *Book Rev, Education Quarterly* 35(3) Jl 1983 p 53-55

Learning activities and the curriculum. Marlow Ediger *Educational Rev* 87(10) Oc 1981 p 193-95

Materialism and scientism in the educational philosophy of Pandit Iswar Chandra Vidyasagar. Sunanda Samaddar and B.R. Purkait *Perspective Education* 2(4) Oc 1986 p 213-20 refs

Philosophical implications in the school curriculum. Marlow Ediger *Teacher Education* 14(10-11) Ja-Ap 1980 p 34-39 refs

Philosophy and education. Michael V. Belok and Joe L. Green, *eds*. Meerut, Anu Prakahan. 227. Rs. 65 *Book Rev, teacher Today* 25 (2) Oc-de 1982 p 99-100

Philosophy of education : An introduction. T.W. Moore. London, Routledge. 1982,142p. £3.95 *Book Rev, Education Quarterly* 35(3) Jl 1983 p 65-66

Philosophy of education and the reading curriculum. Marlow Ediger *Indian Education* 10(8) Mr 1980 p 8-11

Philosophy of education and the social studies. Marlow Ediger *Experiments in Education* 9(5) Jl 1981 p 82-84

Philosophy of education and the teacher. V.K. Rai *Educational Rev* 85(6) Je 1979 p 101-03 refs

The philosophy of schooling. Robin Barrow. Sussex, Weatheaf Bks, 1981. 211p. £3.95 *Book Rev, Education Quarterly* 34(2) Ap 1982 p 51-52

Pre-determimism in education. Jyoti Prasad Banerjee *Our Education* 1 Jl 1980 p 35-40 refs

Providing for individual differences. Marlow Ediger *Progress of Education* 55(1) Ag 1980 p 15-18

Research in philosophy of education. C. Sheshdadri *Indian Educational Rev* 18(4) Oc 1983 p 99-105

Teachers educational philosophic orientation in relation to some personal

variables : A study. A.R. Bisht *Bharatiya Shiksha Shodh Patrika* 4(1) Ja-Je 1985 p 65-68 refs

What is the philosophy of education? V.K. Rai *Educational Rev* 89(11) Nv 1983 p 193-95

Education : Psychology

See

Educational Psychology

Education : Research

See

Educational Research

Education : Russia

Prolonged day school plus aesthetic education (Experiment in a Soviet school), Mikhail Sidur. *Progress of Education* 54(4-5) Nv-De 1979 p 91-93

The role of education in eradicating distinctions between town and countryside and between physical and intellectual labour. *Bulletin of Non-formal Education* 2(3) Ja 1985 p 1-17

School in 2000 : The Soviet model. Bestazhev Lada *Progress of Education* 55(9) Ap 1981 p 241-42

School reform in USSR. D.C. Upreti *Rajasthan Board J Education* 20(4)-21(1) Oc 1984-Mr 1985 p 21-29

Soviet education : Theory and practice. Jaweed Ashraf. New Delhi, Sterling. 1978, 200p. Rs.45 *Book Rev, Education Quarterly* 30(3) Oc 1978 p 41-42; *J Higher Education* 4(1) Mon 1978 p 121-24; *National J Education* 20(1) Se 1979 p 62-63; *Teacher Today* 22(3) Ja-Mr 1980 p 100-02

Soviet school looks into the future, Zoya Malkova *Progress of Education* 57(2) Jl 1983 p 285-87

The Soviet school. V.S. Aransky *Indian Education* 10(7) Oc 1980 p 10-12

Values in Soviet education. K.R.P. Singh *Primary Teacher* 11(3) Jl 1986 p 1-3

Education : Saudi Arabia

Education today in Saudi Arabia. M.I. Kazi *Progress of Education* 60(6) Ja 1986 p 143-44

Education : Simulation Methods

See

Microteaching

Education : Social Aspects

A case for social philosophy of education. Jayshree Mathur *J Indian Education* 8(5) Ja 1983 p 17-20

Challenges in education, culture and social welfare. S. Nurul Hasan. New Delhi, Allied. vol. 1. 1977, 358p. Rs.60 *Book Rev, Teacher Today* 21(3) Ja-Mr 1979 p 103-04

Culture, politics and critical academics. Asoke Basu Allahabad, Archana Pra. 106p. Rs.50 *Book Rev, J Higher Education* 9(1) Mon 1983 p 149-52

Education and culture for liberation. Patrick Van Rensburg *Indian J Adult Education* 44(10) Oc 1983 p 6-15

Education and cultural deprivation. Monica Misra *New Frontiers in Education* 10(2) Ap-Je 1980 p 1-13 refs

Education and cultural development. M.S.V. Chari *Educational Rev* 89(4) Ap 1983 p 75-76

Education and modern society. S.B. Malik *Primary Teacher* 10(2) Ap 1985 p 9-10

Education and social change; editorial. *J Indian Education* 5(4) Nv 1979 p 1-2

Education and social justice in telematic societies. Jack Culbertson *Teacher Education* 18(24-25) Jl-Oc 1983 p 25-43 refs

Education for social development. R. Dhandapani *Experiments in Education* 10(4) Jl 1982 p 74-76 +

Indian education : The anti-cultural involution. Dinesh Mohan *J Higher Education* 9(1) Mon 1983 p 21-34 refs

Linking culture and education. Chandran Deanesan *New Frontiers in Education* 10(3) Jl-Se 1980 p 78-82

School as a socialising agent : A preliminary study. C. Raghava *et al J Indian Education* 6(6) Mr 1981 p 16-19

Teaching in a poly-cultural context : Lessons from concept, trends and developments in some relevant foundation disciplines. M. Kundu *J Higher Education* 8(2) Aut 1982 p 191-98 refs

Universal education and social development. D.S. Hoods *Education Quarterly* 35(3) Jl 1983 p 12-13

See also

Socialism and Education

Education : Standards

An appraisal of the standards in education. Gurpal Singh Jarial *Teacher Today* 23(1) Jl-Se 1980 p 26-35 refs

Are the educational standards deteriorating? M. Sree Rama Murthy *Indian Educational Rev* 15(2) Ap 1980 p 36-49 tabs

Cost-quality relations in education. S.L. Jena *J Indian Education* 6(4) Nv 1980 p 8-12

Criteria and influential factors in standards of education. K. Adinarayana *Experiments in Education* 8(2) Ap 1980 p 37-40

Decentralised curriculum and quality of education. Bager Mehdi *Primary Teacher* 9(2) Ap 1984 p 1-3

Devaluation of education : A quantitive analysis. P.R. Panchamukhi *J Higher Education* 1(1) Mon 1975 p 15-30 tabs

Education and its standards : A study into the problem. M.D. Deousker *Progress of Education* 54(9) Ap 1980 p 170-77

Education, quality and culture : An analysis. C. Seshadri *J Higher Education* 3(3) Spr 1978 p 315-19 refs

Innovative inset strategies for quality in education. M. Raj Chilana *Rajasthan Board J Education* 15(2) Ap-Je 1979 p 51-58

Quality control in education through "control chart" technique. B.B. Pandit *Progress of Education* 56(6) Ja 1982 p 132-35 + tabs

Quality education : Review of the concept and empirical dimensions. Arvind K. Sinha *Indian Educational Rev* 20(4) Oc 1985 p 1-19 refs

Quality education through academic programmes. S. Audinarayana Moorthy *Educational Rev* 84(11) Nv 1978 p 201-02

Quality in education and its relevance. R.P. Singh *Education Quarterly* 35(1) Ja 1983 p 5-8

Quality in education; editorial. *J Indian Education* 5(5) Ja 1980 p 1-2

Quest for quality in education. G.L. Arora *Education Quarterly* 38(1) Spr 1986 p 5-7

This problem of standards in education. S.K. Nanda *Educational Rev* 86(9) Se 1980 p 178-79

Education : Tanzania

Mass education in Tanzania. Nazar Gerves Nyoni *Indian Education* 10(9-10) De 1980-Ja 1981 p 20-22

Education : Thailand : History

Culture and education in Thailand : Historical antecendents. S.N. Katiyar *Teacher Today* 22(3) Ja-Mr 1980 p 71-80

Education : United States

Education as a industry. Joseph T. Froomkin and others, *eds*. Cambridge, Ballinger Pub Co. 1976, 480p. *Book Rev, J Indian Education* 5(4) Nv 1979 p 71-72

The educationally disadvantaged in the USA and the U.K. M. Raghuram-singh *Experiments in Education* 10(5) Jl 1982 p 79-89 refs

Issues and advances in education. U.S. Chaudhari. Delhi, Ajanta Books Int. 1986, 230p. Rs.125 *Book Rev, Teacher Today* 29(1) Jl-Se 1986 p 106-07

Education : Yugoslavia

Recurrent education in Yogoslavia. Mikse Nikola Soljan, *ed.* Zegrab, Preglad Jugsolovenshi. 1987. 116p. *Book Rev, J Higher Education* 9(3) Spr 1984 p 418-19

Education, Agricultural

See

Agricultural Education

Education, Art

See

Art : Study and Teaching

Education, Basic

See

Basic Education

Education, Business

See

Business Education

Education, Character

See

Moral Education

Education, Civic

Concepts of civic education. G.N.S. Raghavan *Indian J Adult Education* 46(9) Se 1985 p 5-9

Mass media for civic education the challenges of research. J.S. Yadav *Indian J Adult Education* 46(9) Se 1985 p 17-21 refs

Mass media for civic education. V.N. Kakar *Indian J Adult Education* 46(9) Se 1985 p 22-26

Education, Comparative

See

Comparative Education

Education, Compulsory

See

School Attendance

Education, Elementary

Elementary education : A study of regional and social disparities; editorial. *J Education and Psychology* 39(4) Ja 1982 p 207-10

Formation and role of place value concepts of the number system at the elementary stage of education. A.K. Sharma *Quest in Education* 17(2) Ap 1980 p 181-87

Quality and its role in universalising elementary education. K. Sudha Rao *Education Quarterly* 37(1) Spr 1985 p 27-31 refs

Role of non-formal education in the context of universalisation of elementary education. Prabina K. Tripathy *Progress of Education* 60(5) De 1985 p 107-10 refs

Systems approach in elementary education. R.N. Agarwal *Primary Teacher* 11(1) Ja 1986 p 7-10

Simulation and gaming in elementary education : An experiment. R.N. Agarwal *Primary Teacher* 11(3) Jl 1986 p 29-32

Universalisation of elementary education : A dream. C. Dharmarajan *Educational Rev* 92(7) Jl 1986 p 105-06

Universalising elementary education. D.V. Chickermane. Res Centre. 1983, 40p. *Book Rev, Progress of Education* 57(6) Ja 1983 p 143

Universalising of elementary education. Sunil Behari Mohanty *Education Quarterly* 35(2) Ap 1983 p 24-32 refs

Education, Elementary : China (People's Republic)

Elementary education in the People's Republic of China, 1949-1975. Ramdev P. Kathuria *Teacher Today* 21(3) Ja-mr 1979 p 6-18 refs

Education, Elementary : Great Britain

Dilemmas of schooling. Ann Berlak and Harold Berlak. London, Methuen. 299p. *Book Rev, Education Quarterly* 34(4) Oc 1982 p 55-56

Elementary education : British pointers; editorial. *Educational Rev* 85(9) Se 1979 p 180

Education, Elementary : India

Challenge of elementary education in India. Rajendra Jayaswal *Bharatiya Shiksha Shodh Patrika* 5(2) Jl-De 1986 p 61-67

Contemporary issues in elementary education. Vajubhai Patel *Experiments in Education* 6(5) Jl 1978 p 88-89

Elementary education in India : Myth, reality alternative. John Kurian. New Delhi, Vikas Pub,1983. *Book Rev, Bulletin of Non-formal Education* 3(1 Je 1985 p 16-19; *Progress of Education* 58(4) Nv 1983 p 98+

Experimental try-out application of tools and techniques for evaluation and monitoring of universalisation of elementary education in India. I.S. Chaudhri *EPA Quarterly Bulletin* 7(3-4) Oc 1984-Ja 1985 p 17-25 refs

Guidelines in the elementary school. E.G. Vedanoyagam *Experiments in Education* 6(6) Ag 1978 p 93-98 refs

Universalisation of elementary education : A difficult task. R.K. Bhandari *Education Quarterly* 31(2) Jl 1979 p 8-11

Universalisation of elementary education in India : Past experiences, future strategies. V.P. Garg *Education Quarterly* 36(2) Ap 1984 p 1-9

Universalisation of elementary education : The alternative strategies. Sarla Rajput *Indian Education* 10(3) Jl 1980 p 24-28

Education, Elementary : India : Andhra Pradesh

Progress of elementary education in Andhra Pradesh : Impact of demographic factors. D.P. Jain. New Delhi, NCERT. 1984, 114p. Rs.15 *Book Rev, Indian Educational Rev* 20(3) Jl 1985 p 113-14

Education, Elementary : India : Assam

Elementary education in Assam. S.C. Barthakur *Educational Rev* 92(8) Ag 1986 p 126-27

Education, Elementary : India : Uttar Pradesh

A study of private costs of schooling girls at the elementary stage. S.L. Gupta *EPA Bulletin* 6(2) Jl 1983 p 31-40 tabs

Education, Elementary : Indonesia

The 'Pamong' elementary education system : An introduction. *Rajasthan Board J Education* 16(1-2) Ja-Je 1980 p 26-29

Education, Elementary : Standards

Towards quality elementary school. Ashwani Kumar *Primary Teacher* 9(4) Oc 1984 p 14-16

Education, Experimental

See

Experimental Education

Education, Higher

Advancement in higher education teaching methods - A review. D. Prabhakara Rao *Educational Rev* 90(2) Fe 1984 p 28-29

Conceptualising higher education as a system. S.P.. Gupta *Progress of Education* 59(12) Jl 1985 p 260-65+

College climates : Explorations of a concept. J. Filella *New Frontiers in Education* 12(3) Jl-Se 1982 p 1-13 refs

Contemporary teaching methods and technologies in higher education : A report of this national seminar. *University News* 21(19) Oc 1983 p 632-33

Effective reorganisation for higher education. P.C. Shejwalkar *Progress of Education* 56(3) Oc 1981 p 71-73

The effectiveness of modular scheduling in higher education. P.J. Gabrial and J.K. Pillai *J Higher Education* 6(1-3) 1980-81 p 128-31 refs

Emerging ward at colleges. Anand P. Srivastava *University News* 24(43) 16 Nv 1986 p 1-3

Evaluation in higher education. Moonis Raza and Amitabh Kundu *J Higher Education* 5(3) Spr 1980 p 359-69 refs

The future of college education. *Educational Rev* 86(5) My 1980 p 87-88

The future of college education. *Educational Rev* 87(2) Fe 1981 p 37-39

Higher education - A comparative and historical perspective. *J Higher Education* 7(3) Spr 1982 p i-v

Higher education and culture. Ungkur Aziz *New Frontiers in Education* 14(1) Ja-Mr 1984 p 81-86

Higher education and training in non-violence : The Shanti Sena of Gandhigram Rural Institute. M. Radha Krishnan *University News* 23(32) 23 Ag 1985 p 5-7

Higher education : Crisis and support : An international perspective. New York, ICED. 134p. *Book Rev, J Higher Education* 5(3) Spr 1980 p 433-35

Higher education in the tribal context. Nirmal Minz *New Frontiers in Education* 12(1) Ja-Mr 1982 p 50-53

Higher education revisited. Lord Robbins. London, Macmillan. 1980, 117 p £ 12 *Book Rev, Educational Quarterly* 32(4) Oc 1980 p 47-48

The higher education system : Academic organisation in cross-national perspective. Burton R. Clark. Berkeley, Univ. of Calif Press. 1983, 315p. *Book Rev, J Higher Education* 9(3) Spr 1984 p 415-18

INSAT-1B and higher education : Rais Ahmed *J Higher Education* 9(3) Spr 1984 p 301-03

Imperative need for value-based higher education. Ramlal Parikh *University News* 23(2) 8 Ja 1985 p 5-6

In higher education : Neglected aspect of good teaching. Navin Chandra Joshi *Education Quarterly* 37(1) Spr 1985 p 1-3

In higher education : The neglected aspect of good teaching. Navin Chandra Joshi *Educational Quarterly* 32(1) Ja 1980 p 8-10

Integration of higher education for effective vocational training. M.R. Bhiday *J Higher Education* 5(3) Spr 1980 p 371-79

Intercultural cooperation in higher education. Ettore Gelpi *J Higher Education* 9(3) Spr 1984 p 323-32 refs

Issues and choices in higher education. Kishore Gandhi. Delhi, B.R. Pub.1977. 195p. Rs 55 *Book Rev, Education Quarterly* 34(2) Ap 1982 p 52-53

Limits in higher education. R.S. Mishra *University News* 23(35) 16 Se 1985 p 11-13 refs

Linkages between teaching and learning in higher education. A.P. Srivastava *National J Education* 7(1) Se 1984 p 1-18 refs

Linkage of higher education with environment. G. Subramania Pillay *J Higher Education* 4(3) Spr 1979 p 373-80

Meritocracy in higher education. Vasant D. Bhat *Education Quarterly* 33(3) Jl 1981 p 14-16 +

Modernising effect of university education. S.L. Sharma. New Delhi, Allied. 1979, 236p. Rs.45 *Book Rev, J Higher Education* 6(1-3) 1980-81 p 161-63

New direction for higher education. Navin Chander Joshi *Teacher Education* 20(30-31) Ja-Ap 1985 p 33-36

Problems of teachers in higher education. Asha Khopkar and Sunanda Karnad *Progress of Education* 60(1) Ag 1985 p 7-9

The remedial approach in college education. Plamthodathil. S. Jacob *New Frontiers in Education* 11(4) Oc-De 1981 p 15-27

Role of research in higher education. M.R. Rangarajan *Educational Rev* 92(5-6) My-Je 1986 p 81-83 refs

Salvaging higher education : Limiting the importance of degrees. John Kurrion *J Higher Education* 9(2) Aut 1985 p 207-16

Some thoughts on higher education. V.K.R.V. Rao *J Higher Education* 6(1-3) 1980-81 p 1-7

Striving for height in higher education. Devdatta Dabhalkar *J Higher Education* 6(1-3) 1980-81 p 41-50

Structure and performance of college education. Rudolf C. Heredia. Bombay, Somaiya Pub. 1981, 192p. Rs.65 *Book Rev, Indian Educational Rev*

17(2) Ap 1982 p 137-38; *J Higher Education* 8(2) Aut 1982 p 254-55

A tool for undergraduate in selecting a specialisation. Asha Rao *Progress of Education* 58(1) Ag 1983 p 19-24

The university as an institution : Present problems and future trends. Dietrich Goldschmdt *J Higher Education* 9(1) Mon 1983 p 65-75 tabs

See also

Higher Education and State
Higher Education of Women
Semester System
Technical Education
Television in Higher Education
Universities and Colleges
University Grants Commission

Education, Higher : Asia

Asian higher education : A new challenges. Paul T. Lauby *New Frontiers in Education* 14(4) Oc-De 1984 p 46-53

Higher education and the labour market in Asia. Bikas C. Sanyal *J Higher Education* 8(2) Aut 1982 p 167-77 refs tabs

Education, Higher : Brazil

Higher education in an authoritarian society : A case study of Brazil. R. Narayanan *J Higher Education* 7(3) Spr 1982 p 219-26 refs

Education, Higher : Canada

Demand and financing of higher education in Canada. K.R. Shah *J Higher Education* 5(2) Aut 1979 p 251-52

The demand for and financing of higher education in Canada. Brahm Prakash *J Higher Education* 3(3) Spr 1978 p 345-55 refs

Education, Higher : China (People's Republic)

Fair access to higher education : Reflections on India's and China's experience of the past thirty years. Mathew Zechariah *J Higher Education* 8(3) Spr 1983 p 311-20

Higher education in China. Gargi Dutt *J Higher Education* 5(2) Aut 1979 p 159-66

Higher education in China. *New Frontiers in Education* 14(1) Ja-Mr 1984 p 90-93

Higher education in China. Shao-xi-shi *University News* 23(14) 8 Ap 1985 p 2-3

Some steps on the reform in higher education. Z.Y. Huo *Teacher Education* 20(30-31) Ja-Ap 1985 p 21-24

Education, Higher : Costs

The cost analysis in higher education. V.P. Garg. New Delhi, Metropolitan. 1985, 216p. Rs.80 *Book Rev, Perspectives in Education* 1(3) Jl 1985 p 205-06

Expenditure on university education : A unit cost analysis. K.S. Chalam *J Higher Education* 4(2) Aut 1978 p 201-24

Institutional costs of university education. G.D. Sharma. New Delhi, Assn. of Indian University. 1980, 165p. Rs.40 *Book Rev, Indian Educational Rev* 15(3) Jl 1980 p 125-26; *J Higher Education* 6(1-3) 1980-81 p 163-64

Pricing of higher education. Neela Shelat and Shribatsa Jena *New Frontiers in Education* 11(3) Jl-Se 1981 p 73-79 refs

Private costs in higher education. U.P. Garg *J Higher Education* 8(2) Aut 1982 p 220-27 tabs

Private cost of post graduate education. B.P. Goel *J Indian Education* 11(2) Jl 1985 p 58-63 refs

Unit cost analysis of higher education in India. Jandhyala B.G. Tilak *J Higher Education* 5(2) Aut 1979 p 183-93

Universities costs and outputs : Studies on education. Donald Verry and Bleddyn Pryce Davies. Elsevier Scientific Pub. vol. 6. 1978 244p. *Book Rev, J Higher Education* 4(1) Mon 1978 p 124-25

Education, Higher : Curricula

Criteria in the higher education curriculum. Marlow Ediger *New Frontiers in Education* 14(4) Oc-De 1984 p 34-39 refs

Curriculum development and instructional organisation in higher education. S.P. Duggal *Educational Rev* 89(7) Jl 1983 p 118-21 refs

Curricular reform in higher education. N.K. Upasani *Quest in Education* 19(2) Ap 1982 p 137-45

Curriculum : A proposal. Buddhadeva Bhattacharya and Janes Patranabis *J Higher Education* 1(1) Mon 1975 p 87-90

Determinants of choice of studies at university level. Ujagar Singh *J Higher Education* 2(2) Aut 1976 p 253-59 tabs

Education, Higher : Developing Countries

Higher education in the third world : Themes and variations. Philip G. Altbach. Singapore, Maruzan Asia. 1982, 28p. *Book Rev, J Higher Education* 9(1) Mon 1983 p 145-48

Education, Higher : Economic Aspects

Economic versus educational viability dilemma in higher education. V.P. Garg *EPA Quarterly Bulletin* 6(2) Jl 1983 p 22-30 refs

Economics of higher education current trends and new priorities. S.M. Israney and K.K. Balachander *University News* 24(42) 8 Nv 1986 p 111-17 refs

Education, Higher : Finance

Financing of higher education in India. Jagdish Lal Azad. New Delhi, Sterling 1975, 214p. Rs.40 *Book Rev, J Higher Education* 3(3) Spr 1978 p 421-22

Is financing Indian higher education equitable? C.B. Padmanabhan *University News* 23(8) 23 Fe 1985 p 25-27

Management and financing of higher education. K.N. Bhatnagar *University News* 23(6) 8 Fe 1985 p 2-4

Education, Higher : France

Higher education in France : Recent trends. Jacques Hallak *J Higher Education* 5(1) Mon 1979 p 1-6

Education, Higher : Great Britain

Developments in British tertiary education. John Egglestone *J Higher Education* 5(3) Spr 1980 p 301-16 refs tabs

Higher education in the United Kingdom, 1980-82. London, Longmans. 326p. £4.95 *Book Rev, Education Quarterly* 33(3) Jl 1981 p 50

The higher education scene in Britain today. Asa Briggs *J Higher Education* 9(1) Mon 1983 p 47-63

Education, Higher : India

All India conference of Vice Chancellors on value orientation in higher education. *University News* 23(2) 8 Ja 1985 p 1-3 +

American influence on higher education in India. M. Shahnaz Suri. New Delhi, Sterling. 88p. Rs.30 *Book Rev, Education Quarterly* 32(1) Ja 1980 p 42-43

A case for autonomy. R.V. Kamat *J Higher Education* 1(1) Mon 1975 p 91-97 refs

A comparative study of the attitudes of social and engineering students to certain aspects of higher education. Jayalakshmi Indiresan *J Higher Education* 5(2) Aut 1979 p 233-36

Crisis in higher education in India. D.P. Pattanayak *J Higher Education* 6(1-3) 1980-81 p 51-54 refs

Crisis in higher education. K. Vikram Sinha Rao *Progress of Education* 57(8) Mr 1983 p 181-83

Economic versus educational viability : Dilemma in higher education. V.P. Garg *EPA Quarterly Bulletin* 6(2) Jl 1983 p 22-30 refs tabs

Equalisation of opportunities in higher education. *J Higher Education* 1(2) Aut 1973 p 269-70

Fair access to higher education : Reflections on India's and China's experience of the past thirty years. Mathew Zechariah *J Higher Education* 8(3) Spr 1983 p 311-20

Far from the main campus. R.K. Yadav *J Higher Education* 1(1) Mon 1975 p 99-102

Federalism and highr education : The Indian experience. Marina Pinta. Bombay, Orient Longman. 1984, 250p. Rs.85 *Book Rev, Perspectives in Education* 1(4) Oc 1985 p 267-68

Higher education and five year plans : Policies, plans and perspectives. S.N. Saraf *University News* 23(3) 16 Ja 1985 p 2-5; 23(5) 1 Fe 1985 p 2-4

Higher education : Frames of reference in existing literature. Sushanta Banerjee and Ashok Malhotra *J Higher Education* 3(3) Spr 1978 p 301-14 refs

Higher education in India. B. Rajaiah *Educational Rev* 91(8) Ap 1985 p 124-25 tabs

Higher education in India : Certain issues. P.K. Sahoo *New Frontiers in Education* 13(3) Oc-De 1983 p 62-68

Higher education in India : Plans and prospects. Satish Chandra *J Higher Education* 1(1) Mon 1975 p 5-18 tabs

Higher education in India : Some issues. Q.U. Khan *J Higher Education* 5(2) Aut 1979 p 167-82

Higher education in India : Survival and revival. M.S. Yadav *et al Indian Educational Rev* 20(3) Jl 1985 p 1-11

Higher education : Kothari Commission and after. A.R. Kamat *J Higher Education* 8(2) Aut 1982 p 141-43 refs

The higher learning in India. Amrik Singh and Philip G. Altbach. Vikas Pub. 1974, 451p. Rs.50 *Book Rev, J Higher Education* 1(1) Mon 1975 p 141-43

Human values in higher education. V. Shanmugasundaram *University News* 22(48) 23 De 1984 5-7 refs

Innovations in undergraduate education. J.N. Kapur *J Higher Education* 1(1) Mon 1975 p 103-09 refs

International cooperation and collaboration in Indian higher education. Vipula Chaturevedi *Indian Education* 18(5-6) Ag-Se 1983 p 19-26

Issues and options in higher education in India. S.C. Goel *New Frontiers in Education* 11(3) Jl-Se 1981 p 26-32

Latent function of higher education in India. Indra Deva *J Higher Education* 7(3) Spr 1982 p 211-17 refs

Management of learning in higher education. N.K. Upasani *Quest in Education* 16(4) Oc 1979 p 267-74; 17(1) Ja 1980 p 13-20

Obstacles to creativity in higher education. *University News* 23(10) 8 Mr 1985 p 5-8

On the state of higher education in India. *New Frontiers in Education* 9(4) Oc-De p 74-78

Oppose Jha Commission report. Pallab Sengupta *Student Action* 2(2) Je 1983 p 7-8

Patterns and problems of higher education. Samuel Mathai *New Frontiers in Education* 11(2) Ap-Je 1981 p 37-72; 11(3) Jl-Se 1981 p 33-72

A perspective on higher education in India - The case of private control. Nirmal Singh *J Higher Education* 5(1) Mon 1979 p 21-31

A philosophical analysis of methods of teaching at the higher education stage. C.D. Indapurkar *J Higher Education* 5(1) Mon 1979 p 7-11

Problems of higher education in India : An approach to structural analysis and reorganisation. K.L. Joshi. Bombay, Popular. 1977. 312p. Rs.18 *Book Rev, Indian Educational Rev* 14(1) Ja 1979 p 152-57; *J Higher Education* 4(2) Aut 1978 p 287-90; *New Frontiers in Education* 9(1) Ja-Mr 1979 p 114-15

Regional imbalance in the growth of higher education in India. M.R. Rabindranathan *J Higher Education* 4(1) Mon 1978 p 33-40

Remoulding Indian higher education. Malcolm S. Adiseshiah *New Frontiers in Education* 12(2) Ap-Je 1982 p 14-20

Social costs of reservation in higher education : A decision theoretic view. B.B. Chatterjee *J Higher Education* 9(1) Mon 1983 p 77-89 refs tabs

Some steps on the reform on higher education. Z.Y. Hua *University News* 23(15) 16 Ap 1985 p 4-5

Student perception of the purposes of higher education. P. Joseph Sathiaraj. *J Higher Education* 9(3) Spr 1984 p 395-97 refs

Teachers in higher education : A review of their problems and status. R.P. Singh *Education Quarterly* 37(1) Spr 1985 p 4-11

Teaching and research in higher education : Some problems. V. Bhaskara Rao *J Higher Education* 4(1) Mon 1978 p 11-22 refs tabs

Toning up of higher education in India. U. Tirupati Rao *Educational Rev* 91(12) De 1985 p 211-14

Towards a meaningful first degree. V.V. John *J Higher Education* 1(1) Mr 1975 p 56-60

Universities and people's education for development. Kishore Sant *J Higher Education* 8(2) Aut 1982 p 185-89 refs

University education today. Shamsuddin *Progress of Education* 59(5) De 1984 p 95-98 +

What determines higher education aspirations? *J Indian Education* 5(4) Nv 1979 p 62-64

Who goes to college? Vimal P. Shah and Tara Patel. Rachna Pra. 1977, 219p. *Book Rev, J Higher Education* 4(3) Spr 1979 p 427-30

Education, Higher : India : Andhra Pradesh

Productivity trends in higher education in Andhra Pradesh. K.S. Chalam *EPA Quarterly Bulletin* 6(3-4) Oc 1983-Ja 1984 p 40-55 refs tab

Education, Higher : India : Assam

Higher education in Assam 1866-1979. Samir Kumar Sutradhar *Educational Rev* 86(9) Se 1980 p 165-71

Education, Higher : India : History

Higher education : Historical and other problems. K.L. Joshi. Bombay, Popular. 1981, 143p. Rs.15 *Book Rev, Education Quarterly* 35(4) Oc 1983 p 68-70; *Indian Educational Rev* 18(2) Ap 1983 p 136-37; *Progress of Education* 57(8) Mr 1983 p 189+

Higher education in India, 1951-71. J.N. Kaul. Simla, IIAS. 1974, 203p. *Book Rev, J Higher Education* 1(2) Aut 1975 p 292-93

Education, Higher : India : Kerala

Higher education in Kerala. C. Paul Verghese *New Frontiers in Education* 12(2) Ap-Je 1982 p 21-24

Turning points in sex differentials in higher education. J. Rajasekharan Nair *J Higher Education* 6(1-3) 1980-81 p 122-28 tabs

Education, Higher : India : Maharashtra

Progress of higher education in Maharashtra. Ram Takawala *Progress of Education* 59(10-11) My-Je 1985 p 218-23 +

Education, Higher : India : Punjab

Interconversion of awards in trimester and traditional systems of education for the P.G. programme. T.A. Ramasubban *et al J Higher Education* 4(2) Aut 1978 p 273-77

Education, Higher : India : Rajasthan

Making undergraduate education more relevant - A moral developed at the University of Rajasthan, Jaipur. M.L. Sisodia and B.M. Agrawal *J Higher Education* 8(2) Aut 1982 p 214-45 appdx

Education, Higher : India : States

Determinants of levels of higher education in states. S.C. Seddey and Ravi Kant Gupta *J Higher Education* 9(1) Mon 1983 p 133-44 refs tabs

Education, Higher : India : Uttar Pradesh

Value structures of higher education and the university teachers. Sunita Gupta *J Higher Education* 9(2) Aut 1983 p 254-59 refs

Education, Higher : India : West Bengal

Graduate employment and higher education in West Bengal. P. Bose and S.P. Mukherjee *J Higher Education* 5(3) Spr 1980 p 281-89 tabs

Education, Higher : Nepal

Higher education in Nepal - At a glance. W.H. Siddiqui and Wizarat Husain *Educational Rev* 88(11) Nv 1982 p 199-201; 89(1) Ja 1983 p 3-4; 89(2) Fe 1983 p 24-25

Education, Higher : Philippines

Higher education and the labour market in the Philippines. Bikas C. Sanyal. Paris, UNESCO; New Delhi, Wiley East. 1981, 316p. *Book Rev, J Higher*

Education 8(2) Aut 1982 p 255-57

Education, Higher : Research

Researches in higher education. D.C. Joshi *J Higher Education* 3(3) Spr 1978 p 399-404 refs

Education, Higher : Russia

Some aspects of higher education in the Soviet Union. R.G. Gidadhubli *J Higher Education* 2(2) Aut 1976 p 149-65 refs tabs

Education, Higher : Standards

Improving quality of higher education. I. Satya Sundaram *Education Quarterly* 38(2) Sum 1986 p 1-4

Education, Higher : State Aid

See

State Aid to Higher Education

Education, Higher : United States

Higher education in the USA. R.P. Singh *J Indian Education* 6(1) My 1980 p 38-41

Some glimpses of American higher education. V. Krishna Moorthy *University News* 23(30) 8 Ag 1985 p 2-4 +

Education, Humanistic

Dear teacher let the relationship be human. S. Lakshmi *Experiments in Education* 6(11) Ja 1979 p 197-200

Education and attention : A basis for the humanities. Douglas Walatara. Delhi, Macmillan. 1980, xii, 125p. Rs.50 *Book Rev, Education Quarterly* 33(3) Jl 1981 p 45-46

Education and human values. D.S. Kothari *Teacher Today* 28(1) Jl-Se 1985 p 1-10

Education for human excellence. K.K.S. Rajendran *Educational Rev* 84(11) Nv 1978 p 210-14

Humanising education. Srinibas Bhattacharya *Quest in Education* 17(3) Jl 1980 p 212-16

In search of humanistic schools. G.L. Arora *J Indian Education* 6(1) My 1980 p 3-7

Need to humanise education. V.S. Mathur *J Indian Education* 6(4) Nv 1980 p 23-25

Education, International

See

International Education

Education, Liberal

See

Education, Humanistic

Education, Manual

See

Manual Training

Education, Military

See

Military Education

Education, Moral

See

Moral Education

Education, Pre-school

A case and programme for pre-primary education. V. Rajasekharan *Experiments in Education* 6(4) Je 1978 p 64-65 refs

Early childhood pre-school education : Importance and need. J.T. Jayaprasada Rao *Indian Education* 12(3-4) Je-Jl 1982 p 31-33

Education of the pre-school child. Indu Pandit *Progress of Education* 54(10-11) My-Je 1980 p 194-98

Harnessing the pre-schooler's potential : An educational imperative. K. Basavaiah *New Frontiers in Education* 9(1) Ja-Mr 1979 p 70-76

How to make pre-primary education more effective. Qamaruddin *Primary Teacher* 6(2) Ap 1981 p 18-23

Need for early childhood education. U. Bevli *Primary Teacher* 8(4) Oc 1983 p 9-13

Perspectives in preschool education. Aruna Thakkar. Bombay, Popular. 1980, 84p. Rs.30 *Book Rev, Education Quarterly* 33(3) Jl 1981 p 50-51

Pre-school education : An Indian perspective. V.J. Kochuthresia *J Indian Education* 11(2) Jl 1985 p 3-10 refs

Priority to pre-primary education. Bir Singh *Education Quarterly* 33(1) Ja 1981 p 8-9

Education, Pre-school : India

Emerging needs and problems of pre-school education in India. B. Mukhopadhyay and T. Datta *Educational Rev* 87(12) De 1981 p 231-33; 88(1) Ja 1982 p 11-14

Emerging of early childhood education in India. B.D. Sharma *J Indian Education* 12(1) My 1986 p 31-40

Origin and development of pre-school education in India. A.N. Patra *Education Quarterly* 31(1) Ap 1979 p 13-14

Education, Pre-school : India : Andhra Pradesh

A study of the effect of pre-school education on primary and secondary school education. R. Srinivasa Rao *Experiments in Education* 8(11) Ja 1981 p 193-97 tabs

Education, Pre-school : India : Gujarat

Experiments in community development through early childhood intervention experiences of the department of child development. Amita Verma *Quest in Education* 19(1) Ja 1982 p 7-20 refs

Education, Pre-school : India : History

Pre-primary education in India from 1949-61 and its related problems. M.N. Ravindranatha *Experiments in Education* 8(5) Jl 1980 p 84-93 refs

Education, Primary

Comprehensive access to primary education. *Primary Teacher* 8(3) Jl 1983 p 1-8

Contemporary educational problems. D.L. Gupta *Primary Teacher* 6(1) Ja 1981 p 26-27

Development schedule for first standard primary students. Hari Datt Sharma *Primary Teacher* 6(4) Oc 1981 p 26-28

Effect of schooling on learning abilities and academic achievement of primary school children. S. Moses and K. Mayuli *Indian Educational Rev* 19(1) Ja 1984 p 120-25

Effecting teaching in primary schools : A strategy. Rajeshwar N. Mathur *Primary Teacher* 6(3) Jl 1981 p 4-10

The effectiveness of two different menthods of teaching reading in primary school children. S. Subramanyam *Experiments in Education* 8(10) De 1980 p 185-87 tabs

Emergence of primary school psychology. R.D. Sharma *Primary Teacher* 9(2) Ap 1984 p 16-18

Environment as a basis for meaningful learning in primary education. *Primary Teacher* 8(3) Jl 1983 p 18-22

Making primary education creative. Bhanwar Lal Magda *Primary Teacher* 8(1) Ja 1983 p 18-19

A new strategy for primary education. Rajeshwar N. Mathur *Indian Education* 12(1-2) Ap-My 1982 p 30-31

Non-formal education as an alternative to universalisation of primary education; editorial. *J Education and Psychology* 44(2-3) Jl-De 1986 p 75-76

On improving the programme of classes I and II. D.S. Panihar *Primary Teacher* 6(1) Ja 1981 p 22-25

Parents and homework for children. Visalaksh Rajagopal *Educational Rev* 85(5) My 1979 p 83-85

Piaget in the context of primary education. A.B. Saxena *Primary Teacher* 5(3) Jl 1980 p 10-17 tabs

Primary education reforms and universalisation of elementary education. B.D. Gururasami *Primary Teacher* 4(3) Ja 1979 p 5-6

Problems in primary education : Some issues. B.N. Biswal and Kabita Biswal *Experiments in Education* 10(2) Ap 1982 p 25-28

Reading, writing and arithematics scopes as predictors of academic success in primary school children. S. Subrahmanyam *Experiments in Education* 13(11) Ja 1986 p 195-200 tabs

Reforming primary education. V. Rajasekaran *Experiments in Education* 7(1) Mr 1979 p 9-13

Relationship of constitutional factors to learning difficulties among primary school children. Bindu Prasad *Indian Educational Rev* 17(2) Ap 1982 p 1-19 refs tabs

States endeavour for primary education. Govindanand Misra *Teacher Education* 18(22-23) Ja-Ap 1983 p 75-76

A strategy for child centred approach. G. Vidyasagar and Y.F.W. Prasada Rao *Primary Teacher* 11(4) Oc 1986 p 1-4

Teaching young minds. Manjit Sengupta *Indian Education* 10(7) Oc 1980 p 3-6

Understanding processes of universalisation of education. I. Grover *Primary Teacher* 11(4) Oc 1986 p 15-16

Universal learning strategy for primary schools. N.K. Jangira *Primary Teacher* 5(1) Ja 1980 p 20-23

Universalisations of primary education. D.S. Parihar *Primary Teacher* 8(1) Ja 1983 p 23-24

Wastage in primary education : A global perspective. I. Grover *J Indian Education* 12(3) Se 1986 p 23-29 refs tabs

Education, Primary : Audio-Visual Aids

Satellite technology for primary education. Jagdish Singh and A.K. Singh *Primary Teacher* 11(1) Ja 1986 p 22-24

Education, Primary : Bangladesh

Objectives of primary education in Bangladesh : Then and now. N.B. Biswas and G.C. Blawl *Educational Rev* 91(5-6) My-Je 1985 p 88-90

Primary education curriculum in Bangladesh : A historical review. Mikunja Behari Biswas *Perspectives in Education* 1(1) Ja 1985 p 5-20 tabs

Education, Primary : China (People's Republic)

Primary education in China. R.P. Kathuria *Primary Teacher* 5(4) Oc 1980 p 5-8

Universal primary education and literacy programmes in China : Some reflections. S.K. Tuteja *Indian J Adult Education* 46(2) Fe 1985 p 4-9 +

Education, Primary : Curricula

Curriculum-based realisation of educational aims in India : With special reference to primary education. M.S. Bawa *Education Quarterly* 38(1) Spr 1986 p 16-20

Education, Primary : France

Primary education in France. K.C. Nautiyal *Primary Teacher* 6(4) Oc 1981 p 35-38

Education, Primary : India

Are we interested in sending our children to primary schools? Jai Prakash Sharma *Teacher Today* 24(4) Ap-Je 1982 p 65-71

Breaking away. Krishna Kumar *Teacher Today* 27(4) Ap-Je 1985 p 1-9

Challenge of education : Face to face with realities. Bhawani Shankar Vyas *Teacher Today* 28(2) Oc-De 1985 p 23-26

Contemporary issues in primary education. C. Gopinath Rao *Experiments in Education* 6(6) Ag 1978 p 99-101

Curriculum-based realisation of educational aims in India : With special reference to primary education. M.S. Bawa *Education Quarterly* 38(1) Spr 1986 p 16-20

Improving primary education. V.S. Mathur *Primary Teacher* 9(3) Jl 1984 p 1-3

Nationalise primary education to eradicate illiteracy. Ranjit Singh *Indian J Adult Education* 46(4) Ap 1985 p 23-25

Needs and significance of leadership study at primary level. Prakash Chandra Shukla *Educational Rev* 87(12) De 1981 p 235

Primary education in rural India. N.T. Taskar *Teacher Education* 20(30-31) Ja-Ap 1985 p 37-39

Primary education in India. *New Frontiers in Education* 10(1) Ja-Mr 1980 p 74-82 tabs

Primary education in the new educational pattern : Towards broader base and stronger foundation. M.R. Chilana *Teacher Today* 24(4) Ap-Je 1982 p 30-43

Return to the roots : An alternative policy frame for primary education. Anil Bordia *Teacher Today* 27(4) Ap-Je 1985 p 72-85 tabs

Universalisation of primary education - A far cry. K.P. Narayanan *Student Action* 2(9) Mr 1984 p 16

Wastage and stagnation : A case for lower primary school. T.K. Leelavathy *EPA Quarterly Bulletin* 6(3-4) Oc 1985-Ja 1984 p 15-21 refs tabs

Wastage in primary education. K. Venkatasubramanian. New Delhi, Orient Longman. 1978. 86p. Rs.15 *Book Rev, Progress of Education* 53(12) Jl 1979 p 238

Whither primary education? Naresh Kumar *Primary Teacher* 7(3) Jl 1982 p 24-25

Education, Primary : India : Andhra Pradesh

The effectiveness of two different methods of teaching reading in primary schools. S. Subramanyam *J Educational Research and Extension* 18(3) Ja 1982 p 129-32 tabs

Education, Primary : India : Haryana

Impact of compulsory primary education legislation on the rural society of Haryana. Raj Singh and M.L. Sharma *Education Quarterly* 31(2) Jl 1979 p 23-25

Education, Primary : India : Madhya Pradesh

Wastage in primary education in Raipur district, M.P. C.K.M. Rao *Indian Education* 10(8) Nv 1980 p 37-40

Education, Primary : India : Maharashtra

Curriculum load and stress at primary level : A study. M.A. Tamboh *Primary Teacher* 11(1) Ja 1986 p 25-28

Education, Primary : India : Maharashtra : History

Development of primary education under local bodies in Maharashtra, 1892-1984. Ambika Jain *Research Bulletin* 16(1-2) Mr-Je 1986 p 3-24 tabs

Education, Primary : India : Rajasthan

A survey of the primary schools of Tonk Phatak (Jaipur) areas. M. Pareek *Educational Rev* 91(7) Jl 1985 p 116-19 tabs

Education, Primary : India : West Bengal

Primary education in rural West Bengal : A survey. H.B. Mazumdar *Primary Teacher* 10(3) Jl 1985 p 16-19

Education, Primary : Nepal

Primary education in Nepal. W.H. Siddiqui *Educational Rev* 87(7) Jl 1981 p 127-30

Education, Primary : Nigeria

The effects of ecological differences on subject preference; academic aspiration and achievement among primary school pupils. E.E. Ezowu and C.C. Anandi *Progress of Education* 60(5) De 1985 p 98-102 refs

Language medium/media choices and their effects on the learning of science-oriented subject (i.e. mathematics) at the primary school level in Ilorin, Kwara state Nigeria. Adedeji Awoniyi *Progress of Education* 58(12) Jl 1984 p 293-300 + refs tabs

Education, Primary : Switzerland

Primary school children in Switzerland : Their achievement in multi-lingual environment. Krishna Maitra *Primary Teacher* 8(2) Ap 1983 p 28-30

Education, Professional

See

Professional education

Education, Rural

Role of media technology in rural education. M.P. Gupta *J Higher Education* 8(2) Aut 1982 p 239-41

See also

Teachers, Rural

Education, Rural : India

Antyodaya education. Bir Singh *Educational Rev* 85(6) Je 1979 p 115-18

Changes in education in rural India. K.K. Das *Educational Quarterly* 31(2) Jl 1979 p 12-14

Education and rural development. Sudha V. Rao. New Delhi, Sage Pub. 334p. Rs.150 *Book Rev, Education Quarterly* 38(3) Aut 1986 p 55-58

Education for rural people. Pravakar Rout *J Indian Education* 12(2) Jl 1986 p 20-23 refs

Education in rural area : Socially relevant and integrated strategy. Lalita Kabra *Teacher Today* 28(4) Ap-Je 1986 p 54-57

Experiments in rural education. D.V. Chickermane. D.V. Chockermana Res Centre in Rural Education. 1979. 86p. Rs.8 *Book Rev, J Indian Education* 7(2) Jl 1979 p 69-70

Functional education and integrated rural development. V.R. Sharma *Our Education* 5 Jl 1984 p 17-22

Improving elementary education in rural areas. Qamaruddin *Primary Teacher* 9(4) Oc 1984 p 8-10

Managing education for rural development : Overall problems and strategies. D.P. Nayar *Education Quarterly* 30(3) Oc 1978 p 15-18

Need for pre-primary education in rural India. B.N. Biswal and Kabita Biswal *Experiments in Education* 9(7) Se 1981 p 121-25

Problems of rural and tribal schools. M.N. Ravindranath *Educational Rev* 88(8) Ag 1982 p 131-32; 88(9) Se 1982 p 149-50

Rural education : An emphasis on weaker section. Azmat Nayeen *Education Quarterly* 32(3) Jl 1980 p 13-17 tabs

Rural primary school. Vikram Rai *Primary Teacher* 4(2) Ap 1979 p 31-33

The rural university : The Jawaja experiment in education innovation. Ravi J. Mattai. Bombay, Popular. xvi, 360p. Rs.150 *Book Rev, Education Quarterly* 38(3) Aut 1986 p 52-54

School education in rural areas : Some ideas and issues. R. Govinda *New Frontiers in Education* 10(4) Oc-De 1980 p 65-72 refs

Education, Rural : India : Karnataka

Education in a rural community : An indepth study of a village in Karnataka. S. Roy and M.N. Ravindranath *Quest in Education* 18(4) Oc 1981 p 265-77

Education in a rural environment. S. Narayana Tara. New Delhi, Ashish Pub H. 1985, 144p. Rs.100 *Book Rev, Education Quarterly* 37(4) Wint 1985 p 66-69

Education in rural areas : Constraints and prospects. A.S. Seetharama and Usha Devi. New Delhi, Ashish Pub H. 1985, 220p. Rs.100 *Book Rev, Education Quarterly* 37(4) Wint 1985 p 60-62

Education, Rural : India : West Bengal

Mass education under panchayati raj : A proposition. G. Haldar *Indian J Adult Education* 47(7) Jl 1982 p 21-24 +

Education, Rural : United States

Towards improving education for the rural youth : The working of two universities in India and America. Ivan D. Muse and Motilal Sharma *J Indian Education* 8(6) Mr 1983 p 20-26

Education, Secondary

A.N. Jha Memorial lecture : Secondary education : Some issue. A.V. Gadgil *Indian Education* 12(11-12) Fe-Mr 1983 p 35-49

Problem behaviour in the secondary school. Bill Gilham, ed. London, Croom Helm. 195p. £5.95 *Book Rev, Education Quarterly* 34(1) Ja 1982 p 46-47

Secondary education : Some issues. A.V. Gadgil *Progress of Education* 57(10) My 1983 p 218-23

Whither secondary schooling? *Teacher Today* 23(1) Jl-Se 1980 p 87-90

Education, Secondary : Curricula

Highlights of Ishwarbhai Patel Committee's report. *Experiments in Education* 6(5) Jl 1978 p 84-87

Selection of courses of study by P.U. (Sc.) students. P.C. Das *J Higher Education* 5(2) Aut 1979 p 236-42

Education, Secondary : India

Adjustment problem at plus two. Prakash Chandra Shukla *Educational Rev* 87(2) Fe 1981 p 36-37 refs tabs

Experimentation in secondary schools. J.C. Goyal and Ajit Singh *Quest in Education* 17(3) Jl 1980 p 228-41 refs

'Higher secondary' - In what sense? N.S. Padmanathan *Educational Rev* 86(10) Oc 1980 p 198-99

Illusion and reality in Indian secondary education. Rajendra K. Verma *et al.* Teakfield Ltd. 1980, i-xvii, 146p. Rs.120 *Book Rev, Indian Education* 6(6) Mr 1981 p 62-63

Is 10+2+3 a failure. D.R. Portia *Educational Rev* 85(3) Mr 1979 p 50-51

The magical formula of education 10+2+3 or 8+4+3 or 7+5+3. P.D. Shukla *Education Quarterly* 30(3) Oc 1978 p 19-20

On understanding youth at higher secondary. Pillo Buch *Progress of Education* 55(4) Nv 1980 p 90-93

Plus two : A panacea or a pandora's box. *Educational Rev* 84(12) De 1978 p 223-25

Review of 10+2 pattern of education in some states : Implementation stage. D.C. Upreti and J.S. Rajput *Teacher Today* 24(1) Jl-Se 1981 p 30-36

Some thoughts on 10+2 system. K.K. Sethi *Education Quarterly* 32(2) Ap 1980 p 30-35

10+2+3 pattern : Its history. B.K. Sahni *Educational Rev* 87(1) Je 1981 p 3-6+; 87(2) Fe 1981 p 31-35

Towards a meaningful first degree. V.V. John *J Higher Education* 1(1) Mon 1975 p 51-60

Education, Secondary : India : Bihar

Effect of school system on the competence of secondary school students. Suddha R. Sinha *Indian Educational Rev* 15(1) Ja 1980 p 62-70 refs tabs

Education, Secondary : India : Delhi

An opinion survey of high school teachers in Delhi regarding 10+2 system of education. P. Mathur and A. Satapathy *Asian J Psychology and Education* 4(1) Ja 1979 p 21-24

Education, Secondary : India : Maharashtra : History

Secondary education in Western Maharashtra : A history of its evolution from 1859 till today. *Research Bulletin* 12(1-2) Mr-Je 1982 p 43-64

Education, Secondary : India : Orissa

New 10+2+3 pattern of education : Its problems with special reference to Orissa. Sura Prasad Pati *Educational Rev* 92(5-6) My-Je 1986 p 84-86

Education, Secondary : India : Rajasthan

Readiness of higher secondary schools in introducting 10+2 system of education in Rajasthan. Pushpa Gupta and S.L. Mathur *Education Quarterly* 32(3) Jl 1980 p 33-36 refs tabs

Education, Secondary : India : Tamil Nadu

Higher secondary scheme in Tamil Nadu : An evaluation after the first year. M. Murgesa Mudaliar *Educational Rev* 85(7) Jl 1979 p 121-22

An opinion survey on selected aspects relating to the restructuring of the school education system as 10+2 in Tamil Nadu. E.G. Vedanayagam *Experiments in Education* 6(1) Mr 1978 p 223-30 tab

Education, Secondary : Nepal

Secondary education in Nepal : A profile. W.H. Siddiqui and Wizarat Husain *Educational Rev* 86(10) Oc 1980 p 194-97

Education, Secondary : Nigeria

A role of the parents-teachers association : A case study of secondary schools in Ikale local government area. Ondostali, Nigeria. R.A. Adeboyeje *Progress of Education* 61(1) Ag 1986 p 13-16 refs

Education, Technical

See

Technical Education

Education, Theological

See

Religious Education

Education, Vocational

See

Vocational Education

Education and Democracy

See

Democracy and Education

Education and Economic Development

See

Education and National Development

Education and Libraries

See

Libraries and Education

Education and National Development

Education and development. B.L. Raina and S.C. Panigrahi *Education Quarterly* 37(2) Sum 1985 p 1-6 refs

Education and development. John M. Thomson *Indian Education* 10(5) Ag 1980 p 5-7

Education and economic development in India : Tamil Nadu - A case study. K. Venkata Subramanian. Delhi, Frank Bros & Co. 1980, xxiii, 243p. Rs. 95 *Book Rev, Indian Educational Rev* 16(1) Ja 1981 p 126-28

Education and rural development in Asia. Udai Pareek. New Delhi, Oxf-IBH. 232p. Book Rev, *New Frontiers in Education* 13(1) Ja-Mr 1983 p 73-74

Education and rural development. Sudha V. Rao. New Delhi, Sage Pub. 1985, 334p. Rs.150 *Book Rev, PR* 2(3) Jl 1986 p 188-90

Education and welfare state. G.A. Patrick *Educational Rev* 87(12) De 1981 p 237-39

Education as a tool for development. R. Gomez *Educational Rev* 88(10) Oc 1982 p 179-81; 88(11) Nv 1982 p 195-98 refs

Education, economic growth and income distribution : Contributions to economic analysis, 112. J.M.M. Ritzen. Amsterdam, North-Holland Pub. xx, 257p. *Book Rev, Indian Educational Rev* 18(2) Ap 1983 p 134-35

Education for development. Challenges. Bangkok, UNESCO 1985, 189p. *Book Rev, Teacher Today* 28(4) Ap-Je 1986 p 126

Education for national development. O.P. Sharma. Meerut, Anu Pra. 162p. Rs.50 *Book Rev, Teacher Today* 24(4) Ap-Je 1982 p 136-37

Education for rural development. H.H.A. Bourai *Quest in Education* 17(3) Jl 1985 p 3-4

Education for rural development. Ramlal Parikh *University News* 23(1) 1 Ja 1980 p 207-11

Education, science and rural development. J.S. Rajput *Education Quarterly* 31(2) Jl 1979 p 20-22

Education, science, technology and integrated development. Hari Narain *Indian J Adult Education* 44(1-2) Ja-Fe 1983 p 33-50

Educational science : Educational aid and development in the third world. Patrick V. Dias *New Frontiers in Education* 14(4) Oc-De 1984 p 54-65

Imbalance of educational opportunities and the implications for national development. Sakha R. Gangopadhyay *Teacher Today* 26(2) Oc-De 1983 p 78-99 refs tabs

Integrating education with development in the community : Role of university teachers. M.S. Yadav *et al New Frontiers in Education* 14(2) Ap-Je 1984 p 43-51

Integration of education with development. N.M. Bhagia *Education Quarterly* 36(1) Ja 1984 p 6-10

Integration of education with economic needs. C.B. Padmanabhan *New Frontiers in Education* 12(1) Ja-Mr 1982 p 37-49

Non-formal education for development : A critique. D.P. Pattanayak *Indian J Adult Education* 40(2) Fe 1979 p 22-26

Parenting on dimensions of economic well-beings culture and education. N.S. Chauhan *et al J Education and Psychology* 39(3) Oc 1981 p 156-62

Planning education for economic development. Jandhyala B.G. Tilak *Perspectives in Education* 1(1) Ja 1985 p 35-47 refs tabs

Relevance of Gandhian economics for national development. T.S. Avinashilingam *J Educational Research and Extension* 16(2) Oc 1979 p 65-71

A report on the commonwealth conference on non-formal education for development. *Indian J Adult Education* 40(2) Fe 1979 p 5-21

Role of education in development of science and technology in India. Ranjana Srivastava *Education Quarterly* 31(3-4) Oc 1979-Ja 1980 p 16-20

The role of education in economic development in India. M.A. Hussain *Indian Educational Rev* 18(4) Oc 1983 p 15-27

Rural development education. M.P. Boraiyan *Experiments in Education* 9(11) Ja 1982 p 201-04

University and national development. R.K. Yadav *Perspectives in Education* 1(2) Ap 1985 p 71-74

Universities and people's education for development in India. Kishore Saint *Teacher Today* 22(3) Ja-Mr 1980 p 64-68

Universities, colleges and the programme of integrated rural development. Malcolm S. Adiseshiah *Teacher Education* 14(10-11) Ja-Ap 1980 p 40-45

Universities role in poverty eradication. Tarlok Singh *Teacher Education* 20(30-31) Ja-Ap 1985 p 6-19

Working papers on 'Socially useful productive work and community service'. *Teacher Education* 13(8-9) Jl-Oc 1979 p 21-25

See also

Adult Education and National Development

Educational Planning

Education and National Integration

The concept of national integration. Bharati Basu and V. Rukuma Rao *Indian Educational Rev* 14(4) Oc 1979 p 78-85 ft-n

Education and national integration. Kapila Vatsayayan *Teacher Today* 27(1) Jl-Se 1984 p 63-67

Integration : What does it involve? Sudesh Mukhopadhyay *Education Quarterly* 37(1) Spr 1985 p 21-26 refs

Language, education and national integration. Renu Debi *Teacher Education* 16(18-19) Ja-Ap 1982 p 72-76 refs

Level integration in the educational process. V.S. Mathur *Education Quarterly* 76(4) Wint 1984 p 1-3

National integration and education. D.D. Tiwari *Teacher Education* 20(30-31) Ja-Ap 1985 p 1-5

The national integration camp. S.N. Tripathi and H.K. Shukla *J Indian Education* 6(1) My 1980 p 26-29

National integration : Role of college. V.S. Mathur *Education Quarterly* 34(2) Ap 1982 p 27-28+

National integration through education. P.D. Puranik. Pune, Vidyarthi Griha Pra. 96p. Rs.15 *Book Rev, Progress of Education* 53(6) Ja 1979 p 119

A study of national integratedness in MSS and non-MSS students. Gyanendra P. Shrivastava *J Education and Psychology* 36(4) Ja 1979 p 192-99

Text books and national integration. G.C. Upadhyay *Experiments in Education* 11(7) Se 1983 p 126-28

Education and Nationalism
See
Nationalism and Education
Education and Politics
See
Politics and Education
Education and Psychology
See
Educational Psychology
Education and Religion
See
Religion and Education
Education and Secularism
See
Secularism and Education
Education and Socialism
See
Socialism and Education
Education and Sociology
See
Educational Sociology
Education and State
Universalisation of education : An experiment. R.P. Kathuria *Primary Teacher* 7(3) Jl 1982 p 12-14
See also
Adult Education and State
Community and School
Politics and Education
Education and State : China (People's Republic)
Chinese educational policy. Jan Ingvar Lofstedt. New York, Humanities Press; Stockholm, Almquist. 1980, 204 p. *Book Rev, J Higher Education* 8(2) Aut 1982 p 251-52
Education and State : India
An apology for new education. Mali Ram Sharma *Teacher Today* 27(4) Ap-Je 1985 p 63-69
Challenge of education : A policy perspective : An approach to education and reorientation. *University News* 23(36) 23 Se 1985 p 2-13
Challenge of education : A policy perspective. *EPA Quarterly Bulletin* 8(1-2) Ap-Jl 1985 p 1-16
Challenge of education : A policy perspective. *Education Quarterly* 37(4) Wint 1985 p 32-40
Challenge of education : A policy perspective. *New Frontiers in Education* 15(3) Jl-Se 1985 p 78-112; 15(4) Oc-De 1985 p 73-107
A challenge of education : A policy perspective. *Primary Teacher* 11(1) Ja 1986 p 34-38
Directive principles of state policy and education in the concurrent list : Some policy implications. K.C. Nautiyal *Teacher Education* 17(20-21) Jl-Oc 1982 p 30-39 refs tabs
Draft national policy on education; editorial. *Rajasthan Board J Education*

15(3) Jl-Se 1979 p I-III

Draft national policy on education, 1979. S.N. Katiyar *Teacher Today* 22(2) Oc-De 1979 p 79-83

Draft national policy on education, 1979 : Some comments. A. Verstraeten *New Frontiers in Education* 10(3) Jl-Se 1980 p 47-58

Draft national policy on education,1979. *Teacher Today* 22(1) Jl-Se 1979 p iii-xvi

Economic education and educational policy reflections of an amateur. Radhika Ramasubban *J Higher Education* 8(2) Jl 1982 p 27-32

Education as a concurrent subject : A new tool for educational reform. K.C. Nautiyal *J Indian Education* 8(2) Aut 1982 p 179-83

Education in India : A perspective on policy perspective. Devdatta Dabhalkar *Perspectives in Education* 2(2) Ap 1986 p 67-76 refs

Education and policy : A few suggestions. Laxmi Kant Mishra *Primary Teacher* 4(3) Jl 1979 p 31-32

Educational policy for modernisation and national development. Debika Bhattacharya *J Indian Education* 12(3) Se 1986 p 6-14

Educational policy. Salma Kuraishy *Education Quarterly* 38(1) Spr 1986 p 1-4

Indore discussion group on new national policy of education. *University News* 23(23) 16 Je 1985 p 3-4

Issues for the national policy on education; editorial. *National J Education* 7(2) My 1985 p I-VIII

Issues in the national policy on education. Malcolm S. Adiseshiah *New Frontiers in Education* 10(3) Jl-Se 1980 p 14-24

Making of our new education policy. Satya Pal Ruhela *University News* 23(16) 23 Ap 1985 p 2-3

National policy on education,1986. *New Frontiers in Education* 16(2) Ap-Je 1986 p 82-105

National policy on education, 1986. *Teacher Today* 28(4) Ap-Je 1986 p 94

National policy on education : Programme of action. *New Frontiers in Education* 16(3) Jl-Se 1986 p 34-116; 16(4) Oc-De 1986 p 1-81

New education policy and the techniques of teaching. Jagat Bahukhandi *Teacher Today* 28(2) Oc-De 1985 p 27-30

The new education policy in India. Raghunath Safaya *Educational Rev* 92(2) Fe 1986 p 26-27

New education policy. K.K. Khullar *Education Quarterly* 38(3) Aut 1986 p 1-3

The new education policy. S.C. Dutta *Indian J Adult Education* 47(7) Jl 1986 p 11-13+

New education policy : Some urgent tasks. Ramlal Parikh *Teacher Education* 20(30-31) Ja-Ap 1985 p 15-18

New education policy : Some urgent tasks. Ramlal Parikh *University News* 23(18) 8 My 1985 p 7-8

New educational policy : A university teachers critical appraisal. S. Chitraputra Nainar *Educational Rev* 92(1) Ja 1986 p 15-17

New educational policy : A view from the grassroots. Plomthodathil S. Jacob *New Frontiers in Education.* 16(3) Jl-Se 1986 p 19-29

Political calculus and educational designs. S.P. Mistry *Progress of Educa-*

tion 59(2) Se 1984 p 31-33

Priorities in national policy on education. G. Rasool *EPA Quarterly Bulletin* 7(1-2) Ap-Jl 1984 p 1-5 refs

Reformulating educational policy in India. Issues in ponder. R.P. Singhal *University News* 23(28) 23 Jl 1985 p 19-24

Reflections on a new national policy on education. T.V. Kunnunkal *New Frontiers in Education* 10(3) Jl-Se 1980 p 25-34

Relevance of national educational policy. B. Rajaiah *Educational Rev* 89(3) Mr 1983 p 48-50

Return to the roots : An alternative policy frame for primary education. Anil Bordia *Teacher Today* 27(4) Ap-Je 1985 p 72-85 tabs

A review of 'draft national policy of education 1979'. B.P. Lulla *Progress of Education* 54(9) Ap 1980 p 182-85 +

A review of draft national policy of education, 1979. B.P. Lulla *Rajasthan Board J Education* 15(4) Oc-De 1979 p 11-14

Role of educational institutions in the implementation of national policies. R. Krishna Rao *Progress of Education* 54(7) Fe 1980 p 136-40

Some comments on the draft national policy on education, 1979. B.M. Udgaonkar *New Frontiers in Education* 10(3) Jl-Se 1980 p 83-91

A tentative balance sheet of the new educational policy. Malcolm S. Adiseshiah *New Frontiers in Education* 16(3) Jl-Se 1986 p 1-10 refs

Towards a national policy on education; editorial. *National J Education* 6(2) My 1984 p I-V

Towards some clean and achievable goals for a national educational programme for India. Paulos Mar Gregorios *New Frontiers in Education* 16(3) Jl-Se 1986 p 11-18

Unscientific approach and irrational thinking of our educational elite. Anil Sadagopal *Indian Education* 12(1-2) Ap-My 1982 p 11-13

Whither national educational policy? B. Rajaiah *Educational Rev* 86(6) Je 1980 p 114-15

Education and State : India : Rajasthan

A policy frame for the development in education in Rajasthan. M.F. Paliwal *Teacher Today* 27(2) Oc-De 1984 p 34-36

Education and State : Nigeria

A critical analysis of the problems of implementing Nigeria's new policy on education. Ose A. Effrakeya *New Frontiers in Education* 16(1) Ja-Mr 1986 p 67-78 refs

Policy determination and control in Nigerian education. J. Okpako Enaohwo *New Frontiers in Education* 14(3) Jl-Se 1984 p 14-23 refs

Education for Nation Building

See

Education and National Development

Education in Five Year Plans

See

Educational Planning

Education of Adults

See

Adult Education

Education of Children

Adult education and schooling of slum children. Jacob Alkara *Indian J Adult Education* 41(8) Ag 1980 p 7-12 refs

The child and the teacher. Bhagat Ramgopal *Primary Teacher* 6(4) Oc 1981 p 19-21

The child : The family and the school. E.G. Parameswaran *Indian Education* 10(3) Je 1980 p 11-18

Children in their primary schools. Henry Pluckrose. Middlesex, Penguin Bks. 1979. 175p. $1.25 *Book Rev, Education Quarterly* 32(3) Jl 1980 p 45-46

Children's media laboratory as a learning resource centre. Jagannath Mohanty *Primary Teacher* 5(2) Ap 1980 p 22-24

Classroom interaction and congnitive development in primary school chiidren. P. Sandeep *Indian Educational Rev* 15(4) Oc 1980 p 63-65

Early childhood education : Foundations and practice. J.S. Grewal. Agra, Nat. Psychology Corpn. 1984, Rs.120 *Book Rev, Teacher Today* 28(1) Jl-Se 1985 p 107-09

The education and development of your child - A guide. A.P. Srivastava. New Delhi, Learning Systems. 1982. 110p. *Book Rev, Education Quarterly* 36(2) Ap 1984 p 74-75

Education of the disadvantaged. J.T. Jayaprasadarao *Education Quarterly* 37(1) Spr 1985 p 15-17

Educational approach to a deprived child. Pramilla Pandit Barooah *Primary Teacher* 4(2) Ap 1979 p 10-14

An educational game for children. G.S. Sangha *Primary Teacher* 5(1) Ja 1980 p 11-13

Educational provisions for the socially disadvantaged children. Muralidhar Dash *Indian Education* 10(9-10) De 1980-Ja 1981 p 30-32

Elementary non-formal education for out of the school children. D.V. Chickermane *Progress of Education* 54(3) Oc 1979 p 67-69

An enquiry into the role of the family and school in leading in children towards the threshold of democratic citizenship. Deb Kumar De *J Education and Psychology* 4(1-2) Ap-Jl 1983 p 17-22

Helping the child to become human. Margaret Verma *Primary Teacher* 4(4) Oc 1979 p 10-14

How to prepare children for examination? Sada Ram Machli *Primary Teacher* 4(5) Jl 1979 p 28-31

In search of the third dimension. Kalyan K. Banerjee *Primary Teacher* 8(1) Ja 1983 p 20-22

Integrated child development in the non-formal system of edcuation. M.D. Usha Devi *Progress of Education* 56(6) Ja 1982 p 143-46

Planning on integrated child welfare programme. H.W. Butt *Indian Education* 9(10-11) Ja-Fe 1980 p 19-26

A psychological view of the child and child education. E.G. Parameswaran *Indian Education* 9(10-11) Ja-Fe 1980 p 16-18

The right of the child to education. *Experiments in Education* 6(12) Fe 1979 p 213-19

Scientific inquiry in children : A review. K. Adinarayana *Experiments in Education* 9(1) Mr 1981 p 3-8 refs

Some of our children : The early education of children with special needs.

M. Chazan. London, Open Bks. 1980. 260p. £12 *Book Rev, J Indian Education* 8(4) Nv 1982 p 52-53

Spare of child. W. David Wills. Penguin Educ (Repr). 1973. 153p. 40d. *Book Rev, Teacher Today* 22(3) Ja-Mr 1980 p 98-100

A study of family and social etiquettes of adolescents. A.W. Oak *et al Research Bulletin* 12(1-2) Mr-Je 1982 p 35-42

The teacher and the inquisitive child. Bhaka Lal Gupta *Primary Teacher* 4(3) Jl 1979 p 25-27

Teaching children from the cradle : What and how? *Progress of Education* 55(1) Ag 1980 p 12-14

Teaching encounter of a third kind. Veena R. Murty *J Indian Education* 6(4) Nv 1980 p 20-30

Teaching the tribal children. K.R. Sharma *Education Quarterly* 35(4) Oc 1983 p 25-28

Training personnel for care and education of young children. Sunita Kaul and Neena Kapoor *Progress of Education* 60(5) De 1985 p 103-06

See also

Education, Elementary
Education, Pre-school
Education, Primary
Educational Toys
Handicapped Children : Education
Montessori Method of Education

Education of Children : Curricula

Building young children's self-concepts through a non-sex it approach to early childhood education curriculum materials. Margaret Verma *Indian Educational Rev* 20(4) Oc 1985 p 20-33

Education of Children : Great Britain

A perspective on the education of Asian children in Britain. Christopher Bagley *Indian Educational Rev* 15(3) Jl 1980 p 1-21

Education of Children : India

Are we interested in sending our children to primary schools? Jai Prakash Sharma *Teacher Today* 24(4) Ap-Je 1982 p 65-71 refs

Child education in India : Present trends and the needed future development. Satya Pal Ruhela *Teacher Today* 28(3) Ja-Mr 1986 p.8-15 refs

Children and their education in India : The following an address by Sri Raja Roy Singh Director, UNESCO Regional Office, for education in Asia and Oceania. *Primary Teacher* 4(4) Oc 1979 p 4-9

Education of Children : India : Bihar

Child literacy in Bihar, 1961-71. R.B. Ram and S.K. Singh *J Indian Education* 8(2) Jl 1982 p 74-78 tabs

Education of Children : India : Delhi

Educational attainment of children in the sweeper community of AIIMS campus : An explanatory study. Om Prakash *Indian Educational Rev* 15(4) Oc 1980 p 97-103

Education of Children : India : Gujarat

An evaluation of effect on participation programme on overall development of children of a municipal nursery school in Baroda. Yogini Pathak and Aruna Dave *Quest in Education* 18(4) Oc 1981 p 278-91

Education of Children : India : Uttar Pradesh

Educational goals and dropout factors in a rural population. Arun Kumar Sharma *Indian Educational Rev* 18(3) Jl 1983 p 1-7 tabs

Education of Children : Russia

School education in USSR. Ada Baskina *Teacher Education* 14(12-13) Jl-Oc 1980 p 71-73

Education of Girls

See

Education of Woman

Education of the Blind

See

Blind : Education

Education of Women

Education adolescent girls. E.M. Chandler, London, Allen and Unwin. 1980, 217p. *Book Rev, Education Quarterly* 33(3) Jl 1981 p 44-45

Educational development of women. R.K. Bhandari *Education Quarterly* 34(3) Jl 1982 p 12-14

Factors influencing the growth of girls education at the elementary stage. S.L. Gupta *Indian Educational Rev* 18(4) Oc 1983 p 77-82

Perspectives on women's education. Suresh Chandra Shukla *National J Education* 3(2) Mr 1981 p 7-16

Woman and her education. R.S. Chainani *Progress of Education* 57(4) Nv 1982 p 77-80

Women and rural development. M.S. Swaminathan *New Frontiers in Education* 12(3) Jl-Se 1982 p 56-63

Women, education and work; A review. Usha Nayar *J Higher Education* 1(2) Aut 1975 p 283-92 refs

See also

Adult Education of Women
Co-education
Medical Education of Women
Professional Education of Women
Women College Students

Education of Women : India

A comparative study of adjustment pattern of girls in co-educational colleges and women colleges. Girish Bala *J Higher Education* 3(3) Spr 1978 p 405-08 refs

Development of women's education. R.T.K. Bhandari *New Frontiers in Eduation* 12(4) Oc-De 1982 p 32-38

Educating women in India : Ends and means. Muriel Wasi *Education Quarterly* 34(4) Oc 1982 p 1-4

Education for women : A five year plan. Kunthala Jayaraman *J Higher Education* 1(2) Aut 1975 p 255-56

Education for women and girls today in cities in India. A. Jacob *Education Quarterly* 34(4) Oc 1982 p 11-13

Education of women in India : Inequalities and bottlenecks. Radha Rani Sharma *Education Quarterly* 34(4) Oc 1982 p 20-27

Educational development of women in India : Problems and suggestions for improvement. Marjorie Fernandes *Prasar* 8(3-4) Oc 1981-Ja 1982 p 26-36

Educational programme for rural women : Lakshahira Das *Educational Rev* 85(8) Ag 1979 p 141-43

Indian women's right to education. V.S. Mathur *Education Quarterly* 31(1) Ap 1979 p 18-20

Literate girls : Impact of family. Mumtaz Ali Khan *Educational Rev* 85(4) Ap 1979 p 75-77 tabs

Reform entails a predefinition process. Chhaya Dey *Progress of Education* 56(4) Nv 1981 p 85-88

Research on women's education in India : A review. Vibha Joshi and Geeta Menon *Perspectives in Education* 2(2) Ap 1986 p 77-78

Secondary education for girls : The what and the now. Rajni Kumar *Education Quarterly* 34(4) Oc 1982 p 31-33

The social context of women's education in India, 1921-81 : Tentative formulations. Karuna Chanana Ahmad *New Frontiers in Education* 15(3) Jl-Se 1985 p 1-36 refs tabs

Socio-personal correlates and gain in the knowledge of correspondence course trainees. Ranjit Singh and R.K. Saini *Indian J Adult Education* 45(4) Ap 1984 p 30-33 tabs

Woman education in India today. Amrit Kaur *Teacher Today* 21(4) Ap-Je 1979 p 9-24 tabs

Education of Women : India : Assam

Problems and priorities in the education of women in Assam. Lakshahira Das *Education Quarterly* 34(2) Ap 1982 p 22-26

Education of Women : India : Bihar

A study of disadvantages associated with different socio-economic groups of girls studying in secondary schools. J. Jha and Bimla Saxena *J Education and Psychology* 41(1-2) Ap-Jl 1983 p 12-16

Education of Women : India : Gujarat

Educate a woman and you educate a family. T.S. Saraswathi and Radhika Gupta *Perspectives in Education* 1(1) Ja 1985 p 49-54 refs tabs

Education of Women : India : Haryana

Girl dropouts in rural Haryana : A socio-economic analysis. M.L. Surana *Indian Educational Rev* 20(2) Ap 1985 p 109-16

Education of Women : India : Punjab

Attitude of the people towards women literacy in Punjab. Kuldeep Kaur *Educational Rev* 91(8) Ag 1985 p 126-29

Participation and interest of rural school going girls in household and farm activities. Shavinder K. Mangat and Sumita Roy *Indian J Extension Education* 19(1-2) Mr-Je 1983 p 69-73

Education of Women : India : Uttar Pradesh

Attitudes of Harijan women towards education : A comparative study of a city and surrounding villages. R.K. Srivastava and B. Rawat *Indian J Adult Education* 43(7) Jl 1982 p 27-31 refs tabs

Education of Workers

See

Labour and Labouring Classes - Education

Educational Accountability

Accountability in Indian education : Perspectives and practices. J.V. D'Cruz and N.M. Bhagia *J Educational Planning and Admininstration* 1(1) Oc 1986 p 1-12 refs

Programme evaluation : A conceptual analysis. P.K. Sahoo *J Educational Planning and Administration* 1(1) Oc 1986 p 34-42 refs

Educational Administration

Action learning and action research in education management. John Elliot-Kemp *J Education and Psychology* 37(3) Oc 1979 p 151-57

Changing concepts and functions of educational management. S.P. Mistry *Progress of Education* 61(3) Oc 1986 p 54-57 refs

The concept of systems approach to educational administration. V.G. Marihal *Educational Rev* 89(3) Mr 1983 p 41-44 refs

Concern for human values in educational administration. B.R. Gupta *Indian Education* 10(12) Mr 1981 p 27-29

Courses in educational administration : New dimensions. V.P. Garg *J Educational Planning and Administration* 1(1) Oc 1986 p 63-66

Decision-making in educational administration. Jamnalal Bayti *Progress of Education* 58(6) Ja 1984 p 132-37 +

Educational administration. S.P. Sukhla. Agra, Vinod Pustak Mandir. 1982, 397p. Rs. 22 *Book Rev, J Indian Education* 12(1) My 1986 p 62-63

Educational management and educational development. John Elliott-Kemp *J Education and Psychology* 37(1) Ap 1979 p 4-9 refs

Educational management : Challenges for professionalisation. M. Mukhopadhyay and K.S. Rao *Perspectives in Education* 1(2) Ap 1985 p 91-98 refs

Educational planning and administration as a discipline in the universities. J.N. Kaul *Indian Education* 10(12) Mr 1981 p 30-34

Human relationship in educational administration. N. Ezekiel *J Indian Education* 8(1) My 1982 p 32-36 refs

Improvement of the organisation and management of education systems as a means of raising efficiency in order to extend the right to education. *Teacher Education* 13(8-9) Jl-Oc 1979 p 45-57

Modern approach in evaluation of training programmes of education management. N.M. Bhajia *Indian Education* 11(1-2) Ap-My 1981 p 53-56

Modernising educational administration at the grassroot level. H.R. Justa *Teacher Today* 27(4) Ap-Je 1985 p 45-56

Private agencies and management of education. D. Sangameswara Rao *Indian Education* 11(1-2) Ap-My 1981 p 95-98

Relevance and problems of the systems theory in education and adminstration. Ukpako Enaekuo *New Frontiers in Education* 15(1) Ja-Mr 1985 p 1-12 refs

Research in management of education. J.L. Azad *Indian Education* 11(1-2) Ap-My 1981 p 18-23

Students participation in educational administration : A view point. G. Hara Gopal *Indian Education* 11(1-2) Ap-My 1981 p 71-75

Systems approach to educational management. M. Malla Reddy and Ravi Shankar *Indian Education* 11(6) Se 1981 p 15-19

Teachers participation in educational administration. E.V. Rathniah *Indian Education* 11(1-2) Ap-My 1981 p 67-70

Towards a programme for educational health. Shardamba Rao and B. Phalachandra *J Indian Education* 7(3) Se 1979 p 38-42

Towards education management. D.R. Darji and D.K. Sharma *Educaion Quarterly* 32(2) Ap 1980 p 8-12

Training of educational administrators. T.K.D. Nair *Indian Education* 11(1-2) Ap-My 1981 p 49-52

See also

School Management and Organisation

Universities and Colleges : Administration

Educational Administration : Developing Countries

Professional preparation of educational administration in developing countries. D.K. Briggs and N.M. Bhagle *EPA Quarterly Bulletin* 8(1-2) Ap-Je 1985 p 80-85 refs

Educational Administration : India

Administration of education in India. P.D. Shukla. New Delhi, Vikas Pub 1983, 216p. Rs.95 *Book Rev, New Frontiers in Education* 13(1) Ja-Mr 1983 p 74-75

Doctoral thesis on educational administration in Indian universities. A.C. Gupta *EPA Quarterly Bulletin* 7(1-2) Ap-Je 1984 p 51-59 refs

Training for educational administrators in India. N.M. Bagia *New Frontiers in Education* 16(4) Oc-De 1986 p 88-94

Educational Administration : India : Rajasthan

Educational administrator in Rajasthan. P.L. Tiwari *Teacher Today* 24(3) Ja-Mr 1982 p 66-68

Educational Adminstration : Research

Research in educational administration : Retrospect and prospect. N.M. Bhagla *Teacher Today* 26(2) Oc-De 1983 p 62-77 refs tabs

Educational Aims and Objectives

See

Education : Aims and objectives

Educational Aspirations

See

Student Aspirations

Educational Associations

Strengthening teacher organisations. P.D. Sachdeva *Indian Education* 11(6) Se 1981 p 29-33

See also

All India Federation of Educational Associations

Indian Adult Education Association

Teacher Unions

Educational Broadcasting

Colleges of education and school broadcasts. D.R. Goel *J Indian Education* 5(5) Ja 1980 p 65-72

Educational broadcasting : Radio and television in education. J. Mohanty. New Delhi, Sterling. 168p. Rs.75 *Book Rev, Education Quarterly* 37(2) Sum 1985 p 78-79; *J Education and Psychology* 42(3) Oc 1981 p 171-72

Effective school broadcast. Sunil Behari Mohanty *Primary Teacher* 10(3) Jl 1985 p 10-12

School broadcasting. C.S. Nagaraja and Usha Ram Kumar *J Indian Educa-*

tion 9(1) My 1983 p 20-24

Teachers and school broadcasts. D.R. Goel *Progress of Education* 54(1) Ag 1979 p 12-20

Educational Broadcasting : India

School broadcasts in India. G.R. Sudama *et al Perspectives in Education* 1(2) Ap 1985 p 123-27

Scripts writers as school broadcasts in India. D.R. Goel *J Indian Education* 6(6) Mr 1981 p 28-35

A study of school broadcasts in India. G.R. Sudama and D.R. Goel *Indian Education* 12(3-4) Je-Jl 1982 p 25-30

Educational Broadcasting : India : Andhra Pradesh

School broadcasts for primary schools in Andhra Pradesh. D.R. Goel *Experiments in Education* 7(8) Oc 1979 p 141-45

Educational Broadcasting : India : Haryana

Headmasters and school broadcasts. D.R. Goel *Progress of Education* 54(12) Jl 1980 p 221-28

School broadcast programme : Some observations. D.R. Goel *J Indian Education* 6(3) Se 1980 p 22-26

Students and school broadcasts. D.R. Goel *Progress of Education* 54(3) Oc 1979 p 50-58

A study of school broadcasts in Haryana. D.R. Goel *Experiments in Education* 7(5) Jl 1979 p 80-86 refs

Educational Broadcasting in Adult Education : Great Britain

Educational broadcasting for adults in the United Kingdom and the lessons for India. Jagannath Mohanty *Education Quarterly* 30(2) Ap 1980 p 18-20

Educational Change

See

Educational Innovations

Educational Discrimination

See

Discrimination in Education

Educational Equalisation

Determinants of rural/urban disparities in the literary role in India. P.K. Bhargava *Indian Educational Rev* 20(2) Ap 1985 p 9-20

Economic dimensions of inequality in India. Shabri Shetty *New Frontiers in Education* 16(2) Ap-Je 1986 p 41-45

Education and equality : A perspecive from the West. Jean Floud *J Higher Education* 1(2) Aut 1975 p 199-209 refs

Education for equality. E.V. Rathnaiah *Indian Education* 10(1-2) Ap-My 1980 p 35-39

Education, equality and society. Bryan Wilson, ed. London, Allen and Unwin. 1975, 200p. *Book Rev, J Indian Education* 5(5) Ja 1980 p 84-86

Education, inequality and industrialisation. Satish Saberwal *J Higher Education* 1(2) Aut 1975 p 189-97 refs

Education, inequality and life chances. Paris, OECD. 2 vols. 1975, 612p; 448p. $23.75 Book Rev, *Indian Educational Rev* 15(2) Ap 1981 p 125-28

Equality in education : An India's profile. V.P. Garg *New Frontiers in Education* 15(2) Ap-Je 1985 p 67-68 refs tabs

Equality of educational opportunity. V. Jaganathan *New Frontiers in Educa-*

tion 16(2) Ap-Je 1986 p 55-59 tabs

Equalisation of educational opportunity - The role of the teacher and government. K. Adinarayana *Progress of Education* 54(6) Ja 1980 p 109-11

The psychological dimensions of inequality. M. Almeida *New Frontiers in Education* 16(2) Ap-Je 1986 p 46-56

A study of equality and the higher learning; editorial. *J Higher Education* 1(2) Aut 1975 p 151-54

Educational Games

Quiz to create lively interest. Benimadhab Mukherji *Primary Teacher* 11(3) Jl 1986 p 18-19

Educational Guidance

See

Personnel Service in Education

Educational Innovations

Creativity and innovation in education. B. Rajaiah *Educational Rev* 92(8) Ag 1986 p 127-29 refs

Development of attitudes towards educational innovations scale (AEIS). Dileep Kumar and S.P. Ahluwalia *Asian J Psychology and Education* 11(1) 1983 p 28-31

Development of attitude towards educational innovations scale (AEIS). Dileep Kumar and S.P. Ahluwalia *Teacher Education* 16(18-19) Ja-Ap 1982 p 33-37 refs tabs

The dilemma of innovative change : An organisational analysis. Rudulf C. Heredia *New Frontiers in Education* 11(1) Ja-Mr 1981 p 12-28 refs tabs

Education and innovation; editorial. *J Indian Education* 5(6) Mr 1980 p 1-2

Educational innovations and their manangement in schools. Sushma Bhagia *Rajasthan Board J Education* 20(1-2) Ja-Je 1984 p 9-14

Educational innovations : Role of educational administration. Shaikh Sabjan *Progress of Education* 60(7) Fe 1986 p 150-55+

Educational innovations : Towards better schooling. M. Mukhopadhyay *Indian Education* 12(1-2) Ap-My 1982 p 5-19

Failure of an innovation in a university : As inventigation. R.P. Jain *New Frontiers in Education* 10(4) Oc-De 1979 p 73-79 refs tabs

Inviting innovation. Earl D. Hanson *Indian Education* 11(5) Ag 1981 p 7-10

Limits to educational changes. P.R. Dalin. London, Macmillan. 112p. £2.95 *Book Rev, Education Quarterly* 31(2) Jl 1979 p 43-44; *Indian Educational Rev* 15(1) Ja 1980 p 125-28

Management of an innovation : A case of a school for a planned change. D.C. Joshi *J Indian Education* 5(5) Ja 1980 p 8-16

Management of innovations in higher education. Sushma Bhagia *New Frontiers on Education* 15(3) Jl-Se 1985 p 73-77 refs

Planned change in education. John Elliott-Kamp *J Education and Psychology* 27(4) Ja 1980 p 216-24 refs

The process of educational innovation - An international perspective. Raymond S. Adam and David Chen. Paris, UNESCO. 1981, 284p. *Book Rev, Indian Educational Rev* 18(3) Jl 1983 p 126-28

Rationalisation of educational system in the scientific and technological age I.V. Ramana Reddy *Experiments in Education* 10(3) Ap 1982 p 23-25

Relevance, renovation and process of change. D.P. Pattanayak *J Higher Education* 1(1) Mon 1975 p 43-48

Researches in innovation and change in education. D.P. Darji and B.R. Panehal *Asian J Psychology and Education* 7(2) Jl 1981 p 16-26

Ring in the new in the past quarter-century. Indu Dave *Teacher Today* 26(1) Jl-Se 1983 p 45-53

See also

Education Technology

Educational Innovations : Developing Countries

Educational innovation in the third world. Martin Carnoy *J Higher Education* 5(2) Aut 1979 p 141-55

Educational Innovations : India

Education innovations and agricultural development : A study of North India. D.P. Chaudhri. New Delhi, Vikas Pub. 1979, 127p. Rs.95 *Book Rev, Education Quarterly* 32(1) Ja 1980 p 45-46

Educational Innovations in India. D.N. Gaind *Rajasthan Board J Education* 16(1-2) Ja-Je 1980 p 16-25

Educational Innovations : India : Andhra Pradesh

Innovations and experiments in education in Andhra Pradesh. P. Adinarayana *Indian Education* 12(1-2) Ap-My 1982 p 13-16

Educational Innovations : India : History

Innovations education : The colonial historical context. Suresh Chandra Shukla *Our Education* 2 Jl 1981 p 15-21 refs

Innovations in education : The colonial historical context. Suresh Chandra Shukla *Teacher Today* 24(2) Oc-De 1981 p 1-19

Educational Innovations : Korea

Educational innovations in the Republic of Korea. Rajasthan *Board J Education* 16(1-2) Ja-Je 1980 p 30-35

Educational Innovations : Pakistan

Educational innovation in Pakistan. L. Habib Khan *Rajasthan Board J Education* 16(1-2) Ja-Je 1980 p 41-54

Educational Innovations : Philippines

Educational reforms and innovations in the Philippines. Felex P. Santos *Rajasthan Board J Education* 16(1-2) Ja-Je 1980 p 55-64

Educational Innovations : Thailand

Some aspects of educational innovations in Thailand. Ekavidya Nathalong *Rajasthan Board J Education* 16(1-2) Ja-Je 1980 p 82-85

Educational Journalism

See

Journalism, Educational

Educational Laws and Legislation

The no-man's land between law and education. Raja Gonesan *Experiments in Education* 8(6) Ag 1980 p 99-102

Educational Laws and Legislation : United States

Implementation of a systems model approach in facilitating passage of school law as contrasted with Kentucky's recent education reform movement. Roger C. Noe *Progress of Education* 60(10-11) My-Je 1986 p 222-32 + tabs

Educational Measurements
See
Educational Tests and Measurements
Educational Media
See
Teaching : Aids and Devices
Educational Photography
See
Photography in Education
Educational Planning
Cost-analysis for educational planning : Some basic issues. V.P. Garg *New Frontiers in Education* 13(4) Oc-De 1983 p 40-49
Development and planning of modern education. J.C. Agarwal. New Delhi, Vikas Pub. 1982, 424p. Rs.95 *Book Rev, J Indian Education* 8(6) Mr 1983 p 78-79
Educational planning for economic development. Romesh Chandra *J Education and Psychology* 36(1-2) Ap-Je 1978 p 26-33 refs
In the mind of men : Psychological foundations of educational planning. I.C. Menon *New Frontiers in Education* 9(4) Oc-De 1979 p 46-57
Innovative educational programmes : Some hurdles. V. Srinivasan *J Indian Education* 10(6) Mr 1985 p 30-32
Institutional planning : An approach to effective learning environment. S.G. Mathur and A.B. Saxena *Educationa Quarterly* 33(1) Ja 1981 p 10-11
Institutional planning. B.R. Deshmukh *Research Bulletin* 14(3-4) Se-De 1984 p 33-49
Management of educational resources : A systems approach R. Srinivasa Rao *Experiments in Education* 7(1) Mr 1979 p 13-15 refs
Nurturing non-academic talent in the school : A challenge. Ashok K. Hota *J Indian Education* 8(6) Mr 1983 p 35-41 refs
Paulo Freire's criticism of educational system. S.N. Prasad *J Indian Education* 11(2) Jl 1985 p 11-18 refs
Resource management for education systems. D.R. Darji and D.K. Sharma *Progress of Education* 55(8) Mr 1981 p 211-13+
Science technology interaction : A systems model for education. M.V. Ananthakrishnan *J Higher Education* 9(2) Aug 1983
System analysis in educational planning. Raghunath Safaya *Educational Rev* 85(5) My 1979 p 89-93 figs
See also
Education and National Development
Educational Administration
Educational Innovations
School Management and Organisation
Educational Planning : Asia
Summary of the principal recommendations. *Experiments in Education* 7(3) My 1979 p 53-57
Educational Planning : Developing Countries
Systems approach to planning new educational media in the developing countries. Santosh K. Panda *Education Quarterly* 35(1) Ja 1983 p 12-15 refs

Educational Planning : France

Educational structure administration and planning in France. K.C. Nautiyal *Teacher Education* 17(20-21) Jl-Oc 1982 p 69-80

Educational Planning : India

Economics of educational planning in India. Ranjana Srivastava *Education Quarterly* 32(2) Ap 1980 p 1-5 ft-n

The Education Commission and after. J.P. Naik. New Delhi, Allied 1982, 258p. Rs.120 *Book Rev, New Frontiers in Education* 13(3) Jl-Se 1983 p 85-96; *Progress of Education* 57(9) Ap 1983 p 213-14

Education in the sixth five year plan. R.K. Bhandari *New Frontiers in Education* 12(3) Jl-Se 1982 p 31-49

Education in the sixth plan. R.S. Uppal *Teacher Education* 15(16-17) Jl-Oc 1981 p 1-29 annex tabs

Education in the sixth plan. S. Ravishankar *Indian Education* 11(7) Oc 1981 p 33-34

Education in the sixth plan. S. Ravishankar *Indian Education* 11(8-9) Nv-De 1981 p 45-47; 11(10) Ja 1982 p 46-47; 11(11-12) Fe-Mr 1982 p 41-42

Education in the seventh five-year plan. V.V. Chiplunkar *Progress of Education* 59(1) Ag 1984 p 2-5+

Educational development during six five year plans : An evaluation. R.K. Bhandari *New Frontiers in Education* 15(2) Ap-Je 1985 p 52-66 tabs

Educational development in the seventh five year plan. R.K. Bhandari *New Frontiers in Education* 13(4) Oc-De 1983 p 50-61

Educational planning at the institution level. K.S. Chalam *Educational Rev* 87(7) Jl 1981 p 124-26

Educational planning in India. Saleshwara Saxena. New Delhi, Sterling. 1979, 202p. Rs.45 *Book Rev, Education Quarterly* 31(2) Jl 1979 p 38

Educational planning. S. Sreedhara Swamy *Indian Education* 10(3) Je 1980 p 19-23

Integration of educational planning with overall planning. E.W. Frankin *Indian Education* 10(1-2) Ap-My 1980 p 10-14

Kothari commission's warning. R.S. Nigam *Educational Rev* 87(1) Ja 1981 p 18-19

An operations research approach to educational planning. J.N. Kapur *Indian Education* 10(1-2) Ap-Je 1980 p 23-28

Planning education for the eighties. M.V. Rajagopal *Indian Education* 10(1-2) Ap-My 1980 p 5-9

Retrospect and prospect of research on educational planning in India. L.P. Singh *National J Education* 2(2) Mr 1980 p 52-58 refs

Sixth plan : Priorities in educational development. J.L. Azad *Indian Education* 10(1-2) Ap-My 1980 p 15-22

Systems approach to educational planning in higher education in India. S.P. Malhotra and S.K. Panda *Quest in Education* 19(3) Jl 1982 p 246-54 refs

Towards excellence, equity and productivity education. *University News* 23(8) 23 Fe 1985 p 13-15

Educational Planning : India : Haryana

The limits of the manpower approach. J.C. Galabawa *Perspectives in Education* 2(4) Oc 1986 p 231-37 refs

Educational Planning : India : States

Programme proposed in the States Sixth Plan for educational development. *Teacher Today* 24(1) Jl-Se 1981 p 95-102 tabs

Educational Planning : Russia

Planning and administration of education in the USSR under the new education policy. Jayashree Jalali *J Educational Planning and Administration* 1(1) Oc 1986 p 76-80

Educational Planning : Tanzania

Planning education for development in Tanzania : The limits of the manpower approach. J.C. Galabawa *Perspectives in Education* 2(4) Oc 1986 p 231-37 refs

Educational Planning : United States

Implementation of a systems model approach in facilitating passage of school law as contrasted with Kentucky's recent education reform movement. Roger C. Noe *Progress of Education* 60(10-11) My-Je 1986 p 222-32 + tabs

Educational Policy

See

Education and State

Educational Programme

See

Educational Planning

Educational Psychology

Academic promise and fulfilment. Rup Nagpal. New Delhi, New Soc Pub. 139p. Rs. 48 *Book Rev, Education Quarterly* 34(2) Ap 1982 p 53-54

Attitude towards education of students, parents and teachers. K. Sivasankara Reddy *J Education and Psychology* 42(4) Ja 1985 p 229-33

The attitudes of convent and general school boys : A comparative study. M.D. Sharma *J Indian Education* 6(3) Se 1980 p 40-43

A case for analysis and development of learning and administrative skills in education. B.K. Passi *J Education and Psychology* 38(4) Ja 1981 p 207-10

A comparative study of alienation from the school among the first generation learners and *vice versa*. V.K. Rai *Educational Rev* 89(8) Ag 1983 p 132-34 refs

Comparative study of attitudes of boys and girls towards education. M.M. Patel and J.C. Parikh *J Education and Psychology* 42(1-2) Ap-Je 1984 p 85-90 refs

Construction and standardisation of the educational leadership behaviour discription questionnaire. P.C. Shukla *J Education and Psychology* 42(1-2) Ap-Jl 1984 p 51-54 refs

The EUE factor of educational psychology. Norman C. Dowseet *Bhartiya Shiksha Shodh Patrika* 1(2) Jl 1982 p 1-4 refs

Education and psychology : Plato, Piaget and scientific psychology. Kievan Egan. London, Methuen. xiii, 210p. £4.95 *Book Rev, Education Quarterly* 38(3) Aut 1986 p 54-55

Educational approach to psychology. K.U. Bhambhra *Teacher Today* 21(4) Ap-Je 1979 p 32-35

Educational psychology from the standpoint of a Marxist. Amiya Kumar Basu *Our Education* 5 Jl 1984 p 29-38 ref

Elementary statistics in psychology and education. A.B.L. Srivastava and K.K. Sharma. New Delhi, Sterling. *Book Rev, J Institute of Educational Research* 10(1) Ja 1986 p 31

Level of satisfaction of teachers and students regarding the traditional and modern systems of education as practised in the two selected home science institutions. Anupama Shah *J Education and Psychology* 31(3) Oc 1983 p 117-25

New directions in educational psychology : Learning and teaching. Noel Entwistle, *ed.* Sussex, Falmer Press. 346p. *Book Rev, Education Quarterly* 37(4) Wint 1985 p 56-57

Personality profile of withdrawing deviance in schools. Saroj Aurora *Indian Educational Rev* 18(3) Jl 1983 p 102-06 refs

Problem behaviour in the secondary school. Bill Gilham, *ed.* London, Croom Helm. 195p. £5.95 *Book Rev, Education Quarterly* 34(1) Ja 1982 p 47

Psychology of education : A pedagogical approach. Edgar Stones. London, Methuen. 490p. £5.95 *Book Rev, Education Quarterly* 37(4) Wint 1985 p 63-64

The role of the teacher in the free progress method of integral education. Indra Sen *Education Quarterly* 36(1) Ja 1984 p 1-5

Some data on the validity of Hindi adaptation of W.A. S.R. verbal section. Dwarka Prasad and S.K. Varma *J Education and Psychology* 40(1-2) Ap-Jl 1982 p 61-65

Stress experience of higher education students. MS. Ramamurthy *J Higher Education* 9(2) Aut 1983 p 245-49 tabs

Students attitude towards study. Sumitra L. Patel *J Education and Psychology* 38(3) Oc 1980 p 181-88 refs tabs

Study habits and underachievement among rural girls. Prem Lata Sharma *J Education and Psychology* 42(3) Oc 1984 p 115-18 ref

Towards development of attitudes : A paradigm. M.J. Ravindranath *Education Quarterly* 35(2) Ap 1983 p 8-11 refs

See also

Ability Grouping in Education
Achievement Motivation
Child Study
Interest : Psychological Aspects
Learning, Psychology of
Listening
Mental Tests
Perception
Piaget Jean
Psychology, Applied
Rewards and Punishment in Education
Students : Psychology

Educational Research

Applying educational research : A practical guide for teachers. Walter R. Borg. New York, Longmans. 1981, $9.95 *Book Rev, Research Bulletin* 16(1-2) Mr-Je 1986 p 58-63

Basic characterstics of a researcher. T.B. Mathur *J Indian Education* 8(6) Mr 1983 p 55-57

Choices for research in education : A note of criteria. A.S. Seetharamu *Indian Educational Rev* 18(1) Ja 1983 p 116-20

Content analysis : An emerging paradigm in educational research. T. Purushathama Rao *Progress of Education* 61(3) Oc 1986 p 58-61

Current research in education : The malady. R.P. Bhatnagar *Indian Education* 11(7) Oc 1981 p 8-12

Development research in the context of instruction : Significance and design. M.S. Yadav and M.B. Menon *National J Education* 6(2) My 1984 p 59-67 refs

Educational research as an inter-disciplinary endeavour. M.S. Yadav *et al New Frontiers in Education* 12(3) Jl-Se 1982 p 14-22

Educational research at the Sri Aurobindo Society. Norman C. Dowsett *Bharatiya Shiksha Shodh Patrika* 4(2) Jl-De 1985 p 13-19

Educational research by Indian research scholars at foreign universities : A review. D.N. Khosla and Neerja Shukla *Indian Educational Rev* 15(2) Ap 1980 p 50-58 appdx

Formative research. Baij Nath Singh *Indian J Adult Education* 39(9) Se 1978 p 16-22 ft-n

Multiple choice items : A framework of educational research. K.L. Kumar and S.D. Palki *Indian Education* 13(3-4) Je-Jl 1983 p 15-16

Paradigm and ideology in educational research : The social functions and the intellectual. Thomas S. Popkewitz. Sussex, Falmer Press. 1984, 208p. £4.25 *Book Rev, Education Quarterly* 36(4) Wint 1984 p 56-57; *Progress of Education* 60(7) Fe 1986 p 169-70

Planning educational research. G.M. Prakash *Indian Educational Rev* 18(3) Jl 1983 p 91-94

Programmatic considerations for facilitating educational research and development. A.A. Akinsanya *Indian Educational Rev* 16(1) Ja 1981 p 37-47

Quantitative and qualitative approaches in educational research. M.S. Yadav *et al J Educational and Psychology* 43(4) Ap 1985 p 5-13

Research and practice in education. Shib K. Mitra *J Indian Education* 8(2) Jl 1982 p 59-64

Research in education. Devika Hiranandani *Teacher Today* 21(2) Oc-De 1978 p 57-59

The scientific method in educational research : Need for rethinking. R. Govinda *et al New Frontiers in Education* 14(4) Oc-De 1984 p 40-45

Social crisis and educational research. Len Barton and Stephen Walker, *eds.* London, Croom Helm. 347p. £8.95 *Book Rev, Education Quarterly* 37(3) Aut 1986 p 63-64

A study of response bases through a questionnaire without questions. S.K. Verma *et al J Education and Psychology* 40(1-2) Ap-Jl 1982 p 74-84

Verified knowledge in education : The need for meta-analysis. Vasant D. Bhat *Perspectives in Education* 1(1) Ja 1985 p 25-33 refs

Wastage at the Ph.D. level. R.C. Yadav and H.P. Singh *New Frontiers in Education* 12(4) Oc-De 1982 p 43-48

Why is'nt educational research more useful? Henry M. Levin *Indian Educa-*

tional Rev 15(1) Ja 1980 p 1-9

See also

United Nations Educational, Scientific and Cultural Organisations

Educational Research : Asia

Regional seminar on education research in relation to educational reform in Asia and Oceania. *J Indian Education* 7(3) Se 1979 p 50-51

Educational Research : Asia : Southeastern

Educational research in South East Asia. R.P. Singh *Indian Educational Rev* 14(4) Oc 1979 p 43-46

Educational Research : Developing Countries

Educational research environments in the developing world. Canada, IDRC. 228p. *Book Rev, Indian J Adult Education* 45(10) Oc 1984 p 17-22

Educational Research : India

Demyslifying educational research. K. Sivadasan Pillai *Teacher Today* 26(4) Ap-Je 1984 p 66-68

Documentation and dissemination of educational research. R.P. Singh *Teacher Today* 24(2) Oc-De 1981 p 26-31

Educational research in India : The need for quality control. N.K. Upasani *Progress of Education* 56(4) Nv 1981 p 78-81 +

See also

National Council of Educational Research and Training

Educational Research : India : Rajasthan

Twenty-five years of educational research in Rajasthan. P.L. Verma *Teacher Today* 26(1) Jl-Se 1983 p 87-100 refs

Educational Research : Latin America

Connecting worlds : A survey of developments in educational research in Latin America. Robert G. Myers. Ottawa, IDRC. 1980. 88p. *Book Rev, Education Quarterly* 34(3) Jl 1982 p 51-52

Educational Research : Mathematical Models

Mathematical models in educational research : Issues, problems and prospects. R. Govinda *Perspectives in Education* 1(4) Oc 1985 p 257-66

Educational Research : Quality Control

Quality control in educational research. S.K. Pal and P.C. Saxena. New Delhi, Metropolitan. 1985, 660p. Rs.250 *Book Rev, Perspectives in Education* 1(4) Oc 1985 p 270-71

Educational Societies

See

Educational Associations

Educational Sociology

Education and social and moral values : Lessons of history. M. Gopalakrishnan *Indian Education* 12(3-4) Je-Jl 1982 p 12-16

Education and social change. Kamlesh Chaudhury *Quest in Education* 18(2) Ap 1981 p 130-38 refs

Education and social justice. N.S. Padmanabhan *Educational Rev* 86(5) My 1980 p 85-87

Education and socialistic pattern of society. Raghunath Safaya *Educational Rev* 87(11) Nv 1981 p 213-14

Education and society. K.G. Rastogi *Primary Teacher* 6(2) Ap 1981 p 24-27

Education and the social process. D.S. Chauhan *Perspectives in Education* 2(4) Oc 1986 p 239-48 refs tabs

Education for community living. Kathita Hatibaruah *Educational Rev* 88(1) Ja 1982 p 4-6; 88(3) Mr 1982 p 47-50 refs

Education in a changing society. Pritam Singh Brar *Educational Rev* 89(11) Nv 1983 p 190-91

The effect of ecological differences on subject preferences, academic aspiration and achievement among primary school pupils. E.E. Ezenu and C.C. Anadi *Progress of Education* 60(5) De 1985 p 98-102 refs tabs

An enquiry into the role of the family and the school in leading the children towards the threshold of democratic citizenship. Deb Kumar De *J Education and Psychology* 41(1-2) Ap-Jl 1983 p 17-22

Inculcation of ethical and social values in education : A proposal for implementation. T.S. Avinashilingam. Coimbatore, Sri Rama Krishna Mission. *Book Rev, Progress of Education* 56(12) Jl 1982 p 305

Literate girls : Impact on family. Mumtaz Ali Khan *Educational Rev* 85(4) Ap 1979 p 75-77

Major deficiencies of hypothetico deductive model in explaining social behaviour. R.R. Singh *Indian Educational Rev* 19(1) Ja 1984 p 93-113

Religious and social behaviour among academics : Some findings of a survey. Rudolf Heredia *New Frontiers in Education* 14(3) Jl-Se1984 p 39-46 refs

Social change and education present and future. M.P. Paliwal. New Delhi, Uppal Pub H. 1984, 354p. Rs.175 *Book Rev, Teacher Today* 28(2) Oc-De 1985 p 123-24

Social change and the educational system. Anne Van Haecht *J Higher Education* 6(1-3) 1980-81 p 105-15 refs

Social crisis and educational research. Len Borton and Stephen, Walker, *eds*. London, Croom Helm. 347p. £8.95 *Book Rev, Education Quarterly* 37(3) Aut 1986 p 63-64

Social demands on the university. R.K. Yadav *National J Education* 3(1) Se 1980 p 1-8 refs

The social impact of education. Kaberi Dey *Educational Rev* 88(8) Ag 1982 p 142-43

Socially useful productive work some thoughts on its implementation in our schools. C.B. Patyal *Asian J Psychology and Education* 6(1) Ja 1980 p 32-34

Society and education. Jagannath Mohanty *Educational Rev* 86(4) Ap 1980 p 65-67

The teacher and the society. Daleep Mukherji *New Frontiers in Education* 9(1) Ja-Mr 1979 p 1-11

Teachers and social change. S. Rajagopalan *Experiments in Education* 7(8) Oc 1979 p 131-36; 7(9) Nv 1979 p 166-70+; 7(10) De 1979 p 176-79; 7(12) Fe 1980 p 220-22 refs

World mindedness as related to personal values and religion of collegeates. Ramji Srivastava and Q.G. Alam *J Education and Psychology* 38(1) Ap 1980 p 33-35 tabs

See also
Education : Aims and objectives

School Environment
Socialism and Education
Students Socio-Economic Status

Educational Sociology : Africa

Educational and society in Africa. Mark Bray *et al.* London, Arnali, Edwar. 1986, 191p. *Book Rev, Perspectives in Education* 2(4) Oc 1986 p 249-50

Educational Sociology : Developing Countries

Education and social values in developing countries. S.C. Nandwani *J Indian Education* 8(3) Se 1982 p 3-8

Educational Sociology : Great Britain

Community service, social education and curriculum. Peter Scrimshow. London, Hodder. 85p. £3.95 *Book Rev, Education Quarterly* 34(4) Oc 1982 p 58-59

Educational Sociology : India

India's challenge : Education for social justice. V.V. John *New Frontiers in Education* 14(2) Ap-Je 1984 p 17-25

Models of education system : Pitfalls of ignoring socio-economic variables. Satyapal Julka *J Higher Education* 7(3) Spr 1982 p 319-21

A sociological approach to Indian education. S.S. Mathur. Agra, Vinod Pustak Mandir. 1985, 452p. Rs.30 *Book Rev, Education Quarterly* 37(3) Aut 1985 p 57-59; *Perspectives in Education* 2(3) Jl 1986 p 187-88

Educational Sociology : India : Gujarat

Social contest of tribal education. Vimal P. Shah and Tara Patel. New Delhi, Concept Pub. 212p. Rs.150 *Book Rev, Education Quarterly* 38(2) Sum 1986 p 49-51

Educational Surveys

Designing class room instruction through students cognitive styles : A practical approach. Subhash Chandra Agarwal *Quest in Education* 19(1) Ja 1982 p 35-41 refs tabs

Educational Technology

The appropriate educational technology. A.B. Saxena *Education Quarterly* 33(2) Ap 1981 p 4-6

Computer technology and the future of education. L.M. Prakash Srivastava *Education Quarterly* 37(3) Aut 1985 p 13-16

The concept of educational technology. S.M. Mehta *Teacher Today* 22(4) Ap-Je 1980 p 48-51

Developing software educational technology. R.M. Agarwal *Primary Teacher* 11(4) Oc 1986 p 8-11

Education, technology and development : A perspective. M.V. Verghese. New Delhi, NIEPA. 29p. *Book Rev, Education Quarterly* 36(4) Wint 1984 p 53-54

Educational development and educational technology. Malla Reddy Mannidi and S. Ravishankar. New Delhi, Sterling. 1984, 380p. Rs.21.50 *Book Rev, Education Quarterly* 37(1) Spr 1985 p 67-68

Educational technology. A.R. Sharma. Agra, Vinod Pustak Mandir. 1985, 225p. Rs.25 *Book Rev, Education Quarterly* 37(4) Wint 1985 p 64-66; *Indian Educational Rev* 20(4) Oc 1985 p 171-72

Educational technology - An approach to systematic learning. S. Umar *Asian J Psychology and Education* 11(2) 1983 p 23-27

Educational technology and communication media. J. Mohanty. Cuttack, Nalanda Pub 188p. Rs.14 *Book Rev, Education Quarterly* 33(3) Jl 1981 p 46-47

Educational technology : Concept, claims and constraints. J.N. Bahukhandi *Teacher Today* 27(1) Jl-Se 1984 p 14-25 refs

Educational technology for creative education. M.N. Deshmukh *J Indian Education* 5(4) Nv 1979 p 3-11 refs

Educational technology for primary schools. Jagannath Mohanty *Primary Teacher* 11(4) Oc 1986 p 5-7

Educational technology for teacher education : An experimental study. D.K. Sharma and R.K. Sharma *J Indian Education* 6(6) Mr 1981 p 36-41 refs

Educational technology. K.T. Mamtora *Educational Rev* 86(1) Ja 1980 p 1-4

Fundamentals of educational technology. Narendra Nath Pangotra. Chandigarh. Int Pub. 103p. Rs.22 *Book Rev, Progress of Education* 56(8) Mr 1982 p 200

Instructional technology. Vishwanath Muddu *Indian Education* 10(9-10) De 1980-Ja 1981 p 13-15

Introduction of educational technology. K. Sampath *et al* New Delhi, Sterling, viii, 292p. Rs.25 *Book Rev, Education Quarterly* 34(1) Ja 1982 p 47-48

Language laboratory : An important innovation in educational technology. Jagannath Mohanty *Education Quarterly* 37(1) Spr 1985 p 12-14

Management of educational technology : New challenge in education. M. Mukhopadyay *Education Quarterly* 37(2) Sum 1985 p 10-18 refs

The need for an educational technology. G. Subramania Pillay *Quest in Education* 17(1) Ja 1980 p 74-80

New educational technology and the teaching of chemistry. R.C. Mehrotra *J Higher Education* 1(1) Mon 1975 p 31-42 refs

The open university in achievement in educational technology. J. Mohanty *Education Quarterly* 31(3-4) Oc 1979-Ja 1980 p 21-23

A peep into Glaser's model of instructional system. G.R. Sharma *Teacher Today* 22(1) Jl-Se 1979 p 36-39

Readings in educational technology. B. Anand Rao and S. Ravishankar, *eds.* Bombay, Himalaya Pub H. 1982, 411p. *Book Rev, Indian Education* 12(7) Oc 1982 p 35-36; *Progress of Education* 57(7) Fe 1983 p 166

Role of educational technology cell in developing countries. M.P. Gupta *Education Quarterly* 33(2) Ap 1981 p 7-8

A study of the use of educational technology in colleges of education in Punjab and its effect on their output. S.P. Gupta *Progress of Education* 57(9) Ap 1983 p 204-07

Teachers versus technology. C. Dharmarajan *Educational Rev* 92(1) Ja 1986 p 7-9

Technology invades education. M. Sengupta *Education Quarterly* 37(2) Sum 1985 p 7-9

See also

Computer in Education

Programmed Instruction

Teaching : Aids and Devices

Educational Technology : History

Educational technology in historical perspective. S. Ravishankar *Indian Education* 10(8) Nv 1980 p 31-32

Educational Technology : India

Curriculum development and educational technology. Malla Reddy Mamida and S. Ravishankar. New Delhi, Sterling. *Book Rev, J Institute of Educational Research* 10(2) My 1986 p 26

Developing educational technology for deprived sections of the Indian society. R.S. Sharma *Bulletin of Non-formal Education* 3(3) De 1985 p 1-17

Educational technology in distance education. Vasant D. Bhat *University News* 24(42) 8 Nv 1986 p 79-82

Educational technology in India : The present and the prospect. Sushma Bhagia *J Indian Education* 8(5) Ja 1983 p 55-59 refs

Trends of research on educational technology in India. C.H.K. Misra *J Institute of Educational Research* 7(3) Se 1983 p 19-25

Educational Technology : Sweden

The rise and fall of educational technology in Sweden. Christer Brushing *Teacher Education* 17(20-21) Jl-Oc 1982 p 23-29 refs

Educational Television

See

Television in Education

Educational Tests and Measurements

Appraisal of internal assessment Lokesh K. Verma *Teacher Education* 14(10-11) Ja-Ap 1980 p 28-33 refs

Attitude of university examiners in arts and science subjects towards spot evaluation. Lokesh K. Verma *J Higher Education* 7(3) Spr 1982 p 286-88 tabs

Central evaluation : A time saving device. M.L. Mishra *J Educational Planning and Administration* 1(1) Oc 1986 p 43-53

A close look at sample 'multiple' - Choice questions of E.T.S. R.D. Godbate *J Higher Education* 7(3) Spr 1982 p 317-19

A comparative study of reliability of true-false items and multiple choice, items. Ram Dutt and Jai Prakash Sharma *Rajasthan Board J Education* 19(2-3) Ap-Se 1983 p 1-5

A comparative study of the opinions of teachers of different faculties of the Sardar Patel University with regard to internal assessment. A.D. Patel *J Education and Psychology* 39(4) Ja 1982 p 248-53

Contributions of memory and speed to psychology honours examination scores. Biranchi N. Puhan and Suresh C. Das *Asian J Psychology and Education* 5(1-3) 1979 p 26-33

A correlational study of internal and external test performance. J.S. Grewal and K.B. Subramaniam *J Educational Research and Extension* 18(2) Oc 1981 p 55-59 refs tabs

Criterion referenced measurement. Mohottige U. Sodore *New Frontiers in Education* 9(1) Ja-Mr 1979 p 52-62 refs

Criterion referenced testing of written expression at degree level. Haribhai G. Desai *J Educational Research and Extension* 20(2) Oc 1983 p 118-24

Criterion *vs* norm-referenced tests. V.K. Rai *Educational Rev* 91(1) Ja 1985 p 3-6 refs

A critical study of an objective type test. Ved Prakash *J Indian Educational Rev* 8(3) Se 1982 p 14-19 tabs

Development of a question bank for a course on educational evaluation, at B.Ed level. M.S. Yadav and M.B. Menon *J Higher Education* 3(3) Spr 1978 p 357-67 refs tabs

Educational evaluation : Trends towards more participating approaches. Steven Klees *et al Perspectives in Education* 2(3) Jl 1986 p 133-53

Educational measurement. Richard H. Lindeman, Bombay, Taraporewala. 1971. 173p. *Book Rev, Teacher Today* 23(2) Oc-De 1980 p 96-97

Effect of simulated information on assessment of cognitive competence : A test of expectancy hypothesis. K.C. Panda and P.C. Dash *Indian Educational Rev* 15(2) Ap 1980 p 22-35 refs

Effect strategy for college students assessment. Mukul Kumar Sharma *Educational Rev* 90(9) Se 1984 p 128-32 refs

Effectiveness of test types on high and low achievers. V.P. Sharma *Indian Educational Rev* 20(4) Oc 1985 p 78-89

Evaluating apperceptive mass in science through word association. Ram Niwas Gupta *Rajasthan Board J Education* 15(2) Ap-Je 1979 p 42-50

Evaluating educational outcomes. Pritam Singh Brar *Primary Teacher* 10(3) Jl 1985 p 23-26

Evaluation : A new concept. Dig Vijaya Singh *Progress of Education* 55(7) Fe 1981 p 192-93

Evaluation and achievement. Marlow Ediger *New Frontiers in Education* 12(4) Oc-De 1982 p 25-31

Evaluation approach for teaching and testing. W.A.F. Hopper *New Frontiers in Education* 13(3) Jl-Se 1983 p 38-41

Evaluation in higher education. E.S. Balachandran and E.G. Vedanayagam *Experiments in Education* 8(4) Je 1980 p 61-64

Evaluation of achievement. Marlow Ediger *Education Quarterly* 33(3) Jl 1981 p 24-25 refs

An evaluation of English medium and Tamil medium pupils at X standard level. A.N. Deenadayala *Experiments in Education* 7(11) Ja 1980 p 304-07 tabs

Evaluation practices in some selected primary and middle schools : A study. P.N. Arora *J Indian Education* 6(6) Mr 1981 p 46-48

An experiment in the subjective assessment of essays. C.Z. Shah *Progress of Education* 55(6) Ja 1981 p 150-54 tabs

An experimental study of the effect of different methods of checking the written work. Kuram Gupta *Educational Rev* 90(11) Nv 1984 p 173-75 refs

An experimental study of the predilections of the examiners correcting the answer books. Sushil K. Behadur *J Education and Psychology* 36(1-2) Ap-Je 1978 p 54-62 refs

Fundamentals of educational assessment : Cregg F. Ingram. New York, Van Nostrand. 1980, 404p, *Book Rev, Teacher Today* 25(3) Ja-Mr 1983 p 106-07

A golden means to internal assessment and external examination. K.T. Mamtora *Progress of Education* 54(3) Oc 1979 p 63-66

Guidelines for continuous assessment. N.S. Gnanapragasam *Educational Rev* 85(12) De 1979 p 231-33

How to engineering students look at internal assessment? A. Venkata Rami Reddy *Asian J Psychology and Education* 7(1) Ja 1981 p 31-39

Human factor in evaluation. S.R. Jayaswal *University News* 24(39) 16 Oc 1986 p 1-3

Implication of formative evaluation. Lokesh Koul and Satish Bhadwal *J Indian Education* 12(4) Nv 1986 p 11-16 refs

Improving evaluation at the elementary stage. Qamaruddin *Primary Teacher* 9(2) Ap 1984 p 11-12

Innovation in student evaluation. K.V. Natarajan *J Indian Education* 5(6) Mr 1980 p 3-5

Innovation in student evaluation. K.V. Natarajan *Quest in Education* 17(1) Ja 1980 p 81-85

Internal assessment and dropouts. G.C. Nagpal *Progress of Education* 53(10-11) My-Je 1979 p 201-02+

Internal assessment : Expectations and experiences. A. Venkata Rami Reddy *Asian J Psychology and Education* 4(2) Jl 1979 p 22-26 refs

Interactional effect of length, style and handwriting on the marking of examiners at postgraduate stage : A study. Bharat Bhushan *J Higher Education* 9(3) Spr 1984 p 392-95 refs tabs

International trends in educational assessment. Patricia Broadfoot *J Higher Education* 7(3) Spr 1982 p 227-35 refs

Maintenance of standards with reference to internal assessment. Sushama A. Keshar *Progress of Education* 56(10) My 1982 p 246-50

Merit list on the basis of 2-scores is not valid. R.D. Godbole *J Higher Education* 9(2) Aut 1983 p 269-71

Modern evaluation technique. Goswami Rambalak *Primary Teacher* 5(4) Oc 1980 p 40-44

A new method of student evaluation. Arvind Sharma *Educational Rev* 87(5) My 1981 p 83-84

Obstacles to evaluation : Teachers' views. Devyani S. Punalekar *Progress of Education* 57(10) My 1983 p 231-34 +

P.G.'s want a change over to internal assessment. V. Venkata Rami Reddy *Asian J Psychology and Education* 13(1) Ja 1984 p 11-19 refs

Pragmatisation of student evaluation. K.V. Natarajan *J Education Research and Extension* 20(30) Ja 1984 p 172-77

Question banks and construction of tests and reporting of results for internal assessment and external examinations. Harinder Nanda Mahajan *J Higher Education* 9(2) Aut 1983 p 235-44 refs

Reducing test tensions. M. Mascarenhas *Rajasthan Board J Education* 15(4) Oc-De 1979 p 38-42

Reliability and usability of measuring instruments. G. Subramania Pillai *Experiments in Education* 10(10) De 1982 p 175-79 refs

Revival of essay testing. B.V. Adkoli *Progress of Education* 58(11) Je 1984 p 266-69

Scaling of examination. R.D. Godbole *Progress of Education* 57(5) De 1982 p 108-10

School self-evaluation : Some initial considerations. Norman Whiting *J*

Education and Psychology 40(3) Oc 1982 p 107-16 ref

Selection, certification and control : Social issues in educational assessment. Patricia Broadfuot, ed. Sussex, Falmer Press. 1984. 275p. *Book Rev, Education Quarterly* 37(2) Sum 1985 p 76-77

Sessional evaluation in colleges : A research study. Radha Rani Sharma *J Higher Education* 7(3) Spr 1982 p 280-86 tabs

A study of internal assessment. J.P. Srivastava and Pradeep Kumar Srivastava *Quest in Education* 16(4) Oc 1979 p 327-32 refs

A study of internal assessment. P. Mehta and R.C. Sharma *J Education and Psychology* 37(3) Oc 1979 p 167-72 refs

Uses and abuses at periodical test system in evaluation of classroom learning. Daveshdutt Pandey *Indian Educational Rev* 18(4) Oc 1983 p 135-42

Variability in evaluation and re-evaluation of answer scripts. Lokesh K. Verma *Experiments in Education* 8(3) My 1980 p 56-58 refs

See also

Ability : Testing

Examinations

Grading and Marking : Students

Mental Tests

Personality Tests

Students : Rating

Educational Tests and Measurements : Great Britain

Oral examination in foreign languages at 16 in the U.K. : A review of test types and assesement, Principles. John D. Hurman *J Indian Education* 11(2) Jl 1985 p 25-34

Educational Tests and Measurements : India

A comparative study of the attitude of post-graduate students of two institutions towards internal assessment. A. Venkata Rami Reddy *J Education and Psychology* 38(1) Ap 1980 p 4-16 refs tabs

Evaluation system in Indian conditions. K.V. Natarajan *J Indian Education* 9(1) My 1983 p 42-44

Inter-examiner variability in assessing answer scripts of engineering sciences. S.A. Balu and G.S. Chandran *J Higher Education* 5(2) Aut 1979 p 224-28

Educational Tests and Measurements : India : Uttar Pradesh

A comparative study of internal and external assessment of post- graduate level. P.K. Srivastava *Progress of Education* 55(12) Jl 1981 p 231-34 tabs

Educational Toys

Lovable toys : A project of educating the handicapped children. Ram Singh Kanchan *Primary Teacher* 9(2) Ap 1984 p 31-33

Toys can also teach. *Primary Teacher* 5(2) Ap 1980 p 26A-26C

Educationists

Doctrines of great educators. Robert R. Rusk and James Scotland. London, Macmillan. 1979 *Book Rev, National J Education* 3(1) Se 1980 p 75

On defining an educationist; editorial. *J Indian Education* 6(2) Jl 1980 p 1-2

Teacher educators effectiveness : A research study. Umma Kulsum and M. Khagapeer *Indian Educational Rev* 20(2) Ap 1985 p 51-57

See also

Teachers

Wirszup, Izaak
Educationists : Russia
See
Stoletov, Vsevolod
Efficiency Rating
See
Teachers : Rating
Eggs : Production
See
Poultry
Eistein, Albert
Einstein and the philosophical problems of 20th century physics. Sergei Syrovatkon, Tr. Moscow, Progress Pub. 1983, 508p. Rs. 11.25 *Book Rev, Teacher Today* 27(4) Ap-Je 1985 p 148-49
Elementary Education
See
Education, Elementary
Elementary School Dropouts : India : Madhya Pradesh
Identification and prevention of potential dropouts at the elementary stage. J.S. Grewal *Primary Teacher* 9(1) Ja 1984 p 16-19
Elementary School Students
See
School Children
Elementary School Teachers
Interests and involvement in continuing education programmes among primary school teachers. K.S. Pillai and G.S.K. Nair *Prasar* 5(1-2) Ap-Jl 1977 p 36-44
Learning disability : Challenge to primary school teachers. Prem Lata Sharma *Primary Teacher* 11(3) Jl 1986 p 20-22
The primary teacher in action. Deanne Boydell. Open Bks Pub. vii, 126p. £1.95 *Book Rev, Education Quarterly* 31(3-4) Oc 1979 - Ja-1980 p 47
The role of rural primary school teacher. N.A. Mudh *Primary Teacher* 5(4) Oc 1980 p 22-23
A study of social cohesion in elementary teachers training institutions and its relationship with their efficiency. N.K. Jangira *EPA Quarterly Bulletin* 6(1) Ap 1983 p 36-42 refs
Elementary School Teachers : Absenteeism
Teacher absenteeism in primary schools. L.S. Sinha *Primary Teacher* 11(2) Ap 1986 p 24-27
Elementary School Teachers : India
The primary school teachers : An instrument of social change. Qamaruddin *Primary Teacher* 4(2) Ap 1979 p 5-9
Elementary School Teachers : India : Nagaland
Creative pupil perception by Angami Nagas serving in elementary schools of Nagaland. A.C. Pachaury *J Educational Research and Extension* 18(4) Ap 1982 p 224-28 refs tabs
Elementary School Teachers : India : Uttar Pradesh
Achievement motivation and job satisfaction in primary school teachers. S.K. Srivastava and Solan Gupta *J Education and Psychology* 43(3-4) Oc

1985-Ja 1986 p 193-96 refs

Effect of the variables of sex and marital status on the level of job satisfaction among primary school teachers. Meera Dixit *J Institute of Educational Research* 9(1) Ja 1985 p 22-24 refs

Primary school teachers as community health workers. A.K. Sen *Teacher Today* 28(2) Oc-De 1985 p 67-70 tabs

Elementary School Teachers : In-service Training

Life long education, in service education programme for primary school teachers. Sunil Behari Mohanty *Experiments in Education* 9(9) Nv 1981 p 6[illegible]-64 refs

Elementary School Teachers : Training : Scotland

Training of primary school teachers and Scotland and its implications for Indian situation. Sunil Behari Mohanty *Primary Teacher* 8(4) Oc 1983 p 1-5

Emancipation of Women

See

Woman : Rights of Women

Emotional Problems in Children

Emotional and social development of pupils of class X. Banamali Mohanty and Bijayashree Pani *Asian J Psychology and Education* 4(1) Ja 1979 p 1-4 refs

Emotionally Disturbed Children

See

Problem Children

Emotions

See

Anxiety

Control : Psychological Aspects

Fear

Frustration

Employee Incentive

See

Incentive in Industry

Employees, Rating of

See

Performance Standards

Employment of Women

See

Women : Employment

Encounter Groups

See

Group Relations Training

Encyclopaedias and Dictionaries

The use of dictionaries. H.L. Chopra *Primary Teacher* 9(1) Ja 1984 p 20-21

Engineering : Study and Teaching

Continuing engineering education. M.L. Jain *J Higher Education* 5(1) Mon 1979 p 51-56

Intellective and non-intellective factors associated with engineering creativity. M. Sengupta *Indian Educational Rev* 17(1) Ja 1982 p 93-98

The role of humanities and social sciences in engineering education. S.

Ambirajan *J Higher Education* 9(3) Spr 1984 p 333-48 refs

Engineering : Study and Teaching : Iran

Study and practice of engineering in Iran. S.M. Mosavi *J Higher Education* 4(1) Mon 1978 p 114-18 refs

Engineering Industry Workers : India : Maharashtra

Education and industrial productivity : A case study of workers and supervisors employed in the engineering industry in Pune metropolitan region. S. Pinto *Research Bulletin* 16(1-2) Mr-Je 1986 p 43-57

Engineering Students : India

Hopes and concerns of engineering students in India. Khalid Ahmed Kazi and Rehana Ghadially *J Higher Education* 5(3) Spr 1980 p 401-09 appdx refs tabs

Engineers, Women

See

Women Engineers

English Language

Indian and British English. Pasoo Nihalain *et al.* New Delhi, OUP. 1979, 260p. Rs. 40 *Book Rev, J Indian Education* 7(3) Se 1979 p 58-59

English Language : Composition and Exercises

Constructions of a battery of objective tests for assessment of proficiency in writing English composition. Amarjit Singh *Indian Educational Rev* 15(1) Ja 1980 p 90-103

English Language : Examinations, Questions, etc.

Monograph on question banking in English language and literature for universities. Assn of Indian Univ. *Book Rev, J Higher Education* 5(1) Mon 1979 p 117-20

O grade English : Should it be assessed internally. *J Indian Education* 5(1) My 1979 p 81-85

The question paper for std XII. S.S. Pundlik *Progress of Education* 56(1) Ag 1981 p 8-9

English Language : Grammar

A study of the pupils knowledge of English grammar and its relationship to their proficiency in English in standards IX. S. Rajagopalan *Experiments in Education* 7(2) Ap 1979 p 21-25

English Language : India

Indian and British English. Paroo Nihalain et al. New Delhi, OUP. 1979, 260p. Rs.40 *Book Rev, J Indian Education* 7(3) Se 1979 p 58

Indian English : Model, identity and use. S.V. Parasher *J Indian Education* 5(1) My 1979 p 68-75 refs

Indian English : Search for an independent standard. V.B. Singh *Teacher Today* 23(3) Ja-Mr 1981 p 73-80 refs

English Language : Inflection

An evaluation of discriminant frames through a programme on English morphology. M.D. Chadha and V.P. Singh *Indian Educational Rev* 18(4) Oc 1983 p 47-57

English Language : Pronunciation

A study of the English pronunciation of the teachers of English. C.D. Indapurkar *Research Bulletin* 15(3-4) Se-De 1985 p 3-20 appdx tabs

English Language : Remedial Teaching

An applied psycholinguistics experiment in remedial teaching of English grammar. I.U. Rungla and Anasuya Pal *Indian Educational Rev* 14(1) Ja 1979 p 136-40 refs

English Language : Study and Teaching

Developmental of an extrinric programme in English grammar and studing its relative effectiveness in relation to the conventional method of teaching. Lalji Tripathi *Asian J Psychology and Education* 11(3) 1983 p 25-31 refs tabs

The discussion on the unilevel English textbook prescribed for std XII. Kishore Bhide *Progress of Education* 56(1) Ag 1981 p 2-4

The effect of knowledge of results on the achievement in English : An investigation. Jamnalal Bayti *Research Bulletin* 15(3-4) Se-De 1985 p 21-29 tabs

An evaluation of discriminant frames through a programme on English morphology. D.K. Chadha and V.P. Singh *Indian Educational Rev* 18(4) Oc 1983 p 47-57

How much lesson does an English teacher require? D.N. Bezboruah *Teacher Today* 24(2) Oc-De 1981 p 34-38

Language laboratory drills and their role in teaching a foreign language English. Rajendra Kothari *Rajasthan Board J Education* 19(2-3) Ap-Se 1983 p 10-14

Methods of teaching in relation to English textbooks for std XII. Sushasini P. Sathe *Progress of Education* 56(1) Ag 1981 p 5-7

New directions in English teaching. Anthony Adams, ed. Sussex, Falmer Press. 1982, 244p. *Book Rev, Education Quarterly* 35(4) Oc 1983 p 63-64

A note in supports of the grammar-translation method. B.N. Patnaik *Indian Educational Rev* 18(3) Jl 1983 p 106-11 refs

Overseas students composition in English studies. J.P. Heaton and J.P. Stocks. London, Longmans. 1978, 340p. 70d *Book Rev, Education Quarterly* 31(1) Ap 1979 p 38-39

A probe into the study of English language. V.S. Sivamohan and R. Israel Mansingh *J Educational Research and Extension* 16(3) Ja 1980 p 174-75

Problems in the analysis and teaching of the structure of the English nominal group. R.S. Pathak *J Indian Education* 5(4) Nv 1979 p 42-45 refs

The question papers for std XII. S.S. Pundlik *Progress of Education* 56(1) Ag 1981 p 8-9

The regional language and English as media of instruction. A. Venkata Rami Reddy and D. Muni Reddy *J Indian Education* 6(4) Nv 1980 p 13-16

The situational approach in teaching English. H.H. Raval *Progress of Education* 56(1) Ag 1981 p 17-18+

Some issues in the pedagogies of the general English studies. Anand Rao Thota *Indian Education* 10(11) Fe 1981 p 40-43

The structural approach : Its shortcomings. J.G. Kulkarni *Progress of Education* 55(5) De 1980 p 129-31 +

Teaching English by correspondence. E.J. Ekambaran *J Higher Education* 5(2) Aut 1979 p 252-55

Teaching English through games. Veen Bahal *Educational Rev* 58(6) Je 1979 p 104-06

Teaching in English : Need to revise objectives. S.H. Josh *New Frontiers in Education* 12(4) Oc-De 1982 p 53-58

The teaching of composition in English. H.H. Raval *Progress of Education* 55(8) Mr 1981 p 214-16

The teaching of English : Men, methods and materials. Jagat Bahukhandi *Teacher Today* 23(2) Oc-De 1980 p 22-29

Teaching of English through correspondence. Inayat Khan *University News* 24(42) 8 Nv 1986 p 45-54 refs

Teaching of structures in English. C.D. Indapurkar *Progress of Education* 56(11) Je 1982 p 265-68+ figs

Un-English expressions in English books. Indira Kulshreshtha *Primary Teacher* 9(3) Jl 1984 p 8-10

English Language : Study and Teaching : Great Britain

The language centre of Birmingham. I.S. Sharma *Primary Teacher* 9(2) Ap 1984 p 21-23

English Language : Study and Teaching : Higher

Rationalising M.A. course in English. M.S.V. Chani *Educational Rev* 85(8) Ag 1979 p 151-53

Teaching of English at degree level : Some new directions. P. Grace Jacob *New Frontiers in Education* 11(4) Oc-De 1981 p 31-41 refs

English Language : Study and Teaching : India

The paradoxical situation of English in India. Ananda Rao Thota *Indian Education* 10(8) Nv 1980 p 23-25

The teaching of English in India. A.N. Mishra *Educational Rev* 16(3) Mr 1980 p 43-44

English Language : Study and Teaching : Primary

Teaching English alphabets : A play-way method. Benimadhab Mukerji *Primary Teacher* 8(2) Ap 1983 p 31-38

Teaching English as a second language. Mamta Agrawal *Primary Teacher* 9(4) Oc 1984 p 21-25

Teaching of correct pronunciation in English at primary level. M. Kunwar *Primary Teacher* 9(2) Ap 1984 p 24-26

Word recongnition techniques in the reading curriculum. Marlow Ediger *Progress of Education* 58(12) Jl 1984 p 282-92 refs

English Language : Study and Teaching : Secondary

Prose teaching in English language at secondary level. Mahesh Bhargava *Rajasthan Board J Education* 19(4) Oc-De 1983 p 22-29

A study of perception of undergraduate and post-graduate students towards the achievement of objective of teaching English at secondary level. B.N. Biswal *Experiments in Education* 6(2) Ap 1978 p 28-31 tabs

English Language : Study and Teaching : Secondary : Curricula

Proposed procedural details of a research study on secondary school English syllabus at masters level. B.N. Biswal *Experiments in Education* 6(1) Mr 1979 p 56-58

English Language : Technical English

Technical English : American and British usage. A.G. Khan *J Indian Education* 5(2) Jl 1978 p 230-33

English Language : Text-books

The discussion on the unilevel English text books prescribed for std XII.

Kishore Bhide *Progress of Education* 56(1) Ag 1981 p 2-4
Methods of teaching in relation to English textbooks for std XII. Suharini P. Sathe *Progress of Education* 56(1) Ag 1981 p 5-7

English Language : Voice
Passivisation : To teach or not to teach. A.G. Khan *J Indian Education* 8(3) Se 1982 p 44-47

English Language : Writing
Importance of developing writing skills in English at the junior college level. Parvathy S. Ayyar and S.K. Somaiya *Progress of Education* 56(7) Fe 1982 p 170-73

Entrepreneur : India : Madhya Pradesh
Creativity as a predictor of entrepreneurial success among tribals. Gurpal Singh Jarial *Experiments in Education* 11(12) Fe 1984 p 110-14 refs

Environment, School
See
School Environment

Environmental Education
See
Ecology : Study and Teaching

Epic Literature : India
See
Ramayana, The

Equal Educational Opportunity
See
Educational Equalisation

Equalisation, Educational
See
Educational Equalisation

Erosion Control
See
Soil Conservation

Essay Writing
Essay writings in primary schools. M.D. Pandey *Primary Teacher* 5(1) Ja 1980 p 33-34

Ethical Education
See
Moral Education
Religious Education

Ethics
See also
Honesty
Literature and Morals
Self-respect
Student Ethics
Worth

Europe
See also
Schools : Europe
Universities and Colleges : Europe

Europe : West

See also

Universities and Colleges : Europe : West

Evaluation of Schools

See

Educational Surveys

Evolution

See also

Heredity

Examinations

An analysis of question bank in mathematics. M.L. Sisodia *et al J Higher Education* 4(3) Spr 1979 p 392-400

Attitude of teachers and students towards the semester. Parveen Akhtar Hassan *Indian Educational Rev* 18(4) Oc 1983 p 116-22

Biochemical consequences of examination stress. M.K. Raina *Indian Educational Rev* 18(2) Ap 1983 p 17-39 refs tabs

Case for a merit examination on a national basis. G. Gunasekaran *University News* 22(2) Ja 1984 p 2-3

Construction and validation of criterion referenced test : An empirical study. B.P. Verma *J Education and Psychology* 41(4) Ja 1984 p 184-92 refs

Development of a question bank for a course on educational evaluation at B.Ed. M.S. Yadav and M.B. Menon *J Higher Education* 3(3) Spr 1978 p 357-67 refs tabs

Educational relevance of external examinations. R.G. Misra *Educational Quarterly* 31(2) Jl 1979 p 27-29

Essay type questions : Their significance and use. Qumaruddin *J Indian Education* 9(1) My 1983 p 25-30

Evaluation of performance of candidates at post-graduate examinations. T. Srinivasaraghavan *J Higher Education* 4(3) Spr 1979 p 410-13

Examination performance and goal displacement. Rudolf C. Heredia *New Frontiers in Education* 10(4) Oc-De 1980 p 1-5 refs

Examinations reforms : Towards an integrated perspective. Jacob Tharu *New Frontiers in Education* 14(8) Ap-Je 1984 p 30-35

The examinee : The neglacted factor in the examination system. J. Indiresan *J Higher Education* 4(2) Aut 1978 p 268-71

Follow up of students who passed SSC/HSC examinations up to 50 per cent marks. R.B. Naik *Research Bulletin* 15(3-4) Se-De 1985 p 42-56 refs tabs

Moderation of examination results. V. Natarajan and Ved Prakash. *J Higher Education* 4(3) Spr 1979 p 407-10

Monitoring : Its role and mechanics in examination management. N.L. Mishra *University News* 24(47) 16 De 1986 p 5-9

Non-detention in schools : An academic exploration. C. Seshadri *Education Quarterly* 36(2) Ap 1984 p 10-23

Objective versus essay examinations. R.D. Godbole *Progress of Education* 57(1) Ag 1982 p 13-15 +

On relative efficiency of examiners. H.R. Singh and C.K. Chatia *Indian Educational Rev* 15(4) Oc 1980 p 35-38

Open book examination. Lokesh K. Verma *National J Education* 2(1) Se 1979 p 57-64 refs

Open book examination system. P.N. Arora *J Indian Education* 8(3) Se 1982 p 40-43

The open book system of examination : An experiment. Lakshmana Rao *Indian Education* 10(9-10) De 1980-Ja 1981 p 33-35

Oral examinations. V. Natarajan *New Frontiers in Education* 9(1) Ja-Mr 1979 p 63-69

A reassessment of home examination. M.N. Razdan *Rajasthan Board J Education* 19(2) Ap-Je 1979 p 20-28

Scrape this examination system. S.S. Jaswal *Educational Rev* 87(11) Nv 1981 p 215-17

Some innovations for the improvement of examinations. Lokesh K. Verma *Indian Educational Rev* 16(3) Ja 1981 p 1-13

Status of examination reforms. Satyapal Julka *Education Quarterly* 33(1) Ja 1981 p 24-25

A study of correlations between performance of academic degree and B.Ed. degree examinations. Leela K. Patel *J Education and Psychology* 39(3) Oc 1981 p 177-83

Which do they want : IA or TS : A comparative study. A. Venkata Rami Reddy and G. Prathapa Simha *J Higher Education* 4(3) Spr 1979 p 400-06

See also

Competitive Examinations

Educational Tests and Measurements

National Talent Search Examination

Students Failure

Subdivision 'Examinations' under subjects, e.g., English Language : Examinations, Questions, etc.

Universities and Colleges examinations

Examinations : India

An agenda for educational reforms of examinations. V.S. Mathur *Education Quarterly* 37(4) Wint 1985 p 15-19

Analysis of re-evaluation cases in Northern universities. Lokesh K. Verma *J Higher Education* 5(2) Aut 1979 p 213-20

Attitude of post-graduate students towards the semester system : A synopsis. Parveen Akhtar Hassan *Indian Education* 11(5) Ag 1981 p 31-34 tabs

The challenge of examination reform. V.S. Mathur *J Indian Education* 6(2) Je 1980 p 52-54

Evaluating the AIU correspondence courses on evaluation methodology and examination. V. Natarajan and Asha Arora *New Frontiers in Education* 10(4) Oc-De 1980 p 15-21

Examination reform and future prospects. R.S. Yadav *Quest in Education* Jl 1981 p 243-62

Examinations : Some new dimensions. V.S. Mathur *Rajasthan Board J Education* 15(4) Oc-De 1979 p 22-25

Examination reforms. J. Joe Prakash *Experiments in Education* 11(12) Fe 1984 p 218-19

Innovations in examinations in India. R.C. Misra *Rajasthan Board J Education* 16(1-2) Ja-Je 1980 p 4-15

Internal *vs* external assessment. K.T. Mamtora *Educational Rev* 85(8) Ag 1979 p 153-55

Introduction of examination reform. V. Natarajan *New Frontiers in Education* 13(3) Jl-Se 1983 p 24-37

Multiple choice and short answer questions : Effect of study habits of students. R.D. Godbole *Progress of Education* 55(7) Fe 1981 p 184-85

National seminar on examination reform. *J Higher Education* 1(2) Aut 1975 p 277-79

Quality education through academic programmes. S. Audinarayana Moorthy *Educational Rev* 84(11) Nv 1978 p 201-02

Radical examination reforms at plus two stage A.P. Committee makes report. *J Indian Education* 6(6) Mr 1981 p 53-56

Relationship between the scores of projects, assignments, unit tests, half-yearly examinations and annual examinations. M.S. Verma *Experiments in Education* 8(11) Ja 1981 p 197-203 refs

Seminar on examination reform as a part of curricular reform; editorial. *Quest in Education* 19(2) Ap 1982 p 95-97

Seminar on examination reform as a part of curricular reform; working paper. Gunvant B. Shah *Quest in Education* 19(1) Ja 1982 p 3-6

They want the new system of evaluation : A. Venkata Rami Reddy and K. Sidda Reddy *Education Quarterly* 32(3) Jl 1980 p 1-4 refs

A two year follow up study on internal assessment. A. Venkata Rami Reddy *J Higher Education* 4(1) Mon 1978 p 47-56 refs tabs

Examinations : India : Andhra Pradesh

Attitudes of teachers toward non-detention system of examinations. S. Padmanabhaiah *Experiments in Education* 7(5) Jl 1979 p 77-80 refs tabs

Radical examination reforms at plus two stage. A.P. Committee makes report. *Indian Education* 10(6) Se 1980 p 29-33

Examinations : India : Karnataka

Achieving better success in examinations. B.G. Barki. Mysore, Smitha Pub. 320p. Rs.35 *Book Rev, J Educational Research and Extension* 18(3) Ja 1982 p 191-92

Examinations : India : Kerala

A statistical analysis of performance in the secondary school leaving certificate examination : Community-wise. J. Rajasekharan Nair *J Institute of Educational Research* 6(3) Se 1982 p 14-19 tabs

Turning point in sex differentials in higher education. J. Rajasekharan Nair *J Higher Education* 6(1-3) 1980-81 p 122-28 tab

Examinations : India : West Bengal

An investigation into the results of the new higher secondary examination in West Bengal. D. Mahanta *Our Education* 1 Jl 1980 p 9-22 refs tabs

Examinations : Malayasia

The Malaysian examinations syndicate. Omar Bin Mohammed Hasim *Rajasthan Board J Education* 16(1-2) Ja-Je 1980 p 36-40

Examinations : Questions

A critical analysis of S.S.L.C. public examination question papers. K. Adinarayana *Experiments in Education* 8(4) Je 1980 p 65-71 tabs

Essay type examinations - Some theoretical issues. C.P.S. Chauhan *Education Quarterly* 36(1) Ja 1984 p 18-22

Have 'question banks' improved the quality of question papers? Jayalakshmi Indiresan and K. Kanakaraj *J Higher Education* 8(2) Aut 1982 p 199-209 refs tabs

Improving the essay test. Banbehari Mukhopadhyay *Educational Rev* 87(3) Mr 1981 p 55-58

Refining the questions. G. Subramania Pillay *J Higher Education* 5(3) Spr 1980 p 422-24

Scoring objective type items : A new method. Ved Prakash *Indian Educational Rev* 20(4) Oc 1985 p 143-50

Examinations : Research

Research in examination : A sociological perspective. L.K. Oad *Quest in Education* 17(1) Ja 1980 p 66-73

Examinations : Sri Lanka

Some trends in the development of examinations in Sri Lanka. L.S. Pereira *New Frontiers in Education* 10(4) Oc-De 1980 p 6-14 refs tabs

Exceptional Children

Exceptional children in schools. S.P. Anand *J Indian Education* 12(1) My 1986 p 3-8 refs

Exceptional children. Uday Shankar. New Delhi, Sterling. 1984, 220p. Rs.75 *Book Rev, Education Quarterly* 37(1) Spr 1985 p 69-70; *Teacher Today* 28(1) Jl-Se 1985 p 109-10

See also

Gifte : Children

Exercise : Physical

Physiological response to exercise. Thankamma Mall *New Frontiers in Education* 13(3) Ap-Je 1980 p 67-77 refs

Preventive, therapeutic and rehabilitative aspects of exercise and sports. N.N. Mall *New Frontiers in Education* 13(2) Ap-Je 1983 p 58-66 refs

See also

Physical Education and Training

Existentialism

Existentialism in education. Angad Singh *Teacher Education* 18(22-23) Ja-Ap 1983 p 69-74 refs

Experimental Education

Experiments and projects. *Experiments in Education* 6(7) Se 1978 p 121-28

Experimental Psychology

See

Psychology, Experimental

Extention Work, Agricultural

See

Agricultural Extension Work

Extra-curricular Activities

See

Student Activities

Extraversion

Extraversion and drive as correlates of substitution reminiscence. Jitendra Mohan and Nalini Munjal *Asian J Psychology and Education* 4(3) Nv 1979 p 1-5 refs

Neuroticism and extraversion of university student dissidents and non-

dissidents. B.S. Wadhwa and C.L. Kundu *Asian J Psychology and Education* 14(1-4) 1984 p 52-56 refs

Relationship between academic achievement, extraversion and neuroticism. Tarlok Singh *J Education and Psychology* 40(4) Ja 1983 p 202-06 refs

Extroversion

See

Extraversion

Fables : Indian

The Panchatantra and Aesope's fables - A study in genre. C.I. Pawate. Delhi, Amar Pra 1986, viii, 122p. Rs.75 *Book Rev, Education Quarterly* 38(3) Aut 1986 p 49-50

Faculty : Education

See

College Teachers

Universities and Colleges : Faculty

Faculty Participation in Administration

See

Teacher Participation in Administration

Faculty-Principal Relationships

See

Teacher-Principal Relationships

Family

See also

Family Life Education

Family Life Surveys

Family : India

Indian family facing inner contradictions. Jose Murichan *New Frontiers in Education* 16(1) Ja-Mr 1986 p 49-66 ft-n

Family Life Education

Family life education. Marie Mignon Mascarenhas *New Frontiers in Education* 14(1) Ja-Mr 1984 p 44-50

Socio-personal correlates and gain in the knowledge of correspondence course trainees. Ranjit Singh and R.K. Saini *Indian J Adult Education* 45(4) Ap 1984 p 30-33 refs

See also

Home Economics

Sex Instruction

Family Life Surveys

Family life of working rural women : A few cases. R. Bhagat *Indian J Extension Education* 16(3-4) De 1980 p 67-70

Family Planning

Attitude of teachers towards small family norm. V. Indira *Experiments in Education* 11(6) Ag 1983 p 109-10+

Family Planning : India

Promoting family planning through non-formal education. K.S. Chalam *Indian J Adult Education* 42(1-2) Ja-Fe 1981 p 25-28

Family Planning : India : Delhi

Differential perception of the characteristics of innovations of farming

couples for high yielding varieties of wheat and family planning practices. J.R. Singh and S.N. Singh *Indian J Extension Education* 16(3-4) De 1980 p 16-21 refs tabs

Farm Crops

See

Field Crops

Farm Mechanisation : India : Punjab

Selected characteristics of farmers in relation to their adaption of farm mechanisation. Ranjit Singh *Indian J Extension Education* 19(3-4) Se-De 1983 p 11-17 refs tabs

Value orientation in relation to adaption of farm mechanisation by the farmers of Ludhiana, Punjab. Ranjit Singh *Indian J Extension Education* 18(3-4) De 1982 p 10-15 refs

Farmers : Education

Agricultural training needs of tribal farmers in Maharashtra. N.B. Shete *Indian J Extension Education* 14(3-4) Jl-De 1978 p 65-67

Construction of attitude scales : Attitude towards improved agricultural practices : Attitude towards adult literacy. N. Venkataiah *Indian J Adult Education* 40(2) Fe 1979 p 27-40 appdx

The correspondence course for farmers as paddy cultivation. O. Abdul Rehiman and A.G.G. Menon *Indian J Extension Education* 14(3-4) Jl-De 1978 p 58-61

Differential dairy farming knowledge and perceived training needs of the trained and untrained farmers. K.D. Kokate and K.C. Tyagi *J Educational Research and Extension* 18(4) Ap 1982 p 201-09 refs tabs

Farmers' functional literacy centres : A case study. B.S. Vasudeva Rao and K. Ganeswara Rao *Indian J Adult Education* 43(6) Je 1982 p 15-18

Farmers functional literacy project, Bhimili study. D.S. Rao *Indian J Adult Education* 40(5) My 1979 p 36-40 tabs

Impact of training and visit system of extension on tribal farms in Hoogly district : A case study. A.K. Ray *et al Indian J Extension Education* 18(1-2) Je 1982 p 59-65 refs tab

Imparting mass training to farmers. G.G. Nandapurkar and K.H. Sirdeshpande *Indian J Adult Education* 41(12) De 1980 p 28-30 refs tabs

Influence of peripatetic training programme on the adoption of recommended farm practices. M. Muthiah *Indian J Extension Education* 14(3-4) Jl-De 1978 p 62-64

Perceptual variability of training needs as views by trained and untrained farmers. K.D. Kokate and K.C. Tyagi *Indian J Extension Education* 18(3-4) De 1982 p 65-67

Relationship of training needs fulfilment with personal characteristics of the farmers. M.P. Singh and S.S. Gill *Indian J Extension Education* 21(3-4) Jl-De 1985 p 89-94 refs tabs

Socio-psychological factors associated with training needs of small and marginal farmers. M. Anatharaman and V.S. Subramanyan *Indian J Extension Education* 18(3-4) De 1982 p 72-73

A study of farmers comprehension of illustrations. D.K. Kaur and P.N. Mathur *Indian J Extension Education* 20(1-2) Je 1984 p 1-6 refs tabs

Training needs of dairy farmers. J.N. Singh *et al Indian J Extension Educa-*

tion 15(3-4) De 1979 p 77-82 tabs

Training needs of farmers in Himachal Pradesh. M.P. Gupta *Indian J Extension Education* 18(3-4) De 1982 p 70-71

Training needs of farmers. N.P. Singh and S.S. Gill *Indian J Extension Education* 18(1-2) Je 1982 p 66-72 tabs

Training needs of tribal farmers. Amar Singh and Suraj Singh *Indian J Extension Education* 17(3-4) Se-De 1981 p 81-88 tabs

Farmers : India

See also

Adoption of Improved Farm Practices

Small Farmers Development Agency

Farmers : India : Andhra Pradesh

Construction of attitude scales : Attitude towards improved agricultural practices : Attitude towards adult literacy. N. Venkataiah *Indian J Adult Education* 40(2) Fe 1979 p 27-40 appdc tabs

Farmers : India : Haryana

Some selected socio-personal economic characteristics of the farmers of progressive and non-progressive dairy villages. Balkishan Singh *et al Indian J Extension Education* 21(3-4) Jl-De 1985 p 101-03 tabs

Farmers : India : Madhya Pradesh

Comparative analysis of adoption behaviour of beneficiaries of farm development programme. Y.C. Sanoria and D.K. Sharma *Indian J Extension Education* 19(1-2) Mr-Je 1983 p 84-86

Farmers : India : Punjab

Information needs of the small and marginal farmers of Punjab state. G.S. Saini *Indian J Extension Education* 17(3-4) Se-De 1981 p 101-02

Need of coordination between small, marginal farmers and agricultural labourers agencies and other concerned departments in Punjab. C.S. Arneja and Surjeet Singh Gill *Indian J Extension Education* 15(1-2) Je 1979 p 63-66

Farmers : India : Tamil Nadu

Differential perception of farm practice : Attributes by progressive and non-progressive farmers. B. Asul Raj and A. John Knight *Indian J Extension Education* 14(1-2) Ja-Je 1978 p 64-65

Factors effecting the knowledge of adopter and non-adopter small farmers. D. Somasundaram and S.N. Singh *Indian J Extension Education* 14(1-2) Ja-Je 1978 p 30-34 refs

Farmers : India : West Bengal

A multiple regression analysis of factors related with attitude of farmers. S. Pathak *Indian J Extension Education* 17(3-4) Se-De 1981 p 73-80 refs tabs

Farmers : Iraq

Farmers information sources at different stages of innovation decision process. Zaki M. Mohammed and Ranjit Singh *Indian J Extension Education* 14(1-2) Ja-Je 1978 p 79-82 refs

Farmers : Psychology

Components of fluency, intelligence and socio-economic status as correlates of the interests in agricultural pursuits. Rajeev Lochan Bhardwaj *J Education and Psychology* 38(4) Ja 1981 p 227-34 refs

Farming
See
Agriculture
Fear
How and why children fear? Kuldeep Kumar *Primary Teacher* 10(4) Oc 1985 p 13-16
Structure of interrelations among fear of success, motivation and personality measures. Satvir Singh and Kiran Vanvaria *Asian J Psychology and Education* 6(2) Jl 1980 p 17-20 refs tabs
A study of fears in adolescents. A.K. Salma Begum *J Institute of Educational Research* 9(3) Se 1985 p 14-16 refs tabs
Fechner's Law
The verification of Fechner's law by method of equal appearing intervals : Some problems. P.H. Lodi *Asian J Psychology and Education* 4(3) Nv 1979 p 23-30
Feedback : Psychological Aspects
Functioning of feedback. Prabhaker Singh *J Indian Education* 12(1) My 1986 p 52-54
Feeding Stuffs
See
Feeds
Feeds : India : Karnataka
Information sources consulted by dairy farmers in the cultivation of green fodders in Tumkur district. H.N. Subba Reddy and M.B. Channagowda *Indian J Extension Education* 18(1-2) Je 1982 p 92-94
Feeling
See
Perception
Female
See
Woman
Feminine Health
See
Woman : Health and Hygiene
Feminism
See
Woman
Fertilizers and Manures : India : Haryana
Fertilizer consumption in Haryana : A determinant of differential agricultural growth. Madan Singh and R.P. Singh *Indian J Extension Education* 19(3-4) Se-De 1983 p 32-39 refs tabs
Fertilizer consumption in Haryana : A determinant of differential agricultural growth. Madan Singh and R.P. Singh *Indian J Extension Education* 20(1-2) Je 1984 p 12-19 refs tabs
Fertilizers and Manures : India : Maharashtra
Shift in use of fertilizers to constraints. M.G. Bhilagaonkar *Indian J Extension Education* 15(3-4) De 1979 p 34-38 tabs
Fertilizers and Manures : India : Tamil Nadu
Role of fertilizer dealers in the transfer of new farm technology V.A. Amalraj

and M.S. Prasad *Indian J Extension Education* 20(3-4) Se-De 1984 p 69-70

Fertilizers and Manures : India : West Bengal

Variables contributing to the level of fertilizer use of the farmers. A.K. Singh and G.L. Ray *Indian J Extension Education* 21(3-4) Jl-De 1985 p 1-10 refs tabs

Field Crops

See also

Bajra
Maize
Rice
Sugar-cane
Wheat

Field Crops : India : Haryana

Cropping pattern in Haryana and Punjab : A temporal analysis. Madan Singh and R.P. Singh, *Indian J Extension Education* 19(1-2) Mr-JE 1983 p 57-61

Field Crops : India : Punjab

Cropping pattern in Haryana and Punjab : A temporal analysis. Madan Singh and R.P. Singh *Indian J Extension Education* 19(1-2) Mr-Je 1983 p 57-61

Field Crops : India : Uttar Pradesh

Constraints to production of crops in Uttar Pradesh. Daulat Singh and V.K. Singh, *eds* Kanpur, U.P. Soc Ext. Educ and Rural Devel. 1983, 118p. Rs.85 *Book Rev, India : Indian J Extension Education* 19(3-4) Se-De 1983 p 97

Field Crops : India : West Bengal

Factors contributing to the farmers productivity of crops. R.L. Sagar and G.L. Ray *Indian J Extension Education* 20(1-2) Je 1984 p 20-28 refs tabs

First Born Children

See

Children, First-born

Fish Culture : India : West Bengal

Factors related to the adoption of recommended species of fish in composite fish culture. Mohammed A. Haque and G.L. Ray *Indian J Extension Education* 19(1-2) Mr-Je 1983 p 74-83

Fish farmers perception of the problems in comparative fish culture and measures suggested by them for increasing the yield of fish. Mohammed A. Haque and G.L. Ray *Indian J Extension Education* 19(3-4) Se-De 1983 p 56-61 refs tabs

Fisheries : India

The summer institute in fisheries : An evaluation. G.R. Desai and P.N. Kaul *J Educational Research and Extension* 18(1) Jl 1981 p 43-50 tabs

Fisheries : India : Kerala

Adoption of improved practices by fish trawler owners in Kerala. S. Balasubramaniam and P.N. Kaul *Indian J Extension Education* 20(3-4) Se-De 1984 p 35-42 refs tabs

Adoption of improved practices by traditional fisherman in Kerala. S. Balasubramaniam and P.N. Kaul *Indian J Extension Education* 21(3-4) Jl-

De 1985 p 80-88 refs

Fishery Products : Preservation

Adoption of improved fish curing practices. S. Balasubramaniam and P.N. Kaul *Indian J Extension Education* 18(3-4) De 1982 p 45-50 refs tabs

Fodder

See

Feeds

Folk-lore of Agriculture : India : Haryana

Folk beliefs associated with dry farming. Hira Nand and Kamlesh Kumar *Indian J Extension Education* 16(3-4) De 1980 p 36-42 refs tabs

Folk-lore of Harvesting

See

Folk-lore of Agriculture

Folk-songs : India

Bakhen : Ritual invocation songs of a primitive community. Sitakant Mahapatra. New Delhi, Prachi Pra. 1979, 71p. Rs.20 *Book Rev, J Indian Education* 7(3) Fe 1979 p 59

Forage Plants

See also

Sorghum

Form Psychology

See

Gestalt Psychology

Foster Family Care

See

Foster Home Care

Foster Home Care : Russia

Foster homes in the USSR. Kira Agafonova *Progress of Education* 55(5) De 1980 p 127-28

Fowls

See

Poultry

France

See also

Education, Higher : France

Education, Primary : France

Educational Planning : France

Free Education : India

How shall free and compulsory primary education succeed? Acharya Dinnanath *Primary Teacher* 5(4) Oc 1980 p 20-21

Freire, Paulo

Literacy and revolution : The padagogy of Paulo Freire. Robert Mackie, ed. London, Pluto Press £3.80 *Book Rev, Teacher Today* 24(1) Jl-Se 1981 p 103-04

Paulo Freire : A revolutionary padagogue. Narasingha Prosad Sil *Indian Educational Rev* 16(1) Ja 1981 p 35-36 refs tabs

Paulo Freire's criticism of educational system. S.N. Prasad *J Indian Education* 11(2) Jl 1985 p 11-18 refs

Frustration

Inter caste differences in frustration among girls of scheduled and non-scheduled castes. Ajay Mohan Misra *et al J Institute of Educational Research* 4(1) Ja 1980 p 13-15 refs

School climate and reactions to frustration. M.P. Uniyal and A.R. Bisht *Indian Educational Rev* 15(2) Ap 1980 p 95-101 appdc refs

A study of the effect of socio-economic status on the frustration reactions of school going children. Ramanath Kundu and Jayantha Ray-Chaudhury *J Institute of Educational Research* 9(1) Ja 1985 p 13-17 refs tabs

Games

See also

Educational Games

Gandhi, Indira : Educational Thought

Exchange of views on education. Indira Gandhi. *J Educational Research and Extension* 20(2) Oc 1983 p 85-91

Indira Gandhi on education. I.N. Sopori *Teacher Today* 27(3) Ja-Mr 1985 p 1-10

Gandhi, Mohandas Karamchand (1869-1948)

Studies on Gandhi. V.T. Patil, New Delhi, Sterling. 1983, 296p. Rs.13 *Book Rev, Education Quarterly* 36(2) Ap 1984 p 73-74

Understanding Gandhi from Marxist angle. *Student Action* 2(6) Oc 1983 p 3-6 +; 2(7) De 1983 p 9-11

Gandhi, Mohandas Karamchand : Economic Ideas

Relevance of Gandhian economics for national development. T.S. Avinashiligam *J Educational Research and Extension* 16(2) Oc 1979 p 65-71

Gandhi, Mohandas Karamchand : Educational Thought

Education for a just social as economic order : The Gandhian approach. D.D. Tewari *Teacher Education* 18(24-25) Jl-Oc 1983 p 1-24 refs

Fundamental bases on Gandhian education. Lakshahira Das *Educationl Rev* 88(2) Fe 1982 p 34-36

The Gandhian alternative in education. D.D. Tewari *Teacher Education* 18(22-23) Ja-Ap 1983 p 55-68

Gandhiji as an educational philosopher. W.H. Siddique and Qamar Jahan *Educational Rev* 87(12) De 1981 p 223-25; 88(1) Ja 1982 p 7-9

Gandhiji on adult education. J.K. Pillai *Indian J Adult Education* 39(10) Oc 1978 p 19-20

Gandhiji and education. *Primary Teacher* 5(4) Oc 1980 p 31-32

Gandhiji on true national education : Some excerpts. *Primary Teacher* 4(1) Ja 1979 p 10-12

Mahatma Gandhi's philosophy of education : Its salient features recalled. H.K. Mehta and H.N. Patel *Progress of Education* 54(3) Oc 1979 p 59-62 + tabs

Modern approaches to management of education and the way of

Mahatama Gandhi. R. Ramaswamy *Experiments in Education* 12(3) My 1984 p 50-56

A study of anxiety : Summer Institute of Gandhian thought. J.K. Pillai and S. Jaleel Saheb *Indian Education* 10(8) Nv 1980 p 16-19

A study of Gandhian education. K.G. Warty. Bombay, Somaiya Pub. 1981, 138p. Rs.10 *Book Rev, Progress of Education* 56(7) Fe 1982 p 177

Gandhi Shikshan Bhavan, Bombay

Gandhi Shikshan Bhavan College of Education; Report of practice teaching, 1978-79. Asha Kalla *Quest in Education* 16(2) Ap 1979 p 149-59

Socially useful productive work in Gandhi Shikshan Bhavan, 1979-80. Shaila Savur *Quest in Education* 17(2) Ap 1980 p 106-11

General Education

Some thoughts on general education. Brijmohan Gupta *Rajasthan Board J Education* 16(4) Oc-De 1980 p 45-53

Stray thoughts on general education in the context of vocationalisation. D. Anjaneyulu *Experiments in Education* 9(2) Ap 1981 p 27-30

See also

Education, Humanistic

General Science : Ability Testing

A comparative study of two item type parallel objective achievement test in general science. Upendra Nath Rout *Experiments in Education* 6(7) Se 1978 p 117-21 tabs

A comparative study of two items type parallel objective achievement tests in general science. Upendra Nath Rout *J Educational Research and Extension* 16(3) Ja 1980 p 176-80

General Science : Study and Teaching : Elementary

Problems of teaching general science for standard VI in Tamil Nadu and their impact on pupil achievement in general science. S. Sundararajan *Experiments in Education* 7(11) Ja 1980 p 193-201; 7(12) Fe 1980 p 211-19; 8(1) Mr 1980 p 6-9 tabs

General Science : Study and Teaching : Secondary : Audio- Visual Aids

An experimental study to compare the effectiveness of lecture and lecture-cum-filmtrip in teaching one unit in general science for std. VII pupils. S. Sundararajan *Experiments in Education* 6(5) Jl 1978 p 78-81 refs

Generation Gap

See

Conflict of Generations

God

Genetics

See also

Heredity

Genius

See also

Gifted Children

Geography : Study and Teaching

Analysis of scholastic aptitudes for learning geography and the higher secondary stage. B.B. Singh *J Education and Psychology* 40(3) Oc 1982 p 127-35

Geography and the school curriculum. Marlow Ediger *Indian Education* 11(6) Se 1981 p 5-9

Geography Teaching : Some observations and suggestions. R.K. Singh Arora *Teacher Today* 21(2) Oc-De 1978 p 85-88

Issues in teaching geography. Marlow Ediger *J Indian Education* 8(6) Mr 1983 p 61-64

Place of surveying in geography curriculum : A reappraisal. Mumtaz Khan *Teacher Today* 24(2) Oc-De 1981 p 45-53 refs

Preparation on tryout of assignments and to study their effect on the achievements of pupils of class V in the subject of geography. Jashbir M. Patel *J Education and Psychology* 38(2) Jl 1980 p 129-34 refs tabs

The relevance of geography as a school subject. M. Mascarenhas *J Indian Education* 6(3) Se 1980 p 31-33

A study of the effect of low and high readability materials in geography on the reading comprehension of students in the context of reading abilities. C.B. Patyal *J Educational Research and Extension* 18(4) Ap 1982 p 193-200 refs tabs

Teaching geography to the blind. Avinash S. Pandit *Progress of Education* 56(10) My 1982 p 241-45

Geography : Text-books

Geographic thought as expressed in Marathi text-books in geography, 1841-1941. S.A. Garsole *Progress of Education* 55(12) Jl 1981 p 325-27

Geography text-books in Gujarat and Maharashtra : A comparative study. K.M. Kulkarni and A.T. Desai *Progress of Education* 59(10-11) My-Je 1985 p 86-98

Geology : Study and Teaching

Geoscience in our educational system. Surendra *J Indian Education* 5(5) Ja 1980 p 55-57

Reorientation of geological education. I.C. Pande *J Higher Education* 4(2) Spr 1979 p 327-32

Geometry

SSA : A new theorem in geometry. Dipalee D. Sathe *Progress of Education* 57(4) Nv 1982 p 91-92

Geometry : Curricula

The changing geometry curriculum. Marlow Ediger *Educational Rev* 88(2) Fe 1982 p 23-25

Geometry : Study and Teaching

Geometry in the school curriculum. Marlow Ediger *Indian Education* 10(7) Oc 1980 p 7-9

SSA : A new theorem in geometry. Dipalee D. Sathe *Progress of Education* 57(9) Nv 1982 p 91-92

Teaching of geometry. How can it be modernised? C. Seshadri *Rajasthan Board J Education* 15(1) Ja-Mr 1979 p 21-23

Germany : East

See also

Education : Germany : East
Teachers : Germany : East
Vocational Education : Germany : East

Germany : West

See also

Education : Germany : West
Universities and Colleges : Germany : West
Vocational Education : Germany : West

Gestalt Psychology

Kohlar comes to the classrooms. Arvind Dave *Teacher Today* 22(4) Ap-Je 1980 p 69-73

Ghana

See also

Adult Education and Universities : Ghana

Gifted Children

Case study of gifted child. Satish Kumar Yadav *J Education and Psychology* 38(1) Ap 1980 p 61-66 refs tabs

The concept of the gifted child. Jamnalal Bayti *Educational Rev* 92(2) Fe 1986 p 30-33

A gifted child; a national asset. K. Srinivasa Murti *Primary Teacher* 10(3) Jl 1985 p 33-34

Importance and role of gifted in society. Umesh C. Vashishtha *Indian Education* 10(5) Ag 1980 p 16-18

An enquiry into the relation of creativity to academic achievement of the intellectually gifted. R.J. Joshi *J Educational Research and Extension* 18(3) Ja 1982 p 142-48

See also

Talented Students

Gifted Children : Education

Educating the gifted child. Jamna Lal Bayti *Primary Teacher* 10(2) Ap 1985 p 6-8

Education of the gifted. Radha Rani Sharma *Teacher Today* 23(2) Oc-De 1980 p 37-43 refs

The gifted and their education. J.P. Gupta *Primary Teacher* 19(1) Ja 1986 p 17-21

Girls

The effect of personality trait variation on the intensity of problems of girls. B.G. Sudha and Lalitha V. Tirath *J Education and Psychology* 37(2) Jl 1979 p 103-14 refs

See also

Adolescent Girls

Delinquent Girls

Women

Girls : Education

See

Coeducation

Education of Women

Girls : Employment

See

Employment of Women

Girls : India : Punjab

Participation and interest of rural school going girls in household and farm activities. Shavinder K. Mangat and Sunita Roy *Indian J Extension Education* 19(1-2) Mr-Je 1983 p 69-73

Goa

See also

Adult Education : India : Goa

Goats : India : Uttar Pradesh

Attitude of farmers towards goats and sheep farming. Baldeo Singh and O.N. Kunzrov *Indian J Extension Education* 21(1-2) Ja-Je 1985 p 86-88 tabs

Gobar Gas Plants : India : Karnataka
Feeding practice of gobar gas plants in Karnataka. M.B. Channegowda and B. Ranganna *Indian J Extension Education* 16(3-4) De 1980 p 94-95
God
Attitude towards God : A study of the generation gap. K. Sivasankara Reddy *Experiments in Education* 11(9) Nv 1983 p 162-64+
Graded Schools
See
Grading and Marking : Students
Grading and Marking : Students
A comparative study of direct and indirect : methods of absolute grading systems. B.D. Tikkiwal and G.C. Tikkiwal *Indian Educational Rev* 16(2) Ap 1981 p 113-18 tabs
The credibility of external examination marks. R.G. Misra *J Indian Education* 5(5) Ja 1980 p 21-26 tabs
Grade system. Ramesh Chandra Kothari *Educational Rev* 91(10) Oc 1985 p 161-63
Marks and marking behaviour of examiners : An observation. Tarlok Singh *Rajasthan Board J Education* 16(4) Oc-De 1980 p 32-34
Runs of identical marks in marksheets and their bearing on the reliability of marking. H.J. Taylor *Indian Educational Rev* 15(3) Jl 1980 p 51-60 appdx
Scaling of examination scores. V.P. Sharma *Indian Educational Rev* 20(4) Oc 1985 p 40-49
Stability of divisions over the college career. Karuna Shankar Misra *Progress of Education* 54(2) Se 1979 p 29-36 + tabs
Graduate Examinations
See
Universities and Colleges : Examinations
Grain Sorghum
See
Sorghum
Gram Sevak
See
Village Level Workers
Grammar : Comparative and General : Study and Teaching
The teaching of grammar through literature. V.K. Joshi *J Indian Education* 6(4) Nv 1980 p 31-33
Great Britain
See also
Adult Education : Great Britain
Education : Great Britain
Education, Elementary : Great Britain
Education, Higher : Great Britain
Education of Children : Great Britain
Educational Broadcasting : Adult Education : Great Britain
Educational Sociology : Great Britain
Educational Tests and Measurements : Great Britain
English Language : Study and Teaching : Great Britain
Handicapped Education : Great Britain

High School Teachers Training : Great Britain
School Management and Organisation : Great Britain
Schools : Great Britain
Single Teachers Schools : Great Britain
Teachers : Great Britain
Television in Education : Great Britain
Unemployment : Great Britain
Vocational Education : Great Britain

Group Reading

Grouping for instruction in the reading curriculum. Marlow Ediger *Progress of Education* 60(3) Oc 1985 p 50-53+

See also

Books and Reading

Group Relations Training

An experimental inquiry into the dynamics of behaviour in a group setting. S.L. Patel *Experiments in Education* 8(5) Jl 1980 p 79-84 refs

Group Teaching

See

Group Work in Education

Group Work in Education

Aims and techniques of group teaching. M.L.J. Abercrombie. Surrey, Univ of survey. 1979. *Book Rev, J Indian Education* 5(4) Nv 1979 p 72-74

Grouping pupils for instruction. Marlow Ediger *Progress of Education* 58(2) Se 1983 p 30-35; 58(3) Oc 1983 p 54-57+

Learning through small group discussion : A study of seminar work in higher education. Jean Rudduck. Univ of Survey. 1978, *Book Rev, J Higher Education* 5(2) aut 1979 p 269-72

Talking to learn : Improving teaching and learning in small groups. M.L.J. Abercrombie and P.M. Jerry. Univ of Survey. 1978, *Book Rev, J Higher Education* 5(1) Mon 1979 p 120-22

Grouping by Ability

See

Ability Grouping in Education

Guidance, Vocational

See

Vocational Guidance

Guidance in Education

See

Personnel Service in Education

Gujarat

See also

Adult Education : India : Gujarat
Agricultural Cooperative Credit Societies : India : Gujarat
Community Development : India : Gujarat
Education : India : Gujarat
Education, Pre school : India : Gujarat
Education of Children : India : Gujarat
Education of Women : India : Gujarat
Educational Sociology : India : Gujarat

High School Principals : India : Gujarat
High School Teachers : India : Gujarat
Illiteracy : India : Gujarat
National Adult Education Programme : India : Gujarat
Mental Tests : India : Gujarat
Radio in Education : India : Gujarat
Reading Ability : India : Gujarat
Rural Youth : India : Gujarat
School Attendance : India : Gujarat
School Management and Organisation : India : Gujarat
Schools : India : Gujarat
Students : India : Gujarat
Students Socio-Economic Status : India : Gujarat
Teachers : India : Gujarat
Teachers Colleges : India : Gujarat
Television Programme : India : Gujarat
Tribes : India : Gujarat
Vocational Interests : India : Gujarat

Guru Nanak Dev University, Amritsar

Dr. Varadarajan addresses convocation of Guru Nanak Dev University. *University News* 23(17) 1 My 1985 p 7-11

Handicapped

Planning for the handicapped. D.P. Nayar *Education Quarterly* 33(4) Oc 1981 p 10-11+

Promoting abilities in the disabled : A case study. M.S. Samer *J Indian Education* 12(1) My 1986 p 55-57

See also

Mentally Handicapped

Handicapped : Education

Classroom instruction : Needs of the disabled. N.K. Jangira and K.B. Rath *Primary Teacher* 9(3) Jl 1984 p 4-7

International year for the handicapped : Education for the disabled. Asoke Mohan Sen *Education Quarterly* 33(3) Jl 1981 p 5-7

National adult education programme and the disabled. N. Venkataiah and P. Adinarayana Reddy *Educational Rev* 88(7) Jl 1982 p 109-10

Special education. Fred Adams. Essex, Longman Group. *Book Rev, Education Quarterly* 38(3) Aut 1986 p 58-60

Handicapped : Education : Great Britain

Special educational needs of the handicapped. *Teacher Today* 23(3) Ja-Mr 1981 p 145-52

Handicapped : Psychology

Preference and tolerance of disability groups as a function of age and educational level. Henry H. Reiter and Audrey L. Kirsch *Our Education* 5 Jl 1984 p 1-3 refs

Handicapped Children

Helping the retarded children to grow. P. Hanumantha Rao *Primary Teacher* 6(2) Ap 1981 p 8-11

Handicapped children : A programme for the parents. Jyoti Parikh and R.

Health Education
Health and population education. S.N. Singh, ed. Varanasi, BHU. 1979, 187p. Rs.35 *Book Rev, J Indian Education* 7(3) Se 1979 p 60
The role of social sciences in health education. M.G. Oswal *J Indian Education* 5(2) Jl 1979 p 23-26

Health Education : India
Health education of youth in India Usha S. Naidu and S. Parasuraman. Bombay, TISS 1982, 67p. *Book Rev, Education Quarterly* 35(3) Jl 1983 p 59-60
Health education programme for adults : Some guidelines. D. Verma *Indian J Adult Education* 43(6) Je 1982 p 3-6 refs
Health Education : India : Assam
A plea for health educational pyramid in Assam. M.K. Sharma *EPA Quar-*

terly Bulletin 6(2) Jl 1983 p 13-21 refs

Health Education : United States

Teaching good health to children. *J Indian Education* 5(1) My 1979 p 80-81

Health of Women

See

Woman : Health and Hygiene

Hens

See

Poultry

Heredity

Mendel and laws of heredity. Nem Kumar Jain *J Indian Education* 5(1) My 1979 p 44-49

High School Education

See

Education, Secondary

High School Libraries

See

School Libraries

High School Principals

Administrative styles as related to headmasters sex. P.C. Shukla *Educational Rev* 92(7) Jl 1986 p 108-09 tabs

Headmaster *vs* teachers : A study. Bir Singh *Educational Rev* 86(2) Fe 1980 p 21-23

An investigation into the pattern of leadership behaviour of the headmasters, headmistressess of Puri district. A.N. Mishra *Experiments in Education* 6(2) Ap 1978 p 31-35 refs

The role of a headmaster. A. Rama Sarma *Indian Education* 11(5) Ag 1981 p 37-38

School climate and its relationship with headmasters leadership behaviour. Motilal Sharma *Teacher Today* 24(3) Ja-Mr 1982 p 42-49 refs

Why teachers tease you, Mr. headmaster? Bir Singh *Progress of Education* 55(3) Oc 1980 p 77-85

High School Principals : India

Headmaster's keyrole in changing climate. Gyan Prakash Gupta *Rajasthan Board J Education* 15(2) Ap-Je 1979 p 59 62

High School Principals : India : Delhi

A study of students expectation of secondary school principals. R.P. Jain *Experiments in Education* 7(5) Jl 1979 p 86-91 refs

A study of students expectations of secondary school principals. R.P. Jain *J Educational Research and Extension* 18(3) Ja 1982 p 133-41 refs tabs

High School Principals : India : Gujarat

Leadership style of school principals. P.B. Dekhtawala *Progress of Education* 61(2) Se 1986 p 40-42 tabs

High School Principals : India : Tamil Nadu

Leadership styles of heads of schools in Madras. *EPA Quarterly Bulletin* 6(2) Jl 1983 p 1-12 refs

High School Principals : United States

Stress on the headmasters family. Robert J. Gerardi and Gary C. Benedict. *EPA Quarterly Bulletin* 6(2) Jl 1983 p 41-47 refs tabs

High School Students

Characteristics of syllabus bond and syllabus free students of class X. Sushil Prakash Gupta *Quest in Education* 19(3) Jl 1982 p 187-93 refs tabs

High school students and teachers interest in yoga as a part of school curriculum. U. Shashikala Devi and B.S. Satyanarayana *Quest in Education* 17(4) Oc 1980 p 352-59 refs

Sense of deprivation among high school students. Usha Upadhyaya. Varanasi, Yojana Pra. 1985, viii, 136p. Rs.75 *Book Rev, J Indian Education* 12(2) Jl 1986 p 60-62

A study of self-concept of high school students at different levels of adjustment and socio-economic status. S.M. Gupta *J Institute of Educational Research* 10(1) Ja 1986 p 21-24 refs tabs

High School Students : Ability Testing

A study of creativity in relation to socio-economic status of high school students. R.C. Pandey *et al J Institute of Educational Research* 10(1) Ja 1986 p 9-12 tabs

High School Students : Attitudes

Anxiety in relation to economic achievement of high school students. Zakia A. Siddiqi and Shamim Akhtar *Indian Educational Rev* 18(4) Oc 1983 p 106-10

A study on the relationship between adjustment and personality characteristics of higher secondary school students. A.K. Basu *et al Our Education* 1 Jl 1980 p 29-34 tabs refs

High School Students : India : Andhra Pradesh

A study of some personality correlates of intelligence and creative abilities among high school students in Andhra Pradesh. Vishwanath Muddu *Indian Education* 10(4) Jl 1980 p 19-23

High School Students : India : Himachal Pradesh

Creative thinking and culture : A comparative study of tribal and non-tribal high school students of Himachal Pradesh. Kulwinder Singh *Progress of Education* 59(1) Ag 1984 p 11-17 refs tabs

High School Students : India : Orissa

A study of attitude of students towards school of Harijans and tribal welfare department high school of Orissa. Bana Behati Kamila *J Education and Psychology* 43(3-4) Oc 1985 -Ja 1986 p 187-92 refs

High School Students : Psychology

Cognitio-effect development of high school students : Piagetion Perspective. T.S. Sandhu *Indian Educational Rev* 20(3) Jl 1985 p 32-36

Personality trait differences : First, second, and third division high school students. G.N. Prakash and S.S. Srivastava *National J Education* 2(1) Se 1979 p 41-49 refs

High School Teachers

Creative teacher personality and classroom teaching behaviour of secondary school teachers. Mathew George *J Educational Research and Extension* 17(3) Ja 1981 p 150-63 refs tabs

High school students and teachers in yoga as a part of school curriculum. U. Shashikala Devi and B.S. Satyanarayana *Quest in Education* 17(4) Oc 1980 p 352-59 refs

An investigation into the problem of job satisfaction among secondary

My 1980 p 24-29 refs tabs

Teacher morale in secondary schools of Gujarat. P.B. Dekhtawala *Quest in Education* 16(2) Ap 1979 p 160-64 refs

High School Teachers : India : Karnataka

A study of the problems of school teachers. B.G. Sudha *et al J Institute of Educational Research* 4(1) Ja 1980 p 37-40 refs

High School Teachers : India : Maharashtra

See also

Maharashtra State Headmasters Conference, 1982

High School Teachers : India : Orissa

A study of the temperament of secondary school teachers of Orissa. Chintamani Somantaray *Experiments of Education* 6(10) De 1978 p 182-84

High School Teachers : India : Rajasthan

A study of motives of secondary school teachers. C.M. Sharma and M. Pareek *Progress of Education* 58(1) My 1984 p 241-45 refs tab

High School Teachers : India : Uttar Pradesh

A comparative study of the personality traits of effective and less effective secondary school teachers. Kamala Chopra *National J Education* 6(1) Se 1983 p 34-39

Socio-personal factors in the job satisfaction of higher secondary school teachers. S.B.K. Tripathi *et al J Education and Psychology* 39(1) Ap 1981 p 57-65 refs

A study of the influence of personal factors on teachers attitude towards their job. Tahira Khatoon and M.R. Verma *J Institute of Educational Research* 6(2) My 1982 p 6-11 refs tabs

High School Teachers : Training : Great Britain

Recent trends of teacher education for secondary schools in U.K. and India. A.K. Chatterjee *Our Education* 6 Jl 1985-86 p 31-41 refs

High School Teachers : Training : India

Recent trends of teachers education for secondary schools in U.K. and India. A.K. Chatterjee *Our Education* 6 Jl 1985-86 p 31-41 refs

Teacher education at the secondary level in North Eastern region. P.C. Das *Teacher Education* 14(12-13) Jl-Oc 1980 p 9-22 tabs

High School Teachers : Training : India : Orissa

Education of secondary school teachers in Orissa. Sunil Behari Mohanty *Teacher Education* 14(10-11) Ja-Ap 1980 p 8-15 refs

High Schools

See also

Education, Secondary

High Schools : Netherlands

Folk high schools in Netherlands. Cees Staple and Martha Lutman *Indian J Adult Education* 44(8-9) Ag-Se 1983 p 34-40 refs

Higher Education

See

Education, Higher

Higher Education and State : India

Government support for higher education and research. J.L. Azad. New Delhi, Concept Pub. 1984, 202p. Rs.80 *Book Rev, Education Quarterly* 37(2) Sum 1985 p 72-73; *Progress of Education* 59(12) Jl 1985 p 271

Higher education and five-year plans, policies, plans and perspectives. S.N. Saraf *University News* 23(4) 23 Ja 1985 p 2-6 tabs

The politics of manpower planning of graduate unemployment and the planning of higher education in India. Tirlok N. Dhar. Calcutta, Minerva. 1974, 284p. Rs.42 *Book Rev, J Higher Education* 1(1) Mon 1975 p 139-41

The role of the University Grants Commission in framing the policy of higher education. A. Mathew *J Higher Education* 9(2) Aut 1983 p 117-95 refs

State grants to collegiate institutions : A study of patterns and procedures. J.L. Azad *J Higher Education* 2(2) Aut 1976 p 243-52 refs tabs

Systems approach to education and planning in higher education in India. S.P. Malhotra and S.K. Panda *Quest in Education* 19(3) Jl 1982 p 246-54 refs

Higher Education and State : Sri Lanka

A review of problems, issues and government policies on higher education in Sri Lanka. D. Thenuwara Gamage *Perspectives in Education* 1(2) Ap 1985 p 75-90 refs ft-n

Higher Education of Women

Higher medical education for women. S. Padmavati *J Higher Education* 1(3) Aut 1975 p 256-58 refs

See also

Professional Education of Women

Higher Education of Women : India

Developmental goals and women's higher education. Lata Murugkar *J Higher Education* 8(3) Spr 1983 p 321-26 refs

Development of women's education at the university stage. M.R. Rabindranathan *J Higher Education* 1(2) Aut 1975 p 258-62 refs

From secondary to higher education : Focus on women. Karuna Chanana Ahmad *J Higher Education* 9(3) Spr 1984 p 349-62 refs

Equity and women's higher education. Karuna Chanana Ahmad *J Higher Education* 5(1) Mon 1979 p 33-49

Higher education and the status of women in India. *J Higher Education* 1(2) Aut 1975 p 270-72

Higher education of women in India. Vina Mazumdar *J Higher Education* 1(2) Aut 1975 p 156-65 tabs

New approaches to higher education for women. Pushpitta John *Education Quarterly* 34(4) Oc 1982 p 28-30

Higher Education of Women : India : Kerala

University education for what? The case of Kerala women. Morilyn Fernandez *New Frontier in Education* 15(1) Ja-Mr 1985 p 82-85

Higher Education of Women : India : Rajasthan

Higher education among women : An analysis of the situation in a district of India. Hem Lata Talesra *Perspectives in Education* 2(2) Ap 1986 p 121-24

Himachal Pradesh

See also

Communication in Agriculture : India : Himachal Pradesh

High School Students : India : Himachal Pradesh

Hindi Language

Factor analysis of language learning abilities in Hindi achievement with special reference to delta class. R.A. Sharma and Geeta Sharma *J Education*

and Psychology 39(1) Ap 1981 p 12-21 refs

Hindi Language : Russia

Popularity of Hindi in the USSR. S.K. Malnahan *Progress of Education* 58(4) Nv 1983 p 93-95

Hindi Language : Study and Teaching

Development of norms for Hindi adaptation of junior-senior HSPQ. G.N. Prakash Srivastava *Asian J Psychology and Education* 9(3) 1982 p 43-47

An experimental study of the effectiveness of audiolingual and cognitive code methods in the teaching of Hindi sentence patterns to non-Hindi speaking students. *J Education and Psychology* 37(4) Ja 1980 p 263-73 refs tabs

Hindi Language : Vocabulary

Effect of sex, academic stream and locality on Hindi vocabulary. Dhiraj K. Jain *J Educational and Psychology* 36(1-2) Ap-Je 1978 p 20-25

History

History : A curse or a boon? H.L. Chopra *J Indian Education* 8(2) Jl 1982 p 84-86

History : Curricula

Preparation of history teachers for new currculum. V.K. Raina *Education Quarterly* 35(3) Jl 1983 p 17-20 refs

History : Examinations

Effects of memory and speed on history honour examination scores. Biranchi N. Puhan and Mahesh P. Mohapatra *J Education and Psychology* 39(2) Jl 1981 p 83-90

Examinations in history : A content analysis of secondary level question papers. Vijay K. Raina *J Indian Education* 8(6) Mr 1983 p 50-54 tab

Experimental verification of various methods of examination in history as the lower and higher stages. Bharat Bhushan Sharma *Indian Eduational Rev* 14(4) Oc 1979 p 47-53

History : Study and Teaching

Behavioural objectives and teaching of history V.K. Raina *J Indian Education* 5(4) Nv 1979 p 23-27 refs

Developments in history teaching. Ian Steele. London, Open Bks. 125p. $ 1.50 *Book Rev, Indian Educational Rev* 16(2) Ap 1981 129-32; *Teacher Today* 22(2) Oc-De 1979 p 92-94

How to teach history? N. Gomati *Educational Rev* 87(5) My 1981 p 84-86

Philosophical implications in the teaching of history. Marlow Ediger *Education Quarterly* 33(1) Ja 1981 p 17-18

Piagetian theory and teaching of history. V.K. Raina *J Indian Education* 5(1) My 1979 p 54-58

The teaching of history. D. Venkata Rao *Indian Education* 12(8-9) Nv-De 1982 p 38-39

Teaching of history from world perspective. D.N. Gaind *Teacher Today* 23(1) Jl-Se 1980 p 1-6

Teaching of history in Indian colleges : Need for a new approach : Surinder Suri *New Frontiers in Educatin* 10(4) Oc-de 1980 p 43-58

Teaching of history, method and techniques. S.M. Patki. Milind Pub. 337p. Rs.30 *Book Rev, Progress of Education* 54(12) Jl 1980 p 239-40

History : Study and Teaching : Audio-Visual Aids

Teaching history through radio vision. Motilal Sharma and C.K. Tripathi *J Indian Education* 6(3) Se 1980 p 48-50

History, Modern : Study and Teaching

See also

Current Events

Holidays

See also

Vacations

Home

See also

Family Life Surveys

Home and Schools

See also

Parent-Teacher Relationships

Home Economics

Home science and work experience. Saroj Bansal *Progress of Education* 55(5) De 1980 p 118-19 +

See also

Dairying

Home Economics : Study and Teaching

Impact of training on concept of home science held by home science students. Pushpa Gupta and Saroj Bansal *Education Quarterly* 34(2) Ap 1982 p 14-16

Level of satisfaction of teachers and students regarding the traditional and modern systems of education as practised in the two selected home science institutions. Anupama Shah and Rita Shah *J Education and Psychology* 41(3) Oc 1983 p 117-25 tabs

Perception of importance and extent of achievement of the identified objectives of home science programme at school level. Pushpa Gupta and S.L. Mathur *Education Quarterly* 33(2) Ap 1981 p 27-30

Reactions of students towards the course mass communication in home science. Anita S. Thomas and Arvinda Chandra *Educational Rev* 92(9) Se 1986 p 153-57 refs

Teachers concept of rural orientation in home science education. A. Malaviya *et al Indian J Extension Education* 21(3-4) Jl-De 1985 p 95-98 tabs

Usefulness of home science programme at school level. Pushpa Gupta and S.L. Mathur *Progress of Education* 57(10) My 1983 p 224-30 + tabs

Home Economics : Study and Teaching : India : Assam

Opinions of college home science students regarding home science education in Assam. Anupama Shah *Progress of Education* 56(11) Je 1982 p 269-74 refs tabs

Home Economics : Study and Teaching : India : Rajasthan

A critical appraisal of physical facilities in teaching home science in higher secondary schools of Rajasthan. Pushpa Gupta and S.L. Mathur *Rajasthan Board J Education* 16(4) Oc-De 1980 p 25-31

Home Economics Students

Life styles of home science graduates. A.W. Oak *Research Bulletin* 14(3-4)

Se-De 1984 p 10-32 tabs

Home Education

See

Correspondence Schools and Courses

Home Science

See

Home Economics

Homework

Homework : Some suggestions. M.N. Prahallada *Primary Teacher* 9(1) Ja 1984 p 1-3

Homework and assignments. Salma Kurashy *Educational Rev* 89(10) Oc 1983 p 179-81

Homework and its correction. K.G. Rastogi *Primary Teacher* 6(4) Oc 1981 p 32-34

Honesty

A cross-sectional development study of belief in honesty. I.S. Singh and A.S. Dash *J Education and Psychology* 39(2) Jl 1981 p 117-20

Horn, H.H.

Dewey versus Horn on education. Marlow Ediger *New Frontiers in Education* 13(3) Jl-Se 1983 p 21-23

Hostility : Psychological Aspects

Construction and standardisation of a group test of general hostility (GTGH) in Indian conditions. H.C. Kocher and S.D. Kapur *J Education and Psychology* 36(3) Ja 1979 p 437-47 tabs

Factor structure of psychoticism in relation to hostility, anxiety neuroticism and ability measures. Satvir Singh and Meena Sehgal *Asian J Psychology and Education* 4(3) Nv 1981 p 18-21

House Sanitation

See

Sanitation, Household

Household Sanitation

See

Sanitation, Household

Household Science

See

Home Economics

Human Behaviour

Behaviour modification : Theory and practice. B.K. Jana *Educational Rev* 86(5) My 1980 p 97-99

A dimension of human behaviour : Biochemical stress. Rishi Dev Anand *J Education and Psychology* 36(1-2) Ap-Je 1978

A dimension of human behaviour : Biochemical stress. Rishi Dev Anand *Teacher Today* 21(4) Ap-Je 1979 p 45-51 refs

Human Ecology : Study and Teaching

Environmental studies in the national curriculum. A.B. Saxena *Education Quarterly* 38(3) Aut 1986 p 8-12

Role of environmental studies in motivating children's learning. J.S. Rajput and J.S. Grewal *Progress of Education* 53(12) Jl 1979 p 228-33 refs

Human Environment
See
Human Ecology
Human Resources Development
See
Manpower Policy
Humanistic Education
See
Education, Humanistic
Humanities
See also
General Education
Humanities : Study and Teaching
Modernisation of our courses and syllabi in the humanities and the social sciences. A.M. Ghose *J Higher Education* 4(1) Mon 1978 p 75-80
Teaching of humanities for the computer age. A.G. Khan *J Indian Education* 12(4) Nv 1986 p 22-26
Hungary
See also
Education : Hungary
Hyderabad : Slums
See
Slums : India : Andhra Pradesh : Hyderabad
Hygiene
See also
Excercise
Physical Education and Training
School Hygiene
Woman : Health and Hygiene

Illiteracy
After literacy, teaching : Paradoxes of post-literacy work. Bernard Dumont *J Indian Education* 5(6) Mr 1980 p 32-42
Concepts and measurement of literacy, semi literacy and illiteracy : A literature review. J.T. Okedara *Indian Educational Rev* 17(3) Jl 1982 p 42-61 refs
Eleven issues in literacy for the 1990's Arthur Gillette and John Ryam *Indian J Adult Education* 45(4) Ap 1984 p 5-19 refs
Factors affecting the retention of literacy among neoliterates. M.G. Mall. Gargoti, Asha Pra. 1979, 200p. Rs.30 *Book Rev, Indian Educational Rev* 15(3) Jl 1980 p 124-25; *J Indian Education* 6(5) Ja 1981 p 53; *Progress of Education* 54(10-11) My-Je 1980 p 214
International literacy day. N. Venkataiah *Experiments in Education* 7(6) Ag 1979 p 103-05
Linguistics in literacy programmes. Shivendera K. Verma *J Indian Education* 5(6) Mr 1980 p 43-49
Linking literacy with development - Some suggestions. Ranjit Singh *Indian J Adult Education* 42(10) Oc 1981 p 11-13
Literacy and development. Rajeshwar Mishra *Indian J Adult Education* 42(9)

Se 1981 p 11-16; 42(10) Oc 1981 p 3-7 refs

Literacy and revolution : The padagogy of Paulo Freire. Robert Mackie, *ed.* London, Pluto Press. $3.50 *Book Rev, Teacher Today* 24(1) Jl-Se 1981 p 103-04

Literacy and world population. U.K. Sahay *J Indian Education* 5(1) My 1979 p 59-63 tabs

Literacy as a communication skill. R.N. Srivastava *Indian J Adult Education* 40(3) Mr 1979 p 1-14 appdx refs tabs

Literacy campaign : A world movement. Kathita Hatibaruah *Educational Rev* 92(1) Ja 1986 p 13-14

Myths and realities of literacy efforts. Manzoor Ahmed *Indian J Adult Education* 41(8) Ag 1980 p 3-6

NAEP and universal literacy : Some suggestions. R. Singh *Indian J Adult Education* 40(5) My 1979 p 41-43

Research on literacy and work among the rural poor. Kenneth J. King *Indian J Adult Education* 41(1-2) Ja-Fe 1980 p 15-23

The role of universities in the eradication of illiteracy. Lakshmi Misra *Educational Rev* 91(8) Ag 1985 p 134-36

With struggle, there is hope for literacy. H.S. Bhola *Indian J Adult Education* 47(7) Jl 1986 p 4-10

World literacy. R.N. Safaya *Educational Rev* 86(10) Oc 1980 p 187-88

See also

Literacy House, Lucknow

Illiteracy : Afghanistan

Organisation of education remote rural areas of Afganistan. M.A. Qayum *Indian J Adult Education* 40(5) My 1979 p 33-35

Illiteracy : Australia

Educating for literacy and numaracy in Australian schools. J.P. Keeves. ACER. 1978. 60p. *Book Rev, Education Quarterly* 31(1) Ag 1979 p 39

Illiteracy : India

The dark areas of literacy : Facts at a glance. *Indian J Adult Education* 41(4) Ap 1980 p 28-29

Determinants of rural/urban disparities in the literacy rate in India. P.K. Bhargava *Indian Educational Rev* 20(2) Ap 1985 p 9-20

Humanising literacy campaign. Tarlok Singh *Indian J Adult Education* 45(4) Ap 1984 p 23-25 +

Hundred per cent literacy : Perspectives and plan. S.C. Dutta *Indian J Adult Education* 46(2) Fe 1985 p 10-13

Inequalities in the levels of literacy in India. Moonis Raza and Y.P. Agarwal. New Delhi, NIEPA. 1983. *Book Rev, Education Quarterly* 36(4) Wint 1984 p 53-54

Linking literacy with development. *Indian J Adult Education* 41(3) Mr 1980 p 22-30

Linking literacy with TRYSEM : An experiment. R. Jaya Gopal *et al Indian J Adult Education* 47(8) Ag 1986 p 15-21 refs

Literacy for tribals. G.S. Rao *Indian J Adult Education* 40(4) Ap 1979 p 1-4 refs

The literacy scene in India. M.V. Sudhakara Reddy and D. Janaradhana Reddy *Indian Education* 12(7) Oc 1982 p 23-26

Magnitude of illiteracy in India-1981. Prem Chand *Indian J Adult Education* 43(1) Ja 1982 p 11-14 annex tabs

A mass movement for functional literacy. P.K. Patnaik *Indian J Adult Education* 47 (2-3) Fe-Mr 1986 p 24-41 +

Motivational problems in functional literacy programmes. C. Rajyalakshmi *Indian J Adult Education* 42(1-2) Ja-Fe 1981 p 7-12

Problems of literacy and the remedial measures. Vimla Mehta *J Indian Education* 5(6) Mr 1980 p 14-19 tabs

Progress of literacy during 1951-80. Jitendra Kumar Sinha *Indian Educational Rev* 17(1) Ja 1982 p 109-19 appdx

Socio-ecclogical and linguistic factors if illiteracy. Mukul Saxena *Indian J Adult Education* 45(10) Oc 1984 p 9-15 tabs

Illiteracy : India : Bihar

Child literacy in Bihar, 1961-71. R.B. Ram and S.K. Singh *J Indian Education* 8(2) Jl 1982 p 74-78 tabs

Illiteracy : India : Gujarat

Economic factors explaining variations in literacy rates in rural areas : A case study of Gujarat. Maya Shah. Baroda, M.S. Univ of Baroda (Economics Services No.7). 1981, 58p. Rs. 10 *Book Rev, Indian J Adult Education* 44(4) Ap 1983 p 40

Illiteracy : India : Kerala

Fighting illiteracy in Kerala. K. Sivadasan Pillai *Indian J Adult Education* 42(1-2) Ja-Fe 1981 p 3-6

Illiteracy : India : Punjab

Attitude of the people towards woman literacy in Punjab. Kuldip Kaur *Educational Rev* 91(8) Ag 1985 p 126-29

Is caste a stigma for acquistion of literacy skills? Tarlok Singh *Quest in Education* 19(2) Ap 1982 p 171-77 refs

Illiteracy : India : Tamil Nadu

Problem-oriental literacy method in practice in Thirukkazhukundarm block of Tamil Nadu. L.S. Saraswathi and D.J. Ravindran *Indian J Adult Education* 41(3) Mr 1980 p 7-13

Illiteracy : Nigeria

Alternative sources of funding the mass literacy campaign in Nigeria : The place of voluntary agencies and social clubs. B.A. Eheazu *New Frontiers in Education* 16(4) Oc-De 1986 p 95-106 ref

Mass literacy campaigns in Nigeria : 1940-1960. Michael Omolewr *Indian J Adult Education* 41(9) Se 1980 p 15-23

Illiteracy : United States

A national disgrace. *Student Action* 1(12) Ap 1983 p 4-5

Illiteracy : Vietnam

How Vietnam tackled illiteracy? A report : M. Khajapeer *Indian J Adult Education* 40(3) Mr 1979 p 39-42 refs tabs

Illustrated Books : Children

Illustrations in children's literature. R.K. Chopra *Primary Teacher* 4(3) Jl 1979 p 7-10

See also

Picture Books for Children

Illustrated Children's Books
See
Illustrated Books : Children
Immediate Memory
See
Short-term Memory
Immunisation : India : Haryana
Mothers compliance with prescribed recommendations on immunisation and their source utilisation pattern. S. Agarwal and T.R. Singh *Indian J Extension Education* 19(3-4) Se-De 1983 p 40-41; 20(3-4) Se-De 1984 p 48-52 refs tabs
Incentives : Psychological Aspects
See also
Reinforcement : Psychological Aspects
Incentives in Education
See
Rewards and Punishment in Education
Incentives in Industry
Incentive in industry. A.B.M. Zahirul Haque *Asian J Psychology and Education* 4(2) Jl 1979 p 51-53
India
See also
Adult Education : India
Adult Education : Research : India
Adult Education, Rural : India
Adult Education and State : India
Adult Education and Universities : India
Adult Education of Women : India
Agricultural Administration : India
Agricultural Colleges : India
Agricultural Education : India
Agricultural Engineering : Research : India
Agricultural Extension Education : India
Agricultural Extension Workers : India
Agricultural Research : India
Agricultural : Periodicals : India
Book Industries : India
Business Education : India
Caste : India
Child Welfare : India
Children : Employment : India
Citizenship : Education : India
College Students : India
College Teachers : India
Community and School : India
Community Development : India
Correspondence Schools and Courses : India
Curriculum Change : India
Curriculum Planning : India

Woman : Employment : India
Women : India
Women, Muslim : India
Women, Rural : India
Women College Students : India
Women Colleges : India
Women Scientists : India
Women Studies : India
Youth : India

India : Cultural Relations : Asia : Southeastern

India and South East Asia : A study in cultural relations. India, Ministry of Educ and Soc Welfare. 1979, 56p. Rs. 8.40 *Book Rev, J Indian Education* 6(3) Se 1980 p 58

India : National Commissions for Teachers

Full text of the resolution of National Commissions for Teachers. *Teacher Education* 18(22-23) Ja-Ap 1983 p 31-32

India, Ancient

See also
Education : India : Ancient

India, Eastern

See also
Universities and Colleges : India : Eastern

India, Northeastern

See also
Education : India : Northeastern

Indian Adult Education Association

Adult education and the last man; editorial. *Indian J Adult Education* 41(11) Nv 1980 p 2-3

Group reports. *Indian J Adult Education* 41(11) Nv 1980 p 31-41

IAEA General Secretary's report (1978-79). V.S. Mathur *Indian J Adult Education* 40(10-11) Oc-Nv 1979 p 39-44

Indian Adult Education Association. *Indian J Adult Education* 40(5) My 1979 p 46+

Report of the General Secretary : Mr V.S. Mathur for 1979-80. *Indian J Adult Education* 41(11) Nv 1980 p 23-30

Indian Adult Education Association : 32 Annual Conference, 1979 Declarations and recommendations of thirty-second IAEA Conference. Ramesh Thanvi *Teacher Today* 22(2) Oc-De 1979 p 87-90

32nd annual conference of IAEA (A brief report). J.L. Sachdeva *Indian J Adult Education* 40(10-11) Oc-Nv 1979 p 56-58

Indian Adult Education Association : 33rd Annual Conference, 1980 A brief report of the Ahmedabad conference. J.S. Sachdeva *Indian J Adult Education* 41(11) Nv 1980 p 7-8

Inaugural address. Narayan Datt Tiwari. *Indian J Adult Education* 41(11) Nv 1980 p 17-21

Statement adopted by the 33rd annual adult education conference. *Indian J Adult Education* 41(11) Nv 1980 p 5-6

Indian Adult Education Association; 34th Annual Conference, Patna, 1981

After Patna, what; editorial. *Indian J Adult Education* 42(1) Nv 1981 p 2-3

A brief report of the Patna conference. J.L. Sachdeva *Indian J Adult Education* 42(1) Nv 1981 p 8-10

The declaration. *Indian J Adult Education* 42(11) Nv 1981 p 4-5

Inaugural session. *Indian J Adult Education* 42(11) Nv 1981 p 11

Presidential address of V.S. Mathur. *Indian J Adult Education* 42(11) Nv 1981 p 12-21

Indian Agricultural Research Institute, New Delhi

Journal communication of IARI theses. P.N. Sandhya and Y.P. Singh *Indian J Extension Education* 18(1-2) Je 1982 p 34-44 tabs

Indian Association of Teacher Educators : XXII, Annual Conference, Kanpur, 1981

Address to XXII Conference of Indian Association of Teacher Educators : On objectives of teacher education. Atmanand Misra *Teacher Education* 15(14-15) Ja-Ap 1981 p 21-29

Indian Association of Teacher Educators, XXII Annual Conference. *Teacher Education* 15(14-15) Ja-Ap 1981 p 124-27

Objectives of teacher education. Kamala Dwivedi *Teacher Education* 15(14-15) Ja-Ap 1981 p 10-16

Objectives of teacher education. Vijay Laxmi Agarwal *Teacher Education* 15(14-15) Ja-Ap 1981 p 17-20

Presidential address. D.D. Tewari *Teacher Education* 15(14-15) Ja-Ap 1981 p 1-9

Report of the XXII Annual Conference, March 8-11, 1981. *Teacher Education* 15(14-15) Ja-Ap 1981 p 115-20

XXII Annual Conference : Indian Association of Teacher Educators, March, 8 to 11, 1981. *Teacher Education* 15(14-15) Ja-Ap 1981 p 121-23

Indian Council of Agricultural Research, New Delhi

First line extension projects of ICAR : A comparative analysis. N.P. Singh and R.P. Singh *J Indian Education* 12(2) Jl 1986 p 24-34

Perception of work environment by agricultural research service scientists of ICAR Institutes. R.K. Samanta *Indian J Extension Education* 21(3-4) Jl-De 1985 p 53-61 refs tabs

Indian Council of Social Science Research : Social Science Documentation Centre

See

National Social Science Documentation Centre

Indian Educational Review (Periodical)

Indian Educational Review through ten year. M.K. Raina and M. Sengupta *Indian Educational Rev* 14(1) Ja 1979 p 56-68

Indian Institute of Science, Bangalore

Activities of the technological forecasting and research management cell of Indian Institute of Science, Bangalore. P.K. Bohatgi *J Higher Education* 4(1) Mon 1978 p 109-11

Indian Journal of Adult Education (Periodical)

The Indian Journal of Adult Education. *Indian J Adult Education* 41(10) Oc 1980 p 29-32

Indian Journal of Extension Education (Periodical) : Content Analysis

Content analysis of Indian Journal of Extension Education. B.S. Siddaramaiah and Raghavendra *Indian J Extension Education* 19(1-2)

Instructional Supervision
See
School Supervision

Instructional Systems Analysis
See
Educational Surveys

Integrated Rural Development Programme
Communication and management of Integrated Rural Development Programme. J.S. Yadava *Indian J Extension Education* 21(1-2) Ja-Je 1985 p 42-47

Integrated Rural Development Programme : Current status. S.C. Verma *Indian J Extension Education* 18(1-2) Je 1982 p 10-15

Monitoring and evaluation of Integrated Rural Development Programme. D.S. Dhillon *et al Indian J Extension Education* 21(1-2) Ja-je 1985 p 48-52

Intellectuals
Some notes on the intelligentsia. Vasanthi Raman *J Higher Education* 1(2) Aut 1975 p 211-22 refs

Intelligence
See
Intellect

Intelligence and Socio-Economic Status
Social intelligence testing : A retrospect. P.K. Ganguli *J Educational Research and Extension* 18(1) Jl 1981 p 51-63

Intelligence Levels
Acquisition of general information : Role of sex and general intelligence. Zafar Umar *Educational Rev* 85(2) Fe 1979 p 25-28 refs tabs

Creativity and its components in relation to different levels of intelligence and academic subjects among high school students. D.N. Sauranwal and Gurpal Jarial *Asian J Psychology and Education* 11(2) 1983 p 9-13

Intelligence Levels : Deaf
Moderating role of intelligence variable in aspirations and deprivations of the institutionalised non-institutionalised sensory handicapped children. Akbar Husain and Afzal Kureshi *J Institute of Educational Research* 9(1) Ja 1985 p 5-9 refs tabs

Intelligence Levels : Testing
See
Mental Tests

Intellect
Free recall of categorised materials : A cross cultural examination of Jenson's theory. Kasturi Jachuk and Jeesur Charandas *Asian J Psychology and Education* 9(3) 1982 p 1-6

Social intelligence *vis-a-vis* abstract and mechanical intelligence. P.K. Ganguli *Asian J Psychology and Education* 11(2) 1983 p 28-32

Interaction Analysis in Education
Appraising the evaluation. Marlow Ediger *Experiments in Education* 10(10) De 1982 p 189-92 refs

Classroom interaction patterns of language teachers functioning at two levels of cognitive development. Amrit Kaur and Basanti Chatterji *Rajasthan Board J Education* 20(1-2) Ja-je 1984 p 21-29

Classroom interaction sequence of categories. A.P. Oza *Progress of Education* 58(3) Oc 1983 p 61-63

Classroom verbal interaction of teachers trained through integrated and conventional approaches : A comparison. Nagendra Singh *Indian Educational Rev* 18(1) Ja 1983 p 129-32 refs tabs

The classroom verbal interaction patterns of effective and ineffective teachers. R.A. Sharma and Vimla Mahesh *J Education and Psychology* 37(2) Jl 1979 p 90-96 refs

A comparison of classroom verbal interaction of trained professional teachers using STOS. S.C. Bhargava and Kamla Kant Sharma *Rajasthan Board J Education* 16(4) Oc-De 1980 p 39-44

Flanders interaction analysis : A critique. R.C. Deva *Educational Rev* 84(11) Nv 1978 p 214-17 refs

Life in the classroom : A research study. F.A. Adeyoyin *J Indian Education* 6(2) Jl 1980 p 3-8 refs tabs

Pattern of teacher class-room behaviour and their relation to students liking in the science classes of secondary schools. R.S. Maini *Educational Rev* 92(9) Se 1986 p 145-48 refs

Students rating of teaching efficiency. R.V. Naidu *Experiments in Education* 7(9) Nv 1979 p 153-56 refs tabs

Teacher sex and classroom interaction. Ajit Singh *J Indian Education* 8(2) Jl 1982 p 48-51 refs tabs

Teacher sex and classroom interaction. Ajit Singh *National J Education* 2(1) Se 1979 p 1-6 refs tabs

Teacher-pupil interaction in different types of schools : A comparative study. James A. Bright *J Educational Research and Extension* 17(3) Ja 1981 p 164-71 refs tabs

Verbal interaction patterns of pre-school teachers through observation technique of equivalent talk categories. (E.T.C.). A.P. Sharma and Kanak Chaturvedi *J Education and Psychology* 30(3) Oc 1978 p 148-53

See also

Communication in Education

Microteaching

Interest : Psychological Aspects

A study of interest and personality patterns of succesful men in different occupations. S.P. Sinha *Indian Educational Rev* 15(4) Oc 1980 p 66-70

Interest : Psychological Aspects : Testing

Evaluation of interests. S.L. Makkar *Primary Teacher* 10(3) Jl 1985 p 27-28

International Education

Education for international understanding. Paul Morren *Education Quarterly* 34(1) Ja 1982 p 25-27

Education for one world : A long term perspective. Bimen Sen *University News* 23(7) 16 Fe 1985 p 3-6

The effect of language barrier on the universalisation of education. V.G. Kulkarni and V.G. Gambhir *Indian Educational Rev* 16(1) Ja 1981 p 48-59

International Education : Curricula

Culture and curriculum : Should there be a common curriculum for universal education. V.K. Rai *Educational Rev* 92(10) Oc 1986 p 166-69

Teaching world studies : An introduction to global perspectives in the

curriculum. David Hicks and Charles Townley, *eds.* Esses, Longmans. 216p. $6.59 *Book Rev, Education Quarterly* 35(2) Ap 1983 p 71-73

Interns : Education

See also

Student Teaching

Interpersonal Attraction

Determinants of interpersonal attraction among boys and girls : An empirical study. P.D. Juyal *J Education and Psychology* 44(3-4) Jl-De 1986 p 148-52

Evaluators physique and self evaluation as moderating variables in opposite sex physique attraction. Afzal Kureshi and Akbar Husain *J Education and Psychology* 43(1) ap 1985 p 37-43 refs

Interpersonal Relations

Effective communication for positive human relations. Marlow Ediger *Primary Teacher* 10(1) Ja 1985 p 1-16

Teacher human relation management. S. Mohan *Experiments in Education* 11(8) Oc 1983 p 145-46

See also

Dependency : Psychological Aspects

Group Relations Training

Interpersonal Attraction

Interviews and Interviewing

On the reliability of ratings in interviews. V. Natarajan *J Educational Research and Extension* 16(3) Ja 1980 p 125-34

See also

Questioning

Introversion

See also

Extraversion

Iran

See also

Engineering : Study and Teaching : Iran

Iraq

See also

Farmers : Iraq

Islam : Education

Pesantrian, Islamic education and community development. Abdur Rahman Wahid *New Frontiers in Education* 14(2) Ap-Je 1984 p 26-29

See also

Women, Muslim : India

Israel

See also

Education : Israel

Jamaica

See also

Curriculum Change : Jamaica

Jammu and Kashmir
See also
Education : India : Jammu and Kashmir

Jammu University
Shri Venkataraman addresses convocation of Jammu University. *University News* 27(24) 23 Je 1985 p 5-6

Japan
See also
Education : Japan
Handicapped Children : Education : Japan
Vocational Education : Japan

Job Analysis
Job involvement of extension supervisors : A factor analysis. V. Veerabhadraiah and K.A. Jaliahal *Indian J Extension Education* 19(3-4) Se-De 1983 p 1-10 refs

Job Performance Standards
See
Performance Standards

Job Satisfaction
Achievement motivation and job satisfaction in primary school teachers. S.K. Srivastava and Solan Gupta *J Education and Psychology* 43(3-4) Oc 1985-Ja 1986 p 193-96 refs

Aptitude in teaching and job satisfaction among teachers. Rita George and B.G. Sudha *J Institute of Educational Research* 10(2) My 1986 p 16-20 refs tabs

Are married teachers more satisfied with their jobs than the unmarried? A Venkata Rami Reddy and O. Babjan *Indian Educational Rev* 16(2) Ap 1981 p 15-18 refs

Construction and standardisation of teachers job satisfaction scale. S.P. Gupta and J.P. Srivastava *J Education and Psychology* 38(1) Ap 1980 p 43-53 refs tabs

Construction and standardisation of teachers job satisfaction scale. S.P. Gupta and J.P. Srivastava *J Educational Research and Extension* 18(3) Ja 1982 p 155-89 refs tabs

Effect of the variables of sex and marital status on the level of job satisfaction among primary school teachers. Mera Dixit *J Institute of Educational Research* 9(1) Ja 1985 p 22-24 refs

Factor effecting job satisfaction of veterinary assistant surgeons of Vijayawada and Hyderabad areas, A.P. V.N. Rao and T.S. Sohal *Indian J Extension Education* 14(1-2) Ja-Je 1978 p 6-8 refs

Grouping effect in rating scales : The case of faculty attitudes. Yoram Neuman *J Education and Psychology* 38(2) Jl 1980 p 76-87 refs tabs

An investigation into the problem of job satisfaction among secondary school teachers. T. Rajammal *Indian Education* 12(8-9) Nv-De 1982 p 40-41

Job content and context factors in job satisfaction of deputy agricultural officers. K.R. Menon *et al Indian J Extension Education* 14(1-2) Ja-Je 1978 p 1-5 refs

Job satisfaction among primary, middle and secondary school teachers.

Gudesh Gakhar *et al J Institute of Educational Research* 8(2) My 1984 p 1-6 refs

Job satisfaction and job performance of agricultural extension officers, of Tamil Nadu. G. Perumal and G.C. Rai *Indian J Extension Education* 14(1-2) Ja-Je 1978 p 73-75

Job satisfaction of college teachers. A. Venkata Rami Reddy *J Education and Psychology* 38(4) Ja 1981 p 211-18 refs tabs

Job satisfaction of college teachers relationship with age and experience and sex differences. N. Muthaiah *Experiments in Education* 8(12) Fe 1981 p 218-20 refs tabs

Job satisfaction of developmental personnel : A catalytic force for rural development. K.M.P. Singh and S. Mulay *Indian J Adult Education* 43(5) My 1982 p 6-12 refs

Job satisfaction of teachers and its relationship to their anger and aggression as rated by them. Debi Prasad Bhattacharyya *J Education and Psychology* 36(3) Oc 1978 p 160-62

Job satisfaction of teachers working under different managements. A. Venkata Rami Reddy *Education Quarterly* 30(3) Oc 1978 p 28-29

Job satisfaction of veterinary assistant surgeons. S.V.N. Rao and T.S. Sohal *Indian J Extension Education* 16(3-4) De 1980 p 74-77 tabs

Job satisfaction versus work role variables. S.P. Anand *Indian Educational Rev* 14(4) Oc 1979 p 106-17 tabs

Measuring job satisfaction of scientists in an ICAR Institute. Usha Anand and T.S. Sohal *Asian J Psychology and Education* 9(4) 1982 p 13-20

Motivation and job satisfaction : A theoretical analysis. Sudesh Gakhar *Indian Educational Rev* 20(3) Jl 1985 p 23-31

Organisational climate in relation to teachers job satisfaction and students achievement. Ravi Kanta Chopra *Indian Educational Rev* 31(3) Oc 1983 p 211-28

Performance in relation to ego-strength and alienation of blue collar industrial workers. A.P. Singh and Sudha Shrivastava *Asian J Psychology and Education* 9(1) Ja 1982 p 34-40 refs

A research study about teachers perception of job satisfaction. Edwin O. McCaskill *et al Indian Educational Rev* 15(3) Jl 1980 p 22-30 refs

A study of the influence of personal factors on teachers attitude towards their job. Tahira Khatoon and M.R. Verma *J Education and Psychology* 41(3) Oc 1983 p 159-67

A study of influence of personal factors on teachers attitude towards their job. Tahira Khatoon and M.R. Verma *J Institute of Educational Research* 6(2) My 1982 p 27-32 refs tabs

A study of job satisfaction among clerks of Saurashtra University. K.U. Lavingia *J Education and Psychology* 39(4) Ja 1982 p 259-61

A study of job satisfaction among secondary school teachers. Kiran Gupta and Badarun Nisha *Asian J Psychology and Education* 4(1) Ja 1979 p 25-30 refs

A study of job satisfaction at three levels of teaching. S.P. Gupta *Indian Educational Rev* 18(2) Ap 1983 p 75-78

A study of relationship between job satisfaction and personality maturity among secondary teachers. S.P. Gupta and J.P. Srivastava *J Education*

Status of educational journalism. G.S. Koshe *Progress of Education* 57(7) Fe 1983 p 151-53

Status of educational journalism in India. A review. D.M. Khosla *J Indian Education* 11(3) Se 1985 p 3-12

Towards a sound journalism in education. Vijay Kumar Gupta *Progress of Education* 57(4) Nv 1982 p 81-83

Training in educational journalism. T. Rama Murthy *J Indian Education* 11(3) Se 1985 p 21-23

Juvenile Delinquency

Assessment of delinquency. Kemal Mukerji and Moitrayee Basu. New Delhi, Wiley Eastern. 1980, 134p. *Book Rev, Asian J Psychological Rev* 7(2) Jl 1981 p 64

Prevention and control of delinquency. Lakshahira Das *Educational Rev* 86(7) Jl 1980 p 133-35 refs

Social and psychological factors influencing juvenile delinquency. Ramanath Kundu and Gita Bhaumik *Our Education* 1 Jl 1980 p 41-47

A study of intelligence, achievement, motivation and adjustment of the juvenile delinquents. Harish Sharma and Sushma *J Institute of Educational Research* 9(3) Se 1985 p 21-26 refs tabs

Who is responsible for criminal mentality in children? Mohammed Raziuddin Muazzam *Primary Teacher* 4(1) Ja 1979 p 21-22

Juvenile Literature

See

Children's Literature

Kakatiya University

Shri Chavan address convocation of Kakatiya University. *University News* 23(29) 1 Ag 1985 p 6-8

Kakatiya University : Students

An investigation into the relative performance levels of English literature students of Kakatiya University in relation to their caste background. S. Parmaji *et al Progress of Education* 60(2) Se 1985 p 34-35

Karan Singh : Educational Thought

Education must take into account the various dimensions of the human individual, says E.M. *J Indian Education* 5(4) Nv 1979 p 61-62

Karnataka

See

Adoption of Improved Farm Practices : India : Karnataka
Adult Education : India : Karnataka
Agricultural Extension Officers : India : Karnataka
Agricultural Innovations : India : Karnataka
Communication in Agriculture : India : Karnataka
Dairying : India : Karnataka
Dropouts : India : Karnataka
Education, Rural : India : Karnataka
Examinations : India : Karnataka
Feeds : India : Karnataka
Gobar Gas Plants : India : Karnataka
High School Teachers : India : Karnataka

York, Philosophical Lib. 184p. $14.95 *Book Rev, Education Quarterly* 38(3) Aut 1986 p 46

Laboratories

Laboratory instruction in science : Its implications in our schools Ved P. Goel *J Indian Education* 5(1) My 1979 p 34-38

Labour and Labouring Classes : Education

Central Board for Workers education - An introduction. A.C. Gupta *Indian J Adult Education* 46(5) My 1985 p 16-19 +

Education and industrial productivity : A case study of workers and supervisors employed in the engineering industry in Pune metropolitan region. S. Pinte *Research Bulletin* 16(1-2) Mr-Je 1986 p 43-57

Seva Credit Union : A success story of workers self-reliance. J.R. Victor Karunan *Indian J Adult Education* 46(5) My 1985 p 37-40 tabs

Trade unions and workers education : International perspective. S.K. Jain *Indian J Adult Education* 46(5) My 1985 p 4-9 +

Training in workers education. B.N. Niranjan Reddy *Indian J Adult Education* 45(4) Ap 1984 p 20-22

The use of qualitative research in workers education. Victor M. Mlekwe *Perspectives in Education* 2(2) Ap 1986 p 99-108 refs

What education workers need? E.A. Ramaswamy *Indian J Adult Education* 46(5) My 1985 p 20-33 ft-n

What is workers education? : An attempt at clarification. *Indian J Adult Education* 46(5) My 1985 p 10-18 +

Worker's education today. V.S. Mathur *Indian J Adult Education* 44(3) Mr 1983 p 3-12

Labour and Labouring Classes : Education : India

Workers education : A trade union representative in view point. T.N. Sidhanta *Indian J Adult Education* 46(5) My 1985 p 14-15 +

Workers education : Need for empirical approach. A.N. Buch *Indian J Adult Education* 46(5) My 1985 p 41-42

Workers education : The contribution of IAEA. S.C. Dutta *Indian J Adult Education* 46(5) My 1985 p 34-36

Labour Incentives

See

Incentives in Industry

Ladakh : Cultural Heritage

Cultural heritage of Ladakh. India, Ministry of Edu and Soc Welfare. 1979, 101p. *Book Rev, J Indian Education* 7(2) Jl 1979 p 68-69

Lady Doak College, Madurai

Autonomy at Lady Doak College. Nirmala Wydiffe *New Frontiers in Education* 12(2) Ap-Je 1982 p 55+

Land Credit

See

Agricultural Credit

Language and Languages

Factors analysis of language learning abilities in Hindi achievement with special reference to delta class. R.A. Sharma *J Education and Psychology* 39(1) Ap 1981 p 22-27 refs tabs

Mehta and D.L. Charles *Experiments in Education* 8(3) My 1980 p 49-53

Handwriting and the purpose. Marlow Ediger *Progress of Education* 58(5) De 1983 p 102-11

Importance of language in answering examinations question. R.D. Godbole *Progress of Education* 58(5) De 1983 p 112-13 +

Listening comprehension in relation to different catagories of readers. D.N. Patel *J Education and Psychology* 40(1-2) Ap-Jl 1982 p 66-73 refs

Language Arts : Curricula

The language arts curriculum : A philosophical perspective. Marlow Ediger *Rajasthan Board J Education* 19(1) Ja-Mr 1983 p 1-5

Language Problem

Language policy in the context of MAPE. G.V. Bhaktapriya *Indian J Adult Education* 40(6) Je 1979 p 25-28 refs

Multilingualism and mother-tongue education. D.P. Pattanayak. New Delhi, OUP. 1981, 185p. Rs. 80 *Book Rev, Progress of Education* 56(11) Je 1982 p 280

Language Teachers

Classroom interaction patterns of language teachers functioning at two levels of cognitive development. Amrit Kaur and Basanti Chatterji *Rajasthan Board J Education* 20(1-2) Ja-je 1984 p 21-29

Latin America

See also

Educational Research : Latin America

Law : Study and Teaching

New pattern of legal education. M.L. Upadhyaya *University News* 22(2) Ja 1981 p 8-9

Law, Educational

See

Educational Law and Legislation

Leadership

Consideration and structure dimensions of leadership behaviour and supervisory effectiveness as determined by managers rating and group productivity. Hamida Akhtar and Mohammed Nurul Anwar *Asian J Psychology and Education* 3(2) Jl 1978 p 40-47 refs

Leadership among youth. G. Rasooi *J Education and Psychology* 38(2) Jl 1980 p 89-93 refs

Marks of leadership among children. Shamsuddin *Education Quarterly* 32(1) Ja 1980 p 28-29

See also

Rural Leadership

Leadership in Education

Leadership styles of heads of schools in Madras. P.S. Balasubramanian *EPA Quarterly Bulletin* 6(2) Jl 1983 p 1-12 refs

Learning, Art of

See

Study, Method of

Learning, Psychology of

An advanced cognitive theory of learning for a curriculum model. R.S. Yadav *Progress of Education* 58(7) Fe 1984 p 155-66 refs

Classification of learners according to their learning styles : A new approach. Tarak Nath Pan *Indian Educational Rev* 20(2) Ap 1985 p 88-95

Criteria to utilise in selecting objectives. Marlow Ediger *Education Quarterly* 32(2) Jl 1980 p 25-26

Criterion-reference testing. Lalit Kishnore *Primary Teacher* 9(3) Jl 1984 p 24-25

Development as learning. Soedjatmoko *Perspectives in Education* 1(4) Oc 1985 p 211-29 refs

The effect of adolescent problems on PA learning : A test of Taylor's drive theory. Madhu Gupta and Prabha Gupta *J Education and Psychology* 36(4) Ja 1979 p 203-09

The effect of imagery on the learnigs of extended passages : A study. Mihir K. Chatterjee *Indian Educational Rev* 15(1) Ja 1980 p 27-34 refs

The effect of intra-task non-specific competition paired associate learning in relation to intelligence and ego-strength. S. Gakhar and Swayam Prabhu *J Education and Psychology* 38(4) Ja 1981 p 235-41 refs

Effect of master learning procedure and text book study. Lalit Kishore *Educational Rev* 91(12) De 1985 p 201-03 refs

Effect of *yoga aasana* on learning : An experiment on primary students. D.K. Sharma Probhit and M.P. Tyagi *J Institute of Educational Research* 4(2) My 1980 p 30-34 refs tabs

Encoding as a function of paradigms and type of materials. N. Hasnain *Asian J Psychology and Education* 6(3) Nv 1980 p 38-41 refs

Identification of learning needs of non-formal learners in the age-group 6-14. P.K. Tripathy *Primary Teacher* 8(4) Oc 1983 p 6-8

Intent, instruction, individual and inspection in mastery learning model. Lalit Kishore *Educational Rev* 88(9) Se 1982 p 147-49 refs

An investigation into the controversial issue on continuity and non-continuity in learning. J.C. Parikh *J Education and Psychology* 40(4) Ja 1983 p 229-33 refs

Learning and teaching concepts : A strategy for testing applications of theory. Herbert J. Klausmeier. New York, Academic Press (N.Y.) 1980, 22p. $22.50 *Book Rev, J Education and Psychology* 89(3) Oc 1981 p 204

Learning for mastery. Muralidhar Dash *Experiments in Education* 8(12) Fe 1981 p 226-28 refs

Learning style : A new area of research. Subhash Chandra Agrawal *J Educational Research and Extension* 17(3) Ja 1981 p 172-77 refs

Learning theories and new social studies. H. Dhand *Educational Rev* 85(3) Mr 1979 p 55-59 refs

Living and learning. Muriel Wasi. Dutta Book Centre. 1978. 107p. Rs.20 *Book Rev, Education Quarterly* 31(1) Ap 1979 p 35-36; *Teacher Today* 21(3) Ja-Mr 1979 p 101-02

Master learning : An application of behavioural theory. Lalit Kishore *Experiments in Education* 11(10) De 1983 p 181-82

Masterly learning. Sunil Behari Mohanty *Experiments in Education* 11(1) Mr 1983 p 15-18

A new aim teaching vs learning. M.P. Bhasin *Educational Rev* 91(10) Oc 1985 p 167-71

Piagets views on learning. Karuna Shankar Misra *J Indian Education* 6(3) Se 1980 p 3-8 refs

The process of learning in a young child. Verghis Chandy *Progress of Education* 55(4) Nv 1980 p 99-101

The psychology of learning and curriculum, Marlow Ediger *Experiments in Education* 7(11) Ja 1980 p 202-04 refs

The role of prior learning, target learning and set in practice inhibition. Kamal Dwivedi *Asian J Psychology and Education* 5(1-3) 1979 p 34-43

Self paced learning for primary school. Lalit Kishore *Primary Teacher* 11(1) Ja 1986 p 11-12

Student learning style and contract activity package. Subhash Chandra Agrawal *Indian Education* 10(4) Jl 1980 p 33-36

Students learning style and contract activity package. Subhash Chandra Agrawal *J Education and Psychology* 39(2) Jl 1981 p 128-31

The teacher and the psychology of learning. Marlow Ediger *Progress of Education* 55(11) JE 1981 p 293-94

See also

Concept Learning
Learning Ability
Learning by Discovery
Motivation in Education
Paired-association Learning
Programmed Instruction
Verbal Learning

Learning, Verbal

See

Verbal Learning

Learning Ability

Classification of learners according to their learning styles : A new approach. Tarak Nath Pan *Progress of Education* 57(9) Ap 1983 p 194-99 refs tabs

A comparison of the learning ability of rural and urban children. Pratibha Dev and H.B. Tripathi *National J Education* 2(1) Se 1979 p 15-23 refs

Discrimination learning among illiterate rural adults as function of their intelligence. Rajender Singh Mann *Progress of Education* 55(7) Fe 1981 p 189-91 + tabs

Effect of incentives on the learning ability of school students. Ashok. K. Kalia and S.S. Mathur *Progress of Education* 60(2) Se 1985 p 26-30 refs tabs

Effect of schooling on learning abilities and academic achievement of primary school children. S. Moses and K. Mayuli *Indian Educational Rev* 19(1) Ja 1984 p 120-25

Evaluating learning : The need. Lalit Kishore *Educational Rev* 92(7) Jl 1986 p 110-11 refs

Learning disability : Challenge to primary school teachers. Prem Lata Sharma *Primary Teacher* 11(3) Jl 1986 p 20-22

Management of learning systems. Suraksha Pal *Indian Education* 13(7) Oc 1983 p 16-18

Relationship of constitutional factors to learning difficulties among primary school children. Bindu Prasad *Indian Educational Rev* 17(2) Ap 1982 p 1-19 refs tabs

Some aspects of scientific assessment of learning achievement and creativity. J.N. Kapur *Indian Education* 10(4) Jl 1980 p 6-10+;10(5) Ag 1980 p 8-12

Learning Ability : Testing

A comparative study of the learning abilities, academic achievement and disposition towards school of the primary school children from progressive and less progressive schools. K. Mayvani and S.V. Reddy *J Educational Research and Extension* 19(3) Ja 1983 p 180-86

Improving students creativity through the application of mastery learning strategy. R.C. Hooda and G.C. Jarilal *J Indian Education* 9(1) My 1983 p 16-19

Learning by Discovery

Reflection of the pupils in guided discovery learning method. Surya Bhan Gupta *Education Quarterly* 33(1) Ja 1981 p 19-21

Leave of Absence

See also

Teachers : Leave of Absence

Lecture Method in Teaching

A comparative study of the efficacy of two teaching methods, the lecture method and the discussion method. A.V. Dak *J Education and Psychology* 36(1-2) Ap-Je 1978 p 85-88

A comparative study of lecture method, guided discovery approach in the teaching of science. R.S. Yadav *J Education and Psychology* 44(1) Ap 1986 p 58-65 refs

An experimental study of contribution of learning objective to achievement scores through lecture and guided discovery methods. R.S. Yadav *Asian J Psychology and Education* 14(1-4) 1984 p 1-14 refs

An experimental study for the validation of guided-discovery method over lecture method at different academic levels on VII grade students. R.S. Yadav *Progress of Education* 57(4) Nv 1982 p 84-90 tabs

Lectures on scientific method. B.N. Ghosh. New Delhi, Sterling. *Book Rev, J Institute of Educational Research* 10(2) My 1986 p 25

On mastery learning instructional plan. M.N. Panjotra and Lalit Kishore *Educational Rev* 92(4) Ap 1986 p 66-69 refs

Left : Political Science Aspects

See

Right and Left : Political Science Aspects

Legal Education

See

Law : Study and Teaching

Lesson Planning

How to correct teaching lessons. Goswami Ram Balak *Primary Teacher* 8(1) Ja 1983 p 34-35

Level of Aspiration

A comparative study of majority and minority communities in India on feeling of security, self-acceptance and level of aspiration. Anwar Jahan Zuberi *Teacher Education* 14(12-13) Jl-Oc 1980 p 34-40 refs

A comparative study of R&D units with special reference to motivation, involvement and level of aspiration. V.S. Shanthamani *Asian J*

Psychology and Education 9(4) 1982 p 1-12

Level of aspiration and locality. Beena Thadani and B.S. Raizada *Educational Rev* 91(8) Ag 1985 p 137-38

The level of aspiration of teacher trainees of rural and urban areas in relation to their achievement. M.P. Uniyal and Beena Sah *Indian Educational Rev* 16(1) Ja 1981 p 60-65

N-achievement hope of success and fear of failure in relation to level of aspiration. Afzal Kureshi *et al Asian J Psychology and Education* 3(3) Nv 1978 p 30-34 refs tabs

Performance of adolescents on a linear programme in relation to their level of aspiration. K.K. Gosain and A.K. Dwivedi *J Institute of Educational Research* 6(1) Ja 1982 p 6-9 refs tabs

See also

Student Aspirations

Liberal Education

Liberal education : A process of man-making. Dibakar Kundu *J Indian Education* 12(4) Nv 1986 p 52-55

Librarians : India

Staff structure for university libraries : A proposal. S.C. Uppal *University News* 24(37) 1 Oc 1986 p 5-8

Teachers professional attitude to library, utilisation. *Educational Rev* 89(9) Se 1983 p 151-52

Libraries

Assistance to libraries overseas. *University News* 24(47) 16 De 1986 p 1-4

See also

Libraries : University and Colleges

School Libraries

Libraries : Branches, Delivery Stations

See also

Rural Libraries

Libraries : India

Centralisations of libraries : Merits and demerits. M. Venkatiah *J Indian Education* 8(5) Ja 1983 p 52-54

See also

Libraries : University and Colleges

Rural Libraries

School Libraries

Libraries : University and College

Staff structure for university libraries : A proposal. S.C. Uppal *University News* 24(37) 1 Oc 1986 p 5-8

University library and documentation service. M. Venkatiah *J Indian Education* 6(1) My 1980 p 19-20

Libraries : University and College : Administration

University libraries in India : Their organisation and administration. S.N. Srivastava and S.C. Verma. New Delhi, Sterling. 1980, 351p. Rs. 75 *Book Rev, Education Quarterly* 33(2) Ag 1981 p 40-41; Teacher Today 24(4) Ap-Je 1982 p 138-39.

Libraries : University and College : India

National policy on university libraries. *University News* 24(40) 23 Oc 1986 p 5-7

University libraries in India; Their organisation and administration. S.N.

Srivastava and S.C. Verma. New Delhi, Sterling. 1980, 351p. Rs.75 *Book Rev, Teacher Today* 24(4) Ap-Je 1982 p 138-39; *Education Quarterly* 33(2) Ag 1981 p 40-41

Libraries : University and College : India : Orissa

Teacher's college libraries in Orissa : A study. P.S. Kawatra *J Indian Education* 6(2) Jl 1980 p 55-58

Libraries : University and College : India : Punjab

Bhai Gurdas Library Guru Nanak Dev University. Kirpal Singh *University News* 24(40) 23 Oc 1986 p 3-4

Libraries, College

See

Libraries : University and College

Libraries, Rural

See

Rural Libraries

Libraries and Adult Education

Role of libraries in adult education. H.J. Naqvi *J Indian Education* 6(1) My 1980 p 48-52

Libraries and Education

Creating library consciousness. C. Dharmarajan *Educational Rev* 87(8) Ag 1981 p 141-43

Libraries and Readers

Philosophy of user education. Girja Kumar and Krishna Kumar. New Delhi, Vikas Pub. 1983, 247p. Rs.125 *Book Rev, J Higher Education* 9(2) Aut 1982 p 289-91

Library Science

New dimensions in library science. T.K.S. Iyengar. Bombay, Allied. 1977, 210p. Rs.45 *Book Rev, J Indian Education* 6(4) Nv 1980 p 59-60

Lifelong Education

See

Adult Education

Life Sciences : Study and Teaching

Concept in the teaching of life sciences. Shahejehan Siddiqui *Indian Education* 11(11-12) Fe-Mr 1982 p 29-30

The role of concepts in the teaching of life sciences. Shahejehan Siddiqui *Educational Rev* 88(2) Fe 1982 p 21-23

Teaching of the life sciences through the environment. Surya Bhan Gupta *Education Quarterly* 32(2) Ap 1980 p 27-29

Life Sciences : Study and Teaching : Higher

Life sciences in Indian universities : Course and curriculum. D.P. Burma *National J Education* 2(1) Se 1979 p 33-40

Life Sciences : Study and Teaching : Primary

Investigatory projects in life sciences for school children. W.A.F. Hopper *Rajasthan Board J Education* 15(4) Oc-De 1979 p 6-10

Linguistics

Pedagogical linguistics. Sidheshwar Dhari Sinha *J Indian Education* 7(3) Se 1979 p 29-31

Listening

Can listening skills be modified? B.V. Patel *J Education and Psychology*

37(4) Ja 1980 p 239-46 refs

Can listening skills be modified? B.V. Patel *Rajasthan Board J Education* 15(4) Oc-De 1979 p 15-21

Developing listening skill in school pupils with the help of audio-tape recorder. K.C. Venugopal *J Indian Education* 12(1) My 1986 p 55-57

An experiment in the teaching of listening comprehension in Gujarati pupils of class VIII. B.V. Patel *J Education and Psychology* 36(3) Oc 1978 p 91-98

An experiment in the teaching of listening comprehension in Gujarati to pupils class IX. B.V. Patel *J Education and Psychology* 39(4) Ja 1982 p 224-31 refs

Listening and the pupil. Marlow Ediger *Experiments in Education* 11(7) Se 1983 p 121-26; 11(8) Oc 1983 p 140-44

Listening comprehension in relation to different categories of readers. D.N. Patel *Progress of Education* 56(12) Jl 1982 p 292-98 refs

Listening in the school curriculum. Marlow Ediger *Educational Rev* 87(6) Je 1981 p 108-10

Literacy

See

Illiteracy

Literacy House, Lucknow

The man with the tin trunk. T. Drieberg *Indian J Adult Education* 40(9) Se 1979 p 41-43

The story of Literacy House. V. Tripathi *Indian J Adult Education* 40(9) Se 1979 p 37-40

Literacy Sketch

See

Essay

Literacy Testing

See

Reading : Ability Testing

Literature : Curricula

Learning activities in the literature curriculum. Marlow Ediger *Experiments in Education* 11(2) Ap 1983 p 33-34

Literature : Moral and Religious Aspects

See

Literature and Morals

Literature and Morals

Literature as moral education in schools. D. Michael and M. Mascarenhas *Teacher Today* 23(1) Jl-Se 1980 p 8-13

Loan Funds, Student

See

Student Loan Funds

Loyola College, Madras

Autonomous programme at Loyola College. J. Kuriakose *New Frontiers in Education* 12(2) Jl-Se 1982 p 26-36

Lucknow University : Students

Attitudes and beliefs of Harijan studens. S.P. Rastogi *J Higher Education* 4(2) Aut 1978 p 251-58 refs

Maharashtra State Headmasters Conference, 1982

Twenty second headmasters conference. M.G. Joshi *Progress of Education* 56(5) De 1981 p 119+

Mahdism

The Mahdewi movement in India. Qamaruddin *Indian Educational Rev* 18(4) Oc 1984 p 88-94

Maize

Adoption of the high yielding varieties of maize by the farmers of Sikkim. H.S.P. Sinha and S.K. Sinha *Indian J Extension Education* 16(1-2) Je 1980 p 46-50 tabs

Maladjusted : Psychological Aspects

See

Adjustment : Psychological Aspects

Maladjusted Children

See

Problem Children

Malaysia

See also

Examinations : Malaysia

Management

See also

Materials Management
School Management and Organisation
Water Resources Management

Management : Study and Teaching

Computer storage and retrieval of MBA admission test items. V. Natarajan and Veena *New Frontiers in Education* 13(1) Ja-Mr 1983 p 20-23

Management education in India : Some reflections. R. Satya Raju *Educational Rev* 90(1) Ja 1984 p 14-15

Off campus MBA programme : Deakin University. Paul Northcott *Indian Education* 12(5-6) Ag-Se 1982 p 14-18

Orientation of teachers and heads of schools to the basic concepts of management : A preliminary exercise in management education. D. Rajaganesan *Experiments in Education* 7(4) Je 1979 p 64-69

Teaching-learning in higher education M.B. style. Rajani R. Shirur *J Higher Education* 7(3) Spr 1982 p 302-06 refs

Manpower

Institutional vitality. J. Filella *New Frontiers in Education* 15(2) Ap-Je 1985 p 34-51

See also

Unemployment, Educated

Manpower, Educated : Employment
See
Unemployment, Educated
Manpower Policy
Education and human resource development. S. Sreedhara Swamy *Progress of Education* 57(11) Je 1983 p 240-49
Education as investment in human resources development. Jagannath Mohanty *Indian Education* 11(10) Ja 1982 p 6-15
Education human resources development. M. Pramod Reddy *Indian Education* 11(11-12) Fe-Mr 1982 p -7-11
Manpower Policy : India
Education as on investment in human resources development. G. Haragopal *Indian Education* 11(7) Oc 1981 p 35-38
Manpower Training Programmes
See
Occupational Training
Manual Training : India
Inplant experience programme. M. Shanmugham *Experiments in Education* 6(5) Jl 1978 p 75-78
Manures
See
Fertilizers and Manures
Map Reading
See
Maps
Maps
Designing maps for school children : Implications of the research on children's congnitive processing and visual perception. B.L. Sukhwal *J Indian Education* 12(3) 1986 p 15-22 refs
Marathi Language : Study and Teaching
Learning Marathi, Kalyan Kala and Anjali Soman Pune, Vishakha Pra. 1986, 231p. Rs.150 *Book Rev, Progress of Education* 61(1) Ag 1986 p 24+
Marathwada University
Naming a University. W.V. Bhave *Progress of Education* 56(6) Ja 1982 p 136-39
Marine Resources
See also
Fisheries
Marking : Students
See
Grading and Marking : Students
Marx, Karl : Educational Thought
Educational ideas of Karl Marx. Harikesh Singh and Surya Nath Singh *National J Education* 6(1) Se 1983 p 20-28
Marxism
Marxism and Christianity. Sebastian Kappan *New Frontiers of Education* 15(2) Ap-Je 1985 p 22-28

Mass Communication

See

Mass Media

Mass Media

Role of mass media in rural development. R. Srinivasa Rao *Experiments in Education* 6(12) Fe 1979 p 205-06

Mass Media : India

Training facilities in mass communication in India. Bhaskara Rao Digumarti *Experiments in Education* 11(2) Ap 1983 p 21-24

Mass Media : Research

Current perspectives in mass communication theory and research. Indu B. Singh *Indian J Extension Education* 16(3-4) De 1980 p 52-66 refs

Mass Media : Study and Teaching

Relationship between knowledge and ability gain in the course : Mass communication in home science. Anita S. Thomas and Arvinda Chandra *Experiments in Education* 13(11) Ja 1986 p 189-94 refs

Mass Media in Education

Media education. N.C. Rajamani *Experiments in Education* 8(11) Ja 1981 p 203-04

Role of mass media in distance education. R.S. Yadav *EPA Quarterly Bulletin* 7(3-4) Oc 1984-Ja 1985 p 37-52 refs

Role of mass media in distance education. V.B. Patel *Quest in Education* 18(4) Oc 1981 p 320-37 refs

Mass Psychology

See

Social Psychology

Master of Education

Evaluation of M.Ed dissertations : How objective are internal examiners. Haribhai G. Desai *J Education and Psychology* 38(1) Ap 1980 p 17-21 tabs

An experiment study in programmed learning for teaching research methodology course at M.Ed level. D.M. Sansanwal *Indian Educational Rev* 14(4) Oc 1979 p 72-77

Materials Management

Material management in special education. S. Mukhopadhyay *Education Quarterly* 38(2) Sum 1986 p 5-7

Maternal Deprivation

Maternal deprivation : A review of literature. P.C. Saxena and Usha Upadhyaya *National J Education* 2(2) Mr 1980 p 15-25 refs

Mathematical Ability

Effect of feedback on the acquisition of algebraic concepts in relation to intelligence and anxiety. J.N. Joshi and Subhash Gakhar *J Education and Psychology* 36(4) Ja 1979 p 180-85

The effect of personality variables and intelligence on the performance of high school students in mathematics. Anand Bhushan and Usha Sharma *Asian J Psychology and Education* 7(2) Jl 1981 p 44-49

Study habits as correlates of achievement in mathematics. N.R. Tuli *J Education and Psychology* 38(3) Oc 1980 p 141-48 tabs

Mathematical Ability : Testing

Achievement motivation and anxiety as related to academic success in mathematics. S.S. Grewal and Kirpal Kaur *Experiments in Education* 8(12) Fe 1981 p 221-24; 10(2) Ap 1982 p 34-37 refs

Attitude of high school boys and girls towards mathematics. Kumkum Srivastava *et al J Institute of Educational Research* 9(1) Ja 1985 p 25-31 refs tabs

A comparative study of attainments in the algebraic concept formation of standard VIII students. S.P. Wani *Research Bulletin* 12(1-2) Mr-Je 1982 p 27-34

Correlation between attitude to and attainment in mathematics. V. Rajasekaran *Experiments in Education* 6(8) Oc 1978 p 143-48

Effect of general and test anxiety on cognitive performance in mathematics. A. Sukumaran Nair *Quest in Education* 17(3) Jl 1980 p 242-49 refs

Evaluating pupils learning in mathematics. V.P. Gupta *Primary Teacher* 8(3) Jl 1983 p 12-17

Intelligence, creativity and achievement in mathematics : A regression analysis. S.C. Gakhar *J Institute of Educational Research* 9(3) Se 1985 p 17-20 refs tabs

Introversion, neuroticism and achievement in mathematics in school going adolescent girls. A.K. Sarkar *Quest in Education* 18(1) Ja 1981 p 13-18

Mathematical achievement among children of working and non-working mothers in relation to parents' encouragement. S.C. Gakhar *Progress of Education* 57(11) Je 1983 p 250-52 tabs

Mathematical concepts learning as determined by feedback and no feedback conditions. S.C. Gakhar *Educational Rev* 89(10) Oc 1983 p 168-70 refs tabs

Mathematical creativity : A teaching model. Bhoodev Singh *Primary Teacher* 9(3) Jl 1984 p 11-13

Mathematical creativity and personality. Mulkh Raj Tuli *J Education and Psychology* 44(1) Ap 1986 p 16-20 refs

Mixed ability teaching in mathematics : A survey of current practices. Evans. 148p. £2.50 *Book Rev, Education Quarterly* 31(1) Ap 1979 p 36

Sex and regional differences in mathematical creativity. Mulkh Raj Tuli *Indian Educational Rev* 17(3) Jl 1982 p 128-34 refs

Sex and regional differences in mathematical creativity. Mulkh Raj Tuli *J Education and Psychology* 39(4) Ja 1982 p 211-47

A study of acquisition of mathematical concepts among 8th grades of different types of schools. S.C. Gakhar *Experiments in Educaiton* 10(9) Nv 1982 p 164-67 refs

A study of learning outcomes in mathematics in relation to classroom to climate and academic motivation. S.P. Gupta and A.K. Bhargava *Rajasthan Board J Education* 19(4) Oc-De 1983 p 9-15

Study of the effect of socio-economic status on the mathematical achievement of English grade children. Subhahi Gakhar *J Institute of Educational Research* 7(2) My 1983 p 12-15

Mathematical Recreation

Inculcating discovery attitude in pupils through arithmatical recreations. M. Subramanya *Primary Teacher* 4(2) Ap 1979 p 19-22

Learning mathematics through lube games. K.J. Srinivasan *Experiments in Education* 11(6) Ag 1983 p 98-100

Mathematics can be fun. Hem Raj Garg *Primary Teacher* 5(2) Ap 1980 p 28-32

Motivation through mathematical games. Gomathi Mani *Experiments in Education* 11(3) My 1983 p 39-41

Motivation through mathematical games. Gomathi Mani *Teacher Today* 27(1) Jl-Se 1984 p 44-47

Mathematical Statistics

See also

Regression Analysis

Mathematics

Ways and practices of writing objectives in mathematics. K. Dorasami and V. Shankaram *Indian Educational Rev* 17(1) Ja 1982 p 43-63 appdx refs

See also

Geometry

Mathematics : Ability Testing

See

Mathematical Ability : Testing

Mathematics : Curricula

Mathematics : Basics versus an activity centred curriculum. Marlow Ediger *Experiments in Education* 10(6) Ag 1982 p 105-08; 10(9) Nv 1982 p 171-72 +

Mathematics experiences in the curriculum. Marlow Ediger *Education Quarterly* 34(2) Ap 1982 p 11-13

Micro computers in the mathematics curriculum. Marlow Ediger *Experiments in Education* 12(4) Je 1984 p 59-63

Philosophy in the matehmatics curriculum. Marlow Ediger *New Frontiers in Education* 14(2) Ap-Je 1984 p 36-42 refs

Philosophy of micro computer use in the mathematics curriculum. Marlow Ediger *New Frontiers in Education* 15(1) Ja-Mr 1985 p 56-76 refs

A study of the relationship between the secondary school science and mathematics curricula of Kerala and Tamil Nadu. K. Krishnan *J Educational Research and Extension* 18(4) Ap 1982 p 210-19 refs tabs

Mathematics : Examinations

Error analysis in mathematics at the S.S.C. examination. B.V. Adkoli *Indian Educational Rev* 17(4) Oc 1982 p 124-38 tabs

Internal and external examination scores in science and mathematics : A study. P.S. Verma *J Indian Education* 5(6) Mr 1980 p 6-10

Some comments on the moderation of question papers in mathematics education. V. Sankaram and K. Dorasami *J Higher Education* 8(2) Aut 1982 p 246-47 refs

Mathematics : Programmed Instruction

Programmed instruction in mathematics. C.H. Vijayalakshmi *Indian Education* 11(11-12) Fe-Mr 1982 p 15-21

Programmed instruction in mathematics. S. Sreedhara Swamy and P.M. Thayaru *Experiments in Education* 10(9) Nv 1982 p 167-69

A study of the effectiveness of programmed learning method to teach modern mathematics to high, normal and low creative students. D.R.

Sharma and Surendra Singh *Experiments in Education* 9(3) My 1981 p 49-54 refs

Mathematics : Study and Teaching

Application of action research in teaching mathematics. C.H. Vijayalakshmi *Indian Education* 12(1-2) Ap-My 1982 p 52-55

Development of concepts in mathematics. Ramachandra Reddy *Experiments in Education* 10(6) Ag 1982 p 108-09 refs

Effect of teachers variables on the acquisition of mathematical concepts. S.C. Gakhar *Experiments in Education* 11(6) Ag 1983 p 105-09 refs tabs

Formation of mathematical signs by fingers. Benimadhab Mukherji *Primary Teacher* 11(4) Oc 1986 p 36-39

Individually guided system of instruction in mathematics. Rajendra P. Gupta and Rajeshwar N. Mathur *J Indian Education* 10(5) Ja 1985 p 44-48

Language errors in a mathematics class. Gomath Mani *Experiments in Education* 7(8) Oc 1979 p 139-41

Mathematical education. C.T. Wain, ed. Von Nostrand Reinhold. 197p. £8.50 *Book Rev, Education Quarterly* 3(3-4) Oc 1979-Ja 1980 p 48

Mathematics education and the structure of intellect. C.P. Singh Chauhan *J Indian Education* 5(1) My 1979 p 39-43

Mathematics education in schools : A management approach. A.K. Das *J Indian Education* 5(1) Ag 1980 p 9-11

Problem of mathematics : A solution. S. Joshi *Progress of Education* 55(1) My 1979 p 22-27

Self-revelation of mathematics. C.V. Bhimasankaran *Progress of Education* 57(11) Je 1983 p 253-54

Teaching of mathematics : A point of view. M.S. Samar. Ajmer, Regional College of Educ. 118p. *Book Rev, Education Quarterly* 33(4) Oc 1981 p 36

Teaching of mathematics in distance education. J.N. Kapur *University News* 24(42) 8 Nv 1986 p 43

Teaching the slow-learners in mathematics. D. Seshagiri Rao *Indian Education* 11(4) Jl 1981 p 29-31

To investigate the effectiveness of educational technology in the teaching of mathematics to deaf and dumb children. Subhash Chandra Agrawal *Progress of Education* 54(9) Ap 1980 p 178-81

Unit plan for teacher education in mathematics, 1978-79. M. Govindarajacharyulu *Experiments in Education* 9(1) Mr 1981 p 9-15

What is mathematics? Sushil Kumar Tyagi *Indian Educational Rev* 20(3) Jl 1985 p 102-10

The Wirszup report. *J Indian Education* 6(2) Jl 1980 p 71-73

Mathematics : Study and Teaching : India : Rajasthan

The uplift of the scholastically backward students in mathematics through socio-metric techniques : A study. Ram Niwas Gupta *J Indian Education* 6(6) Mr 1981 p 20-27 refs

Mathematics : Study and Teaching (Elementary)

Teaching elementary school mathematics. Rakesh Chilana *Primary Teacher* 9(4) Oc 1984 p 30-31

Mathematics : Study and Teaching (Higher)

An experimental study of the multi media approach to instruction in modern

mathematics at B.Ed level. *J Educational Research and Extension* 19(3) Ja 1983 p 167-72

On university mathematics. U. Shukla *J Higher Education* 2(2) Aut 1976 p 261-64

Mathematics : Study and Teaching (Primary)

Mathematics teaching at primary levels. V.P. Gupta *Primary Teacher* 9(2) Ap 1984 p 13-15

Mathematics : Study and Teaching (Primary) : India : Kerala

Teaching of science and mathematics in primary classes of Kerala. T.K.D. Nair *J Indian Education* 7(3) Se 1979 p 3-9 annex

Mathematics : Study and Teaching (Secondary)

An investigation into the difficulties encountered by the secondary grade teachers in teaching mathematics in standard VIII in Madras city schools. J. Davies and V. Natarajan *J Educational Research and Extension* 18(2) Oc 1981 p 15-21 refs

Modernisation of mathematics instruction at secondary school : A development of project. M.S. Yadav and Malathi Seshadri *Indian Educational Rev* 19(1) Ja 1984 p 36-51

Some social-familial variables causing under achievement in secondary school mathematics. A. Sukumaran Nair *J Educational Research and Extension* 18(2) Oc 1981 p 10-14 refs tabs

A study of effectiveness of non-traditional methods for teaching mathematics to class X. S.P. Wani *Research Bulletin* 12(3-4) Se-de 1982 p 30-43

Mathematics : Text-books

Compartive evaluation of mathematics text book. Bhoodev Singh *Experiments in Education* 9(12) Fe 1982 p 217-22 tabs

Mathematics Teachers

Logico-mathematical reasoning of mathematics teachers. A.C. Pachaury *J Educational Research and Extension* 16(2) Oc 1979 p 80-88 tabs

Maturation : Psychological Aspects

See also

Social Maturity Scales

Mechanisation in Agriculture

See

Farm Mechanisation

Medical Colleges : Faculty

Organisation culture, its perception and the medical faculty. Somnath Chattopadhyay and K.G. Agrawal *J Higher Education* 4(2) Aut 1978 p 245-50

Medical Colleges : India

Health care services, medical education and social science research. I. Qadeer *J Higher Education* 4(1) Mon 1978 p 105-08 refs

Medical Colleges : India : Andhra Pradesh

Caste levels and performance during medical training. S. Paramaji *Indian Education* 12(5-6) Ag-Se 1982 p 10-13

Medical Education

See also

Medical Colleges

Medical Education : India

What ails medical education in India. Problems and solutions? C.M. Francis *New Frontiers in Education* 10(1) Ja-Mr 1980 p 1-13 refs

Medical Education for Women

Higher medical education for women. S. Padmavati *J Higher Education* 1(2) Aut 1975 p 256-58 refs

Medical Personnel : Education

See

Medical Education

Medical Schools

See

Medical Colleges

Medium of Instruction

Attitude of students towards introduction of regional medium at the post-graduate level. A. Venkata Rami Reddy and T. Chandra Reddy *Education Quarterly* 32(1) Ja 1980 p 16-18

Attitudes of parents towards English medium and non-English medium schools. J.S. Jha *J Educational Research and Extension* 16(2) Oc 1979 p 115-24 refs

The case for and against English as medium of instruction in higher secondary schools. T.R. Natarjan *Experiments in Education* 8(1) Mr 1980 p 10-12

Do students achieve better in regional medium than in English medium. A. Venkata Rami Reddy *Indian Educational Rev* 19(2) Ap 1984 p 79-90

The effect of the medium of instruction on the achievement of the students. B.A. Parikh *J Education Research and Extension* 17(3) Ja 1981 p 137-41 refs

From English to regional languages. Muthyalayya Naidu *Educational Rev* 89(10) Oc 1983 p 175-77

Media of education. Raghuvir Sahay Nigam *Educational Rev* 85(7) Jl 1979 p 127-28

Students reactions towards English and regional media : A comparative study A. Venkata Rami Reddy *J Higher Education* 5(1) Mon 1979 p 101-08 refs tabs

Meerut

See also

Student Activities : India : Meerut

Meghalaya

See also

Tribal Education : India : Meghalaya

Memory

The brain, memory and languages. Vladimir Konovatov *Progress of Education* 58(1) Ag 1983 p 17-18 +

Contributions of memory and speed to psychology honours examinations scores. Biranchi N. Puhan and Suresh C. Das *Asian J Psychology and Education* 5(1-3) 1979 p 26-33 refs tabs

Proactive inhibition : A cause for forgetting. Vibha Premchand *Experiments in Education* 9(6) Ag 1981 p 107-09 refs

Retenties of subject matter in physics : Individualised system of instruction

and lecture model. Lalit Kishore *J Indian Education* 10(5) Ja 1985 p 40-43 refs

Semantic retrievals in creative products. K.N. Sharma *Asian J Psychology and Education* 5(1-3) 1979 p 9-20 refs

Span of memory : Links with intelligence and personality. Umesh Agarwal *Educational Rev* 86(3) Mr 1980 p 45-48 refs tabs

A study of retention curve. R.M. Saraswat *et al Experiments in Education* 9(6) Ag 1981 p 102-07

Why do children forget? Hari Shankar Sharma *Primary Teacher* 8(3) Jl 1983 p 34-36

See also

Short-term Memory

Mendel, Gregor Johann (1922-1984)

See

Mendel's Laws

Mendel's Law

Mendel and laws of heredity. Nem Kumar Jain *J Indian Education* 5(1) My 1979 p 44-49

See also

Heredity

Menon, T.K.N.

A tribute to the late Professor T.K.N. Menon *Teacher Education* 17(20-21) Jl-Oc 1982 p 1-6

Mental Tests

Construction and standardisation of a performance test-battery of general mental ability of the children of age groups 6 to 10 years. S.C. Chakraborty *Our Education* 3-4 Jl 1983 p 59-67 refs

Construction of diagonestic test in physics for class VII. V.K. Gautam *Indian Education* 11(4) Jl 1981 p 22-23

Developing competence in the skill of asking questions at different levels. M.S. Bawa *J Indian Education* 11(2) Jl 1985 p 45-54

Differential personality traits of tribal and non-tribal adolescents at different levels of intelligence and socio-economic status. Sudarsan C. Panigrahi *J Education and Psychology* 44(1) Ap 1986 p 51-57 refs

Fluency intelligence and socio-economic status as correlates of the interests in scientific pursuits. R.L. Bhardwaj and R.P. Gupta *Asian J Psychology and Education* 6(3) Nv 1980 p 23-31 refs

An investigation of sex difference in general intellectual ability in rural and urban children. R.L. Worlson and A.G. Linford *J Education and Psychology* 37(1) Ap 1979 p10-18 refs

Need of Piagetian testing for intellectual assessment. Tarak Nath Pan *J Indian Education* 8(1) My 1982 p 37-39 ft-n

Relationship of home and school environments to intellectual performance. Karuna Shankar Mishra *J Indian Education* 20(3) Ag 1983 p 174-86

A study of family background intellectual abilities of educationally advantaged and disadvantaged group. Govind Tiwari and Rama Pal *Asian J Psychology and Education* 7(1) Ja 1981 p 40-43

See also

Educational Tests and Measurements

Mental Tests : India : Gujarat

Comparative factorial structure of haven's standard progressive matrics, Cattell's culture fair scale and Desai Bhatt group tests of intelligence on samples of various sub-cultures of Gujarat. K.G. Desai *J Education and Psychology* 39(1) Ap 1981 p 4-11

Mentally Handicapped : Care and Treatment

Diognc stic verbal test of mentally retardents. Subimal Deb and Varasha M. Shah *Our Education* 5 Jl 1984 p 5-16 refs

Mentally Handicapped : Education

Diagonsis of mental retardation. Usha Rama and M.H. Palsane *J Education and Psychology* 38(2) Jl 1980 p 94-98 refs

Education and care of the mentally retarded. Anima Sen *Indian Education* 11(8-9) Nv-De 1981 p 18-20

Mentally Handicapped : India

The place of the mentally retarded in Indian society. N.Y. Reddy *Indian Education* 9(10-11) Ja-Fe 1980 p 12-24 refs

Mentally Handicapped Children

Age and sex distribution in institutionalised mentally deficient children. Pushpa Murari and V. Sinha *Asian J Psychology and Education* 3(3) Nv 1978 p 9-11 refs tabs

Diagnosing mentally retarded children. Janak Verma *Primary Teacher* 10(4) Oc 1985 p 30-32

Information processing and conservation of quantity among the mentally retarded children. A. Grewal and Sarojini Gupta *J Institute of Educational Research* 7(3) Se 1983 p 10-14

Mentally retarded and normal children. Manju Biswas. New Delhi, Sterling. 158p. Rs.45 *Book Rev, Teacher Today* 26(4) Ap-Je 1984 p 94-95

My problems : A mentally retarded child speaks. A.S. Narayana Pillai *Teacher Today* 23(3) Ja-Mr 1981 p 23-26

A study of the personality characterstics of mentally retarded and normal children. S.P. Ahluvalia and M. Deouskfer *Our Education* 5 Jl 1984 p 57-67 refs

Mentally Handicapped Children : Education

Children's attitudes towards mentally retarded peers. Aneeta Gupta and Adarsh Sharma *Indian Educational Rev* 18(4) Oc 1983 p 28-36

Education of the mentally retarded children. Lakshahira Das *Educational Rev* 85(12) De 1979 p 225-29

Effect of training the mentally retarded children on certain tasks. Avinash Grewal and Saroj Gupta *Research Bulletin* 12(1-2) Mr-Je 1982 p 19-26 refs

Mentally retarded : Their education. B.G. Barki *Educational Rev* 87(11) Nv 1981 p 201-03

Mentally Retarded Children

See
Mentally Handicapped Children

Method of Study

See

Study, Method of

Microteaching

An adaptation of 'effective questioning' for preservice and inservice teachers in India. Iris Paintal *Indian Educational Rev* 17(4) Oc 1982 p 1-19 refs tabs

Carry over effect of micro-teaching on student-teachers from college of education to regular school teaching. S.P. Malhotra and R.M. Syad *Progress of Education* 55(8) Mr 1981 p 208-10 tab

A comparative study of the effect of different types of feedback in micro teaching. S.K. Sharma and A.K. Gupta *Asian J Psychology and Education* 9(1) Ja 1982 p 41-44 refs tabs

A comparative study of the effect of micro teaching and Diod model to improve teaching competency of pre-service teachers. R.N. Syaq *et al J Institute of Educational Research* 6(1) Ja 1982 p 38-41 refs tabs

A comparative study of the effectiveness of feedback given by peer and audio tape under micro teaching setting. Shalini Bhouraskar *National J Education* 2(2) Mr 1980 p 6-14 refs tabs

Development and tryout of multi media package an effective questioning in the context of micro teaching. S.G. Shah *Indian Education* 10(9-10) De 1980-Ja 1981 p 16-19

Differential effectiveness of micro-teaching components. R.C. Das *et al Indian Educational Rev* 14(1) Ja 1979 p 69-84 refs

Differential personality factors of high and low feedback acceptance groups in micro-teaching. Kamala Rai and Pritty Gandhi *J Institute of Educational Research* 4(1) Ja 1980 p 33-36 refs

The effect of micro-teaching and integration of skills on teaching self-concept of student teachers. Mathew George *J Educational Research and Education* 18(2) Oc 1981 p 31-39; 19(3) Ja 1983 p 129-37 refs tabs

Effect of training in selected teaching skills using micro-teaching on the teaching competence of social education teachers : A field study. N.K. Jangira *et al J Indian Education* 8(4) Nv 1982 p 9-14 refs tabs

Effective teaching practice : A micro-teaching approach. Lal Pratap Singh *Teacher Today* 21(3) Ja-Mr 1979 p 71-76 refs

Effectiveness of micro-teaching on the development of psychomotor skills. L.P. Singh and Jagdishwar Dwivedi *Teacher Today* 16(18-19) Ja-Ap 1982 p 21-29 tabs

Effectiveness of skills-based instructional materials synchronised with micro-teaching approach in the acquistion of the skill of illustrating with examples. Sneha Joshi *Indian Educational Rev* 16(3) Jl 1981 p 69-74

An experiment to study the effect of training in micro-teaching skills on the teacher competence of primary teachers. V. Seth Kaushik and Panna Desai *Progress of Education* 53(10-11) My-Je 1979 p 194-200 tabs refs

An experimental study of improvement in the teaching skills under micro-teaching among the student-teachers. Charudatta Parshuram Kadam *Progress of Education* 58(10) My 1984 p 246-48 refs tab

Impact of different feedback sources on acquistion of teaching skills im microteaching situation. K. Rai and B.L. Katiyar *National J Education* 2(1)

Se 1979 p 24-31 refs tabs

Improving college instruction through self instructional micro-teaching. G.M. Palted and V.R. Suryavanshi *Indian Educational Rev* 18(4) Oc 1981 p 66-71

Micro-teaching : A handbook for teachers. Iris Panital. New Delhi, OUP. 1980, x, 147p. Rs. 12 *Book Rev, Edcuation Quarterly* 33(2) Ap 1981 p 38-39; *Progress of Education* 56(7) Fe 1982 p 177

Micro-teaching : A novel teacher training technique. K.C. Venugopal *J Indian Education* 7(3) Se 1979 p 20-23

Micro-teaching : A appraisal. Subhash Chandra Agarwal *Indian Education* 11(3) Ag 1981 p 13-16

Micro-teaching and teacher education. Fareeda Khatoon *Indian Education* 12(10) Ja 1983 p 13-15

Micro-teaching as an innovation in teacher education. Surendra Pratap Singh *Teacher Education* 15(14-15) Ja-Ap 1981 p 73-79

Micro-teaching at pre-service level. K.K. Sharma *J Indian Education* 7(3) Se 1979 p 24-28

Micro-teaching-2. Arvind Dave *Progress of Education* 53(10-11) My-Je 1979 p 203-07

Micro-teaching. George Brown. Methuen. 1978, 163p. Rs.77.30 : £4.20 *Book Rev, Teacher Today* 22(4) Ap-Je 1980 p 96-98

Micro-teaching in higher education : Research, development and practice. Elizabeth Parrott. Guildford, Soc Res Higher Educ. 1977, 107p. *Book Rev, Indian Educational Rev* 15(4) Oc 1980 *J Higher Education* 5(2) Aut 1979 p 266-68 113-16

Micro-teaching : Ragunath Safaya *Educational Review* 86(12) De 1980 p 227-34 refs

Micro-teaching. Ramdev P. Kathuria. New Delhi, Vikas Pub. *Book Rev, Educational Review* 85(8) Ag 1979 p 158

Micro-teaching. S.S. Washikar. Pune, Nutan Pra. 74p. Rs. 7 *Book Rev, Progress of Education* 56(6) Ja 1982 p 153

Modifying and extending basic skills programme : Encounter with micro-teaching. L.M. Shivanerkar *Research Bulletin* 15(3-4) Se-De 1985 p 30-41 refs

Organising micro-teaching programme in teacher training institutions. V.P. Gupta *Indian Education* 11(11-12) Fe-Mr 1982 p 37-41

Our first experiments with micro-teaching. Joseph M. Dias *Progress of Education* 57(11) Je 1973 p 255-57 +

Reactions of our students to micro-teaching. Joseph M. Dias *Progress of Education* 57(12) Jl 1983 p 279-81 + tabs

The relative impact of micro-teaching and conventional teaching. M. Malla Reddy *Indian Education* 10(5) Ag 1980 p 31-41

Shift of learned teaching skills from micro to micro-teaching selling : A study A.R. Bisht *J Institute of Educational Research* 7(2) My 1983 p 8-11

Skill of reinforcement : Programme for implementation. Pijush Kanti Chatterjee *Progress of Education* 53(6) Ja 1981 p 161-64

Some issues in micro-teaching. C.S. Shukla *Teacher Education* 15(14-15) Ja-Ap 1981 p 83-89

Students perception of the micro-teaching programme. Hansraj Pal

Progress of Education 55(8) Mr 1981 p 204-07 tabs

A study of micro-teaching in the context of methods, subjects, sex and I.Q. C.B. Patel *J Educational Psychology* 44(1) Ap 1986 p 21-28 refs

A study of the comparative effects of micro-teaching under simulated and mixed conditions upon general teaching competence and attitude towards teaching. L.P. Singh and T. Singh *J Educational Research and Extension* 16(3) Ja 1980 p 142-52 refs tabs

A study of the effect of skill based instructional materials synchronised with micro teaching technique on the attitude towards teaching. Sneha Joshi *Progress of Education* 55(10) My 1981 p 255-60 tabs refs

Teaching styles of student teachers exposed to micro-teaching approach and traditional approach. K.A. Gandhi *Experiments in Education* 10(1) Mr 1982 p 3-6 refs

To study the effectiveness of Peers managed micro teaching programme under simulated conditions. D.K. Sharma *Experiments in Education* 10(8) Oc 1982 p 150-54 + refs

Teacher training : The role of micro-teaching. B. Niranjan Reddy and M.V. Lakshmi Reddy *J Indian Education* 12(4) Nv 1986 p 17-21

Military Administration

Family background and military leadership qualities. R.P. Gautam *J Indian Education* 8(6) Mr 1983 p 27-34 refs tabs

Military Education : India

Sainik schools : Perceptions and reflections. R.C. Wadhera *J Indian Education* 8(4) Nv 1982 p 43-47

Scenario of Sainik schools. R.C. Wadhera *J Indian Education* 12(2) Jl 1986 p 15-19

Military Law

See also

Military Administration

Military Schools

See

Military Education

Military Service as a Profession

General awareness of military career among rural and urban students. R.P. Gautam *Indian Educational Rev* 14(1) Ja 1979 p 123-30

Military Training

See

Military Education

Milk Production : India : Haryana

Correlates of level of aspiration of high and low milk producers. J.P.S. Chouhan and K.N.K. Chouhan *Indian J Extension Education* 18(3-4) De 1982 p 40-44 refs

Milk Supply

See also

Milkmen

Milk Trade

See also

Milkmen

Milkmen

A study of the job activities of the milk procurement personnel. M.N. Sinha *et al Indian J Extension Education* 16(1-2) Je 1980 p 82-83

Mind

See

Intellect

Minnesota Multiphasic Personality Inventory

Indian norms of the Minnesota teacher attitude inventory. Agya Jit Singh *Indian Educational Rev* 14(4) Oc 1979 p 24-32 refs tabs

Minorities : Education

Constitutional protection of minority educational institutes in India. Anwarul Yaqlin. New Delhi, Deep and Deep Pub. 390p. Rs.100 *Book Rev, New Frontiers in Education* 12(4) Oc-De 1982 p 59-60

See also

Muslims in India : Education

Minorities : India

A comparative study of majority and minority communities in India on feeling of security, self-acceptance and level of aspiration. Anwar Jahan Zuberi *Teacher Education* 14(12-13) Jl-Oc 1980 p 34-40 refs

Meaning and implications of minority rights. E.D. Devadasan *New Frontiers in Education* 12(2) Ap-Je 1982 p 25-29

Mizoram

See also

Adult Education : India : Mizoram

Mobile Schools

The brain-drain : A British exercise in early morning mobile education. *J Indian Education* 6(1) My 1980 p 71-73

The brain train : An exercise in mobile education. D'Este Bond *Educational Rev* 86(4) Ap 1980 p 73-74

Modernisation

Modernisation and the autocratic tradition in China. Philip Shen *New Frontiers in Education* 14(2) Ap-Je 1984 p 10-16 ft-n

Modernisation and the Korean experience. Yung Chung Kim *New Frontiers in Education* 14(2) Ap-Je 1984 p 1-9 refs

Montessori Method of Education

Effect of tape recorder as a medium of instruction upon the memorising ability and pronunciation of the nursery students. S.P. Malhotra and Neelam Bhamija *Progress of Education* 56(5) De 1981 p 114-16 refs

Moral Education

Attitude development for moral judgement. Raghunath Safaya *Educational Rev* 92(10) Oc 1986 p 163-65

Can we teach children to be good? P. Snelders and C. Wringe, eds. London, Allen and Unwin. 1982. 115p. *Book Rev, Teacher Today* 27(11) Jl-Se 1984 p 93-94

Character building : The basic structure of education. A. Sundara Mahalingam *Experiments in Education* 10(7) Se 1982 p 127-28 refs

The concept of morale. P.B. Dekhawala *New Frontiers in Education* 12(3) Jl-Se 1982 p 53-55

Contemporary significance of value education. N.N. Prahallada *J Indian*

Education 8(6) Mr 1983 p 56-60

Dynamics of moral development. H.H.A. Bourai *Rajasthan Board J Education* 16(4) Oc-De 1980 p 21-24

Education : A medium of transmitting values. Nagendra Singh *Primary Teacher* 9(4) Oc 1984 p 17-20

Education and ethics. Mahendra N. Pandia *Progress of Education* 60(10-11) My-Je 1986 p 233-38

Education and values : Need for integration. P.T. Chandy *New Frontiers in Education* 14(1) Ja-Mr 1984 p 29-30

Education for social, moral and spiritual values. S.R. Jayaswal *Bhartiya Shiksha Shodh Patrika* 1(2) Jl 1982 p 5-8 refs

Education *vis-a-vis* life values. P.N. Mathur *National J Education* 7(2) My 1985 p 1-8

Ethics in education. R.S. Chainani *Progress of Education* 56(7) Fe 1982 p 163-64

The importance of moral education at the high school level. Ashok K. Kalia *Educational Rev* 90(10) Oc 1984 p 158-60

Inculcation of ethical and social values in education. K. Kulandaivel *J Educational Research and Extension* 17(3) Ja 1981 p 191-94

Inculcating ethical and social values in education : Proposal for implementation. T.S. Avinashilingam. Coimbatore, Sri Ramakrishna Mission. *Book Rev, Progress of Education* 56(12) Jl 1982 p 305

Key to value orientation. S.N. Ghosh *New Frontiers in Education* 14(1) Ja-Mr 1984 p 38-43

Methods of moral education. Shamsuddin *Progress of Education* 56(12) Jl 1982 p 289-91

Moral and religious education. Raghunath Safaya *Educational Rev* 88(10) Oc 1982 p 173-75; 88(11) Nv 1982 p 190-92+; 88(12) De 1982 p 209-13

Moral development and moral education. R.S. Peters. London, Allen and Unwin. 1981, 187p. $4.50 *Book Rev, Progress of Education* 57(2) Se 1982 p 46

Moral education : A challenge. Surinder K. Bhullar *Educational Rev* 92(10) Oc 1986 p 177-78

Moral education : A unique experiment. R.P. Singh *Primary Teacher* 8(1) Ja 1983 p 5-6

Moral education : Approach and perspective. J.V. Joshi *Progress of Education* 57(3) Oc 1982 p 50-52

Moral education at the primary level : An attitudinal study. P. Subramaniyam and B.G. Sudha *Quest in Education* 18(1) Je 1981 p 27-38 refs

Moral education in schools. K.G. Rastogi *Primary Teacher* 5(2) Ap 1980 p 33-36

Moral education. Raghunath Safaya *Educational Rev* 87(12) De 1981 p 229

Moral education : Some comparative considerations. Suresh Chandra Shukla *National J Education* 3(1) Se 1980 p 9-16

Moral education : Some points to ponder. C. Seshadri *Education Quarterly* 34(3) Jl 1982 p 1-4

Morality : Can it be taught. Uma Doraiswamy *Indian Education* 12(7) Oc 1982 p 15-19

The need for ethical and social values in education. Swami

Raghunathananda *J Educational Research and Extension* 20(1) Jl 1983 p 37-84
A new approach to moral development. P.K. Barua *J Indian Education* 5(2) Jl 1979 p 27-30
Problems in moral education. J.V. Joshi *Progress of Education* 57(2) Se 1982 p 31-34 +
Programme form moral education. J.V. Joshi *Progress of Education* 57(5) De 1982 p 98-102 +
Psycho-philosophical perspective of value oriental education. Baqer Mehdi *J Indian Education* 12(2) Jl 1986 p 35-38
Reasons for decreasing importance of values in education. Vibha Premchand *Educational Rev* 87(11) Nv 1981 p 203-05
A quest for values in education. H.B. Majumder *J Indian Education* 8(5) Ja 1983 p 25-29
The school and moral education. Narendarnath Pangotra *Progress of Education* 54(8) Mr 1980 p 154-59
Some issues in moral education. George Lobs *New Frontiers in Education* 10(2) Ap-Je 1980 p 79-96
Some reflections on value education. Abhay Pethe *New Frontiers in Education* 14(1) Ja-Mr 1984 p 51-54
A study of n-Achievement and anxiety of school adolescents with respect to their sex and socio-economic status. S.C. Sahoo and S.K. Panda *Progress of Education* 56(7) Fe 1982 p 165-69 + refs
Teachers and value education : C. Seshadri *New Frontiers in Educaiton* 14(1) Ja-Mr 1984 p 31-37
Techniques of moral education. J.V. Joshi *Progress of Education* 57(6) Ja 1983 p 122-29 +
Value-based education. T.V. Kunnunkal *New Frontiers in Education* 14(1) Ja-Mr 1984 p 19-25
Value-oriented education. Archie J. Bahm *Progress of Education* 56(11) Je 1982 p 256-60; 56(12) Jl 1982 p 284-88+; 57(1) Ag 1982 p 2-7; 57(2) Se 1982 p 26-30
Value-oriented education. C.A. Abraham. *New Frontiers in Education* 9(4) Oc-de 1979 p 41-45
Value-oriented education in schools. Sushma Bhagia *Rajasthan Board J Education* 22(1) Ja-Mr 1986 p 1-7
See also
Religious Education
Student Ethics

Moral Education : Asia
Moral education in Asia. *Teacher Today* 25(2) Oc-De 1982 p 79-94

Moral Education : China (People's Republic)
Socialist moral education in China. Chan Fang *Indian Education* 12(8-9) Nv-De 1982 p 18-19

Moral Education : Curricula
Values and the curriculum. Marlow Ediger *New Frontiers in Education* 12(3) Jl-Se 1982 p 23-27 refs
Values and the curriculum. Marlow Ediger *Research Bulletin* 12(3-4) Se-De 1982 p 3-9

Values : Foundation of curriculum. Saroj Bansal *Educational Rev* 87(4) Ap 1981 p 61-66 refs

Moral Education : India

A comparative study of moral judgement in children. Narendra Pratap Singh *Educational Rev* 90(4) Ap 1984 p 61-65 refs tabs

Moral and religious education in colleges. J. Filellia *New Frontiers in Education* 12(2) Ap-Je 1982 p 1-13 refs

Need for national policy on moral education. N.N. Prahallada *J Indian Education* 10(5) Ja 1985 p 25-28

Value education through children's literature. Indira Kulshreshtha *Education Quarterly* 38(3) Aut 1986 p 18--27

Morale

See also

Teacher Morale

Morales and Literature

See

Literature and Morals

Motivation : Psychological Aspects

See also

Conflict : Psychological Aspects

Need : Psychological Aspects

Risk-taking : Psychological Aspects

Self-actualisation : Psychological Aspects

Motivation in Education

Congnitive complexity and approval motivation. N.K.M. Tripathi *J Education and Psychology* 37(4) Ja 1980 p 225-30 refs

A comparative study of R&D units special reference to motivation involvement and level of aspiration. V.S. Shanthamani *Asian J Psychology and Education* 9(4) 1982 p 1-12

Cultural determinants of motivation. M.K. Tripathi *National J Education* 3(2) Mr 1981 p 24-32 refs

Factor structure of correlates of graphic expression measure of N-achievement among rural children. Satvir Singh *et al Asian J Psychology and Education* 7(2) Jl 1981 p 55-59

Motivators and job satisfaction : A theoretical analysis. Sudesh Gakhar *Indian Educational Rev* 20(3) Jl 1985 p 23-31

Motivation development in the classroom. S.P. Gupta *Educational Review* 87(4) Ap 1981 p 67-68 refs

Motivation in education. K.S. Venkataramu *Educational Rev* 88(3) Mr 1982 p 41-42

Persistence, sex-differences and educational peformance. R.S. Dubey *Asian J Psychology and Education* 9(3) 1982 p 24-29

See also

Achievement Motivation

Motor Ability : Testing

Effect of stress and anxiety on psycho-motor performance. Sunil Abrol *Asian J Psychology and Education* 11(1) 1983 p 32-35

Moving-pictures in Education : India : Andhra Pradesh

A study of the effectiveness of the use of motion pictures as aids in the

Music, Vocal
See
Vocal Music

Music in Education
Importance of music in elementary education. Jagmohan Sharraja *Primary Teacher* 6(3) Jl 1981 p 16-18
The stage and music in primary schools. Sushil Kudesia *Primary Teacher* 5(2) Ap 1980 p 40-42

Musical Education
See
Music : Instruction and Study

Musical Instruction
See
Music : Instruction and Study

Muslim Education
See
Islam : Education

Muslim Women
See
Women : Muslim

Muslims : India : Education
Education of a national minority : A case of the Indian Muslims. Krishnan Dev Sharma. New Delhi, Kalamkar Pra. 263p. Rs.50 *Book Rev, J Indian Education* 5(5) Ja 1980 p 86
Educational survey report on Muslim managed schools and colleges in India with special emphasis on science education. S. Shamim Shah, New Delhi, Hamdard Educ. Soc. 226p. *Book Rev, Education Quarterly* 37(2) Sum 1985 p 69-71

Muslims : India : Uttar Pradesh : Education
Equality of educational opportunity and Muslims. Bishan Swarup Gupta *Indian Educational Rev* 18(2) Ap 1983 p 84-91

Nagaland
See also
Elementary School Teachers : India : Nagaland
Science : Study and Teaching : India : Nagaland

Nagarjuna University
Shri Venkataraman addresses convocation : Nagarjuna University. *University News* 23(18) 8 My 1985 p 9-10

Nanak Dev, Guru : Educational Thought
Educational concepts of Guru Nanak in Japaji Sahib. T.S. Sodhi and Kamaljeet Kaur. Ludhiana, Mukand Pub. 1980, 40p. Rs.5 *Book Rev, J Indian Education* 8(6) Mr 1983 p 76-77

Narsimharao, P.V. : Thoughts
On the front now : an interview with Shri P.V. Narasimha Rao *Teacher Today* 29(1) Jl-se 1986 p 1-8

National Adult Education Programme : India
Concept and objectives of National Adult Education Programme. P.C. Sharma *Progress of Education* 53(12) Jl 1979 p 218-22

Conceptual basis of the National Adult Education Programme. Anand Kashyap *Prasar* 7(3-4) Oc 1980-Ja 1981 p 31-37

An effective approach for the success of adult education programme. Sant Prakash *Education Quarterly* 35(2) Ap 1983 p 12-15

Elites' resistance to NAEP. Markandey Rai and Harikesh Singh *Indian J Adult Education* 42(10) Oc 1981 p 9-10+

Evaluation of National Adult Education Programme. K.G. Rastogi *Indian J Adult Education* 39(11-12) Nv-De 1978 p 53-59 tabs

Evaluation of National Adult Education Programme. P.K. Sahoo *Indian Education* 13(8-9) Nv-De 1983 p 8-11

Implementation of NAEP : A look back. J.D. Sharma *Indian J Adult Education* 40(10-11) Oc-Nv 1979 p 59-63

Implementation of the NAEP (A short review). J.D. Sharma *Indian J Adult Education* 40 (10-11) Oc-Nv 1979 p 52-54

Involvement of teachers and students in the national adult education programme. Raghuveer Singh *Prasar* 7(1-2) Ap-Jl 1980 p 33-38

Language policy in the context of NAEP. G.V. Bhaktapriya *Indian J Adult Education* 40(6) Je 1979 p 25-28 refs

Launching of national adult education programme. *Indian J Adult Education* 39(11-12) Nv-De 1978 p 65-67

NAEP : A strategy. T.R. Nagappa *Indian J Adult Education* 40(7) Jl 1979 p 44-46

NAEP and universal literacy : Some suggestion. R. Singh *Indian J Adult Education* 40(5) My 1979 p 41-43

NAEP and the University Grants Commission. M.L. Mehta *Prasar* 7(1-2) Ap-Jl 1980 p 11-26

NAEP : Conditions for its success. R. Bala Tripura Sundari. *Education Quarterly* 31(3-4) Oc 1979-Ja 1980 p 9-10

NAEP : Some suggestions. N. Kumar *Indian J Adult Education* 40(9) Se 1979 p 31

NAEP : The national and regional objectives. P.C. Sharma *Indian J Adult Education* 40(6) Je 1979 p 42-44

National Adult Education Programme : An appraisal of the first year. *New Frontiers in Education* 10(1) Ja-Mr 1980 p 50-74 refs

National Adult Education Programme : An appraisal. R.K. Bhandari *New Frontiers in Education* 13(2) Ap-Je 1983 p 1-16

National Adult Education Programme and integrated rural development. S.P. Ahluwalia and M.D. Deouskar *Indian J Adult Education* 39(11-12) Nv-De 1978 p 41-49 tabs

National Adult Education Programme and teacher educators : The strategy for implementation. R.N. Patil *Progress of Education* 54(6) Ja 1980 p 98-100

National Adult Education Programme and the role of voluntary organisations. J.D. Sharma *Indian J Adult Education* 39(9) Se 1978 p 38-41

National Adult Education Programme : Strategies of implementation. B.S. Gupta and J.S. Rajput *Education Quarterly* 32(1) Ja 1980 p 1-3

National Adult Education Programme : *vis-a-vis* rural development. P.K. Dongre and Dig Vijai Singh *National J Education* 3(1) Se 1980 p 33-39 refs tabs

National programme for adult education. Gunada Majumdar *Indian J Adult Education* 39(11-12) Nv-De 1978 p 60-64

Non-formal education and the NAEP. A.B. Shah and Susheela Bhan. eds. New Delhi, OUP. 1980, viii, 245p. Rs.65 *Book Rev, Education Quarterly* 33(2) Ap 1981 p 39-40; *J Education and Psychology* 39(3) Oc 1981 p 204; *Progress of Education* 56(5) De 1981 p 122

People's participation in National Adult Education Programme. Baij Nath Singh *Indian J Adult Education* 39(10) Oc 1978 p 3-7

Perceptions of the key functionaries about NAEP - A critical appraisal. G. Haragopal and A. Ravinder *Indian J Adult Education* 41(5) My 1980 p 36+

Quick appraisal of projects under NAEP. S.N. Mehrotra *Indian J Adult Education* 30(10) Oc 1978 p 27-33

The software for the NAEP. V.D. Singh *Indian J Adult Education* 41(1-2) Ja-Fe 1980 p 9-13

Whither the National Adult Education Programme. R. Devadas *Indian J Adult Education* 40(10-11) Oc-Nv 1979 p 21-38

National Adult Education Programme : India : Assam

National Adult Education Programme in Assam. R. Debi *Indian J Adult Education* 40(4) Ap 1979 p 11-15 refs

National Adult Education Programme : India : Audio-Visual Aids

Communication support to the National Adult Education Programme. B.B. Mohanty *Indian J Adult Education* 40(8) Ag 1979 p 30-34

National Adult Education Programme : India : Gujarat

A quick appraisal of the National Adult Education Programme in Gujarat. J.P. Naik *Indian J Adult Education* 40(2) Fe 1979 p 1-4

National Adult Education Programme : India : Tamil Nadu

National Adult Education Programme in Tamil Nadu. R. Gomez *Experiments in Education* 7(9) Nv 1979 p 160-65

National Awards for Teachers : India

National awardee teachers travel abroad. Anil *Primary Teacher* 11(1) Ja 1986 p 4-6

National Commissions for Teachers : India

See

India : National Commissions for Teachers

National Council for Teacher Education

NCTE : An introduction. D.R. Vij *Educational Rev* 88(1) Ja 1982 p 14-17

National Council of Educational Research and Training, New Delhi

NCERT is 20 years old. Bir Singh *Educational Rev* 87(8) Ag 1981 p 148-49

National Development and Adult Education

See

Adult Education and National Development

National Development and Education

See

Education and National Development

National Integration

The concept of national integration. Bharti Basu and V. Rukma Rao *Indian Educational Rev* 14(4) Oc 1979 p 78-85 tabs

National integration : A view point. S.C. Mathur *University News* 23(34) 8 Se 1985 p 3 +

National integration : An analysis. A. Agaiah Acharya *Teacher Education* 14(12-13) Jl-Oc 1980 p 1-8

National integration and the role of Indian academics. Surya Nath Singh *National J Education* 3(2) Mr 1981 p 1-6 refs

National Integration and Education

See

Education and National Integration

National Merit Scholarship Qualifying Tests

Merit list on the basis of 2-scores is not valid. R.D. Godbole *J Higher Education* 9(2) Aut 1983 p 269-71

National Service Scheme

Action research : An integral part of policy and implementation in N.S.S. S.K. Huble and A.S. Jacob *Prasar* 9(1-4) Ap-Ag 1983 p 9-19

Evaluation of NSS programme : Alternative approaches. N.K. Dave *Prasar* 9(1-4) Ap 1982-Ja 1983 p 20-32

NSS : Some issue areas. Mamta Jaitly *Prasar* 9(1-4) Ap 1982-Ja 1983 p 47-50

Preparing training material from ongoing field experience in NSS. N.F. Kailobad *Prasar* 9(1-4) Ap 1982-Ja 1983 p 1-8

National Social Science Documentation Centre, New Delhi

Social Science Documentation Centre. S.P. Agrawal. *Experiments in Education* 10(7) Se 1982 p 129-34

Social Science Documentation Centre. S.P. Agrawal *Experiments in Education* 11(2) Ap 1983 p 34-36

Social Science Documentation Centre. S.P. Agrawal *Experiments in Education* 11(3) My 1983 p 52-54

Social Science Documentation Centre. S.P. Agrawal *Progress of Education* 57(5) De 1982 p 111-14

Social Science Documentation Centre. S.P. Agrawal *J Educational Research and Extension* 19(4) Ap 1983 p 239-48

Social Sciences Documentation Centre. S.P. Agrawal. *Indian J Extension Education* 19(1-2) Je 1983 p 109-11.

Social Science Documentation Centre-ICSSR : Its activities and services. S.P. Agrawal *J Institute of Educational Research* 8(2) My 1984 p 38-44

National Social Science Documentation Centre. S.P. Agrawal. *University News* 24(36) Se 23 1986 p 9-12.

Nationalism and Education

Can education strengthen the cohesive bonds of the nations. R.S. Trivedi *J Education and Psychology* 41(3) Oc 1983 p 168-71

Need : Psychological Aspects

A study of perceived need satisfaction at middle and bottom levels. Asha Nahta *Asian J Psychology and Education* 6(2) Jl 1980 p 8-11 refs

Nehru, Jawaharlal

Jawaharlal Nehru : A internationalist, apostle of peace. S.S. Bhatia *Educational Rev* 90(5-6) My-Je 1984 p 91-93

Nepal

See also

Education : Nepal

Education, Higher : Nepal

Education, Primary : Nepal
Education, Secondary : Nepal

Netherlands

See also

High Schools : Netherlands

Neurosis

Neurosis : Developing a measuring scale. M.P. Unial and A.R. Bisht *J Educational Research and Extension* 16(3) Ja 1980 p 162-67 refs tabs

Neuroticism and extraversion of university student dissidents and nondissidents. B.S. Wadhwa and C.L. Kundu *Asian J Psychology and Education* 14(1-4) 1984 p 52-56 refs

Neurosis : Programmed Instructions

Programmed and expository instructional treatments effectiveness in relation to neuroticism. A. Kumar *J Education and Psychology* 41(1-2) Ap-Je 1983 p 84-87

New Left

See

Right and Left : Political Science Aspects

Newspapers : Kenya

Printing works in a van will publish newspapers in Kenya's rural areas? *J Indian Education* 6(1) My 1980 p 73-75

Nigeria

See also

Adult Education : Nigeria
Adult Education and State : Nigeria
Agricultural Extension Work : Nigeria
Blind : Education : Nigeria
Business Education : Nigeria
College Teachers : Nigeria
Education : Nigeria
Education, Primary : Nigeria
Education, Secondary : Nigeria
Education and State : Nigeria
Illiteracy : Nigeria
Science : Study and Teaching : Nigeria
Teachers : Training : Nigeria
Teaching : Nigeria
Vocational Guidance : Nigeria

Nigeria : Social Conditions

Male-female social relationship in Nigeria : The impact of Western education. Elden U.I. Anwana *J Indian Education* 12(4) Nv 1986 p 59-64 refs

Noise

Anxiety, personality types and sex as the determine of the influence of the noise distractibility in reversal shifts. Ramji Srivastava *Asian J Psycholgy and Education* 4(3) Nv 1979 p 9-13 refs

Personality, noise and performance. R.V.R. Malhotra and Jitendra Mohan *Asian J Psychology and Education* 4(2) Jl 1979 p 27-37

Nutrition : Study and Teaching

Impact of nutritional education imparted to rural house wives under the applied nutrition programme. Neelam Mahajan and S. Bajaj *Indian J Extension Education* 19(3-4) Se-De 1983 p 90-93 tabs

Imparting nutrition education to rural school children : Impact of the dramatisation method. Ajit Randhava *et al Indian Educational Rev* 20(2) Ap 1985 p 1-8

Nutrition education in adult education programme. R.D. Sharma *Indian J Adult Education* 47(7)Jl 1986 p 22-28 refs

Nutrition Extension Work

Gain and retention of nutritional knowledge by the members of ladies Charcha Mandals by the use of selected extension teaching methods. Rajinder Kaur Manchanda and B.S. Hansara *Indian J Extension Education* 19(3-4) Se-De 1983 p 94-96

Nutrition of Children

See

Children : Nutrition

Occult Sciences

See also

Superstition

Occupational Aspirations

See

Vocational Interests

Occupational Mobility : India : Tamil Nadu

Occupational mobility among a special group of scheduled castes in Tamil Nadu : A survey. R. Jayagopal *Indian J Adult Education* 47(1) Ja 1986 p 8-12

Occupational Training

Integration of higher education for effective vocational training. M.R. Bhiday *J Higher Education* 5(3) Spr 1980 p 371-79

Occupations

Construction and standardisation of a two-way classificatory system of occupations. S.S. Chadha *et al J Education and Psychology* 39(3) Oc 1981 p 148-55 refs

One Teacher Schools

See

Single Teacher Schools

Open Classroom Approach to Teaching

See

Open Plan Schools

Open Education

See

Open Plan Schools

Open Plan Schools

Distance teaching. Vatsala Vedantam *University News* 23(11) 16 Mr 1985 p 2-3

The open elementary school : Congnitive and the nomenological correlates. Lee A. Morris *et al Education Quarterly* 32(4) Oc 1980 p 30-34

See also
Individualised Instruction
Open Universities : India
Designing the instructional system for the open university : A perspective. M.B. Menon and Vibha Joshi *University News* 24(42) 8 Nv 1986 p 37-41 refs figs
Open university and gram swaraj. Sandhya Gandhi *Indian Educaiton* 13(8-9) Nv-De 1982 p 5-8
Open university at door step. Pradeep Kumar Srivastava *University News* 23(25) 1 Jl 1985 p 5-7
Open university : Problems and prospects. S. Shreedhara Swamy *Progress of Education* 57(8) Mr 1983 p 170-72 +
The open university system. Biswanath Bhattacharya *Teacher Education* 20(30-31) Ja-Ap 1985 p 11-14
See also
Andhra Pradesh Open University
Oral Interpretation
See also
Story-telling
Oral Reading
A study into the silent versus oral reading performance of good and poor comprehenders. G.C. Ahuja *J Education and Psychology* 37(1) Ap 1979 p 57-61 refs
Originality
Intelligence, fixation, frustration, and economic status as correlates of the originality. R. Bhardawaj and A.D. Sharma *J Education and Psychology* 44(3-4) Jl-De 1986 p '58-61
Orissa
See also
Adoption of Improved Farm Practices : India : Orissa
Adult Education : India : Orissa
Dropouts : India : Orissa
Education, Secondary : India : Orissa
High School Students : India : Orissa
High School Teachers : India : Orissa
High School Teachers : Training : India : Orissa
Libraries, University and College : India : Orissa
Rice : India : Orissa
School Management and Organisation : India : Orissa
Student Teaching : India : Orissa
Students Socio-Economic Status : India : Orissa
Tribes : India : Orissa
Vocational Interests : India : Orissa
Orissa University of Agriculture and Technology
Shri Burney addresses convocation of Orissa University of Agriculture and Technology. *University News* 23(32) 23 Ag 1985 p 8-11
Orthography
See
Spelling Reforms

Osmania University : Administration

The changing pattern of University academic control over affiliated colleges. Mehtab Giri *J Higher Education* 6(1-3) 1980-81 p 151-53

Outside Reading

See

Supplementary Reading

Paired Associates

See

Paired-Association Learning

Paired-Association Learning

Visual and auditory effects on recall performance to individual components of the compound stimulus in paired associate learning. Khan Dildar and Mohammed Ghufram *J Institute of Educational Research* 4(1) Ja 1980 p 8-12 refs tabs

Pakistan

See also

Educational Innovations : Pakistan

Television in Education : Pakistan

Panchayat Raj

See

Panchayats

Panchayats : India : Rajasthan

Role perception and role performance of Sarpancha (Chairman of Gram Panchayats) in Rajasthan. S.I. Intodia and G.S. Shaktawat *Indian J Extension Education* 16(1-2) Je 1980 p 64-68 tabs

Panjab University

Giani Zail Singh addresses convocation of Panjab University. *University News* 23(23) 16 Je 1985 p 7-8

Parent and Child

Correlates of chidren's attitudes towards their parents. A.K. Sarkar *Quest in Education* 19(1) Ja 1982 p 21-34 refs tabs

Children and parental role perception. B.P. Lulla *Progress of Education* 53(4) Nv-De 1978 p 79-85

The role of parents in moulding the child's behaviour. Sarla Rajput *Primary Teacher* 5(3) Jl 1980 p 31-35

See also

Conflict of Generations

Parent-Student Counsellor Relationships

Impact of parents vocations and education upon the interest of pupils. K.M. Shah *J Education and Psychology* 44(3-4) Jl-De 1986 p 153-57

Parent-Teacher Relationships

Attitude of parents towards English medium and non-English medium schools. J.S. Jha *J Educational Research and Extension* 16(2) Oc 1979 p 115-24 refs

What parent want, Mr. Teacher : A study? Bir Singh *Educational Review* 86(8) Ag 1980 p 145-50

Chand Bhadwal *J Indian Education* 12(3) Se 1986 p 23-29 refs tabs

See also

College and School Periodicals

Under the title of individual periodicals

Periodicals : Education

See

College and School Periodicals

Under the titles of individual periodical e.g. Indian Educational Review (Periodical)

Personality

Contributions to the concept of a dissociative personality. S.N. Dhondiyal *National J Education* 3(1) Se 1980 p 55-74 refs

Differential personality factors of high and low feedback acceptance groups in micro-teaching. Kamala Rai and Pretty Gandhi *J Institute of Educational Research* 4(1) Ja 1980 p 33-36 refs tabs

The effect of personality trait variation on the intensity of problems of girls. B.G. Sudha and Lalitha V. Tirth *J Education and Psychology* 37(2) Jl 1979 p 103-14 refs

Effects of sex, training and experience on the personality development of teachers. S.K. Pande and R.K. Mishra *Indian Educational Rev* 18(4) Oc 1983 p 106-10

Musical preference in relation to discrimination between notes and certain personality variables. Aruna Suri and S.P. Suri *J Education and Psychology* 36(3) Oc 1978 p 123-32 refs

Personality correlates of approval motive. Narendra K.M. Tripathi and Devendra K.M. Tripathi *J Educational Psychology* 40(3) Oc 1982 p 143-46

Personality : Marxist concepts and practices. Sukumar Bose *Our Education* 5 Jl 1984 p 47-53 refs

Personality, noise and performance. R.V.R. Malhotra and Jitendra Mohan *Asian J Psychology and Education* 4(2) Jl 1979 p 27-37 refs

Problem levels and personality patterns. R.K. Arora *J Indian Education* 8(6) Mr 1983 p 13-19 refs

Relationship between personality of the heads of institutions and organisational climate of their schools. Sheshi Kala Deshpande *J Education and Psychology* 43(1) Ap 1985 p 44-49

Sociometric approach to personality. S.K. Shukla *J Institute of Educational Research* 7(2) My 1983 p 24-30

A study of anxiety in relation to parental acceptance and peer acceptance. G. Ansari and Z. Rahman *J Education and Psychology* 39(3) Oc 1981 p 189-96

A study of interest and personality patterns of successful men in different occupation. S.P. Sinha *Indian Educational Rev* 15(4) Oc 1980 p 66-70

See also

Frustration

Personality Assessment

Rigidity : Psychological Aspects

Personality, Disorders of

See also

Frustration

Personality and Academic Achievement

An investigation into the effect of teachers sex on the students achievement in science. Harbana Singh *J Education and Psychology* 41(1-2) Ap-Jl 1983 p 64-66

Relationship between personality factors and academic achievement of students. Arvinda Chandra and Raj Kala Kundu *J Educational Research and Extension* 18(1) Jl 1981 p 1-7 refs

A study of personality trait differences of low and high achiever students of higher secondary. G.N. Prakash Srivastava and Rajeswari Dubey *J Education and Psychology* 40(3) Oc 1982 p 149-51

Personality and Intelligence

See also

Personality and Academic Achievement

Personality Assessment

College teachers compared with engineers, doctors, and lawyers in personality factors. J. Stephen and S. Satthiagirirajan *J Educational Research and Extension* 18(3) Ja 1982 p 187-90 refs tabs

Comparison of the personality profiles of over, under and equal achiever. S. Chatterji and M. Mukherjee *J Education and Psychology* 43(1) Ap 1985 p 14-21 refs

Concept of social intelligence. P.K. Ganguli *Quest in Education* 17(2) Ap 1980 p 188-94

Generation gap : A comparative study of parent and children on a measure of authoritarianism. T.N. Raina *Indian Educational Rev* 19(2) Ap 1984 p 37-50

A study of the personality profiles of teachers and pupil-teachers. V.K.D. Tripathi *J Education and Psychology* 36(1-2) Ap-Je 1978 p 63-70

See also

Personality Tests

Personality Diagnosis

See

Personality Assessment

Personality Tests

A comparative study of engineers, doctors, and university teachers in relation to intelligence, level of frustration, extraversion introversion and neuroticism. M.L. Lidhoo *Indian Educational Rev* 17(2) Ap 1982 p 108-18 refs

Projective inventory : A new approach to personality assessment. Biranchi N. Puhan and Pratap K. Rath *Asian J Psychology and Education* 7(1) Ja 1981 p 16-24

See also

Rosschach Test

Personnel Management

See also

Incentives in Industry

Interviews and Interviewing

Personnel Records in Education

See also

Grading and Marking (Students)

Personnel Service in Education

Counselling in personnel and guidance service in schools. S.P. Anand *Education Quarterly* 32(3) Jl 1980 p 5-9 refs

Group guidance programme in schools. S.P. Anand *J Indian Education* 9(1) My 1983 p 31-37

Guidance and counselling. Prem Pasricha *New Frontiers in Education* 11(4) Oc-De 1981 p 46-47; 12(1) Ja-Mr 1982 p 1-36

Guidance for slow learners in school. S.P. Anand *Our Education* 3-4 Jl 1983 p 47-57 refs

Guidances in primary school : A felt need. *Primary Teacher* 10(4) Oc 1985 p 1-5

Guidance services at primary school level : Some suggestions. Ashok K. Kalia *Educational Rev* 92(1) Ja 1986 p 5-6

Guiding creative talent : The role of the counseller. Khorshed A. Wadia *J Indian Education* 8(4) Nv 1982 p 15-19 refs

In the guest of guidance in education. S.P. Anand *Education Quarterly* 33(3) Jl 1981 p 8-11 refs

The need for guidance services at primary stage. Daya Pant *Primary Teacher* 9(4) Oc 1984 p 5-7

Organisation of guidance services in schools. M. Raghuram Singh *Experiments in Education* 9(5) Jl 1981 p 77-82

See also

Counselling
Dropouts
Group Guidance in Education
Parent-student Counsellor Relationships
Teacher Participation in Personnel Service
Vocational Guidance

Personnel Service in Education : India

Problems in the dissemination of educational and occupational information to secondary school pupils. Perin H. Mehta *J Indian Education* 5(6) Mr 1980 p 52-57 refs

Personnel Service in Higher Education : India

Guidance and counselling in colleges and universities. S.K. Kochhar. New Delhi, Sterling. 1984, 462p. Rs. 26 *Book Rev, J Indian Education* 10(5) Ja 1985 p 53-55

Philippines

See also

Adult Education, Rural : Philippines
Education, Higher : Philippines
Educational Innovations : Philippines
Population : Study and Teaching : Philippines

Philosophers

See also

Russell, Bertrand

Philosophers : Indian

See also

Krishnamurti, J.

Philosophy
See also
Consciousness
Philosophy : Curricula
Philosophy in the school curriculum. Marlow Ediger *J Indian Education* 6(5) Ja 1981 p 13-16
Philosophy : Indian
Impact of Indian thought in developing a value pattern in education. L.K. Oad *J Indian Education* 6(3) Ja 1981 p 8-12
Philosophy of Teaching
See
Education : Philosophy
Photography in Education
Discover the power of photography in working with handicapped children. Jyan Nath *Our Education* 5 Jl 1984 p 55-58
The use of still photography as learning assistance for the language handicapped in the classroom. Jyan Nath *Our Education* 6 Jl 1985-86 p 27-30
Physical Education and Training
Mass media for promotion of sports and physical education. P.D. Sharma *Primary Teacher* 11(2) Ap 1986 p 28-30
Statistics in physical education. K.J. Srinivasan *Experiments in Education* 8(4) Je 1980 p 71-74
Teaching physical sciences in secondary schools. S.K. Gupta. New Delhi, Sterling. 1981, vi, 184p. *Book Rev, J Indian Education* 8(2) Jl 1982 p 92-93
See also
Posture
Physical Education and Training : Developing Countries
Physical education and sport in the developing countries. I.A. Salama *Student Action* 2(2) Je 1983 p 10-11 +
Physical Education and Training : India
Physical education and sports programming in schools. Agya Jit Singh *J Indian Education* 8(1) My 1982 p 56-60
The role of mass media in the promotion of sports and physical education in the country. P.D. Sharma *Progress of Education* 61(4-5) Nv-De 1986 p 89-91
Physical Education and Training : Primary
Physical education and primary school curriculum. Satish Kumar Yadav *Primary Teacher* 5(1) Ja 1980 p 4-7
Physical education in primary schools. Neerja Shukla *Primary Teacher* 5(1) Ja 1980 p 8-10
Physical Education and Training : Russia
The system of physical education in the USSR. G.I. Kukushkin, *ed.* Moscow, Roduge Pub. 1983, 321p. Rs. 6.25 *Book Rev, Progress of Education* 60(10-11) My-Je 1986 p 256
Physical Training
See
Physical Education and Training

Physically Handicapped Children : Education

They need your help. Subhash Chandra Agarwal *Educational Review* 87(1) Ja 1981 p 1-3 refs

Physics : Ability Testing

Construction of diagnostics test in physics for class VII. V.K. Gautam *Indian Education* 11(4) Jl 1981 p 22-23

Construction of an achievement test in physics. V.T. Deshpande and V.K. Gautam *Progress of Education* 35(6) Ja 1981 p 165-66 refs

Physics : Philosophy

Eistein and the philosophical problems of 20th century physics. Sargal Syrovalkin, Tr. Moscow, Progress Pub. 1983, 508p. Rs.11.25 *Book Rev, Teacher Today* 27(4) Ap-Je 1985 p 148-49

Physics : Study and Teaching

Cognition of learning or definitions of physical concepts. J.K. Mohapatra *J Education and Psychology* 44(3-4) Jl-De 1986 p 118-23

An experiment with individually guided system of instruction in physics. Lalit Kishore *Experiments in Education* 13(12) Fe 1986 p 211-14 refs

Integration on physics education. S.K. Gupta *J Indian Education* 11(2) Jl 1985 p 64-66

Physics and its applications : Some teaching experiments. M.V. Ananthakrishnan *J Higher Education* 5(3) Spr 1980 p 351-57 refs tabs

Retenties of subject matter in physics : Individualised system of instruction and lecture model. Lalit Kishore *J Indian Education* 10(5) Ja 1985 p 40-43 refs

Physics : Study and Teaching : Secondary

An investigation into the diagnostic study of the remedial programme with a view to identifying the conceptual errors and gaps in the learning of thermal expansion in standard IX, physics. R. Sukumaron Nair *Experiments in Education* 11(5) Jl 1983 p 75-79 refs tabs

An investigation into the relative effectiveness of inductively and deductively sequenced modes of teacher-centred presentation in secondary school physics. R. Sukumaron Nair *Experiments in Education* 12(7) Se 1984 p 113-23; 12(8) Oc 1984 p 138-39 refs tabs

Teaching physics at the higher secondary stage : A study. S. Swetharonyam *Experiments in Education* 9(10) De 1981 p 169-72

Piaget, Jean

Cognitio-affecto development of high school students : Piagetian perspective. T.S. Sandhu *Indian Educational Rev* 20(3) Jl 1986 p 32-36

Developing primary school science curriculum based on Piage's theory. R.P. Singh *Primary Teacher* 6(2) Ap 1981 p 12-15

Development of Piagetian operational comprehension among school adolescents. G.S. Sodhi and Tejinder Mohini *J Institute of Educational Research* 10(3) Se 1986 p 21-23 refs

Jean Piget : A tribute; editorial. *J Indian Education* 6(3) Se 1980 p 1-2

Jean Piaget on congnitive development of child. D.N. Prakash Srivastava *Asian J Psychology and Education (Special)* 10(1-4) 1982 p 40-44 refs

Piaget : A reappraisal in an educational perspective. S.M. Menon *New Frontiers in Education* 13(4) Oc-De 1983 p 1-6 ft-n

Piaget in the context of primary education. A.B. Saxena *Primary Teacher*

5(3) Jl 1980 p 10-17 tabs
Piaget on play. G.N. Prakash Srivastava *Primary Teacher* 10(3) Jl 1985 p 5-9
The Piagetian journey from Molluska through Mohpets to Methaphor, 1896-1980. N. Vaidya *Indian Educational Rev* 15(4) Oc 1980 p 1-14 refs ft-n
Piagetian theory and teaching of history. V.K. Raina *J Indian Education* 5(1) My 1979 p 54-58
Piaget's developmental psychology and its implication in the teaching of sciences. Shajehan Siddique *Educational Rev* 92(7) Jl 1986 p 113-14 refs
Piaget's views on learning. Karuna Shankar Misra *J Indian Education* 6(3) Se 1980 p 3-8 refs
Piaget's work and the learning of science. R.C. Jain *Teacher Today* 28(3) Ja-Mr 1986 p 31-36 refs

Picture Books for Children
Impact of pictorials on children. V.M. Mohanraj *Primary Teacher* 10(1) Ja 1985 p 28-31
NBT's gift to preschoolers. R. Muralidharan *Primary Teacher* 11(2) Ap 1986 p 31-32
See also
Illustrated Books : Children

Planned Parenthood
See
Family Planning

Planning, Curriculum
See
Curriculum Planning

Planning, Educational
See
Educational Planning

Plato : Educaational Thought
Platonic system of education. D. Bhaskara Rao *Educational Rev* 39(4) Ap 1983 p 68-71

Play
Authority and freedom in play. K. Rajagopalan *Primary Teacher* 8(3) Jl 1983 p 9-11
Importance of play for creativity. Girijesh Kumar *Primary Teacher* 10(1) 1985 p 14-15
Let our children play and learn. Jagannath Mohanty *Primary Teacher* 9(2) Ap 1984 p 19-20
Piaget on play. G.M. Prakash Srivastava *Primary Teacher* 10(3) Jl 1985 p 5-9
See also
Drama in Education

Playgrounds
See also
Vacation Schools

Poland
See also
Youth : Poland
Political Parties
See also
Right and Left : Political Science Aspect
Political Science
See also
Right and Left : Political Science Aspect
Political Science : Study and Teaching : India
Discipline of political science in India. G. Banerjee *University News* 23(11) 16 Mr 1985 p 6-7
Politics : Practical
See also
Teachers : Political Activity
Politics and Education
Education for political leadership. R.N. Vyas. Ambika Pub. 1976, 92p. Rs. 30 *Book Rev, Teacher Today* 22(2) Oc-de 1979 p 91-92
Politicisation of education. Kokila S. Thangasamy *Indian Educaiton* 12(3-4) Je-Jl 1982 p 17-19
Politics and education. B.S. Hundal *Educational Rev* 89(5-6) My-Je 1983 p 99-100
Politics and Education : India
Education and political culture in India : The limits of schooling system and political socialisation. Ehsanul Haq. New Delhi, Sterling. 1981, 174p. Rs.60 *Book Rev, Indian Educational Rev* 17(2) Ap 1982 p 136-37; *J Indian Education* 8(1) My 1982 p 79-80; *Teacher Today* 24(4) Ap-Je 1982 p 137-38
Politics and Students
See
Students : Political Activity
Pollution
See also
Noise Pollution
Population
Population growth : Ecology and environment pollution. S. Sreedhara Swamy *Indian Education* 13(12) Mr 1984 p 16-18
Searching links between population, family size and quality of life. Ramesh Chandra *Teacher Today* 27(1) Jl-Se 1984 p 49-58
A study of pre-university students awareness of population problems. Manohar Deshmukh *Experiments in Education* 8(10) De 1980 p 188-89
See also
Family Planning
Population : Study and Teaching
Developing population education programme for teacher training colleges. Ramesh Chandra *Teacher Education* 13(8-9) Jl-Oc 1979 p 62-69 refs
Dimensions of population education. I. Satya Sundaram *Education Quarterly* 35(2) Ap 1983 p 16-19 ft-n
Education for parenthood in the 80's. Satya Swadeshi *Educational Rev*

86(5) My 1980 p 90-91

Effective communication in population education. Chandrakala Dave *Progress of Education* 60(3) Nv 1985 p 81-82+

Health and population education. S.M. Singh, *ed.* Varanasi, BHU. 1979, 187p. Rs. 35 *Book Rev, J Indian Education* 7(3) Se 1979 p 60

A macroscopic view of population education. T. Das *Educational Rev* 92(4) Ap 1986 p 70-71 refs

Material production for out of school population education. Ansar Ali Khan *Indian J Adult Education* 43(7) Jl 1982 p 3-8 refs

Need and scope of population study. G. Thangavelu *Experiments in Education* 8(8) Oc 1980 p 148-52 tabs

Population and population education in India. B.S. Parakh *Teacher Education* 18(22-23) Ja-Ap 1983 p 20-30

Population education : A contemporary concern. Unesco. 1978, 118p. *Book Rev, Teacher Today* 21(4) Ap-Je 1979 p 86-87

Population education and school curriculum. K.T. Mamtora *Educational Rev* 84(11) Nv 1978 p 207-09

Population education and the new secondary school. V.S. Mathur *J Indian Education* 12(3) Se 1986 p 3-5

Population education : Concepts and aims. H. Visvesvaran *Experiments in Education* 7(6) Ag 1979 p 95-102

Population education corner : A promising innovation. Saroj Yadav *Primary Teacher* 10(2) Ap 1985 p 1-3

Population education for developing countries. K.R. Sarkar. New Delhi, Sterling. 1986, 224p. Rs.125 *Book Rev, Education Quarterly* 38(3) Aut 1986 p 51-52; *J Institute of Educational Research* 10(1) Ja 1986 p 32

Population education for national reconstruction. D.K. Chadha and V.P. Singh *J Indian Education* 6(6) Mr 1981 p 42-45

Population education for quality of life. M.M. Mascarenhas. New Delhi, Oxf-IBH. 362p. Rs.54 *Book Rev, New Frontiers in Education* 12(3) Jl-Se 1982 p 77-79

Population education for rural adults. H.D. Dwarakanath *Education Quarterly* 31(3-4) Oc 1979-Ja 1980 p 11-12

Population education in education institutes. Purnima Sharma *Rajasthan Board J Education* 22(1) Ja-Mr 1986 p 8-17

Population education. R.G. Kothari *Educational Rev* 89(9) Se 1983 p 159-61

Population education - The problem of teacher orientation. V.S. Mathur *Education Quarterly* 34(3) Jl 1982 p 5-8

Population growth : Role of education. V.S. Mathur *Rajasthan Board J Education* 16(4) Oc-De 1980 p 14-20

Psycho-social aspects of population education. M. Sreeramamruthy *Progress of Education* 59(5) De 1984 p 99-102+

Renewed relevance of population education. V.S. Mathur *J Indian Education* 5(2) Jl 1979 p 52-55

A scale to measure teachers attitude towards population education in secondary schools. Neelam Srivastava and Devki Tewari *J Education and Psychology* 41(1-2) Ap-Jl 1983 p 30-36

School teachers role in national population education programme. Manohar

deshmukh *Indian Education* 11(6) Se 1981 p 20-23

Socio-psychological implications in population education. Rajani R. Shirur *Experiments in Education* 8(1) Mr 1980 p 14-15

Population : Study and Teaching : Bangladesh

Population education curriculum development in Bangladesh. Abu Hamid Latif *Rajasthan Board J Education* 16(1-2) Ja-Je 1980 p 1-3

Population : Study and Teaching : Curricula

Curriculum for population education. R.S. Sharma *Rajasthan Board J Education* 15(2) Ap-Je 1979 p 1-12 refs

Curriculum innovation through population education. J.E. Jayasuriya. Colombo, Associated Educ Pub. 1978, 121p. Rs.45; £3 *Book Rev, Indian Educational Rev* 14(4) Oc 1979 p 145-46

Population : Study and Teaching : India

Coordination between education and population policies : A case study of India. S.P. Chawla. New Delhi, NCERT 1978, 151p. *Book Rev, Education Quarterly* 31(2) Jl 1979 p 43

In-school population education programme in India. M. Ubaidullah *Educational Rev* 92(7) Jl 1986 p 103-04

Indian population situation and population education. D.P. Jain *Rajasthan Board J Education* 19(1) Ja-Mr 1983 p 17-21

Introduction of population education as a subject in secondary schools. G. Thangavelu *Experiments in Education* 8(9) Nv 1980 p 166-72 refs tabs

School teachers role in national population education programme. Manohar Deshmukh *J Education and Psychology* 41(1-2) Ap-Jl 1983 p 43-46

A study of the attitude of secondary school teachers during and after emergency period towards the need of population education. Neelam Srivastava and Devaki Tewari *J Education and Psychology* 37(2) Jl 1979 p 115-20 refs tabs

Training methodology of population education for NAEP functionaries. M. Ubaidullah *Educational Rev* 89(10) Oc 1983 p 165-68

Population : Study and Teaching : Philippines

Population education in the Philippines. Remedios M. Cayari *Rajasthan Board J Education* 16(1-2) Ja-Je 1980 p 65-71

Posture

Posture education in Indian schools. P.D. Sharma *J Indian Education* 7(2) Jl 1979 p 48-51

Poultry : India : Tamil Nadu

Spatial distribution of poultry farms and constraints in poultry development. G. Ayyadurai and A. John Bright. *Indian J Extension Education* 17(3-4) Se-de 1981 p 103-06 tab

Time lag in adoption of poultry farming. R. Subramaniam *et al Indian J Extension Education* 16(1-2) Je 1980 p 59-60

Power : Psychological Aspects

See

Control : Psychological Aspects

Prediction of Creative Ability

Nature and concepts of regression analysis and prediction. Z.M. Quraishi *Quest in Education* 16(3) Jl 1979 p 195-201

Prediction of Scholastic Success

Prediction of success in Bachelor's degree examinations in arts, science, and commerce. Shashi Lata Kaushik and Atmanand Sharma *Indian Educational Rev* 14(4) Oc 1979 p 128-44 appdx

Structure of intellect abilities as predictors of achievement in tenth grade algebra. C.P.S. Chauhan *Indian Educational Rev* 19(2) Ap 1984 p 19-27

Security-insecurity, adjustment, socio-economic status and family structure as the predictors of academic achievement of intermediate students. S.K. Jindal and Netranand Pradhan *Indian Educational Rev* 18(4) Oc 1983 p 58-65

Premchand, Munshi

Premchand. Nagendera, *ed.* Delhi, Bansal and Co. 221p. Rs.80 *Book Rev, Education Quarterly* 35(2) Ap 1983 p 77-79

Premchand, Munshi : Educational Thought

Premchand on education. *Primary Teacher* 5(4) Oc 1980 p 33-34

Preschool Education

See

Education, Preschool

Primary Education

See

Education, Primary

Primary School Students

See

School Children

Principal-Teacher Relationships

See

Teacher-principal's Relationships

Principals : High School

See

High School Principals

Principals : School

See

School Superintendents and Principals

Private Schools

See also

Boarding Schools

Private Schools : India

Coaching institutions in India. A survey. Satvir Singh *J Indian Education* 8(4) Nv 1982 p 33-40 refs tabs

A note on the private sector in education. Mathew Zachariah *Indian Educational Rev* 15(1) Ja 1980 p 104-09

Private agencies and minority institutions. John Villamattam *New Frontiers in Education* 10(3) Jl-Se 1980 p 67-70

Private agencies in Indian education. T.A. Mathias *New Frontiers in Education* 10(3) Jl-Se 1980 p 59-66

Probation Officers

Personality patterns of officers of correctional adminstration and faculty members. N. Muthiah *Experiments in Education* 10(6) Ag 1982 p 99-101 refs

Problem Children

Helping the maladjusted child. Denis H. Scott. Milton Kegnes. Open Univ. Press. 126p. *Book Rev, Education Quarterly* 35(3) Jl 1983 p 54-57

Reduction of abusive behaviour as a function of types of reinforcement in scheduled and non-scheduled caste children. Pradeep Kumar Khattri and Prabha Gupta *J Educational and Psychology* 37(4) Ja 1980 p 255-62 refs tabs

Some adjustment traits of behavioural problem students. V.D. George and H. Somsananda Raj *J Institute of Educational Research* 7(3) Se 1983 p 38-42

Professional Education

Evaluation in professional courses. Santosh Sharma *J Indian Education* 12(1) My 1986 p 49-51

On selection of candidates for professional education. B.K. Bhattacharya *J Higher Education* 8(3) Spr 1983 p 290-96

Students problems in different streams of profession courses : A comparative study. R.K. Arora *J Education and Psychology* 44(2-3) Jl-De 1986 p 96-104

Professional Education of Women : India

Trends in professional education among women. S.C. Seddey *J Higher Education* 8(3) Spr 1983 p 327-34

See also

Medical Education for Women

Professions

See also

Agriculture as a Profession

Professors

See

College Teachers

Programmed Instruction

Anxiety and step size as correlates of performance through programmed instruction. Harish Chandra Sharma and Malvindar Ahuja *J Education and Psychology* 36(4) Ja 1979 p 173-79

The effect of schedules of reinforcement and extroversion on programmed instruction achievement. R.F. Sharma and M.N. Verma *Indian Educational Rev* 14(4) Oc 1979 p 33-42 refs tab

Effects of achievement motivation on learning outcomes following programmed instructional material. B.D. Verma *Indian Educational Rev* 20(3) Jl 1985 p 37-46

Effects of immediate and delayed feedback on performance in programmed instruction. B.P. Verma *J Institute of Educational Research* 7(2) My 1983 p 20-23

An experimental study of programmed instruction method of teaching chemistry on high and low achievers. Arun Kumar Gupta and Pramod Kumar Gupta *J Education and Psychology* 36(4) Ja 1979 p 186-91

An experimentation in the use of programmed learning material for revision purpose. D.N. Sansanwal *Experiments in Education* 7(6) Ag 1979 p 109-10+

Programmed instruction (PI) : Significance and implications. M. Malla Reddy

See also
Adjustment : Psychological Aspects
Adolescent : Psychological Aspects
Attitude : Psychological Aspects
Cognition
Concepts
Consciousness
Control : Psychological Aspects
Educational : Psychological Aspects
Extraversion
Gestatt : Psychological Aspects
Hostility : Psychological Aspects
Human Behaviour
Intellect
Interest : Psychological Aspects
Memory
Motivation : Psychological Aspects
Perception
Personality
Risk Taking : Psychological Aspects
Social : Psychological Aspects

Psychology : Experiments
See also
Psychology, Experimental

Psychology, Applied
See also
Clinical Psychology

Psychology, Child
See
Child Study

Psychology, Clinical
See
Clinical Psychology

Psychology, Comparative
See also
Play

Psychology, Educational
See
Educational Psychology

Psychology, Experimental

Experimenter expectancy effect and internal-external locus of control of experimenters and subject. Hamida Akhtar Begum, and Manfura Shams *Asian J Psychology and Education* 7(2) Jl 1981 p 27-33 refs

The verification of Fachner's law by method of equal appearing intervals : Some problems. P.H. Lodi *Asian J Psychology and Education* 4(3) Nv 1979 p 23-30

Psychology, Industrial

Attitude towards work environment and its relation with personality traits and choice of leisure time activities among a group of executives. Anima Sen

Rural Youth Club : India : Punjab
Student Teaching : India : Punjab
Students : India : Punjab
Teachers : India : Punjab
Teachers Colleges : India : Punjab
Television in Agriculture : India : Punjab
Veterinarians : India : Punjab
Village Level Workers : India : Punjab
Women in Agriculture : India : Punjab

Punjabi University : Examinations

Toppers in the post-graduate examinations of Punjabi University : A study. T.R. Sharma *Indian Educational Rev* 19(1) Ja 1984 p 1-17

Punjabrao Krishi Vidyapeeth, Akola

Evaluation of foundation course organised by Punjabrao Krishi Vidyapeeth, Akola for village development officers under T & V system. O.P. Ingle *et al* *Indian J Extension Education* 19(1-2) Mr-je 1983 p 41-45

Pupil-Teacher Relationships

See
Teacher-student Relationships

Puppets and Puppet-plays in Education

Pupils creativity in different types of institutional climates. Arun K. Gupta and Suresh K. Sharma *J Indian Education* 6(3) Ja 1981 p 27-33 refs

Use of puppets as audio-visual aids. Naresh Kumar *Primary Teacher* 8(3) Jl 1983 p 29-30

Questioning

Putting questions in the classroom. N.K. Jangira *Primary Teacher* 6(3) Jl 1981 p 19-21

Value of open ended evaluation. Gomathi Mani *Experiments in Education* 9(7) Se 1981 p 125-27

Questionnaires

Construction of a locus of control questionaire. Ved Prakash *J Indian Education* 6(1) My 1980 p 53-57 refs tabs

Questions and Answers

Blue print in designing test. Subhash Chandra Moharana Experiments in Education 8(7) Se 1980 p 119-23 refs tabs

Facility value and discrimination index of supply type questions. V. Natarajan and Ved Prakash *Indian Educational Rev* 15(2) Ap 1980 p 102-08

How good are long answer questions : A lay man's analysis. Haribhai G. Desai *Asian J Psychology and Education* 4(2) Jl 1979 p 38-45 tabs

Internal vs-external choices in question-papers. Lokesh K. Verma *J Indian Education* 6(1) My 1980 p 21-25

Scoring objectives type items : A new method. Ved Prakash *Indian Educational Rev* 20(4) Oc 1985 p 143-50

A short training programme in question-writing for college teachers. D. Raja Ganesan *J Higher Education* 5(2) Aut 1979 p 255-60

Toward building up a question bank. G. Subramaniam *Experiments in Education* 7(7) Se 1979 p 113-17

See also
Examinations

Radio and Women
See also
Radio Programms for Women

Radio Education
See
Radio in Education

Radio in Adult Education
Role of the radio and newspaper in R/A OP. B. Malikarjun *Indian J Adult Education* 40(3) Mr 1979 p 43-45
See also
Educational Broadcasting in Adult Education

Radio in Agriculture
Factors associated with effectiveness of farm broadcast. S.N. Pandey and N.K. Roy *Indian J Extension Education* 14(1-2) Ja-Je 1978 p 54-56
A study of the farm school on the air. R. Sundarajan *et al Indian J Extension Education* 14(1-2) Ja-Je 1978 p 48-49

Radio in Agriculture : India : Assam
Listening behaviour of the radio owning farmers in Assam. R.K. Talukdar and S.S. Pawar *Indian J Extension Education* 18(1-2) Je 1982 p 90-91

Radio in Agriculture : India : Punjab
Farmers opinion about the rural broadcast of AIR Jullundar, Punjab. G.S. Momi *et al Indian J Extension Education* 19(1-2) Mr-Je 1983 p 87-91 tabs

Radio in Agriculture : India : Tamil Nadu
Small farmers preference for radio programmes and modes of their presentation. A. John Knight and D. Somesundaram *Indian J Extension Education* 16(3-4) De 1980 p 90-93 tabs

Radio in Education
Distance education. Gunvant B. Shah *Teacher Today* 24(1) Jl-Se 1981 p 16-20
Instruction through radio vision : A comparative study. Motilal Sharma and Meena Oberai *Indian Educational Rev* 18(4) Oc 1983 p 37-46
Radio and school education. S.M Mehta *Teacher today* 21(3) Ja-Mr 1979 p 39-43
Radio for educational development. Dean T. Jamison and Emile G. Mcananny. London, Sage Pub. 1985, 221p. 14 *Book Rev, J Indian Education* 12(2) Jl 1986 p 62
Radio for formal education and for development communication. *J Indian Education* 5(1) My 1979 p 76-79
Radio for non-formal education. Neena Oberai *Progress of Education* 55(2) Jl 1981 p 335-37 +
Radio vision as an educational medium. Motilal Sharma *Indian Education* 12(10) Ja 1983 p 17-20
Radio vision in and out of the classroom. Motilal Sharma and Neena Oberai *Education Quarterly* 34(2) Ap 1982 p 17-21
Radiovision in biology class : An exploratory study. Motilal Sharma and C.K. Tripathi *Progress of Education* 55(2) Se 1980 p 45-50

Using radio for classroom instruction. *J Indian Education* 5(1) My 1979 p 78-80

See also

Educational Broadcasting

Educational Broadcasting in Adult Education

Radio in Adult Education

Radio in Education : India : Gujarat

A study of school broadcasts in Gujarat. D.R. Goel *Educational Rev* 85(11) Nv 1979 p 203-05

Radio in Education : India : Haryana

Students and school broadcasts in Gujarat. D.R. Goel *Progress of Education* 54(3) Oc 1979 p 50-58

Radio Programmes for Women

Content analysis of Tiranjan programme of AIR Jullunder. D.K. Sandhu and A.N. Shukla *Indian J Extension Education* 17(3-4) Se-De 1981 p 7-16 refs

Rajasthan

See also

Adoption of Improved Farm Practices : India : Rajasthan

Adult Education : India : Rajasthan

Adult Education, Rural : India : Rajasthan

Agricultural Extension Work : India : Rajasthan

Agricultural Extension Workers : India : Rajasthan

Agricultural Innovations : India : Rajasthan

Agriculture : India : Rajasthan

Agriculture : Information Services : India : Rajasthan

Children, First-born : India : Rajasthan

College Students : India : Rajasthan

Correspondence Schools and Courses : India : Rajasthan

Education : India : Rajasthan

Education, Higher : India : Rajasthan

Education, Primary : India : Rajasthan

Education, Secondary : India : Rajasthan

Education and State : India : Rajasthan

Educational Administration : India : Rajasthan

Educational Research : India : Rajasthan

High School Teachers : India : Rajasthan

Higher Education of Women : India : Rajasthan

Home Economics : Study and Teaching : India : Rajasthan

Panchayat : India : Rajasthan

Mathematics : Study and Teaching : India : Rajasthan

School Children : India : Rajasthan

School Management and Organisation : India : Rajasthan

Students : India : Rajasthan

Teachers : India : Rajasthan

Teachers : Training : India : Rajasthan

Vacation Schools : India : Rajasthan

Vocational Interests : India : Rajasthan

Women : India : Rajasthan

Rajasthani Literature

History of Rajasthani literature. Hiralal Maheshwari. New Delhi, Sahitya Acad, 187p. Rs.25 *Book Rev, Education Quarterly* 33(3) Jl 1981 p 49-50

Ramayana, The

The *Ramayana* tradition in Asia. V. Raghavan, ed. New Delhi, Sahitya Acad. 1980, 707p. Rs.75 *Book Rev, Education Quarterly* 34(1) Ja 1982 p 51-52

Ranchi University : Students

Sterotypes of tribal students of Ranchi University towards people of fifteen old Indian states. Pushpa Chandra *Asian J Psychology and Education* 4(1) Ja 1979 p 14-20

Rating of Students

See

Students, Rating of

Rating of Teachers

See

Teachers, Rating of

Readers and Libraries

See

Libraries and Readers

Reading

Dynamic reading skills. Venkata Iyer. New Delhi, Sterling. vi, 175p. Rs.70 *Book Rev, Education Quarterly* 38(3) Aut 1986 p 61-62

The effectiveness of two different methods of teaching reading in primary school children. S. Subramanyam *Experiments in Education* 8(10) De 1980 p 185-87 refs

A group experiment in teaching reading to beginners. L.M. Shivanekar and S.V. Kelkar *Research Bulletin* 12(3-4) Se-De 1982 p 10-20 refs tabs

An investigation into the reading efficiency in English of students of standards XI in Aurangabad city and measures to improve it. Shabbir Hussain Josh *Research Bulletin* 15(1-2) Mr-Je +1985 p 3-9

Mobilising family forces for worldwise reading success. Haray W. Sartain, ed. New York, IRA. 1981, vi, 86p. *Book Rev, Education Quarterly* 34(1) Ja 1982 p 48-49

Models of efficient reading. Karen M. Cohen. Delaware, Inst Reading Assn. 1978, viii, 70p.*Book Rev, Indian Educational Rev* 16(2) Ap 1981 p 125-28

Plans of reading instruction. Marlow Ediger *Rajasthan Board J Education* 20(1-2) Ja-Je 1984 p 30-37

Reading and the pupil. Marlow Ediger *Education Quarterly* 32(2) Ap 1980 p 23-24

Reading : The basics *vs* problem solving. Marlow Ediger *Educational Rev* 87(9) Se 1981 p 168-70 refs

Roads to reading. Ralph C. Staiger. UNESCO. 1979, 141p. $5 *Book Rev, J Indian Education* 6(5) Ja 1981 p 51-53

The relative importance of some selected factors on reading achievement of primary school children. S. Subrahmanyam *J Institute of Educational Research* 7(2) My 1983 p 31-36

A study of reading achievement in relation to sex attitude and anxiety. I.A. Vora *J Education and Psychology* 36(1-2) Ap-Je 1978 p 41-53 refs

Teaching reading skills through the newspapers. Arnold B. Cheyney. Int Reading Assn. 50p. *Book Rev, Education Quarterly* 31(2) Jl 1979 p 40

Towards better reading in English in India. Varmala T. Bhamwari *Educational Rev* 92(12) De 1986 p 211-13

See also

Oral Reading

Silent Reading

Supplementary Reading

Reading : Ability Testing

Development of reading ability among the students of class VI to X. Vijay Laxmi Sinha *Rajasthan Board J Education* 21(2) Ap-Je 1985 p 9-14

Differential characteristics of good and poor readers in the range of 9-14. S. Subrahmanyam *Experiments in Education* 11(6) Ag 1983 p 95-97

Home environment and reading achievement in primary school children. S. Subrahmanyam *Experiments in Education* 7(3) My 1979 p 39-42 refs

An enquiry into the reading ability of the bright students. D.N. Patel *Progress of Education* 56(4) Nv 1981 p 89-90+ tabs

Improvement of reading skills. S. Rajagopalan *Experiments in Education* 8(10) De 1980 p 175-80

Measurement of reading efficiency. Shabbir Hussain Josh *Education Quarterly* 32(3) Jl 1980 p 23-24

Reading ability and intelligence. K.P. Krishna and Vijaya Rani Agarwal *Indian Educational Rev* 18(1) Ja 1983 p 33-39 refs

Reading ability and maladjustment. K.P. Krishna and Vijaya Rani Agarwal *Asian J Psychology and Education* 9(4) 1982 p 42-44

Reading ability of over and under-achievers. D.S. Shivananda and G.P. Usha *Indian Educational Rev* 20(2) Ap 1985 p 95-100

Reading ability test for elementary school dropouts. Kailash Khanna and G.P. Malhotra *Indian J Adult Education* 44(2) Ap 1983 p 23-30 refs tabs

A study of reading ability in relation to certain cognitive and non-cognitive factors. Vijaya Rani Agrawal *Indian J Psychology and Education* 11(3) 1983 p 41-44

A study of the effect of low and high readability materials in geography on the reading comprehension of students in the context of reading abilities. C.B. Patyal *J Educational Research and Extension* 18(4) Ap 1982 p 193-200 refs tabs

A study of the effect of low and high readability materials on the reading comprehension of students in the context of reading abilities. C.B. Patyal *J Institute of Educational Research* 4(2) My 1980 p 35-38 refs tabs

Reading : Curricula

Reading in the curriculum. Marlow Ediger *Rajasthan Board J Education* 16(4) Oc-De 1980 p 10-13

Reading : Psychological Aspects

Neuropsychological and cognitive processes in reading. Francis J. Pirozzolo and Merlin C. Wittcock, eds. New York, Academic Press. 1981. *Book Rev, J Education and Psychology* 40(4) Ja 1983 p 242-44

A study of effects of anxiety and attitude in reading achievement. I.A. Vora *J Education and Psychology* 38(1) Ap 1980 p 36-42 tab

See also
Reading : Remedial Reading

Reading : Remedial Reading

The teaching of reading. R.P. Srivastava. New Delhi, Bahari Pub. 1979, 144p. Rs.45 *Book Rev, J Indian Education* 5(6) Mr 1980 p 65; *National J Education* 3(1) Se 1986 p 77

Vocalisation : A malady. G.C. Ahuja *Progress of Education* 53(8) Mr 1979 p 156-59 refs

Reading, Aloud

See
Oral Reading

Reading, Choice of

See
Books and Reading

Reading, Oral

See
Oral Reading

Reading (Adult Education)

Evaluation of reading and writing skills of learners. D. Janardhana Reddy *Educational Rev* 91(10) Oc 1985 p 164-66

Reading materials for neo-literates. M. Venkataiah *Experiments in Education* 7(8) Oc 1979 p 136-39 refs

Reading materials for neo-literates. N. Venkataiah *Indian J Adult Education* 40(9) Se 1979 p 8-10

Reading (Elementary Education)

Reading problems of children in the age range of 9-14. S. Subrahmanyam *Experiments in Education* 12(8) Oc 1984 p 140-44 tabs

Reading (Secondary Education)

Increasing the reading speed in English at the higher secondary level. Khazan Singh *Rajasthan Board J Education* 19(2-3) Ap-Se 1983 p 15-21

Reading Comprehension

A comparative study of some personal and physiological variables and reading comprehension. J.H. Shah *J Education and Psychology* 39(2) Jl 1981 p 97-105

Impact of readability levels, writing styles grade and reading ability upon pupils comprehension. D.N. Patel *J Education and Psychology* 41(1-2) Ap-Jl 1983 p 49-54

Reading comprehension as a function of self concept. B.V. Patel *J Education and Psychology* 44(2-3) Jl-De 1986 p 92-95

Reading comprehension of correspondence trainees. Shavinder Kaur and Amarjit Singh Dhaliwal *Indian J Extension Education* 20(1-2) Je 1984 p 73-75 refs tabs

A study of the effect of low and high readability materials in geography on reading comprehension in the context of I.Q. C.B. Patyal *Asian J Psychology and Education* 3(3) Nv 1978 p 17-21 refs tabs

Testing reading comprehension in English. Mamta Agrawal *Primary Teacher* 11(4) Oc 1986 p 29-31

Reading Disability

How to come over reading disability. Chinna Oommen *Primary Teacher*

11(1) Ja 1986 p 29-33

Impaired language mechanisms involoved in specific reading disability. P.G. Patel *Indian Educational Rev* 10(2) Ag 1981 p 46-49 refs

Reading Habits

See

Books and Reading

Reading Interests

An investigation into the study habits of 10 to 12 years of children with regard to their parental profession. S.S. Chauhan and Harbans Singh *Indian Educational Rev* 17(2) Ap 1982 p 118-22

A survey of interest in reading of the pupils of secondary and higher secondary schools of Bhavanagar city. J.D. Bhal *J Education Research and Extension* 18(1) Jl 1981 p 8-11

Reading Interests of Children

See

Books and Reading for Children

Reading Readiness

Reading readiness and the learners. Marlow Ediger *J Indian Educaiton* 10(5) Ja 1985 p 6-11

Reasoning : Child Psychology Aspects

Comparative effect of different school environments on reasoning of primary school children. Shakuntla Banga and J.P. Sharma *Progress of Education* 58(4) Nv 1983 p 78-80 refs tabs

Reasoning : Psychological Aspect

See also

Intellect

Recreation

See also

Vacations

Reacreations, Mathematical

See

Mathematical Recreations

Refractive Index

A simple method of determining the refractive : Indexes of a liquid. L.S. Prabhumirashi *Progress of Education* 53(9) Ap 1979 p 170-73 refs figs

Regression Analysis

Nature and concepts of regression analysis and prediction. Z.M. Quraishi *Quest in Education* 16(3) Jl 1979 p 195-201 refs

Reinforcement : Psychological Aspects

Study of alpha-beta process in perceiving reinforced social situation. Subimal Deb *Our Education* 3-4 Jl 1983 p 35-38 refs tabs

Religion

See also

Superstition

Religion and Education

Education : Viewpoints of religion and philosophy. Ram Shakal Pandey *Educational Rev* 85(5) My 1979 p 81-82 refs

Religion and education. P.R. Chakraborty *J Indian Education* 8(2) Se 1982 p 33-39

Religion and Sex
See
Sex and Religion
Religion in Literature
See also
Literature and Morals
Religious Education
Attitude of primary school teachers towards religious education. V.K. Rao and Malti Mishra *Experiments in Education* 11(5) Jl 1983 p 89-92 refs
Do all students in departments of studies in religion constitute a single population. Arvind Sharma *J Higher Education* 4(1) Mon 1978 p 86-91 appdx refs
Moral and religious education in colleges. J. Filella *New Frontiers in Education* 12(2) Ap-Je 1982 p 1-13 refs
Reflections of the current controversy on the teaching of comparative religion in Queensland schools. Arvind Sharma *Progress of Education* 56(9) Ap 1982 p 204-09
Theology and education. Stephen Moon *New Frontiers in Education* 12(4) Oc-De 1982 p 14-24
Religious Education : India
Religious education for children : An action programme. Kalipada Bandyapadhyay *Primary Teacher* 5(4) Oc 1980 p 16-19
Remedial Reading
See
Reading : Remedial Reading
Remedial Teaching
Bridging the gap : An experiment in remedial education. Seetha Srinivasan *New Frontiers in Education* 15(1) Ja-Mr 1985 p 86-90
Priming for remedial education. P.S. Jacob *New Frontiers in Education* 13(4) Oc-De 1983 p 12-16
Remedial education at Spicer Memorial College. Ralph H. Jones *New Frontiers in Education* 13(3-4) Oc-De 1983 p 27-39
Remedial education : With reference to reading. E.G. Vedanayagam *New Frontiers in Education* 13(4) Oc-De 1983 p 17-26
See also
Reading : Remedial Reading
Renaissance : India
The Indian renaissance. Samuel Mathai *New Frontiers in Education* 11(4) Oc-De 1981 p 1-7
Research
Breaking inter-science barriers. Pierreite Posmowski *Educational Rev* 84(12) De 1978 p 231-35
Case study method in research on instructional process. M.B. Menon and P.K. Sahoo *New Frontiers in Education* 14(4) Oc-De 1984 p 26-33 refs
The climate of research in colleges of education. Sharada Manvikar *Progress of Education* 56(6) Ja 1982 p 140-42
An investigation into the problem of research scholars. G. Vijayalakshmi *Experiments in Education* 12(4) Je 1984 p 69-71
Meta analysis : Quantitive approaches in review of research findings.

Vasant D. Bhat *J Indian Education* 11(1) My 1985 p 42-51 refs
Pursuit of quality in postgraduate studies and research in education. G.M. Patted *Quest in Education* 18(2) Ap 1981 p 108-16
Qualities of an ideol researchers as perceived by the research supervisors. N. Venkatiah and P. Adinarayana Reddy *Experiments in Education* 11(10) De 1983 p 177-80
Research for human central development. M.B. Mura *J Indian Education* 10(6) Mr 1985 p 15-23 refs
Scientific research in universities : Need for a policy. A. Vasantha *Progress of Education* 53(3) Mr 1979 p 149-55 +
Should implications be incorporated in research reports. B.K. Passi *et al Teacher Education* 16(18-19) Ja-Ap 1982 p 9-16 refs
University research. D.P. Verma *University News* 24(41) 1 Nv 1986 p 1-4
See also
Agricultural Research
Dairy Research
Educational Research
Social Science Research

Research : India
Post graduate education and research : cost analysis. R.P.S. Rana *J Higher Education* 6(1-3) 1980-81 p 155-60 tabs
Science, technology, development and the universities. R.C. Mehrotra *J Higher Education* 6(1-3) 1980-81 p 25-39 tabs
Scientific research in universities : Need for a policy. A. Vasantha *Progress of Education* 53(8) Mr 1979 p 149-55 +
UGC's policy and the programme for improvement of research in the universities. *University News* 22(48) 23 De 1984 p 1-4

Research : Management
Management of research in universities. R. Srinivasa Rao *Experiments in Education* 8(2) Ap 1980 p 25-26 refs
Case study as a method of research. P.K. Sahoo *J Institute of Educational Research* 7(2) My 1983 p 37-42
Case study method in research on instructional process. M.B. Menon and P.K. Sahoo *New Frontiers in Education* 14(4) Oc-De 1984 p 26-33 refs

Research : Programmed Instruction
An experimental study in programmed learning for teaching research methodology course at M.Ed level. D.N. Sensanwal *Indian Educational Rev* 14(4) Oc 1979 p 72-77

Research, Industrial : India : Haryana
See also
Dairy Research : India : Haryana

Residence and Education
See also
Boarding Schools

Retarded Children
See
Mentally Handicapped Children

Retention : Psychological Aspects
See also
Memory
Rewards and Punishment in Education
Effects of extrinsic rewards on performance : A review. Kailas Nath Tripathi *J Education and Psychology* 38(4) Ja 1981 p 242-52 refs
Rice : Fertilizers and Manures
Adoption of NPK and nutrients in rice crop in Punjab. Tarlochan Singh Randhawa *Indian J Extension Education* 21(1-2) Ja-Je 1985 p 91-93
Rice : India : Andhra Pradesh
Communication behviour of extension personnel with regard to modern rice technology. A. Ramesh Babu and B.P. Sinha *Indian J Extension Education* 21(3-4) Jl-De 1985 p 11-15 tabs
Rice : India : Orissa
Constrants in adoption of H.Y. rice technology in coastal Orissa. A. Tripathi *et al Indian J Extension Education* 18(1-2) Je 1982 p 51-58 refs tabs
Right and Left : Political Science Aspects
Mrs. Gandhi and the Indian Left. N. Rajasekharan Reddy *Student Action* 2(8) Ja 1984 p 12-13 +
Rights of Women
See
Women : Rights of Women
Rigidity : Psychological Aspects
An experimental investigation of the relationalship between creativity and regidity. P. Anantha Krishanan *J Institute of Educational Research* 4(2) My 1980 p 39-41 tabs refs
Risk-taking : Psychological Aspects
A correlational study of risk-taking and creativity with special reference to sex differences. Saroj Agarwal and Sushila Kumari *Indian Educational Rev* 17(3) Jl 1982 p 104-10 refs tabs
Effect of socio-economic status and academic achievement on risk taking behaviour of student teachers. R.C. Hooda and H.R. Paul *J Institute of Educational Research* 10(2) My 1986 p 1-3 refs
Role Playing
Development of creativity through the techniques of role playing. R.C. Hooda and Gurpal Singh Jarial *Rajasthan Board J Education* 19(4) Oc-De 1983 p 16-21
Rorschach Test
Anxiety and achievement : A Rorschach study of high and low achievers. C.R. Jindal and S.K. Panda *Indian Educational Rev* 17(4) Oc 1982 p 118-24 refs tabs
A study of Rorschach's indices of intelligence. Ratra Mookerjee *Asian J Psychology and Education* 9(1) Ja 1982 p 8-14 refs
Rumania
See also
Agricultural Extension Work : Rumania
Rural Credit
See
Agricultural Credit

Rural Economic Development

See

Community Development

Rural Education

See

Education, Rural

Rural Leadership

A socio-psychological study of the leaders of village panchayats. Ram Kumar and G.C. Rai *Indian J Extension Education* 15(3-4) De 1979 p 39-45 refs tabs

Rural Libraries : India

Rural library movement in India. T.R. Nagappa *Indian J Adult Education* 40(9) Se 1979 p 17-21

Village library and the primary teacher. Satypal Bharat Bhushan. *Primary Teacher* 5(3) Jl 1980 p 42-43

Rural Leadership : India : Bihar

Farm leadership in relation to age. N.K. Sinha and B.K. Bimal *Indian J Extension Education* 14(1-2) Ja-Je 1978 p 76-78

Rural Schools

See also

Education, Rural

Rural Schools : India

Whither our single teacher schools? D.N. Khosla *Teacher Today* 22(4) Ap-Je 1980 p 33-39

Rural Schools : India : Andhra Pradesh

Rural schools and enrolment : A case study of Andhra Pradesh. D.P. Jain *J Indian Education 6(4)* Nv 1980 p 40-42

Rural Schools : Russia

Village school in the USSR - Specific features and problems. Viktor Korotov *Progress of Education* 55(2) Se 1980 p 33-35

Rural Technology

See

Technology, Rural

Rural Youth Club

Rural Youth : Employment

See also

Training of Rural Youth for Self Employment

Rural Youth : India

Differential interest areas of rural youth and non-school going youth club members. P.N. Jha and J.K. Jain *Indian J Extension Education* 15(1-2) Je 1979 p 39-48 refs tabs

Rural Youth : India : Gujarat

Occupational socialisation of rural youth. N.P. Singh and P.M. Singh *Indian J Extension Education* 14(1-2) Ja-Je 1978 p 35-42 tabs

Rural Youth : India : Tamil Nadu

A dialogue with the rural youth : Chinglepet study. R.R. Sharur and R. Thetagraj *Indian J Adult Education* 40(7) Jl 1979 p 24-27

Rural Youth Club : India : Punjab

Communication of information through Rural Youth Club leaders. G.S. Saini

Ag-Se 1982 p 23-29

Attitudes and beliefs of Harijan students. S.P. Rastogi *J Higher Education* 4(2) Aut 1978 p 251-58

Background variables of the scheduled castes and tribes college students : A comparative study. M.S. Ameerjan *Indian Educational Rev* 19(2) Ap 1984 p 28-36

A comparative study of academic achievement of the scheduled castes and tribes students of agriculture. M.S. Ameerjan *J Education and Psychology* 37(2) Jl 1979 p 121-29 refs tabs

Conditions of scheduled castes and tribes. Anita Horsey *New Frontiers in Education* 11(2) Ap-Je 1981 p 1-36 refs

Constitution law and reservation. Aruna Sundaresh *New Frontiers in Education* 16(2) Ap-Je 1986 p 33-40

Developing educational technology for deprived sections of the Indian society. R.S. Sharma *Bulletin of Non-formal Education* 3(3) De 1985 p 1-17

Educating Harijans. Bhagat Ram Goyal. Gurgaon, Academic Press (India). 129p. Rs.50 *Book Rev, Progress of Education* 56(8) Mr 1982 p 200-01; *Quest in Education* 19(1) Ja 1982 p 90-94

Educating the disadvantaged : A few suggestions. R.P. Varma *National J Education* 6(2) My 1984 p 1-6 refs

Education, earning and occupation of weaker castes. Alexander V. Verghese *J Higher Education* 9(3) Spr 1984 p 373-81 refs

Education of the scheduled castes. Suma Chitnis *J Higher Education* 1(2) Aut 1975 p 167-78 tabs

Educational attainment of children in the sweeper community at AIIMS Campus : An exploratory study. Om Prakash *Indian Educational Rev* 15(4) Oc 1980 p 97-103

Educational development of the scheduled castes. M.S. Swaminathan *J Indian Education* 8(1) My 1982 p 40-55 tabs

Educational equality and economic opportunities : A comparative study of scheduled castes and non-scheduled castes. Kusum K. Premi *J Higher Education* 9(3) Spr 1984 p 363-72 refs tabs

Educational facilities for scheduled castes. G. Khurana *Educational Quarterly* 31(3-4) Oc 1979-Ja 1980 p 31-35

Educational problems in scheduled castes. M.N. Ravindranatha *Educational Rev* 87(4) Ap 1981 p 69-74

Educational problems of scheduled caste college students in Karnataka. Satyanarayana *J Higher Education* 7(3) Spr 1982 p 253-60 refs tabs

Enrolment of the scheduled castes in general colleges : A case study of Tamil Nadu. G.R. Sudame and A.P. Thiagarajan *Experiments in Education* 9(4) Je 1981 p 63-69 tabs

Equalisation of educational opportunities for scheduled castes and scheduled tribes. K.C. Nautiyal and Y.D. Sharma. new Delhi, NCERT. 1979. *Book Rev, J Indian Education* 6(1) My 1980 p 78-79

Harijan wasti. Marion J. Rice *Progress of Education* 55(2) Se 1980 p 51-57

Higher education and the scheduled castes. Malvika Karlekar *J Higher Education* 1(2) Aut 1975 p 179-87 refs tabs

The impact of constitutional provision upon the uplift of Harijans S.P.

Rastogi *Indian Educational Rev* 15(4) Oc 1980 p 76-80

Improving the quality of tribal education. Khemraj Sharma *Educational Quarterly* 32(4) Oc 1980 p 22-26

Minority rights and reservation policy : Towards coherence and consistence. Rudi Heredia *New Frontiers in Education* 16(2) Ap-Je 1986 p 60-63

New horizons and scheduled castes. C. Pasvathamma. New Delhi, Ashish Pub H. 184p. Rs.100 *Book Rev, Education Quarterly* 38(2) Sum 1986 p 51-52

Occupational status of parents of Harijan and tribal welfare department high school students of Orissa. Banu Behari Kamila *National J Education* 6(1) Se 1983 p 56-64 refs tabs

Post-matric scholarship for scheduled castes and scheduled tribes students. P.S.K. Menon *J Higher Education* 1(2) Aut 1975 p 263-66

The problem of reservations : Economic backwardness or social injustice. D.L. Sheth *Indian J Adult Education* 47(5) My 1986 p 9-15; 47(6) Je 1986 p 4-7+; 47(7) Jl 1986 p 14-21

Problems of school dropouts : A study with a special reference to scheduled castes and scheduled tribes in Andhra Pradesh. S. Subrahmanyam *Education Quarterly* 38(3) Aut 1986 p 28-32

Regional educational disparity among scheduled castes of Punjab. Amrit Kaur and Tarlok Singh *Indian J Adult Education* 46(4) Ap 1985 p 7-10+ tabs

Research review on implementation of the educational schemes of scheduled castes. S.K. Yadav *Indian Educational Rev* 18(3) Jl 1983 p 112-22 refs

Reservations in Hr. education and jobs. B. Rajaiah *Educational Rev* 88(3) Mr 1982 p 55-58

Reservations in Higher education and jobs. B. Rajaiah *Experiments in Education* 10(9) Nv 1982 p 159-63

Role of achievement anxiety, alienation and value discrepancy in achievement of scheduled caste students. Renu Sood *J Higher Education* 6(1-3) 1980-81 p 117-22 refs tabs

Scheduled caste college students in Rajasthan. Shiv Kumar Lal *J Higher Education* 1(2) Aut 1975 p 244-50 refs

Scheduled castes and higher education : A study of college students in Bombay. Jacob Aikara. Pune, Dastana Rama Chandra. 1980, 112p. Rs.35 *Book Rev, Education Quarterly* 33(3) Jl 1981 p 48-49

Scheduled castes and tribes in higher education in Tamil Nadu. Malcolm S. Adiseshiah *J Higher Education* 1(2) Aut 1975 p 241-44

Scheduled tribes and equality of educational opportunity. K.R. Sharma *Indian Education* 12(10) Ja 1983 p 10-13

Self-concept of Harijan students and attitudes of other students towards them. Haribhai G. Desai and D.A. Uchat *Indian Educational Rev* 16(3) Jl 1981 p 44-50

Some demographic variables influencing the attitudes of scheduled caste towards the measrues adopted for their welfare : An empirical study. P.D. Juyal *Progress of Education* 61(4-5) Nv-De 1986 p 85-88 refs

A study of attitude of students towards school of Harijans and tribal welfare departement high school of Orissa. Bana Behari Kamila *J Education and*

Psychology 43(3-4) Oc 1985-Ja 1986 p 187-92 refs

A study of attitude towards learning of science among scheduled caste students. Ajay M. Misra *et al J Education and Psychology* 41(3) Oc 1983 p 112-16

A study of personality syndromes and congnitive characteristics of scheduled castes, backward classes and non-scheduled castes students. L.P. Gupta *J Higher Education* 4(3) Spr 1979 p 381-87

A study of the scheduled castes awareness about the schemes for their educational progress. S.K. Yadav *Indian Educational Rev* 17(1) Ja 1981 p 85-93

A study of the scheduled castes students in some secondary schools of Tamil Nadu. A.P. Thiagarajan *Indian Education* 11(5) Ag 1981 p 22-26 tabs

Scheduled Castes and Scheduled Tribes : Employment

Occupational mobility among a special group of scheduled castes in Tamil Nadu. A survey. R. Jayagopal *Indian J Adult Education* 47(1) Ja 1986 p 8-12

Scheduled Castes and Scheduled Tribes : Occupations

Inter-generations mobility among the scheduled castes. *J Indian Education* 5(4) Nv 1979 p 61

Scheduled Castes and Scheduled Tribes : Reservation Issue

The problem of reservations : Economic backwardness or social injustice. D.L. Seth *Indian J Adult Education* 47(5) My 1986 p 9-15+; 47(6) Je 1986 p 4-7+; 47(7) Jl 1986 p 14-21

Scholarships

See also

Student Loan Funds

Scholastic Success

See

Academic Achievement

School Adjustment

See

Student Adjustment

School Administration

See

School Management and Organisation

School Adminstrators

Motivation and the administrator. Marlow Ediger *EPA Quarterly Bulletin* 8(3-4) Oc 1985-Ja 1986 p 7-11

School Administrators : India : Andhra Pradesh

Personality characteristics of educational administrators. D. Bhaskara Rao *et al J Institute of Educational Research* 9(3) Se 1985 p 8-13 refs tabs

School Administrators : India : Karnataka

Functions and problems of deputy directors of public instruction in Karnataka state. H.M.Kasinath *EPA Quarterly Bulletin* 8(3-4) Oc 1985- Ja 1986 p 1-6 refs

School and Community

See

Community and School

The communication behaviour of school heads : Self perceptions versus faculty perceptions. A. Subhalakchumi *Experiments in Education* 11(8) Oc 1983 p 134-37

School Attendance

Projection of school enrolment. Adeyemi Akinsanya *Primary Teacher* 10(3) Jl 1985 p 20-22

Should attendance be compulsory? C. Dharmarajan *Educational Rev* 91(3) Mr 1985 p 46-47

A study of truancy in relation to security-insecurity parental acceptance and peer-acceptance. Ghazala Ansari and Wadudul Haque Siddequi *J Education and Psychology* 40(3) Oc 1982 p 169-74

See also

Dropouts

Educational Law and Legislation

Vacations

School Attendance : India : Andhra Pradesh

Why don't they go to school? P.S. Geethanath *Experiments in Education* 10(9) Nv 1982 p 169-71 tabs

School Attendance : India : Gujarat

Construction of a scale for measuring the attitude of boys and girls towards compulsion of attendance at postgraduate level. Ranjana Dhingra *Experiments in Education* 7(2) ap 1979 p 34-36

School Attendance : India : Uttar Pradesh

A study of truancy in relation to security-insecurity, parental acceptance and peer acceptance. Wodudul Haque Siddiqui *J Institute of Educational Research* 4(2) My 1980 p 9-12 refs

School Boards

See also

School Superintendents and Principals

School Books

See

Text-books

School Buildings : India

Investment shyness in elementary school buildings. K.C. Nautiyal *J Indian Education* 7(3) Se 1979 p 43-49 refs

School Children

Behavioural problems in school children : Implication for teacher training programme. V.N. Rao *et al Experiments in Education* 12(3) My 1984 p 41-46 refs tabs

Causes of general backwardness among school children. Shamsuddin *Indian Education* 10(8) Nv 1980 p 33-36

Causes of general backwardness among school children. Shamsuddin *Primary Teacher* 11(3) Jl 1986 p 9-12

Classroom interaction and congnitive development in primary school. P. Sandeep *Indian Educational Rev* 15(4) Oc 1980 p 62-65

Development of creative thinking in the primary school children. S. Kumar and M.J. Ravindranath *Primary Teacher* 4(1) Ja 1979 p 5-9

Development of self-confidence among primary school children. M.L. Kaul *Primary Teacher* 8(1) Ja 1983 p 25-28 tabs

A study of some intellectual correlates of scholastic attainment of VII class children. S. Subrahmanyam *J Education and Psychology* 44(3-4) Jl-Oc 1986 p 112-17

School Children : Food

Relative effectiveness of graphic aids and projected aids enriched with museum experiences in teaching food and digestion to VIII standard students of Navredna Higher Secondary School, Baroda 1982-83. Anupama Shah and Neera Chetenlal *Experiments in Education* 11(9) Nv 1983 p 151-59 refs tabs

School Children : Health and Hygiene

Child to child programme. Duncan Guthrie *Primary Teacher* 4(1) Ja 1979 p 13-20

Health education programme for primary schools. Harish Chandra *Primary Teacher* 6(4) Oc 1981 p 9-14

Physical needs of children. Kuldip Kumar *Primary teacher* 10(4) Oc 1985 p 6-8

School Children : India : Andhra Pradesh

A study of some socio-metric choices of socially backward, socially non-backward primary school children. V. Bharathi and P.V. Ramamurthi *J Institute of Educational Research* 6(3) Se 1982 p 33-40 refs tabs

School Children : India : Rajasthan

Comparative effect of different school environments on reasoning of primary school children. Shakuntla Banga and J.P. Sharma

Progress of Education 58(4) Nv 1983 p 78-80 refs tabs

School Children : Psychology

Primary school children : Development of their congnitive abilities. M. Pushpa *Primary Teacher* 6(4) Oc 1981 p 5-8

School Costs

See

Education : Costs

School Discipline

Disciplinary education in the present social setup. Vimla Mehta *Teacher Education* 13(8-9) Jl-Oc 1979 p 58-61

Discipline and the school curriculum. Marlow Ediger *Experiments in Education* 10(5) Jl 1982 p 93-96 refs

Establishing cross-cultural validity of disciplined-indisciplined scale. (D-1 scale). Ravi Wangu *Indian Educational Rev* 20(4) Oc 1985 p 34-39

Indiscipline : Teachers point of view. Bir Singh *Educational Rev* 85(8) Ag 1979 p 144-48

A structural framework for multi-disciplinary studies. Vasantha Ramkumar *Indian Educational Rev* 14(1) Ja 1979 p 85-91 refs

School Dropouts

See

Dropouts

School Environment

Ideal school atmosphere. Pritam Singh Brar *Educational Rev* 86(4) Ap 1980 p 69-71

School Evaluation
See
Educational Surveys
School Filing Systems
See
Schools : Records and Correspondence
School Finance
See
Education : Finance
School Houses
See
School Buildings
School Hygiene
National foundation : Better school health. Mukesh Raghav *Teacher Today* 25(2) Oc-De 1982 p 66-71
Toning up primary school health programme. N.N. Prahallada *Primary Teacher* 11(3) Jl 1986 p 13-15
See also
Posture
School Law
See
Educational Law and Legislation
School Libraries
International association of school librarianship. *Experiments in Education* 9(9) Nv 1981 p 104-06
Renovating school libraries. G.S. Thaker and I.V. Malhan *J Indian Education* 11(1) My 1985 p 71-75
School library in the modern concept of education. Janakraj Sharma *Teacher Today* 29(1) Jl-Se 1986 p 64-71 refs
School Libraries : Administration
Organisation of libraries in schools and their effectiveness use. C.D. Sharma *Teacher Today* 25(2) Oc-De 1982 p 44-50 refs
School Libraries : India
The role of school libraries in primary and secondary schools. Maya K. Vora *Indian Educational Rev* 14(1) Ja 1979 p 92-99
School Management and Organisation
Attitudes of secondary school teachers towards educational adminstration. Kiran Deep *Educational Rev* 90(12) De 1984 p 197-201 refs
A comparative study of organisational climate of government and non-government schools. S. Gakhar and Abha Tripathi *J Institute of Educational Research* 7(3) Se 1983 p 32-37
A comparative study of personality factors of effective and ineffective teachers in different types of school organisational climate. Y.K. Gupta and M. Swaroop *Progress of Education* 55(11) Je 1981 p 300-02 refs tabs
Decision-making : A framework for educational institutions. T.K.A. Naidu *Indian Education* 13(10-11) Ja Fe 1984 p 17-19
Decision-making in school administration. Jamnalal Bayti *Indian Education* 13(8-9) Nv-De 1983 p 23-26
Dimension of organisational climate. Arvind K. Sinha *Indian Educational*

Rev 18(4) Oc 1983 p 1-14

Head of the school. B.S. Hundal *Educational Rev* 88(11) Nv 1982 p 185-88

The headmaster and organiser. S.G. Kapadia *Progress of Education* 53(12) Jl 1979 p 234-36

The human aspect of systems design in school management. Shobha Deane *J Indian Education* 8(2) Jl 1982 p 44-47

Human relationship and modern high schools administration. Shamsuddin *Indian Education* 11(1-2) Ap-My 1981 p 64-66

Management and nonformal and adult education. J.S. Rajput *Indian Education* 11(1-2) Ap-My 1981 p 59-63

Moral and school administration. S.P. Duggal *Progress of Education* 55(7) Fe 1981 p 181-83 refs

Organisation development and the technology of school self-evaluation. John Elliott-Kemp *J Education and Psychology* 41(1-2) Ap-Jl 1983 p 5-11

Organisational climate of schools and work alienation : A comparative analysis. K.A. Gandhi *J Educational Research and Extension* 18(2) Oc 1981 p 22-30 refs tabs

Perspective leadership. Colin Moyle *EPA Quarterly Bulletin* 8(1-2) Ap-Je 1985 p 17-25 refs

The problems of sub-deputy inspectors of schools. Prakash Chandra Shukla *Progress of Education* 53(8) Mr 1981 p 217-18

Recollections of a reluctant administrator. V.V. John *Teacher Today* 26(1) Jl-Se 1983 p 133-43

Relationship between personality of the heads of institutions and organisational climate of their schools. Shashi Kala Deshpande *J Education and Psychology* 43(1) Ap 1985 p 44-49

Risk reduction and the management of change. Warren L. Mellor *Indian Education* 11(1-2) Ap-My 1981 p 5-12

School climate and its relationship with headmasters leadership behaviour. Motilal Sharma *Teacher Today* 24(3) Ja-Mr 1982 p 42-49 refs

School climate and teacher absenteeism. K.A. Gandhi *J Education and Psychology* 40(1-2) Ap-Jl 1982 p 90-95

The school inspection - A plea for evolving new strategies. M.R. Kamatkar *Progress of Education* 57(8) Mr 1983 p 184-86

School management : A old idea with new significance. D.R. Darji and B.R. Panchal *Progress of Education* 55(12) Jl 1981 p 315-20

School organisation and teachers. B. Rajaiah *Educational Rev* 86(4) Ap 1980 p 63-64

Staff associations : Line of authority and responsibility. K. Adinarayana *Indian Education* 10(7) Oc 1980 p 29-32

Streamlining curriculum administration. B.P. Lulla *Indian Education* 11(1-2) Ap-My 1981 p 76-80

Systems in school administration. Mahtab Singh *Educational Rev* 87(3) Mr 1981 p 47-50 refs

Using basic psychology in school administration. Douglas J. Thom *Indian Education* 13(12)_ Mr 1984 p 1-2

See also

Ability Grouping in Education

Classroom Management

Educational Adminstration
See also
Elementary School Teachers : Absenteeism
High School Principals
School Discipline
School Superintendents and Principals
School Supervision
Schools : Records and Correspondence
Teacher Participation in Adminstration
Teachers : Selection and Appointment

School Management and Organisation : Great Britain

School inspection in Scotland (U.K.) and Orissa (India). Sunil Behari Mohanty *EPA Quarterly Bulletin* 7(1-2) Ap-Jl 1984 p 30-40 refs

School Management and Organisation : India

Creating creative atmosphere in our educational institutions. Sharada Manvikar *Progress of Education* 56(3) Oc 1981 p 69-70

Effective change in secondary school administration. L.P. Singh *J Indian Education* 6(2) Jl 1980 p 14-18; 6(4) Nv 1980 p 3-7

Organisational climate in relation to teachers job satisfaction and students achievement. Ravi Kanta Chopra *Indian Educational Rev* 31(3) Oc 1983 p 211-28

Study of educational administration in India. R.C. Srivastava *EPA Quarterly Bulletin* 8(1-2) Ap-Je 1985 p 67-69 refs

Turn to the basics VII : Checking proliferating government control and centralisation editorial. *Indian Education* 11(5) Ag 1981 p 3-6; 11(6) Se 1981 p 3-4 +

School Management and Organisation : India : Gujarat

Personality characteristics of teaching staff and organisational climate of schools. K.A. Gandhi *Experiments in Education* 10(6) Ag 1982 p 110-16 refs

The quality of school life and pupil control ideology. K.A. Gandhi *J Educational Research and Extension* 17(3) Ja 1981 p 142-49 refs tabs

School Management and Organisation : India : Maharashtra

Application of Getzel's model to the rapport-based programme of school improvement. V.K. Kalpande *Research Bulletin* 12(1-2) Mr-Je 1982 p 3-10 tabs

Inspection and supervision of primary schools in Maharashtra with special reference to Aurangabad region. N.B. Kulkarani *Research Bulletin* 15(3-4) Se-De 1985 p 47-57

School Management and Organisation : India : Orissa

Management of educational institutions by private bodies in Orissa : Some observations. B. Biswal *EPA Quarterly Bulletin* 5(3-4) Oc 1982-Ja 1983 p 26-35

School inspection in Scotland (U.K.) and Orissa (India). Sunil Behari Mohanty *EPA Quarterly Bulletin* 7(1-2) Ap-Je 1984 p 34-40 refs

School Management and Organisation : India : Rajasthan

Dimensions of school climate. Motilal Sharma *Indian Educational Rev* 15(1) Ja 1980 p 35-45 refs tabs

School Management and Organisation : India : Tamil Nadu

Leadership styles of heads of schools in Madras. P.S. Balasubramanian *EPA Quarterly Bulletin* 6(2) Jl 1983 p 1-12 refs

Size and structure of educational organisations. R. Krishnaraj and P.S. Balasubramanian *J Education and Planning Administration* 1(1) Oc 1986 p 21-27 refs

School Management and Organisation : India : Uttar Pradesh

A correlational study of organisational climate and teacher attitudes. M.K. Tripathi *National J Education* 6(2) My 1984 p 21-32 refs tabs

Organisational climate and teacher attitude : A study of relationship. Madhu Kanta Tripathi *Indian Educational Rev* 15(1) Ja 1980 p 85-94 tabs

School Management and Organisation : Papua New Guinea

Personnel involvement and government at the school level : Theory and practice in Papua New Guniea. Mark Bray *Perspectives in Education* 2(2) Ap 1986 p 109-20 refs

School Organisation

See

School Management and Organisation

School Periodicals

See

College and School Periodicals

School Personnel Management

See also

College Personnel Management

Teacher Morale

Teacher-Principal Relationships

School Principals

See

High School Principals

School Superintendents and Principals

School Records

See

Schools : Records and Correspondence

School Reports

See also

Grading and Marking : Students

School Superintendents and Principals

Behavioural characteristics of school principals. M.R. Kansal and P.L. Gupta *EPA Quarterly Bulletin* 7(1-2) Ap-Jl 1984 p 24-29 refs

The principal. V. Ramachandran *Indian Education* 11(1-2) Ap-My 1981 p 56-58

Superintendents : Movers or stayers. Robert J. Gerardi *J Educational Research and Extension* 18(3) Ja 1982 p 170-74

Superintendents : Movers or stayers? Robert J. Gerardi *Progress of Education* 55(3) Oc 1980 p 74-76

See also

High School Principals

School Supervision

School Supervision

Challenging tasks of educational supervisor. R. Krishan Rao and R. Papa *Primary Teacher* 10(1) Ja 1985 p 32-34

Clinical supervision : A New technique. G.L. Mehta *Educational Rev* 87(8) Ag 1981 p 154-55 refs

Inspection and supervision of the future. T.K.D. Nair *New Frontiers in Education* 16(1) Ja-Mr 1986 p 79-84

Management of supervision of schools : A pragmetic and functionally useful approach. P. Adinarayana *Indian Education* 11(1-2) Ap-My 1981 p 81-83

School supervision : A measure of qualitative improvement in education : editorial. *Rajasthan Board J Education* 22(1) Ja-Mr 1986 p I-II

Staff and student supervision. Dorothy E. Petters. London, Allen and Unwin. 1979, 157p. $2.95 *Book Rev, Education Quarterly* 32(1) Ja 1980 p 42

A study of the supervisory tasks. Mehtab Singh Mamel *Educational Rev* 85(10) Oc 1979 p 189-95

School Supervision : India

Supervision in secondary schools. Abdul Haq Khan. Delhi, Arya Book Depot. 1980, 61p. Rs.15 *Book Rev, J Indian Education* 6(2) Jl 1980 p 78

School Supervision : India : Maharashtra

What is wrong with the formal educational institution; editorial comments. *J Education and Psychology* 40(3) Oc 1982 p 103-06

School Surveys

See

Educational Surveys

Schools

Improving schools : Using what we know? Rolf Lehning and Michael Kane. California, Sage Pub. *Book Rev, Teacher Today* 27(4) Ap-Je 1985 p 145-47

Reschooling not deschooling. Jagannath Mohanty *J Indian Education* 6(3) Se 1980 p 44-47

The school of future. Nilakantha Mishra *Educational Rev* 86(8) Ag 1980 p 140-43

The school perception. M.P. Bhasin *Primary Teacher* 9(1) Ja 1984 p 4-8

Schools without failure. William Glasser. New York, Harper. 1969, 266p. *Book Rev, Teacher Today* 23(3) Ja-Mr 1981 p 155-59

What is a progressive school? Shib K. Mitra *Indian Education* 11(4) Jl 1981 p 15-18

See also

Art Schools
Boarding Schools
Correspondence Schools and Courses
Education
Open Plan Schools
Private Schools
Professional Education
Single Teacher Schools
Teachers Colleges
Vacation Schools

Schools : Accounting
See also
Education : Costs
Schools : Curricula
See
Education : Curricula
Schools : Europe
The teenager and the school in Europe. Torsten Husen *Teacher Today* 26(2) Oc-De 1983 p 1-17 refs
Schools : Finance
See
Education : Finance
Schools : Great Britain
The comprehensive school in the United Kingdom. Verghis Chandy *Educational Rev* 90(3) Mr 1984 p 41-43
Improving primary schools. *Teacher Today* 27(3) Ja-Mr 1985 p 87-93
A visit to a British single teacher school. Sunil Behari Mohanty *Indian Education* 10(4) Jl 1980 p 39-40
Schools : India
Folk high schools for India. S.C. Dutta *Indian J Adult Education* 44(8-9) Ap-Se 1983 p 22-24
Problems of rural and tribal schools. M.N. Ravindranatha *Educational Rev* 88(8) Ag 1982 p 131-32; 88(9) Se 1982 p 149-50
Strategy for changing the school climate. K.A. Gandhi *Quest in Education* 16(3) Jl 1979 p 202-08 refs
What schools can do to promote national integration. R.P. Singhal *Education Quarterly* 33(2) Ap 1981 p 1-3
Schools : India : Bihar
Effect of school system on the competence of secondary school students. Sudha R. Sinha *Indian Educational Rev* 15(1) Ja 1980 p 62-77 refs tabs
Schools : India : Delhi
See also
Balwadi Schools : India : Delhi
Schools : India : Gujarat
Readiness programmes for schools : A search for a viable model. Prarana Mohiti *Quest in Education* 16(4) Oc 1979 p 314-26
Schools : India : Madhya Pradesh
An MP experiment in school complex. Bir Singh *Education Quarterly* 33(2) Ap 1981 p 21-23
Schools : India : Maharashtra
A study of fulfilment of minimum needs of the schools coming under the school complex centre. S.P. Wani *Research Bulletin* 15(1-2) Mr-Je 1985 p 10-18 refs tabs
Village school an agent of social change. P.L. Gauade *Progress of Education* 61(4-5) Nv-De 1986 p 74-76 +
Schools : India : Uttar Pradesh
A study of physical facilities in educational institutions of Garhwal division. K.B. Budhuri *Indian Educaitonal Rev* 18(2) Ap 1983 p 110-19 refs tabs

Schools : Inspection
See
School Management and Organisation : School Supervision
Schools : Records and Correspondence
Maintaining school records. Shamsuddin *Primary Teacher* 11(4) Oc 1986 p 23-26
Suggestions for maintaining school records. Shamsuddin *Progress of Education* 53(6) Ja 1981 p 157-60
Schools : Russia
New programmes of Soviet schools. Le Tsesarsky *Progress of Education* 56(9) Ap 1982 p 221-22
Soviet school looks into the future. Zoya Malkova *Progress of Education* 57(12) Jl 1983 p 285-87
Soviet schools : Today and tomorrow. M.A. Prokoflev *Student Action* 2(4) Ag 1983 p 24
A study of educational leadership in relation to location of the schools. P.C. Shukla *Progress of Education* 57(7) Fe 1983 p 161-63 refs tabs
Schools : Sanitary Affairs
See
School Hygiene
Schools : Time Tables
Planning school time table. K.M. Gupta *Primary Teacher* 10(2) Ap 1985 p 18-20
Schools : United States
The U.S. School system - Some recent trends. John E. Owen *Educational Rev* 87(11) Nv 1981 p 209-11
Schools, Community
See
Community schools
Schools, Military
See
Military Education
Schools, Neighbourhood
See
Community Schools
Schools, Travelling
See
Mobile Schools
Science
Peer review in science. Kailash Chandra Garg *J Higher Education* 7(3) Spr 1982 p 321-23 refs
Science : Ability Testing
Attitude of high school pupils towards their teachers and its relationship with achievement in science. Sarah S. Williams *J Educational Research and Extension* 18(1) Jl 1981 p 21-23
A comparative study of vocational interests of high and low achievers of science and intermediate level. B.P. Singh *et al Experiments in Education* 11(1) Mr 1983 p 11-15
Constellations of personality traits, intelligence and achievement in relation

to scientific creativity. Didar Singh Jhaj *Asian J Psychology and Education* 11(1) 1983 p 13-20

Construction and administration of scientific attitude scale. Y.K. Shinde *Research Bulletin* 15(1-2) Mr-Je 1985 p 26-31

Correlation between scientific attitude and achievement in science. Akaram Ramachary *Experiments in Education* 10(7) Se 1982 p 123-27 refs tabs

Developing scientific aptitudes in students : The role of science teachers. Damyanta S. Moses *Primary Teacher* 9(2) Ap 1984 p 27-30

Environmental factors related to under achievement in science. Shajehan Siddiqui *Educational Rev* 89(11) Nv 1983 p 185-89 tabs

Evaluating students learning in science : A challenge to science educators. Karuna Shankar Misra *Quest in Education* 18(2) Ap 1981 p 139-49

The gains of special coaching on science aptitude of the pupils preparing for the NSTS examination. D.N. Agarwal *Indian Educational Rev* 18(3) Jl 1983 p 8-16 refs tabs

Innovative evaluation procedures in science. Marlow Ediger *J Education and Psychology* 41(4) Ja 1984 p 178-83 refs

Intelligence and originality among science and art students at + 2 stage : A comparative study. A. Kumar *Asian J Psychology and Education* 14(1-4) 1984 p 15-18

Intelligence as a correlate of achievement in science across different levels of socio-economic status. Harnek S. Kaile and Parminder S. Bajwa *J Institute of Educational Research* 9(1) Ja 1985 p 18-21 refs

Relationship between creative structures of high school science students. R.A. Sharma and Krishna Kumali *J Education and Psychology* 41(3) Oc 1983 p 133-37

Relationship between scientific creativity and generalised attitude towards science. A. Grewal *J Education and Psychology* 78(2) Jl 1980 p 399-403

A study of attitude towards learning of science among scheduled caste students. Ajay M. Misra *et al J Education and Psychology* 41(3) Oc 1983 p 112-16

A study of interest and ability of the secondary schools students in science. B.B. Senapati and G.B. Kapat *Our Education* 2 Jl 1981 p 39-44 refs ft-n

Study of observing process in science in relation to certain socio-economic and congnitive variables. S.N.L. Bhargava *Research Bulletin* 14(1-2) Mr-Je 1984 p 22-28 ref

A study of science achievement in relation to intelligence. M.C. Das *J Education and Psychology* 44(1) Ap 1986 p 11-15 refs

A study of scientific creativtiy of boys in two institutional settings. Karuna Shankar Misra *Experiments in Education* 7(12) Fe 1980 p 223-24 tabs

A study of sex difference in science achievement of secondary school pupils. Kamala S. Pillai *J Educational Research and Extension* 19(4) Ap 1983 p 249-58 refs

A study of some personality of talented students in science. O.P. Verman and K. Yadav *J Educational Research and Extension* 16(2) Oc 1979 p 89-93 refs tabs

A study of the measuring process in scince in relation to certain cognitive and social variables. S.N.L. Bhargava *J Institute of Educational Research* 10(2) My 1986 p 4-7 refs tabs

Science : Curricula

An evaluative study of science syllabus in secondary schools of Tamil Nadu. V. Rajesekaran *Experiments in Education* 6(10) De 1978 p 169-77 refs tabs

An evaluative study of the new science curriculum and upper primary level in Andhra Pradesh. Bhaskara Rao Digmarti *Experiments in Education* 10(8) Oc 1982 p 147-49 refs

Improving the science curriculum. Marlow Ediger *Experiments in Education* 9(4) Je 1981 p 69-71 refs

Improving science curricula. Marlow Ediger *Experiments in Education* 10(3) My 1982 p 52-54 refs

Problem solving in the science curriculum. Marlow Ediger *Rajasthan Board J Education* 2(7) Jl-Se 1984 p 17-19

The science curriculum and the learner. Marlow Ediger *Experiments in Education* 8(6) Ag 1980 p 111-13

Science curriculum materials for the disadvantaged children. R.M. Kalra *J Indian Education* 8(1) My 1982 p 3-9 tabs

The science curriculum : Process of product. Marlow Ediger *Educational Rev* 87(5) My 1981 p 99

Science teachers in the upper primary schools and the new science syllabus. Vasant D. Bhatt *Experiments in Education* 9(6) Ag 1981 p 110-12 +

A study of the relationship between the secondary school science and mathematics curricula of Kerala and Tamil Nadu. K. Krishnan *J Educational Research and Extension* 18(4) Ap 1982 p 210-19 refs tabs

Science : Examinations

Internal and external examination scores in science and mathematics : A study. P.S. Verma *J Indian Education* 5(6) Mr 1980 p 6-10 tabs

Reshaping science examination in our schools. I.P. Aggarwal *Quest in Education* 18(3) Jl 1981 p 220-27

Science : India

Taking science and technology to the rural sector. Sant Prakash *Education Quarterly* 30(3) Oc 1978 p 21-23

Science : International Cooperation

New directions for international scientific cooperation. B.M. Udgaonkar *J Higher Education* 2(2) Aut 1976 p 167-83 refs

Science : Language

Role of language in the development of concepts in science. Krishna Maitra *Progress of Education* 60(4) Nv 1985 p 86-90 refs

Science : Programmed Instruction

Programmed instruction in the learning of science : A new perspective. P. Arun Kumar *et al J Indian Education* 5(1) My 1979 p 3-10 refs tabs

Science : Study and Teaching

Advances in science and technology as a motivational factor for science education. R.M. Kalra *Education Quarterly* 36(2) Ap 1984 p 24-28

Behavioural objectives in science instruction. Vishwanath Muddu *Indian Education* 11(7) Oc 1981 p 31-32

Brain science and science education. Munawar Ahmad Anis *J Education and Psychology* 39(1) Ap 1981 p 28-34 refs

A comparative study of lecture method, guided discovery approach and discovery approach in the teaching of science. R.S. Yadav *J Education and Psychology* 44(1) Ap 1986 p 58-65 refs

Development of scientific attitude through the teaching of sciences. M.B. Menon and P. Arun Kumar *Education Quarterly* 31(1) Ap 1979 p 15-17 refs

Distant study systems in science education. S.K. Gupta *EPA Quarterly Bulletin* 8(3-4) Oc 1985-Ja 1986 p 39-44

Education and scientific temper. Malcolm S. Adiseshiah *New Frontiers in Education* 14(1) Ja-Mr 1984 p 55-58

Effective use of community resources in the teaching of science. J.P.S. Malik *Progress of Education* 54(6) Ja 1980 p 116-18

An endeavour towards anatomy of science education. Rishi Anand and V. Shankaram *J Higher Education* 2(2) Aut 1976 p 197-202 refs

Hoshangabad science teaching experiment for improving teachers training. J.P. Sharma and R.N. Syag *Progress of Education* 55(10) My 1981 p 261-63

Inquiry-based science teaching : A few approaches. M.J. Ravindranath and V.D. Bhatt *Education Quarterly* 33(3) Jl 1981 p 21-23

Issues in teaching science. Marlow Ediger *Experiments in Education* 11(5) Jl 1983 p 82-85 refs

Integrated approach of science teaching. I.P. Aggarwal *Teacher Today* 22(1) Jl-Se 1979 p 29-34

An investigation into the effect of teachers sex on the student achievement in science. Harbans Singh *J Education and Psychology* 41(1-2) Ap-Jl 1983 p 64-66

A learner centred science curriculum. Marlow Ediger *Educational Rev* 88(7) Jl 1982 p 111-13

Nuffied science teaching project. Sunthamma Raju *Progress of Education* 55(6) Ja 1981 p 155-56 refs

The philosophy of inter-disciplinary approach in science education. S. Paramaji and V. Sudhakar *Indian Education* 12(1-2) Ap-My 1982 p 23-26

Piagets developmental psychology and its implication in the teaching of science. Shajehan Siddiqui *Educational Rev* 92(7) Jl 1986 p 113-14 refs

Piagets work and the learning of science. H.C. Jain *Teacher Today* 28(3) Ja-Mr 1986 p 31-36 refs

Process of science instruction : A model. P. Arun Kumar *et al J Indian Education* 10(5) Ja 1985 p 34-39 refs

Revamping science education. R.C. Deva *Educational Rev* 85(4) Ap 1979 p 61-63

Role of philosophy in the teaching of science. Marlow Ediger *New Frontiers in Education* 15(2) Ap-Je 1985 p 29-33 refs

STOS : A technique for evaluation of science teaching. S.C. Bhargava and Sunder Lal Mathur *Rajasthan Board J Education* 20(1-2) Ja-Je 1984 p 15-20

Science education : Objectives. M.M. Shah *et al Experiments in Education* 7(7) Se 1979 p 121-28

Science education what is'nt and what it is? R.D. Anand and C. Seshadri *Teacher Today* 26(4) Ap-Je 1984 p 70-80 refs

Science for all. R.M. Kalra *Teacher Today* 27(2) Oc-De 1984 p 50-55

Science teaching and the nature of science. Jagesh Kumar Kadiyar *Educational Rev* 86(2) Fe 1980 p 28-30

Science teaching observation : A need for tools. M.S. Padma *Progress of Education* 55(5) De 1980 p 122-23 + refs

A simplified teaching in science. R.N. Gupta *J Indian Education* 5(1) My 1979 p 11-21 refs

Social and personal adjustment in relation to teaching success in science. K.V. Radha *National J Education* 7(2) My 1985 p 31-37 refs

A study of attitude towards learning of science among scheduled castes students. Ajay M. Mishra *et al J Education and Psychology* 41(3) Oc 1983 p 112-16 refs tabs

Supervision in science education. B.K. Jana *Educational Rev* 86(12) De 1980 p 235-39; 87(1) Ja 1981 p 11-13

The Wirszup report. *J Indian Education* 6(2) Jl 1980 p 71-73

World views of science education. U.N. Wanchoo, ed. New Delhi, Oxf-IBH, 414p, Rs 90 *Book Rev, Education Quarterly* 34(4) Oc 1982 p 57-58; *Indian Educational Rev* 18(3) Jl 1983 p 123-26

Science : Study and Teaching : Audio-Visual Aids

Differential effects of using a projected and non-projected visual media in teaching science. R. Srinivasa Rao and V. Suguna *Experiments in Education* 7(9) Nv 1979 p 157-59 refs

A study of relative effectiveness of hand synchronised OHP-tape, isolated tape and isolated OHP : Presentation of a science program to non-science teachers at two levels of protest performance. K. Ramachandrachar *Quest in Education* 19(3) Jl 1982 p 194-205 refs tabs

Science : Study and Teaching : Developing Countries

Science, society and trends in science education : A search for relevance in the developing countries. J.K. Sood *Teacher Today* 24(2) Oc-De 1981 p 19-25 refs

Science : Study and Teaching : India

Needed research in science education in India. Anil K. Saxena *Teacher Today* 22(4) Ap-Je 1980 p 61-66

Role of education in development of science and technology in India. Ranjana Srivastava *Education Quarterly* 31(3-4) Oc 1979-Ja 1980 p 16-20

Science education in India. Viswanath Muddu *Indian Education* 12(1-2) Ap-My 1982 p 31-33

Science teaching in Indian schools; editorial. *J Indian Education* 5(1) My 1979 p 1-2

Science teaching in rural India : An experiment. Prabuddha Ganguli *J Higher Education* 1(2) Aut 1975 p 266-67 refs

Status of science education in India. H.C. Jain *J Indian Education* 10(5) Ja 1985 p 12-17

A study of attitudes towards science and scientists among certain groups of students and teachers in India. J.K. Sood *Indian Educational Rev* 14(4) Oc 1979 p 61-66

Science : Study and Teaching : India : Kerala

See also

Kerala Sastra Sahitya Parishad

Science : Study and Teaching : India : Nagaland

Exploration of local resources for science teaching. K.K. Sharma and Mary Abraham *Experiments in Education* 7(2) Ap 1979 p 31-34

Science : Study and Teaching : Nigeria

Science educators perception of readiness for learning science in Nigerian secondary schools. T.O. Odunsi *Perspective in Education* 2(3) Jl 1986 p 171-77 refs

Science : Study and Teaching (Elementary)

Elementary education and science. J.S. Rajput *Primary teacher* 4(3) Jl 1979 p 11-14

Science education in elementary schools. Vasant D. Bhatt and M.J. Ravindranath *Indian Education* 10(12) Mr 1981 p 18-22

Micro-evaluation in elementary science. Pritam Singh *J Indian Education* 5(5) Ja 1980 p 47-54

Science : Study and Teaching (Higher)

Use of semi-programmed learning material for teaching demonstration method in science to B.Ed. students. M.L. Pandya *Progress of Education* 59(12) Jl 1985 p 256-59 tabs

Science : Study and Teaching (Primary)

Creativity and teaching of science at the primary level. A.B. Saxena *Primary Teacher* 8(3) Jl 1983 p 23-26

Developing nuturant effect strategy for environment-oriented primary science education programme. B.K. Jana *Experiments in Education* 8(6) Ag 1980 p 102-08; 8(7) Se 1980 p 126-29

Developing primary school science curriculum based on Piagets theory. R.P. Singh *Primary Teacher* 6(2) Ap 1981 p 12-15

The growth of logical thinking in science during adolescence. Narendra Vaidya. New Delhi, Oxf-IBH Pub. 1979, 215p. Rs.15 *Book Rev, J Indian Education* 5(1) My 1979 p 90

Learning science through environment. A. Elizabeth *Primary Teacher* 8(1) Ja 1983 p 7-10

Modern science for children : Need for a rational education. Narendra Prasad Das *J Indian Education* 5(1) My 1979 p 28-33

The role of science learning centres for primary school children. Anil K. Saxena *Primary Teacher* 6(2) Ap 1981 p 5-7

Science in pre-primary schools. K. Adinarayana *Primary Teacher* 6(1) Ja 1981 p 35-39

Science teaching through local environment. Chunnilal Saluja *Primary Teacher* 5(4) Oc 1980 p 35-37

Scientific inquiry in children : A review. K. Adinarayana *Experiments in Education* 9(1) Mr 1981 p 3-8 refs

Teaching primary science. B.L. Young. London, Orient Longman. 1984, 217p. *Book Rev, Teacher Today* 28(2) Oc-De 1985 p 121-23

Science : Study and Teaching (Primary) : Asia

Primary science education with local resources in Asia. Keith Warren *Primary Teacher* 5(2) Ap 1980 p 4-10

Science : Study and Teaching (Primary) : India : Kerala

Teaching of science and mathematics in primary classes of Kerala. T.K.D. Nair *J Indian Education* 7(3) Se 1979 p 3-9 annex

Science : Study and Teaching (Primary) : India : Maharashtra

Primary school science curriculum of Maharashtra. T.M. Das *Primary Teacher* 9(1) Ja 1984 p 13-15

Science : Study and Teaching (Secondary)

Effective teaching and learning of science in higher secondary schools. M. Raghuram Singh *Experiments in Education* 6(11) Ja 1979 p 191-96 refs

An investigation into the relationship between socio-economic status, intelligence, science aptitude and science interest of secondary school pupils. R. Sukumaran Nair *Experiments in Education* 11(4) Je 1983 p 57-62 tabs

Science at 2 stage : A few problems. K. Adinarayana and Jyothi Prakash *Educational Rev* 87(6) Je 1981 p 103-05

Scientific attitudes of experienced science teachers at secondary school level. Digumarti Bhaskara Rao *et al Educational Rev* 92(4) Ap 1986 p 61-65 tabs refs

Teaching of science in secondary schools. New Delhi, NCERT. 1982, Rs.21.80 *Book Rev, Indian Educational Rev* 18(3) Jl 1983 p 123-26; *J Indian Education* 8(5) Ja 1983 p 65-66

Teaching science art the plus two stage : A few problems. K. Adinarayana and Jyothi Prakash *Experiments in Education* 10(2) Ap 1982 p 28-31

Science : Teacher Training

The dynamics of science teacher education. J.K. Sood *Education Quarterly* 36(2) Ap 1984 p 29-33

Hoshangabad science teaching experiment for improving teachers training. J.P. Sharma and R.N. Syag *Progress of Education* 55(10) My 1981 p 261-63

Science and Civilisation

Impact of emerging sciences and technologies on society, excerpts from Shanti Swarup Bhatnagar Memorial Oration. Y. Nayudamma *New Frontiers in Education* 13(3) Jl-Se 1983 p 72-78

Science Research

See

Research

Science Students

Significance of innate factors and sex differences among science students. Jyoti Prakash Bagchi *National J Education* 6(2) My 1984 p 68-74 refs

Study of values of science undergraduates at different levels of socio-economic status. Ashok Kumar *J Educational Research and Extension* 18(3) Ja 1982 p 175-82 refs tabs

Science Teachers

Analysis of classroom transactions of science teacher. P.R. Shukla *Experiments in Education* 12(11) Ja 1985 p 192-98 refs

Developing scientific aptitude in students : The role of science teachers. Damyanti S. Moses *Primary Teacher* 9(2) Ap 1984 p 27-30

In-service education of science teachers. K.S. Rao *Educational Rev* 85(11) Nv 1979 p 216-19

An investigation into the questioning behaviour of science teachers. S. Kumar *Experiments in Education* 6(9) Nv 1978 p 163-66

Lack of science orientation in rural primary school teachers : A crucial problem. Harikesh Singh *National J Education* 5(1) Se 1982 p 39-45 refs

Personality traits of creative science teachers. Karuna Shankar Misra *J Indian Education* 5(5) Ja 1980 p 27-30 refs

Personality traits of flexible science teachers. Karuna Shankar Misra *Quest in Education* 17(3) Jl 1980 p 269-75

Science teachers and educational reconstruction. A.B. Saxena *J Indian Education* 8(2) Jl 1982 p 65-68

Science teachers in the upper primary schools and the new science syllabus. Vasant D. Bhatt *Experiments in Education* 9(6) Ag 1981 p 110-12

Scientific attitudes of experienced science teachers at secondary school level. Digumarti Bhaskara Rao *et al Educational Rev* 92(4) Ap 1986 p 61-65 refs tabs

A study of verbal classroom pattern of high school science teachers. B. Ramachandra *Indian Education* 10(8) Nv 1980 p 12-15

Science Teachers : India

A study of attitudes towards science and scientists among certain groups of students and teachers in India. J.K. Sood *Indian Educational Rev* 14(4) Oc 1979 p 61-66

Science Teachers : Psychology

Personality traits of successful science teachers. J.S. Malik *Progress of Education* 59(10-11) My-Je 1985 p 235-39

Verbal classroom behaviour of high school science teachers - Social extraverts vs social introverts. B. Ramachandra Reddy *J Education and Psychology* 40(1-2) Ap-Jl 1982 p 18-28 refs

Scientific Apparatus and Instruments

Service and maintenance of sophisticated scientific instruments in universities. Mohinder Singh *J Higher Education* 4(2) Aut 1978 p 279-80

Scientific Expeditions

Fourth Indian scientific expedition to Antarctica, 1984-85. B.B. Bhattacharya *University News* 23(33) 1 Se 1985 p 6-8

Scientific Research

See

Research

Scientists

See also

Einstein, Albert

Mandel, Gregor Johann (1922-1984)

Woment Scientists

Scientists : India

Measuring job satisfaction of scientists in an ICAR Institute. Usha Anand and T.S. Sohal *Asian J Psychology and Education* 9(4) 1982 p 13-20

Scotland

See also

Elementary School Teachers : Training : Scotland

Sea-fisheries
See
Fisheries
Secondary Education
See
Education, Secondary
Secondary School Principals
See
High School Principals
Secondary School Teachers
See
High School Teachers
Secondary Schools
See
Private Schools
Secularism and Education
The concept of secularism in education. Sunil Behari Mohanty *Educational Rev* 88(8) Ag 1982 p 140-41 refs
Cultural pluralism and education. Subhash Chandra Agrawal *Educational Rev* 86(1) Ja 1980 p 12-14
Education and secular morality. M. Mascarenhas *Teacher Today* 25(2) Oc-De 1982 p 14-18 refs
Security : Psychological Aspects
A study of security and insecurity in respect to the academic achievement. Umesh Agrawal and R.M. Saraswat *J Educational Research and Extension* 18(4) Ap 1982 p 247-53 refs tabs
Segregation in Education
See also
Discrimination in Education
Selection of Nonbook Materials
Selection of media for instruction. Malay K. Basu and Karuna Shankar Misra *Education Quarterly* 32(2) Ap 1980 p 25-26
Self-actualisation : Psychological Aspects
Sex differences in self-actualisation. P. Mathur and A. Satapathy *J Institute of Educational Research* 4(2) My 1980 p 13-17 refs tabs
Self-assurance
See
Self-reliance
Self-concept
See
Self-perception
Self-confidence
See
Self-reliance
Self-disclosure
Effect of self-disclosure on different cultural settings. Amlya Kumar Basu *J Education and Psychology* 37(1) Ap 1979 p 31-34 refs
Self-disclosure and occupational persona. Ratna Mookerjee *J Educational Research and Extension* 20(2) Oc 1983 p 113-17

Self-esteem
See
Self-respect

Self-perception

Achievement motivation and self-concept in the settings. Neelu Srivastava *Asian J Psychology and Education* 4(1) Ja 1979 p 5-9

An analysis of the development of self-concepts among children belonging to an orphanage. A. Suriakanthi *J Educational Research and Extension* 18(3) Ja 1982 p 149-54 refs tabs

Building young children's self-concepts through a non-sex, approach to early childhood education curriculum materials. Margaret Verma *Indian Educational Rev* 20(4) Oc 1985 p 20-33

Development of self-concept during adolescence. V.V. Jogawar *Asian J Psychology and Education* 9(1) Ja 1982 p 3-7 refs tabs

Measurement of self-concept. Haribhai G. Desai and D.A. Uchat *Indian Educational Rev* 17(1) Ja 1982 p 1-11 refs

Reading comprehension as a function of self-concept. B.V. Patel-1 *J Education and Psychology* 442-3) Jl-De 1986 p 92-95

Relationship between self-concept and academic achievement. B. Jeyakantham *Experiments in Education* 7(3) My 1979 p 42-46 refs

Self-concept and achievement. Vasantha Ramkumar *J Higher Education* 1(1) Mon 1975 p 124-26 refs

Self-concept and adjustment as factors in academic achievement. Radha Rani Sharma *Indian Educational Rev* 18(2) Ap 1983 p 46-59 refs tabs

The self-concept and scholastic achievement of the socially disadvantaged. S. Ushasree *J Institute of Educational Research* 10(1) Ja 1986 p 17-20 refs

Self-concept in relation with locus of control, socio-economic status and intelligence of pupils in private and government schools. Arun Kumar Gupta and Suresh Sharma *Indian Educational Rev* 15(3) Jl 1980 p 78-80 refs tabs

Self-concept of female students of single sex colleges and co-education colleges : A comparative study. D.A. Uchat and H.G. Desai *J Institute of Educational Research* 6(2) My 1982 p 33-36 refs tabs

Self-concept of high achieving and low achieving students of first year classes of colleges. H.G. Desai and D.A. Uchat *J Educational Research and Extension* 19(3) Ja 1983 p 155-61

Self-concept of student-teachers of colleges of education. M.D. Trivedi *J Education and Psychology* 39(3) Oc 1981 p 169-75

Self-concept of student teachers of colleges of education. M.D. Trivedi *Teacher Education* 15(14-15) Ja-Ap 1981 p 37-44 refs tabs

Self-perception among high and low groups. Kusum K. Bhatt *J Education and Psychology* 36(1-2) Ap-Je 1978 p 34-40 refs

Student problems; self-concepts and level of aspiration : A comparative study. R.K. Arora *Indian Educational Rev* 20(3) Jl 1985 p 12-22

A study of academic achievement in relation to motivation and self-concept. R. Shanmuga Sundaram *J Educational Research and Extension* 18(2) Oc 1981 p 40-48 refs tabs

A study of relationship between the self-concept of student teachers and

The semester system. Dibakar Kundu *J Indian Education* 8(3) Se 1983 p 20-25

The semester system. Parveen Akhtar Hassan *J Higher Education* 7(3) Spr 1982 p 306-09 refs

Trimester system of education : As perceived by students. G. Rajaguru *et al J Higher Education* 3(3) Spr 1978 p 386- 89 tabs

Senior High School Teachers

See

High School Teachers

Senses and Sensation

See also

Fechner's Law

Sensitivity Training

See

Group Relations Training

Set Theory : Programmed Instruction

An experimental study of a programme in set theory. Kanti Prasad *et al Bhartiya Shiskhsha Shodh Patrika* 1(2) Jl 1982 p 10-24 refs tabs

Sex : Study and Teaching

See

Sex Instruction

Sex and Religion

Religiousity as function of age and sex. Govind Tiwari *et al Asian J Psychology and Education* 6(2) Jl 1980 p 36-40 refs

Sex Differences

Sex differences in expression of aggression. S.C. Prasad *Asian J Psychology and Education* 6(2) Jl 1980 p 33-35

Sex Education

See

Sex Instruction

Sex Instruction

Adolescents attitude towards sex education. C. Beena *J Institute of Educational Research* 7(2) My 1983 p 1-7

Impact of sex education of the social adjustment of individuals. K.G. Desai and Chandra Mohini *J Indian Education* 8(5) Je 1983 p 47-51 refs

Sex education. K.T. Mamtora *Educational Rev* 88(2) Fe 1982 p 30-33

Sex education. Lakshmi Shankar. New Delhi, Sterling. 1978, 168p. Rs.50 *Book Rev, Education Quarterly* 31(2) Je 1979 p 42

Sex Instruction for Girls

Sex knowledge of schools girls and their mothers. Pushpa Gupta and Indu Gupta *Progress of Education* 58(6) Ja 1984 p 138-42 tabs

Short Stories

See also

Story-telling

Short Term Memory

A developmental study of short-term recall of numeral sequence. V.K. Kool and Rita Agarwal *Asian J Psychology and Education* 5(1-3) 1979 p 44-50 refs tabs

Proactive inhibition in short-term-memory. N. Hasnain *Asian J Psychology*

and Education 5(1-3) 1979 p 1-8 refs tabs

Sikkim

See also

Adoption of Improved Farm Practices : India : Sikkim

Silent Reading

Vocalisation in silent reading : How to avoid? G.C. Ahuja *Educational Rev* 85(6) Je 1979 p 113-15 refs

Single Teacher Schools

Social benefits and economics of single teachers schools. M.G. Mall. Kolhapur, Gargoti. 1979, 66p. *Book Rev, J Indian Education* 6(3) Se 1980 p 58-59

Single Teacher Schools : Great Britain

A day in a single-teacher school in Carrington. Sunil Behari Mohanty *Primary Teacher* 5(4) Oc 1980 p 9-11

Single Teacher Schools : India : Maharashtra

Social benefits and economics of single teacher schools. M.G. Mali *J Educational Research and Extension* 16(3) Ja 1980 p 183-84

Single Woman

See also

Divorcees

Sketch, Literacy

See

Essay

Sleep

See also

Dreams

Slow Learning Children

Educational provisions for slow learners. Sunil Behari Mohanty *Experiments in Education* 11(5) Jl 1983 p 79-82 refs

Slums : India : Andhra Pradesh : Hyderabad

Attitude of literate women of Hyderabad slums. K. Padma *Experiments in Education* 11(8) Oc 1983 p 138-40

Small Farmers Development Agency

Beneficiaries of Small Farmers Development Agency. V.G. Salankhe *Indian J Extension Education* 16(1-2) Je 1980 p 61-63

Multivariate regression analysis of involvement of small farmers in SFDA. V.G. Salunkhe *Indian J Extension Education* 16(3-4) De 1980 p 71-73

Small Groups

See also

Group Relations Training

Social Acceptance

Current status of studies on approval motive : A critical appraisal. B.N. Tewari and Girishwar Misra *J Education and Psychology* 37(3) Oc 1979 p 203-12 refs

Social Adjustment

Home adjustment patterns of adolescent boys and girls at various levels of socio-economic status and general intelligence. B.K. Mattoo *J Education and Psychology* 40(3) Oc 1982 p 136-42

See also
Social Acceptance

Social Approval
See
Social Acceptance

Social Classes
Social class and marital status as correlates of modernisation. Roma Pal and Ashok K. Dixit *Asian J Psychology and Education* 14(1-4) 1984 p 25-33 refs

Social Conflict
See also
Conflict of Generations

Social Education
How to accelerate the programme of social education. H.K. Mehta and N.H. Patel *Progress of Education* 53(4) Nv-De 1978 p 74-78
Social education of the child. Vimla Mehta *Teacher Education* 14(10-11) Ja-Ap 1980 p 65-68

Social Interaction
See also
Group Relations Training

Social Maturity Scales
An investigation into social maturity as a function of area and modernisation. I.A. Vora *J Education and Psychology* 40(1-2) Ap-Jl 1982 p 58-61 refs
Social maturity of children in India. Pramila Phatak *Indian Educational Rev* 18(1) Ja 1983 p 1-11 tabs

Social Problems
See also
Woman : Social and Moral Questions

Social Problems in Education
See
Educational Sociology

Social Psychology
Disruption in communication at social occasions : An essay in social psychology. Proshanta K. Nandi *Indian Educational Rev* 18(1) Ja 1983 p 120-28 refs
See also
Leadership

Social Research
See
Research
Social Science Research

Social Science Documentation Centre
See
National Social Science Documentation Centre

Social Science Research : Asia
Issues and experiences in participatory research in Asia. Rajesh Tandon *Teacher Today* 22(3) Ja-Mr 1980 p 55-60

Social Science Research : India
See also
Indian Council of Social Science Research
Social Science Research : Methodology
An introduction to research methods in social sciences. C.C. Pattanshetti. Coimbatore, Rainbow Pub. 1981, 166p. Rs.36 *Book Rev, Progress of Education* 56(4) Nv 1981 p 98+
Social Science Teachers
Problems and perceptions of social science teachers in higher education. G. Haragopal and K. Jagannadha Rao *J Higher Education* 4(1) Mon 1978 p 67-74 refs tabs
Social Sciences : Canada
Analysis of projects in social studies education in Canada, 1971-1980. Harry Dhand *Educational Rev* 91(11) Nv 1985 p 186-87
Social Sciences : Curricula
Social sciences : New trends in curriculum. D.N. Gaind *Education Quarterly* 35(3) Jl 1983 p 14-16
Social Sciences : Periodicals
A study of the image of Indian journals on management and social sciences in the international academic community. Anand S. Dhawle and Amitabha Ghose *J Higher Education* 4(3) Spr 1979 p 313-26
Social Sciences : Study and Teaching
Issues and problems in the social studies. Marlow Ediger *Experiments in Education* 10(8) Oc 1982 p 141-44
Issues in the social studies. Marlow Ediger *Education Quarterly* 33(4) Oc 1981 p 22-23 +
Jurisprudential way of teaching social sciences. S.P. Malhotra *Progress of Education* 60(7) Fe 1986 p 161-66
Learning theories and new social studies. H. Dhand *Educational Rev* 85(3) Mr 1979 p 55-59 ft-n
Modernisation of our courses and syllabi in the humanities and social sciences. A.M. Ghore *J Higher Education* 4(1) Mon 1978 p 75-80
Philosophy of education and the social studies. Marlow Ediger *Experiments in Education* 9(5) Jl 1981 p 82-84
Social sciences and social studies. Marlow Ediger *Educational Rev* 87(1) Ja 1981 p 7-11 refs
Social studies : Processes versus products. Marlow Ediger *New Frontiers in Education* 13(1) Ja-Mr 1983 p 13-19 refs
Social studies projects. H. Dhand *Educational Rev* 85(5) Je 1979 p 85-88 refs
Teaching of social sciences. S.K. Kochar. New Delhi, Sterling. 1979, 389 p. Rs. 50 *Book Rev, Education Quarterly* 32(3) Jl 1980 p 47-48
Teaching of social sciences. Surinder Suri *New Frontiers in Education* 10(4) Oc-De 1980 p 27-42
Social Sciences : Study and Teaching : Audio-Visual Aids
The differential effects of using projected and non-projected visual media in the teaching of social studies. R. Srinivasa Rao *Experiments in Education* 6(10) De 1978 p 178-81 refs tabs

Social Sciences : Study and Teaching : Canada

Canadian trends in social studies. H. Dhand *Educational Rev* 85(10) Oc 1979 p 185-89 refs tabs

Social Sciences : Study and Teaching : Primary

A study of the effect of integration approach to teaching social studies in the primary schools. Pratibha Veerkar *Research Bulletin* 12(1-2) Mr-Je 1982 p 11-18

Social Sciences : Study and Teaching : Secondary

Undergraduate curricula in social sciences. Arun Bose *J Higher Education* 1(1) Mon 1975 p 61-75 ft-n

Social Status

See also

Students Socio-Economic Status

Social Surveys

See also

Family Life Surveys

Socially Handicapped Children : Education

Educational problems of socially disadvantaged children. A. Joseph *J Indian Education* 11(1) My 1985 p 14-19.

Relationships between achievement motivation and level of aspiration of socially deprived students. Beena Thadani and B.S. Raizada *Educational Rev* 90(7-8) Jl-Ag 1984 p 119-21 tab.

Society and Education

See

Educational Sociology

Socio-Economic Status of Students

See

Students Socio-Economic Status

Socialism and Education

Education for socialism, secularism and democracy. Sahitya Nand Jha. Delhi, Amar Pra. 134p. Rs.80 *Book Rev, Educational Rev* 91(11) Nv 1985 p 198.

Sociology

See also

Educational Sociology

Family

Sociology : India

See also

Caste : India

Sociology : Study and Teaching

The teaching of sociology. Radhika Ramasubhan *J Higher Education* 1(1) Mon 1975 p 77-86.

Sociology, Educational

See

Educational Sociology

Sociology, Rural

See also

Gram Sevaks

Soil Conservation : India : Bihar

A study of attitude of farmers of Chhota Nagpur towards soil conservation programme. H.S.P. Sinha *et al Indian J Extension Education* 20(3-4) Se-De 1984 p 9-18 refs tabs

Soil Erosion

See also

Soil Conservation

Sophia College, Bombay

Sophia : Wisdom is her name. Palty Tobin *New Frontiers in Education* 14(2) Ap-Je 1984 p 85-96

Sorghum

Adoption of new technologies in dry land sorghum crop production. L.B. Kunnal *et al Indian J Extension Education* 20(3-4) Se-De 1984 p 60-62

Sounds

The world of sound. Cathy Spagnoli *Primary Teacher* 5(2) Ap 1980 p 18-21

Speech : Disorders

Helping the autistic child. Verghis Chandy *Educational Rev* 86(9) Se 1980 p 173-74

Speech Defects

See

Speech : Disorders

Spelling : Psychological Aspects

See also

Spelling Ability

Spelling Ability

Teaching of spelling. Varmala T. Bhamwari *Educational Rev* 89(12) De 1983 p 205-11 refs which word should pupils learn to spell? Marlow Ediger *Educational Rev* 86(12) De 1980 p 222-25 refs

Spelling Reform

Developmental and cognitive aspects of learning to spell a reflection of word knowledge. Edmund H. Henderson and James W. Beers, *eds*. New York, IRA 148p. *Book Rev, Education Quarterly* 34(1) Ja 1982 p 45-46

Learning spellings meaningfully. P.R. Saluja *Primary Teacher* 5(1) Ja 1980 p 31-32

Neet to take extra care for spelling teaching. Qaiser Zoha Alam *Primary Teacher* 10(1) Ja 1985 p 10-13

Promoting spelling proficiency. Bir Singh *Educational Rev* 85(2) Fe 1979 p 34-36 refs

Psychology and pedagogy of spelling. B.B. Bhattacharyya *Our Education* 1 Jl 1980 p 23-28 refs

Reinforcement programme package to reduce orthographical errors : A dilemma. L.M. Shivanekar *Research Bulletin* 15(1-2) Mr-Je 1985 p 41-52 refs tabs

Sports

Mass media for promotion of sports and physical education. P.D. Sharma *Primary Teacher* 11(2) Ap 1986 p 28-30

Sports : India

Our cultural fabric : Popular sports and pastimes of India. New Delhi, India, Ministry of Education and Social Welfare. 1978, 62p. Rs. 12.30 *Book Rev,*

J Indian Education 7(3) Se 1979 p 59

Sri Aurobindo Society, Pondicherry

Educational research at the Sri Aurobindo Society. Norman C. Dowsett *Bharatiya Shiksha Shodh Patrika* 4(2) Jl-De 1985 p 13-19 refs

Sri Krishna Devaraya University

Shri Pant addresses convocation of Sri Krishna Devaraya University. *University News* 23(35) 16 Se 1985 p 17-19

Sri Lanka

See also

Adult Education : Sri Lanka

Curriculum Planning : Sri Lanka

Examinations : Sri Lanka

Higher Education and State : Sri Lanka

Smt. Surajaba College of Education, Bombay

Gandhi Shikshan Bhavan's Smt. Surajaba College of Education : A report. P. Parikh *Quest in Education* 19(2) Ap 1982 p 110-17

Gandhi Shikshan Bhavan's Smt. Surajaba College of Education : Report of content enrichment through projects during, 1981-82. Usha Murugan *Quest in Education* 19(3) Jl 1982 p 179-86

Gandhi Shikshan Bhavan's Smt. Surajaba College of Education : Socially useful productive work. *Quest in Education* 19(2) Ap 1982 p 106-09

Report of the practice teaching programme at Gandhi Shikshan Bhavan's Smt. Surajaba College of Education, 1981-82. Kamal A. Patankar *Quest in Education* 19(2) Ap 1982 p 98-105

Standard and Standardisation in Education

See

Education : Standards

State Aid to Education

See also

State Aid to Higher Education

State Aid to Higher Education : India

State grants to collegiate institutions : A study of patterns and procedures. J.L. Azad *J Higher Education* 2(2) Aut 1976 p 243-52 refs tabs

State and Adult Education

See

Adult Education and State

State and Education

See

Education and State

State Grants for Higher Education

See

State Aid to Higher Education

States : India

See also

Education, Higher : India : States

Educational Planning : India : States

Statistics

Elementary statistics in psychology and education. A.B.L. Srivastava and K.K. Sharma. New Delhi, Sterling. 1985 *Book Rev, J Institute of*

Educational Research 10(1) Ja 1986 p 31

A new method for the computation of average deviation from a frequency distribution. Sailendra Kumar Ghosh *Our Education* 1 Jl 1980 p 48-53 refs

Statistical methods : Concepts, applications and computation. Y.P. Aggarwal. New Delhi, Sterling. 1986. *Book Rev, J Educational Planning and Adminstration* 1(1) Oc 1986 p 89-90

See also

Regression Analysis

Stock and Stock Breeding

See also

Animal Husbandry

Cattle Breeding

Feeds

Stoletov, Vsevolod

Interview with Vsevolod Stoletov, President of the USSR Academy of Educational Sciences. Inna Rudenko *Teacher Education* 14(12-13) Jl-Oc 1980 p 68-70

Story-telling

The art of story-telling. Gopal Sharma *Primary Teacher* 10(3) Jl 1985 p 35-36

Sane Guruji Kathamala : An organisation trying to make children emotionally literate. Yadunath Thatte *Progress of Education* 57(9) Ap 1983 p 200-01+

Strategic Defence Initiative

Star wars and star peace. Arthur C. Clarke *New Frontiers in Education* 16(4) Oc-De 1986 p 107-16

Stress : Physiological Aspects

Effect of stress and anxiety on psychomotor performance. Sunil Abrol *Asian J Psychology and Education* 11(1) 1983 p 32-35

How to avoid tensions. D. Bhaskara Rao *Educational Rev* 91(3) Mr 1985 p 49-50

Stress : Psychological Aspects

See

Stress : Physiological Aspects

Structural Psychology

See

Gestalt Psychology

Student Activities

A comparative study of academic achievement of active and regular participants in co-curricular activities and that of non-participants. Ram Chander *J Educational Research and Extension* 16(3) Ja 1980 p 135-41 refs

Ideological orientation of student activitism. Jacob Alkara *et al.* Pune, Dastane Ramchandra. 1977, 133p. Rs. 37 *Book Rev, J Higher Education* 4(2) Aut 1978 p 291-92

Relationship of student activism and personality adjustment. G.S. Aswal and G.U. Srinagar *J Institute of Educational Research* 6(3) Se 1982 p 20-23 refs

Societal and institutional magnitudes of activism. M.P. Uniyal and R.R.

Sharma *Indian Educational Rev* 20(4) Oc 1985 p 133-36

See also

Students : Political Activity

Student Unions

Student Activities : India : Uttar Pradesh : Meerut

A differential study of planning and administration of the co-curricular activities of Meerut University adolescents. L.P. Gupta *J Educational Research and Extension* 19(4) Ap 1983 p 220-23

Student Adjustment

Adjustment of XI grade students in relation to neuroticism and extraversion. Agyajit Singh *J Education and Psychology* 36(1-2) Ap-Je 1978 p 78-84 refs

Adjustment of secondary school girls studying in co-education and segregated institutions in relation to their socio-economic status. Kamala Rai *National J Education* 7(2) My 1985 p 46-55

Adjustment problems of college students preparing for four selected professions : A comparative study. G.R. Sharma *Indian Educational Rev* 17(4) Oc 1982 p 68-78 refs tabs

Adjustment problems of non-professional college students. G.R. Sharma *J Higher Education* 4(2) Aut 1978 p 262-66

A comparative study in the areas of adjustment between intellectually bright and average higher secondary adolescents. Anirudh Pandey *Indian Educational Rev* 15(2) Ap 1980 p 120-24 refs tabs

A comparative study of adjustment problems of professional and non-professional college students. G.R. Sharma *J Education and Psychology* 37(2) Jl 1979 p 130-38 refs tabs

A correlational study of adjustment and academic achievement of XI grade students. Agyajit Singh *Quest in Education* 18(1) Ja 1981 p 46-52 refs

The effect of practical behaviour of parents upon the class adjustment of pre-adolescent students. Kshama Garg *Asian J Psychology and Education* 11(2) 1983 p 19-22

Physical environment and class adjustment. Kshama Garg *Educational Rev* 86(3) Mr 1980 p 50-54

Problem levels and personality patterns. R.K. Arora *J Indian Education* 8(6) Mr 1983 p 13-19 refs

Relative effect of co-educational and single sex schooling an academic adjustment of secondary school pupils. I.V. Ramana Reddy *J Education and Psychology* 44(1) Ap 1986 p 5-10 refs tabs

School adjustment and its relation to academic achievement of socially disadvantaged children. B.N. Sujatha *J Education and Psychology* 43(3-4) Oc 1985-Ja 1986 p 197-205 tabs

School adjustment : Part of learning milieu. M.P. Bhasin *Primary Teacher* 11(2) Ap 1986 p 17-20

Self-situational deprivations in the school adjustment of tribal children. Shivendra Kumar Kulshreshtha *J Indian Education* 5(2) Jl 1979 p 41-47

Sociometric study of stars and isolates in relation to their adjustment. Hariprasad O. Joshi *Progress of Education* 57(2) Se 1982 p 41-44 tabs

Stability of nominee status of adolescent boys and girls. Ramanath Kundu and Chandidas Biswas *Our Education* 3-4 Jl 1983 p 13-19 refs

A study of adjustment problems of the students of plus two levels. Prakash Chandra Shukla *Progress of Education* 55(9) Ap 1981 p 232-33 tabs

A study of relationship between adjustment and perceived parental behaviour among the male and female college students. T.K. Chatterjee and V. Shah *Our Education* 2 Jl 1981 p 45-49 refs tabs

Which school shall I choose for my child? : A study of adjustment among students studying in co-educational schools and in single sex schools : M.Le symbol and substance : Indian youth in development. Prabha Krishnan. New Delhi, Vishwa Yuvak Kendra. 1980, 119p. Rs. 15 *Book Rev, J Higher Education* 7(3) Spr 1982 p 332-33

Youth problems adjustment and scholastic performance : A comparative study. J.S. Jha and D.K. Saxena *J Educational Research and Extension* 18(2) Oc 1981 p 49-54 refs tabs

Student Adjustment : India : Andhra Pradesh

Adjustment problems of primary school children : A survey in Andhra Pradesh. S. Subrahmanyam *Education Quarterly* 37(7) Spr 1985 p 32-37

Student Adjustment : India : Kerala

The Calicut University adjustment inventory. R.S. Nair *J Educational Research and Extension* 18(1) Jl 1981 p 22-42 tabs

Student Adjustment : India : Uttar Pradesh

Creativity in relation to adjustment. R.P. Singh *Question Education* 19(3) Jl 1982 p 227-33 refs tabs

Relationship of student activism and personality adjustment G.S. Aswal and G.U. Srinagar *J Institute of Educational Research* 6(3) Se 1982 p 20-23 refs

Student Aid

See also

Student Loan Funds

Student Aspirations

Student aspirations for their future position in life. R.V. Naidu *Indian Education* 10(6) Se 1980 p 34-39

Students problems, self-concept, and level of aspiration : comparative study. R K. Arora *Indian Educational Rev* 20(3) Jl 1985 p 12-22

Student Aspirations : India

Educational and vocational aspirations of Hindu and Muslim school students : A comparative study. M.W. Khan *Indian Educational Rev* 20(4) Oc 1985 p 66-77

Student Attitudes

See

Students : Attitudes

Student Counsellor-Parent Relationships

See

Parent-Student Counsellor Relationships

Student Discipline

Problems of students discipline. Sheikh Imtiaz Ali *Teacher Education* 20(30-31) Ja-Ap 1985 p 25-29

Problems of students discipline. Sheikh Imtiaz Ali *University News* 23(13) 1 Ap 1985 p 3-4+

A study of causes of indiscipline among students as viewed by teachers and

students. Awadesh Kumar Sinha and Suresh Prasad Shahi *J Education and Psychology* 38(3) Oc 1980 p 159-65

A study of the attitudes of high school students towards discipline. T.S. Sodhi *Quest in Education* 16(4) Oc 1979 p 236-44 refs

See also

Student Unrest

Student Ethics

Development of moral judgement in boys and girls and two age levels. A.S. Sethi and Deepti Gupta *J Education and Psychology* 42(1-2) Ap-Jl 1984 p 41-44 refs

A study of sex differences among university students towards different types of values. Swarn Pratap *J Education and Psychology* 42(4) Ja 1985 p 219-22 refs

Student Evaluation of Teachers

A sample study of evaluation of teacher by students. Gomathi Mani *J Higher Education* 5(2) Aut 1979 p 228-32

Student evaluation of instructors as a function of expected and obtained performance. Christopher Orpen *J Higher Education* 9(1) Mon 1983 p 89-94 refs

Teacher student mutual linking at different grade levels. S.P. Malhotra *Indian Educational Rev* 18(3) Jl 1983 p 95-101 refs

Teaching evaluation : Are student comments redundant? Harold C. Ratzlaff *Progress of Education* 58(3) Oc 1983 p 68-70 tabs

Student Failure

See

Students Failure

Student Federation of India

Atul anjari demands permanent coordination Committee between AISF and SFI. *Student Action* 2(9) Mr 1984 p 3-4

Student Guidance

See

Personnel Service in Education

Vocational Guidance

Student Loan Funds

The use of student loans in the finance of higher education : A summary of Western experience. Maureen Woodhall *J Higher Education* 5(3) Spr 1980 p 417-21 refs tabs

Student Movements

See

Student Unrest

Student Participation in Administration

College administration : The study of faculty and student participation in college administration. R.C. Srivastava. New Delhi, Metropolitan Book Co. 1980, 308p. Rs. 75 *Book Rev, Indian Educational Rev* 15(3) Jl 1980 p 126-27; *J Higher Education* 6(1-3) 1980-81 p 166-67

Faculty and student status in adminstration. R.C. Srivastava *J Higher Education* 4(2) Aut 1978 p 225-44

Participation, faculty satisfactors and perceived institutional climate. R.C. Srivastava *J Higher Education* 9(1) Mon 1983 p 94-107 refs tabs

Student Participation in Adminsitration : India

Student participation in college adminstration. B. Rajaiah *Experiments in Education* 12(3) My 1984 p 46-49

Students participation in the management of education systems : A preliminary analysis of emerging trend in India. Swaraj Bandyopadhyay and Nilanjana Kundu *J Higher Education* 8(3) Spr 1983 p 342-48 refs

Student participation in university adminstration. Rajeshwar Upadhyaya *National J Education* 2(2) Mr 1980 p 45-51 refs

Student Periodicals

See

College and School Periodicals

Student Political Activities

See

Students, Political Activity

Student Protest

See

Student Unrest

Student Rating of Teachers

See

Student Evaluation of Teachers

Student-Teacher Relationships

See

Teacher-Students Relationships

Student Teachers

The effect of micro-teaching and integration of skills on teaching self-concept of student teachers. Mathew George *J Educational Research and Extension* 19(3) Ja 1983 p 129-37

Effect of varying sources of feedback upon the general teching competence of student teacher under micro-teaching situation. Vimla Mahesh and J.P. Srivastava *Indian Educational Rev* 16(3) Jl 1981 p 51-58

Impact of training on the educational beliefs of secondary teacher trainees. M. Rama Mohana Rao and D.S.N. Sastry *Experiments in Education* 10(10) De 1982 p 179-83 tabs

Personality traits of student teachers of an army run and a government managed institution : A comparative study. S.P. Ahluwalia and Pratibha Pandeya *J Education and Psychology* 43(1) Ap 1985 p 27-33 refs tabs

Student teachers and the teaching profession. R.D. Sharma *Experiements in Education* 12(8) Oc 1984 p 145-49; 12(11) Ja 1985 p 199-201 refs tabs

Student Teachers : India

Attitude of teacher trainees towards games and sports. Satish Kumar Yadav *Progress of Education* 55(4) Nv 1980 p 102-04+

Comparison of Hindu and Muslim student teachers responses to a measure of authoritarianism in India. T.N. Raina *Indian Educational Rev* 15(4) Oc 1980 p 15-23 refs tabs

Personality adjustment of creative and non-creative student teachers in India. R.J. Singh *Indian Educational Rev* 15(4) Oc 1980 p 49-55

Value orientations of creative and non-creative student-teachers in India. R.J. Singh *Quest in Education* 17(4) Oc 1980 p 318-26 refs

Student Teachers : India : Andhra Preadesh

An inquiry into the study habits of B.Ed students. D. Bhaskara Rao *Educational Rev* 92(8) Ag 1986 p 134-35

Student Teachers : India : Gujarat

Self-concept of student teachers of colleges of education. M.D. Trivedi *Teacher Education* 15(14-15) Ja-Ap 1981 p 37-44 refs tabs

Student-Teachers : India : Haryana

Attainments of students-teachers in education theory : A factorial view. R.C. Hooda *Indian Educational Rev* 17(4) Oc 1982 p 101-08 refs tabs

An attitudinal study of experienced and non-experienced B.Ed. teachers towards their profession. P.K. Sharma and V.K. Gupta *Progress of Education* 55(1) Jl 1981 p 321-24 tabs

A study of social cohesion in secondary training institutions and attitude of student teachers. R.C. Hooda and Krishna Dhaka *J Education and Psychology* 42(3) Oc 1984 p 109-14 refs

Student Teachers : India : Punjab

A study of personality differences among student teachers. K. Anwarjit Singh *J Institute of Educational Research* 9(3) M 1985 p 1-3 refs tabs

A study of the relationship between attitude of teacher trainees of private and government B.Ed Colleges towards profession and their teaching competence. Geeta Devi G. Patil *Research Bulletin* 16(1-2) Mr-Je 1986 p 27-34 tabs

A study of relationship between the self concept of student teachers and their supervisors ratings. Meenu Gupta *Teacher Education* 16(18-19) Ja-Ap 1982 p 38-47 refs tabs

Student Teachers : India : Uttar Pradesh

Relating creative thinking abilities with academic achievement and teaching skills of student teachers. R.J. Singh *J Indian Education* 10(5) Ja 1985 p 49-51

A study of biographical attributes of high and low creative student-teachers. Subhash Chandra Agarwal and Sushi Prakash Gupta *Indian Education* 12(8-9) Nv-De 1982 p 25-27

A study of student disciplinary practices and teacher effectiveness in relation to classroom anxiety among student teachers. Karuna Shankar Misra *Experiements in Education* 8(8) Oc 1980 p 142-45 refs tabs

Student Teachers : Psychology

Sex differences in the personality profiles of student-teacher. S.P. Ahluwalia and Pratibha Pandeya *Indian Educational Rev* 20(2) Ap 1985 p 21-27

A study of personality differences among student teachers. K. Anwarjit Singh *J Institute of Educational Research* 9(3) Se 1985 p 1-3 tabs

Student Teachers : Rating

A strategy for the professional self : improvement of teachers-Paper presented at the SITU Council of educational research, Madras on 11.3.1978. M.S. Lalitha *Experiments in Education* 6(2) Ap 1978 p 21-26 refs

Student Teachers : Socio Economic Status

Effect of socio-economic status and academic achievement on risk taking behaviour of student teachers. R.C. Hooda and H.R. Paul *J Institute of Educational Research* 10(2) My 1986 p 1-3

Student Teaching

Adoption in student teaching : A Try out. Madhu Shah *et al Experiements in Education* 9(9) Nv 1981 p 156-59

Adoption in student teaching programme : A try out. Madhu Shah *et al Experiments in Education* 10(2) Ap 1982 p 38-40

An antomy of student teaching. Shribatsa I. Jena *Education Quarterly* 32(3) Jl 1980 p 10-12

An assessment of the relation between teacher-trainees' attitudes and performance in theory and practice of teaching. Sunanda Ghosh *Indian Educational Rev* 17(4) Oc 1982 p 20-30 refs tabs

Attitude of teacher trainees and their parents towards teaching. S.B. Kokkar *Asian J Psychology and Education* 13(2-4) 1984 p 49-51

Attitude of teaching trainees towards teaching during pre and post student teaching period : A differential study. Shashi Kant *Asian J Psychology and Education* 3(3) Nv 1978 p 1-4

Carry over effect of micro-teaching on student teachers from college of education to regular school teaching. S.P. Malhotra and R.N. Syag *Progress of Education* 53(8) Mr 1981 p 208-10 tabs

Clinical approach to student teaching. V.K. Rai *Educational Rev* 88(2) Fe 1982 p 28-29

Comparative study of modular teaching and traditional teaching methods at B.Ed. level the subject of civics. J.P. Sharma *Progress of Education* 57(9) Ap 1983 p 202-03+

A comparative study of the effect of micro-teaching and Diod model to improve teaching competency of pre-service teachers. R.N. Syag *et al J Institute of Educational Research* 6(1) Ja 1982 p 38-41 refs tabs

A comparative study of the evaluation of student teaching by teacher educators and the supervising school teachers at the secondary level. Gomathi Mani *Experiments in Education* 8(12) Fe 1981 p 213-17 refs tabs

Content-cum-methodology theory and practice. R.C. Hooda and R.N. Syag *Experiments in Education* 9(12) Fe 1982 p 221-22+ tabs

Creativity in relation to teaching subjects offered by student teachers. R.P. Goyal *J Education and Psychology* 41(4) Ja 1984 p 209-14 refs

The effect of micro-teaching and integration of skills on teaching self-concept of student teachers. Mathew George *J Educational Research and Extension* 18(2) Oc 1981 p 31-39 refs tabs

Effect of practice on teaching efficiency and teaching attitude of B.Ed. students. Vimla Mahesh and Alka Saxena *Indian Educational Rev* 18(1) Ja 1983 p 109-15 tabs

The effect of practice teaching on teaching competence and attitude towards teaching of preservice teachers, Bhoodev Singh *J Institute of Educational Research* 10(1) Ja 1986 p 13-16 refs tabs

Effect of strategies developed through micro-teaching with integration of teaching skills using summative model upon student teachers teaching competences. P.K.S. Ray *Teacher Education* 14(12-13) Jl-Oc 1980 p 27-33 refs tabs

Expected performance of pupil teachers and their actual performance during practice teaching. N.S. Kapruan *Quest in Education* 18(2) Ap 1981 p 150-87

An experiment study of improvement in the teaching skills under micro-teaching among the student teachers. Charudatta Parasharam Kadam *Educational Rev* 91(4) Ap 1985 p 69-72 refs

An experimental study of improvement in the teaching skills under micro-teaching among the student teachers. Charudatta Parshuram Kadam *Progress of Education* 58(10) My 1984 p 246-48 refs tabs

Innovation in student teaching. N.A. Shelat and S.B. Mohanty *Educational Rev* 89(4-6) My-Je 1983 p 94-95

Innovations in student teaching : Some considerations. Piloo Buch *New Frontiers in Education* 11(1) Ja-Mr 1981

Inservice teachers and student teachers : A comparative study attitude towards teaching. V.K. Raina *J Education and Psychology* 41(3) Oc 1983 p 138-45

Personality needs and student teaching competency. Sushil Prakash Gupta *Proress of Education* 58(9) Ap 1984 p 210-12 tabs

Practice school programme at BITS - A new concept in higher education. R. Manuvalan *J Higher Education* 8(2) Aut 1982 p 235-38 tabs

Practice teaching : Its supervision. Shamsuddin *Asian J Psychology and Education* 4(1) Ja 1979 p 31-34

Prediction of student teaching success. R.C. Dave *J Education and Psychology* 37(2) Jl 1979 p 139-47 refs

Printing of the practising teacher. G.P. Kulshrestha *Rajasthan Board J Education* 15(2) Ap-Je 1979 p 29-34

Problems in practice teaching. N. Venkataiah *Indian Education* 10(9-10) De 1980-Ja 1981 p 7-12

Problems of student teaching : An opinion survey. V.K. Ravi *Experiments in Education* 11(8) Oc 1983 p 134-37 Relationship of attainments in theory papers with student teaching in secondary teachers training programme. R.C. Hooda and R.N. Syag *J Education and Psychology* 40(4) Ja 1983 p 220-24 refs

Reorganisation in practice teaching. Jagannath Mohanty *Rajasthan Board J Education* 15(1) Ja-Mr 1979 p 11-16

Skill-based approach to student teaching. Sneha Joshi and Eknath Ekbote *New Frontiers in Education* 11(2) Ap-Je 1981 p 81-85 refs

The student teaching programme : A review of researches. Sunil Behari Mohanty *Progress of Education* 56(10) My 1982 p 228-35 refs

Student teaching programmes in colleges of education : Some suggestions. S.M. Divekar *J Indian Education* 5(5) Ja 1980 p 3-7

A study of teaching behaviour of teachers in relation to their personality adjustment. Rama Mishra *Progress of Education* 59(8) Mr 1985 p 186-89

A study of the relationship between teaching efficiency attitude towards teaching profession and academic achievement of the trainees (U.T.C.). U.K. Gupta *et al Educational Rev* 91(11) Nv 1985 p 196-97 refs

System of evaluation in student teaching programme. M.B. Menon and S. Kumar *National J Education* 6(1) Se 1983 p 7-19

Teaching styles of student-teachers exposed to micro-teaching approach and traditional approach. K.A. Gandhi *Experiments in Education* 10(1) Mr 1982 p 3-6 refs

Theory into practice : An analysis of B.Ed theory and practice marks. V.K.

Raina *Indian Educational Rev* 17(4) Oc 1982 p 134-40 refs tabs

Vitalising practice teaching. Rashmin Thakore *Educational Rev* 86(7) Jl 1980 p 121-26

Vitalising practice teaching. Rashmin Thakore *Progress of Education* 55(5) De 1980 p 133-39 refs

Student Teaching : Aids and Devices

The effects of feedback, supervisor, tape recorder and peer supervisor on a teaching skill : Stimulus variation. A.K. Gupta and S.K. Sharma *Experiments in Education* 7(4) Je 1979 p 69-72 refs tabs

Student Teaching : India

Organising practice teaching. R.R. Ashar *Teacher Today* 22(4) Ap-Je 1980 p 54-58

Review of studies and literature on student teaching and other practical work in B.Ed. programme in India. T.N.S. Bhatnagar *Quest in Education* 19(3) Jl 1982 p 206-26

Student teaching and other practical work in the B.Ed. programme in India : Review of studies and literature. T.N.S. Bhatnagar *Indian Educational Rev* 18(3) Jl 1983 p 17-32 refs

Student Teaching : India : Haryana

An attitudinal study of experienced and non-experienced B.Ed. teachers towards their profession. P.K. Sharma and V.K. Gupta *Progress of Education* 55(12) Jl 1981 p 321-24 tab

Student Teaching : India : Madhya Pradesh

Evolvement of an instructional strategy at B.Ed. level for teaching learning. D.N. Sansanwal and Anuradha Joshi *J Educational Research and Extension* 18(2) Oc 1981 p 1-9

Student Teaching : India : Maharashtra

Practice teaching in college of education. W.V. Bhave *Progress of Education* 55(12) Jl 1981 p 328-30

A study of attitude of B.Ed. Pupil teachers towards teaching profession. K.T. Mehare and Geeta Devi Patil *J Institute of Educational Research* 10(2) My 1986 p 8-11 refs

Student Teaching : India : Orissa

Innovation in student teaching through NSS in Orissa state. Sunil Behari Mohanty *Educational Rev* 90(2) Fe 1984 p 21-24 refs

Student Teaching : India : Punjab

Teaching practice in training course : An evaluation. S.S. Mann *Experiments in Education* 6(4) Je 1978 p 57-60

Student Teaching : India : Uttar Pradesh

The effect of practice teaching on teaching competance and attitude towards teaching of preservice teachers. Bhoodev Singh *J Institute of Educational Research* 10(1) Ja 1986 p 13-16 refs tabs

Student Unions

Intelligence, creativity and indisciplined behaviour in student union activities among the university students. J.B.S. Mard and Bheema Manral *Progress of Education* 60(3) Nv 1985 p 83-85 tabs

The students bodies in the universities. Virendra Singh *J Higher Education* 8(2) Aut 1982 p 228-33 tabs

Student Unrest

Approval/disapproval of strikes culture : A sample survey of students guardians and teachers. Abha Gani bisht *J Higher Education* 7(3) Spr 1982 p 272-77 refs

An historical review of struggles for student power : Where the oppressed of all ages once became the apparent. D. Thenurara Gomage *Perspectives in Education* 21(4) Oc 1986 p 195-212 refs

Misconduct of students. Arun Bhattacharjee. New Delhi, Deep & Deep Pub. 440 p. Rs. 125 *Book Rev, New Frontiers in Education* 12(3) Jl-Se 1982 p 76-77

Student protest : biomedical perspective. Steven A. Peterson and Albert Somit *J Higher Education* 3(3) Spr 1978 p 333-44 refs ft-n tabs

Student unrest : A psychoanalysis. P.N. Sahi *Teacher Today* 24(1) Jl-Se 1981 p 61-68

Student Unrest : India

The campus unrest : Students perception. Malka Raj Tuli *J Education and Psychology* 43(1) Ap 1985 p 59-64 refs

Revolt activism and apathy : Reflections on socio-political expectations of student in India. Anil Baran Ray *J Higher Education* 4(3) Spr 1979 p 301-12

Student unrest in an unplanned university : A case study. Swaraj Bandyopadhyay and Swapan K. Bhattacharya *J Higher Education* 3(3) Spr 1978 p 381-86 refs tabs

Youth unrest in contemporary Indian university. Bhupendra Kumar Nagla *J Higher Education* 8(3) Spr 1983 p 289-98 refs

Students

Obscurantism among the university students. Harikesh Singh *J Higher Education* 4(1) Mon 1978 p 91-98 refs tabs

Status perception of the faculty. C.B. Dwivedi *et al Asian J Psychology and Education* 4(3) Nov 1979 p 14-17 refs

Student perception of leadership characteristics. P. Joseph Satharaj *J Indian Education* 8(1) My 1982 p 15-18 refs tabs

Student : Environmental awareness. P. Mohan Raju *Indian Education* 10(5) Ag 1980 p 19-22

Student welfare services : Problems and prospects. R. Krishna Rao and D. Nageswara Rao *J Indian Education* 10(6) Mr 1985 p 55-60

See also

All India Students Federation
College Students
Engineering Students
High School Students
Home Economics Students
Science Students
Student Federation of India
Talented Students
Underachivers

Students : Attitudes

Anxious attitude of students in relations to some backward variables. M.K. Satyarthi *Asian J Psychology and Education* 4(1) Ja 1979 p 35-39 refs

Attitudes in vital areas. M.D. Sharma *J Indian Education* 8(3) Se 1982 p 9-13 tabs

Students attitude towards study. Sumitra I. Patel *J Education and Psychology* 38(3) Oc 1980 p 181-88 refs tabs

Students attitudes towards school. Louis Vernal *Indian Educational Rev* 14(4) Oc 1979 p 1-12 refs ft-n

A study of the effect of economic status on students attitude towards school experience. M.K. Satyarthi *Asian J Psychology and Education* 9(3) 1982 p 7-10

Values as a function of caste. S.S. Mathur and Ashok K. Kalia *J Education and Psychology* 42(1-2) Ap-Jl 1984 p 36-40 refs

Students : Ethics

See

Student Ethics

Students : Failure

Failures, pillars of success or breeders of despondency and criminality. B.G. Tiwari *Rajasthan Board J Education* 20(3) Jl-Se 1984 p 8-12

Who fails, student or the system? Mali Ram Sharma *Rajasthan Board J Education* 20(3) Jl-Se 1984 p 1-7

Students : Foreign : (in India)

Foreign students : A study. D.R. Goel *Experiments in Education* 8(4) Je 1980 p 74-76; 8(5) Jl 1980 p 93-96; 8(6) Ag 1980 p 108-11

Students : India

Selection of courses of study by P.U. (SC) students. P.C. Das *J Higher Education* 5(2) Aut 1979 p 236-42

Selected social norms of the home science students : A. Chandra and Aparna H. Khaund *J Higher Education* 8(3) Spr 1983 p 356-63

Student perception of the purposes of higher education P. Joseph Sathiaraj *J Higher Education* 9(3) Spr 1984 p 395-97 refs

Students and social life : A study. D.R. Goel *Experiments in Education* 7(4) Je 1979 p 73-74

Students and youth convention. *Student Action* 2(4) Ag 1983 p 14+

A study of national integratedness in NSS and non-NSS students. Gyanendra P. Shrivastava *J Education and Psychology* 35(4) Ja 1979 p 192-99

A study of students expectations of secondary school principals of Delhi. R.P. Jain *Progress of Education* 55(4) Nv 1980 p 107-13

Why students shun studies. S.S. Jaswal *Educational Rev* 86(1) Ja 1980 p 11-12

Students : India : Gujarat

A comparative study of vocational interest of home science students in relation to the selected variables. Naina Talati and Uma Joshi *Progress of Education* 61(4-5) Nv-De 1986 p 92-95 refs

Students : India : Punjab

A study of time utilisation by rural school and college students during summer vacation. Raghbir Singh and Surjit Singh Gill *J Higher Education* 4(1) Mon 1978 p 81-86 refs tabs

Students : India : Rajasthan

Profiles of Jaipur students : Their expectation of education and institution. S.S. Nathwat *Prasar* 9(1-4) Ap 1982-Ja 1983 p 51-58

Students : India : Uttar Pradesh

Some psycho-social attributes of student leaders : A differential study. P.C. Sharma *J Higher Education* 6(1-3) 1980-81 p 136-48 refs tabs

Personality characteristics of urban and rural adolescent, students. R.S. Gaur *Indian Educational Rev* 15(1) Ja 1980 p 119-22

A study of motivational aspects of occupational choice of the Indian students of graduate studies. A.K. Srivastava *National J Education* 6(1) Se 1983 p 40-47 refs tabs

Students : India : West Bengal

Bengal's student movement. Gautam Chattopadhyay *Student Action* 2(10) My 1984 p 6+; 2(11) Je 1984 p 2-3+

Students : Indian : (in Foreign Countries)

Indian students and trainees in scientific and technical fields who went abroad during 1965-75. B.K. Nayar *et al J Higher Education* 4(2) Aut 1978 p 171-85

Students : Indian : (in Foreign Countries) : United States

Indian students in the United States. Victor Jesudason *Indian Educational Rev* 14(1) Ja 1979 p 1-21 refs tabs

Students : Medical Examinations

A study of physical health and fitness problems of students. T.S. Sodhi and Surya Bala *Quest in Education* 17(4) Oc 1980 p 338-51 refs

Students : Personality

See

Students : Psychology

Students : Political Activity

Attitude and political and protest behaviour. C.L. Kundu and B.S. Wadhwa *J Education and Psychology* 42(1-2) Ap-Jl 1984 p 15-22 refs

Student politics in the third world. Philip C. Altbach *New Frontiers in Education* 14(2) Ap-Je 1984 p 66-84

Students : Psychology

Attitude and political and protest behaviour. C.L. Kundu and B.S. Wadhwa *J Educational and Psychology* 42(1-2) Ap-Jl 1984 p 15-22 refs

Attitude of students towards English and regional media. A. Venkata Rami Reddy *Quest in Education* 18(3) Jl 1981 p 205-19

A comparative study of personality syndromes of scheduled castes and non-scheduled castes. L.P. Gupta *Teacher Education* 13(8-9) Jl-Oc 1979 p 83-84

Contact personality factors of science, agricultural science and agricultural engineering under-graduate students. Usha Kumamat and G.C. Rai *Indian J Extension Education* 19(3-4) Se-De 1983 p 26-31 refs

Critical factors in human assessment : A plea for evaluating non-scholastic aspects of students growth. N.K. Upasani *Progress of Education* 56(3) Oc 1981 p 54-61 refs

Development of social competence schools obligation to children and adolescents. Prema Sharma *Quest in Education* 17(3) Jl 1980 p 217-27 refs

Effect of anxiety and original thinking of students indifferent streams at +2 stage. A. Kumar and S. Sharma *J Education and Psychology* 40(3) Oc 1982 p 157-61

Identifying the changing students. Har Govind Gupta *J Indian Education* 5(4) Nv 1979 p 35-37

An investigation into existing and expected personal characteristic image patterns of secondary school going children. Anil K. Saxena *Quest in Education* 17(1) Ja 1980 p 59-65 refs

An investigation into social maturity as a function of area and modernisation. I.A. Vora *J Education and Psychology* 40(1-2) Ap-Jl 1982 p 53-61 refs

Personality characteristics of activist students. G.S. Aswal *Progress of Education* 58(8) Mr 1984 p 183-86 refs

Prevention of disruptive behaviour. Sushma Sharma *Primary Teacher* 10(4) Oc 1985 p 37-39

Relationship of disciplined and indisciplined behaviour with academic achievement of adolescent students. Zakia A. Siddiqui and R. Fatima Bilgrami *J Education and Psychology* 42(3) Oc 1984 p 119-22

Relationship of student activism personality needs. G.S. Aswal *J Education and Psychology* 41(1-2) Ap-Jl 1983 p 37-42

Relationship of student and activism and personality adjustment. G.S. Aswal and G.U. Srinagar *J Institute of Educational Research* 6(3) Se 1982 p 20-23 refs

Self-expression of blind students. Prabhakar Singh *Primary Teacher* 11(4) Oc 1986 p 12-14

Social behaviour of teachers and their impact on the social behaviour of students : A socio-econometric study. Ashok K. Kalia and S.S. Mathur *Progress of Education* 59(2) Se 1984 p 34-37 refs tabs

Socio-metric study of personality traits. Akthar Bano and B.S. Satyanarayana *J Institute of Educational Research* 6(2) My 1982 p 17-22 refs tabs

Some psychological correlates the sense of responsibility. Sarla Kumari Pandey *Progress of Education* 60(1) Ag 1985 p 2-6 refs

A study of attitude of college and university students towards drug abuse. Kulwinder Singh *J Institute of Educational Research* 7(3) Se 1983 p 1-6

Students : Part Time

An examination of the role of the part time education in Indian educational system. M.N. Ravindranatha *Experiments in Education* 9(11) Ja 1982 p 194-201

The role of part-time education in our educational system M.N. Ravindranatha *J Indian Education* 6(5) Ja 1981 p 37-40

Students : Rating

An alternative approach of measuring students' performance for different recruitments. A.C. Bora *J Higher Education* 8(2) Aut 1982 p 215-20 refs

A correlational study of students performance. J.A. Christian *J Institute of Educational Research* 4(1) Ja 1980 p 16-19 refs tabs

A correlational study of the student ratings of instruction with examination performance. M.P. Patel *J Education and Psychology* 40(3) Oc 1982 p 117-26

See also

Educational Tests and Measurements

Grading Marking (Students)

Students : Religious Life

The religiosity questionnaire. Asha Gupta *Indian Educational Rev* 18(4) Oc 1983 p 123-31

World mindness as related to personal values and religion of collegiates. Ramji Srivastava and Q.G. Alam *J Education and Psychology* 38(1) Ap 1980 p 33-35 tabs

Students : Socio-Economic Status

A comparative study of value patterns of science and commerce undergraduates. Ashok Kumar and Darshan Anand *J Higher Education* 7(3) Spr 1982 p 277-80 tabs

Creativity, intelligence and socio-economic status. Arun Kumar Gupta and Suresh K. Sharma *Indian Educational Rev* 17(1) Ja 1982 p 64-70 refs

Counselling of the socially disadvantaged child. Nidhu Mohan *Asian J Psychology and Education* 11(2) 1983 p 1-8

Current status of studies on approval motive : A critical appraisal. Girishwar Misra and B.N. Tiwari *J Education and Psychology* 42(3) Oc 1984 p 154-62 refs

Degree of the sense of responsibility in relation to some socio-economic variables. Sarla Kumari Pandey and Rajeshwar Upadhyay *Progress of Education* 59(7) Fe 1985 p 150-56 tabs

Differential personality traits of tribal and non-tribal adolescents at different levels of intelligence and socio-economic status. Sudarsan C. Panigrahi *J Education and Psychology* 44(1) Ap 1986 p 51-57 refs

Economic status as a determinant of tension among youths. Shamsur Rehman Khan *Asian J Psychology and Education* 13(1) Ja 1984 p 4-6

The effect of socio-economic deprivation upon the intelligence of the school going children. Ramesh C. Dixit and Janki D. Moorjani *J Education and Psychology* 40(4) Ja 1983 p 214-19 refs

Effect of socio-economic status on the academic achievement of XI grade students. Lal Singh *J Education and Psychology* 42(4) Ja 1985 p 223-28 refs

An exploratory study of quality of school life, relationship with sex, socio-economic status and the type of school. M.K. Raina and Arunima Vats *Perspective in Education* 2(3) Jl 1986 p 161-69 refs

Home adjustment patterns of adolescent boys and girls at various levels of socio-economic status and general intelligence. B.K. Mattoo *J Education and Psychology* 40(3) Oc 1982 p 136-42

Intelligence in relation to different levels of socio-economic studies. P.O. Pappachan *J Institute of Educational Research* 7(3) Se 1983 p 15-18

Psychological factors associated with the socio-economic status. Sushma and V.V. Upmanyu *Asian J Psychology and Education* 4(2) Jl 1979 p 1-10 refs tabs

The relationship between economic status and value patterns of adolescents. S. Sathappan *Asian J Psychology and Education* 4(2) Jl 1979 p 46-50 refs

Relationship between socio-economic status and academic achievement. V. Rajasekaran *Experiments in Education* 6(1) Mr 1978 p 233-36 refs tabs

Relationship between sociometric index N-ach and rated pupil characteristics. Namita Panda *J Educational Research and Extension*

19(4) Ap 1983 p 224-32

Relationship of vocational choice to self concept and socio-economic status. Pratibha Deo and Vasudha Kamat *Research Bulletin* 14(1-2) Mr-Je 1984 p 40-47 refs

School achievement of pupils belonging to different levels of socio-economic status. Rita Krishnan *Asian J Psychology and Education* 9(3) 1982 p 11-17

Social and emotional adjustment patterns of adolescent boys and girls at various levels of socio-economic status and general intelligence. B.K. Mattoo *Indian Educational Rev* 15(1) Ja 1980 p 110-14 refs tabs

Social isolates in classrooms. M.K. Sarma *Educational Rev* 87(1) Ja 1981 p 15-17

Social relations of school pupils in a multi-religious secular society. Pratibha Deo and Namita Roy-Choudhury. *Indian Educational Rev* 18(3) Jl 1983 p 33-46 refs tabs

Social status in relation to some variables. Charulata H. Bedami *J Education and Psychology* 41(4) Ja 1984 p 205-08 refs

Socio-economic status 'urban' and academic achievement. K. Jagannadhan *J Education and Psychology* 44(3-4) Jl-De 1986 p 128-34

Socio-metric study of personality traits. Akthar Bano and B.S. Satyanarayana *J Institute of Educational Research* 6(2) My 1982 p 17-22 refs tabs

Structure of sociometric status in relation to personality characteristics and intelligence. Sushma Upmanyu and V.V. Upmanyu *J Institute of Educational Research* 6(1) Ja 1982 p 23-28 refs tabs

Students' problems of economic and material facilities : A study. T.S. Sodhi and Surya Bala *Indian Educational Rev* 17(3) Jl 1982 p 10-22 appdx refs tabs

A study of locus of control of high and low creative of high school students and different levels of socio-economic status. Lokesh K. Verma *J Education and Psychology* 38(2) Jl 1980 p 99-104 refs

A study of socio-economic status of the first year college students of M.S. University, Baroda in relation to the academic achievement. M.M. Shah *Experiments in Education* 11(3) My 1983 p 44-47

A study of the effect of economic status on students attitude towards school experience. M.K. Satyarthi *Asian J Psychology and Education* 9(3) 1982 p 7-10

Study of the effect of socio-economic status on the mathematical achievement of English grade children. Subhali Gorkhar *J Institute of Educational Research* 7(2) My 1983 p 12-15

A study of the effects of socio-economic status (SES) and sex on the levels of self concept, anxiety and adjustment. Papiya Ghose and Kiran Khurana *J Education and Psychology* 44(3-4) Jl-De 1986 p 141-47

A study of the socio-economic status variables. J.A. Christian *Progress of Education* 54(2) Se 1979 p 37-46

Values as a function of caste. S.S. Mathur and Ashok K. Kalla *J Education and Psychology* 42(1-2) Ap-Jl 1984 p 36-40 refs

See also

College Students Socio-Economic Status

Students : Socio-Economics Status : India

Value systems and value preference patterns of Indian youths belonging to different socio-metric levels. A. Bhushan and M. Ahuja *J Institute of Educational Research* 4(3) Se 1980 p 7-14 refs tabs

Students : Socio-Economic Status : India : Andhra Pradesh

Impact of Socio-economic status (Rural) and academic achievement. K. Jagannadhan *J Institute of Educational Research* 9(3) Se 1985 p 27-31 refs tabs

Students : Socio-Economic Status : India : Gujarat

A study of the comparison of socio-metric scoring techniques H.O. Joshi *Progress of Education* 61(2) Se 1986 p 43-44 refs

Students : Socio-Economic Status : India : Karnataka

A study of awareness to the Indian social problems an evinced by the postgraduate students of Bangalore University. M.S. Lalitha and Sawaranjit Toor *J Higher Education* 5(1) Mon 1979 p 96-101

Students : Socio-Economic Status : India : Orissa

Relationship between sociometric index N-Ach and rated pupil characteristics. Namita Panda *J Educational Research and Extension* 19(4) Ap 1983 p 224-32 refs tabs

Socio-economic profile of technical graduates in Orissa University of Agriculture and Technology. B. Mohanty and C. Satapathy *J Higher Education* 8(3) Spr 1983 p 363-73 refs

Students : Socio-Economic Status : India : Uttar Pradesh

Socioeconomic status of the family and social acceptability of the students among their classfellows. S.L. Chopra *National J Education* 6(2) My 1984 p 40-47 refs

Students : Socio-Economic Status : India : West Bengal

A study of the effect of socio-economic status on the frustation reactions of school going children. Ramanath Kundu and Jayanthi Ray-Chaudhuri *J Institute of Educational Research* 9(1) Ja 1985 p 13-17 refs tabs

Students : Tribal

Effect of school environment on the attitudes of Santal students. Rajiv Ranjan Singh and Shaitendra Kumar Ojha *J Institute of Educational Research* 10(3) Se 1986 p 28-31 refs

Students : Women : India

Women students in India : Status and personality. Savitri Sharma. New Delhi, Concept Pub. 1979 172p. Rs. 50 *Book Rev, Education Quarterly* 32(2) Jl 1980 p 46-47; *Indian Education* 9(12) Mr 1980 p 45-47; *Indian Educational Rev* 15(2) Ap 1980 p 128-29; *Teacher Today* 23(1) Jl-Se 1980 p 103

See also

Women College Students : India

Study, Courses of

See

Education : Curricula

Study, Method of

Exploiting cramming for teaching composition and essay type answers. Gopal Prasad Kulshreshtha *Rajasthan Board J Education* 21(2) Ap-Je 1985 p 1-8

Group-based learning experiences. M.B. Menon and Vasant Bhat *New Frontiers in Education* 13(1) Ja-Mr 1983 p 58-61

Relationship of study habits of home science under-graduate students with academic achievement and residence. Suman Bhatnagar and Sadhana Bordia *Progress of Education* 58(6) Ja 1984 p 143-45

See also

Homework

Study Habits

Developing self study habits. I. Satya Sundaram *Primary Teacher* 10(3) Jl 1985 p 13-15

Developing study skills in secondary schools. Harold L. Herber, *ed.* Int Reading Assn. 169p. *Book Rev, Education Quarterly* 31(2) Jl 1979 p 44-45

Encouraging self-study habits. I. Satya Sundaram *Rajasthan Board J Education* 20(1-2) Ja-Je 1984 p 43-46

The impact of study-habits of intellectually backward pupils upon their academic achievement. D. Patel *Quest in Education* 18(4) Oc 1981 p 335-43 refs

Inculcating study habits among children. Kuldip Kumar *Primary Teacher* 10(4) Oc 1985 p 24-26

An investigation into the study habits of adolescents of employed and non-employed mothers. Harbans Singh *J Institute of Educational Research* 10(1) Ja 1986 p 5-8 refs tabs

An investigation into the study habits of scheduled and non-scheduled caste adolescents. S.S. Chauhan and Harbans Singh *J Institute of Educational Research* 10(2) My 1986 p 21-24 tabs

Subconsciousness

See also

Dreams

Substitution : Psychological Aspects

Extraversion and drive as correlates of substitution reminiscence. Jitendra Mohan and Nalini Munjal *Asian J Psychology and Education* 4(3) Nv 1979 p 1-5 refs

Success

See

Academic Achievement

Sugarcane : India

Assessment of gain in knowledge of sugarcane development workers after a 4-month training course. R.P. Verma *et al Indian J Extension Education* 20(1-2) Je 1984 p 66-68

Summer Schools : Elementary

See

Vacation Schools

Superstition

Supersititions among school children. Sumitra L. Patel *Educational Rev* 90(4) Ap 1984 p 74-76; 90(5-6) My-Je 1984 p 88-90 tabs

Supervision of Schools

See

School Supervision

Supplementary Reading

Preparing exercises for supplementary readers in English. Mamta Agrawal *Teacher Today* 21(3) Ja-Mr 1979 p 56-70

Sweden

See also

Adult Educationa : Sweden
Educational Technology : Sweden

Switzerland

See also

Education, Primary : Switzerland

Talented Children

See

Gifted Children

Talented Students

National talent search : Some issues. C.P.S. Chauhan *National J Education* 7(1) Se 1984 p 61-64 refs tabs

Personality characteristics of academically talented students. J. Virk *J Education and Psychology* 44(1) Ap 1986 p 41-46

A study of some personality patterns of talented students in science. O.P. Verman and K. Yadav *J Educational Research and Extension* 16(2) Oc 1979 p 89-93 refs tabs

See also

Gifted Children
National Talent Search Examination

Talking

See

Conversation

Tamil Nadu

See also

Adoption of Improved Farm Practices : India : Tamil Nadu
Adult Education : India : Tamil Nadu
Adult Education, Rural : India : Tamil Nadu
Agricultural Administration : India : Tamil Nadu
Agricultural Extension Work : India : Tamil Nadu
Agricultural Extension Workers : India : Tamil Nadu
Agricultural Innovations : India : Tamil Nadu
Children : Nutrition : India : Tamil Nadu
College Students : India : Tamil Nadu
College Teachers : India : Tamil Nadu
Communication in Agriculture : India : Tamil Nadu
Dairying : India : Tamil Nadu
Education : India : Tamil Nadu
Education, Secondary : India : Tamil Nadu
Farmers : India : Tamil Nadu
Fertilizers and Manures : India : Tamil Nadu
High school Principals : India : Tamil Nadu
Illiteracy : India : Tamil Nadu
National Adult Education Programme : India : Tamil Nadu

Teacher Participation in Personnel Service

Teachers as a counsellor. V.N. Rao and B. Parthasarathy *Educational Rev* 90(12) De 1984 p 185-87 refs tabs

Teacher Participation in the Community

See

Teachers and Community

Teacher Placement

See

Teacher : Selection and Appointment

Teaher-Principal Relationships

Teacher perception of their principals PCI and rating of the principals. Ikponmwosa Owie *J Education and Psychology* 41(1-2) Ap-Jl 1983 p 26-29

Teacher-Pupil Interaction

See

Interaction Analysis in Education

Teacher Selection

See

Teachers : Selection and Appointment

Teacher-Student Relationships

Expected performance of pupil teachers and their actual performance during practice teaching. N.S. Kapruan *Quest in Education* 18(2) Ap 1981 p 150-57

Creative pupil perception by Angami Nagan serving in elementary schools of Nagaland. A.C. Pachaury *J Educational Research and Extension* 18(4) Ap 1982 p 224-28 refs tabs

Human relationships in schools. Pritam Singh Brar *Educational Rev* 86(6) Je 1980 p 117-19

Improving pupil responses in the classroom. N.K. Jangira *Primary Teacher* 6(4) Oc 1981 p 15-18

Inter-relations between a teacher and a child. Harishankar Sharma *Primary Teacher* 4(4) Oc 1979 p 28-30

An investigation into the relationship between teachers factual knowledge of teaching practice and their classroom verbal interactions. Sushma Goel *J Education and Psychology* 38(3) Oc 1980 p 166-71 refs tabs

Life in the classroom : A research study. F.A. Adeyyian *J Indian Education* 6(2) Jl 1980 p 3-8 refs tabs

Relationship of sex and age of the teacher with liking of boys and girls for their teachers, at different grade levels S.P. Malhotra *J Education and Psychology* 38(3) Oc 1980 p 172-80 refs tabs

Responsibility feelings of teachers and its relationship with their students adjustment and achievement. Kailash Chandra Vashistha *Experiments in Education* 9(5) Jl 1981 p 89-92

Student's attitude to teachers. Vimala Srinivasan *Educational Rev* 86(6) Je 1980 p 105-06

Students image of satisfied and dissatisfied teachers. K.U. Lavingia *Quest in Education* 16(3) Jl 1979 p 209-16

A study of correlation between classroom verbal and non-verbal behaviour components. Rakesh Jain *Educational Rev* 90(3) Mr 1984 p 56-58 refs

A study of students expectations of secondary school principals. R.P. Jain *J Educational Research and Extension* 13(3) Ja 1982 p 133-41 refs tabs

The teacher and the student. Claude D'Souza *New Frontiers in Education* 9(1) Ja-Mr 1979 p 39-51

Teacher behaviour and student characteristics. S.B. Kakkar *Indian Educational Rev* 17(1) Ja 1982 p 71-79 refs

Teacher classroom behaviour in the classes of boys and girls at different grade levels in relation to teachers sex and age. S.P. Malhotra *J Educational Research and Extension* 16(2) Oc 1979 p 100-14 refs tabs

Teacher effects and perceived behaviour changes in students. Sahab Singh *National J Education* 5(1) Se 1982 p 53-61 refs tabs

Teacher expectation effects on sociometric indices : Interpretation of findings. N.C. Dhoundiyal and V. Dhoundiyal *Progress of Education* 59(2) Se 1984 p 26-36 refs

Teachers, students and parents. Shamsuddin *Indian Education* 10(12) Mr 1981 p 8-12

Verbal classroom behaviour of high school science teachers : Social extraverts *vs* social introverts. *J Education and Psychology* 40(1-2) Ap-Jl 1982 p 16-28 refs

See also

Interaction Analysis in Education

Student Evaluation of Teachers

Teacher-Student Relationship : History

The teacher pupil relationship during Upanishadic period and its relevance to modern education. Sharda Maunikar *Progress of Education* 55(11) Je 1981 p 287-92 refs

Teacher Training

See

Teachers : Training

Teachers

Are married teachers more satisfied with their jobs than the unmarried. A. Venkata Rami Reddy and O. Babijan *Indian Educational Rev* 16(2) Ap 1981 p 15-18 refs

A comparative study of personality factors of effective and ineffective teachers in different types of school organisational climate. *Progress of Education* 55(11) Je 1981 p 300-02 tabs

Construction and standardisation of teachers job satisfaction scale. S.P. Gupta and J.P. Srivastava *J Educational Research and Extension* 18(3) Ja 1982 p 155-89 refs tabs

Democracy and the teacher. G.R. Sharma *Teacher Today* 22(4) Ap-Je 1980 p 28-31

Developing communication skills in teachers. Hans Raj Pal *Education Quarterly* 32(3) Jl 1980 p 27-29 refs

Developing social skills of teachers. Hans Raj pal *Experiments in Education* 7(2) Ap 1979 p 26-28 refs

Development of the educand : The role of the teacher. S.L. Makkar *J Indian Education* 12(4) Nv 1986 p 56-58

Dimensions of teacher adjustment. S.K. Mangal. Kurukshetra, Vishal Pub. 1985. Rs.60 *Book Rev, Research Bulletin* 15(1-2) Mr-Je 1985 p 53-56

An exploratory study of role conception of teachers. Surrendra Kumar Pattnaik *Asian J Psychology and Education* 6(2) Jl 1980 p 12-16

The ideal teachers. G.P. Sohoni. Pune, Nutan Pra. 160p. Rs.10 *Book Rev, Progress of Education* 56(9) Ap 1982 p 224

The international recommendations adopted by the special inter-governmental conference on the status of teachers in Paris, on October 5, 1966. *Teacher Today* 26(1) Jl-Se 1983 p 159-62

Is there anything like teachers will? Mali Ram Sharma *Teacher Today* 24(1) Jl-Se 1981 p 50-57

Job satisfaction of teachers and its relationship to their anger and aggression as rated by them. Debi Prasad Bhattacharyya *J Education and Psychology* 36(3) Oc 1978 p 160-62

Job satisfaction of teachers working under different managements. A. Venkata Rami Reddy and N. Krishna Reddy *Education Quarterly* 30(3) Oc 1978 p 28-29

Making of good teachers. Pritam Singh Brar *Educational Rev* 90(11) Nv 1984 p 165-67

Modification of teacher behaviour : Non-verbal cues as a feedback device. Rakesh Jain *J Indian Education* 12(1) My 1986 p 44-48

A new look on nation builders. Shamsuddin *Primary Teacher* 10(3) Jl 1985 p 1-4

Noble calling but poor returns. Shamsuddin *J Indian Education* 10(5) Ja 1985 p 29-33

Preparing better teachers. K.R.P. Singh *J Indian Education* 12(2) Jl 1986 p 3-7

A research study about teachers perceptions of job satisfaction. Edwin O. McCaskill *et al Indian Educational Rev* 15(3) Jl 1980 p 22-30 refs

Role of teachers. B.S. Hundal *Educational Rev* 90(1) Ja 1984 p 3-5

The role of teachers in a changing society. Shamsuddin *Education Quarterly* 36(2) Ap 1984 p 38-39

The role of teachers in changing society. Shamsuddin *Indian Education* 10(7) Oc 1980 p 17-20

The role of teachers in a changing society. Shamsuddin *J Indian Education* 12(4) Nv 1986 p 49-51

Role of teachers. N. Venkatiah *Educational Rev* 85(1) Ja 1979 p 9-10

The role of the teacher. Rajammal P. Devadas *J Educational Research and Extension* 20(1) Jl 1983 p 30-36

A scale to measure individual modernity of teachers. Shashi Kala Deshpande *J Institute of Educational Research* 8(2) My 1984 p 30-37 appdx refs tabs

A study of professional values among teachers in different organisational climates at 10+2 stage. Arun K. Gupta and D.R. Kapoor *EPA Quarterly Bulletin* 6(3-4) Oc 1983-Ja 1984 p 22-31 refs tabs

A study of the relationship between organisational climate and teachers job satisfaction. Balendu Sharma and S.P. Gupta *J Educational Research and Extension* 19(3) Ja 1983 p 143-49

Teacher : A practical context. Sarla Rajput *Primary Teacher* 6(1) Ja 1981 p 19-21

The teacher and the society. Daleep Mukherji *New Frontiers in Education* 9(1) Ja-Mr 1979 p 1-11

The teacher and the society. M.D. Pandey *Primary Teacher* 4(3) Jl 1979 p 32-33

The teacher : As behavioural and perceptualist. M.P. Bhasi *J Indian Education* 10(6) Mr 1985 p 48-54

The teacher as consultant. Verghis Chandy *Educational Rev* 92(9) Se 1986 p 149-50

Teacher-educators effectiveness : A research study. Umma Kulsum and M. Khazapeer *Indian Educational Rev* 20(2) Ap 1985 p 51-53

The teacher in a democratic set up. Pritam Singh Brar *Educational Rev* 89(5-6) My-Je 1983 p 86-89

Teacher planning : Cognitive information processing approach. Mihir K. Chatterjee *Indian Education Rev* 19(1) Ja 1984 p 27-35

Teacher. Sylvia Ashton-Warner. Middlesex, Penguin Books. 1986. *Book Rev, Teacher Today* 24(1) Jl-De 1981 p 104-06

Teachers and social change. S. Rajagopalan *Experiments in Education* 7(8) Oc 1979 p 131-36; 7(9) Nv 1979 p 166-70+; 7(10) De 1979 p 176-79; 7(12) Fe 1980 p 220-22 refs

Teachers as builders of a new nation. Shamsuddin *Education Quarterly* 35(4) Oc 1983 p 14-16 refs

Teachers, professional and class : A study of organised teachers. Jennifer Ozga and Martin Lawsn. London, Falmer Press. 1981, 153p. *Book Rev, Education Quarterly* 35(1) Ja1983 p 44-45

Teachers role in education. S.L. Makkar *Primary Teacher* 11(3) Jl 1986 p 16-17

Teachers values and job satisfaction. S.P. Anand *Indian Educational Rev* 15(4) Oc 1980 p 24-34 refs

When the teacher becomes a student. M. Subhramanya *Primary Teacher* 56(4) Oc 1979 p 15-17

Who told them to be teacher? R.S. Chainani *Progress of Education* 56(2) Se 1981 p 30-32+

See also

Art Teachers
Biology Teachers
College Teachers
Educational Associations
Elementary School Teachers
High School Teachers
Language Teachers
Mathematics Teachers
Science Teachers
Single Teacher Schools
Social Science Teachers
Student Teachers
Teachers : Part-time
Teachers : Rural

Teachers : Appointment
See
Teachers : Selection and Appointment
Teachers : Attitudes
Attitude of teachers towards contemporary socio-economic-political issues in India. D.C. Upreti *Teacher Today* 25(2) Oc-De 1982 p 19-43 tabs
Dimensions of teacher classroom behaviour and their relationship with demographic and professional factors — A review of researches. S.P. Malhotra *Progress of Education* 54(2) Se 1979 p 26-28
A scale to measure teachers attitude towards population education in secondary schools. Neelam Srivastava and Devki Tewari *J Education and Psychology* 41(1-2) Ap-Jl 1983 p 30-36
Social behaviour of teachers and their impact on the social behaviour of students : A socio-metric study. Ashok K. Kalia and S.S. Mathur *Progress of Education* 59(2) Se 1984 p 34-37 refs
A study of the effect of anxiety on teacher behaviour. Shashikala Despande and Lalitha V. Tirth *Indian Educational Rev* 15(2) Ap 1980 p 1-10 refs
A study of the influence of personal factors on teachers attitude towards their job. Tahira Khatoon and M.R. Verma *J Education and Psychology* 41(3) Oc 1983 p 159-67
Teacher behaviour as correlates of non-verbal creativity. K.P. Baranwal *Educational Rev* 91(4) Ap 1985 p 75-79 refs
Teachers professional attitude to library utilisation. P.S. Kawatra *Educational Rev* 89(9) Se 1983 p 151-52
Verbal and non-verbal classroom behaviours as related to teachers first and second order factors of personality. A.R. Bisht *Indian Educational Rev* 20(3) Jl 1985 p 79-90
Teachers : Awards
See also
National Awards for Teachers : India
Teachers : Conferences
See also
Indian Association of Teacher Educators, XXII, Annual Conference, Kanpur, 1981
Teachers : Germany : East
Social position of teachers in the German Democratic Republic. *Indian Education* 10(5) Ag 1980 p 27-30
Teachers : Great Britain
Teachers centres : The British model. Audrey Griggs *Rajasthan Board J Education* 15(4) Oc-De 1979 p 1-5
Teachers : High School
See
High School Teachers
Teachers : India
Bonus to the teachers : An analytical essay. R. Balapradad *Educational Rev* 88(9) Se 1982 p 151-52
The changing teachers. G.P. Singh *Teacher Today* 27(2) Oc-De 1984 p 21-25
Construction and standardisation of teachers job satisfaction scale. S.P

Gupta and J.P. Srivastava *J Education and Psychology* 38(1) Ap 1980 p 43-53 refs tabs
Effect of type of management and sex on job satisfaction of teachers. S. Venkata Rami Reddy and O. Babijan *Quest in Education* 17(4) Oc 1980 p 309-17 refs
National teachers commission. I and II. R.P. Singh *Teacher Today* 27(4) Ap-Je 1985 p 18-20
Problems of teachers working in tribal areas. D.L. Prasad Rao and P. Venkata Rao *Educational Rev* 89(2) Ag 1983 p 139-41
A study of the relationship between organisation climate and teachers job satisfaction. Balendu Sharma and S.P. Gupta *Educational Rev* 88(10) Oc 1982 p 177-79 refs
Teachers unrest. Kiran Prabha Jain *Educational Rev* 85(2) Fe 1979 p 29-31
Teachers unrest. Kiran Prabha Jain *Progress of Education* 54(1) Ag 1979 p 7-11
Unification of teachers movement in India. V.P. Raghavachari *Indian Education* 11(7) Oc 1981 p 18-24
See also
India : National Commissions for Teachers

Teachers : India : Gujarat
Creative pupil perception by the Gujarati teachers. A.C. Pachaury *J Education and Psychology* 43(3-4) Oc 1985-Ja 1986 p 153-57 refs

Teachers : India : Haryana
An attitudinal study of experienced and non-experienced B.Ed. teachers towards their profession. P.K. Sharma and V.K. Gupta *Progress of Education* 55(12) Jl 1981 p 321-34 tabs
Measuring adjustment of the teacher. S.K. Mengal *J Education and Psychology* 42(3) Oc 1984 p 134-39 refs

Teachers : India : Karnataka
Aptitude in teaching and job satisfaction among teachers. Rita George and B.G. Sudha *J Institute of Educational Research* 10(2) My 1986 p 16-20 refs tabs

Teachers : India : Maharashtra
A study of educational qualifications of teachers of StdX from selected districts of Marathwada. S.B. Gogale *Progress of Education* 58(10) My 1984 p 231-33 refs tabs

Teachers : India : Punjab
Job satisfaction among primary, middle and secondary school teachers. Sudesh Gakhar *et al J Institute of Educational Research* 8(2) My 1984 p 1-6 refs

Teachers : India : Rajasthan
Values of successful teachers. Sahab Singh *National J Education* 3(1) Se 1980 p 17-24 refs tabs

Teachers : India : Tamil Nadu
Teacher role : A study. K. Adinarayan *Experiments in Education* 9(12) Fe 1982 p 207-13 refs

Teachers : India : Uttar Pradesh
A correlational study of organisational climate and teacher attitudes. M.K. Tripathi *National J Education* 6(2) My 1984 p 21-32 refs tabs

Organisational climate and teacher attitudes : A study of relationship. Madhu Kanta Tripathi *Indian Education Rev* 15(1) Ja 1980 p 85-94 tabs

Problems of probationary teachers. H.N. Singh and L.P. Singh *Teacher Education* 14(10-11) Ja-Ap 1980 p 16-17 tabs

A study of educational leadership in relation to sex of the schools. P.C. Shukla *Indian Education* 12(8-9) Nv-De 1982 p 20-24 tabs

A study of educational leadership in relation to teachers attitudes. P.C. Shukla *EPA Quarterly Bulletin* 7(1-2) Ap-Je 1984 p 15-23 refs

A study of influence of personal factors on teachers attitude towards their job. Tahira Khatoon and M.R. Verma *J Institute of Educational Research* 6(2) My 1982 p 27-32 refs tabs

Work load of teacher educators. D.C. Samant *Progress of Education* 53(6) Ja 1979 p 96-101

Teachers : In-service Training

An assessment of the relation between teacher-trainees attitude and performance in theory and practice of teaching. Shunanda Ghosh *Indian Educational Rev* 17(4) Oc 1982 p 20-30 refs

Communication needs to strengthen the educational base : Correspondence courses for primary school teachers. Mulk Raj Chilona *Indian Education* 11(7) Oc 1981 p 38-44

Effect of training on attitude towards creative teaching and learning. M.K. Raina and Arunima Vats *Indian Educational Rev* 18(1) Ja 1983 p 109-10 refs

In-service continuing education of teachers — Some new dimensions. G.L. Narang *Progress of Education* 55(3) Oc 1980 p 70-73

In-service education of teachers at the centres of continuing education. G.S. Grewal *J Indian Education* 8(2) Jl 1982 p 69-73

In-service teacher education. Aziza Hanafi *Educational Rev* 92(10) Oc 1986 p 161-63

In-service teacher education. Paris, UNESCO. 1985, 214p. *Book Rev, J Indian Education* 12(1) My 1986 p 63-64

Inservice teacher education : Programmes and perspectives. Ajit Singh *J Indian Education* 12(1) Nv 1986 p 38-42 refs

Inservice training of teachers. Qamruddin *Primary Teacher* 8(2) Ap 1983 p 26-27

Innovative inset strategies for quality in education. M. Raj Chilana *Teacher Today* 22(2) Oc-De 1979 p 56-65

Revitalising educational extension services. C.S. Subba Rao *Progress of Education* 54(8) Mr 1980 p 160-62

Some thoughts on in-service education of teachers. Sushma Bhagia *New Frontiers in Education* 12(2) Ap-Je 1982 p 61-67

Teachers : In-service Training : Audio-Visual Aids

Radio-cum-correspondence in service teacher training courses in India. B.R. Goel *Experiments in Education* 10(3) My 1982 p 54-57

Teachers : In-service Training : India

Motivating the teacher for in-service education. P. Raghavendra Rao *Progress of Education* 58(12) Jl 1984 p 301-05

Teachers : Leaves of Absence

School climate and teacher absenteeism. K.A. Gandhi *Progress of*

Education 57(6) Ja 1983 p 137-41 refs tabs

Teachers : Mental Illness

Mental health of teacher promotes effective teaching and learning in classroom. B.P. Lulla *Indian Education* 10(12) Mr 1981 p 4-7

A study of mental health of school teachers. S.P. Anand *J Education and Psychology* 44(3-4) Jl-De 1986 p 105-11

Teachers : Political Activity

Politicisation of teachers in India. Shabbir H. Josh *Progress of Education* 61(2) Se 1986 p 33-36

Teachers : Psychology

Burnout : Implications for teacher motivation. Monica Misra *New Frontiers in Education* 13(3) Jl-Se 1983 p 48-55 refs

The concept of alienation : View of Marx and Durkhem. Amita Shukla *Indian Educational Rev* 12(5-6) Ag-Se 1982 p 19-22

Cognitive behaviour of teachers in the classroom. N.K. Jangira and Madhu Raizada *J Indian Education* 7(3) Se 1979 p 32-37 refs tabs

A comparative study of level of aspiration and modes of frustration reactions among prospective teachers. Penni Jain and Saroj Saxena *National J Education* 7(2) My 1985 p 38-45 refs tabs

Different types of observation schedules for specific skills. S.K. Sharma *Progress of Education* 54(6) Ja 1980 p 101-08

Effect of sex, training and experience on the personality development of teachers. S.K. Panda and R.K. Mishra *Indian Educational Rev* 18(4) Oc 1983 p 106-10

An estimate of the teachers aggressiveness in schools : A critical approach. Mahendra Kumar Goyal *Rajasthan Board J Education* 21(2) Ap-Je 1985 p 15-22

Incidence of anxiety among teachers. Karuna Shankar Misra *Asian J Psychology and Education* 4(1) Ja 1979 p 44-47

Indian norms of the Minnosota teacher attitude inventory. Agya Jit Singh *Indian Educational Rev* 14(4) Oc 1979 p 24-32 tabs

An investigation into social maturity as a function of area and modernisation. I.A. Vora *J Education and Psychology* 40(1-2) Ap-Jl 1982 p 53-61 refs

Personality profile of experienced teachers and teacher trainees. Amar Kumar *Teacher Education* 15(14-15) Ja-Ap 1981 p 90-94 refs tabs

Personality studies of teachers : A critique of research in India. S.P. Ahluwalia and Pratibha Pandeya *J Institute of Educational Research* 8(2) My 1984 p 25-29 refs

Personality traits of democratic and *laissez faire* type of teachers. K.G. Sharma and Aryendra Kumar Sharma *Indain Educational Rev* 15(2) Ap 1980 p 109-13 refs tabs

Relationship between teacher characteristics and teacher behaviour. *J Education and Psychology* 27(1) Ap 1979 p 42-50

School climate and teachers attitude. Saroj Pandey *Teacher Education* 14(12-13) Jl-Oc 1980 p 41-47 refs tabs

Some personal traits of a good teachers. S.L. Makkar *Primary Teacher* 8(3) Jl 1983 p 37-38

A study of graduate teachers adjustment and its relationship with student

academic achievement. Surender Wadhwa *J Education and Psychology* 35(3) Oc 1978 p 118-23 refs

A study of job satisfaction in relation to leadership style. P.C. Shukla *J Education and Psychology* 41(1-2) Ap-Jl 1983 p 59-63

Teacher adjustment as related to his classroom behaviour. S.P. Malhotra *Asian J Psychology and Education* 9(4) 1982 p 36-41

The teacher and the psychology of learning. Marlow Ediger *Progress of Education* 55(11) Je 1981 p 293-94

Teachers behaviour and its effects on pupils. Kuldip Kumar *Primary Teacher* 10(4) Oc 1985 p 17-23

Values correlates with effective teachers. Shanti P. Bohra *Asian J Psychology and Education* 13(1) Ja 1984 p 7-10 refs

Teachers : Part Time

Why not part-time teachers? M.S.V. Chari *Educational Rev* 86(1) Se 1980 p 19

Teachers : Rating

Academic learning time model of classroom instruction. Siba P. Bhattacherya *Our Education* 3-4 Jl 1983 p 31-34 refs

Certain psychological correlates of teacher effectiveness. Pramod Kumar and Dinesh Narain Mutta *J Education and Psychology* 41(3) Oc 1983 p 106-11 refs ft-n

A cluster analysis of some operational measure of pupil-teachers performance at the B.Ed level. K. Ramachandrachar *Indian Educaitonal Rev* 14(1) Ja 1979 p 140-47

A comparative study of the personality structure of the teachers trainees at high and low level of intelligence. S. Agarwall and R.K. Srivastava *J Education and Psychology* 41(4) Ja 1984 p 229-35 refs

Competency-based teaching : Some issues. Kamlesh Chaudhury *Progress of Education* 55(9) Ap 1981 p 22-26

Creativity and teacher effectiveness. S. Masih *Quest in Education* 16(2) Ap 1979 p 165-71

Dogmatism and teaching experience as determinants of pupil control ideology. K.A. Gandhi *J Education and Psychology* 38(3) Oc 1980 p 189-93 refs tabs

Effect of different techinques of feedback upon the attainment of teaching skills related to stimulus variation among teachers. Krishnan Kumar Sharma *Indian Educational Rev* 14(4) Oc 1979 p 54-60

Effect of training in selected teaching skills using micro-teaching on the teaching competence of social teachers : A field atudy. N.K. Jangira *et al J Indian Education* 8(4) Nv 1982 p 9-14 tabs

Evaluating teacher aptitudes. V. Natarajan and Ved Prakash *New Frontiers in Education* 12(3) Jl-Se 1982 p 50-52

Evaluation of teachers. C. Dharmarajan *Educational Rev* 92(4) Ap 1986 p 65-66

A factor analytic study of a preschool teacher rating scale. Rama Das and A. Srikanta Dash *Asian J Psychology and Education* 7(3) 1981 p 23-27 refs tabs

Grouping effect in rating scales : The case of faculty attitudes. Yoram Neumann *J Education and Psychology* 38(2) Jl 1980 p 76-87 refs tabs

Improvement of teachers professional competency in the use of classroom techniques. C.B. Patel *Progress of Education* 58(4) Nv 1983 p 81-84 appdx tabs

The making of a successful teacher. K.V. Natarajan *J Indian Education* 12(1) My 1986 p 22-25

Mental health of teacher promotes effective teaching and effective learning in classroom. B.P. Lulla *Progress of Education* 56(2) Se 1981 p 46-48

Personality and attitude patterns of good and poor teachers working in secondary school. S.P. Patnaik and K.C. Panda *J Education and Psychology* 39(4) Ja 1982 p 232-40 refs tabs

Personality correlates of creativity in prospective female teachers. R.P. Goyal *J Educational Research and Extension* 20(3) Ja 1984 p 188-96

Process-Process apprasing scale of teacher effectiveness. Anil G. Bhalwanker and Anant N. Joshi *Research Bulletin* (Suppl) 15(1-2) Mr-Je 1985 p I-VIII

Quality of teachers. S.B. Adval. Allahabad, Amitabh Pra. 1979, 180p. Rs.82.50 *Book Rev, National J Education* 2(2) Mr 1980 p 59-60

Research on assessing teacher effectiveness in developing countries. P.N. Dave *Perspectives in Education* 1(3) Jl 1985 p 195-204 refs

Sixteen personality factor qualification grid for teacher effectiveness. S.S. Srivastava and R.C. Gupta *National J Education* 5(1) Se 1982 p 15-28 refs

A study in the evaluation of teacher educators by their students under training in the B.Ed., summer school-cum-correspondence course. R.P. Kathuria and V.P. Gupta *Quest in Education* 18(4) Oc 1981 p 292-301

A study of emotive aspects of work perceived by effective and ineffective teachers. Dinesh Chandra *Quest in Education* 17(2) Ap 1980 p 173-80

A study of the relationship of certain selected variables of the teachers to their academy success. N. Venkataiah and K. Jayachandrama Naidu *J Education and Psychology* 43(3-4) Oc 1985-Ja 1986 p 174-82 refs

A study of the reliability and validity of the process appraising scale of teacher effectiveness. A.G. Bhalwankar *Research Bulletin* 15(1-2) Mr-Je 1985 p 32-40

A study of the teacher effectiveness as a function of age, sex, area and qualification. K.J. Patel and P.A. Dasa *J Education and Psychology* 42(1-2) Ap-Jl 1984 p 91-98 refs

Teacher competence and pupil performance : The effect of self craft, anxiety and motivation, S.P. Patnaik *J Indian Education* 12(1) My 1986 p 16-21 refs

Teacher creativity and family background : A study of relationship. R.J. Singh *Asian J Psychology and Education* 6(3) Nv 1980 p 42-48 refs

Teacher effectiveness : A resume of research. C.L. Kundu *National J Education* 3(2) Mr 1981 p 30-52 refs

Teacher effectiveness. Hariprasad O. Joshi *J Educational Research and Extension* 20(3) Ja 1984 p 153-57

Teacher effectiveness in schools. S.P. Anand *J Indian Education* 8(6) Mr 1983 p 3-12

Teacher effectiveness. Sunil Behari Mohanty *Research Bulletin* 14(3-4) Se-De 1984 p 3-9

Teacher effectiveness on related with valued orientation and secondary level teaching. Pramod Kumar and Dinesh Muthe *J Education and Psychology* 43(1) Ap 1985 p 22-26 refs

Towards a model for integration of teaching skills. N.K. Jangira *Teacher Education* 15(16-17) Jl-Oc 1981 p 46-56

Towards the making of a better teacher. K.S. Zoseph *Teacher Education* 16(18-19) Ja-Ap 1982 p 53-60

A usable criterion of teaching effectiveness. R.C. Deva *Educational Rev* 86(1) Ja 1980 p 5-10

Who is a good teacher? Asmat Hushain *Primary Teacher* 4(3) Jl 1979 p 33-35

See also

Student Evaluation of Teachers

Student Teachers : Rating

Teachers : Rating : India

Some pesonality and adjustment correlates of teaching effectiveness. Pratibha Deo *J Institute of Educational Research* 4(2) My 1980 p 1-8 refs tabs

Teachers : Rural : India

Rural teachers of their problems. M.N. Ravindranatha *Educational Rev* 87(10) Oc 1981 p 184-90

Teachers : Selection and Appointment

Teacher selection. Gilbert De Landsheer *J Indian Education* 8(2) Jl 1982 p 52-58 refs ft-n

Teachers : United States

Lets have a national retirement program for mobile educations. Robert J. Geradi *Progress of Education* 55(11) Je 1981 p 303-04

Teachers : Training

Art : The case of teacher education. Maqbool Ahmad *Teacher Today* 24(2) Oc-De 1981 p 67-73

Behavioural problems in school children : Implication for teacher training programme. V.N. Rao *et al Experiments in Education* 12(3) My 1984 p 41-46 refers tabs

Changing trends in teacher education. Prakash Chandra Shukla *Progress of Education* 55(10) My 1981 p 246-48

Community work in teacher education programme. J.S. Rajput *Teacher Today* 24(2) Oc-De 1981 p 40-43

Community work in teacher education programmes. J.S. Rajput *University News* 21(21) Nv 1983 p 711-12

A comparative study of relationship of attitudes towards teaching, teaching competence and role-performance among teachers trained through integrated and traditional methods. Nagendra Singh *Progress of Education* 60(5) De 1985 p 111-15 + tabs

Content-cum-methodology strategy. J.P. Sharma and R.C. Hooda *Progress of Education* 56(2) Se 1981 p 45+

Correspondence courses in teacher education. Subbarao Chaganti *Teacher Education* 16(18-19) Ja-Ap 1982 p 17-20

Correspondence courses in teacher education. Subbarao Chaganti *Progress of Education* 59(8) Mr 1985 p 181-83

Earning competences through CBTE : A study of some correlates. M. Mukhopadhyay and Sushila Balaguruswamy *Indian Education* 11(7) Oc 1981 p 13-15

Educational technology for teacher education : An experimental study. D.K. Sharma and R.K. Sharma *J Indian Education* 6(6) Mr 1981 p 36-41 refs

An emerging concept of teacher education. Shree Chinamani Samantaray *Experiments in Education* 6(6) Ag 1978 p 102-03

Evaluation of practice teaching : A simple tool. M.N. Deshmukh *Teacher Education* 15(16-17) Jl-Oc 1981 p 57-63

An experiment to study the effect of training in microteaching skills on the teacher competence of primary teachers. V. Seth Kaushik and Panna Desai *Progress of Education* 53(10-11) My-Je p 194-200 refs tabs

Gaps in teacher eduction. G. Subramania Pillay *Experiments in Education* 11(12) Fe 1984 p 215-18

Improving teacher education. V.V. Malaviya *Indian Education* 12(11-12) Fe-Mr 1982 p 32-34

Innovative proneness of teacher education. B.R. Panchal and D.R. Darji *J Education and Psychology* 39(1) Ap 1981 p 66-72 refs

Institutional plan of the integrated teacher education programme proposed for B.Ed course. Mathew George *Quest in Education* 18(1) Ja 1981 p 53-60

Intake criteria for teacher trainees : A study. P.C. Sharma *Indian Education* 10(3) Je 1980 p 29-32

An investigation into students motivity for joining B.Ed course. V.K. Rai and Asha Srivastava *Educational Rev* 88(7) Jl 1982 p 119-21 refs tabs

Issues in teacher education. M. Malla Reddy and Rhoda Philip *Indian Education* 10(3) Je 1980 p 40-50

Mini-Teaching : A new experiment in teacher education. *Education Quarterly* 33(1) Ja 1981 p 39

Mini teaching : A new experiment in teacher education. S.P. Kulshrestha. DAV (PG) College. 1979, 29 p. Rs. 5 *Book Rev, Teacher Today* 22(4) Ap-Je 1980 p 78

Micro teaching : A novel teacher training technique. K.C. Venugopal *J Indian Education* 7(3) Se 1979 p 20-23

Microteaching and teacher education. Fareeda Khatoon *Indian Education* 12(10) Ja 1983 p 13-15

Microteaching at pre-service level. K.K. Sharma *J Indian Education* 7(3) Dr 1979 p 24-28

Modelling in teacher training. M.S. Padma *Indian Educational Rev* 15(4) Oc 1980 p 56-61 refs tabs

The myth of staff development at the tertiary level of education. Michael D'Hara *J Higher Education* 7(3) Spr 1982 p 297-302

New directions in teacher education. A.R. Rather *Primary Teacher* 9(1) Ja 1984 p 22-25

New directions in teacher education. A.R. Rather *Progress of Education* 59(8) Mr 1985 p 177-80 refs

Operational challenge of teacher education. S.P. Duggal *Educational Rev* 92(3) Mr 1986 p 50-55 refs

Organising micro teaching programme in teacher training institutions. V.D. Gupta *Indian Education* 11(11-12) Fe-Mr 1982 p 37-41

Orientation course for teachers of institutions for the handicapped. Parvin Akhtar Hassan *Experiments in Education* 9(9) Nv 1981 p 159-61

Perceptual change in teacher trainees : A personal perspective. K.K. Sharma and S. Walia *Progress of Education* 53(9) Ap 1979 p 176-86 refs

Philosophical implications in teacher education. Marlow Ediger *Progress of Education* 54(6) Ja 1980 p 112-15

Prediction of teaching efficiency through teachers' attitude towards professional training. Y.K. Gupta *Educational Rev* 88(3) Mr 1982 p 43-45

Prep Index : Proficiency in educational practice. Gomathi Mani *Experiments in Education* 7(11) Ja 1980 p 207-08+

Professional enculturation : Innovative experiments in teaching and training. N.K. Jangira. New Delhi Bookworth India. 1985, 99p. Rs. 70 *Book Rev, Progress of Education* 60(5) De 1985 p 122

The programme in secondary training schools. Surendra Kumar Pattnaik *Educational Rev* 86(2) Gr 1980 p 24-27

Qualitative improvement of teacher education and research. K.K. Vasishtha *Progress of Education* 55(1) Ag 1980 p 19-23

Relationship of attainments in theory papers with student teaching in secondary teachers training programme. R.C. Hooda and R.N. Syag *J Education and Psychology* 40(4) Ja 1983 p 13-15

The relative impact of micro-teaching and conventionaal teaching. M. Malla Reday *Indian Education* 10(5) Ag 1980 p 31-41

Review of the existing arrangements of preservice and in-service training for teachers and suggestions for improvement. V.S. Rokade and S.A. Anarasa *Education Quarterly* 35(4) Oc 1983 p 17-19

The role of teacher education in integrating women into development. Prabha Johari *Teacher Education* 14(10-11) Ja-Ap 1980 p 50-56

Simulation techniques in teacher training. D. Brahadeeswaran *Educational Rev* 86(7) Jl 1980 p 131-33

Some salient issues in teacher education. B.K. Passi *et al National J Education* 6(2) My 1984 p 7-20 refs

Studies in teacher education : An overview. R.P. Singh. New Delhi, Bahri Pub. 1980, 104p. Rs. 40 *Book Rev, Education Quarterly* 32(4) Oc 1980 p 46-47; *J Indian Education* 6(3) Se 1980 p 59-60

A study of teaching behaviour of teachers in relation to their personality adjustment. Rama Mishra *Progress of Education* 59(8) Mr 1985 p 186-89

A study of the achievement in theory and teaching competence of teacher trainees. B.B. Pandit *Progress of Education* 56(11) Je 1982 p 275-77

A study of the attitude of teachers towards teacher education programme. H.R. Joshi and D.R. Darji *Progress of Education* 56(1) Ag 1981 p 22-24

Supervision in teacher education : A counselling and pedagogical approach. Edger Stones. London, Methuen. 1984. 163p. £ 4.95 *Book Rev, Progress of Education* 61(2) Se 1986 p 46+

Systems analysis : Its application to teacher education. Krishna Sehgal *Quest in Education* 18(3) Jl 1981 p 197-204 refs

Systems approach to education and training. S.N. Sharma *Teahcer Education* 16(18-19) Ja-Ap 1982 p 3-8 refs

Teacher education : A brief survey of its weakness. S. Subbarao Chayanty *Progress of Education* 55(10) My 1981 p 249-50

Teacher education : A continuing process. *Indian Education* 12(8-9) Nv-De 1982 p 23-25

Teacher education : A futurology, the new dimensions of teacher educator. S. Sekhar *J Educational Research and Extension* 16(2) Oc 1979 p 72-76

Teacher education and promotion of international understanding P.R. Chakraborty *Primary Teacher* 9(1) Ja 1984 p 9-12

Teacher education and social change : A crucial issue. Lal Pratap Singh *Teacher Education* 14(12-13) Jl-Oc 1980 p 57-62

Teacher education for early childhood. Prerana Mohite and Neena Mukul *Educational Rev* 92(9) Se 1986 p 141-44

Teacher-education for schools in transition. N.K. Upasani *Quest in Education* 16(3) Jl 1979 p 222-35

Teacher education for the future. Chitra Naik *Progress of Education* 59(8) Mr 1985 p 102-07+

Teacher education Goal identification and strategies. Asha Pandey *J Indian Education* 12(3) Se 1986 p 58-62 refs

Teacher education in the next decade : A resume of the capabilities of teachers of the future. N.R. Barde *Progress of Education* 59(8) Mr 1985 p 184-86

Teacher education. R.V. Naidu *Experiments in Education* 11(10) De 1983 p 167-71

Teacher education. S. Chandra Sekhara Sarma *Indian Education* 13(5-6) Ag-Se 1983 p 16-19

Teacher education : The drift and its reversal. S. Parmaji *Indian Education* 10(1-2) Ap-My 1980 p 53-58

Teacher training : A re-education process. S. Sundaramurthy *Education Quarterly* 34(1) Ja 1982 p 12-14

Teacher training : Traditional and developmental learning-teaching and field dependence independence styles. Amiya Kumar Basu *Our Education* 2 Jl 1981 p 23-29 refs tabs

Teacher preparation in non-conventional areas : Especially in technical and vocational fields. M.R. Santhanam *Experiments in Education* 9(8) Oc 1981 p 133-38 refs

Teacher training : The role of micro-teaching. B. Niranjan Reddy and M.V. Lakshmi Reddy *J Indian Education* 12(4) Nv 1986 p 17-21

Teachers as builders of a new nation. Shamsuddin *Progress of Education* 59(8) Mr 1985 p 168-70+

Teachers teaching skills and the teacher education programme. D.L. Sharma *Progress of Education* 55(8) Mr 1981 p 202-03 ref

Teachers' training in higher education. Navin Chandra Joshi *Rajasthan Board J Education* 15(1) Ja-Mr 1979 p 8-10

Teaching skills and teacher education. D.I. Sharma *Education Rev* 86(8) Ag 1980 p 151-53

Towards task-oriented teacher education. T.S. Rao *Teacher Education* 16(18-19) Ja-Ap 1982 p 30-32

Training personnel for care and education of young children. Sunita Kaul and Neena Kapoor *Progress of Education* 603 De 1985 p 103-06

Training teachers to think. Lynne Ames *Indian Education* 13(7) Oc 1983 p 14-16

Unending task of teacher education. P.S. Sindhu *Educational Rev* 87(2) Fe 1981 p 27-30 refs

Unit cost os teacher training for primary schools. C.K.M. Rao *Progress of Education* 55(10) My 1981 p 264-66

Values and the teaching learning process : An integrated approach. J. Filella *New Frontiers in Education* 14(1) Ja 1984 p 1-18

Vitalising teacher education. N.N. Pangotra *Educational Rev* 89(2) Mr 1983 p 55-57 refs

Who will teach the teacher? K.N. Pandey *Teacher Education* 20(30-31) Ja-Ap 1985 p 40-42

Work experience of teacher education. S.V.V. Raghavacharyulu *Indian Education* 10(3) Ag 1981 p 11-13

See also

Bachelor of Education
College Teachers : Training
Comparative Education
Elementary School Teachers : Training
High School Teachers : Training
Master of Education
Microteaching
Student Teaching
Teachers : In-service Training
Teachers Colleges
Teaching Demonstrations

See also

Subdivision 'Teacher Training' under specific subjects, e.g., Adult Education : Teacher Training

Teachers : Training : Aids and Devices

Preparing teaching-learning materials for adult education. Rafat S. Shafi *Indian J Adult Education* 41(5) My 1980 p 15-18

Teachers : Training : Curricula

Can we help ourselves teach better : A case study of series of teaching workshops at BITS, Pilanil, P.N. Dave *J Higher Education* 4(1) Mon 1978 p 108-09

Community work in teacher education, C.S. Subba Rao *Teacher Education* 13(8-9) Jl-Oc 1979 p 16-20

Community service in the school and teacher training curriculum. Tej Bahadur Mathur *Teacher Today* 22(4) Ap-Je 1980 p 41-45

Curriculum and courses with special references to MCTE framework. D.R. Darji *Teacher Education* 15(14-15) Ja-Ap 1981 p 51-72 refs

Developing population education programme for teacher training colleges. Ramesh Chandra *Teacher Education* 13(8-9) Jl-Oc 1979 p 62-69 refs ft-n

New dimensions in the curriculum of teacher education programme. Indravadan M. Gor *Progress of Education* 53(8) My 1979 p 159-66

The place of philosophy in teacher education. Sudarsan C. Panigrahi *Educational Rev* 89(9) Se 1983 p 153-55 refs

Problem oriented Corriculum and its procedural arrangement in a college of

p. Rs. 125 *Book Rev, National J Education* 6(1) Se 1983 p 65-66

Effective teacher education in the eighties : A new suggestions. V.B. Pathak *Teacher Education* 20(30-31) Ja-Ap 1985 p 19-20

Future-oriented education for teachers. N.M. Bhagia *Teacher Today* 28(2) Oc-De 1985 p 72-78

High priority to teacher education. Bir Singh *Teacher Education* 17(20-21) Jl-Oc 1982 p 65-68

Improving teacher education in India. S.P. Duggal *Educational Rev* 85(4) Ap 1979 p 66-68 refs

Innovations in teacher education. C. Madhukar *Educational Rev* 86(10) Oc 1980 p 184-87

Integration of skills in real classroom. S.P. Malhotra and S.K. Sharma *Progress of Education* 55(4) Nv 1980 p 105-06

Job satisfaction versus work role variables. S.P. Anand *Indian Educational Rev* 14(4) Oc 1979 p 106-07 tabs

Management of teacher education in India. S. Krishna Murty *Indian Education* 11(1-2) Ap-My 1981 p 92-95

Need to revitalise teacher education. V.S. Mathur *Education Quarterly* 35(4) Oc 1983 p 8-13

New dimensions in teacher education. A.R. Rather *Teacher Education* 18(24-25) Jl-Oc 1983 p 44-48 refs

Objectives of teacher education : A feedback. S.P. Singh *Teacher Education* 15(14-15) Ja-Ap 1981 p 45-47

Perspectives on teacher education. G. Ramanathan *Quest in Education* 19(2) Ap 1982 p 118-36

Presidential address. S.K. Dasgupta *Teacher Education* 14(10-11) Ja-Ap 1980 p 3-7

Recommendations of the UGC panel on teacher education. R.M. Mehrotra *J Higher Education* 1(1) Mon 1975 p 127-30

"Recruitment and processing in teacher training programme : An appraisal". Subhash Chandra Agarwal *Educational Rev* 86(9) Se 1980 p 161-64

Research experimentation and innovation in teacher education : Some considerations. Baqer Mehdi *Teacher Education* 15(14-15) Ja-Ap 1981 p 80-82

Revitalising educational extension services. C.S. Subba Rao *Progress of Education* 54(8) Mr 1980 p 160-62

State boards of teacher education : Some urgent tasks ahead. C.S.S. Rao *Education Quarterly* 31(2) Jl 1979 p 15-16

State of teacher education in India. Subba Rao Chaganty *Teacher Education* 16(18-19) Ja-Ap 1982 p 64-71

State of teacher education in India. Subba Rao Chaganty *Progress of Education* 58(6) Ja 1984 p 126-31+

A study of relationship among teaching efficiency, attitude towards teaching profession and adjustment of trainee teachers. Umesh Agrawal *et al Progress of Education* 55(4) Nv 1980 p 94-98

Teacher education at cross roads. Prabhakar Singh *Teacher Education* 15(14-15) Ja-Ap 1981 p 30-36 refs

Teacher education in India : Need for radical revitalisation. Harikesh Singh *J Indian Education* 11(2) Jl 1985 p 35-39

Teacher education in India : Some considerations. Baqer Mehdi *Teacher Education* 15(14-15) Ja-Ap 1981 p 112-14

Teacher education in the context of 10+2 pattern : A case study. J.C. Goyal and R.K. Chopra *Quest in Education* 19(1) Ja 1982 p 42-57 refs tabs

Teacher education in the context of the new education policy, Piloo Buch *New Frontiers in Education* 16(4) Oc-De 1986 p 82-87

Teacher education : The continuing debate. C. Seshadri *J Indian Education* 12(4) Nv 1986 p 3-10

Teacher training needs overhauling. Bir Singh *Progress of Education* 55(10) My 1981 p 67-69+

Teacher education in India. K.K. Vashistha. New Delhi, Concept Pub. 1979, 159 p. Rs. 54 *Book Rev, Education Quarterly* 32(2) Ap 1980 p 53; *J Higher Education* 7(3) Spr 1982 p 327-30; *Teacher Education* 14(10-11) Ja-Ap 1980 p 75-76 *Teacher Today* 22(3) Ja-Mr 1980 p 96-98

Test and testing in teacher education in India. R.P. Singh and Neerja Shukla *Indian Educational Rev* 14(1) Ja 1979 p 3035 refs appdx

Theory and practice of teacher education in India. R.S. Srivastava and K. Bose. Allahabad, Chugh Pub. 1978, 344 p. Rs. 65 *Book Rev, J Higher Education* 7(3) Spr 1982 p 327-30

Working with the community as a part of the teacher education programme. Ramdev P. Kathuria *Teacher Education* 13(8-9) Jl-Oc 1979 p 79-82

See also

National Council for Teacher Education

Teachers : Training : India : Andhra Pradesh

An investigation into the attitude of teacher trainees towards practical aspects of B.Ed. programme. G. Srinivasacharyulu *Experiments in Education* 7(7) Se 1979 p 145-48 refs tabs

Pedagogical training for college teachers in Andhra Pradesh. I.V. Radhakrishna Murthy *J Educational Research and Extension* 20(2) Oc 1983 p 123-38

Teachers, Training of : Audio-visual aids : Nepal teacher training via radio in Nepal. *J Indian Education* 5(2) Jl 1979 p 62-64

Teachers : Training : India : Haryana

A study of attitude towards teaching profession among teacher trainees. Satish Kumar Yadav *Progress of Education* 55(10) My 1981 p 251-54 tabs

Teachers : Training : India : Karnataka

Development of teacher education in Mysore district, from 1956 to 1976. B.N. Sujatha *Experiments in Education* 12(7) Se 1984 p 123-31

A study of wastage in teacher training institutions in Karnataka. K.M. Kasinath *Progress of Education* 60(7) Fe 1986 p 156-60 + tabs

Teachers : Training : India : Madhya Pradesh

MP modernises teachers training. Bir Singh *Educatyion Quarterly* 34(1) Ja 1982 p 15-16

Teachers : Training : India : Maharashtra

Defining teaching effectiveness. Sham Lal Sufat *Educational Rev* 86(6) Je 1980 p 108-10

Evaluation of training colleges. K.T. Mehare *Educational Rev* 86(5) My 1980 p 81-84

Future of the colleges of education in the state of Maharashtra. D.G. Samant *Porogress of Education* 54(8) Mr 1980 p 146-53

Improvement in classroom practices. Ajit Singh *Educational Rev* 86(10) Oc 1980 p 181-83

The need for innovation in library services in the colleges of education. M.N. Mahale *Progress of Education* 54(12) Jl 1980 p 231-37

On implementation of a mastery learning strategy. Rajeshwar N. Mathur *J Higher Education* 4(3) Spr 1979 p 337-41

A philosophical analysis of methods of teaching at the higher education stage. C.D. Indapurkar *J Higher Education* 5(1) Mon 1979 p 7-11

The problem of effectiveness in teaching. M.N. Ravindranath *Educational Rev* 85(12) De 1979 p 221-23

Report of the practice teaching programme at Gandhi Shikshan Bhavan's Smt Surajaba College of Education, 1981-82. *Quest in Education* 19(2) Ap 1982 p 98-105

A study of relationship among teaching efficiency, attitude towards teaching profession and adjustment of trainee teachers. Umesh Agrawal *et al* *Progress of Education* 55(4) Nv 1980 p 94-98

Survey of teacher education in Maharashtra. N.S. Marker *Indian Education Rev* 15(1) Ja 1980 p 78-84

What is involved in teaching a subject? K.H. Lawson *Indian J Adult Education* 41(5) My 1980 p 25-27

Teachers : Training : India : Rajasthan

A critical study of the development of teacher education in Rajasthan. G.N. Bhardwaj *Indian Educational Rev* 14(4) Oc 1979 p 66-72

Restructuring teacher education in Rajasthan. S.M. Nayyar and C.M. Karnawat *Teacher Today* 25(2) Oc-De 1982 p 54-61

Teachers : Training : India : Tamil Nadu

Training of teachers. H. Visvesvaran *Experiments in Education* 7(4) Je 1979 p 59-63 refs

Teachers : Training : India : Uttar Pradesh

B.Ed. admissions : Non-academic criteria. P.D. Juyal *Educational Rev* 87(5) My 1981 p 90-93 refs tabs

Dogmatism in relation to sex and caste among the teacher trainees. Harikesh Singh *National J Education* 3(1) Se 1980 p 25-32 refs tabs

Innovated practice teaching programme at the faculty of education, Banaras Hindu University, Varanasi. T. Singh *Teacher Education* 15(14-15) Ja-Ap 1981 p 106-11

Opportunity costs of teacher education. S.K. Dasgupta *Teacher Education* 17(20-21) Jl-Oc 1982 p 51-64 refs tabs

Quality of the output of the teacher education programme. V.B. Pathak *Teacher Education* 15(14-15) Ja-Ap 1981 p 100-05 tabs

Who go for teacher education in Eastern U.P. Vijay Bahadur Pathak *National J Education* 2(2) Mr 1980 p 26-37 tabs

Teachers : Training : Methodology

Content-based methodology and method-based content strategies for pre-service teachers training. J.P. Sharma and R.C. Hooda *Experiments in Education* 9(4) Je 1981 p 59-63 refs

Teachers : Training : Nigeria

Teacher education in Nigeria : A historical perspective. Erogua C. Osuala *Indian Education* 13(3-4) Je-Jl 1983 p 21-23; 13(5-6) Ap-Se 1983 p 26-28

Teachers : Training : United States

Secondary classroom teaching in the US and teacher education. Chhaya Dey *Progress of Education* 56(2) Se 1981 p 40-44

Sociology in U.S. teacher training. John E. Owen *Educational Rev* 88(9) Se 1982 p 153-55

Trends in teacher education in the United States of America. Louise M. Berman *Teacher Education* 15(16-17) Jl-Oc 1981 p 30-45 refs

Teacher and Community

Working with the community and teacher education. R.N. Syag and R.C. Hooda *Experiments in Education* 10(8) Oc 1982 p 144-46

Teachers and Principals

See

Teacher-Principal Relationships

Teachers Colleges

Colleges of education and school broadcasts. D.R. Goel *J Indian Education* 5(5) Ja 1980 p 65-72

Innovating proneness in the secondary teachers' training colleges. B.R. Panchal and D.R. Dorji *Indian Educational Rev* 16(3) Jl 1981 p 14-20

Teachers Colleges : Entrance Requirements

Admission in colleges of education. V.B. Mehta *Teacher Education* 16(18-19) Ja-Ap 1982 p 61-63

Teachers Colleges : India

Functions of colleges of education. S. Santhanam *J Educational Research and Extension* 16(2) Oc 1979 p 77-79

Innovations and teachers colleges. Hariprasad Jagannath *Educational Rev* 87(8) Ag 1981 p 143-47 tabs

Non-enforcement of conditions of affiliation in colleges of education : A study of reasons. J.C. Goyal and Ajit Singh *Indian Educational Rev* 17(3) Jl 1982 p 62-74 refs

Teachers Colleges : India : Gujarat

Diffusion of innovation among training college of India. T. Singh Jaunpur, Bharat Bharati Prakashan. 1978, 139 p. Rs. 30 *Book Rev, J Indian Education* 7(2) Jl 1979 p 70

Teachers Colleges : India : Haryana

Haryana education colleges at the cross-road. Y.P. Aggarwal *Teacher Education* 15(14-15) Ja-Ap 1981 p 95-99

Teachers Colleges : India : Punjab

A study of leadership style and achieving index of the colleges of education in Punjab. S.P. Gupta *Progress of Education* 58(2) Se 1983 p 36-42 tabs

Teachers Socio-Economic Status

The influence of socio-economic factors on teachers career. Shamsuddin *Indian Education* 10(3) Je 1980 p 33-39

The status of the teachers. Govindanand Misra *Teacher Education* 18(24-25) Jl-Oc 1983 p 53-60

See also

Student Teachers Socio-Economic Status

Teachers Unions : India

Teachers organisation in India. Swami S. Sreedhara. Hyderabad, AIFEA. 1980, 241 p. Rs. 35 *Book Rev, Indian Education* 11(6) Se 1981 p 38-40

Teaching

Academic learning time model of classroom instruction. Siba P. Bhattacharya *Our Education* 3-4 Jl 1983 p 31-34 refs

An alternative teaching experience. J. Gabriel. *New Frontiers in Education* 11(4) Oc-De 1981 p 42-46 refs

Anatomy of teaching. D.G. Samant and C.V. Bhimasankaran *Progress of Education* 57(5) De 1982 p 103-07

Aptitude in teaching and job satisfaction among teachers. Rita George and B.G. Sudha *J Institute of Educational Research* 10(2) My 1986 p 16-20 tabs

The art of teaching : An analysis. K.K. Sharma *Educational Rev* 89(9) Se 1983 p 145-47 refs

Behavioural objectives : A missing link in teaching. Mukti Chakraberti *National J Education* 7(2) My 1985 p 25-30 refs

Choosing teaching as a career. Shrihasta Lanchhan Jena *Indian Education* 10(4) Jl 1980 p 24-25

Competency-based teaching : Some issues. Kamlesh Chaudhury *Progress of Education* 55(9) Ap 1981 p 222-29

Cooper Foundation awards for excellence in teaching USA, Nebraske Deptt. of Education. *Book Rev, Progress of Education* 59(6) Ja 1985 p 133

Creative teacher personality and classroom teaching behaviour of secondary school teachers. Mathew George *J Educational Research and Extension* 17(3) Ja 1981 p 150-63 refs tabs

Curriculum and teaching : Some opposing views. Marlow Ediger *New Frontiers in Education* 14(1) Ja-Mr 1984 p 59-63

Cypernatic approach to teaching. Prabhakar Singh *Progress of Education* 58(10) My 1984 p 238-40+

Dear teacher do you really teach? Mali Ram Sharma *Teacher Today* 24(3) Ja-Mr 1982 p 75-80

Development of teaching competence. M. Mukhopadhyay *et al Indian Educational Rev* 17(1) Ja 1982 p 12-21 refs

Don't teach : Let them learn? R.N. Kabra *Teacher Today* 23(3) Ja-Mr 1981 p 137-40

Effect of different techniques of feedback upon the attainment of teaching skills related to stimulus variation among teachers. Krishnan Kumar Sharma *Indian Educational Rev* 14(4) Oc 1979 p 54-60

Effect of language barrier on the univerlisation of education. V.G. Gambhir *Indian Educational Rev* 16(1) Ja 1981 p 48-59

Effect of Megha teaching approach in acquisition of teaching skills. S.K. Sharma *J Education and Psychology* Ap-Jl 1982 p 48-52 refs

Effect of training on attitude towards creative teaching and learning. M.K. Raina and Arunima Vats *Indian Educational Rev* 18(1) Ja 1983 p 104-09 refs

Effectiveness of two basic : The Diode and additive models of teaching skills : A comparative study. G.C. Bhattacharyya and C.S. Shukla *National J Education* 5(1) Se 1982 p 24-32 refs

The ethics of teaching. C.V. Bhimasankaram *Progress of Education* 56(8) Mr 1982 p 180-83+

Evaluating teaching performance in higher education. N.K. Upasani *Quest in Education* 18(1) Ja 1981 p 67-80

Evaluating teaching performance. Marlow Ediger *Education Quarterly* 34(3) Jl 1982 p 15-17

Evaluation approach for teaching and testing. W.A.F. Hopper *New Frontiers in Education* 13(3) Jl-Se 1983 p 38-41

Evaluation of teaching performance. N.K. Upasani *Quest in Education* 17(4) Oc 1980 p 283-07

Examining the attitude of teachers towards classroom teaching in relation to some socio-personal variables. P. Som *Our Education* 3-4 Jl 1983 p 138-45 refs

Functional teaching. D.G. Samant and C.V. Bhimasankaram *Progress of Education* 56(5) De 1981 p 102-07

In higher education : The neglect aspect of good teaching. *Education Quarterly* 32(1) Ja 1980 p 8-10

In-service teachers and student teachers : A comparative study of attitude towards teaching. V.K. Raina *J Education and Psychology* 41(3) Oc 1983 p 138-45 refs

Inquiry training model of teaching : An overview. R.S. Mani *Indian Educational Rev* 20(4) Oc 1985 p 50-65

Laws of teaching. D.G. Samat *Progress of Education* 56(1) Ap 1981 p 10-13

Life skills teaching : Barrie Hopson and Mike Scally Maidenhead, McGraw-Hill. 556 p. *Book Rev, Education Quarterly* 34(1) Ja 1982 p 50

The meaning of teaching : An examination of the critical books of teaching. Frank U. Machke *Perspectives in Education* 2(4) Oc 1986 p 221-30

The measuring of teaching : An examination of the theoretical basis of teaching. Frank U. Madike *Perspectives in Education* 2(4) Oc 1986 p 221-30 refs

Mental health of teacher promotes effective teaching and learning in classroom. B.P. Lulla *Indian Education* 10(12) Mr 1981 p 4-7

Microanalysis of teaching skills : An illustration of prompting. B.K. Passi and Ajit Singh *J Indian Education* 5(5) Ja 1980 p 17-20 refs

The models approach to teaching. N.K. Upasani *Quest in Education* 17(2) Ap 1980 p 141-51

Models of teaching. Bruce Joyce and Marsha Weil. New Delhi, Prentice-Hall of India. e2. 1985, 499 p. Rs. 48 *Book Rev, Perspectives in Education* 1(4) Oc 1985 p 268-70

Multiple class teaching and education of disadvantaged groups. Bangkok, UNESCO. 1982. 98 p. *Book Rev, Teacher Today* 26(3) Ja-Mr 1984 p 102-08

A new aim teaching *vs* learning. M.P. Bhasin *Educational Rev* 91(10) Oc 1985 p 167-71

The pedogogy of behaviour simulation. Udai Pareek *Indian Educational Rev* 16(1) Ja 1981 p 1-24

Philosophical models of teaching. Ram Shakal Pandey *Teacher Today* 21(3) Ja-Mr 1979 p 19-24

Piagetian perspective for pre-schools : A thinking book for teachers. Ruth

Saunders and Ann M. Bingham-Newan. New Jersey, Prentice-Hall. 1984 *Book Rev, Teacher Today* 27(4) Ap-Je 1985 p 147-48

Preparation for teaching profession from school stage. Edward Alesin *Educational Rev* 88(11) Nv 1982 p 188-19; *Progress of Education* 57(5) De 1982 p 115-16

Professional enculturation : Innovation experiments in teaching and training. N.K. Jangira. New Delhi, Bookworth India. 1985. 99p. Rs. 70 *Book Rev, Progress of Education* 60(3) De 1985 p 122

Reorientation in teaching, learning and evaluation. Rais Ahmad *J Higher Education* 5(3) Spr 1980 p 331-33

Research as a tool in the under-graduate teaching learning process : The experience of an autonomous college. M. Casimir Raj and A. Raman *Progress of Education* 61(2) Se 1986 p 29-32

The role of the teachers in the free progress method of integral education. Indra Sen *Education Quarteriy* 36(1) Ja 1984 1-5

Seeking a model of good teaching. G.R. Sharma *J Indian Education* 7(2) Se 1979 p 15-19

Search for teacher behaviour. Ajit Singh *Teacher Today* 23(3) Ja-Mr 1986 p 1-5 refs

Self-criticism technique : A boon or a bane. C.V. Bhimasankaram *Progress of Education* 55(7) Fe 1981 p 186-88

Shift of learned teaching skills from micro to macroteaching : A study. A.R. Bisht *J Institute of Educational Research* 7(2) My 1983 p 8-11

Some recent studies on teaching and teaching bebaviour. M.R. Santhanam *Experiments in Eduction* 6(3) My 1978 p 39-50; 6(4) Je 1978 p 66-71 refs

A study of job satisfaction at three levels of teaching. S.P. Gupta *Indian Educational Rev* 18(2) Ap 1983 p 75-78

A study of some factors considered to be helpful in class teaching. R.P. Gupta *Bharatiya Shiksha Shodh Patrika* 4(2) Jl-De 1985 p 35-42 refs

A study of teachers attitude towards teaching as a career and education : A synopsis. J. Jha and Vidya Rani Roy *Indain Education* 11(5) Ag 1981 p 27-30

A study of the comparative effects of microteaching under simulated and mixed conditions upon general teaching competence and attitude towards teaching. L.P. Singh and T. Singh *J Educational Research and Extension* 163 Ja 1980 p 142-52 refs tabs

Systematic observation in understanding instruction : A review and some rethinking. Syamdass B. Menon and Vasant D. Bhatt *New Frontiers in Education* 14(3) Jl-Se 1985 p 36-46 refs

Talking to learn — Improving teaching and learning in small groups. M.L.J. Abercrombie and P.M. Terry Univ. of Surrey. 1978. *Book Rev, J Higher Education* 5(1) Mon 1979 p 120-22

Tasks for schools. M. Sree Rama Murthy *Education Quarterly* 32(4) Oc 1980 p 8-9

Teacher efficiency as a function of class obtained at professional degree and social maturity. B.V. Patel and I.A. Vora *J Education and Psychology* 42(3) Oc 1984 p 163-70 refs

Teacher planning : Congitive information processing approach. Mihir K. Chatterjee *Indian Educational Rev* 19(1) Ja 1984 p 27-35

Teacher student interaction and classroom performance of high school students. Biranchi N. Puhan and Santosh K. Patra *Asian J Psychology and Education* 3(2) Jl 1978 p 42-51 refs

Teachers decision-making : A new and exciting approach to research on teaching. Mihir K Chatterjee *Teacher Today* 23(2) Oc-De 1980 p 76-82 figs

Teacher effectiveness as related with value orientation at secondary level teaching. Pramod Kumar and Dinesh Muthe *J Education and Psychology* 43(1) Ap 1985 p 22-26

Teachers teaching skills and the teacher education programme. D.L. Sharma *Progress of Education* 56(8) Mr 1981 p 202-03

Teaching as a conserving activity. Neil Postman. London, Melbourne House. £ 6.50 *Book Rev, Teacher Today* 23(3) Ja-Mr 1981 p 153-55

Teaching function of teaching and teaching competence. R.P. Shukla *Educational Rev* 90(11) Nv 1984 p 177-79 refs

Teaching in secondary school. Joseph F. Callahan and Leonard H. Clark. London, Macmillan. 1977, 347p. $7.25 *Book Rev, Teacher Today* 21(4) Ap-Je 1979 p 87-88

Teaching laboratory-cum-clinic. Biswanath Roy *J Indian Education* 6(4) Nv 1980 p 43-52

Teaching learning at school : A new approach. Kailash Chandra Bansal *Primary Teacher* 8(2) Ap 1983 p 13-17

Teaching-learning in classroom. Hemchandra Deka *Educational Rev* 87(9) Se 1981 p 170-73 refs

Teaching learning process : The desired approach. Anand P. Srivastava *University News* 24(39) 16 Oc 1986 p 4

Teaching of imperatives when and where. J.S. Thankur *Primary Teacher* 8(1) Ja 1983 p 11-13

Teaching : Promise and performance. R. Venkataraman *Experiments in Education* 7(6) Ag 1979 p 106-07

Teaching styles of city teachers. M. Sree Ramamurthy *Teacher Education* 13(8-9) Jl Oc 1979 p 70-78 tabs

Teaching through environment. *Primary Teacher* 5(2) Ap 1980 p 11-14

Teaching well-how they do it in Japan. N. Narasimhan *Primary Teacher* 11(1) Ja 1986 p 1-3

Teaching young minds. Manjit Sengupta *Indian Education* 10(7) Oc 1980 p 3-6

Testing for teaching. Frank Spooncer Kent. London, Hodder. 148p. £ 3.45 *Book Rev, Education Quarterly* 38(2) Sum 1986 p 40-42

Towards more effective teaching : A managerial perspective. John Elliott-Kemp *J Education and Psychology* 39(3) Oc 1981 p 142-47 refs

Training teaching techniques. K.R. Khamborkar. Akola, Deshmukh, L.W. 104p. Rs.22.80 *Book Rev, Education Quarterly* 33(1) Ja 1981 p 39-40

See also

Classroom Management
College Teaching
Dictation : Educational Method
Education of Children
Educational Psychology

Examinations
Group Work in Education
High School Principals
Lecture Method in Teaching
Lesson Planning
Medium of Instruction
Micro Teaching
Montessori Method of Education
Questioning
Remedial Teaching
School Management and Organisation
School Superintendents and Principals
School Supervision
Student Teaching
Teacher-Students Relationships
Teachers : Rating
Teachers : Training
Teaching Teams
Tutors and Tutoring

Teaching : Aids and Devices

A collection of teaching aids. B.S. Bandivedekar and P.A. Kulkarni *Progress of Education* 53(6) Ja 1979 p 115-16

Comparison of instructional strategy with traditional teaching. D.N. Sansanwal and Anuradha Joshi *Experiments in Education* 7(12) Fe 1980 p 225-26 tabs

A comparative study of the relative effectiveness of four methods of teaching literacy to adults. R. Krishna Rao *Indian Educational Rev* 17(1) Ja 1982 p 80-85

Computer guided instructional systems. S. Ravishankar *Indain Education* 10(11) Fe 1981 p 44-45

Contemporary teaching methods and technologies in higher education : A report of the national seminar. *University News* 21(9) Oc 1983 p 632-33

Conventional methods of teaching in universities. V. Natarajan and P.K. Malhan *New Frontiers in Education* 14(1) Ja-Mr 1984 p 62-70

Developing instructional strategies. J.S. Tarang *Indian Educational Rev* 17(1) Ja 1982 p 28-42 refs

Different styles of writing instructional material. D.N. Sansanwal and M.Guddhisagar *Progress of Education* 56(7) Fe 1982 p 158-62 refs

Education via satellites. S.K. De *Educational Rev* 85(1) Ja 1979 p 1-3

Effectiveness of multimedia instructional system. Ashok Kumar *Rajasthan Board J Education* 19(2-3) Ap-Se 1983 p 6-9

The efficiency of teaching through environment at primary level. V.G. Jadhao *et al J Indian Education* 6(4)Nv 1980 p 34-39

An efficient approach to the use of audio-visual aids in the classrooms. Dhirendra Verma *Education Quarterly* 30(3) Oc 1978 p 24-27

Electronic link for distant teachers and pupils. Elaine Williams *Progress of Education* 56(4) Nv 1981 p 82-83

Evaluation of instruction and materials. P. Prema *New Frontiers in Education* 13(2) Ap-Je 1983 p 55-57

Instruction through radio vision : A comparative study. Motilal Sharma and Meena Oberai *Indian Educational Rev* 18(4) Oc 1983 p 37-46

Instructional media for distance education. Dinesh Kumar Verma *Indian Educational Rev* 20(3) Jl 1985 p 72-78

Instructional resources in collegiate education. K. Bhakta Vatsal Rao *Indian Education* 11(5) Ag 1981 p 20-21

Instructional skills : A new perspective. M.B. Menon *et al Teacher Education* 18(22-23) Ja-Ap 1983 p 6-19 refs

Low cost teaching aids in schools. Suresh Chandra Barthakur *Educational Rev* 87(9) Se 1981 p 179

Need for instructional material. Pravakar Rout *Teacher Education* 13(8-9) Jl-Oc 1979 p 26-31

Objective-based learning materials : Why and how? S.P. Mullick *Primary Teacher* 8(1) Ja 1983 p 31-33

A personalised instructional design. Lalit Kishore *University News* 72(2) Ja 1984 p 9

Plants help teaching learning process. S.B. Malik *Primary Teacher* 10(1) Ja 1985 p 25-27

Rate centred instruction : Feasibility aspect. Lalit Kishore *Educational Rev* 90(10) Oc 1984 p 161-62

The role of communication media in effective teaching. A. Mohan Singh *J Indian Education* 5(5) Ja 1980 p 31-34

A study of the role of audio visual aids in secondary school teaching. S. Ravishankar *Indian Education* 10(6) Se 1980 p 24-28

Teaching literacy through media. P.V. Krishnamoorthy *Indian J Adult Education* 41(10) Oc 1980 p 24-26

Teaching methods that ensure the learning situation. K.C. Peter *New Frontiers in Education* 10(1) Ja-Mr 1980 p 44-49

Teaching methodology in higher education. P. Arjun Rao *Indian Education* 13(3-4) Je-Jl 1983 p 28-31

Teaching skills : Identification and developing instructional material for it : An analytical views. P.C. Sharma and Ram Dev Sharma *Educational Rev* 91(5-6) My-Je 1985 p 94-95

Teaching values in the class : Jurisprudential technique. S.P. Malhotra *Education Quarterly* 36(4) Wint 1984 p 9-11

Technological aids in teaching — Learning process. S. Ravishankar *Educational Rev* 87(8) Ag 1981 p 156-58

Tools and techniques of guidance in schools. S.P. Anand *Education Quarterly* 36(4) Wint 1984 p 413

See also

Educational Technology
Moving-pictures in Education
Programmed Instruction
Radio in Adult Education
Radio in Education
Television in Education

Teaching : Audio-Visual Aids

See

Teaching : Aids and Devices

Teaching : Nigeria

An appraisal of teaching practice by student interns in Nigerianl Universities. Eric A. Arubayi *Progress of Education* 61(4-5) Nv-De 1986 p 77-84 refs tabs

Teaching : Vocational Guidance

See

Teaching as a Profession

Teaching as a Profession

An analytical study of the motives of primary school teacher trainees for choosing teaching as a career. B.B. Pandit *Progress of Education* 55(9) Ap 1981 p 227-31 tabs

Attitude of university college teachers towards teaching as a career. N.S. Sandhu and Rashmi Jain *Teacher Education* 17(20-21) Jl-Oc 1982 p 40-45 tabs

Development of a scale in Hindi to measure teachers attitude towards teaching profession. P.C. Shukla *Educational Rev* 91(3) Mr 1985 p 53-54 refs

Improvement of teachers professional competency in the use of classroom techniques. C.B. Patel *J Education and Psychology* 41(4) Ja 1984 p 246-53 appdx

Improving professional status of teachers. N. Venkataiah *Educational Rev* 85(7) Jl 1979 p 136-38

National address on objectives of teaching profession. Sheila Kaul *J Educational Research and Extension* 20(2) Oc 1983 p 92-102

Socio-economic status : As related to the students attitude towards teaching profession. P.C. Shukla and Nasreen Ara *Educational Rev* 90(7-8) Jl-Ag 1984 p 111-14 refs tabs

A study of factors in the choice of teaching profession in Afghanistan and India : A comparative study. G.N. Prakash Srivastava and A.J. Wafadar *National J Education* 6(1) Se 1983 p 48-55 refs tabs

A study of professional values among teachers in different organisational climates at 10+2 stage. Arun K. Gupta and D.R. Kapoor *EPA Quarterly Bulletin* 6(3-4) Oc 1983-Ja 1984 p 22-31 refs tabs

A study of relationship between vocational anxiety and attitude towards teaching profession among teacher trainees. S.K. Yadav *Progreess of Education* 57(8) Mr 1983 p 177-80 tab

A study of teacher trainees motives for the choice of teaching career and achievement in teaching skills. B.B. Pandit *J Education and Psychology* 40(3) Oc 1982 p 152-56

Teaching as a profession : Foundations, problems and potentialities. Jamnalal Bayti *J Indian Education* 8(5) Ja 1983 p 30-35

Teaching Demonstrations

An experimental study of effectiveness of demonstration methods over lecture method in terms of learning objectives on VI grade students. R.S. Yadav *Asian J Psychology and Education* 9(3) 1982 p 30-42

Teaching Materials

See

Teaching : Aids and Devices

Teaching Teams

Team teaching, Committee work and educational concerns, Marlow Ediger *Experiments in Education* 9(3) My 1981 p 44-45

Team Teaching

See

Teaching Teams

Techincal Education

Decision-making and organisational health in an technical education system. D.K. Sharma *Experiments in Education* 12(8) Oc 1984 p 133-37 refs tabs

Diversification of teachnical education. M.K. Khanijo *Education Quarterly* 37(4) Wint 1985 p 22-27

Gaps in technical education at training. K.V. Natarajan *J Indian Education* 6(6) Mr 1981 p 9-11

Leadership in technical education institutions. O.N. Wokhlu and G.L. Labhru *Indian Educational Rev* 19(1) Ja 1984 p 159-60

The new technician education, John Heywood, *ed.* Surey, Soc for Res Univ of Survey. 1980, 157p. £ 8.25 *Book Rev, Teacher Today* 25(2) Oc-De 1982 p 104

New perspectives for technical education-industry interaction. L.S. Chandrakant *et al J Higher Education* 7(3) Spr 1982 p 201-10

Technical-vocational education. Dhirendra Verma *J Indian Education* 6(5) Ja 1981 p 23-26

See also

Agricultural Education

Correspondence Schools and Courses

Manual Training

Occupational Training

Professional Education

Vocational Education

Technical Education : Curricula

A new approach to curriculum design in technical education. Dhirendra Verma *J Indian Education* 5(4) Nv 1979 p 28-34 refs

Research in curriculum for technical education. P.C. Jain *Quest in Education* 18(4) Oc 1981 p 307-19

Technical Education : India

Education in the VI five year paln science and technology and education. S. Ravishankar *Indain Education* 12(3-4) Je-Jl 1982 p 37-38

Foreign aided : IIT education. Sheilu Sreenivasan *J Higher Education* 4(2) Aut 1978 p 187-200

Regional distribution of selected technical educational facilities in India. K.K. Rudra and S.P Rastogi *J Higher Education* 4(1) Mon 1978 p 23-31 refs tabs

Technical and vocational education in India. *New Frontiers in Education* 10(1) Ja-Mr 1980 p 82-96

Technical Education : India : Andhra Pradesh

General and technical education in Andhra Pradesh. P. Ramachandra Pillai. Hyderabad, Educ Telugu Akad. 1981, 181p. Rs.7.50 *Book Rev, Indian Educational Rev* 17(2) Ap 1982 p 133-35

Technical Education : Kenya

Kenyas help themselves to technical education and a job. *J Indian Education* 6(4) Nv 1979 p 64-66

Technical Education : Research

Research needs in technical education. M.S. Yadav and S.B. Menon *J Indian Education* 6(4) Nv 1980 p 17-22

Technical Education (Higher)

International perspectives of collaboration in higher technical education. Vipula Chaturvedi and Mahesh C. Chaturvedi *Education Quarterly* 35(4) Oc 1983 p 1-7 refs

Technical Education (Primary)

Importance of technical education at primary levels. Ehtsamul Hassan Rizvi *Primary Teacher* 5(1) Ja 1980 p 30-31

Technical Education (Primary) : Russia

Creative technology for school children. Yuri Stolyarvo *Primary Teacher* 8(2) Ap 1983 p 4-9

Technical Schools

See

Technical Education

Technological Change in Agriculture

See

Agricultural Innovations

Technological Change in Education

See

Educational Innovations

Technological Forecasting

Activities of the technological forecasting and research management cell of Indian Institute of Science, Bangalore. P.K. Rohatgi *J Higher Education* 4(1) Mon 1978 p 109-11

Technology

Science-technology interaction : A systems model for education. M.V. Ananthakrishan *J Higher Education* 9(2) Aut 1983 p 229-34 refs tabs

Technology : India

Education, science, technology and integrated development. Hari Narain *Indian J Adult Education* 44(1-2) Ja-Fe 1983 p 33-50

Science, technology development and the universities. R.C. Mehrotra *J Higher Education* 6(1-3) 1980-81 p 25-39 tabs

Technology : Social Aspects

Technological and social complexity. Maurice M. Richter. Albany, State Univ of N.Y. Press.1982. 120p. $ 34.50 *Book Rev, J Higher Education* 9(1) Mon 1983 p 148-49

Technology, Educational

See

Educational Technology

Technology, Rural : India

Strategies for development of appropriate rural technologies and their extension. Maheshwar Dayal *New Frontiers in Education* 14(4) Oc-De 1984 p 10-17

Taking science and technology to the rural sector. Sant Prakash *Education*

Quarterly 30(3) Oc 1978 p 21-23

Technology for rural development. T.S. Avinaghilingam *J Educational Research and Extension* 19(4) Ap 1983 p 193-206

Teen-age

See

Adolescence : Youth

Teen-age Girls

See

Adolescent Girls

Television

Differences in TV viewers and non-viewers in relation to their adjustment and leisure time activities. Vanita Leki *Experiments in Education* 12(11) Ja 1985 p 189-92

Television and Youth

Students and the STV programme. G.R. Sudama and D.R. Goel *Experiments in Education* 12(10) De 1984 p 174-80

Television and students. A.B. Phatak and V.V. Singh *J Indian Education* 12(3) Se 1986 p 39-43

Television Authorship

Writing for educational television. Jagannath Mohanty *Indian Education* 11(6) Se 1981 p 26-28

Television Broadcasting : India : Delhi

TV broadcast in Delhi : A restropective view. R.C. Jha and B.P. Sinha *Indian J Extension Education* 16(3-4) De 1980 p 32-35 tabs

Television in Adult Education

A perspective survey on television viewing and community learning needs. V. Nagarajan and S. Selvam *Indian J Adult Education* 40(4) Ap 1979 p 37-42 refs tabs

See also

Educational Broadcasting in Adult Education

Television in Agriculture

Effectiveness of television and its combinations in transferring technological know-how to farmers. N.K. Chauhan and B.P. Sinha *Indian J Extension Education* 15(1-2) Je 1979 p 9-18 tab

Television in Agriculture : India : Delhi

Some correlates of farm talecast viewing by Delhi farmers. B.P. Sinha *et al* *Indian J Extension Education* 14(3-4) Jl-De 1978 p 51-57

Television in Agriculture : India : Punjab

Credibility of television as a source of information. G.S. Sangha and M.P. Gupta *Indian J Extension Education* 21(1-2) Ja-Je 1985 p 74-76 tabs

Personal traits and viewing behaviour of rural TV owners of Punjab. M.P. Gupta and G.S. Sangha *Indian J Extension Education* 16(1-2) Je 1980 p 87-89 tabs

Television in Education

Distance education. Motilal Sharma *Teacher Today* 27(2) Oc-De 1984 p 44-48

Educational TV programme. Gopal Saksena *Education Quarterly* 38(1) Spr 1986 p 21-23

Educational television programmes under INSAT. Jagannath Mohanty

Education Quarterly 35(1) Ja 1983 p 16-18

Evaluation of educational television programmes. Jagannath Mohanty *Indian Education* 9(12) Mr 1980 p 23-26

Hardware educational technology : An experiment with television in structure. D.K. Sharma and Yash Pal Singh *Experiments in Education* 9(10) De 1981 p 176-82 refs

Instruction through radio vision : A comparative study. Motilal Sharma and Meena Oberai *Indian Educational Rev* 18(4) Oc 1983 p 37-46

A study on television instruction. D.K. Sharma and Yash Pal Singh *J Institute of Educational Research* 6(1) Ja 1982 p 17-22 refs tabs

Television and the class-room reading programme. George J. Becker. Int Reading Assn. 1971. 32p. *Book Rev, Education Quarterly* 31(2) Jl 1979 p 42-43

Television as an educational medium. S. Ravishankar *Teacher Today* 24(4) Ap-Je 1982 p 50-56 refs

Television programmes through INSAT : A national innovations. Jagannath Mohanty *Indian Education* 12(1-2) Ap-My 1982 p 33-35

See also

Educational Broadcasting

Satellite Instruction Television Experiment

Television in Adult Education

Television in Higher Education

Television in Education : China (People's Republic)

Television for entertainment and education in China. *Indian Education* 11(7) Oc 1981 p 25-26

Television in Education : Great Britain

Electronic link for distant teachers and pupils. Elaine Williams *Progress of Education* 56(4) Nv 1981 p 82-83

Television in Education : India

Development of educational television in India. Sohanvir Singh Chaudhary *Progress of Education* 60(8) Mr 1986 p 183-87+

ETC programme for the children in the age group 9-11 under INSAT. Jagannath Mohanty and Sadasiba Maharana *J Educational Planning and Administration* 1(1) Oc 1986 p 54-62 tabs

Educational television in India : Organisation and utilisation. G.R. Sudama and D.R. Goel *EPA Quarterly Bulletin* 8(1-2) Ap-Je 1985 p 45-58 refs

A study of the ETV programmes under INSAT for the children in the age group 5-8. K.C. Dalal and P.K. Tripathy *EPA Quarterly Bulletin* 8(3-4) Oc 1985-Ja 1986 p 21-28 refs

Teacher education programmes under INSAT. Jagannath Mohanty and S.C. Behera *EPA Quarter Bulletin* 8(1-2) Ap-Je 1985 p 59-66 refs

Television in Education : India : Tamil Nadu

Effects of TV viewing on achievement. Sunanda Ghosh and K.V. Sampoornam *J Institute of Educational Research* 6(2) My 1982 p 30-36 refs tabs

Television in Education : Pakistan

ETC in Pakistan : A glimpse. Moneez Hashmi *Primary Teacher* 11(3) Jl 1986 p 4-5

Television in Higher Education

Educational television and higher education. D.C. Surana *University News* 24(36) 21 Se 1986 p 1-5

Television Programme : India : Gujarat

TV viewing behaviour of urban women : A study. Anita S. Thomas and Namrata Tiwari *Indian J Adult Education* 47(5) My 1986 p 19-23 +

Television Writing

See

Television Authorship

Telugu Language : Text-books

Sex role stereotyping in language texts. R. Srinivasa Rao and S. Sree Lakshmi Devi *Experiments in Education* 7(3) My 1979 p 50-53 refs

Tension

See

Anxiety

Tests

See

Examinations

Tests and Measurements in Education

See

Educational Tests and Measurements

Text-books

Alternatives to the traditional text book. *J. Indian Education* 5(6) Mr 1980 p 58-63

Development of books for professional subjects. B. Ghosh *University News* 21(24) De 1983 p 868

Text book : Does it require a periodic change? Ban Behari Mukhopadhyay *Progress of Education* 56(1) Ag 1981 p 14-16 refs

Text-books : A perspectival overview. D. Dikshit *Education Quarterly* 37(2) Sum 1985 p 22-26

Text-books and national integration. G.C. Upadhyay *Experiments in Education* 11(7) Se 1983 p 126-28

Text books must install patriotism in school children. M.A. Srinivasa Iyengar *Educational Rev* 89(12) De 1983 p 217

Values in text-books : A research perspective. U.S. Chaudhari *Quest in Education* 19(3) Jl 1982 p 255-59 refs

Values in text-books : A research perspective. U.S. Chaudhuri *University News* 23(9) 1 Mr 1985 p 4-5 refs

Writing school text-books : Pedogogical dimensions. L.S. Sharma *J Indian Education* 10(6) Mr 1985 p 33-38 refs

Text-books : India

Attempts to improve school text-books. I.S. Chaudhri *J Indian Education* 8(3) Se 1982 p 26-28

Changing impages of males and females : How of feminist sex role liberation in Indian school text-books. Narendra Nath Kalia *Indian Education* 13(10-11) Ja-Fe 1984 p 10-16

A note on school education and text-books. I.H. Latif *Progress of Education* 58(8) Mr 1984 p 178-80+

Policy for the periodic change of text-books in India. I.S. Sharma *J Indian*

Education 8(6) Mr 1983 p 42-45 tabs
Text-book production in the Indian context. M. Manjusha *Progress of Education* 60(6) Ja 1986 p 135-38
Text-books — A neglected field of research in India. Banbehari Mukhopadhyay *Educational Rev* 86(6) Je 1980
What will I be when I grow up : Equalising occupational choices in India's text books. Narendra Nath Kalia *Educational Rev* 90(9) Se 1984 p 135-38; 90(11) Nv 1984 p 168-69 tabs

Text-books : India : Madhya Pradesh
Book bank schemes of M.P. Bir Singh *Educational Rev* 88(10) Oc 1982 p 165-67

Thailand
See also
Adult Education : Thailand
Education : Thailand
Educational Innovations : Thailand

Theatre : Botswana
Encouraging participation in development : Laedza Batanani case studies. R. Kidd and M.L. Byram *Indian J Adult Education* 40(8) Ag 1979 p 17-29 refs

Theological Education
See
Religious Education

Theosophy
See also
Yoga

Theses
See
Dissertations, Academic

Thompson, John M.
Biography of John M. Thompson. *Experiments in Education* 9(7) Se 1981 p 130

Thought and Thinking
Towards teaching for thinking. G.L. Arora *J Indian Education* 5(4) Nv 1979 p 38-41

Time Tables
See
Schools : Time Tables

Tobacco : India : Andhra Pradesh
Adoption of improved technology of flue-cured Virginia (FCV) tobacco in Andhra Pradesh. M.J. Wilson and J. Chaturvedi *Indian J Extension Education* 21(3-4) Jl-Oc 1985 p 108-09

Trade Unions
See also
Teachers Unions

Traditions
See
Superstition

Training, Manual
See
Manual Training
Training, Occupational
See
Occupational Training
Training, Physical
See
Physical Education and Training
Training, Vocational
See
Occupational Training
Training Colleges for Teachers
See
Teachers Colleges
Training of Children
See
Children : Management
Training of Rural Youth for Self-Employment Programme
Management of TRYSEM programme : A critical analysis. G. Anuradha and B.P. Sinha *Indian J Extension Education* 21(1-2) Ja-Je 1985 p 36-41
Tree Plantation
Knowledge gained about agro-forestry plantation in various training programmes. P. Das and B.K. Sharma *Indian J Extension Education* 21(1-2) Ja-Je 1985 p 89-90
Tribal Eduction
Concept of 'Raska' implications for tribal education. M. Kundu *New Frontiers in Education* 12(2) Ap-Je 1982 p 42-46
Educational programme for tribal population : An alternative strategy. S.C. Dutta *Indian J Adult Education* 44(4) Ap 1983 p 11-14
Equality for tribals : The role of education. V. Sudarsen and B.V. Subba Reddy *Experiments in Education* 9(12) Fe 1982 p 213-15
Higher education in the tribal context. Nirmal Minz *New Frontiers in Education* 12(1) Ja-Mr 1982 p 50-53
Literacy for tribals. G.S. Rao *Indian J Adult Education* 40(4) Ap 1979 p 1-4 refs
Preparing 'readers' for tribal adult learners — Some viable topics. M. Kundu *Indian J Adult Education* 42(9) Se 1981 p 21-24 refs
The problem of cultural integration of the tribals education as the chief instrument of change. M.N. Ravindranathan *Education Quarterly* 35(4) Oc 1983 p 20-24
Problems of teachers working in tribal areas. D.L. Prasada Rao and P. Venkata Rao *Educational Rev* 89(8) Ag 1983 p 139-41
Social context of tribal education. Vimal P. Shah and Tara Patel. New Delhi, Concept. 212 p. Rs.150 *Book Rev, Education Quarterly* 38(2) Sum 1986 p 49-51
Sociological problems in tribal education — A case study. Rajni Srivastava *Indian Educational Rev* 17(3) Jl 1982 p 110-13
A study of educational backwardness of tribal students. K.R. Sharma

Education Quarterly 35(2) Ap 1983 p 33-38

A study of language development, scholastic achievement and tribal students. K.R. Sharma *Research Bulletin* 14(1-2) Mr-Je 1984 p 3-21 tabs

A study of parent child interaction and achievement motivation among tribal high school students. M. Sowaid *et al J Institute of Educational Research* 10(3) Se 1986 p 24-27 refs

Tribal culture and educations response : Search for a model of education for the tribal people. S.A.B.D Hans *New Frontiers in Education* 16(1) Ja-Mr 1986 p 1-47 appdx

Tribal Education : India : Andhra Pradesh

Study of creative abilities of tribal children in relation to their sex and socio-economic status. P. Krishna Kumari *et al J Institute of Educational Research* 10(1) Ja 1986 p 1-4 refs

Educational problems of tribal children of forest and hill areas. Bhaskara Rao Digumastha *Experiments in Education* 12(1) Mr 1984 p 15-18

Educational wastage and stagnation among tribal children. G.C. Ahuja *J Indian Education* 6(1) My 1980 p 58-70 refs tabs

A new approach to State Non-Formal Education Centre in tribal area for all age groups. Upendra Nath Rout *Experiments in Education* 6(4) Je 1978 p 60-63

Non-formal education for adult tribes. N. Venkataiah *Experiments in Education* 8(3) My 1980 p 54-56

Tribal education in India : An effective pedagogy. Manmatha Kundu *J Indian Education* 12(4) Nv 1986 p 43-48 refs

Tribal students and role of schools. K.R. Sharma *Primary Teacher* 9(4) Oc 1984 p 11-13

Tribal Education : India : Madhya Pradesh

Self-situational deprivations in the school adjustment of tribal children. Shivendra Kumar Kulshreshta *J Indian Education* 5(2) Jl 1979 p 41-47

Tribal Education : India : Maharashtra

The second change education for the tribals of Vidarbha. S.K. Jha and H.R. Barde *Progress of Education* 58(11) Je 1984 p 270-72

Tribal Education : India : Meghalaya

Sex differences in creativity among the tribe of Meghalaya. Gitika Dutta *J Institute of Educational Research* 6(2) My 1982 p 23-26 refs tabs

Tribal Education : India : Uttar Pradesh

Parental deprivation in relations to academic achievement of denotified tribes. M.A. Khan *Indian Education Rev* 14(4) Oc 1979 p 95-98

Tribal Education : Research

Perspectives of research in tribal education. M.N. Ravindranatha *Experiments in Education* 9(1) Mr 1981 p 15-18; 9(2) Ap 1981 p 21-26

Tribes : India

A study of social and personal problems of tribal youth. Jitendra Mohan and Narender Kumar *Asian J Psychology and Education* 6(1) Ja 1980 p 5-8

Traditional beliefs of tribal Mundas associated with cattle husbandry. R.M. Srivastava and R.L. Kharde *Indian J Extension Education* 19(3-4) Se-De 1983 p 77-82 refs tabs

Tribal development : The concept and the frame. B.D. Sharma. New Delhi, Prachi Prakashan. 1978, 220p. Rs.36 *Book Rev, J Indian Education* 7(2)

Jl 1979 p 70; *Teacher Today* 25(2) Oc-De 1982 p 102-03

See also

Mundas, The

Tribes : India : Andhra Pradesh

Training needs of tribal farmers. Amar Singh and Suraj Singh *Indian J Extension Education* 17(3-4) Se-De 1981 p 81-88 Tabs

Tribes : India : Arunachal Pradesh

Tribes of Arunachal Pradesh. P. Thankappan Nair. Guwahati, Spectrum Pub. 1985, 319p. Rs.165 *Book Rev, Teacher Today* 28(2) Oc-De 1985 p 124-25

Tribes : India : Bihar

An analysis of tribal loanees in repayment of loans. H.S.P. Sinha and R. Ranjan *Indian J Extension Education* 17(3-4) Se-De 1981 p 54-65 refs tabs

Tribes : India : Gujarat

Economic differentiation and tribal identity : A case study of Chaudharis. Ghanashyam Shah. Delhi, Ajanta. 1984, 152p. Rs.80 *Book Rev, Perspectives in Education* 1(2) Ap 1985 p 129-31

Tribes : India : Madhya Pradesh

Creativity as a prediction of entrepreneurial success among tribals. Gurpal Singh Jarial *Experiments in Education* 11(12) Fe 1984 p 110-14 refs

Tribes : India : Orissa

Occupational status of parents of Harijans and tribal welfare department high school students of Orissa. Banu Behari Kamila *National J Education* 6(1) Se 1983 p 56-64 refs tabs

Tribes : India : Uttar Pradesh

Effect of parental deprivation on personality adjustment : With special reference to the denotified tribes of U.P. *Indian Educational Rev* 17(1) Ja 1982 p 99-109

Socio-psychological make-up of Tharu and Boksa adolescents. Ram Swarup Verma *Bharatiya Shiksha Shodh Patrika* 4(2) Jl-De 1985 p 27-33

Some psychological problems of tribals of Mirzapur : A case study. Rajni Srivastava *Indian Educational Rev* 18(2) Ap 1983 p 106-10 tabs

Trimester Plan

See

Semester System

Trnancy : Schools

See

School Attendance

Tuition

See

Universities and Colleges : Finance

Tuitions : Private

See

Tutors and Tutoring

Tuitions : Students

See

Tutors and Tutoring

Tutors and Tutoring
Effectivness of coaching and self study in schools. M. Shanmugham and M.K. Sivagamsundari *Experiments in Education* 8(8) Oc 1980 p 145-48 refs tabs
Reactions of students towards private tuitions. D.R. Goel *Experiments in Education* 8(9) Nv 1980 p 161-66 tabs
Reactions of students towards private tuitions. D.R. Goel *Progress of Education* 54(4-5) Nv-De 1979 p 78-84+
See also
Group Work in Education
Individualised Instruction
Remedial Teaching
Typewriting
Creativity in typing. Prabhakar Raizada *Primary Teacher* 10(3) Jl 1985 p 29-32
Typewriter draws designs and maps. Prabhakar Raizada *Primary Teacher* 10(2) Ap 1985 p 15-17

Underachievers
Under-achievement synarome among high ability high school boys. Haribhai G. Desai *J Education and Psychology* 35(1-2) Ap-Je 1978 p 4-14 refs
Underdeveloped Areas
See
Developing Countries
Undergraduates
See
College Students
Underprivileged Children
See
Socially Handicapped Children
Unemployment : Great Britain
In place of work : Policy and provision for the young unemployed. Rob Fiddy, *ed.* Sussex, Falmar Press. 193p. *Book Rev, Education Quarterly* 35(4) Oc 1983 p 66-67
Unemployment, Educated
Degree-job delink. M.R. Santhanam *Education Quarterly* 38(1) Spr 1986 p 9-14
Delinking degrees from jobs. Navin Chandra Joshi *Education Quarterly* 33(1) Ja 1981 p 22-23
Education and jobs. S. Parmaji. Delhi, Leeladevi Pub. 1979, 118p. Rs.45 *Book Rev, Education Quarterly* 32(4) Oc 1980 p 48; *Indian Educational Rev* 10(5) Ag 1980 p 44-45; *Indian J Extension Education* 16(3-4) De 1980 p 96-97; *J Education and Psychology* 39(1) Ap 1981 p 73-74; *J Higher Education* 5(3) Spr 1980 p 432-33; *New Frontiers in Education* 12(1) Ja-Mr 1982 p 80-81
Education and manpower development. M. Malla Reddy *Indian Education* 10(1-2) Ap-My 1980 p 29-34
Education, work and employment. Jacques Hallak and Francoise Calliods. Paris, UNESCO. 322p. $ 17 *Book Rev, Teacher Today* 26(1) Jl-Se 1981 p 181-84

Employment problems of university graduates. C. Parvathamma. New Delhi, Ashish Pub H. 159p. Rs.100 *Book Rev, Education Quarterly* 37(3) Aut 1985 p 60-61

Employment to educated masses. R.S. Gaur *Education Quarterly* 31(3-4) Oc 1979-Ja 1980 p 28-30; *Teacher Education* 13(8-9) Jl-Oc 1979 p 32-38

A probe into the problems of educated job Seekers. M.L. Jha *J Indian Education* 8(4) Nv 1982 p 20-23

Problem of unemployment among the educated. *New Frontiers in Education* 15(1) Ja-Mar 1985 p 104-08

Training and employment of educated youth : The twentieth point of the 20-point programme. Prabhakar Raizada *J Indian Education* 10(6) Mr 1985 p 24-29

Unemployment and education. R.S. Nigam *Educational Rev* 86(8) Ag 1980 p 143-44

Unutilised manpower of educated unemployed. Peri Subbarayan *Educational Rev* 85(1) Ja 1979 p 11-15

Unemployment, Educated : Developing Countries

Education and employment problems in developing countries. Mark Blang. New Delhi, Macmillan. 89p. Rs.25 *Book Rev, Education Quarterly* 32(4) Ap 1980 p 49

Unemployment, Educated : India

Delinking of degrees from jobs : Getting jobs without degrees. R.C. Misra *Education Quarterly* 32(1) Ja 1980 p 30-31

Education and employment in India : The policy nexus. Trilok N. Dhar *et al.* Minerva. 1976, 137p. Rs.40 *Book Rev, J Higher Education* 5(2) Aut 1979 p 265-66

Unemployment, Educated : India : West Bengal

Graduate employment and higher education in West Bengal. P.K. Bose and S.P. Mukherjee *J Higher Education* 5(3) Spr 1980 p 281-99 ft-n tabs

Union Public Service Commission

Findings by UPSC Chairman. R.S. Nigam *Educational Rev* 86(11) Nv 1980 p 214-15

Unions : Student

See

Student Unions

United Nations Educational Scientific and Cultural Organisation

India and the UNESCO. *New Frontiers in Education* 16(1) Ja-Mr 1986 p 85-91

United States

See also

Adult Education : United States

Curriculum Planning : United States

Education : United States

Education, Higher : United States

Education, Rural : United States

Educational Law and Legislation : United States

Educational Planning : United States

Health Education : United States

High School Principals : United States

Illiteracy : United States
Municipal Universities and Colleges : United States
Schools : United States
Students : Indian (in the United States)
Teachers : United States
Teachers : Training : United States
Vocational Education : United States

Universities and Colleges

College climates : Explorations of a concept. J. Filella *New Frontiers in Education* 12(3) Jl-Se 1982 p 1-13 refs

Extension service in universities. Janardhana Reddy *Indian Education* 11(7) Oc 1981 p 16-18

Probing mechanics of open university. Pradep Kumar Srivastava *Educational Rev* 91(8) Ag 1985 p 121-23

Role of universities in international cooperation for development. Malcolm S. Adiseshiah *New Frontiers in Education* 14(2) Ap-Je 1984 p 55-65

Universities and national development : Linkage with environment L.R. Shah *Education Quarterly* 31(2) Jl 1979 p 17-19

The university as an institution : Present problems and future trends. Dietrich Goldschmidt *J Higher Education* 9(1) Mon 1983 p 65-75 appdx refs

University as a sanctuary for international awakening and peace. S.N. Prasad *Progress of Education* 60(6) Ja 1986 p 139-42+

See also

Co-education
Dissertations : Academic
Education, Higher
Medical Colleges
Municipal Universities and Colleges
Open Universities
Semester System
Teacher Colleges
University of Agricultural Sciences

Universities and Colleges : Administration

Administration of higher education : An overview. Kumaresh Chakravarty *J Higher Education* 2(2) Aut 1978 p 223-32 refs

The amidget bureaucratic phenomenon : Reflection as system transformations in universities. Y. Raghaviah *J Higher Education* 9(2) Aut 1983 p 157-76 refs

The application of modern scientific management principles to the development of the university administration in developing countries. A.H. Hommadi *EPA Quarterly Bulletin* 6(2) Jl 1983 p 48-50

Aspects and modes of external influence in the university administration. D.K. Ghosh *EPA Quarterly Bulletin* 7(3-4) Oc 1984-Ja 1985 p 26-36

Autonomy in university administration. S.S. Mathur *J Educational Planning and Administration* 1(1) Oc 1986 p 13-20 refs

College climates : A psycho-social matrix model. J Filella *New Frontiers in Education* 13(1) Ja-Mr 1983 p 1-12 refs tabs

Conducting staff meetings in colleges. D.B. Desai *New Frontiers in*

Education 13(3) Jl-Se 1983 p 42-47

Decision-making and faculty participation. D.R. Darji and D.K. Sharma *J Higher Education* 7(3) Spr 1982 p 266-72 refs tabs

Decisional participation in university governance. D.R. Darji and D.K. Sharma *Quest in Education* 19(2) Ap 1982 p 160-68 refs

Democratisation and decentralisation of university administration. V. Venkateshwara Rao *Indian Education* 13(7) Oc 1983 p 19-22

Developing unit structure in university organisation : A study of alternative approach. Swapan K. Bhattacharya *J Higher Education* 5(2) Aut 1979 p 243-50

Dimensions of organisational climate : A case study of university departments. Arvinda K. Sinha *Indian Educational Rev* 18(4) Oc 1983 p 1-14

Effective management of universities and research. D.K. Sharma Purohit and D.R. Darji *J Higher Education* 5(1) Mon 1979 p 112-16

Environment and the challenge of educational management. S.C. Dube *J Higher Education* 6(1-3) 1980-81 p 9-14

Faculty-administration relations. J. Macia *New Frontiers in Education* 9(1) Ja-Mr 1979 p 12-26

Human relations in college administration. Narendra Singh *Educational Rev* 86(7) Jl 1980 p 136-39

Management information systems in university administration. Swapan K. Bhattacharya and Manabendra Nath Pal *J Higher Education* 2(2) Aut 1976 p 213-21 refs tabs

Management of a university. D.K. Sharma and D.R. Darji *Educational Rev* 92(10) Oc 1986 p 169-71

Management of universities in India : Need for structural reforms. V. Venkateshwara Rao *Indian Education* 12(8-9) Nv-De 1982 p 9-12

The need for autonomous boards of under-graduate courses. S. Radha Krishna Moorthy *J Higher Education* 6(1-3) 1980-81 p 154-55

Need for scientific management of universities in India. Y.S. Kiranmayi *University News* 24(43) 16 Nv 1986 p 4-7

An open and participatory college administration. C.T. Kurien *J Higher Education* 2(2) Aut 1976 p 203-11

Organisation and functioning of universities in India. Sushila Singhal *J Higher Education* 1(2) Aut 1975 p 223-40 refs tabs

Organisational health and decision-making in higher education : A comparative study. D.K. Sharma *University News* 24(38) 8 De 1986 p 3-5

Policy analysis as an adjunct tool in the prevention or resolution of managerial crisis in higher education. C. Joanne Garrett and Larry N. Gerrett *J Higher Education* 5(1) Mon 1979 p 13-19

Riding an unbridled horse. S.D. Bahuguna *J Higher Education* 2(2) Aut 1976 p 264-67

Structure and performance of college education in India : An organisational analysis of arts and science colleges in Bombay. Rudolf C. Heredia *New Frontiers in Education* 10(2) Ap-Je 1980 p 21-33

A study of conflict in a university. Mohindera Sharma *J Higher Education* 4(1) Mon 1978 p 1-10 refs ft-n

University administration in India : Some critical issues. G. Ram Reddy

Indian Education 11(1-2) Ap-My 1981 p 24-34

The university community and its autonomy. J.N. Kaul *Indian Education* 11(1-2) Ap-My 1981 p 35-37

University system : Organisational context, structure and performance. Omer Bin Sayeed and Ravi Kumar Varma *J Higher Education* 5(3) Spr 1980 p 409-15 refs tabs

See also

College Personnel Management
Departmental Chairman : Universities
Personnel Service in Education
Students Participation in Administration
Teachers Participation in Administration
University Autonomy
Vice-chancellors

See also

Subdivision 'Administration' under the name of individual university, e.g., Osmania University : Administration

Universities and Colleges : Admission

Admission to universities — A miscellany. Bir Singh *J Higher Education* 5(2) Aut 1979 p 260-63

Long term predictive validity of college admission measures. B.R. Bhadra and P.R. Girija *J Education and Psychology* 38(3) Oc 1980 p 149-58 refs

Universities and Colleges : Admission : India : Tamil Nadu

Enrolment of the scheduled castes in general colleges : A case study of Tamil Nadu. G.R. Sudama and A.P. Thiagarajan *Experiments in Education* 9(4) Je 1981 p 63-69 tabs

Universities and Colleges : Bangladesh

See also

Bangladesh Agricultural University

Universities and Colleges : Belgium

Louvain-La-Neuve (Belgium) : A new town built by and for a university. Michel Woitrin *J Higher Education* 5(2) Aut 1979 p 203-10

Universities and Colleges : Developing Countries

The university as centre and periphery. Philip G. Altbach *J Higher Education* 4(2) Aut 1978 p 157-69

Universities and Colleges : Electronic Data Processing Department

University computer centre : Structure, functions and management. D. Sankara Narayan *J Higher Education* 5(1) Mon 1979 p 108-12

Universities and Colleges : Europe

Change in universities of the European tradition. David Teather *New Frontiers in Education* 14(1) Ja-Mr 1984 p 71-80

Universities and Colleges : Europe : West

The functions and problems of the urban university in the West; A comparative perspective. Frederich Waraser *J Higher Education* 8(3) Spr 1983 p 365-81

Universities and Colleges : Examinations

Attitudes of the professional and non-professional students towards entrance examinations. N. Venkataiah *J Education and Psychology* 40(4) Ja 1983 p 195-201 refs tabs

Failure of an innovation in a university : An investigation. R.P. Jain *Experiments in Education* 10(1) Mr 1982 p 15-20; 10(2) Ap 1982 p 32-34 tabs

Estimation of average proportion of failures at a university examination : A numerical approach. A.K. Sinha and P.C. Sinha *Indian Educational Rev* 15(4) Oc 1980 p 104-05

Opinions of university examiners towards spot evaluation. Lokesh K. Verma *Progress of Education* 56(4) Nv 1981 p 95-97

Origin and diffusion of external examiner system in the conduct of university examination. J.T. Okadara *Indian Educational Rev* 16(2) Ap 1981 p 29-45 refs

Question banks in Indian universities : Potential uses and some psychometric issues. Harinder Nanda Mahajan *J Higher Education* 7(3) Spr 1982 p 310-15 refs

Revaluation at the university examination : Its effect on the results of candidates. Pratibha Deo *J Higher Education* 6(1-3) 1980-81 p 83-103 refs tabs

Universities and Colleges : Faculty

Faculty — administration relations. J. Macia *New Frontiers in Education* 9(1) Ja-Mr 1979 p 12-26

Faculty and student status in administration. R.C. Srivastava *J Higher Education* 4(2) Aut 1978 p 225-44

Faculty development. R.P. Jain *New Frontiers in Education* 13(2) Ap-Je 1983 p 49-54 refs

Faculty improvement programmes. K.C. Peter *New Frontiers in Education* 13(3) Jl-Se 1983 p 56-67

Motivation of the faculty. Hemalata Prabhu *New Frontiers in Education* 9(1) Ja-Mr 1979 p 27-30

Performance appraisal of faculty in higher education in institutions. Rajani R. Shirur *EPA Quarterly Bulletin* 5(3-4) Oc 1982-Ja 1983 p 36-41

Universities and Colleges : Faculty : Heads of Departments

Rotation of leadership and Deanship in universities. M.V. Naidu *Indian Education* 11(5) Ag 1981 p.42-44

Universities and Colleges : Finance

An approach to financial management in education with special reference to colleges in India. C.B. Padmanabhan *J Higher Education* 7(3) Spr 1982 p 293-97

Economics of universities finances : Basic principles and practice. P.R. Panchamukhi. Dharwar, Karnatak Hist Res Soc. 1977, 238p. Rs.22 *Book Rev, Indian Educational Rev* 15(4) Oc 1980 p 117-19; *J Higher Education* 4(1) Mon 1978 p 125-26

The financial aspect of college autonomy. T.A. Mathias *New Frontiers in Education* 10(1) Ja-Mr 1980 p 40-43

Financial management of colleges : Issues and suggestions. J. Jagjit Singh *EPA Quarterly Bulletin* 8(1-2) Ap-Je 1985 p 26-39

Financial management of universities and colleges in India. C.B. Padmanabhan *Indian Education* 11(1-2) Ap-My 1981 p 43-48

Financial management of universities and colleges in India. C.B. Padmanabhan *New Frontiers in Education* 10(4) Oc-De 1980 p 59-64

Financial management of universities in India. C.B. Padmanabhan *J Higher Education* 9(2) Aut 1983 p 282-85

Financing the universities. Bir Singh *New Frontiers in Education* 9(4) Oc-De 1979 p 63-65

University and college finance. Amrik Singh and G.D. Sharma, *eds.* New Delhi, Assn. of Indian Univ. 246p. Rs.45 *Book Rev, Indian Education* 12(5-6) Ag-Se 1982 p 40-42; *Indian Educational Rev* 18(1) Ja 1983 p 136-37

University budgetary reforms for sound financial management. C.B. Padmanabhan *New Frontiers in Education* 15(3) Jl-Se 1985 p 65-72

Working of university finances. D.M. Nanjundappa. New Delhi, Sterling. 1976, 163p. Rs.70 *Book Rev, J Higher Education* 3(3) Spr 1978 p 424-25

See also

State Aid to Higher Education

University Grants Commission : India

Universities and Colleges : Germany : West

The German University : A heraic ideal in conflict with the modern world. Daniel Fallon. Boulder, Colorado, Associated Univ. Press. 1980, xii, 14p. $ 7.95 *Book Rev, J Higher Education* 8(2) Aut 1982 p 252-54

Universities and Colleges : Graduate Work

Continuing education and the role of universities. Lakshmi Misra *Indian Education* 9(12) Mr 1980 p 19-22

Universities and Colleges : India

The changing character of university : Government relations in India. Y. Raghaviah *Indian Education* 11(1-2) Ap-My 1981 p 38-43

College development wing : An appraisal. K.M. Pathusha *University News* 23(1) 1 Ja 1985 p 5-6+

Commentaries on the human frontier. G. Ramanathan *Quest in Eucation* 16(3) Jl 1979 p 175-94

The dynamics of change. Amrik Singh *J Higher Education* 9(2) Aut 1983 p 197-206

Indian universities. Champa Tickoo. New Delhi, Orient Longman. 1980, 197p. Rs.50 *Book Rev, J Higher Education* 6(1-3) 1980-81 p 164-66

Institutional quality, student input and output : Analysis of six Indian universities. M.A. Khadar and Sushila Singhal *J Higher Education* 9(1) Mon 1983 p 34-45 refs tabs

Our universities are not super markets. R.S. Trivedi *Quest in Education* 17(1) Ja 1980 p 27-34

The third dimension of universities. D. Jagannatha Reddy *Experiments in Education* 10(4) Je 1982 p 69-70

Traditional institutions, universities and their coordination. Bansidhar Bhatt *J Indian Education* 12(3) Se 1986 p 35-38 refs

Universities and people's education for development in India. Kishore Sain *Teacher Today* 22(3) Ja-Mr 1980 p 64-68

Universities : Perspectives and problems. Rais Ahmed *J Higher Education* 7(3) Spr 1982 p 177-87

University and national development : Linkage with the environment. M.S. Yadav and S. Roy *New Frontiers in Education* 10(3) Oc-De 1980 p 22-26 refs

than agricultural universities) in the state of Maharashtra. *Progress of Education* 59(3-4) Oc-Nv 1984 p 50-52

Colleges and community : A case study of Ahmednagar College. Plamthodathil S. Jacob *New Frontiers in Education* 13(1) Ja-Mr 1983 p 24-30

State level conference on Maharashtra Universities Draft Act, 1984, V.M. Dandekar *Progress of Education* 59(3-4) Oc-Nv 1984 p 53+

Universities and Colleges : India : Tamil Nadu

Tamil Nadu Bill on private colleges. *New Frontiers in Education* 13(1) Ja-Mr 1983 p 76-82

Universities and Colleges : India : Uttar Pradesh

University administration in Uttar Pradesh. P.C. Shukla *Indian Education* 12(3-4) Je-Jl 1982 p 20-24

Universities and Colleges : Students

See

College Students

University Autonomy

Academic freedom in India. O.P. Sharma *Teacher Today* 24(3) Ja-Mr 1982 p 27-32

Autonomous colleges. Chips of the old block. J. Filella *New Frontiers in Education* 10(1) Ja-Mr 1980 p 14-27

Autonomous colleges experiment : At what price? C. Dharmarajan *Educational Rev* 87(3) Mr 1981 p 50-51

Autonomous programme at Loyola College. J. Kuriakose *New Frontiers in Education* 12(2) Jl-Se 1982 p 26-30

Autonomy at Lady Doak College. Nirmala Wydiffe *New Frontiers in Education* 12(2) Ap-Je 1982 p 55+

Autonomy in education. M.K. Singh *Educational Rev* 87(6) Je 1981 p 101-02

Dynamics of autonomy in education and Banasthali experiment. P.N. Mathur *Rajasthan Board J Education* 16(4) Oc-De 1980 p 1-9

Four years of autonomy at American College. A.R. Venkitaraman *New Frontiers in Education* 12(2) Ap-Je 1982 p 47-51

Implementation of autonomy at St. Joseph's College. C.K. Swamy *New Frontiers in Education* 12(2) Ap-Je 1982 p 61-67

Implementation of college autonomy. R.P. Rais and A.R. Venkitaraman *New Frontiers in Education* 10(1) Ja-Mr 1980 p 28-34

Motivation and curricular relevance in the context of college autonomy. Chandran Devanesan *New Frontiers in Education* 10(2) Ap-Je 1980 p 44-51

Our experience as an autonomous college. N. Casimir Raj *Educational Rev* 91(4) Ap 1985 p 61-65 refs

Three years of college autonomy. N.S. Gnanapragasam *Educational Rev* 87(9) Se 1981 p 164-65

University autonomy in the contemporary context. S.N. Singh and O.P. Tandon *National J Education* 2(1) Se 1979 p 7-14 ref

Working of autonomy of MCC : An appraisal. Mithra Augustine *New Frontiers in Education* 12(2) Ap-Je 1982 p 52-54

See also
Universities and Colleges : Administration

University Autonomy : India

College autonomy : Its impact on higher education and national life. M. Abel *New Frontiers in Education* 10(1) Ja-Mr 1980 p 35-39

The financial aspect of college autonomy. T.A. Mathias *New Frontiers in Education* 10(1) Ja-Mr 1980 p 40-43

Preparing a college for autonomy. M.A. Thangaraj *New Frontiers in Education* 10(2) Ap-Je 1980 p 34-43

Some reflections on college autonomy. *Student Action* 1(12) Ap 1983 p 4-5

University Autonomy : India : Tamil Nadu

College autonomy : An appraisal. D. Albert *New Frontiers in Education* 12(4) Oc-De 1982 p 49-52

University Extension

See also
Correspondence Schools and Courses

University Extension : India

University system and extension as the third dimension. G. Chaurasia *J Educational Planning and Administration* 1(1) Oc 1986 p 28-33

University Grants Commission : India

NAEP and the University Grants Commission. M.L. Mehta *Prasar* 7(1-2) Ap-Jl 1980 p 11-26

New year gift from UGC. *Student Action* 2(8) Ja 1984 p 5-11+

Role of the University Grants Commission in framing the policy of higher education. A. Mathew *J Higher Education* 9(2) Aut 1983 p 177-95 refs

25 years of UGC : Dilemmas and difficulties. K.L. Joshi *J Higher Education* 6(1-3) 1980-81 p 63-68 refs

The University Grants Commission : A personal view. Samuel Mathai *J Higher Education* 6(1-3) 1980-81 p 55-61

University Libraries

See
Libraries : University and College

University of Agricultural Sciences, Karnataka

Extension role expectation and perception of research workers. C.M. Dudhani and K.A. Jalihal *Indian J Extension Education* 21(3-4) Jl-De 1985 p 68-72 refs

University of Bombay

Air Chief Marshall I.H. Latif addresses convocation of Bombay University. *University News* 23(20) 23 My 1985 p 7-9

University of Delhi

Cost and efficiency of the different techniques of education in Delhi University. Ruddar Datt *J Higher Education* 6(1-3) 1980-81 p 71-82 tabs

University of Kerala : Finance

University finance in India : A case study of the University of Kerala. E.T. Mathew. New Delhi, Sterling. 1980, 120 p. Rs. 32 *Book Rev, Education Quarterly* 33(1) Ja 1981 p 40-41

University of Rajasthan

Making undergraduate education more relevant : A model developed at the University of Rajasthan, Jaipur. M.L. Sisodia and B.M. Agrawal *J Higher*

Education 8(2) Aut 1982 p 241-45 approx

University Students

See

College Students

University Teachers

See

College Teachers

Unnat Krishi (Periodical)

A measurement of a farm magazine effectiveness. Prakash Khandekar and P.N. Mathur *Indian J Extension Education* 16(3-4) De 1980 p 82-87 tabs

Urban Schools

See

Community Schools

Urban Universities

See

Municipal Universities and Colleges

Utkal University : Examinations

Internal assessment in relation to external marks of B.A. (Hons.) students of Utkal University : A statistical study. Lokesh K. Verma and Toshar Kanta Goya *Indian Educational Rev* 17(2) Ap 1982 p 27-34 tabs

Uttar Pradesh

See also

Adoption of Improved Farm Practices : India : Uttar Pradesh
Adult Education : India : Uttar Pradesh
Agricultural Extension Work : India : Uttar Pradesh
Agricultural Innovations : India : Uttar Pradesh
College Students : India : Uttar Pradesh
College Teachers : India : Uttar Pradesh
Dropouts : India : Uttar Pradesh
Education : India : Uttar Pradesh
Education, Elementary : India : Uttar Pradesh
Education, Higher : India : Uttar Pradesh
Education of Children : India : Uttar Pradesh
Education of Women : India : Uttar Pradesh
Educational Tests and Measurements : India : Uttar Pradesh
Elementary School Teachers : India : Uttar Pradesh
Field Crops : India : Uttar Pradesh
Goats : India : Uttar Pradesh
High School Teachers : India : Uttar Pradesh
School Attendance : India : Uttar Pradesh
School Management and Organisation : India : Uttar Pradesh
Schools : India : Uttar Pradesh
Student Adjustment : India : Uttar Pradesh
Student Teachers : India : Uttar Pradesh
Student Teaching : India : Uttar Pradesh
Students : India : Uttar Pradesh
Students Socio-economic Status : India : Uttar Pradesh
Teachers : India : Uttar Pradesh
Teachers : Training : India : Uttar Pradesh

Tribal Education : India : Uttar Pradesh
Tribes : India : Uttar Pradesh
Universities and Colleges : India : Uttar Pradesh
Vocational Interests : India : Uttar Pradesh
Women, Rural : India : Uttar Pradesh
Women in Agriculture : India : Uttar Pradesh

Vacation Schools : India : Rajasthan
Working holidays in Rajasthan schools. S.A. Dulani *Educational Rev* 85(8) Ag 1979 p 148-50 tabs
Vacations
A plea for utilisation of vacations. Subhashini Passi *Experiments in Education* 10(3) My 1982 p 57-58
Values
See
Worth
Verbal Behaviour
Academic grades and verbal behaviour. Harswarup Sharma *J Educational Research and Extension* 18(1) Jl 1981 p 16-20 tabs
See also
Verbal Learning
Verbal Learning
Delinquent tendencies in the adolescent girls at different age levels and their effect on verbal learning. Madhu Gupta *Asian J Psychology and Education* 4(3) Nv 1979 p 6-8
Effect of context stimuli in verbal learning. G.S. Dwivedi and Sri Chandra *Asian J Psychology and Education* 5(1-3) 1979 p 21-25
Isolation effects in verbal learning. S.W. Deshpande *Indian Educational Rev* 17(4) Oc 1982 p 48-67 refs
Verbal learning : A study of correlates. Madhu Gupta and Prabha Gupta *J Education and Psychology* 38(2) Jl 1980 p 111-20; 39(1) Ap 1981 p 42-51 refs
Veterinarians : India : Andhra Pradesh
Job satisfaction of veterninary assistant surgeons, S.V.M. Rao and T.S. Sohal *Indian J Extension Education* 16(3-4) De 1980 p 74-77 tabs
Veterinarians : India : Assam
Problems in professional socialisation as faced by agriculture and veterinary graduates in Assam. K.K. Saharia *J Education and Psychology* 44(2-3) Jl-Oc 1986 p 135-40
Veterinarians : India : Punjab
Role performance of veterninary assistant surgeons working in Veterninary hospitals of Punjab. Ram Kumar and V.K. Dubey *Indian J Extension of education* 20(1-2) Je 1984 p 69-70 tabs
Veterinary Medicine as a Profession
See
Veternarians
Veterinary Surgeons
See
Veterinarians

Vice-chancellors
Vice-chancellor and the statutory bodies of a university. K. Guna Sekaran *EPA Quarterly Bulletin* 6(3-4) Oc 1983-Ja 1984 p 22-39 ft-n
Vidyasagar, Ishwarchand : Educational Thought
Materialism and scientism in the educational philosophy of Pandit Iswar Chandra Vidyasagar. Sunanda Samadhar and B.R. Purkait *Perspectives in Education* 2(4) Oc 1986 p 213-20
Vietnam
See also
Adult Education : Vietnam
Illiteracy : Vietnam
Village Level Workers
Role performance of Village Level Workers in agriculture production. R.L. Kharde and B.M. Sahay *Indian J Extension Education* 15(1-2) Je 1979 p 87-89 tabs
Village Level Workers : India : Haryana
Role performance of Village Level Workers in agriculture production. R.L. Kharde and B.M. Sahay *Indian J Extension Education* 15(1-2) Je 1979 p 67-69 tabs
Village Level Workers : India : Punjab
Use of communication media by village level workers. M.P. Gupta *Indian J Extension Education* 16(3-4) De 1980 p 88-89 tabs
Village Level Workers : India : Tamil Nadu
Subject-matter training of Gram Sevaks. R. Ganeshan *et al Indian J Extension Education* 16(1-2) Je 1980 p 51-54 tabs
Village Libraries
See
Rural Libraries
Villages
See also
Community Development
Panchayat
Virtue
See also
Worth
Visiting Teachers
See also
Schools, Travelling
Visual Aids
Relative use of non-projected visual aids at the school level. M.S. Sandhu and Adarsh Bala *J Indian Education* 6(1) My 1980 p 44-47
Visual Education
Visual thinking and education. Arunima Vats *Primary Teacher* 11(2) Ap 1986 p 13-16
See also
Audio-visual Education
Moving-pictures in Education
Visual Perception
Visual thinking : Its physiological bases and educational significance.

Arunima Vats *Indian Educational Rev* 18(2) Ap 1983 p 60-68 refs

Visually Handicapped

Inactivity : The bane of schools for the visually handicapped. Ramesh P. Saxena *Teacher Today* 23(1) Jl-Se 1980 p 49-53

Know visually impaired child in your class. S. Mukhopadhyay *Primary Teacher* 11(3) Jl 1986 p 23-25

Visually Handicapped Children : Education

See

Blind : Education

Vocabulary

Vocabulary : Its importance and techniques of teaching. Ashok Mathur *Rajasthan Board J Education* 15(1) Ja-Mr 1979 p 17-20

Vocal Music

Psychological implications in vocal education. S.A. Durga *Experiments in Education* 7(6) Ag 1979 p 107-08

Voice culture. S.A.K. Durga. Baroda, Indian Musicological Soc. Rs. 25 *Book Rev, Experiments in Education* 8(1) Mr 1980 p 5

Vocational Education

Aptitudes of vocationalisation of education. D. Raja Ganesan *Experiments in Education* 7(1) Mr 1979 p 16-18 refs

Complementary occupational education. R.N. Joshi *EPA Quarterly Bulletin* 5(3-4) Oc 1982-Ja 1983 p 14-25 refs

From manual training to productive work. W.V. Bhave *Indian Education* 10(8) Nv 1980 p 4-7

Secondary education should be mainly vocational; an interview with Prof. Ramanthan *Rajasthan Board J Education* 15(1) Ja-Mr 1979 p 59-63

Technical-vocational education. Dhirendra Verma *J Indian Education* 6(5) Ja 1981 p 23-26

Trends in work education. S.L. Mathur *Rajasthan Board J Education* 20(4)-21(1) Oc 1984-Mr 1985 p 16-20

Vocational education and technological development of a nation. Raph N. Oranu *Indian Education* 12(3-4) Je-Jl 1982 p 5-11

Vocational education. C. Pankajam *Educational Rev* 87(3) Mr 1981 p 41-46 refs

Whither vocationalism. S. Sundaramurthy *Education Quarterly* 35(3) Jl 1983 p 26-28

See also

Agricultural Education
Blind : Education
Education, Basic
Engineering : Study and Teaching
Manual Training
Occupational Training
Professional Education
Technical Education
Vocational Guidance

Vocational Education : Curricula

Socially useful productive work and the school curriculum; editorial. *J Indian Education* 5(2) Jl 1979 p 1-2

Vocational Education : Germany : East

Future-oriented training and education in GDR. *Student Action* 2(9) Mr 1984 p 37+

Vocational Education : Germany : West

West Germany's occupational education. R.P. Singhal *J Indian Education* 5(1) My 1979 p 64-67

Vocational Education : Great Britain

Post secondary vocational education in England and Wales. P. Raizada *J Indian Education* 5(2) Jl 1979 p 18-22

Vocational Education : India

Education for self-employment. Chakradhari Agarwal *New Frontiers in Education* 15(3) Jl-Se 1985 p 61-66

Employment-oriented education. Bir Singh *Progress of Education* 55(9) Ap 1981 p 234-36

Evaluation of SUPW : A model. Arun Kumar Gupta *J Indian Education* 5(2) Jl 1979 p 8-12

Implant experience programme. N. Shanmugam *Experiments in Education* 6(5) Jl 1978 p 75-78

Perspectives of vocational education. Meena Budhisagar *Progress of Education* 61(2) Se 1986 p 37-39

Potential for SUPW teaching in our schools. T.N. Bajpai and C. Seshagiri Rao *J Indian Education* 5(5) Ja 1980 p 43-46

Socially useful productive work. Gurpal Singh Jarial *Experiments in Education* 6(11) Ja 1979 p 187-90

Socially useful productive work. L.K. Oad *J Indian Education* 5(2) Jl 1979 p 3-7

Towards work-oriented education. M.B. Buch and P.A. Patil. Ahmedabad, Gujarat Vidyapith. 1979, 137 p. Rs. 16 *Book Rev, J Indian Education* 7(2) Jl 1979 p 68-69

Vocational education — Needs and limitations. S.S. Bhati *Teacher Today* 22(1) Jl-Se 1979 p 22-27

Vocational education : Needs and scope at +2 stage. P.K. Sahoo *Experiments in Education* 6(12) Fe 1979 p 207-12 refs

Vocational education : Needs and scope at +2 stage. P.K. Sahoo *Experiments in Education* 8(9) Nv 1980 p 155-60 refs

Vocational education programme for schools. M.P. Kakar and K.R. Chandhoke *Rajasthan Board J Education* 21(3-4) Jl-De 1985

Vocationalisation at +2 stage. B. Venkat Ram Reddy *Indian Education* 10(4) Jl 1980 p 3-5

Vocationalisation of education : A perspective. A.K. Dhote *J Indian Education* 6(1) My 1980 p 14-18

Vocationalisation of education at higher secondary stage in India : psychological impediments, consequences and implications. K. Sudha Rao *Perspectives in Education* 2(3) Jl 1986 p 153-60 tabs

Vocationalisation of education : Experience and imperatives. Arun K. Mishra *New Frontiers in Education* 15(3) Jl-Se 1985 p 48-60

Vocationalisation of education : Some issues. I. Satya Sundaram *J Indian Education* 5(6) Mr 1980 p 25-31

Vocationalisation of education. Verghis Chandy *Educational Rev* 88(3) Mr 1982 p 45-46

Vocationalisation of secondary education. Thiru V. Rajasekaran *Experiments in Education* 6(3) My 1978 p 51-54

Work education in India : Experiences and plans. A.K. Dhote *J Indian Education* 10(5) Ja 1985 p 18-24

Work experience and teacher education S.V.V. Raghavacharyulu *Indian Education* 11(5) Ag 1981 p 11-13

Vocational Education : India : History

History of vocationalisation : A review. M.S. Padma *Teacher Today* 21(4) Ap-Je 1979 p 39-44 refs

Vocationalisation of education historical perspective. S.R. Gangopadhyay *Teacher Today* 29(3) Ja-Mr 1985 p 53-58

Vocational Education : India : Karnataka

Vocationalisation of education in Karnataka : A fellow up study by NCERT. *J Indian Education* 5(2) Jl 1979 p 59-62

Vocational Education : India : Madhya Pradesh

Earn while you learn projects in Madhya Pradesh. *J Indian Education* 6(2) Jl 1980 p 74-76

An M.P. experiment in work experience. Bir Singh *Education Quarterly* 22(4) Oc 1980 p 15-16; *Indian Education* 10(4) Jl 1980 p 41-43

Vocational Education : India : Maharashtra

An approach to vocationalisation of higher secondary education in the state of Maharashtra. K.M. Gedam *Education Quarterly* 38(1) Spr 1986 p 24-27

Vocational Education : India : Tamil Nadu

An elementary study on the introduction and implementation of three specific vocational courses in three city higher secondary schools. R. Athmaraman *Experiments in Education* 9(8) Oc 1981 p 138-44

Vocational Education : India : West Bengal

The present position of work education programme in the secondary schools of West Bengal. Agamorani Lahiri *Our Education* 3-4 Jl 1983 p 21-26 refs tabs

Vocational Education : Japan

Recent important developments in vocational education in Japan. *Teacher Education* 18(22-23) Ja-Ap 1983 p 1-5

Vocational Education : Teacher Training

Training of teachers for engineering based vocations. M. Sengupta *Teacher Today* 21(4) Ap-Je 1979 p 25-31 refs

Vocational Education : Thailand

Non-formal vocational education programme of Thailand : An overview. Thongpleu Chomcheun *Perspectives in Education* 1(1) Ja 1985 p 55-60

Vocational Education : United States

Jobs corps — Dreams can come true. Carl E. Lindgren *Educational Rev* 87(12) De 1981 p 227

Vocational Guidance

Comparison of vocational aspiration of urban and rural adolescents. S.S. Chadha *et al J Education and Psychology* 41(3) Oc 1983 p 101-05

General awareness of military career among rural and urban students. R.P. Gautam *Indian Educational Rev* 14(1) Ja 1979 p 123-30

Guidance and counselling and education, vocational and personal needs of the students. Pushpa Chaudhry *J Education and Psychology* 42(4) Ja 1983 p 202-08 refs

Guidance and counselling programmes in schools. R. Seetharam *Asian J Psychology and Education* 4(2) Jl 1979 p 17-21

Guidance in choosing one's career. Aimi Sukamyogi *Progress of Education* 56(8) Mr 1982 p 198

The role of vocational guidance. G.A. Woghalikar *J Indian Education* 9(1) My 1983 p 7-11

Strengthening guidance services and programmes for career development. Perin H. Mehta *J Indian Educational* 8(2) Jl 1982 p 12-25 refs

Vocational guidance at plus-two stage. Banbehari Mukhopadhyay *Educational Rev* 92(1) Ja 1986 p 9-11 refs

See also

Counselling

Personnel Service in Education

Vocational Interests

Vocational Guidance : India

Guidance services in India towards the end of 1981 : Report of a status survey. Perin H. Mehta *Indian Educational Rev* 18(2) Ap 1983 p 1-16 refs tabs

What will I be when I grow up : Equalising occupational choices in India's text books. Narendra Nath Kalia *Educational Rev* 90(10) Oc 1984 p 147-49; 90(11) Mr 1984 p 168-69+

Vocational Guidance : Nigeria

Career development of Nigerian students : Implications for guidance counsellors. Esogwa C. Osuala *Quest in Education* 18(2) Ap 1981 p 165-76

Vocational Interests

An analytical study of interest inventories. P.S.S. Bhasin *Indian Educational Rev* 18(2) Ap 1983 p 79-83

College going girls : Their occupational choices, goals and problems. Sunita Srivastava *J Indian Education* 11(2) Jl 1985 p 40-44

A comparative study of vocational interest of high and low achievers of science at intermediate level. B.P. Singh *et al Experiments in Education* 11(1) Mr 1983 p 11-15

Comparison of vocational aspiration of urban and rural adolescence. S.S. Chadha *et al J Education and Psychology* 41(3) Oc 1983 p 101-05 refs tabs

Development of an interest inventory. Uma Sinha *et al Indian Educational Rev* 18(3) Jl 1983 p 47-62 refs tabs

An exploration into occupational choices of higher secondary students. K.V. Sheth and K.R. Patel *Progress of Education* 56(6) Ja 1982 p 147-50 + tabs

Job preference of home science graduates. Suman Bhatnagar and Puspa Gupta *Indian J Extension Education* 16(3-4) De 1980 p 78-81 tabs

Occupational aspirations of the achievers and underachievers in mathematics. Didar Singh Jhaj and J.S. Grewal *Asian J Psychology and Education* 11(1) 1983 p 36-39

Occupational choice of agricultural students. N.C. Patel *et al Prasar* 7(3-4) Oc 1980-Ja 1981 p 18-25 refs

Relationship of vocational choice to self concept and socio-economic status. Pratibha Deo and Vasudha Kamat *Research Bulletin* 14(1-2) Mr-Je 1984 p 40-47 refs

Scholastic achievements and vocational interests as correlated to prolonged deprivation. V.P. Sharma and R.R. Kathuria *J Education and Psychology* 41(1-2) Ap-Jl 1983 p 69-76

The study of aspirations and achievement motivation of scheduled castes student teachers. A.B. Pathak and Rajesh Prasad Shukla *J Education and Psychology* 42(4) Ja 1985 p 196-201 refs

A study of relationship between values and vocational preferences of adolescents. Raj Kumar Yadav *Quest in Education* 17(2) Ap 1980 p 165-72 refs

A study of the interests of high school students. S. Jaleel Saheb *Quest in Education* 16(4) Oc 1979 p 307-13

A study of vocational interest of adolescent girls in relation to their level of aspiration and intelligence. B.P. Singh and Shushuma Jaiswal *Experiments in Education* 10(10) De 1983 p 172-77 refs

A study of vocational perceptions of high school boys. s. Jaleel Saheb *Asian J Psychology and Education* 4(2) Jl 1979 p 11-16 ft-n

A survey on vocational expectations of junior college students. P.L. Nankar *Research Bulletin* 12(3-4) Se-De 1982 p 44-48

Vocational Interests : India

Knowledge of military career as a determinant of its choice by higher secondary students. R.P. Gautam *J Indian Education* 6(1) My 1980 p 8-13 appdx

Vocational Interests : India : Delhi

Effect of personality factors on the level of occupational aspirations of higher secondary school students of Delhi : A study in sex differences. J.S. Gaur and Punima Mathur *Asian J Psychology and Education* 3(2) Jl 1978 p 1-14 refs tab

An investigation of the relationship between creativity, personality and vocational interest of 12th grade students of a Delhi school. N.K. Chadha and Arun K. Sen *Our Education* 2 Jl 1981 p 31-37 refs tabs

Vocational Interests : India : Gujarat

A comparative study of vocational interest of home science students in relation to the selected variables. Naina Talati and Uma Joshi *Progress of Education* 61(4-5) Nv-De 1986 p 92-95 tabs

Vocational Interests : India : Orissa

Vocational preferences of tenth grade boys and girls. P.K. Sahoo *Experiments in Education* p 32-36 tabs

Vocational Interests : India : Rajasthan

Dominant job values and preferences of undergraduate students. U. Kamawat and G.C. Rai *National J Education* 7(1) Se 1984 p 39-50 refs tabs

Vocational Interests : India : Tamil Nadu

Self concept and vocational aspirations among girls. Sunanda Ghosh and Marie Gordon *J Educational Research and Extension* 18(1) Jl 1981 p 24-27 refs tabs

Vocational Interests : India : Uttar Pradesh

A study of motivational aspects of occupational choice of the Indian students of graduate studies. A.K. Srivastava *National J Education* 6(1) Se 1983 p 40-47 refs tabs

Vocational Training

See

Occupational Training

Volunteer Workers in Education

The voluntary agency and adult education. Muriel Wasi *Education Quarterly* 30(3) Oc 1978 p 1-3

Wastage in Education

Composite index of wastage and stagnation. M.G. Joshi and D.U. Dandwate *Research Bulletin* 15(1-2) Mr-Je 1985 p 19-25 tabs

Educational wastage : A field study. V.P. Garg and J.R. Das *Primary Teacher* 9(3) Jl 1984 p 20-23

Educational wastage and stagnation among tribal children. G.C. Ahuja *J Indian Education* 6(1) My 1980 p 58-70 refs tab

School characteristics and incidence of stagnation in rural primary schools. Ramesh Chandra Sharma *Primary Teacher* 8(4) Oc 1983 p 18-22 refs

Stagnation at the elementary stage. *J Indian Education* 5(5) Ja 1980 p 76-78

Wastage in education in India : A case study in Andhra Pradesh. Jandhyala B.G. Tilk *Indian Educational Rev* 17(2) Ap 1982 p 58-85 refs tabs

Wastage in education; letter to the editor. *Progress of Education* 54(7) Fe 1980 p 141-42+

Wastage in primary education in Raipur district, (M.P.) C.K.M. Rao *Indian Education* 10(8) Nv 1980 p 37-40

Waste in Indian higher education. V. Krishna Kumar *Educational Rev* 85(11) Nv 1979 p 201-02

Water Resources Management

An evaluation of the Summer Institute on Water management in black soils. M.K. Setharao *et al Indian J Extension Education* 16(1-2) Je 1980 p 69-72 refs tabs

Weaning of Infants

See

Infants : Weaning

Weber-Fechner Law

See

Fechner's Law

West Bengal

See also

Agricultural Extension Work : India : West Bengal
Agriculture : Information Services : India : West Bengal
Agricultural Credit : India : West Bengal
Communication in Agriculture : India : West Bengal
Education : India : West Bengal
Education, Higher : India : West Bengal

Education, Primary : India : West Bengal
Education, Rural : India : West Bengal
Examinations : India : West Bengal
Farmers : India : West Bengal
Fertilizers and Manures : India : West Bengal
Field Crops : India : West Bengal
Fish Culture : India : West Bengal
Students : India : West Bengal
Students Socio-Economic Status : India : West Bengal
Unemployment, Educated : India : West Bengal
Vocational Education : India : West Bengal

Wheat : India : Madhya Pradesh

Constraints in adoption of wheat technology by the tribal farmers of Madhya Pradesh. S.K. Waghmare and V.K. Pandit *Indian J Extension Education* 18(1-2) Je 1982 p 95-98

Wirszup, Izaak

The Wirszup report. *J Indian Education* 6(2) Jl 1980 p 71-73

Woman

Women's struggle for the new roles. Madhukanta Tripathi *National J Education* 7(2) My 1985 p 56-60 appdx refs

See also

Radio Programmes for Women

Woman : Education

See

Education of Women
Higher Education of Women

Woman : Employment

Exploitation and utilisation of educated women power. Bina Agarwal *J Higher Education* 2(2) Aut 1976 p 185-95 refs tabs

Women, education and work : A review. Usha Nayar *J Higher Education* 1(2) Aut 1975 p 283-92 refs

Woman : Employment : India

Women and work in India : Continuity and change. Joyee Lebra *et al.* New Delhi, Promilla. 310p. Rs. 250 *Book Rev, New Frontiers in Education* 16(2) Ap-Je 1986 p 106-08

Woman : Health and Hygiene

Women and health. *Prasar* 8(3-4) Oc 1981-Ja 1982 p 18-25

Woman : Occupations

See

Woman : Employment

Woman : Professional Education

See

Professional Education of Women

Woman : Rights of Women

Changing images of males and females : How of feminist sex role liberation in Indian school text books. Narendra Nath Kalia *Indian Education* 13(10-11) Ja-Fe 1984 p 10-16

Women : Sex Instruction

See

Sex Instruction for Girls

Women : Single

See

Divorcees

Woman : Social and Moral Questions

Development of women's social freedom scale : A report. L.I. Bhushan *Asian J Psychology and Education* 7(2) Jl 1981 p 34-38

The dual role of women. J.K. Pillai *New Frontiers in Education* 12(4) Oc-De 1982 p 39-42

Women

Women and the media : A case for critical correction. Kumud Sharma *Indian J Adult Education* 46(9) Se 1985 p 27-30

Women : India

Indian women's battle for freedom. Kamladevi Chattopadhyaya. New Delhi, Abhinav Pub. 1983, 184 p. Rs. 45 *Book Rev, New Frontiers in Education* 13(1) Ja-Mr 1983 p 72-73

Women : India : Andhra Pradesh : Hyderabad

See

Slums : India : Andhra Pradesh : Hyderabad

Women : India : Rajasthan

A comparative study of time utilisation pattern of tribal and nontribal women in Rajasthan. Daya Saxena and Suman Rani Bhatnagar *Indian J Extension Education* 21(1-2) Ja-Je 1985 p 83-85 tabs

Women of Rajasthan : A demographic profile. Meenakshi Hooja *Prasar* 8(3-4) Oc 1981-Ja 1982 p 1-17 tabs

Women : Muslim : India

Muslim educated women in North India. Mayawanti Rallia Ram *J Higher Education* 1(2) Aut 1975 p 250

Women : Rural

Modernisation and the rural women. S.N. Katiyar *Teacher Today* 24(3) Ja-Mr 1982 p 20-26 refs

Women : Rural : Employment : Bangladesh

Women labourers in Bangladesh villages. Abdul Halim *Indian J Extension Education* 20(1-2) J 1984 p 38-46 refs tabs

Women : Rural : Employment : India : Haryana

Existing linkages among various agencies for self-employment activities for rural women of Haryana. T. Verma and Suraj Kaur *Indian J Extension Education* 21(1-2) Ja-Je 1985 p 65-68 tabs

Women : Rural : India

The influence of sexist bias on female role in rural areas. K. Nischol *J Indian Education* 8(3) Se 1982 p 29-32

Leadership development among rural women. *New Frontiers in Education* 13(2) Ap-Je 1983 p 78-104

Women : Rural : India : Andhra Pradesh

Actual and desired type of participation by rural women in selected areas of decision making. Jhansi Rani and Asha M. Bhave *Indian J Extension Education* 18(1-2) Ja 1982 p 83-89 tabs

Measurement of values of rural women. Laxmi Devi Achanta *Indian J Extension Education* 19(3-4) Se-De 1983 p 83-89 refs tabs

Women : Rural : India : Delhi

Family life of working rural women : A few cases. R. Bhagat *Indian J Extension Education* 16(3-4) De 1980 p 67-70

Mass media and changing life style of farm women in Delhi territory. R. Bhagat and P.N. Mathur *Indian J Extension Education* 21(3-4) Jl-De 1985 p 37-42 refs tabs

Women : Rural : India : Haryana

Characteristics of rural women, key communications. Damyanti and Hira Nand *Indian J Extension Education* 19(3-4) Se-De 1983 p 47-55 refs tabs

Rural women's level of knowledge and persuation for the acceptance of solar cooker device. S. Sharma and T.R. Singh *Indian J Extension Education* 20(1-2) Je 1984 p 47-51 refs

Training needs of rural women : An action research. T. Verma and S. Verma *Indian J Extension Education* 21(3-4) Jl-De 1985 p 104-07 tabs

Women : Rural : India : Uttar Pradesh

Attitude towards working women : A depth study in rural Kumaon. G.C. Upadhyay *Experiments in Education* 9(10) De 1981 p 172-76

Sex consciousness among rural women. Seema Sirohi and Rajendra *Indian J Extension Education* 17(3-4) Se-De 1981 p 107-11 tabs

Women as Farmers

See

Women in Agriculture

Women College Students

A correlational study of students performance. J.A. Christian *J Institute of Educational Research* 4(1) Ja 1980 p 16-19 refs

Self-concept of female students of single sex colleges and co-education colleges : A comparative study. D.A. Uchat and H.R. Desai *J Institute of Educational Research* 6(2) My 1982 p 33-36 refs

Women College Students : India

Women students in India : Status and personality. Savitri Sharma. Concept Pub. New Delhi, 1979 171 p. Rs. 80 *Bool Rev. Indian Education* 9(12) Mr 1980 p. 45-47

See also

Studying : Women : India

Women College Students : India : Maharashtra

Women students programme in co-educational context : A case study. Plamthodothil S. Jacob *New Frontiers in Education* 15(1) Ja-Mr 1985 p 77-81

Women Engineers

Problems faced by the women engineers of today. Ranjani Subrahmonia *Progress of Education* 59(5) Ja 1985 p 124-31 refs figs tabs

Women in Agriculture : India : Andhra Pradesh

Role expectation and role performance of rural women in farm activities. A. Laxmi Devi and S. Venku Reddy *Indian J Extension Education* 20(3-4) Se-De 1984 p 27-34 refs tab

Time utilisation pattern of rural farm women. A. Laxmi Devi *Indian J Adult Education* 47(1) Ja 1986 p 13-16 tabs

Women in Agriculture : India : Madhya Pradesh

The decision-making by farm women regarding improved agricultural practices. Rashila Malik *Indian J Extension Education* 15(3-4) De 1979 p 64-69 tabs

Women in Agriculture : India : Punjab

Utilisation of households knowledge by farm women. Neeru Bala and Sumita Roy *Indian J Extension Education* 15(3-4) De 1979 p 22-26 tabs

Women in Agriculture : India : Uttar Pradesh

Involvement of rural women in farming. Seema Sirohi *Indian J Extension Education* 21(3-4) Jl-De 1985 p 110-11

Women in Social Services

A study of attitudes of teacher trainees towards women's participation in social activities and professions. P.C. Verma and B.K. Srivastava *Asian J Psychology and Education* 11 (1) 1983 p 21-27

Women Scientists

Women scientists : The road to liberation. Derek Richter, ed. New York, Macmillan. £10 *Book Rev, Teacher Today* 24(1) Ap-Je 1982 p 135-36

Women Scientists : India

The status of women in science in India. Mathreyi Krishna Raj *J Higher Education* 5(3) Spr 1980 p 381-93 tabs

Women in Science and Technology. Kamla Kumar and Sadhana Khitha *Education Quarterly* 34(4) Oc 1982 p 8-10 refs

Women Studies : India

Women studies in India. Savitri Sharma. New Delhi, Concept. Pub. 1979, 181p. Rs. 50 *Book Rev, Teacher Education* 14(10-11) Ja-Ap 1980 p 76-77

Women's Colleges : India

A separate university for women. Hemant V. Inamdar *Progress of Education* 59(5) De 1984 p 90-94 +

Women's Education

See

Education of Women

Women's Employment

See

Woman : Employment

Women's Liberation

See

Woman : Rights of Women

Words Association Test

Teaching of words through cards. A.B.A. Papali *Primary Teacher* 5(2) Ap 1980 p 37-40

Work Experience

See

Vocational Education

Work Performance Standards

See

Performace Standards

Workers Education
See
Labour and Labouring Classes : Education
Working Women
See
Woman : Employment
Worth
Different views on the stages of moral development. V. Dayakera Reddy and P.S. Geethanath *Experiment in Education* 11(4) Je 1983 p 68-71 refs
Directions and degrees of polarisation of value domains. R.P. Gupta *Bharatiya Shiksha Shodh Patrika* 5(2) Jl-De 1986 p 15-28 refs tabs
Education, sex and cultural background as correlates of values : Aesthetic as social. Kamal Dwivedi *J Education and Psychology* 36(4) Ja 1979 p 219-27
Impact of Indian thought in developing a value-pattern in education. L.K. Oad *J Indian Education* 6(8) Ja 1981 p 8-12
Measurement of values of rural women. Laxmi Devi Achanta *Indian J Extension Education* 19(3-4) Se-De 1983 p 83-89 refs tabs
Search for new human values. Prem Kirpal *Teacher Today* 24(4) Ap-Je 1982 p 13-21
A study of prominent trends in value sensitivity profiles of some educated sections of Indian society. R.P. Gupta *Bharatiya Shiksha Shodh Patrika* 4(1) Ja-Je 1985 p 53-62 refs tabs
A study of relation between value development and exposure to an ideal environment. Deb Kumar De *Quest in Education* 19(1) Ja 1982 p 64-68 refs tabs
A study of values in the process of social change. Debkumar De *Our Education* 3-4 Jl 1983 p 15-20 refs tabs
Study of values of science undergraduates at different levels of socio-economic status. Ashok Kumar *J Educational Research and Extension* 18(3) Ja 1982 p 175-81 refs tabs
Teacher school and community variables coming in the way of value inculations process among the children. M.N. Ravindranatha *Experiments in Education* 11(9) Nv 1983 p 159-62
To live or not to live with values. M. Pla Nagàrath and Maria E. Waples. New Delhi, AIACS. 1980, 143 p. Rs. 28 *Book Rev, Education Quarterly* 23(2) Ap 1981 p 41-42
Using value-clarifying strategies in the classroom. N.K. Jangira *Primary Teacher* 8(2) Ap 1983 p 18-21
Value clarifying strategies. N.N. Jangira *J Indian Education* 11(2) Jl 1985 p 19-24 refs
Value system in the personality of urban and rural adolescents. R.S. Gaur *J Indian Education* 5(6) Mr 1980 p 11-13 refs
Value systems and value preference patterns of Indian youths belonging to different socio-metric levels. A. Bhushan and M. Ahuja *J Institute of Educational Research* 4(3) Se 1980 p 7-14 refs tabs

Values in Soviet education. K.R.P. Singh *Primary Teacher* 11(3) Jl 1986 p 1-3

Values in text-books : A research perspective. U.S. Chaudhari *Quest in Education* 19(3) Jl 1982 p 255-59 refs

World culture and global values. T.A. Mathias *New Frontiers in Education* 15(4) Oc-De 1985 p 1-27 refs

Writing

Balance the basics : Let them write. Donald H. Graves. New York, Ford Foundation. 1978, 32p. $ 2 *Book Rev, J Indian Education* 6(4) Nv 1980 p 58-59

Handwriting *vis-a-vis* writing appliances. Ravindra Agnihotri *Quest in Education* 19(1) Ja 1982 p 69-82 refs

Psychology and pedagogy of handwriting. Bhujanga Bhusan Bhattacharyya *Our Education* 2 Jl 1981 p 51-61 refs

Writing alphabet and numerals. Benimadhab Mukherji *Primary Teacher* 10(2) Ap 1985 p 23-27

See also

Children : Writing

Typewriting

Writing : Ability Testing

Written expression : Different aspects. I.S. Sharma *Primary Teacher* 8(1) Ja 1983 p 14-17

Yoga

Effect of yoga asan on learning : An experiment on primary students. D.K. Sharma Purohit and M.P. Tyagi *J Institute of Educational Research* 4(2) My 1980 p 30-34 refs tabs

High school students and teachers in yoga as a part of school curriculum. U. Shashikala Devi and B.S. Satyanarayana *Quest in Education* 17(4) Oc 1980 p 352-59 refs

The integral system of education. Sita Ram Jayaswal *Teacher Education* 13(8-9) Jl-Oc 1979 p 9-15 refs

Modern education and training in yoga. Shamsuddin *Progress of Education* 60(8) Mr 1986 p 188-90 +

Peace education through yoga. Gunvant N.B. Shah *Teacher Today* 27(2) Oc-De 1984 p 38-41

Relevance of yoga philosophy in education : A critical evaluation. Ashok K. Kalia *Educational Rev* 89(11) Mr 1983 p 195-97

Transcendental meditation in school curriculum. Ben Behari Mukhopadhyay *Indian Education* 10(7) Oc 1980 p 21-25

Yoruba Language : Study and Teaching

A comparative study of the effects of two methods (i.e., alphabetic method and phonic syllable-word method) on the teaching of reading in Yoruba to beginners. Adedell Awonlyl *Progress of Education* 59(1) Ag 1984 p 6-10 refs

Youth

International Youth Year, 1985 : Youth and social development. *Teacher*

Today 27(2) Oc-De 1984 p 67-84

Leadership among youth. G. Rasool *J Education and Psychology* 38(2) Jl 1980 p 88-93

National Council resolutions passed at Nagpur. *Student Action* 2(9) Mr 1984 p 22-23 +

The out of school youth. V.E. Reddy and K.S. Bhat. Sterling. 299p. *Book Rev, J Higher Education* 4(2) Aut 1978 p 290-91

Sociology of youth. Rajendra Pandey. New Delhi, Sterling. 1984, 187p. Rs. 100 *Book Rev, Perspectives in Education* 1(4) Oc 1985 p 272-73

See also

Rural Youth

Rural Youth Club

Student Unrest

Youth Clubs

Youth : Czechoslovakia

From the annals of the Czechoslovak youth movement. *Student Action* 2(9) Mr 1984 p 38-39

Youth : Developing Countries

Youth and values in developing countries. R.M. Kalra *Education Quarterly* 35(2) Ap 1983 p 43-47

Youth : Health and Hygiene

Health situation of youth in India. Usha S. Naidu and S. Parasuraman. Bombay, TISS. 1982, 67p. *Book Rev, Education Quarterly* 35(3) Jl 1983 p 59-60

Youth : India

A study of social and personal problems of tribal youth. Jitendra Mohan and Narender Kumar *Asian J Psychology and Education* 6(1) Ja 1980 p 5-8

The symbol and substance : Indian youth in development. Prabha Krishnan. New Delhi, Vishwa Yuvak Kendra. 1980, 119p. Rs. 15 *Book Rev, J Higher Education* 7(3) Spr 1982 p 332-33

Youth problems : A causative analysis in Indian setting. Rajkumari Chandrasekaran *Experiments in Education* 7(2) Ap 1979 p 28-31

Youth : Poland

The Polish Youth Movement. *Student Action* 2(9) Mr 1984 p 21

Youth : Political Activity

See also

Students : Political Activity

Youth : Psychology

See

Adolescent Psychology

Youth : Rural

See

Rural Youth

Youth Clubs

A study of the profile of Yuv Das's (Youth Clubs) members. G.S. Saini and S.S. Pawar *Indian J Extension Education* 18(1-2) Je 1982 p 99-101

Yugoslavia

See also

Education : Yugoslavia

Zakir Husain : Educational Thought

Educational philosophy of Zakir Husain. Qamar Jahan and W.H. Siddiqui *Educational Rev* 88(8) Ag 1982 p 135-37; 88(9) Se 1982 p 157-58

Educational thought of Dr. Zakir Husain : A critique. K.R.P. Singh *Indian Educational Rev* 20(4) Oc 1985 p 109-15

INDIAN WRITINGS ON EDUCATION 1979 to 1986

An Indicator to Indian Educational Journals Grouped by 2465 Subject Descriptors

PART II

AUTHOR APPROACH

S.P. AGRAWAL

CONCEPT PUBLISHING COMPANY, NEW DELHI 110059

Indian Writings on Education Part II

ISBN 81-7022-381-4

First Published 1992

Published and Printed by
Ashok Kumar Mittal
Concept Publishing Company
A/15-16, Commercial Block, Mohan Garden
NEW DELHI 110059 (India)

Lasertypeset by
Microtech Advance Printing Systems (Pvt.) Ltd.
H-13, Bali Nagar,
NEW DELHI 110015

Abdul Halim

Women labourers in Bangladesh villages. *Indian J Extension Education* 20(1-2) Je 1984 p 38-46 refs tabs

Abdul Rehman, O. and Menon, A.G.G.

The correspondence course for farmers on paddy cultivation. *Indian J Extension Education* 14(3-4) Jl-De 1978 p 58-61

Abel, M.

College autonomy : Its impact on higher education and national life. *New Frontiers in Education* 10(1) Ja-Mr 1980 p 35-39

Abercrombie, M.L.J

Aims and techniques of group teaching. Surrey, Univ. of Surrey. 1979. *Book Rev, J Indian Education* 5(4) Nv 1979 72-74

Abercrombie, M.L.J. and Terry, P.M.

Talking to learn : Improving teaching and learning in small groups. Surrey, Univ of Surrey. 1978. *Book Rev, J Higher Education* 5(1) Mon 1979 p 120-22

Abraham, C.

Value oriented education. *New Frontiers in Education* 19(4) Oc-De 1979 p 41-45

Abraham, Mary

See

Sharma, K.K. *jt. auth.*

Abraham, Mecry and Prasanna, K.C.

Rating scale of motivation for adult learners. *Indian J Adult Education* 47(1) Ja 1986 p 23-29 appdx refs tabs

Abrol, Sunil

Effect of stress and anxiety on psychomotor performance. *Asian J Psychology and Education* 11(1) 1983 p 32-35

Mental health in industry : An Indian scene. *Asian J Psychology and Education* 4(1) Ja 1979 p 10-13 refs

Psychomotor performance as a function of temperature variation and task difficulty. *Asian J Psychology and Education* 4(3) Nv 1979 p 27-31

Abu Hamid Latif

Population education curriculum development in Bangladesh. *Rajasthan Board J Education* 16(1-2) Ja -Je 1980 p 1-3

Achanta, Laxmi Devi

Measurement of values of rural Women. *Indian J Extension Education* 19(3-4) Se-De 1983 p 83-89 refs tabs

Acharya, A.A.

See

Agaiat Acharya, A

Adams, Anthony, *ed.*

New directions in English teaching. Sussex, Falmer Press. 1982. 244p. *Book Rev, Education Quarterly* 35(4) Oc 1983 p 63-64

Adams, Fred

Special education. Essex, Longman Group. *Book Rev, Education Quarterly* 38(3) Aut 1986 p 58-60

Adams, Raymond S. and Chen, David

The process of educational innovation - An international perspective. Paris, UNESCO. 1981. 284p. *Book Rev, Indian Educational Rev* 18(3) Jl 1983 p 126-28

Adarsh Bala

See

Sandhu, N.S. *jt. auth.*

Adaval, S.B.

Quality of teachers. Allahabad, Amitabh Pra. 1979, 180p. Rs. 82.50 *Book Rev, National J Education* 2(2) Mr 1980 p 59-60

Adaval, S.B. *et al*

An analytical study of teacher education in India. Allahabad, Amitabh Pra. 1984, 137p. Rs. 87.50 *Book Rev, Perspectives in Education* 1(1) Ja 1985 p 64-66

Adeyemi, Akinsanya

See

Akinsanya, Adeyemi

Adeyoyin, F.A.

Life in the classroom : A research study. *J Indian Education* 6(2) Jl 1980 p 3-8 refs tabs

A role of the parents-teachers association : A case study of secondary schools in Ikale local government area. Ondostali, Nigeria. *Progress of Education* 61(1) Ag 1986 p 13-16 refs

Adhaoo, S.H. and Vanjari, S.S.

Agricultural engineering research and the role of agricultural universities in India. *J Higher Education* 8(3) Spr 1983 p 381-85 refs

Adinarayana, K.

Criteria and influential factors in standards of education. *Experiments in Education* 8(2) Ap 1980 p 37-40

A critical analysis of S.S.L.C. public examination question papers. *Experiments in Education* 8(4) Je 1980 p 65-71 tabs

Equalisation of educational opportunity - The role of the teacher and government. *Progress of Education* 54(6) Ja 1980 p 109-11

Organising co-curricular activities. *Educational Rev* 86(9) Se 1980 p 175-77

Planning and implementing procedures of action research in schools. *Experiments in Education* 7(1) Mr 1979 p 3-9 refs

Planning and implementing procedures of action research in schools *Quest in Education* 17(3) Jl 1980 p 250-59 refs

Science in pre-primary schools. *Primary Teacher* 6(1) Ja 1981 p 35-39

Scientific inquiry in children : A review. *Experiments in Education* 9(1) Mr 1981 p 3-8 refs

Staff associations : Line of authority and responsibility. *Indian Education* 10(7) Oc 1980 p 29-32

Teachers role : A study. *Experiments in Education* 9(12) Fe 1982 p 207-13 refs

See also

Shah, M.M. *et al jt. auths.*

Adinarayana, K. and Jyothi Prakash

Science at two stage : A few problems. *Educational Rev* 87(6) Je 1981 p 103-05

Teaching science at the plus two stage : A few problems. *Experiments in Education* 10(2) Ap 1982 p 28-31

Adinarayana Reddy, P.

Characteristics of an effective instructor : A study. *Indian J Adult Education* 46(2) Fe 1985 p 27-29

Innovations and experiments in education in Andhra Pradesh. *Indian Education* 12(1-2) Ap-My 1982 p 13-16

Management and supervision of schools : A pragmetic and functionally useful apporach. *Indian Education* 11(1-2) Ap-My 1981 p 81-83

Non-formal education in the context of universalisation of primary education in Andhra Pradesh. *Bulletin of Non-formal Education* 1(1) 1 Je 1983 p 21-29

See also

Venkatiah, M. *jt. auth.*

Adinarayana Reddy, P. and Kumaraswamy, T.

Qualities of an effective adult education organisers from supervisors point of view. *Experiments in Education* 12(1) Mr 1984 p 10-15 tabs

Adiseshiah, Malcolm S.

Adult education and inequality. *Prasar* 9(1-4) Ap 1982- Ja 1983 p 33-46 refs

Adult education and the urban poor. *Indian J Adult Education* 41(8) Ag 1980 p 13-18+

Adult education and urban poor. *Teacher Today* 24(3) Ja-Mr 1982 p 1-13 refs

Adult education development and the NAEP. *Indian J Adult Education* 40(10-11) Oc-Nv 1979 p 15-19

Dar es Salaam inperspective : The role of adult education in development. *Indian J Adult Education* 40(8) Ag 1979 p 1-5

Education and scientific temper. *New Frontiers in Education* 14(1) Ja-Mr 1984 p 55-58

Highlights of the international council of adult education. *Indian J Adult Education* 40(8) Ag 1979 p 6

International council of adult education. *Indian J Adult Education* 41(6-7) Je-Jl 1980 p 31

Issues in the national policy on education. *New Frontiers in Education* 10(3) Jl-Se 1980 p 14-24

Non-formal adult education cadres — what, whom and how? *Indian J Adult Education* 41(6-7) Je-Jl 1980 p 10-13+

Non-formal education for development. *Indian J Adult Education* 41(4) Ap 1980 p 3-5

Remoulding Indian higher education. *New Forntiers in Education* 12(2) Ap-Je 1982 p 14-20

Role of adult education in promoting and effective functioning of rural institutions and organisations. *Indian J Adult Education* 42(12) De 1981 p 5-9

Role of universities in international cooperation for development. *New Frontiers in Education* 14(2) Ap-Je 1984 p 55-65 tabs

Scheduled castes and tribes in higher education in Tamil Nadu. *J Higher Education* 1(2) Aut 1975 p 241-44

Some thoughts on the concepts and forms of distance education. *University News* 24(42) 8 Nv 1986 p 7-9

A tentative balance-sheet of the new educational policy. *New Frontiers in Education* 16(3) Jl-Se 1986 p 1-10 refs

U.S. community colleges and Indian colleges : Some relevant issues. *Indian J Adult Education* 41(9) Se 1980 p 24-25

Universities, colleges and the programme of integrated rural development. *Teacher Education* 14(10-11) Ja-Ap 1980 p 40-45

Adkoli, B.V.

Error analysis in mathematics at the S.S.C. examination. *Indian Educational Rev* 17(4) Oc 1982 p 124-38 tabs

Revival of essay testing. *Progress of Education* 58(11) Je 1984 p 266-69

Agafonova, Kira

Foster homes in the USSR. *Progress of Education* 55(5) De 1980 p 127-28

Agaiah Acharya, A.

National integration : An analysis. *Teacher Education* 14(12-13) Jl-Oc 1980 p 1-8

AGARWAL - AGARWALA - AGGARWAL - AGRAWAL

Agrawal, A.

Motivating achievement in rural children. *Quest in Education* 17(1) Ja 1980 p 52-58 refs

Agrawal, B.M.

See

Sisodia, M.L. *jt. auth.*

Agarwal, Bina

Exploitation utilisation of educated woman power. *J Higher Education* 2(2) Aut 1976 p 185-95 tabs

Agarwal, Chakradhari

Education for self-employment. *New Frontiers in Education* 15(3) Jl-Se 1985 p 61-66

Agarwal, D.N.

The gains of special coaching on science aptitude of the pupils preparing for the NSTS examination. *Indian Educational Rev* 18(3) Jl 1983 p 8-16 refs tabs

Aggarwal, I.P.

Integrated approach of science teaching. *Teacher Today* 22(1) Jl-Se 1979 p 29-34

Non-formal adult education programme : An aid to rural development. *Education Quarterly* 31(1) Ap 1979 p 1-3

Reshaping science examination in our schools. *Quest in Education* 18(3) Jl 1981 p 220-27

Aggarwal, J.C.

Development and planning of modern education. New Delhi, Vikas Pub. 1982, 424p. Rs. 95 *Book Rev, J Indian Education* 8(6) Mr 1983 p 78-79

Agrawal, K.G.
Work satisfaction and mental health. *Indian Educational Rev* 14(1) Ja 1979 p 22-29 refs
See also
Chaudhry, P.N. *jt. auth.*

Agrawal, Mamta
Preparing exercises for supplementary readers in English. *Teacher Today* 21(3) Ja-Mr 1979 p 56-70
Teaching English as a second language. *Primary Teacher* 9(4) Oc 1984 p 21-25
Testing reading comprehension in English. *Primary Teacher* 11(4) Oc 1986 p 29-31

Agarwal, R.N.
Developing software educational technology. *Primary Teacher* 11(4) Oc 1986 p 8-11
Simulation and gaming in elementary education : An experiment. *Primary Teacher* 11(3) Jl 1986 p 29-32
Systems approach in elementary education. *Primary Teacher* 11(1) Ja 1986 p 7-10

Agarwal, Rita
See
Kool, V.K. *jt. auth.*

Agarwal, S. and Singh, T.R.
Mothers compliance with prescribed recommendations on immunisation and their source utilisation pattern. *Indian J Extension Education* 19(3-4) Se-De 1983 p 40-46; 20(3-4) Se-De 1984 p 48-52 refs tabs

Agarwal, S. and Srivastava, R.K.
A comparative study of the personality sturcture of the teachers trainees at high and low level of intelligence. *J Education and Psychology* 41(4) Ja 1984 p 229-35 refs

Agrawal, S.P.
Social Science Documentation Centre. *Experiments in Education* 10(7) Se 1982 p 129-34
Social Science Documentation Centre. *Experiments in Education* 11(2) Ap 1983 p 34-36
Social Science Documentation Centre. *Experiments in Education* 11(3) My 1983 p 52-54
Social Science Documentation Centre. *Progress of Education* 57(5) De 1982 p 111-14
Social Science Documentation Centre. *J Educational Research and Extension* 19(4) Ap 1983 p 239-48
Social Science Documentation Centre. *Indian J Extension Education* 19(1-2) Je 1983 p 109-11
Social Science Documentation Centre-ICSSR : Its activities and services. *J Institute of Educational Research* 8(2) My 1984 p 38-44
National Social Science Documentation Centre. *University News* 24(36) Se 23 1986 p 9-12
See also
Biswas, A. *jt. auth.*

Agrawal, S.P., Gen. ed.

Indian education index (1948-78), New Delhi Manasayan. 1200p. 950 $ 100 *Book Review Progress of Education* 56(5) De 1981 p 123

Theory and principles of education. New Delhi, Vikas pub. 38lp. Rs.25 *Book Rev, Educational Rev* 87(9) Se 1981 p 177-78

Agarwal, Saroj and Sushila Kumari

A correlational study of risk-taking and creativity with special reference to sex differences. *Indian Educational Rev* 17(3) Jl 1982 p 104-10 refs tabs

Agrawal, Subhash Chandra

Cultural pluralism and education. *Educational Rev* 86(1) Ja 1980 p 12-14

Designing class room instruction through students cognitive styles : A practical approach. *Quest in Education* 19(1) Ja 1982 p 35-41 refs tabs

Learning style : A new area of research. *J Educational Research and Extension* 17(3) Ja 1981 p 172-77 refs

Microteaching : An appraisal. *Indian Education* 11(3) Ag 1981 p 14-16

Student learning style and contract activity package. *Indian Education* 10(4) Jl 1980 p 33-36

Students learning style and contract activity package. *J Education and Psychology* 39(2) Jl 1981 p 128-31

Teaching arithmetic to the deaf and dumb. *Educational Rev* 87(6) Je 1981 p 106-08 refs

They need your help. *Educational Rev* 87(1) Ja 1981 p 1-3 refs

To investigate the effectiveness of educational technology in the teaching of mathematics to deaf and dumb children. *Progress of Education* 54(9) Ap 1980 p 178-81

Agrawal, Subhash Chandra and Gupta, Sushi Prakash

A study of biographical attributes of high and low creative students-teachers. *Indian Education* 12(8-9) Nv-De 1982 p 25-27

Agrawal Sushila

War mindedness and aggression amongst Indian university students. *Bharatiya Shiksha Shodh Patrika* 5(2) Jl-De 1986 p 47-52 refs

Agrawal, Umesh

Span of memory : Links with intelligence and personality. *Educational Rev* 86(3) Mr 1980 p 45-48 refs tabs

See also

Saraswat, R.M. *et al jt. auths.*

Agrawal, Umesh and Gupta, Y.K.

Adjustment differences among the high intelligent and low intelligent adolescent students. *J Institute of Educational Research* 8(2) My 1984 p 12-15 refs tabs

Agrawal, Umesh and Saraswat, R.M.

A study of security and insecurity in respect to the academic achievement. *J Educational Research and Extension* 18(4) Ap 1982 p 247-53 refs tabs

Aggarwal, Veena

See

Sharma, Harish *jt. auth.*

Agarwal, Vijay Laxmi

Objectives of teacher education. *Teacher Education* 15(14-15) Ja-Ap 1981 p 17-20

Agrawal, Vijaya Rani
A study of reading ability in relation to certain cognitive and non-cognitive factors. *Indian J Psychology and Education* 11(3) 1983 p 41-44
See also
Krishna, K.P. *jt. auth.*
Aggarwal, Y.P.
Haryana education colleges at the cross-road, *Teacher Education* 15(14-15) Ja-Ap 1981 p 95-99
Statistical methods : Concepts, applications and computation. New Delhi, Sterling. 1986 *Book Rev, J Educational Planning and Administration* 1(1) Oc 1986 p 89-90
See also
Moonis Raza *jt. auth.*
Aggarwala
See
Agarwal
Aggarwal
See
Agarwal
Agnihotri, Ravindra
Handwriting vis-a-vis writing appliances. *Quest in Education* 19(1) Ja 1982 p 69-82 refs
Agnihotry, Rekha
Effects of sub-culture affiliation and sex of self-confidence. *J Education and Psychology* 44(3-4) Jl-Se 1986 p 124-27
Agyajit Singh
Adjustment of XI grade students in relation to neuroticism and extraversion. *J Education and Psychology* 36(1-2) AP-Je 1978 p 78-84 refs
A correlational study of adjustment and academic achievement of XI grade students. *Quest in Education* 18(1) Ja 1981 p 46-52
Indian norms of the Minnesota teacher attitude inventory. *Indian Educational Rev* 14(4) Oc 1979 p 24-32 refs tabs
Physical education and sports programming in schools. *J Indian Education* 8(1) My 1982 p 56-60
Ahluwalia, S.P.
See
Dileep Kumar *jt. auth.*
Ahluwalia, S.P. and Deouskar, M.D.
National Adult Education Programme and integrated rural development. *Indian J Adult Education* 39(11-12) Nv-De 1978 p 41-49 refs tabs
A study of the personality characteristics of mentally retarded and normal children. *Our Education* 5 Jl 1984 p 51-67 refs
Ahluwalia, S.P. and Jain, Rakesh
Measurement of non-verbal communication in the classroom; a review article. *J Institute of Educational Research* 10(1) Ja 1986 p 25-30 refs tabs
Ahluwalia, S.P. and Kala, Ashok K.
Emerging needs and preparation of non-formal education teachers for rural areas. *Educational Rev* 91(1) Ja 1985 p 7-10

Ahluwalia, S.P. and Pandeya, Pratibha

Personality studies of teachers : A critique of research in India. *J Institute of Educational Research* 8(2) My 1984 p25-29 refs

Personality traits of student teachers of an army run and a government managed institution : A comparative study. *J Educational and Psychology* 43(1) Ap 1985 p 27-33 refs

Sex differences in the personality profiles of student-teachers. *Indian Educational Rev* 20(2) Ap 1985 p 21-27

Ahmad, Aqueil

See

Aqueil Ahmaa

Ahmad, Karuna (Chanana)

Equity and women's higher education. *J Higher Education* 5(1) Mon 1979 p 33-49

From secondary to higher education : Focus on women. *J Higher Education* 9(3) Spr 1984 p 349-62 refs

Ahmad, S.A.

Overhead projector : Its role in adult education. *Indian J Adult Education* 43(7) Jl 1982 p 25-26+

Ahuja

See also

Hooja

Ahuja, G.C.

Educational wastage and stagnation among tribal children, *J Indian Education* 6(1) My 1980 p58-70 refs tabs

A study into the silent versus oral reading performance of good and poor comprehenders. *J Education and Psychology* 37(1) Ap 1979 p 51-61 refs

Vocalisation : A malady. *Progress of Education* 53(8) Mr 1979 p 156-59 refs

Vocalisation in silent reading : How to aviod *Educational Rev* 85(6) Je 1979 p 113-15 refs

Ahuja, Malvinder

See

Bhusan, A. *jt. auth*

Sharma, Harish Chandra *jt. auth.*

Aikara, Jacob *et al*

Ideological orientation of student activism. Pune, Dastane Ramchandra. 1977. 113p. Rs.37 *Book Rev, J Higher Education* 4(2) Aut 1978 p 291-92

Ajit Singh

In-sevice teacher education : Programmes and perspectives. *J Indian Education* 12(4) Nv 1986 p 38-42 refs

Search for teacher behaviour. *Teacher Today* 28(3) Ja-Mr 1986 p 1-5 refs

Secondary school teachers attitude towards teaching in relations to their classroom behaviour : A study. *J Indian Education* 6(6) Mr 1981 p 12-15 refs

Secondary school teachers classroom behaviour in relation to their perceived self : A study. *J Indian Education* 5(6) Mr 1980 p 20-24 refs tabs

Teacher sex and classroom interaction. *J Indian Education* 8(2) Jl 1982 p 48-51 refs tabs

Teacher sex and classroom interaction. *National J Education* 2(1) Se 1979 p 1-6 refs tabs

See also

Goyal, J.C. *jt. auth.*

Akbar Husain

See

Kureshi, Afzal *jt. auth.*

Akbar Husain and Kureshi, Afzal

Moderating role of intelligence variable in aspirations and deprivations of the institutionalised, non-institutionalised sensory handicapped children. *J Institute of Educational Research* 9(1) Ja 1985 p 5-9 refs tabs

Akhtar, Hamida and Mohammed Nurual Anwar

Consideration and structure dimensions of leadership behaviour and supervisory effectiveness as determined by managers rating and group productivity. *Asian J Psychology and Education* 3(2) Jl 1978 p 40-47 refs

See also

Hamida Akhtar Begum

Akhtar Bano and Satyana Rayana, B.S.

Socio-metric study of personality traits. *J Institute of Educational Rsearch* 6(2) My 1982 p 17-22 refs tabs

Akhtar Hassan, Parveen

Attitude of post-graduate students towards the semester system : A synopsis. *Indian Education* 11(5) Ag 1981 p 31-34 tabs

Attitude of teachers and students towards the semester. *Indian Educational Rev* 18(4) Oc 1983 p 116-22

Credit course system under the semester system. *Experiments in Education* 9(3) My 1981 p 54-56

Orientation course for teachers of institutions for the handicapped. *Experiments in Education* 9(9) Nv 1981 p 159-61

The semester system. *J Higher Education* 7(3) Spr 1982 p 306-09 refs

Akinsanya, Adeyemi

The drop-out and industrial arts programme. *J Indian Education* 8(4) Nv 1982 p 24-27

Programmatic considerations for facilitating educational research and development. *Indian Educational Rev* 16(1) Ja 1981 p 37-47

Projection of school enrolment. *Primary Teacher* 10(3) Jl 1985 p 20-22

Alam, Qaiser Zoha

Need to take extra care for spelling teaching. *Primary Teacher* 10(1) Ja 1985 p 10-13

Alamina, J.I.

Congition development and learning. *Progress of Education* 58(9) Ap 1984 p 214-20 refs tabs

Albert, D.

College autonomy : An appraisal. *New Frontiers in Education* 12(4) Oc-De 1982 p 49-52

Alesin, Edward

Preparation for teaching profession from school stage. *Educational Rev* 88(11) Nv 1982 p 188-89; *Progress of Education* 57(5) De 1982 p 115-16

Alkara, Jacob

Adult education and schooling of slum children. *Indian J Adult Education* 41(8) Ag 1980 p 7-12 tabs

Almeida, M.

The psychological dimensions of inequality. *New Frontiers in Education* 16(2) Ap-Je 1986 p 46-56

Altbach, Philip G.

The crisis of professoriate. *J Higher Education* 5(3) Spr 1980 p 317-30 refs

Higher education in the third world : Themes and variations. Singapore, Maruzan Asia. 1982, 28p. *Book Rev, J Higher Education* 9(1) Mon 1983 p 145-48

Student politics in the third world. *New Frontiers in Education* 14(2) Ap-Je 1984 p 66-84 ft-n

See also

Amrik Singh *jt. auth.*

Alwar Das

57th All India Education Conference, Visakhapatnam, address by Sri Alwar Das. *Indian Education* 13(5-6) Ap-Se 1983 p9-10

Amaladass, G. and Sathiyagirirajan, S.

Need gratification of college teachers. *J Educational Research and Extension* 18(4) Ap 1982 p 236-46 refs tabs

Amalraj, V.A. and Prasad, M.S.

Role of fertilizer dealers in the transfer of new farm technology. *Indian J Extension Education* 20 (3-4) Se-De 1984 p 69-70

Amar Kumar

Personality profile of experienced teachers and teacher trainees. *Teacher Education* 15(14-15) Ja-Ap 1981 p 90-94 refs tabs

Amar Singh and Prasad, C.

Morale of personnel in agricultural universities. *Indian Educational Rev* 15(4) Oc 1980 p 91-96

Amar Singh and Suraj Singh

Training needs of tribal farmers. *Indian J Extension Education* 17(3-4) Se-De 1981 p 81-88 tabs

Amarjit Singh

Constructions of a battery of objective tests for assessment of proficiency in writing English composition. *Indian Educational Rev* 15(1) Ja 1980 p 90-103

Ambastha, C.K.

Communication pattern of farm scientists. *Indian J Extension Education* 16(1-2) Je 1980 p 34-38 tabs

Ambastha, C.K. and Singh, K.N.

An analysis of inter system communication pattern. *Indian J Extension Education* 15(1-2) Je 1979 p1-8 tabs

Interpersonal communication pattern in client system : A path analysis. *Indian J Extension Education* 14(1-2) Ja-Je 1978 p 9-16 refs

Interpersonal communication pattern of extension personnel. *Indian J Extension Education* 14(3-4) Jl-De 1978 p 8-15 refs

Interpersonal communication patterns of extension system : A path analysis. *Indian J Extension Education* 16(3-4) De 1980 p 10-15 refs tabs

Ambirajan, S.
The role of humanities and soical sciences in engineering education. *J Higher Education* 9(3) Spr 1984 p 333-48 refs

Ameerjan, M.S.
Academic achievement of rural and urban students of agriculture : An analysis. *Asian J Psychology and Education* 6(1) Ja 1980 p 17-22 refs tabs
Background variables of the scheduled castes and tribe college students : A comparative study. *Indian Educational Rev* 19(2) Ap 1984 p 28-36
A comparative study of academic achievement of the scheduled castes and tribes students of agriculture. *J Education and Psychology* 37(2) Jl 1979 p 121-29 refs tabs
A schematic model of the departments of academic achievement. *J Education and Psychology* 39(2) Jl 1981 p 111-16

Ameerjan, M.S. and Thimmappa, M.S.
Academic achievement of the scheduled castes and tribal students : An analysis. *J Education and Psychology* 44(1) Ap 1986 p 29-35 refs

Ameerjan, M.S. *et al*
Academic achievement and its relation to general mental ability, academic adjustment and neuroticism. *J Education and Psychology* 36(3) Oc 1978 p 107-12

Ames, Lynne
Training teachers to think. *Indian Education* 13(7) Oc 1983 p 14-16

Amrik Singh
The dynamics of chnage. *J Higher Education* 9(2) Aut 1983 p 197-206
Stray thoughts on education in India. *Indian Education* 12(7) Oc 19(2 p 9-14

Amrik Singh and Altbach, Philip G.
The higher learning in India. Vikas Pub. 1974, 41p. Rs.50 *Book Rev, J Higher Education* 1(1) Mon 1975 p 141-43

Amrik Singh and Sharma, G.D., *eds*.
University and college finance. New Delhi, Assn of Indian Univ. 246p. Rs.45 *Book Rev, Indian Educational Rev* 18(1) Ja 1983 p 136-37

Amrit Kaur
Adult education programmes for illiterate women in the age group 15-35. *Indian J Adult Education* 40(12) De 1979 p 19-32
Role of universities in training research and evaluation of adult education. *Indian J Adult Education* 40(5) My 1979 p 13-22 refs
Self education. *Prasar* 5(1-2) Ap-Jl 1977 p 25-35 refs
Universities involvement in NAEP. *Indian J Adult Education* 39(10) Oc 1978 p 43-44
Women education in India today. *Teacher Today* 21(4) Ap-Je 1979 p 9-24 tabs

Amrit Kaur and Chatterji, Basanti
Classroom interaction patterns of language teachers functioning at two levels of cognitive development. *Rajasthan Board J Education* 20(1-2) Ja-Je 1984 p 21-29

Amrit Kaur and Tarlok Singh
Regional educational disparity among scheduled castes of Punjab. *Indian J*

Adult Edcuation 46(4) Ap 1985 p 7-10+ tabs

Amritavalli, R.

Role of audio-visual aids in distance education. *University News* 24(42) 8 Nv 1986 p 85-90 refs

Anand, C.L. and Sudhir Kumar, M.A.

Developing a modernity attitude scale. *Indian Educational Rev* 17(3) Jl 1983 p 29-41 refs tabs

Anand, Darshan

See

Ashok Kumar *jt. auth.*

Anand, R.D. and Seshadri, C.

Science education : What is'nt and what it is? *Teacher Today* 26(4) Ap-Je 1984 p 70-80 refs

Anand, Rishi and Shankaram, V.

An endeavour towards anatomy of science education. *J Higher Education* 2(2) Aut 1976 p 197-202 refs

Anand, Rishi Dev

A dimension of human behaviour : Biochemcial stress. *J Education and Psychology* 36(1-2) Ap-Je 1978 p 15-19 refs

A dimension of human behaviour : Biochemical stress. *Teacher Today* 21(4) Ap-Je 1979 p 45-51 refs

Anand, S.P.

Behaviour problems in schools. *Quest in Education* 16(4) Oc 1979 p 299-306

Counselling in personnel and guidance services in schools. *Education Quarterly* 32(3) Jl 1980 p 5-9 refs

Exceptional children in schools. *J Indian Education* 12(1) My 1986 p 3-8 refs

Group guidance programme in schools. *J Indian Education* 9(1) My 1983 p 31-37

Guidance for slow learners in school. *Our Education* 3-4 Jl 1983 p 47-57 refs

In the quest of guidance in education. *Education Quarterly* 33(3) Jl 1981 p 8-11 refs

Job satisfaction versus work role variables. *Indian Educational Rev* 14(4) Oc 1979 p 106-17 tabs

A psychological approach on the curriculum. *J Indian Education* 6(5) Ja 1981 p 17-22

School teaching profession : Reasons for joining and job satisfaction. *Quest in Education* 17(3) Jl 1980 p 260-68 refs

Special education : Evolution and practices. *Education Quarterly* 36(1) Ja 1984 p 11-17

A study of mental health of school teachers. *J Education and Psychology* 44(3-4) Jl-De 1986 p 105-11

Teacher effectiveness in schools. *J Indian Education* 8(6) Mr 1983 p 3-12

Teachers values and job satisfaction. *Indian Educational Rev* 15(4) Oc 1980 p 24-34 refs

Tools and techniques of guidance in schools. *Education Quarterly* 36(4) Wint 1984 p 43

Anand, Usha and Sohal, T.S.
Measuring job satisfaction of scientists in an ICAR institute. *Asian J Psycholcgy and Education* 9(4) 1982 p 13-20

Anand Bhushan
Values among high and low achieving M.Ed. correspondence students belonging to different socio-economic status. *Quest in Education* 17(2) Ap 1980 p 152-64 refs

Anand Bhushan and Sharma, Usha
The effect of personality variables and intelligence on the performance of high school students in mathematics. *Asian J Psychology and Education* 7(2) Jl 1981 p 44-49

Anandi, C.C.
See
Ezewu, E.E. *jt. auth.*

Anandrao, B. and Ravishankar, S., *eds.*
Readings in educational technology. Bombay, Himalaya Pub H. 1982, 411p. *Book Rev, Indian Education* 12(7) Oc 1982 p 35-36; *Progress of Education* 57(7) Fe 1983 p 166

Ananthakrishnan, M.V.
Physics and its applications : Some teaching experiments. *J Higher Education* 5(3) Spr 1980 p 351-57 refs figs
Science technology interaction : A systems model for education. *J Higher Education* 9(2) Aut 1983 p 229-34 refs figs

Anantha Krishnan, P.
An experimental investigation of the relationship between creativity and rigidity. *J Institute of Educational Research* 4(2) My 1980 p 39-41 refs tabs

Ananthanarayana, H.S.
Evaluation of adult literacy materials in Kannada. *Indian J Adult Education* 40(8) Ag 1979 p 7-15 refs

Anantharaman, M. and Subramanyan, V.S.
Socio-psychological factors associated with training needs of small and marginal farmers. *Indian J Extension Education* 18(3-4) De 1982 p 72-73

Ananthasayanam, R.
See
Jayagopal, R. *et al jt. auth.*

Anarasa, S.A.
See
Rokade, V.S. *jt. auth.*

Angad Singh
Existentialism in education. *Teacher Education* 18(22-23) Ja-Ap 1983 p 69-74 refs

Anil
National awardee teachers travel abroad. *Primary Teacher* 11(1) Ja 1986 p 4-6

Anjaneyulu, D.
Stray thoughts on general education in the context of vocationalisation. *Experiments in Education* 9(2) Ap 1981 p 27-30

Ansari, Ghazala and Rahman, Z.
A study of anxiety in relation to parental acceptance and Peer acceptance. *J Educational and Psychology* 39(3) Oc 1981 p 189-96

Ansari, Ghazala and Siddiqui, Wadudul Haqq
A study of truancy in relation to security-insecurity parental-acceptance and Peer-acceptance. *J Education and Psychology* 40(3) Oc 1982 p 169-74

Ansari, M.M.
Educational expenditure : Inflation and economic growth : An empirical analysis. *Perspectives in Education* 1(2) Ap 1985 p 111-22 refs tabs

Ansari, N.A.
Adult education in India : Some aspects. *Teacher Education* 14(10-11) Ja-Ap 1980 p 60-64

Anuradha, G. and Sinha, B.P.
Management of TRYSEM programme : A critical analysis. *Indian J Extension Education* 21(1-2) Ja-Je 1985 p 36-41

Anwana, Elden U.I.
Male-female social relationship in Nigeria : The impact of Western education. *J Indian Education* 12(4) Nv 1986 p 59-64 refs

Anwarjit Singh, K.
A study of personality differences among student teachers. *J Institute of Educational Research* 9(3) Nv 1985 p 1-3 refs tabs

Anwarul, Yaqlin
Constitutional protection of minority educational institutes in India. New Delhi, Deep and Deep Pub. 390p. Rs.100 *Book Rev, New Frontiers in Education* 12(4) Oc-De 1982 p 59-60

Apparao, Gummadi
Agro-social status and adoption of farm innovation in two villages. *Indian Extension Education* 19(3-4) Se-De 1983 p 62-65
The strength of communication dyads and differential adoption in two villages. *Indian J Extension Education* 17(3-4) Se-De 1981 p 31-38 refs tabs

Apparao, Gummadi and Rogers, Everett, M.
Caste and formal education in interpersonal diffusion of an innovation in two Indian villages. *Indian J Extension Education* 16(3-4) De 1980 p 1-9 refs tabs

Apparao, Gummadi *et al*
Interpersonal relations in diffusion of an innovation in two Indian villages. *Indian J Extension Education* 16(1-2) Je 1980 p 19-24 refs

Aqueil Ahmad
The agricultural university as a multi-functional system. *J Higher Education* 5(1) Mon 1979 p 57-73

Aranganayagam, Thiru C.
Inaugural address. *Indian J Adult Education* 41(6-7) Je-Jl 1980 p 14-16

Aransky, V.S.
The Soviet school. *Indian Education* 10(7) Oc 1980 p 10-12

Arjunrao, P.
Teaching methodology in higher education. *Indian Education* 13(3-4) Je-Jl 1983 p 28-31

Arneja, C.S. and Gill, Surjeet Singh
Need of coordination between small, marginal farmers and agricultural labourers agencies and other concerned departments in Punjab. *Indian J Extension Education* 15(1-2) Je 1979 p 63-66
Arora, Asha
See
Natarajan, V. *jt. auth.*
Arora, G.L.
Curriculum and creativity. *J Indian Education* 8(6) Mr 1983 p 49+
Designing school curriculum for the future. *Rajasthan Board J Education* 21(3-4) Jl-De 1985 p 10-15
In search of humanistic schools. *J Indian Education* 6(1) My 1980 p 3-7
National core curriculum for Indian schools. *Education Quarterly* 37(2) Sum 1985 p 27-29
Relationship of sex with creativity general anxiety, vocational anxiety and teaching success. *J Education and Psychology* 36(3) Oc 1978 p 133-39
Social influence on curriculum. *J Indian Education* 9(1) My 1983 p 38-41
Towards teaching for thinking. *J Indian Education* 5(4) Nv 1979 p 38-41
Arora, G.L., *ed.*
Reflections on curriculum. New Delhi, NCERT. 1984, 98p. Rs.8 *Book Rev. Indian Educational Rev* 20(2) Ap 1985 p 142-43
Arora, P.N.
Evaluation practices in some selected primary and middle schools : A study. *J Indian Education* 6(6) Mr 1981 p 46-48
Open book examination system. *J Indian Education* 8(3) Se 1983 p 40-43
Arora, R.K.
Geography teaching : Some observations and suggestions. *Teacher Today* 21(2) Oc-De 1978 p 85-88
Problem levels and personality patterns. *J Indian Education* 8(6) Mr 1983 p 13-19 refs
Students problems in different streams of professional courses : A comparative study. *J Education and Psychology* 44(2-3) Jl-De 1986 p 96-104
Students problems, self-concepts, and level of aspiration : A comparative study. *Indian Educaitonal Rev* 20(3) Jl 1985 p 12-22
Arora, Saroj
Personality profile of withdrawing deviance in schools. *Indian Educational Rev* 18(3) Jl 1983 p 102-06 refs
Arubayi, Eric A.
An appraisal of teaching practice by student interns in Nigerian universities. *Progress of Education* 61(4-5) Nv-De 1986 p 77-84 refs tabs
Arun Kumar, Devangana
See
Menon, M.B. *et al jt. auths.*
Arun Kumar, P.
Development of scientific attitude through the teaching of science. *Education Quarterly* 31(1) Ap 1979 p 15-17
See also
Sudama, G.R. *et al jt. auth.*

Arun Kumar, P. *et al*

Process of science instruction : A model. *J Indian Education* 10(5) Ja 1985 p 34-39 refs

Programmed instruction in the teaching of science : A new perspective. *J Indian Education* 5(1) My 1979 p 3-10 tabs

Arvindra Chandra

See

Thomas, Anita S. *jt. auth.*

Arvindra Chandra and Kundu, Raj Kala

Relationship between personality factors and academic achievement of students. *J Education and Psychology* 39(1) Ap 1981 p 35-41; *J Educational Research and Extension* 18(1) Jl 1981 p 1-7 refs

Asha, C.B.

Creativity and academic achievement among secondary school children. *Asian J Psychology and Education* 6(1) Ja 1980 p 1-4 refs

Ashok Kumar

Effectiveness of multi media instructional system. *Rajasthan Board J Education* 19(2-3) Ap-Se 1983 p 6-9

Study of values of science undergraduates at different levels of socio-economic status. *J Educational Research and Extension* 18(3) Ja 1982 p 175-82 refs tabs

Ashok Kumar and Anand, Darshan

A comparative study of value patterns of science and commerce under graduates. *J Higher Education* 7(3) Spr 1982 p 277-80 tabs

Ashton-Warner, Sylvia

Teacher. Middlesex, Penguin Books. 1966. *Book Rev, Teacher Today* 24(1) Jl-Se 1981 p 104-06

Ashwani Kumar

Early education of the handicapped. *Primary Teacher* 9(2) Ap 1984 p 8-10

Towards quality elementary school. *Primary Teacher* 9(4) Oc 1984 p 14-16

Asiedu, Kobina

Demand on university based education in Ghana : A review. *Indian J Adult Education* 47(6) Je 1986 p 13-20 refs

Asmat Hussain

Who is a good teacher? *Primary Teacher* 4(3) Jl 1979 p 33-35

Aswal, G.S.

Personality characteristics of activist students. *Progress of Education* 58(8) Mr 1984 p 183-86 refs

Relationship of student activism and personality needs. *J Education and Psychology* 41(1-2) Ap-Jl 1983 p 37-42

Aswal, G.S. and Srinagar, G.U.

Relationship of student activism and personality adjustment. *J Institute of Educational Research* 6(3) Se 1982 p 20-23 refs

Athma Raman, R.

An elementary study on the introduction and implementation of three specific vocational courses in three city higher secondary schools. *Experiments in Education* 9(8) Oc 1981 p 138-44

Attinson, G.B.J.

The economics of education. London, Hodder. 1983, 150p. £5.95 *Book Rev,*

Perspectives in Education 2(4) Oc 1986 p 253-56

Audinarayana Moorthy, S.

Quality education through academic programmes. *Educational Rev* 84(11) Nv 1978 p 201-02

Augustine, Mithra

Working of autonomy of MCC : An appraisal. *New Frontiers in Education* 12(2) Ap-Je 1982 p 52-54

Aurora

See

Arora

Avinashilingam, T.S.

Inculation of ethical and soical values in education : A proposal for implementaiton. Coimbatore, Sri Ramakrishna Mission. *Book Rev, Progress of Education* 56(12) Jl 1982 p 305

Non-formal education : To earn more and live better. *Indian J Adult Education* 39(11-12) Nv-De 1978 p 13-15

Relevance of Gandhian economics for national development. *J Educational Research and Extension* 16(2) Oc 1979 p 65-71

Technology for rural development. *J Educational Research and Extension* 19(4) Ap 1983 p 193-206 refs

Avtar Singh

Education in the Andaman and Nicobar Islands, 1951-79 : Elementary and secondary levels. *Education Quarterly* 33(1) Ja 1981 p 26-30

Awoniyi, Timsthy Adedeji

An analysis of primary five pupils attitude of alternative language media for class room learning and interaction. *Progress of Education* 58(7) Fe 1984 P 150-54 refs tabs

A comparative study of the effects of two methods (i.e. alphabetic method and phonic syllable-word method) on the teaching of reading in Yoruba to beginners. *Progress of Education* 59(1) Ag 1984 p 6-10 refs

Language medium/media choices and their effects on the learning of science-oriented subject (i.e. mathematics) at the primary school level in Ilorin, Kwara state Nigeria. *Progress of Education* 58(12) Jl 1984 p 293-300+ refs tabs

Ayyadurai, G. and Bright, A. John

Spatial distribution of poultry farms and constraints in poultry development. *Indian J Extension Education* 17(3-4) Se-De 1981 p 103-06 refs tabs

Ayyar, Parvathy S. and Somaiya, S.K.

Importance of developing writing skills in English at the Junior college level. *Progress of Education* 56(7) Fe 1982 p 170-73

Azad, J.L.

Financing distance education. *University News* 24(42) 8 Nv 1986 p 105-10 refs

Financing of higher education in India. New Delhi, Sterling. 1975, 214p. Rs.40 *Book Rev, J Higher Education* 3(3) Spr 1978 p 421-22

Government support for higher education and research. New Delhi, Concept Pub. 1984, 202p. Rs.80 *Book Rev, Education Quarterly* 37(2) Sum 1985 p 72-73; *Progress of Education* 59(12) Jl 1985 p 271

Research in management of education. *Indian Education* 11(1-2) Ap-My 1981 p 18-23

Research needs and priorities in financing of education. *Quest in Education* 18(4) Oc 1981 p 328-34 refs

Sixth Plan : Priorities in educational development. *Indian Education* 10(1-2) Ap-My 1980 p 15-22

State grants to collegiate institutions : A study of patterns and procedures. *J Higher Education* 2(2) Aut 1976 p 243-52 refs tabs

Aziz, Ungku

Higher education and culture. *New Frontiers in Education* 14(1) Ja-Mr 1984 p 81-86

Azmat Nayeem

Rural education : An emphasis on weaker section. *Education Quarterly* 32(3) Jl 1980 p 13-17 refs tabs

Babjon, A.Q.

See

Venkata Rami Reddy, jt, auth.

Babu

See under

full surname, e.g., Ramesh Babu, A.

Bacchus, M.K.

Structural change and transformation. *Indian J Adult Education* 40(8) Je 1979 p 1-8 refs

Bachhotia, H.L.

Learner's interest in adult education. *J Indian Education* 12(1) My 1986 p 41-43

Badami, Gharulata H.

A developmental study of some locomotor skills during early childhood. *J Education and Psychology* 36(4) Ja 1979 p 210-18 refs

Badarun Nisha

See

Gupta, Krian *jt. auth.*

Badhera, Gijubhai

Divaswapna. *Teacher Today* 26(3) Ja-Mr 1984 p 60-83

Bagchi, Jyoti Prakash

Significance of innate factors and sex differences among science students. *National J Education* 6(2) My 1984 p 68-74 refs

Bagley, Christopher

A perspective on the education of Asian children in Britain. *Indian Education Rev* 15(3) Jl 1980 p 1-21 refs

Bahadur, Sushil K.

An experimental study of the predilections of the examiners correcting the answer books. *J Education and Psychology* 36(1-2) Ap-Je 1978 p 54-62 refs

Bahal, R.

See

Sethy, B. *et al jt. auths.*

Bahal, Veena
Teaching English through games. *Educational Rev* 58(6) Je 1979 p 104-06
Bahm, Archie J.
Value-oriented education. *Progress of Education* 56(11) Je 1982 p 256-60; 56(12) Jl 1982 p 284-88+; 57(1) Ag 1982 p 2-7; 57(2) Se 1982 p 26-30
Bahuguna, S.D.
Riding an unbridled horse. *J Higher Education* 2(2) Aut 1976 p 264-67
Bahukhandi, J.N.
Educational technology : Concept, claims and constraints. *Teacher Today* 27(1) Jl-Se 1984 p 14-25 refs
Bahukhandi, Jagat
New edcuation policy and the techniques of teaching. *Teacher Today* 23(2) Oc-De 1985 p 27-30
The teaching of English : Men, methods and materials. *Teacher Today* 23(2) Oc-De 1980 p 22-29
Baij Nath Singh
Formative research. *Indian J Adult Education* 39(9) Se 1978 p 16-22 refs
People's participation in National Adult Education Programme. *Indian J Adult Education* 39(10) Oc 1978 p 3-7
Bajaj, S.
See
Mahajan, Neelam *jt. auth.*
Bajpai, J.N. and Seshagiri Rao, C.
Potential for SUPW teaching in our schools. *J Indian Education* 5(5) Ja 1980 p 43-46
Bajwa, Parminder S.
See
Kaile, Harnek S. *jt. auth.*
Bakhshish Singh
World conference on correspondence education. *J Higher Education* 4(2) Aut 1978 p 267-68
Bala
See
under full name, Adarsh Bala
Balachander, K.K.
See
Israney, S.M. *jt. auth.*
Balachandran, E.S. and Vedanayagam, E.G.
Evaluation in higher education. *Experiments in Education* 8(4) Je 1980 p 61-64
Balaguruswamy, Sushila
See
Mukhopadhyay, M. *jt. auth.*
Balak, Goswami Ram
How to correct teaching lessons. *Primary Teacher* 8(1) Ja 1983 p 34-35
Balakrishna Reddy, P.
See
Venkata Rami Reddy, A. *jt. auth.*

Balaprasad, R.

Bonus to the teachers : An analytical essay. *Educational Rev* 88(9) Se 1982 p 151-52

Balasubramaniam, P.S.

Leadership styles of heads of schools in Madras. *EPA Quarterly Bulletin* 6(2) Jl 1983 p 1-12 refs

See also

Krishnaraj, K. *jt. auth.*

Balasubramaniam, R. and Knight, A. Johan

Bottlenecks in modern dairying. *Indian J Extension Education* 18(1-2) Je 1982 p 102-05 refs tabs

Balasubramaniam, S. and Kaul P.N.

Adoption of improved fish curing practices. *Indian J Extension Education* 18(3-4) De 1982 p 45-50 refs tabs

Adoption of improved practices by fish trawler owners in Kerala. *Indian J Extension Education* 20(3-4) Se-De 1984 p 35-42 tabs

Adoption of improved practices by traditional fishermen in Kerala. *Indain J Extension Education* 21(3-4) Jl-De 1985 p 80-88 refs

Balasubramaniam, Saraswathi

The status of correspondence courses in India. *University News* 24(42) 8 Nv 1986 p 13-15

Bala Tripura Sundari, R.

NAEP : Conditions for its success. *Education Quarterly* 31(3-4) Oc 1979-Ja 1980 p 9-10

Baldev Singh and Kunzroo, O.N.

Attitude of farmers towards goats and sheep farming. *Indian j Extension Education* 21(1-2) Ja-Je 1985 p 86-88 tabs

Balkishan Singh *et al*

Some selected socio-personal economic characteristics of the farmers of progressive and non progressive dairy villages. *Indian J Extension Education* 21(3-4) Jl-De 1985 p 101-03 tabs

Balu, S.A. and Chandran, G.S.

Inter examiner variability in assessing answer scripts of engineering sciences. *J Higher Education* 5(2) Aut 1979 p 224-28

Bandyopadhyaya, Kalipada

Religious education for children : An action programme. *Primary Teacher* 5(4) Oc 1980 p 16-19

Bandyopadhyay, Swaraj and Bhattacharya, Swapan K.

Student unrest in an unplanned university : A case study. *J Higher Education* 3(3) Spr 1978 p 381-86 refs tabs

Bandyopadhyay, Swaraj and Kundu, Nilanjana

Students participation in the management of education systems : A preliminary analysis of emerging trend in India. *J Higher Education* 8(3) Spr 1983 p 342-48 refs

Bandivedekar, B.S. and Kulkarni, P.A.

A collection of teaching aids. *Progress of Education* 53(6) Ja 1979 p 115-16

Banerjee, Gautam

Counselling in the context of distance education. *University News* 24(42) 8 Nv 1986 p 63-67

Discipline of political science in India. *University News* 23(11) 16 Mr 1985 p 6-7

Banerjee, Jyoti Prasad

Pre-determinism in education. *Our Education* 1 Jl 1980 p 35-40 refs

Banerjee, Kalyan K.

Colour and colour combination. *Primary Teacher* 5(3) Jl 1980 p 18-22

In search of the third dimension. *Primary Teacher* 8(1) Ja 1983 p 20-22

Banerjee, Sushanta and Malhotra, Ashok

Higher education : Frames of reference in existing literature. *J Higher Education* 3(3) Spr 1978 p 301-14 refs

Banga, Shakuntla and Sharma, J.P.

Comparative effect of different school environments on reasoning of primary school children. *Progress of Education* 58(4) Nv 1983 p 78-80 refs tabs

Bansal, Kailash Chandra

Teaching learning at school : A new approach. *Primary Teacher* 8(2) Ap 1983 p 13-17

Bansal, Saroj

Home science and work experience. *Progress of Education* 55(5) De 1980 p 118-19+

Values : Foundation of curriculum. *Educational Rev* 87(4) AP 1981 p 61-66 refs

See also

Gupta, Pushpa *jt. auth.*

Baqer Mehdi

Decentralised curriculum and quality of education. *Primary Teacher* 9(2) Ap 1984 p 1-3

Psycho-philosophical perspective of value oriental education. *J Indian Education* 12(2) Jl 1986 p 35-38

Research experimentation and innovation in teacher education : Some considerations. *Teacher Education* 15(14-15) Ja-Ap 1981 p 80-82

Teacher education in India : Some considerations. *Teacher Education* 15(14-15) Ja-Ap 1981 p 112-14

Barde, M.R.

Teacher education in the next decade : A resume of the capabilities of teachers of the future. *Progress of Education* 59(8) Mr 1985 p 184-86

See also

Jha, S.K. *jt. auth.*

Barthakur, Suresh Chandra

Elementary education in Assam. *Educational Rev* 92(8) Ag 1986 p 126-27

Low cost teaching aids in schools. *Educational Rev* 87(9) Se 1981 p 179

Barua, P.K.

A new approach to moral development. *J Indian Education* 5(2) Jl 1979 p 27-30

Basavaiah, K.

Harnessing the pre-schooler's potential : An educational imperative. *New Frontiers in Education* 9(1) Ja-Mr 1979 p 70-76

Bashiruddin, S.

Educational journals : Guidelines for writing, reporting and editing. *Indian Education* 11(3) Je 1981 p 15-17

Baskaran, K and Parveen, C.

Adoption of improved dryland agricultural technology in an integrated dryland agricultural development project in Andhra Pradesh. *Indian J Extension Education* 18(3-4) De 1982 p 32-39 tabs

Baskina, Ada

School education in USSR. *Teacher Education* 14(12-13) Jl-Oc 1980 p 71-73

Bastia, K.C. and Sudame, G.R.

National adult education programme : Role of Indian universities. *Experiments in Education* 8(2) Ap 1980 p 29-32 refs

Basu, A.K. *et al*

A study on the relationship between adjustment and personality characteristics of higher secondary school students. *Our Education* 1 Jl 1980 p 29-34 refs tabs

Basu, Amiya Kumar

Educational psychology from the standpoint of a Marxist. *Our Education* 5 Jl 1984 p 29-38 refs

Effect of self-disclosure on different cultural settings. *J Education and Psychology* 37(1) Ap 1979 p 31-34 refs

Teacher training : Traditional and developmental learning teaching and field dependence independence styles. *Our Education* 2 Jl 1981 p 23-29 refs tabs

Basu, Aparna

Essays in the history of Indian education. New Delhi, Concept Pub. 1982, x, 108p. Rs.60 *Book Rev, Progress of Education* 58(3) Oc 1983 p 71

Basu, Asoke

Culture, politics and critical academics. Allahabad, Archana Pra. 106p. Rs.50 *Book Rev, J Higher Education* 9(1) Mon 1983 p 149-52

Basu, Bharati and Rukma Rao, V.

The concept of national integration. *Indian Educational Rev* 14(4) Oc 1979 p 78-85 ft-n

Bawa, M.S.

Developing competence in the skill of asking questions at different levels. *J Indian Education* 11(2) Jl 1985 p 45-54

Bayti, Jamnalal

The concept of the gifted child. *Educational Rev* 92(2) Fe 1986 p 30-33

Decision-making in school administration. *Indian Education* 13(8-9) Nv-De 1983 p 23-26; *Progress of Education* 58(6) Ja 1984 p 132-37 +

Educating the gifted child. *Primary Teacher* 10(2) Ap 1985 p 6-8

The effect of knowledge of results on the achievement in English : An investigation. *Research Bulletin* 15(3-4) Se-De 1985 p 21-29 tabs

Teaching as a profession : Foundations, problems and potentialities. *J Indian Education* 8(5) Ja 1983 p 30-35

Becker, George J.
Television and the class room reading programme. Int. Reading Assn. 1971. 32p. *Book Rev, Education Quarterly* 31(2) Jl 1979 p 42-43

Bedami, Charulata H.
Social status in relation to some variables. *J Education and Psychology* 41(4) Ja 1984 p 205-08 refs

Beena, C.
Adolescents attitude towards sex education. *J Institute of Educational Research* 7(2) My 1983 p 1-7

Beers, James W., *ed.*
See
Henderson, Edmund H., ed.

Behera, S.C.
See
Mohanty, Jagannath *jt. auth.*

Belok, Michael V. and Greeen, Joe L, *eds.*
Philosophy and education. Meerut, Anu Pra. 227p. Rs.65 *Book Rev, Teacher Today* 25(2) Oc-De 1982 p 99-100

Benedict, Gary C.
See
Gerardi, Robert J. *jt. auth.*

Benedict, Gary C. and Gerardi, Robert J.
The future of curriculum in America : Facing conflicting expectations. *J Education and Psychology* 40(4) Je 1983 p 186-94 refs

Benseman, John
Study circles in Sweden; A participants viewpoint. *Indian J Adult Education* 41(10) Oc 1980 p 15-19 refs tabs

Berg, Ivar
The great train robbery. Penguin Bks. 1973, 197p. *Book Rev, Teacher Today* 22(3) Ja-Mr 1980 p 97-98

Berlak, Ann and Berlak, Harold
Dilemmas of schooling. London, Methuen. 299p. *Book Rev, Education Quarterly* 34(4) Oc 1982 p 55-56

Berlak, Harold
See
Berlak, Ann *jt. auth.*

Berman, Louise M.
Trends in teacher education in the United States of America. *Teacher Education* 15(16-17) Jl-Oc 1981 p 30-45 refs

Bernbaum, Gerald, *ed.*
Schooling in decline. London, Macmillan. 1979, 240p. £3.95 *Book Rev, Education Quarterly* 33(1) Ja 1981 p 41-42

Bevli, U.
Need for early childhood education. *Primary Teacher* 8(4) Oc 1983 p 9-13
See also
Bharati, K. *jt. auth.*

Bezboruah, D.N.
A closer look at the tower of babel. *Teacher Today* 21(2) Oc-De 1978 p 49-56 refs

How much lesson does an English teacher require? *Teacher Today* 24(2) Oc-De 1981 p 34-38

Bhadra, B.R. and Girija, P.R.

Long term predictive validity of college admission measures. *J Education and Psychology* 38(3) Oc 1980 p 149-58 refs

Bhadwal, Satish Chandra

See

Koul, Lokesh *jt. auth.*

Bhagat, Rekha

Family life of working rural women : A few cases. *Indian J Extension Education* 16(3-4) De 1980 p 67-70

Bhagat, Rekha and Koshy, S.

Profile of nutritional status of children of the marginal farmers and agricultural labourers in Delhi villages. *Indian J Extension Education* 20(3-4) Se-De 1984 p 43-47 tabs

Bhagat, Rekha and Mathur, P.N.

Mass media and changing lifestyle of farm women in Delhi territory. *Indian J Extension Education* 21(3-4) Jl-De 1985 p 37-42 refs tabs

Bhagia, N.M.

Future-oriented education for teachers. *Teacher Today* 28(2) Oc-De 1985 p 72-78

Integration of education with development. *Education Quarterly* 36(1) Ja 1984 p 6-10

Modern approach in evaluation of training programmes of education management. *Indian Education* 11(1-2) Ap-My 1981 p 53-56

Promoting attitudes and values through environmental studies. *Teacher Today* 23(2) Oc-De 1980 p 9-21 refs figs

Research in educational administration : Retrospect and prospect. *Teacher Today* 26(2) Oc-De 1983 p 62-77 refs ft-n

Training for educational administrators in India. *New Frontiers in Education* 16(4) Oc-De 1986 p 88-94

See also

Briggs, D.K. *jt. auth.*

D'Cruz, J.V. *jt. auth.*

Bhagia, Sushma

Developments in non-formal education. *Rajasthan Board J Education* 21(3-4) Jl-De 1985 p 16-26

Educational innovations and their management in schools. *Rajasthan Board J Education* 20(1-2) Ja-Je 1984 p 9-14

Educational technology in India : The present and the prospect. *J Indian Education* 8(5) Ja 1983 p 55-59 refs

Some thoughts on in-service education of teachers. *New Frontiers in Education* 12(2) Ap-Je 1982 p 61-67

Value-oriented education in schools. *Rajasthan Board J Education* 22(1) Ja-Mr 1986 p 1-7

Bhagwat, P.

Evaluation of condensed courses of education for adult women. *J Adult Education* 42(10) Oc 1981 p 17-20 refs

Bhaktapriya, G.V.

Language policy in the context of NAPE. *Indian J Adult Education* 40(6) Je 1979 p 25-28 refs

Bhaktavatsal Rao, K.

Instructional resources in collegiate education. *Indian Education* 11(5) Ag 1981 p 20-21

New dimensions in education. *Indian Educaion* 10(4) Jl 1980 p 37-38

Bhal, J.D.

A study of the effectiveness of the programme for improvement of children's hand writing. *Progress of Education* 60(8) Mr 1986 p 174-78 + tabs

A survey of interest in reading of the pupils of secondary and higher secondary schools of Bhavnagar city. *J Educational Research and Extension* 18(1) Jl 1981 p 8-11

Bhalwanker, A.G.

Continuing education : Search for identity. *Progress of Education* 60(2) Se 1985 p 44-46

A study of the reliability and validity of the process appraising scale of teacher effectiveness. *Research Bulletin* 15(1-2) Mr-Je 1985 p 32-40 tabs

Bhalwanker, A.G. and Joshi, Anant N.

Process-Processes appraising scale of teacher effectiveness. *Research Bulletin (Suppl)* 15(1-2) Mr-Je 1985 p I-VIII

Bhambhre, K.U.

Educational approach to psychology. *Teacher Today* 21(4) Ap-Je 1979 p 32-35

Bhamwari, Varmala T.

Teaching of spelling. *Educational Rev* 89(12) De 1983 p 205-11 refs

Towards better reading in English in India. *Educational Rev* 92(12) De 1986 p 211-13

Bhan, Susheela, *ed.*

See

Shah, A.B. *jt. auth.*

Bhandari, R.K.

Crisis in education in India. *New Frontiers in Educaiton* 14(3) Jl-Se 1984 p 74-81

Development of women's education. *New Frontiers in Education* 12(4) Oc-De 1982 p 32-34

Education in the Sixth Five Year Plan. *New Frontiers in Education* 12(3) Jl-Se 1982 p 31-49

Education in the Sixth Plan. *Education Quarterly* 33(3) Jl 1981 p 1-4 tabs

Educational development in the Seventh Five Year Plan. *New Frontiers in Education* 13(4) Oc-De 1983 p 50-61

Educational development of women. *Education Quarterly* 34(3) Jl 1982 p 12-14

Financing of education. *Education Quarterly* 34(1) Ja 1982 p 1-6 tabs

Investment in education. *New Frontiers in Education* 14(2) Ap-Je 1984 p 97-111

National Adult Education Programme : An appraisal. *New Frontiers in Education* 13(2) Ap-Je 1983 p 1-16 tabs

Universalisation of elementary education : A difficult task. *Education*

Quarterly 31(2) Jl 1979 p 8-11

Bhansali, Kamalini H.

Sign-posts for a learning society. Nashik, Gokhale Educ Soc. 146p. Rs.36 *Book Rev, Indian J Adult Education* 46(3) Mr 1985 p 25-27

Bhanu Pratap Singh

Educational aims in British in India. *Educational Rev* 85(10) Oc 1979 p 196-97

Bharat Bhusan, Satyapal

Agricultural research and primary teacher. *Primary Teacher* 4(4) Oc 1979 p 27-28

Village library and the primary teacher. *Primary Teacher* 5(3) Jl 1980 p 42-43

Bharathi, V. and Ramamurthi, P.V.

A study of some socio-metric choices of socially backward socially non-backward primary school children. *J Institute of Educational Research* 6(3) Se 1982 p 33-40 refs tabs

Bharati, K. and Bevli, U.

Causal thinking in Indian children : A study. *Indian Educational Rev* 19(2) Ag 1984 p 9-18

Bhardwaj, G.N.

A critical study of the development of teacher education in Rajasthan. *Indian Educational Rev* 14(4) Oc 1979 p 66-72

Bhardwaj, Neelam and Hansra, B.S.

Effectiveness of some selected modes of communication in imparting knowledge to the members of ladies *charcha mandals* of Ludhiana district. *Indian J Extension Education* 19(1-2) Mr-Je 1983 p 99-103 tabs

Bhardwaj, R.L.

Components of fluency, intelligence and socio-economic status as correlates of the interests in agricultural pursuits. *J Education and Psychology* 38(4) Ja 1981 p 227-34 refs

Bhardwaj, R.L. and Gupta, R.P.

Fluency, intelligence and socio-economic status as correlates of the interests in scientific pursuits. *Asian J Psychology and Education* 6(3) Nv 1980 p 23-31 refs

Bhardwaj, R.L. and Sharma, A.D.

Intelligence, fixation, frustration, and economic status as correlates of the originality. *J Education and Psychology* 44(3-4) Jl-De 1986 p 158-61

Bhargava, A.K.

See

Gupta, S.P. *jt. auth.*

Bhargava, Mahesh

Prose teaching in English language at secondary level. *Rajasthan Board J Education* 19(4) Oc-De 1983 p 22-29

See also

Sharma, V.P. *jt. auth.*

Bhargava, Mahesh and Marwah, Madhu

Academic performance as a function of prolonged deprivation. *Indian Educational Rev* 17(3) Jl 1982 p 114-22 refs tabs

Bhargava, P.K.

Determinants of rural/urban disparities in the literacy rate in India. *Indian Educational Rev* 20(2) Ap 1985 p 9-20

Bhargava, S.C.

Role of chemistry in socially useful productive work and community services. *Rajasthan Board J Education* 20(4)-21(1) Oc 1984-Mr 1985 p 52-55

Bhargava, S.C. and Mathur, Sunder Lal

STOS : A technique for evaluation of science teaching. *Rajasthan Board J Education* 20(1-2) Ja-Je 1984 p 15-20

Bhargava, S.C. and Sharma, Kamala Kant

A comparison of classroom verbal interaction of trained professional teachers and untrained professional teachers using STOS. *Rajasthan Board J Education* 16(4) Oc-De 1980 p 39-44

Bhargava, S.N.L.

Study of observing process in science in relation to certain socio-economic and congnitive variables. *Research Bulletin* 14(1-2) Mr-Je 1984 p 22-28 refs

A study of the measuring process in science in relation to certain congnitive and social variables. *J Institute of Educational Research* 10(2) My 1986 p 4-7 refs tabs

Bhasin, M.P.

A new aim : Teaching vs learning. *Educational Rev* 91(10) Oc 1985 p 167-71

School adjustment : Part of learning milieu. *Primary Teacher* 11(2) Ap 1986 p 17-20

The school perception. *Primary Teacher* 9(1) Ja 1984 p 4-8

The teacher : As behaviourial and perceptualist. *J Indian Education* 10(6) Mr 1985 p 48-54

Bhasin, P.S.S.

An analytical study of interest inventories. *Indian Educational Rev* 18(2) Ap 1983 p 79-83

Bhaskara, S.

Reduction of congnitive; affective imbalance : An experiment. *Experiments in Education* 6(11) Ja 1979 p 200-01

See also

Bhatt, Vasant D. *jt. auth.*

Bhaskaran, C.

See

Sethurao, M.K. *et al jt. auths.*

Bhaskaran, C. and Sethurao M.K.

Correlates of interpersonal communication behaviour of farmers in differentially progressive villages. *Indian J Extension Education* 21(3-4) Jl-De 1985 p 16-22 refs tabs

Bhaskara Rao, D.

How to avoid tensions. *Educational Rev* 91(3) Mr 1985 p 49-50

An inquiry into the study habits of B.Ed. students. *Educational Rev* 92(8) Ag 1986 p 134-35

Platonic system of education. *Educational Rev* 89(4) Ap 1983 p 68-71

Bhaskara Rao, D. and Sundara Rao, G.

A study of the reactions of teacher trainees towards the evaluation procedure followed at B.Ed. level. *Experiments in Education* 12(12) Fe1985 p 216-19

Bhaskara Rao, D. *et al*

Personality characteristics of educational administrators. *J Institute of Educational Research* 9(3) Nv 1985 p 8-13 refs tabs

Scientific attitudes of experienced science teachers at secondary school level. *Educational Rev* 92(4) Ap 1986 p 61-65 refs tabs

Bhaskara Rao, P.

UGC study centres : Nature and performance : A case study of Andhra University centres. *University News* 23(23) 16 Je 1985 p 5-8

Bhaskara Rao, V.

Teaching and research in higher education : Some problems. *J Higher Education* 4(1) Mon 1978 p 11-22 refs tabs

BHAT - BHATT

Bhatt, Bansidhar

Traditional institutions, universities and their coordination. *J Indian Education* 12(3) Se 1986 p 35-38 refs

Bhatt, G.K.

See

Tilak, J.B.G. *jt. auth.*

Bhatt, Kusum K.

Self perception among high and low groups. *J Education and Psychology* 36(1-2) Ap-Je 1978 p 34-40 refs

Bhat, Vasant D.

Educational technology in distance education. *University News* 24(42) 8 Nv 1986 p 79-82

Meritocracy in higher education. *Education Quarterly* 33(3) Jl 1981 p 14-16+

Meta analysis : Quantitive approaches in review of research finding. *J Indian Education* 11(1) My 1985 p 42-51 refs

Science teachers in the upper primary schools and the new science syllabus. *Experiments in Education* 9(6) Ag 1981 p 110-12+

Verified knowledge in education : The need for meta-analysis. *Perspectives in Education* 1(2) Ja 1985 p 25-33 refs

See also

Menon, M.B. *et al jt. auths.*

Ravindranath, M.J. *jt. auth.*

Bhat, Vasant D. and Bhaskara, S.

Education for creativity through simulation. *Education Quarterly* 35(3) Jl 1983 p 7-11 refs

Bhat, Vasant D. and Ravindranath, M.J.

Science education in elementary schools. *Indian Education* 10(12) Mr 1981 p 18-22

Bhatia, S.C. *ed.*

Some critical considerations in adult education. Delhi, Univ. of Delhi. 1980, 64p. *Book Rev, Education Quarterly* 33(4) Oc 1981 p 35-36

Bhatia, S.S.

Jawaharlal Nehru : An internationalist, apostle of peace. *Educational Rev* 90(5-6) My-Je 1984 p 91-93

Bhatnagar, G.S.

Channels of communication in rural communities of Uttar Pradesh. *Indian J Extension Education* 14(3-4) Jl-De 1978 p 34-38

Bhatnagar, K.N.

Management and financing of higher education. *University News* 23(6) 8 Fe 1985 p 2-4

Bhatnagar, R.P.

Current research in education : The malady. *Indian Education* 11(7) Oc 1981 p 8-12

Bhatnagar, Suman

See

Saxena, Daya *jt. auth.*

Bhatnagar, Suman and Bordia, Sadhana

Relationship of study habits of home science undergraduate students with academic achievement and residence. *Progress of Education* 58(6) Ja 1984 p 143-45

Bhatnagar, Suman and Gupta, Pushpa

Job preference of home science graduates. *Indian J Extension Education* 16(3-4) De 1980 p 78-81 refs tabs

Bhatnagar, Suman and Singhal, Asha

Attitude of women participants towards integrated child development services (ICDS). *Indian J Extension Education* 20(3-4) Se-De 1984 p 67-78 refs tabs

Bhatnagar, T.N.S.

Review of studies and literature on student teaching and other practical work in B.Ed programme in India. *Quest in Education* 19(3) Jl 1982 p 206-26 refs

Student teaching and other practical work in the B.Ed. programme in India : Review of studies and literature. *Indian Educational Rev* 18(3) Jl 1983 p 17-32

Bhatt

See

Bhat

BHATTACHARJEE - BHATTACHARYA - BHATTACHARYYA

Bhattacharjee, Arun

Misconduct of students. New Delhi, Deep & Deep Pub. 440p. Rs.125 *Book Rev, New Frontiers in Education* 12(3) Jl-Se 1982 p 76-77

Bhattacharya, B.B.

Fourth Indian scientific expedition to Antarctica, 1984-85. *University News* 23(33) 1 Se 1985 p 6-8

Psychology and pedagogy of spelling. *Our Education* 1 Jl 1980 p 23-28; 2 Jl 1981 p 51-61 refs

Bhattacharyya, B.K.

On selection of candidates for professional education. *J Higher Education* 8(3) Spr 1983 p 390-96

Bhattacharya, Bishnubrata
Education for India. Calcutta, Banerjee, Mohit Kumar 74p. Rs.8 *Book Rev, Progress of Education* 57(2) Se 1982 p 46

Bhattacharya, Biswanath
The Open University system. *Teacher Education* 20(30-31) Ja-Ap 1985 p 11-14

Bhattacharya, Budhadeva and Patranabis, Janes
Curriculum : A proposal. *J Higher Education* 1(1) Mon 1975 p 87-90

Bhattacharyya, Debi Prasad
Job satisfaction of teachers and its relationship to their anger and aggression as rated by them. *J Education and Psychology* 36(3) Oc 1978 p 160-62

Bhattacharya, Debika
Educational policy for modernisation and national development. *J Indian Education* 12(3) Se 1986 p 6-14

Bhattacharyya, G.C. and Shukla, C.S.
The diode and additive models of teaching skills : A comparative study. *National J Education* 5(1) Se 1982 p 24-32 refs

Bhattacharya, S. and D'sleneida, Fleur
The caste system and discrimination in historical perspective. *New Frontiers in Education* 16(2) Ap-Je 1986 p 25-32 tabs

Bhattacharya, Siba P.
Academic learning time model of classroom instruction. *Our Education* 3-4 Jl 1983 p 31-34 refs
Alienation in the school system : A factor analytic model for empirical study. *Our Education* 6 Jl 1985-86 p 21-26 refs tabs

Bhattacharya, Srinibas
Humanising education. *Quest in Education* 17(3) Jl 1980 p 212-16

Bhattacharya, Swapan K.
See
Bandyopadhyay, Swaraj *jt. auth.*

Bhattacharya, Swapan K. and Pal, Manabandra nath
Management information systems in university administration *J Higher Education* 2(2) But 1976 p 213-21 refs

Bhaumik, Gita
See
Kundu, Ramanath *jt. auth.*
Patel, Bhasker *jt. auth.*

Bhave, Asha M.
See
Jansi Rani *jt. auth.*

Bhave, W.A.
From manual training to productive work. *Indian Education* 10(8) Nv 1980 p 4-7
Naming a university. *Progress of Education* 56(6) Ja 1982 p 136-39
Pracitce teaching in college of education. *Progress of Education* 55(12) Jl 1981 p 328-30

Bhide, Kishore
The discussion on the uni level English textbook prescribed for std. XII. *Progress of Education* 56(1) Ag 1981 p 2-4

Bhide, M.R.

Integration of higher education for effective vocational training. *J Higher Education* 5(3) Spr 1980 p 371-79

Bhilugaonkar, M.G.

Shift in use of feritilizers to constraints. *Indian J Extension Education* 15(3-4) De 1979 p 34-38 tabs

Bhima Rao, T.

Efficacy of inductive and deductive approaches in teaching biological sciences. *Indian Education* 10(7) Oc 1980 p 33-37

Bhimasankaram, C.V.

The ethics of teaching. *Progress of Education* 56(8) Mr 1982 p 180-83 +

Functional teaching *Progress of Education* 56(5) De 1981 p 102-07

Self-criticism technique : A boon or a bane. *Progress of Education* 55(7) Fe 1981 p 186-88

Self-revelation of mathematics. *Progress of Education* 57(11) June 1983 p 253-54

See also

Samant, D.G. *jt. auth.*

Bhimaya, Suriya

Symbol systems in the school programme. *Education Quarterly* 36(4) Wint 1984 p 12-16

Bhllegsonkar, M.G. and Dakh, A.M.

A study of mobile farm advisory service. *Indian J Extension Education* 14(1-2) Ja-Je 1978 p 62-63

Bhoite, H.S.

See

Sawant, G.K. *jt. auth.*

Bhola, H.S.

With struggle, there is hope for literacy. *Indian J Adult Education* 47(7) Jl 1986 p 4-10

Bhoodev Singh

Comparative evaluation of mathematics textbook. *Experiments in Education* 9(12) Fe 1982 p 217-22 tabs

The effect of practice teaching on teaching competence and attitude towards teaching of pre-service teacher. *J Institute of Educational Research* 10(1) Ja 1986 p 13-16 refs tabs

Mathematical creativity : A teaching model. *Primary Teacher* 9(3) Jl 1984 p 11-13

Bhouraskar, Shalini

A comparative study of the effectiveness of feedback given by Peer and audio tape under micro teaching setting. *National J Education* 2(2) Mr 1980 p 6-14 refs tabs

Bhullar, Surinder K.

Moral education : A challenge. *Educational Rev* 92(10) Oc 1986 p 177-78

Bhushan

See also

under full name, e.g., Anand Bhushan

Bhusan, A. and Ahuja, M.

Value systems and value preference patterns of Indian youths belonging to different socio-metric levels. *J Institute of Educational Research* 4(3) Se 1980 p 7-14 refs tabs

Bhushan, L.I.

Development of women's social freedom scale : A report. *Asian J Psychology and Education* 7(2) Jl 1981 p 34-38

Bilgrami, R. Fatima

See

Siddiqi, Zakia A. *jt. auth.*

Bimal, B.K.

See

Sinha, N.K. *jt. auth.*

Bindal, V.R.

See

Chaudhary, U.S. *jt. auth.*

Bingham-Newan, Ann M.

See

Saunders, Ruth *jt. auth.*

Bir Singh

Antyodaya education. *Educational Rev* 85(6) Je 1979 p 115-18

Book bank schemes of M.P. *Educational Rev* 88(10) Oc 1982 p 165-67

Education for the unwilling. *Educational Rev* 86(11) Nv 1980 p 213-14

Education in 1980s. *Education Quarterly* 33(1) Ja 1981 p 3-7

Employment oriented education. *Progress of Education* 55(9) Ap 1981 p 234-36

Environmental education. *Education Quarterly* 34(3) Jl 1982 p 9-11

Higher priority to teacher education. *Teacher Education* 17(20-21) Jl-Oc 1982 p 65-68

Improving reading through self-selection. *Educational Rev* 87(12) De 1981 p 221-22

Indiscipline : Teachers point of view. *Educational Rev* 85(8) Ag 1979 p 144-48

An M.P. experiment in school complex. *Education Quarterly* 33(2) Ap 1981 p 21-23

An M.P. experiment in work experience. *Education Quarterly* 22(4) Oc 1980 p 15-16; *Indian Education* 10(4) Jl 1980 p 41-43

MP modernises teachers training. *Education Quarterly* 34(1) Ja 1982 p 15-16

NCERT is 20 years old. *Educational Rev* 87(8) Ag 1981 p 148-49

Priority to pre-primary education. *Education Quarterly* 33(1) Ja 1981 p 8-9

Promoting spelling proficiency. *Educational Rev* 85(2) Fe 1979 p 34-36 ref

Teacher training needs overhauling. *Progress of Education* 55(10) My 1981 p 267-69 +

To stop copying : Examinees suggestions. *Educational Rev* 85(3) Mr 1979 p 48-49

What parents want, Mr. teacher : A study? *Educational Rev* 86(8) Ag 1980 p 145-50

Why teachers tease you, Mr. Headmaster? *Progress of Education* 55(3) Oc 1980 p 77-85

Bisht, A.R.

Approval/disapproval of strikes culture : A sample survey of students guardians and teachers. *J Higher Education* 7(3) Spr 1982 p 272-77 refs

Dropping out phenomenon in adult education. *Indian J Adult Education* 44(5) My 1983 p 25-26

Sex-wise and age-wise difference in some educationally significant variables : Institutional stress, academic stress, need for academic achievement, school climate, and academic achievement. *National J Education* 6(2) My 1984 p 33-39 ref

Shift of learned teaching skills from micro to macro teaching : A study. *J Institute of Educational Research* 7(2) My 1983 p 8-11

Teachers educational philosophic orientation in relation to some personal variables : A study. *Bharatiya Shiksha Shodh Patrika* 4(1) Ja-Je 1985 p 65-68 refs

Verbal and non-verbal classroom behaviours as related to teachers first and second order factors of personality. *Indian Educational Rev* 20(3) Jl 1985 p 79-90

See also

Uniyal, M.P. *jt. auth.*

Bisht, A.R. and Pathani, R.S.

Educating visually handicapped children. *Educational Rev* 92(10) Oc 1986 p 178-79

Biswal, B.N.

Extension input in curriculum for undergraduates. *Quest in Education* 18(4) Oc 1981 p 302-06

Management of educational institutions by private bodies in Orissa : Some observations. *EPA Quarterly Bulletin* 5(3-4) Oc 1982-Ja 1983 p 26-35

Proposed procedural details of a research study on secondary school English syllabus at masters level. *Experiments in Education* 6(1) Mr 1978 p 230-33

A study of perception of undergraduate and post-graduate students towards the achievement of objective of teaching English at secondary level. *Experiments in Educaiton* 6(2) Ap 1978 p 28-31 refs tabs

A study of reactions of the students of correspondence education : A synopsis. *Indian Education* 11(7) Oc 1981 p 27-39

Biswal, B.N. and Biswal, Kabita

Need for pre-primary education in rural India. *Experiments in Education* 9(7) Se 1981 p 121-25

Problems in primary education : Some issues. *Experiments in Education* 10(2) Ap 1982 p 25-28

Biswal, Kabita

See

Biswal, B.N. *jt. auth.*

Biswas, A. and Agrawal, S.P.

Development of education in India : A historical survey of educational documents before and after independence. New Delhi, Concept, 1986. xv, 936p Rs.700 *Book Rev, Education Quarterly* 39(2) Sum 1987 p 52-56

Biswas, Chandidas
See
Kundu, Ramanath *jt. auth.*

Biswas, Manju
Mentally retarded and normal children : A comparative study. New Delhi, Sterling. 1980 153p. Rs.45 *Book Rev, Education Quarterly* 33(3) Jl 1981 p 47-48; *Teacher Today* 26(4) Ap-Je 1984 p 94-95

Biswas, N.B.
Primary education curriculum in Bangladesh : A historical review. *Perspectives in Education* 1(1) Ja 1985 p 5-20 refs
See also
Blawal, G.C. *jt. auth.*

Biswas, N.B. and Blawal, G.C.
Objectives of primary education in Bangladesh : Then and now. *Educatinal Rev* 91(5-6) My-Je 1985 p 88-90

Blawal, G.C. and Biswas, N.B.
Self-esteem and children's academic achievement : A cross cultural study. *Experiments in Education* 12(12) Fe 1985 p 220-22

Blang, Mark
Education and employment problems in developing countries. New Delhi, Macmillan. 89p. Rs.25 *Book Rev, Education Quarterly* 32(4) Ap 1980 p 49

Bohatgi, P.K.
Activities of the technological forecasting and research management cell of Indian Institute of Science, Bangalore. *J Higher Education* 4(1) Mon 1978 p 109-11

Bohra, Shanti P.
Values correlates with effective teachers. *Asian J Psychology and Education* 13(1) Ja 1984 p 7-10 refs

Bollnow, Otto F.
On the virtues of the education. *Teacher Today* 27(1) Jl-Se 1984 p 1-13 refs

Bond, D'Este
The brain train : An exercise in mobile education. *Educational Rev* 86(4) Ap 1980 p 73-74

Bonanni, C.
Education for human needs. New Delhi, Indian Adult Educ. Assn. (Series No. 139). 1982, 170p. Rs.15 *Book Rev, Indian J Adult Education* 44(4) Ap 1983 p 39-40

Bora, A.C.
An alternative approach of measuring students' performance for different recruitments. *J Higher Education* 8(2) Aut 1982 p 215-20 refs

Bora, Surabhi
Adolescents with educational and family adjustment problems. *J Indian Education* 12(2) Jl 1986 p 39-41

Boraiyan, M.A.
Rural development education. *Experiments in Education* 9(11) Ja 1982 p 201-04

Bordia, Anil
Co-ordination between non-formal adult education and development programme. *Indian J Adult Education* 10(1) Ja 1979 p 1-8 refs

Return to the roots : An alternative policy frame for primary education. *Teacher Today* 27(4) Ap-Je 1985 p 72-85 tabs

Bordia, Sadhana

See

Bhatnagar, Suman *jt. auth.*

Borg, Walter, R.

Applying educational research : A practical guide for teachers. New York, Longmans. 1981, $9.95 *Book Rev, Research Bulletin* 16(1-2) Mr-Je 1986 p 58-63

Borton, Len and Walker, Stephen, *eds.*

Social crisis and educational research. London, Croom Helm. 347p. £8.95 *Book Rev, Education Quarterly* 37(3) Aut 1986 p 63-64

Bose, Arun

Undergraduate curricula in social sciences. *J Higher Education* 1(1) Mon 1975 p 61-75

Bose, K.

See

Srivastava, R.S. *jt. auth.*

Bose, Kshanika

Developing superior ability. *Education Quarterly* 32(3) Jl 1980 p 18-21

Bose, Nirmal

57th All India Education Conference, Visakhapatnam : Address by Prof. Nirmal Bose. *Indian Education* 13(5-6) Ag-Se 1983 p 5-8

Bose, P.K. and Mukherjee, S.P.

Graduate employment and higher education in West Bengal. *J Higher Education* 5(3) Spr 1980 p 281-89 refs tabs

Bose, Sukumar

Personality : Marxist concepts and practices. *Our Education* 5 Jl 1984 p 47-53 refs

Bourai, H.H.A.

Dynamics of moral development. *Rajasthan Board J Education* 16(4) Oc-De 1980 p 21-24

Education for rural development. *Quest in Education* 17(3) Jl 1980 p 207-11

Boydell, Deanne

The primary teacher in action. Open Bks. Pub. vii, 126p. £1.95 *Book Rev, Education Quarterly* 31(3-4) Oc 1979-Ja 1980 p 47

Boyle, J.P.

Listening in education and forcing language learning. *New Frontiers in Education* 15(1) Ja-Mr 1985 p 51-55 refs

Brahm Prakash

The demand for and financing of higher education in Canada. *J Higher Education* 3(3) Spr 1978 p 345-55 refs

See also

Chaturvedi, V. *jt. auth.*

Brahmankar, E.B.

Patterns of commerce education in Indian Universities. *University News* 23(33) 1 Se 1985 p 4-5 +

Brar, Pritam Singh

Children and creativity. *Educational Rev* 88(7) Jl 1982 p 115-18

Education for democracy. *Educational Rev* 85(3) Mr 1979 p 43-45
Education in a changing society. *Educational Rev* 89(11) Nv 1983 p 190-91
Efficient classroom management. *Educational Rev* 88(1) Ja 1982 p 1-3
Evaluating educational outcomes. *Primary Teacher* 10(3) Jl 1985 p 23-26
Ideal school atmosphere. *Educational Rev* 86(4) Ap 1980 p 69-71
Love and respect for the child. *Educational Rev* 87(10) Oc 1981 p 181-83
Making of good teachers. *Educational Rev* 90(11) Nv 1984 p 165-67
The teacher in a democratic set up. *Educational Rev* 89(5-6) My-Je 1983 p 86-89

Bray, Mark
Personnel involvement and government at the school level : Theory and practice in Papua New Guinea. *Perspectives in Education* 2(2) Ap 1986 p 109-20 refs

Bray, Mark *et al*
Education and society in Africa. London, Annali, Edward. 1986, 191p. *Book Rev, Perspectives in Education* 2(4) Oc 1986 p 249-50

Briggs, Asa
The higher education scene in Britain today. *J Higher Education* 9(1) Mon 1983 p 47-63

Briggs, D.K. and Bhagia, N.M.
Professional preparation of educational administration in developing countries. *EPA Quarterly Bulletin* 8(1-2) Ap-Je 1985 p 80-85

Bright, A. John
See
Ayyadurai, G. *jt. auth.*

Bright, James A.
Teacher-pupil interaction in different types of schools : A comparative study. *J Educational Research and Extension* 17(3) Ja 1981 p 164-71 refs tabs

Broadfoot, Patricia
International trends in educational assessment. *J Higher Education* 7(3) Spr 1982 p 227-35 refs

Brookfield, Stephen
Adult learners, adult education and the community. Stratford, Open Univ Press. 1983, 229p. *Book Rev, Education Quarterly* 37(2) Sum 1985 p 73-75

Brown, George
Microteaching. Methuen. 1978, 163p. £4.20 *Book Rev, Teacher Today* 22(4) Ap-Je 1980 p 96-98

Brusling, Christer
The rise and fall of educational technology in Sweden. *Teacher Education* 17(20-21) Jl-Oc 1982 p 23-29 refs

Buch, A.N.
Workers education : Need for empirical approach. *Indian J Adult Education* 46(5) My 1985 p 41-42

Buch, M.B. and Patil, P.A.
Towards work-oriented education. Ahmedabad, Gujarat Vidyapith 1979, 137p. Rs.16 *Book Rev, J Indian Education* 7(2) Jl 1979 p 68-69

Buch, P.M. *et al*
A study of self-concept, intelligence and achivement of IX grade students. *J*

Educational Research and Extension 16(2) Oc 1979 p 94-99 refs tabs

Buch, Piloo

Innovations in student teaching : Some considerations. *New Frontiers in Education* 11(1) Ja-Mr 1981 p 69-72

On understanding youth at higher secondary. *Progress of Education* 55(4) Nv 1980 p 90-93

Socially useful productive work : An innovation in school curriculum. Baroda, Shweta Pub. 42p, Rs.6 *Book Rev, National J Education* 2(1) Se 1979 p 63-64

Teacher education in the context of the new education policy. *New Frontiers in Education* 16(4) Oc-De 1986 p 82-87

Buckman, Peter, *ed.*

Education without schools. New Delhi, Rupa. 1973. 134p. Rs.10 *Book Rev, Teacher Today* 24(3) Ja-Mr 1982 p 118-20

Budhisagar, Meena

Perspectives of vocational education. *Progress of Education* 61(2) Se 1986 p 37-39

See also

Sansanwal, D.N. *jt. auth.*

Budhori, K.B.

A study of physical facilities in educational institutions of Garhwal division. *Indian Educational Rev* 18(2) Ap 1983 p 110-19 refs tabs

Burke, To By

Special education of handicapped. *Educational Rev* 86(10) Oc 1980 p 189-90

Burma, D.P.

Life sciences in Indian universities : Course and curriculum. *National J Education* 2(1) Se 1979 p 33-40

Bute, D.N.

See

Ingle, O.P. *et al jt. auth.*

Butt, H.W.

Planning an integrated child welfare programme. *Indian Education* 9(10-11) Ja-Fe 1980 p 19-26

Bwatwa, Y.D.M.

The training of adult education manpower at home and abroad : The Eastern African scene. *Perspectives in Education* 1(2) Ap 1985 p 99-109 tabs

Byram, M.L.

See

Kidd, R. *jt. auth.*

Byra Reddy, H.N.

See

Nagaraj, N. *jt. auth.*

Callahan, Joseph F. and Clark, Leonard H.

Teaching in secondary school. London, Macmillan. 1977, 347p. $7.25 *Book Rev, Teacher Today* 21(4) Ap-Je 1979 p 87-88

Calliods, Francoise
See
Hallak, Jacques *jt. auth.*

Carnoy, Martin
Educational innovation in the third world. *J Higher Education* 5(2) Aut 1979 p 141-55
Socialist development and educational reform in Cuba, 1959-1980. *Perspectives in Education* 1(4) Oc 1985 p 237-56 refs

Cass, Alan F.
Profile of Indian child. *Asian J Psychology and Education (Special Issue)* 10(1-4) 1982 p 13-16

Cayari, Remedios M.
Population education in the Philippines. *Rajasthan Board J Education* 16(1-2) Ja-Je 1980 p 65-71

Chadha, D.K. and Singh, V.P.
An evaluation of discriminant frames through a programme on English morphology. *Indian Educational Rev* 18(4) Oc 1983 p 47-57
Population education for national reconstruction. *J Indian Education* 6(6) Mr 1981 p 42-45

Chadha, N.K. and Sen, Arun K.
Creativity as a function of intelligence, socio-economic status and sex among 12th grade school students. *J Education and Psychology* 39(1) Ap 1981 p 52-56 refs
An investigation of the relationship between creativity personality and vocational interest of 12th grade students of a Delhi school. *Our Education* 2 Jl 1981 p 31-37 refs tab

Chadha, S.S. *et al*
Comparison of vocational aspiration of urban and rural adolescents. *J Education and Psychology* 41(3) Oc 1983 p 101-05
Construction and standardisation of a two way classificatory system of occupations. *J Education and Psychology* 39(3) Oc 1981 p 148-55 refs

Chaganti, Subbarao
Correspondence courses in teacher education. *Progress of Education* 59(8) Mr 1985 p 181-83
Correspondence courses in teacher education. *Teacher Education* 16(18-19) Ja-Ap 1982 p 17-20
State of teacher education in India. *Teacher Education* 16(18-19) Ja-Ap 1982 p 64-71
State of teacher education in India. *Progress of Education* 58(6) Ja 1984 p 126-31+
Teacher education : A brief survey of its weakness. *Progress of Education* 55(10) My 1981 p 249-50

Chainani, R.S.
Ethics in education. *Progress of Education* 56(7) Fe 1982 p 163-64
Who told them to be teacher? *Progress of Education* 56(2) Se 1981 p 30-32 +
Woman and her education. *Progress of Education* 57(4) Nv 1982 p 77-80

CHAKRABARTI - CHAKRABARTY - CHAKRABORTY - CHAKRAVARTY

Chakravarty, Kumaresh
  Administration of higher education : An overview. *J Higher Education* 2(2) Aut 1978 p 223-32 refs
Chakrabarti, Mukli
  Behavioural objectives : A missing link in teaching. *National J Education* 7(2) My 1985 p 25-30 refs
Chakraborty, P.R.
  Religion and education. *J Indian Education* 8(3) Se 1982 p 33-39
  Teacher education and promotion of international understanding. *Primary Teacher* 9(1) Ja 1984 p 9-12
Chakrabarty, S.C.
  Construction and standardisation of a performance test-battery of general mental ability of the children of age groups 6 to 10 years. *Our Education* 3-4 Jl 1983 p 59-67 refs tabs
Chakrabarti, Sharmistha
  Academic achievement of primary school children. *Progress of Education* 60(9) Ap 1986 p 209-15 tabs
Chalam, K.S.
  Educational planning at the institution level. *Educational Rev* 87(7) Jl 1981 p 124-26
  Expenditure on university education : A unit cost analysis. *J Higher Education* 4(2) Aut 1978 p 201-24
  Financial strategy for the development of education in India. *EPA Quarterly Bulletin* 8(3-4) Oc 1985-Ja 1986 p 29-39 tabs
  Productivity trends in higher education in Andhra Pradesh. *EPA Quarterly Bulletin* 6(3-4) Oc 1983-Ja 1984 p 40-55 refs
  Promoting family planning through non-formal education. *Indian J Adult Education* 42(1-2) Ja-Fe 1981 p 25-28
  See also
    Ramesh Babu, M. *jt. auth.*
Chalam, K.S. and Sudarsana Rao, R.
  Correspondence education as an agency of continuing education for weaker sections. *Indian J Adult Education* 43(5) My 1982 p 13-17
Chalapati Rao, I.V.
  Glimpses of education in ancient India. *Indian Education* 11(10) Ja 1982 p 25-32
Chamala, Shankarish *et al*
  A new look at adopter categories and an alternative proposal for target grouping of farming community. *Indian J Extension Education* 16(1-2) Je 1980 p 1-18 refs
Chan, Anthony B.
  Programme planning for new immigrants and refugees. *Indian J Adult Education* 44(3) Mr 1983 p 13-20 refs
Chanana, Karuna
  See
    Ahmad, Karuna

Chander
See
under full name, e.g., Ram Chander
Chandler, E.M.
Educating of adolescent girls. London, Allen & Unwin. 1980, 217p. *Book Rev, Education Quarterly* 33(3) Jl 1981 p 44-45
Chandra
See also
under full name, e.g., Mohini Chandra
Chandra, A. and Khaund, Aparna H.
Selected social norms of the home science students. *J Higher Education* 8(3) Spr 1983 p 356-63 refs tabs
Chandrakant, L.S.
New perspectives for technical education : Industry interaction. *J Higher Education* 7(3) Spr 1982 p 201-10
Chandra Reddy, T.
See
Venkata Rami Reddy, A. *jt. auth.*
Chandrasekharan, Rajkumari
Appropriate learning techniques in the sector of non-formal education for school dropouts and non-starters. *Experiments in Education* 9(3) My 1981 p 46-49
Aspects of adult education. Madras, New Era Pub. 1982, viii, 151p. Rs.60 *Book Rev, Education Quarterly* 35(1) Ja 1983 p 47-48
Designing curriculum and technology for women's adult education programmes. *Indian J Adult Education* 41(4) Ap 1980 p 19-24
Different methods of literacy teaching. *Experiments in Education* 7(5) Jl 1979 p 92+
Guidelines for adult education programme : A blue print for action at the micro-level. *Education Quarterly* 30(3) Oc 1978 p 13-14
University adult education and national development. *Indian J Adult Education* 39(9) Se 1978 p 32-37 refs
Youth problems : A causative analysis in Indian setting. *Experiments in Education* 7(2) Ap 1979 p 28-31
Chadrasekhara Sarma, S.
Teacher education. *Indian Education* 13(5-6) Ag-Se 1983 p 16-19
Chandrashekaran, M.K.
Teaching chronobiology in Indian universities. *J Higher Education* 5(3) Spr 1980 p 343-49 refs
Chandwani, Anita
Job analysis of Balwadi workers of Delhi : A case study. *Indian J Extension Education* 15(1-2) Je 1979 p 70-74 tabs
Chandy, P.T.
Education and values : Need for integration. *New Frontiers in Education* 14(1) Ja-Mr 1984 p 29-30
Chandy, Verghis
The comprehensive school in the United Kingdom. *Educational Rev* 90(3) Mr 1984 p 41-43
Dimensions of classroom behaviour. *Experiments in Education* 6(2) Ap 1978

p 26-27
Dimensions of classroom behaviour. *Experiments in Education* 10(7) Se 1982 p 134+
Helping the artistic child. *Educational Rev* 86(9) Se 1980 p 173-74
Moral education and citizenship. *Educational Rev* 86(3) Mr 1980 p 59
The process of learning in a young child. *Progress of Education* 55(4) Nv 1980 p 99-101
The teacher on consultant. *Educational Rev* 92(9) Se 1986 p 149-50
Vocationalisation of education. *Educational Rev* 88(3) Mr 1982 p 45-46

Chang Fang
Socialist moral education in China. *Indian Education* 12(8-9) Nv-De 1982 p 18-19

Channegowda, C.
See
Patel, S. Subhashchandra *jt. auth.*

Channegowda, M.B.
Interaction between researchers and farmers in Bangalore district of Karnataka. *Indian J Extension Education* 19(3-4) Se-De 1983 p 66-68 refs
See also
Nataraju, M.S. *jt. auth.*
Subha Reddy, H.N. *jt. auth.*

Channegowda, M.B. and Jalihal, K.A.
Indirect influence of print information under different communication situation on non-participant literate and illiterate farmers. *Indian J Extension Education* 20(1-2) Je 1984 p 62-65 refs tabs

Channegowda, M.B. and Ranganna, B.
Feeding pracitce of gobar gas plants in Karnataka. *Indian J Extension Education* 16(3-4) De 1980 p 94-95

Charandas, Jeesur
See
Jachuk, Kasturi *jt. auth.*

Chari, Ahalya
J. Krishnamurti : Freedom and education. *J Indian Education* 6(2) Jl 1980 p 9-11

Chari, M.S.V.
Education and cultural development. *Educational Rev* 89(4) Ap 1983 p 75-76
Rationalising M.A. course in English. *Educational Rev* 85(8) Ag 1979 p 151-53
Stray thoughts on education. *Educational Rev* 85(5) My 1979 p 94-95

Chark, Leonard H.
See
Callahan, Joseph F. *jt. auth.*

Charles, D.L.
See
Mehta, S.J. *jt. auth.*

Chatia, C.K.
See
Singh, H.R. *jt. auth.*

CHATTERJEE - CHATTERJI

Chatterjee, A.K.

Recent trends of teacher education for secondary schools in U.K. and India. *Our Education* 6 Jl 1985-1986 p 31-41 refs

Chatterjee, B.B.

Dimensions of language learning by adults. *Indian J Adult Education* 40(5) Mr 1979 p 23-27 refs

Social costs of reservation in higher education : A decision theoretic view. *J Higher Education* 9(1) Mon 1983 p 77-89 tab

Chatterji, Basanti

See

Amrit Kaur *jt. auth.*

Chatterjee, Bishwa B. and Das, Basanta Kumar

Factors structure of projective outputs. *Asian J Psychology and Education* 3(2) Jl 1978 p 19-34 refs

Chatterjee, Mihir K.

Adaptation of vividness of visual imagery questionnaire scale for Bengali children. *Indian Educational Rev* 18(2) Ap 1983 p 40-45 refs tabs

The effect of imagery on the learnings of extended passages : A study. *Indian Educational Rev* 15(1) 1980 p 27-34 refs

Teacher planning : Cognitive information processing approach. *Indian Educational Rev* 19(1) Ja 1984 p 27-35

Teachers decision-making : A new and exciting approach to research on teaching. *Teacher Today* 23(2) Oc-De 1980 p 76-82 figs

Chatterjee, Pigush Kanti

Skill of reinforcement : Programme for implementation. *Progress of Education* 53(6) Ja 1981 p 161-64 tabs

Chatterji, S. and Mukherjee, M.

Comparison of the personality profiles of over, under and equal achiever. *J Education and Psychology* 43(1) Ap 1985 p 14-21

Chatterjee, T.K. and Shah, V.

A study of relationship between adjustment and perceived parental behaviour among the male and female college students. *Our Education* 2 Jl 1981 p 45-49 refs tabs

CHATTOPADHYAYA - CHATTOPADHYAY

Chattopadhyay, Gautam

Bengal's student movement. *Student Action* 2(10) My 1984 p 6+; 2(11) Je 1984 p 2-3+

Chattopadhyay, Kamladevi

Indian women's battle for freedom. New Delhi, Abhinav Pub. 1983, 184p. Rs.45 *Book Rev, New Frontiers in Education* 13(1) Ja-Mr 1983 p 72-73

Chattopadhyay, Samnath and Agrawal, K.G.

Organisation culture, its perception and the medical faculty. *J Higher Education* 4(2) Aut 1978 p 245-50

Chaturvedi, J.
See
Wilson, M.J. *jt. auth.*

Chaturvedi, Kanak
See
Sharma, A.P. *jt. auth.*

Chaturvedi, Mahesh C.
See
Chaturvedi, Viplula *jt. auth.*

Chaturvedi, S.C.
Development of school for special education in Japan. *National J Education* 7(1) Se 1984 p 19-28 refs

Chaturvedi, Vipula
International cooperation and collaboration in Indian higher education. *Indian Education* 18(5-6) Ag-Se 1983 p 19-26

Chaturvedi, Viplula and Braham Prakash
Impact of functional literacy programme in rural areas near Delhi. *Indian J Adult Education* 44(3) Mr 1983 p 31-35 ref tab

Chaturvedi, Viplula and Chaturvedi, Mahesh C.
International perspectives of collaboration in higher technical education. *Education Quarterly* 35(4) Oc 1983 p 1-7 refs

CHAUDHRI - CHAUDHURY - CHAUDHARY - CHAUDHURI - CHAUDURY - CHOWDHRY

Chaudhri, D.P.
Education innovations and agricultural development : A study of North India. New Delhi, Vikas Pub. 1979, 127p. Rs.95 *Book Rev, Education Quarterly* 32(1) Ja 1980 p 45-46

Chaudhri, I.S.
Attempts to improve school text books. *J Indian Education* 8(3) Se 1982 p 26-28
Experimental try-out application of tools and techniques for evaluation and monitorinig of universalisation of elementary education in India. *EPA Quarterly Bulletin* 7(3-4) Oc 1984-Ja 1985 p 17-25 refs

Chaudhary, Kamlesh
Competency based teaching : Some issues. *Progress of Education* 55(9) Ap 1981 p 222-26

Chaudhri, M.M.
Educational technology and system design for the production of educational material for adult education programme : A case study. *J Adult Education* 41(1-2) Ja-Fe 1980 p 25-34

Chaudhary, P.N. and Agrawal, K.G.
Professional obsolescence and the role of continuing education. *Indian Educational Rev* 15(1) Ja 1980 p 10-26 refs

Chaudry, Pushpa
Guidance and counselling and education, vocational and personal needs of the students. *J Education and Psychology* 42(4) Ja 1983 p 202-08 refs

Chowdhry, S.K. and Shukla, P.K.
Adult education in Vietnam and Thailand : A study-visit report *Indian J Adult Education* 44(10) Oc 1983 p 19-23
Chaudhary, Sohanvir Singh
Development of educational television in India. *Progress of Education* 60(8) Mr 1986 p 183-87 +
Chaudhary, Sankarrao Kranti Chandra
Revolutionary livable education system. *Educational Rev* 87(6) Je 1981 p 115-16
Chaudhuri, U.S.
Issues and advances in education. Delhi, Ajanta Books Int. 1986, 230p. Rs.125 *Book Rev, Teacher Today* 29(1) Jl-Se 1986 p 106-07
Values in text-books : A research perspective. *Quest in Education* 19(3) Jl 1982 p 255-59 refs
Values in text books : A research perspective. *University News* 23(9) 1 Mr 1985 p 4-5 refs
Chaudhury, U.S. and Bindal, U.R.
Experimental attitude and creativity : A correlational study.
Bhartiya Shiksha Shodh Patrika 1(2) Jl 1982 p 29-32 refs tabs

CHAUHAN - CHOUHAN

Chauhan, C.P. Singh
Computational ability as a determinant of achievement in tenth grade algebra. *Indian Educational Rev* 16(1) Ja 1981 p 43-47
Essay type examinations : Some theoretical issues. *Education Quarterly* 36(1) Ja 1984 p 18-22
Mathematics education and the structure of intellect. *Indian Education* 5(1) My 1979 p 39-43
National talent search : Some issues. *National J Education* 7(1) Se 1984 p 61-64 refs tabs
Structure of intellect abilities as predictors of achievement in tenth grade algebra. *Indian Educational Rev* 18(2) Ap 1984 p 19-27
Chauhan, D.S.
Education and the social process. *Perspectives in Education* 2(4) Oc 1986 p 239-48 tabs
Chauhan, J.P.S. and Chouhan, K.N.K.
Correlates of level of aspiration of high and low milk producers. *Indian Extension Education* 18(3-4) De 1982 p 40-44 refs
Chouhan, K.N.K.
See
Chauhan, J.P.S. *jt. auth.*
Chauhan, M.K. and Sinha, B.P.
Effectiveness of television and its combinations in transfering technological know-how to farmers. *Indian J Extension Education* 15(1-2) Je 1979 p 9-18 refs tabs
Chauhan, M.S. *et al*
Parenting on dimensions of economic well-being, culture and education. *Asian J Psychology and Education* 6(3) Nv 1980 p 17-22 refs

Parenting on dimensions of economic well-beings, culture and education. *J Education and Psychology* 39(3) Oc 1981 p 156-62

Chauhan, S.S.

A textbook of programmed instruction. New Delhi, Sterling. 1978, 186p. Rs.40 *Book Rev, J Indian Education* 5(1) My 1979 p 89-90

Chauhan, S.S. and Harbans Singh

An investigation into the study habits of scheduled and non-scheduled caste adolescents. *J Institute of Educational Research* 10(2) My 1986 p 21-24 refs tabs

An investigation into the study habits of 10 to 12 years of children with regard to their parental profession. *Indian Educational Rev* 17(2) Ap 1982 p 118-22 refs

Chauhan, Sheelendra *et al*

Creative and old age. *Asian J Psychology and Education* 11(3) 1983 p 1-4 refs

Chouhan, V.L. and Rai, G.C.

Attitude of tribal and non-tribal farmers towards adult literacy and improved agricultural practices : A study. *Indian J Adult Education* 45(3) Mr 1984 p 26-31 refs tabs

Chaurasia, G.

From Stockholm to Tbillisi to Jabalpur for environmental education. *Indian Education* 12(11-12) Fe.Mr 1983 p 9-12

Second national seminar on educational journalism, April 10-11, 1981. *Indian Education* 11(3) Je 1981 p 6-7

University system and extension as the third dimension. *J Educational Planning and Administration* 1(1) Oc 1986 p 28-33

Chawla, S.P.

Coordination between education and population policies : A case study of India. New Delhi, NCERT. 1978, 151p. *Book Rev, Education Quarterly* 31(2) Jl 1979 p 43

Chazan, M.

Some of our children : The early education of children with special needs. London, Open Bks. Pub. 1980, 260p. £12 *Book Rev, J Indian Education* 8(4) Nv 1982 p 52-53

Chen, David

See

Adams, Raymond S. *jt. auth.*

Chetenlal, Neera

See

Shah, Anupma *jt. auth.*

Cheyney, Arnold B.

Teaching reading skills through the newspapers. Int Reading Assn. 50p. *Book Rev, Education Quarterly* 31(2) Jl 1979 p 40

Chhabra, Rami

Establishing linkages between women's literacy programmes, status issues and access to family planning. *Indian J Adult Education* 41(4) Ap 1980 p 6-9

Chickermane, D.V.

Elementary non-formal education for out of the school children. *Progress of Education* 54(3) Oc 1979 p 67-69

Experiments in rural education. D.V. Chakermane Res Centre in Rural Education, 1979, 86p. Rs.8 *Book Rev, J Indian Education* 7(2) Jl 1979 p 69-70

Universalising elementary education. Res. Centre, 1983, 40p. *Book Rev, Progress of Education* 57(6) Ja 1983 p 143

Chilana, Mulk Raj

Communication needs to strengthen the educational base : Correspondence courses for primary school teachers. *Indian Education* 11(7) Oc 1981 p 38-44

Innovative inset strategies for quality in education. *Rajasthan Board J Education* 15(2) Ap-Je 1979 p 51-58

Law and the national policy for child welfare : Focus on education and promotional services. *Teacher Today* 25(3) Ja-Mr 1983 p 77-85

Life-long education as the master concept for educational policies. *Education Quarterly* 31 (1) Ap 1979 p 9-10

Primary education in the new educational pattern : Towards broader base and stronger foundation. *Teacher Today* 24(4) Ap-Je 1982 p 30-43

Prominent practices : Baffling dilemmas. *Teacher Today* 21(2) Oc-De 1978 p 76-84

Chilana, Rakesh

Teaching elementary school mathematics. *Primary Teacher* 9(4) Oc 1984 p 30-31

Chiplunkar, V.V.

Education in the Seventh Five Year Plan. *Progress of Education* 59(1) Ag 1984 p 2-5+

Chitnis, Suma

Education of the scheduled castes. *J Higher Education* 1(2) Aut 1975 p 167-78 tabs

Chitraputranarinar, S.

New Educational policy : A university teacher's critical appraisal. *Educational Rev* 92(1) Ja 1986 p 15-17

Chole, R.R. and Rahudkar, W.D.

Source credibility pattern among small and big farmers. *Indian J Extension Education* 14(1-2) Ja-Je 1978 p 50-53

Chomcheun, Thongpleu

Non-formal vocational education programme of Thailand : An overview. *Perspectives in Education* 1(1) Ja 1985 p 55-60

Chopra, H.L.

History : A curse or a boon? *J Indian Education* 8(2) Jl 1982 p 84-86

The use of dictionaries. *Primary Teacher* 9(1) Ja 1984 p 20-21

Chopra, Kamala

A comparative study of the personality traits of effective and less effective secondary school teachers. *National J Education* 6(1) Se 1983 p 34-39

Chopra, R.K.

Child and art education. *Primary Teacher* 4(2) Ap 1979 p 15-18

Identifying creative potential through arts. *Primary Teacher* 10(1) Ja 1985 p 19-24
Illustrations in children's literature. *Primary Teacher* 4(3) Jl 1979 p 7-10
Trends in art education : A perspective. *Primary Teacher* 5(3) Jl 1980 p 27-30
See also
Goyal, J.C. *jt. auth.*
Chopra, Ravi Kanta
Organisational climate in relation to teachers job satisfaction and students achievement. *Indian Educational Rev* 31(3) Oc 1983 p 211-28
Chopra, S.L.
Socio-economic status of the family and social acceptability of the students among their classfellows. *National J Education* 6(2) My 1984 p 40-47 refs
Chouhan
See
Chauhan
Chowdhry
See
Chaudhri
Christian, J.A.
A correlational study of students performance. *J Institute of Educational Research* 4(1) Ja 1980 p 16-19 refs tabs
A study of achievement motivation and its related varibles. *Indian J Psychology and Education* 4(1) Ja 1979 p 58-56 refs
Christian, Jyoti
Dimensions of class-room management. *Educational Rev* 69(7) Jl 1983 p 105-06
Study habits as a function of need achievements (n. Ach). *Asian J Psychology and Education* 11(1) 1983 p 6-12
Clark, Burton R.
The higher education system : Academic organisation in cross national perspective. Berkeley, Univ. of Calif Press. 1983, 315p. *Book Rev, J Higher Education* 9(3) Spr 1984 p 415-18
Clarke, Arthur C.
Star wars and star peace. *New Frontiers in Education* 16(4) Oc-De 1986 p 107-16
Cochrone, N.J.
A cross-cultural comparison of J.R. Kidd's contribution to adult education. *Indian J Adult Education* 46(3) Mr 1985 p 3-13 refs
Cohen, Karen M.
Models of efficient reading. Delaware, Inst. Reading Assn. 1978, viii, 70p. *Book Rev, Indian Educational Rev* 16(2) Ap 1981 p 125-28
Contractor, B.M.
A study of some background factors underlying scholastic performance. *J Education and Psychology* 41(4) Ja 1984 p 215-19 refs
Coombs, Philip H.
Future critical world issues in education : A provisional report of findings. Essex, ICED. 1981. 80p. *Book Rev, Education Quarterly* 34(3) Jl 1982 p 49-51

The world crisis in education : The view from the eighties. New York, OUP. 1985, 353p. *Book Rev, Indian J Adult Education* 47(6) Je 1986 p 31-32; *Progress of Education* 61(3-4) Nv-De 1986 p 101-02

Cross, Jack

Funding the academic scene in the British way. *Progress of Education* 60(10) Ag 1985 p 10-12

Culbertson, Jack

Education and social justice in telematic societies. *Teacher Education* 18(24-25) Jl-Oc 1983 p 25-43 refs

Dabholkar, Devdatta

Education in India : A perspective on policy perspective. *Perspectives in Education* 2(2) Ap 1986 p 67-76 refs

Striving for height in higher education. *J Higher Education* 6(1-3) 1980-81 p 41-50

Dak, A.V.

A comparative study of the efficacy of two teaching methods, the lecture method and the discussion method. *J Education and Psychology* 36(1-2) Ap-Je 1978 p 85-88

Dakh, A.M.

See

Bhllegsonkar, M.G. *jt. auth.*

Dalal, K.C. and Tripathy, P.K.

A study of the ETV programmes under INSAT for the children in the age group, 5-8. *EPA Quarterly Bulletin* 8(3-4) Oc 1985-Ja 1986 p 21-28

Dalin, P.R.

Limits to educational changes. London, Macmillan. 112p. £2.95 *Book Rev, Educational Quarterly* 31(2) Jl 1979 p 43-44; *Indian Educational Rev* 15(1) Ja 1980 p 125-28

Damija, Neelam

See

Malhotra, S.P. *jt. auth.*

Damodharan, G.R.

Presidential address. *Indian J Adult Education* 41(6-7) Je-Jl 1980 p 17

Damyanti and Hira Nand

Characteristics of rural women, key communicators. *Indian J Extension Education* 19(3-4) Se-De 1983 p 47-55 refs tabs

Dandapani, S.

Regular colleges and correspondence courses. *Experiments in Education* 9(5) Jl 1981 p 88-89

Dandekar, V.M.

State level conference on Maharashtra Universities Draft Act, 1984. *Progress of Education* 59(3-4) Oc-Nv 1984 p 53+

Dandiya, Chandra Kanta

National adult education policy approach : Contradictions in assumptions and implementation. *Prasar* 5(3-4) Oc 1977-Ja 1978 p 41-47

Profile of the adult educators in India. *Prasar* 5(1-2) Ap-Je 1977 p 3-14 tabs

Dandwate, D.U.
Composite index of wastage and stagnation. *Research Bulletin* 15(1-2) Mr-Je 1985 p 19-25 tabs
Darji, D.R.
Curriculum and courses with special reference to NCTE frame work. *Teacher Education* 15(14-15) Ja-Ap 1981 p 51-72 tabs
Research curriculum. *J Institute of Educational Research* 4(1) Ja 1980 p 1-7 refs
See also
Joshi, H.R. *jt. auth.*
Panchal, B.R. *jt. auth.*
Shah, Madhu *et al jt. auth.*
Sharma, D.K. *jt. auth.*
Darji, D.R. and Panchal, B.R.
Researches in innovation and change in education. *Asian J Psychology and Education* 7(2) Jl 1981 p 16-26
School management : An old idea with new significance. *Progress of Education* 55(12) Jl 1981 p 315-20
Darji, D.R. and Sharma, D.K.
Decision making and faculty participation. *J Higher Education* 7(3) Spr 1982 p 266-72 refs tabs
Decision and participation in university governance. *Quest in Education* 19(2) Ap 1982 p 160-68 refs
Environmental awareness and education systems. *J Education and Psychology* 40(4) Ja 1983 p 234-38
Resource management for education systems. *Progress of Education* 55(8) Mr 1981 p 211-13+
Towards education management. *Education Quarterly* 32(2) Ap 1980 p 8-12

DAS - DASS
See also
under full name, e.g., Alwar Das
Das, A.K.
Mathematics education in schools : A management approach. *J Indian Education* 5(1) My 1979 p 22-27
Das, Basanta Kumar
See
Chatterjee, Bishwa B. *jt. auth.*
Das, F.S.
Adult education in Rajasthan. *Indian J Adult Education* 40(7) Jl 1979 p 28-30
Dass, J.P. *et al*
Simultaneous and successive congnitive processes. New York, Academic Press. 1979. £17.50 *Book Rev, Indian Educational Rev* 17(4) Oc 1982 p 147-52
Das, J.R.
See
Garg, V.P. *jt. auth.*

Das, K.K.

Changes in education in rural India. *Education Quarterly* 31(2) Jl 1979 p 12-14

Communication media and professional education. *Educational Rev* 86(7) Jl 1980 p 127-29

Das, Lakshahira

Education of the mentally retarded children. *Educational Rev* 85(12) De 1979 p 225-29

Educational programme for rural women. *Educational Rev* 85(8) Ag 1979 p 141-43

Fundamental bases of Gandhian education. *Educational Rev* 88(2) Fe 1982 p 34-36

Prevention and control of delinquency. *Educational Rev* 86(7) Jl 1980 p 133-35 refs

Problems and priorities in the education of women in Assam. *Education Quarterly* 34(2) Ap 1982 p 22-26

Das, N.C.

A study of science achievement in relation to intelligence. *J Education and Psychology* 44(1) Ap 1986 p 11-15 refs

Das, Navendra Prasad

Modern science for children : Need for rational education. *J Indian Education* 5(1) My 1979 p 28-33

Das, P. and Sharma, B.K.

Knowledge gained about agro-forestry plantation in various training programmes. *Indian J Extension Education* 21(1-2) Ja-Je 1985 p 89-90

Das, P.C.

Restructing of courses at degree level. *Progress of Education* 57(3) Oc 1982 p 60-64 + tabs

Selection of courses of study by P.U. (SC) students. *J Higher Education* 5(2) Aut 1979 p 236-42

Teacher education at the secondary level in North Eastern region. *Teacher Education* 14(12-13) Jl-Oc 1980 p 9-22 tabs

Das, R.C. *et al*

Differential effectiveness of micro-teaching components. *Indian Educational Rev* 14(1) Ja 1979 p 69-84 refs

Das, Rama and Dash A. Srikanta

A factor analytic study of a pre-school teacher rating scale. *Asian J Psychology and Education* 7(3) 1981 p 23-27 refs

Das, Rekha

Writing of children's literature can shape the life of a child. *Primary Teacher* 5(4) Oc 1980 p 12-14

Das, Suresh C.

See

Puhan, N. *jt. auth.*

Das, T.

A macroscopic view of population education. *Educational Rev* 92(4) Ap 1986 p 70-71 refs

Das, T.N.

Curriculum theories. *National J Education* 7(1) Se 1984 p 57-60 refs

Primary school science curriculum of Maharashtra. *Primary Teacher* 9(1) Ja 1984 p 13-15

Dasa, P.A.

See

Patel, K.J. *jt. auth.*

Dasgupta, S.K.

Presidential address. *Teacher Education* 14(10-11) Ja-Ap 1980 p 3-7

Dasgupta, S.P.

Opportunity costs of teacher education. *Teacher Education* 17(20-21) Jl-Oc 1982 p 51-64 refs tabs

Dash, A. Srikanta

See

Rama Das *jt. auth.*

Singh, I.S. *jt. auth.*

Dash, Jagannath

Objective-based evaluation. *Educational Rev* 90(5-6) My-Je 1984 p 81-83 refs

Dash, Muralidhar

Educational provisions for the socially disadvantaged children. *Indian Education* 10(9-10) De 1980-Ja 1981 p 30-32

Learning for mastery. *Experiments in Education* 8(12) Fe 1981 p 226-28 refs

Dash, P.C.

See

Panda, K.C. *jt. auth.*

DATT - DATTA - DUTT - DUTTA

See also

under full name surname, e.g., Ruddar Dutt

Datta, Bhabatosh

Social science research : Universities and autonomous institutions. *J Higher Education* 6(1-3) 1980-81 p 15-24

Dutt, Gargi

Higher education in China. *J Higher Education* 5(2) Aut 1979 p 157-66

Dutta, Gitika

Sex differences in creativity among the tribe of Meghalaya. *J Institute of Educational Research* 6(2) My 1982 p 23-26 refs tabs

Dutt, M.L.

Life long education : A conceptual analysis. *Experiments in Education* 10(3) My 1982 p 50-52; *Progress of Education* 57(3) Oc 1982 p 58-59 refs tabs

A study of achievement motivation in relation to sex, intelligence and socio-economic status. *Progress of Education* 58(1) Ag 1983 p 6-12 refs tabs

Which school shall I choose for my child : A study of adjustment among students studying in co-educational schools and in single sex schools? *J Education and Psychology* 41(3) Oc 1983 p 153-58; *Progress of Education* 58(4) Nv 1983 p 87-90 refs tabs

Dutt, N.K.
The psychology of adult learning. *Teacher Today* 25(2) Oc-De 1982 p 72-76 refs
The morale of teachers. *Teacher Today* 27(1) Jl-Se 1984 p 31-34
Datt, Ruddar
Cost and efficiency of the different techniques of education in Delhi University. *J Higher Education* 6(1-3) 1980-81 p 71-82 tabs
Dutta, S.C.
Acknowledgement of the award. *Indian J Adult Education* 47(2-3) Fe-Mr 1986 p 43-47
Develop non-formal structures to educate women. *Indian J Adult Education* 46(4) Ap 1985 p 11-13
Educational programme for tribal population : An alternative strategy. *Indian J Adult Education* 44(4) Ap 1983 p 11-14
Environmental programme for tribal population : A alternative strategy. *Indian J Adult Education* 44(11) Nv 1983 p 8-9+
Folk high schools for India. *Indian J Adult Education* 44(8-9) Ap-Se 1983 p 22-24
General Secretary's report, 1977-78. *Indian J Adult Education* 39(11-12) Nv-De 1978 p 9-12
Hundred per cent literacy : Perspectives and plan. *Indian J Adult Education* 46(2) Fe 1985 p 10-13
The New Education Policy. *Indian J Adult Education* 47(7) Jl 1986 p 11-13+
Training for cadres for adult education : An outline. *Indian J Adult Education* 41(12) De 1980 p 5-8
Workers education : The contribution of IAEA. *Indian J Adult Education* 46(5) My 1985 p 34-36
Dutta, T.
The deprived and neglected child. *Primary Teacher* 10(4) Oc 1985 p 27-29
Dutta, Tapati
Parental involvement in the teaching of handicapped children. *Primary Teacher* 8(3) Jl 1983 p 39-41
Datta, Vibha
Developing an ascendance-submission reaction scale for Hindi - speaking adolescent population. *Indian Educational Rev* 17(4) Oc 1982 p 31-39 refs
Daulat Singh and Singh, V.K., *eds.*
Constraints to production of crops in Uttar Pradesh. Kanpur, U.P. Soc Ext. Education and Rural Devel. 1983. 118p. Rs.85 *Book Rev, Indian J Extension Education* 19(3-4) Se-De 1983 p 97
Dave, Aruna
See
Pathak, Yogini *jt. auth.*
Dave, Arvind
Kohlar comes to the classrooms. *Teacher Today* 22(4) Ap-Je 1980 p 69-73
Micro-teaching-2. *Progress of Education* 53(10-11) My-Je 1979 p 203-07
Dave, Chandrakala
Effective communication in population education. *Progress of Education* 60(3) Nv 1985 p 81-82 +

Dave, Indu

Ring in the new in the past quarter-century. *Teacher Today* 26(1) Jl-Se 1983 p 45-53

Dave, N.K.

Evolution of NSS programme : Alternative approaches. *Prasar* 9(1-4) Ap 1982-Ja 1983 p 20-32

Dave, P.N.

Can we help ourselves teach better : A case study of series of teaching workshops at BITS, Pilani. *J Higher Education* 4(1) Mon 1978 p 108-09

Research on assessing teacher effectiveness in developing countries. *Perspectives in Education* 1(3) Jl 1985 p 195-204 refs

Davies, Bleddyn Pryce

See

Verry, Donald *jt. auth.*

Davies, J. and Natarajan, V.

An investigation into the difficulties encountered by the secondary grade teachers in teaching mathematics in standard VIII in Madras city, schools. *J Educational Research and Extension* 18(2) Oc 1981 p 15-21 refs tabs

Dayakera Reddy, V. and Geethanath, P.S.

Different views on the stages of moral development. *Experiments in Education* 11(4) Je 1983 p 68-71 refs

Dayal

See

under full name/surname, e.g., Maheshwar Dayal

DE - DEY

Dey, Chhaya

Reform entails a predefintion process. *Progress of Education* 56(4) Nv 1981 p 85-88

Secondary classroom teaching in the U.S. and teacher education.

Progress of Education 56(2) Se 1981 p 40-44

De, Deb Kumar

An enquiry into the role of the family and school in leading in children towards the threshold of democratic citizenship. *J Education and Psychology* 41(1-2) Ap-Jl 1983 p 17-22

A study of relation between value development and exposure to an ideal environment. *Quest in Education* 19(1) Ja 1982 p 64-68 refs tabs

A study of values in the process of social change. *Our Education* 3-4 Jl 1983 p 15-20 refs tabs

A test of efficacy of composite social interaction model of teaching first language. *Quest in Education* 19(3) Jl 1982 p 260-68 refs

Dey, Kaberi

The social impact of education. *Educational Rev* 88(8) Ag 1982 p 142-43

Dey, Pradip Kumar

Channels preference for agricultural messages. *Indian J Extension Education* 17(3-4) Se-De 1981 p 17-21 refs tabs

Differential availability and utilisation of agricultural publications : Haringhata study. *Indian J Adult Education* 40(7) Jl 1979 p 36-43 refs tabs

Differential extension contacts. *Indian J Extension Education* 16(3-4) De 1980 p 22-31 refs

De, S.K.

Education via satellites. *Educational Rev* 85(1) Ja 1979 p 1-3

Normal development and growth of human personality. *Educational Rev* 88(8) Ag 1982 p 125-29

Deane, Shobha

The human aspect of systems design in school management. *J Indian Education* 8(2) Jl 1982 p 44-47

Deb, S.R.

Improving school education : The role of magazines. *J Indian Education* 11(3) Se 1985 p 55-57

Deb, Subimal

Study of alpha-beta process in perceiving reinforced social situation. *Our Education* 3-4 Jl 1983 p 35-38 refs tabs

Deb, Subimal and Shah, Varasha M.

Diognostic verbal test of mentally retardents. *Our Education* 5 Jl 1984 p 5-16 refs

Debi

See also

under full name, e.g., Renu Debi

Debi, R.

National Adult Education Programme in Assam. *Indian J Adult Education* 40(4) Ap 1979 p 11-15 refs

D'Cruz, J.V. and Bhagia, N.M.

Accountability in Indian education : Perspectives and practices. *J Educational Planning and Administration* 1(1) Oc 1986 p 1-12 ref

Deenadayala, A.N.

An evaluation of English medium and Tamil medium pupils at X standard level. *Experiments in Education* 7(11) Ja 1980 p 304-07 refs tabs

Deka, Hemchandra

Review of researches in creativity and achievement. *J Educational Research and Extension* 18(3) Ja 1982 p 182-86

Teaching-learning in classrooms. *Educational Rev* 87(9) Se 1981 p 170-73 refs

Deka, Ucharan

Pupil achievement in successive school examinations. *Asian J Psychology and Education* 7(3) 1981 p 33-42 refs figs tabs

Dekhtawala, P.B.

The concept of morale. *New Frontiers in Education* 12(3) Jl-Se 1982 p 53-55

How to improve staff morale? *Asian J Psychology and Edcuation* 11(3) 1983 p 38-40

How to improve staff morale? *Progress of Education* 57(2) Se 1982 p 39-40 +

Leadership style of school principals. *Progress of Education* 61(2) Se 1986 p 40-42 tabs

The measurement of staff morale. *Experiments in Education* 10(9) Nv 1982 p 157-59

Teacher morale in secondary schools of Gujarat. *Quest in Education* 16(2) Ap 1979 p 160-64 refs

Dekhtawala, Pramila

Teacher morale in schools. *Asian J Psychology and Education* 3(3) Nv 1978 p 22-25 refs

De Landsheer, Gilbert

See

Landsheer, Gilbert De

Deo, Pratibha

Revaluation at the university examination : Its effect on the results on candidates. *J Higher Education* 6(1-3) 1980-81 p 83-103 refs tabs

Some personality and adjustment correlates of teaching effectiveness. *J Institute of Educational Research* 4(2) My 1980 p 1-8 refs tabs

Deo, Pratibha and Kamat, Vasudha

Relationship of vocational choice to self concept and socio-economic status. *Research Bulletin* 14(1-2) Mr-Je 1984 p 40-47 refs

Deo, Pratibha and Roy Choudhury, Namita

Social relations of school pupils in a multi-religious secular society. *Indian Educational Rev* 18(3) Jl 1983 p 33-46 refs tabs

Deo, Pratibha and Tripathi, H.B.

A comparison of the learning ability of rural and urban children. *National J Education* 2(1) Se 1979 p 15-23 refs

Deouskar, M.D.

Education and its standard : A study into the problem. *Progress of Education* 54(9) Ap 1980 p 170-77

Non-formal education and rural development through higher education. *Indian J Adult Education* 44(4) Ap 1983 p 31-38 ref

See also

Ahluwalia, S.P. *jt. auth.*

De Rebello, Dasphane M.

Formal schocling and personal efficacy. Sterling, xi, 151p. Rs.45 *Book Rev, Education Quarterly* 31(3-4) Oc 1979-Ja 1980 p 46-47

Desai, A.T.

See

Kulkarni, K.M. *jt. auth.*

Desai, D.B.

Conducting staff meetings in colleges. *New Frontiers in Education* 13(3) Jl-Se 1983 p 42-47

Desai, G.R. and Kaul, P.N.

The summer institute in fisheries : An evaluation. *J Educational Research and Extension* 18(1) Jl 1981 p 43-50 tabs

Desai, G.R. and Rao, M.K.S.

Information sources for technology transfer : A study. *Indian J Adult Education* 44(10) Oc 1983 p 29-31 refs tab

Profile of block demonstration participant farmers : Dharwad study. *Indian J Adult Education* 40(6) Je 1979 p 35-38 refs tabs

Desai, Haribhai G.

Bloom's taxonomy : Review of researches. *Indian Educational Rev* 14(1) Ja 1979 p 115-22 refs

Curriculum development. *Teacher Today* 21(3) Ja-Mr 1979 p 1-5 ref

Criterion referenced testing of written expression at degree level. *J Educational Research and Extension* 20(2) Oc 1983 p 118-24

Evaluation of M.Ed dissertations : How objective are internal examinations. *J Education and Psychology* 38(1) Ap 1980 p 17-21 tabs

How good are long answer questions : A lay man's analysis. *Asian J Psychology and Education* 4(2) Jl 1979 p 38-45 tabs

Psychological needs of college teachers. *J Higher Education* 1(2) Aut 1975 p 250-53 refs

Style manual for dissertations theses. Rajkot, Sourashtra Univ. 1979. 99p. *Book Rev, J Higher Education* 7(3) Spr 1982 p 327-30

Under-achievement syndrome among high ability high school boys. *J Education and Psychology* 35(1-2) Ap-Je 1978 p 4-14 refs

See also

Uchat, D.A. *jt. auth.*

Desai, Haribhai G. and Uchat, D.A.

Measurement of self-concept. *Indian Educational Rev* 17(1) Ja 1982 p 1-11 refs

Self-concept of Harijan students and attitudes of other students towards them. *Indian Educational Rev* 16(3) Jl 1981 p 44-50

Self concept of high achieving and low achieving students of first year classes of colleges. *J Educational Research and Extension* 19(3) Ja 1983 p 155-61

Desai, K.G.

Comparative factorial structure of Raven's standard progressive matrics, Cattell's culture fair scale and Desai-Bhatt group tests in intelligence on samples of various sub-cultures of Gujarat. *J Education and Psychology* 39(1) Ap 1981 p 4-11

Desai, K.G. and Mohini, Chandra

Impact of sex education of the social adjustment of individuals. *J Indian Education* 8(5) Je 1983 p 47-51 refs

Desai, Panna

See

Kaushik, V. Seth *jt. auth.*

Desai, Shanta S.

Defence mechanisms. *Progress of Education* 53(8) Mr 1979 p 10 +

Deshmukh, B.R.

Institutional planning. *Research Bulletin* 14(3-4) Se-De 1984 p 33-49

Deshmukh, K.G.

Genesis and the growth of distance education. *University News* 24(42) 8 Nv 1986 p 3-6

Deshmukh, M.N.

Educational technology for creative education. *Education Quarterly* 32(2) Ap 1980 p 13-17 refs

Educational technology for creative education. *J Indian Education* 5(4) Nv 1979 p 3-11 refs

Evaluation of practice teaching : A simple tool. *Teacher Education* 15(16-17) Jl-Oc 1981 p 57-63

Future education : Some reflections. *Asian J Psychology and Education* 3(3)

Nv 1978 p 42-45

Taxonomy of objections for creative teaching. *Quest in Education* 18(3) Jl 1981 p 235-42 refs

Deshmukh, Manohar

School teachers role in national population education programme. *Indian Education* 11(6) Se 1981 p 20-23; *J Education and Psychology* 41(1-2) Ap-Jl 1983 p 43-46

A study of pre-university students awareness of population problems. *Experiments in Education* 8(10) De 1980 p 188-89

Deshmukh, P.P.

User instructions in effective use of university library in teaching agricultural education and research. *University News* 23(22) 8 Je 1985 p 4-7

Deshpande, K.N. and Mali, A.I.

History of education in middle ages. Pune, Nutan Prakashan. 1985, 124p. Rs. 17.50 *Book Rev, Progress of Education* 61(3-4) Nv-De 1986 p 100

Deshpande, S.W.

Isolation effects in verbal learning. *Indian Educational Rev* 17(4) Oc 1982 p 48-67 refs

Deshpande, S.W. and Kawane, S.D.

Anxiety and serial verbal learning : A test of the Verkes- Dodson law. *Asian J Psychology and Education* 9(3) 1982 p 18-23

Deshpande, Shashi Kala

Relationship between personality of the heads of institutions and organisational climate of their schools. *J Educational and Psychology* 43(1) Ap 1985 p 44-49

A scale to measure individual modernity of teachers. *J Insititute of Educational Research* 8(2) My 1984 p 30-47 refs tabs

Deshpande, Shashi Kala and Tirth, Lalitha V.

A study of the effect of anxiety on teacher behaviour. *Indian Educational Rev* 15(2) Ap 1980 p 1-10 refs

Deshpande, V.T. and Gautam, V.K.

Construction of an achievement test in physics. *Progress of Education* 55(6) Ja 1981 p 165-66 refs

Deva, Indra

Latent function of higher education in India. *J Higher Education* 7(3) Spr 1982 p 211-17 refs

Deva, R.C.

Flanders interaction analysis : A critique. *Educational Rev* 84(11) Mr 1978 p 214-17 refs

Prediction of student teaching success. *J Education and Psychology* 37(2) Jl 1979 p 139-47 refs

Revamping science education. *Educational Rev* 85(4) Ap 1979 p 61-63

Devadas, R.

Whither the National Adult Education Programme. *Indian J Adult Education* 40(10-11) Oc-Nv 1979 p 21-28

Devadas, Rajammal P.

The role of the teacher. *J Educational Research and Extension* 20(1) Jl 1983 p 30-36

Devadasan, E.D.
Meaning and implications of minority rights. *New Frontiers in Education* 12(2) Ap-Je 1982 p 25-29

Devanesan, Chandran
Linking culture and education. *New Frontiers in Education* 10(3) Jl-Se 1980 p 78-82
Motivation and curricular relevance in the context of college autonomy. *New Fontiers in Education* 10(2) Ap-Je 1980 p 44-51
Selectivity and egalitarianism. *New Frontiers in Education* 10(3) Jl-Se 1980 p 71-77

Devi
See under full surname, e.g., Laxmi Devi, A.

Dewal, Onkar Singh
Understanding adults for teaching. *J Indian Education* 6(2) Jl 1980 p 25-29
Understanding adults. *Indian J Adult Education* 41(8) Ag 1980 p 19-22 +

Dhakam, Naaz S.
See
Kesawalla, Gulistan J. *jt. auth.*

Dhaka, Krishna
See
Hooda, R.C. *jt. auth.*

Dhaliwal, Amarjit Singh
See
Savinder Kaur *jt. auth.*

Dhand, Harry
Analysis of projects in social studies education in Canada, 1971-1980. *Educational Ref* 91(11) Nv 1985 p 186-87
Canadian trends in social studies. *Educational Rev* 85(10) Oc 1979 p 185-89 refs tabs
Learning theories and new social studies. *Educational Rev* 85(3) Mr 1979 p 55-59 refs
Social studies projects. *Educational Rev* 85(5) Je 1979 p 85-88 refs
Trends in social studies education : Theses in Canada, 1971-77. *Indian Educational Rev* 16(2) Ap 1981 p 19-28 ft-n

Dhandapani, R.
Education for social development. *Experiments in Education* 10(4) Je 1982 p 74-76 +

Dhar, Trilok N.
The politics of manpower planning : Graduate unemployment and the planning of higher educaiton in India. Calcutta, Minerva. 1974, 284p. Rs.42 *Book Rev, J Higher Education* 1(1) Mon 1975 p 139-41

Dhar, Trilok N. *et al*
Education and employment in India : The policy nexus. Minerva. 1976, 137p. Rs.40 *Book Rev, J Higher Education* 5(2) Aut 1979 p 265-66

Dharmarajan, C.
Autonomous colleges experiment : At what price? *Educational Rev* 87(3) Mr 1981 p 50-51
Creating library consciousness. *Educational Rev* 87(8) Ag 1981 p 141-43
Evaluation of teachers. *Educational Rev* 92(4) Ap 1986 p 65-66

Should attendance be compulsory? *Educational Rev* 91(3) Mr 1985 p 46-47
Teacher versus technology. *Educational Rev* 92(1) Ja 1986 p 7-9
Universalisation of elementary education : A dream. *Educational Rev* 92(7) Jl 1986 p 105-06

Dhatiwal, G.S. and Gursharan Kaur
Problems of pre-adolescence. *Progress of Education* 55(3) Oc 1980 p 62-66

Dhawle, Anand S. and Ghose, Amitabha
A study of the image of Indian journals on management and social sciences in the international academic community. *J Higher Education* 4(3) Spr 1979 p 313-26

Dhillon, D.S. *et al*
Monitoring and evaluation of Integrated Rural Development Programme. *Indian J Extension Education* 21(1-2) Ja-Je 1985 p 48-52

Dhingra, Ranjana
Construction of a scale for measuring the attitude of boys and girls towards complusion of attendance at post graduate level. *Experiments in Education* 7(2) Ap 1979 p 34-36

Dhote, A.K.
SUPW and its implementation. *Rajasthan Board J Education* 20(4)-21(1) Oc 1984-Mr 1985 p 30-35
Vocationalisation of education : A perspective. *J Indian Education* [illegible](1) My 1980 p 14-18
Work education in India : Experiences and plans. *J Indian Education* 10(5) Ja 1985 p 18-24

Dhoundiyal, N.C. and Dhoundiyal, V.
Teacher expectation effects on sociometric indices : Interpretation of findings. *Progress of Education* 59(2) Se 1984 p 26-36 refs

Dhoundiyal, S.N.
Contributions to the concept of a dissociative personality. *National J Education* 3(1) Se 1980 p 55-74 refs

Dhoundiyal, V.
See
Dhoundiyal, N.C. *jt. auth.*

Dias, J.B.
See
Misra, Ajya M. *et al jt. autns.*

Dias, Joseph M.
Our first experiments with micro-teaching. *Progress of Education* 57(11) Je 1983 p 255-57 +
Reactions of our students to micro-teaching. *Progress of Education* 57(12) Jl 1983 p 279-81 + tabs

Dias, Patrick V.
Educational scene : Educational aid and development in the third world. *New Frontiers in Education* 14(4) Oc-De 1984 p 54-65

Dibona, Joseph
One teacher, one school : The Adam's reports on indigenous education in 19th century India. New Delhi, Biblia Impex. 1983, 309p. Rs.150 *Book Rev, Education Quarterly* 36(2) Ap 1984 p 70-72

Digvijaya Singh
Evaluation : A new concept. *Progress of Education* 55(7) Fe 1981 p 192-93
See also
Dongre, P.K. *jt. auth.*
Digvijaya Singh and Mehta, B.N.
Nature of origin need achievement or achievement motivation. *Teacher Education* 15(16-17) Jl-Oc 1981 p 64-68 refs
Dighe, Anita
Promoting adult literacy through mobile creches. *Indian J Adult Education* 41(10) Oc 1980 p 5-14 tabs
Digozzi, Mary Joy
See
Mclachlan, Milla *et al jt. auths.*
Digumasti, Bhaskara Rao
Development of creativity among students. *Experiments in Education* 11(6) Ag 1983 p 100-03 refs
Educational problems of tribal children of forest and hill areas. *Experiments in Education* 12(1) Mr 1984 p 15-18
An evaluative study of the new science curriculum at upper primary level in Andhra Pradesh. *Experiments in Education* 10(8) Oc 1982 p 147-49 refs
Training facilities in mass communication in India. *Experiments in Education* 11(2) Ap 1983 p 21-24

DIKSHIT - DIXIT

Dixit, Ashok K.
See
Pal, Roma *jt. auth.*
Dikshit, D.
Text-books : A perspectival overview. *Education Quarterly* 37(2) Sum 1985 p 22-26
Dixit, Meera
Effect of the variables of sex and marital status on the level of job satisfaction among primary school teachers. *J Institute of Educational Research* 9(1) Ja 1985 p 22-24 ref
Dixit, Ramesh C. and Moorjani, Janki D.
The effect of socio-economic derivation upon the intelligence of the school going children. *J Education and Psychology* 40(4) Ja 1983 p 214-19 refs
Dixit, V.B. *et al*
Adequacy of coverage of extension education course contents in relation to the job of agriculture development officers. *Indian J Extension Education* 21(3-4) Jl-De 1985 p 73-79 tabs
Dileep Kumar and Ahluwalia, S.P.
Development of attitudes towards educational innovations scale (AEIS). *Asian J Psychology and Education* 11(1) 1983 p 28-31
Development of attitudes towards educational innovations scale (S). *Teacher Education* 16(18-19) Ja-Ap 1982 p 33-37 ref
anath, Acharya
'low shall free and compulsory primary education succeed? *Primary*

Teacher 5(4) Oc 1980 p 20-21

Dinesh Chandra

A study of emotive aspects of work perceived by effective as ineffective teachers. *Quest in Education* 17(2) Ap 1980 p 173-80

Dinesh Mohan

Indian education : The anti-cultural involution. *J Higher Education* 9(1) Mon 1983 p 21-34 refs

Divaker, S.M.

Education in modern India : National goals. *J Indian Education* 11(1) My 1985 p 20-24

Student teaching programmes in colleges of education : Some suggestions. *J Indian Education* 5(5) Ja 1980 p 3-7

Diwakaran, R.

A framework for environmental education : An overview. *New Frontiers in Education* 10(2) Ap-Je 1980 p 14-20 refs

Dixit

See

Dikshit

Dnotia, N.C.

Achievement and errors in book keeping of regular and correspondence students of Rajasthan : A comparative study. *Indian Educational Rev* 14(4) Oc 1979 p 99-106 refs tabs

Dodge, C.P.

Non-formal education and rural development : A case from rural Tamil Nadu. *Indian J Adult Education* 41(10) Oc 1980 p 20-23

Dongre, G.S.

Adult education, continuing education and national development. *Teacher Today* 22(3) Ja-Mr 1980 p 23-26

Dongre, P.K. and Digvijaya Singh

Adult education : Problems and solutions. *Indian Education* 10(6) Se 1980 p 10-13

National Adult Education Programme *vis-a-vis* rural development. *National J Education* 3(1) Se 1980 p 33-39 refs tabs

Doraiswamy, Uma

Morality : Can it be taught. *Indian Education* 12(7) Oc 1982 p 15-19

Dorasami, K.

See

Sankaram, V. *jt. auth.*

Dorasami K. and Shankaram, V.

Ways and practices of writing objectives in mathematics. *Indian Educational Rev* 17(1) Ja 1982 p 43-63 refs appdx

Dowsett, Norman C.

The EUE factor of educational psychology. *Bhartiya Shiksha Shodh Patrika* 1(2) Jl 1982 p 1-4 refs

Educational research at the Sri Aurobindo Society. *Bhartiya Shiksha Shodh Patrika* 4(2) Jl-De 1985 p 13-19 refs

Drahman, Tom

See

Levinger, Beryl *jt. auth.*

Drieberg, T.
The man with the tin trunk. *Indian J Adult Education* 40(9) Se 1979 p 41-43

D'Sleneida, Fleur
See
Bhattacharya, S. *jt. auth.*

D'Souza, Claude
The teacher and the student. *New Frontiers in Education* 9(1) Ja-Mr 1979 p 39-51

DUBE - DUBEY

Dubey, R.S.
Persistence, sex-differences and educational performance. *Asian J Psychology and Education* 9(3) 1982 p 24-29

Dubey, Rajeswari
See
Srivastava, G.N. Prakash *jt. auth.*

Dube, S.C.
Environment and the challenge of educational management. *J Higher Education* 6(1-3) 1980-81 p 9-14
Significance of non-formal education. *Indian J Adult Education* 41(4) Ap 1980 p 11-12

Dubey, V.K.
See
Sukhbir Singh *jt. auth.*
Ram Kumar *jt. auth.*

Dubey, V.K. *et al*
A study of the technical knowledge of the stockmen of the ICDPIS. *Indian J Extension Education* 15(3-4) De 1979 p 60-63 tabs

Dudhani, C.M. and Jalihal, K.A.
Extension role expectation and perception of research workers. *Indian J Extension Education* 21(3-4) Jl-De 1985 p 68-72 refs

Duggal, S.P.
Curriculum development and instructional organisation in higher education. *Educational Rev* 89(7) Jl 1983 p 118-21 refs
Improving teacher-education in India. *Educational Rev* 85(4) Ap 1979 p 66-68 refs
Moral and school administration. *Progress of Education* 55(7) Fe 1981 p 181-83 refs
Operational challenge of teacher education. *Educational Rev* 92(3) Mr 1986 p 50-55 refs

[illegible]ulani, S.A.
[illegible]king holidays in Rajasthan schools. *Educational Rev* 85(8) Ag 1979 [illegible]

[illegible]g : Paradoxes of post-literacy work. *J Indian Education* [illegible]42

[illegible]c education. *Experiments in Education* 6(12) Fe 1979

p 219-20 +

Psychological implications in vocal education. *Experiments in Education* 7(6) Ag 1979 p 107-08

Voice culture. Baroda, Indian Musicological Soc. Rs. 25 *Book Rev, Experiments in Education* 8(1) Mr 1980 p 5

Dutt-Dutta

See

Datta

Dwarka Prasad and Verma, S.K.

Some data on the validity of Hindi adaptation of W.A.S.R. verbal section. *J Education and Psychology* 40(1-2) Ap-Jl 1982 p 61-65

Dwarakanath, H.D.

Population education for rural adults. *Education Quarterly* 31(3-4) Oc 1979-Ja 1980 p 11-12

Dwivedi, A.K.

See

Gosain, K.K. *jt. auth.*

Dwivedi, C.B. *et al*

Status pereption of the faculty. *Asian J Psychology and Education* 4(3) nv 1979 p 14-17 refs-ft-n

Dwivedi, Jagdishwar

See

Singh, L.P. *jt. auth.*

Dwivedi, Kamal

Education, sex and cultural background as correlates of values : Aesthetic and social. *J Education and Psychology* 36(4) Ja 1979 p 219-27

Objectives of teacher education. *Teacher Education* 15(14-15) Ja-Ap 1981 p 10-16

The role of prior learning, target learning and set in practice inhibition. *Asian J Psychology and Education* 5(1-3) m1979 p 34-43

Dwivedi, T.N.

See

Sahoo, P.K. *jt. auth.*

Ediger, Marlow

The administrator and the curriculum. *New Frontiers in Education* 14(3) Jl-Se 1984 p 24-35

Administrators and the curriculum. *Experiments in Education* 11(9) Nv 1983 p 149-51

Appraising pupil achievement. *Experiments in Education* 9(7) Se 1981 p 127-29

Appraising the evaluators. *Experiments in Education* 10(10) De 1982 p 189-92 refs

The changing geometry curriculum. *Educational Rev* 88(2) Fe 1982 p 23-25

The community and the curriculum. *Educational Rev* 88(10) Oc 1982 p 170-72 refs

Computer in the curriculum. *Experiments in Education* 11(3) My 1983 p 48-49

Computers and education. *New Frontiers in Education* 13(2) Ap-Je 1983 p 40-44

Criteria in the higher education curriculum. *New Frontiers in Education* 14(4) Oc-De 1984 p 34-39 refs

Criteria to utilise in selecting objectives. *Education Quarterly* 32(2) Jl 1980 25-26

Curriculum and teaching : Some opposing views. *New Frontiers in Education* 14(1) Ja-Mr 1984 p 59-63

Curriculum improvement. *Progress of Education* 57(3) Oc 1982 p 65-68

A curriculum of classics. *New Frontiers in Education* 16(2) Ap-Je 1986 p 1-24

Dewey verses Horns on education. *New Frontiers in Education* 10(9) Jl 1982 p 93-96 refs

Discipline and the school curriculum. *Experiments in Education* 13(3) Jl-Se 1983 p 21-23

Educational objectives and the pupil. *Indian Education* 10(6) Se 1980 p 14-18

Effective communication for positive human relations. *Primary Teacher* 10(1) Ja 1985 p 1-6

Evaluating the curriculum. *Experiments in Education* 12(1) Mr 1984 p 8-9

Evaluating teaching performance. *Education Quarterly* 34(3) Jl 1982 p 15-17

Evaluation and achievement. *New Frontiers in Education* 12(4) Oc-De 1982 p 25-31

Evaluation and the curriculum. *Experiments in Education* 8(12) Fe 1981 p 224-26 refs

Evaluation of achievement. *Education Quarterly* 33(3) Jl 1981 p 24-25 refs

Evaluation of achievement in language arts. *Education Quarterly* 37(2) Sum 1985 p 30-34 refs

Geography and the school curriculum. *Indian Education* 11(6) Se 1981 p 5-9

Geometry in the school curriculum. *Indian Education* 10(7) Oc 1980 p 7-9

Grouping for instruction in the reading curriculum. *Progress of Education* 60(3) Oc 1985 p 50-53 +

Grouping pupils for instruction. *Progress of Education* 58(2) Se 1983 30-35; 58(3) Oc 1983 p 54-57 +

Handwriting and the pupil. *Progress of Education* 58(5) De 1983 p 102-11

Improving the science curriculum. *Experiments in Education* 9(4) Je 1981 p 69-71; 10(3) My 1982 p 52-54

Innovative evaluation procedures in science. *J Education and Psychology* 41(4) Ja 1984 p 178-83 refs

Interest of learners and the curriculum. *Experiments in Education* 9(8) Oc 1981 p 147-48 +

Issues and problems in the social studies. *Experiments in Education* 10(8) Oc 1982 p 141-44

Issues in curriculum development. *Indian Education* 10(3) Je 1980 p 5-10 refs

Issues in teaching geography. *J Indian Education* 8(6) Mr 1983 p 61-64

Issues in teaching science. *Experiments in Education* 11(5) Jl 1983 p 82-85 refs

Issues in the social studies. *Education Quarterly* 33(4) Oc 1981 p 22-23+

Issues in the writing curriculum. *Indian J Adult Education* 42(10) Oc 1981 p 21-24 refs

The language arts curriculum : A philosophical perspective. *Rajasthan Board J Education* 19(1) Ja-Mr 1983 p 1-5

Leadership in curriculum development. *Experiments in Education* 9(12) Fe 1982 p 215-17 refs

Leadership in the curriculum. *New Frontiers in Education* 11(4) Oc-De 1981 p 28-30

The learner and the curriculum. *Experiments in Education* 8(7) Se 1980 p 117-19

A learner centered science curriculum. *Educational Rev* 88(7) Jl 1982 p 111-13 refs

Learning activities and the curriculum. *Educational Rev* 87(10) Oc 1981 p 193-95 refs

Learning activities in the literature curriculum. *Experiments in Education* 11(2) Ap 1983 p 33-34

Listening and the pupil. *Experiments in Education* 11(7) Se 1983 p 121-26; 11(8) Oc 1983 p 140-44

Listening in the school curriculum. *Educational Rev* 87(6) Je 1981 p 108-10

The literature curriculum. *Progress of Education* 58(9) Ap 1984 p 202-07

Mastery learning and the curriculum. *Experiments in Education* 8(3) My 1980 p 47-49 refs

Mathematics : Basics versus an activity centred curriculum. *Experiments in Education* 10(6) Ag 1982 p 105-08; 10(9) Nv 1983 p 171-72+

Mathematics experiences in the curriculum. *Education Quarterly* 34(2) Ap 1982 p 11-13

Micro computers in the mathematics curriculum. *Experiments in Education* 12(4) Je 1984 p 59-63

Mini calculators and the learner. *Experiments in Education* 11(6) Ag 1983 p 103-04

Motivation and the administrator. *EPA Quarterly Bulletin* 8(3-4) Oc 1985-Ja 1986 p 7-11

Objectives and creativity in the curriculum. *Experiments in Education* 9(11) Ja 1982 p 191-94

Objectives and the pupil. *New Frontiers in Education* 13(4) Oc-De 1983 p 7-11

Objectives in the curriculum. *Educational Rev* 88(1) Ja 1982 p 8-10 refs

Objectives in the curriculum. *Progress of Education* 56(2) Se 1981 p 38-39 refs

Organising the curriculum. *Experiments in Education* 8(10) De 1980 p 180-85 refs

Organising the curriculum. *Experiments in Education* 11(12) Fe 1984 p 207-09

Philosophical considerations and committee work in the curriculum. *Indian Educational Rev* 15(3) Jl 1980 p 94-96

Philosophical implications in the school curriculum. *Progress of Education*

57(2) Se 1982 p 35-38

Philosophical implications in the school curriculum. *Teacher Education* 14(10-11) Ja-Ap 1980 p 34-39 refs

Philosophical implications in the teaching of history. *Education Quarterly* 33(1) Ja 1981 p 17-18

Philosophy and goals in the curriculum. *Education Quarterly* 35(1) Ja 1983 p 19-23

Philosophy in the mathematics curriculum. *New Frontiers in Education* 14(2) Ap-Je 1984 p 36-42 refs

Philosophy in the school curriculum. *J Indian Education* 6(5) Ja 1981 p 13-16

Philosophy of education and the reading curriculum. *Indian Education* 10(8) Nv 1980 p 8-11

Philosophy of education and the social studies. *Experiments in Education* 9(5) Jl 1981 p 82-84

Philosophy of micro computer use in the mathematics curriculum *New Frontiers in Education* 15(1) Ja-Mr 1985 p 56-76 refs

Plans of reading instruction. *Rajasthan Board J Education* 20(1-2) Ja-Je 1984 p 30-37

The principal and the curriculum. *Progress of Education* 57(7) Fe 1983 p 159-60

Problem solving in the science curriculum. *Rajasthan Board J Education* 20(3) Jl-Se 1984 p 17-19

Providing for individual differences. *Progress of Education* 55(1) Ag 1980 p 15-18

The psychology of learning and curriculum. *Experiments in Education* 7(11) Ja 1980 p 202-04 refs

Reading and the pupil. *Education Quarterly* 32(2) Ap 1980 p 23-24

Reading in the curriculum. *Rajasthan Board J Educaiton* 16(4) Oc-De 1980 p 10-13

Reading readiness and the learner. *J Indian Education* 10(5) Ja 1985 p 6-11

Reading : The basic vs problem solving. *Educational Rev* 87(9) Se 1981 p 168-70 refs

Role of philosophy in the teaching of science. *New Frontiers in Education* 15(2) Ap-Je 1985 p 29-33 refs

School curriculum in philosophical perspective. *Indian Education* 10(12) Mr 1981 p 13-17

The science curriculum and the learner. *Experiments in Education* 8(6) Ag 1980 p 111-13

The science curriculum : Process of product. *Educational Rev* 87(5) My 1981 p 99

Selecting objectives in the curriculum. *Indian Education* 11(4) Jl 1981 p 11-14

Sequence in the curriculum. *Experiments in Education* 8(2) Ap 1980 p 27

Social sciences and social studies. *Educational Rev* 87(1) Ja 1981 p 7-11 refs

Social studies : Processes versus products. *New Frontiers in Education* 13(1) Ja-Mr 1983 p 13-19 refs

Structural ideas versus creativity in the curriculum. *Experiments in*

Education 10(1) Mr 1982 p 12-14 refs

The teacher and the curriculum. *Experiments in Education* 7(9) Nv 1979 p 151-53 refs

The teacher and the psychology of learning. *Progress of Education* 55(11) Je 1981 p 293-94

Team teaching, committee work and educational concerns. *Experiments in Education* 9(3) My 1981 p 44-45

Values and the curriculum. *New Frontiers in Education* 12(3) Jl-Se 1982 p 23-27; *Research Bulletin* 12(3-4) Se-De 1982 p 3-9

Vocabulary development and the pupil. *Primary Teacher* 9(1) Ja 1984 p 26-32

Which word should pupils learn to spell? *Educational Rev* 86(12) De 1980 p 222-25 refs

World recognition techniques in the reading curriculum. *Progress of Education* 58(12) Jl 1984 p 282-92 refs

Effrakeya, Ose A.

A critical analysis of the problems of implementing Nigeria's new policy on education. *New Frontiers in Education* 16(1) Ja-Mr 1986 p 67-78 refs

Egan, Kievan

Education and psychology : Plato, Piaget and scientific psychology. London, Methuen, xiii, 210p. £4.95 *Book Rev, Education Quarterly* 38(3) Aut 1986 p 54-55

Egglestone, John

Developments in British tertiary education. *J Higher Education* 5(3) Spr 1980 p 301-16 refs tabs

Eheazu, B.A.

Alternative sources of funding the mass literacy campaign in Nigeria : The place of voluntary agencies and social clubs. *New Frontiers in Education* 16(4) Oc-De 1986 p 95-106 refs

Ehsanul Haq

Education and political culture in India : The limits of schooling system and political socialisation. New Delhi, Sterling. 1981, 174p. Rs.60 *Book Rev, Indian Educational Rev* 17(2) Ap 1982 p 136-37; *J Indian Education* 8(1) My 1982 p 79-80; *J Higher Education* 7(3) Spr 1982 p 3330-32

Ekambaram, E.J.

Teaching English by correspondence. *J Higher Education* 5(2) Aut 1979 p 252-55

Ekboti, Eknath

See

Joshi, Sneha *jt. auth.*

Elias, M.

Towards a broader concept of adult education. *Indian J Adult Education* 42(1-2) Ja-Fe 1981 p 21-24

Elizabeth, A.

Learning science through environment. *Primary Teacher* 8(1) Ja 1983 p 7-10

Elliot-Kemp, John

Action learning and action research in education management. *J Education and Psychology* 37(3) Oc 1979 p 151-57 refs

Educational management and educational development. *J Education and Psychology* 37(1) Ap 1979 p 4-9 refs

Organisation development and the technology of school self-evaluation. *J Education and Psychology* 41(1-2) Ap-Jl 1983 p 5-11

Planned change in education. *J Education and Psychology* 27(4) Ja 1980 p 216-24 refs

Towards more effective teaching : A managerial perspective. *J Education and Psychology* 39(3) Oc 1981 p 142-47 refs

Enaohwo, J Okpako

Policy determination and control in Nigerian education. *New Frontiers in Education* 14(3) Jl-Se 1984 p 14-23 refs

Relevance and problems of the system theory in education and administration. *New Frontiers in Education* 15(1) Ja-Mr 1985 p 1-12 refs

Etherington, A.

No education is neutral. *Indian J Adult Education* 40(9) Se 1979 p 1-7

Ezewu, E.E. and Anandi, C.C.

The effects of ecological differences on subject-preference : Academic aspiration and achievement among primary school pupils. *Progress of Education* 60(5) De 1985 p 98-102 refs

Ezikiel, N.

Human relationships in educational administration. *J Indian Education* 8(1) My 1982 p 32-36 ft-n

Fallon, Daniel

The German University : A heroic ideal in conflict with the modern world. Boulder, Colorado Assoc Univ Press. 1980, xii, 14p. £7.95 *Book Rev, J Higher Education* 8(2) Aut 1982 p 252-54

Fareeda Khatoon

Concept of man machine system in education. *Indian Education* 13(8-9) Nv-De 1983 p 12-14

Micro-teaching and teacher education. *Indian Education* 12(10) Ja 1983 p 13-15

Fasokan, Thomas O.

Development of adult education in Nigeria. *Indian J Adult Education* 42(1-2) Ja-Fe 1981 p 13-19 refs tabs

Faust, Paula J., *ed.*

An introduction to fund raising. Washington, CASE. 1983, 92p. $16.50 *Book Rev, Progress of Education* 58(11) Je 1984 p 279

Febbro, Eduardo

Rural development : A common sense approach. *University News* 23(24) 8 Se 1985 p 2+

Educational development of women in India : Problems and suggestions for improvement. *Prasar* 8(3-4) Oc 1981-Ja 1982 p 26-36

Fernandez, Marilyn

University education for what? The case of Kerala women. *New Frontiers in Education* 15(1) Ja-Mr 1985 p 82-85

Fiddy, Rob, *ed.*

In place of work : Policy and provision for the young unemployed. Sussex,

Falmer Press. 193p. *Book Rev, Education Quarterly* 35(4) Oc 1983 p 66-67

Filella, J.

Autonomous colleges : Chips of the old block. *New Frontiers in Education* 10(1) Ja-Mr 1980 p 14-27

College climate : A psycho-social matrix model. *New Frontiers in Education* 13(1) Ja-Mr 1983 p 1-12 refs tabs

College climate : Explorations of a concept. *New Frontiers in Education* 12(3) Jl-Se 1982 p 1-13 refs

College teaching in India : A academic function, a personal relationship or coaching for examinations. *J Higher Education* 3(3) Spr 1978 p 321-31 refs tabs ft-n

Five models of education : A challenge to education. *New Frontiers in Education* 12(4) Oc-De 1982 p 1-13

Institutional vitality. *New Frontiers in Education* 15(2) Ap-Je 1985 p 34-51

Moral and religious education in colleges. *New Frontiers in Education* 12(2) Ap-Je 1982 p 1-13 refs

Values and the teaching learning process : An integrated approach. *New Frontiers in Education* 14(1) Ja 1984 p 1-18

Floud, Jean

Education and equality : A perspective from the West. *J Higher Education* 1(2) Aut 1975 p 199-209 refs

Foat, Patrica Broad, *ed.*

Selection, certification and control : Social issues in educational assessment. Sussex, Falmer Press. 1984, 275p. *Book Rev, Education Quarterly* 37(2) Sum 1985 p 76-77

Fordham, Paul

Participation, learning and change. London, Pall Mall. 1980, 223p. £5 *Book Rev, Indian Educational Rev* 17(1) Ja 1982 p 12-24

Fozdar. Ameeta and Mistry, Veena R.

Evaluative criteria for story books for the age group six to ten years. *Quest in Education* 16(2) Ap 1979 p 142-48

Francis, C.M.

What ails medical education in India : Problems and solutions? *New Frontiers in Education* 10(1) Ja-Mr 1980 p 1-13 refs

Franklin, E.W.

Integration of educational planning with overall planning. *Indian Education* 10(1-2) Ap-My 1980 p 10-14

Froomkin, Joseph T. and others, *eds.*

Education as an industry. Cambridge, Ballinger Pub Co. 1976, 480p. *Book Rev, J Indian Education* 5(4) Nv 1979 p 71-72

Fussell, D. and Quarmby, A.

Study service : A practical interaction of formal and non-formal education. *Indian J Adult Education* 40(4) Ap 1979 p 5-10

Gabriel, P.J.

An alternative teaching experience. *New Frontiers in Education* 11(4) Oc-De 1981 p 42-46 refs

Gabrial, P.J. and Pillai, J.K.

The effectiveness of modular scheduling in higher education. *J Higher Education* 6(1-3) 1980-81 p 128-31 refs

The new structure of Nigerian educational system. *EPA Quarterly Bulletin* 7(3-4) Oc 1984-Ja 1985 p 8-16 refs

Gadewar, A.U. *et al*

Awareness of farm technology among small farmers. *Indian J Adult Education* 43(7) Jl 1982 p 9-12 refs

Gadgil, A.V.

A.N. Jha Memorial Lecture : Secondary education : Some issues. *Indian Education* 12(11-12) Fe-Mr 1983 p 35-49

Educational journalism in India. *Indian Education* 11(3) Je 1981 p 13-15

Perceptions of the middle class young women. *Research Bulletin* 16(1-2) Mr-Je 1986 p 25-34

Secondary education : Some issues. *Progress of Education* 57(10) My 1983 p 218-23

Gaind, D.N.

Educational innovations in India. *Rajasthan Board J Education* 16(1-2) Ja-Je 1980 p 16-25

Social sciences : New trends in curriculum. *Education Quarterly* 35(3) Jl 1983 p 14-16

Teaching of history from world perspective. *Teacher Today* 23(1) Jl-Se 1980 p 1-6

Gajanayake, Jaya

People's participation in rural development : The rationale and significance. *Indian J Adult Education* 45(3) Mr 1984 p 13-16 +

GAKHAR - GAKHER

Gakhar, S.

Mathematical concepts learning as determined by feedback and non-feedback conditions. *Educational Rev* 89(10) Oc 1983 p 168-70 refs tabs

Study of the effect of socio-economic status on the mathematical achievement of English grade children. *J Institute of Educational Research* 7(2) My 1983 p 12-15

Gakhar, S. and Tripathi, Abha

A comparative study of organisational climate of government and non-government schools. *J Institute of Educational Research* 7(3) Se 1983 p 32-37

Gakhar, S.C.

Effect of teachers variables on the acquisition of mathematical concepts. *Experiments in Education* 11(6) Ag 1983 p 105-09 refs tabs

Intelligence, creativity and achievement in mathematics : A regression analysis. *J Institute of Educational Research* 9(3) Se 1985 p 17-20 refs tabs

Mathematical achievement among children of working and non-working mothers in relation to parents encouragement. *Progress of Education* 57(11) Je 1983 p 250-52 refs tabs

A study of acquisition of mathematical concepts among 8th graders of different types of schools. *Experiments in Education* 10(9) Nv 1982 p 164-67 refs

Gakher, Subhash

See

Joshi, J.N. *jt. auth.*

Gakhar, Sudesh

Motivators and job satisfaction : A theoretical analysis. *Indian Educational Rev* 20(3) Jl 1985 p 23-31

See also

Sharnajit Kaur *jt. auth.*

Gakhar, Sudesh and Jagdip Kaur

Figural creativity and concrete operational logic as correlates of school achievement in IV, V, and VI grade children. *J Education and Psychology* 40(3) Oc 1982 p 162-68

Gakhar, Sudesh and Prabhu, Swaym

The effect of intro-task non-specific competition paired associate learning in relation to intelligence and ego-strength. *J Education and Psychology* 38(4) Ja 1981 p 235-41 refs

Gakhar, Sudesh *et al*

Job satisfaction among primary middle and secondary school teachers. *J Institute of Educational Research* 8(2) My 1984 p 1-6 refs

Galabawa, J.C.

The limits of the manpower approach *Perspectives in Education* 2(4) Oc 1986 p. 231-37 refs

Planning education for development in Tanzania : The limits of the manpower approach. *Perspectives in Education* 2(4) Oc 1986 p 231-37 refs

Gamage, D. Thenuwara

An historical review of struggles for student power : Where the oppressed of all ages once became the opporessed. *Perspectives in Education* 2(4) Oc 1986 p 195-212 refs

A review of problems, issues and government policies on higher education in Sri Lanka. *Perspectives in Education* 1(2) Ap 1985 p 75-90 refs ft-n

Gambhir, V.G.

See

Kulkarni, V.G. *jt. auth.*

Ganapathy, M. and Raghuram Singh, M.

The impact of socio-economic conditions on achievement. *Experiments in Education* 9(8) Oc 1981 p 144-47 tabs

Gandhi, Indira

Exchange of views on education. *J Educational Research and Extension* 20(2) Oc 1983 p 85-91

Gandhi, K.A.

Dogmatism and teaching experience as determinants of pupil control ideology. *J Education and Psychology* 38(3) Oc 1980 p 189-93 refs tabs

The impact of pupil control ideology, teachers locus of control and quality of school life on academic achievement of pupils. *Experiments in Education* 10(10) De 1982 p 184-89 refs tabs

Organisational climate of schools and work alienation : A comparative analysis. *J Educational Research and Extension* 18(2) Oc 1981 p 22-30 refs tabs

Personality characteristics of teaching staff and organisational climate of schools. *Experiments in Education* 10(6) Ag 1982 p 110-16 refs

The quality of school life and pupil control ideology. *J Educational Research and Extension* 17(3) Ja 1981 p 142-49 refs tabs

School climate and teacher absenteeism. *J Education and Psychology* 40(1-2) Ap-Jl 1982 p 90-95

School climate and teacher absenteeism. *Progress of Education* 57(6) Ja 1983 p 137-41 refs tabs

Strategy for changing the school climate. *Quest in Education* 16(3) Jl 1979 p 202-08 refs

A study of academic performance in relation to teacher-pupil-relations. *Progress of Education* 56(5) De 1981 p 110-13 refs tabs

Teaching styles of student-teachers exposed to microteaching approach and traditional approach. *Experiments in Education* 10(1) Mr 1982 p 3-6 refs

Gandhi, K.L.

Unfair means in examinations. *J Indian Education* 8(4) Nv 1982 p 28-32

Gandhi, Kishore

Issues and choices in higher education. Delhi, B.R. Pub. 1977, 195p. Rs.55 *Book Rev, Education Quarterly* 34(2) Ap 1982 p 52-53

Gandhi, Pritty

Academic achievement in relation to achievement motive, affiliation motive and power motive. *EPA Quarterly Bulletin* 6(1) Ap 1983 p 29-35

See also

Rai, Kamala *jt. auth.*

Gandhi, Sandhya

Open University and gram swaraj. *Indian Education* 13(8-9) Nv-De 1982 p 5-8

GANESAN - GANESHAN

Ganeshan, R. *et al*

Subject-matter training of Gram Sevaks. *Indian J Extension Education* 16(1-2) Je 1980 p 51-54 tabs

Ganeshan, Raja

The no-man's land between law and education. *Experiments in Education* 8(6) Ag 1980 p 99-102

Ganesan, Vadagiri

Contributions of Wallach and Kogan to creative research. *Indian Educational Rev* 14(1) Ja 1979 p 131-35

Ganeswara Rao, K.

See

Vasudeva Rao, B.S. *jt. auth.*

Gangopadhyay, S.R.

Choices in African education. *Teacher Today* 21(2) Oc-De 1978 p 70-75

Imbalance of educational opportunities and the implications for national development. *Teacher Today* 26(2) Oc-De 1983 p 78-99 refs tabs

Vocationalisation of education : Historical perspective. *Teacher Today* 27(3) Ja-Mr 1985 p 53-58

Ganguli, P.K.

Anxiety and academic achievement. *Asian J Psychology and Education* 7(2) Jl 1981 p 39-43

Anxiety and academic achievement. *J Educational Research and Extension* 19(4) Ap 1983 p 233-38 refs

Concept of social intelligence. *Quest in Education* 17(2) Ap 1980 p 188-94

Programmed learning : Potential in India. *Educational Rev* 85(9) Se 1979 p 170-73

Social intelligence testing : A retrospect. *J Educational Research and Extension* 18(1) Jl 1981 p 51-63

Social intelligence vis-a-vis abstract and mechnical intelligence. *Asian J Psychology and Education* 11(2) 1983 p 28-32

Ganguli, P.K. *et al*

Adult education in Bihar : An appraisal. *Indian J Adult Education* 46(2) Fe 1985 p 14-20

Ganguli, Prabuddha

Science teaching in rural India : An experiment. *J Higher Education* 1(2) Aut 1975 p 266-67 refs

Garden, R., *ed.*

Teacher education in developing countries : Prospects for the eighties. London, Univ of London, *Book Rev, Progress of Education* 56(11) Je 1982 p 281

Garg, Chandra

See

Sharma, D.K. *jt. auth.*

Garg, Hem Raj

Developing cleanliness habits among children. *Primary Teacher* 9(3) Jl 1984 p 29-30

Mathematics can be fun. *Primary Teacher* 5(2) Ap 1980 p 28-32

New challenge in teaching arithmetic. *Primary Teacher* 10(2) Ap 1985 p 31-32

Garg, Kailash Chandra

Peer review in sciences. *J Higher Education* 7(3) Spr 1982 p 321-23 refs

Garg, Kshama

The effect of practical behaviour of parents upon the class adjustment of pre-adolescent students. *Asian J Psychology and Education* 11(2) 1983 p 19-22

Physical environment and class adjustment. *Educational Rev* 86(3) Mr 1980 p 50-54

Self-esteem and academic achievement among adolescents. *Progress of Education* 55(6) Ja 1981 p 146-49 refs tabs

Garg, Mithlesh

Manipulative drive and rearing behaviour. *Asian J Psychology and Education* 3(2) Jl 1978 p 15-18 refs

Garg, V.P.

Budget formulation for educational planning. *EPA Quarterly Bulletin* 7(1-2) Ap-Jl 1984 p 41-50 refs

Cost-analysis for educational planning : Some basic issues. *New Frontiers in Education* 13(4) Oc-De 1983 p 40-49

The cost analysis in higher education. New Delhi, Metropolitan. 1985, 216p. Rs.80 *Book Rev, Perspectives in Education* 1(3) Jl 1985 p 205-06

Courses in educational administration : New dimensions. *J Educational Planning and Administration* 1(1) Oc 1986 p 63-66

Economic versus educational viability : Dilemma in higher education. *EPA Quarterly Bulletin* 6(2) Jl 1983 p 22-30 ref

Futuristic scenario of educational system : A viewpoint. *J Indian Education* 5(4) Nv 1979 p 56-60 refs

Personalising education : A perspective. *Teacher Today* 22(2) Oc-De 1979 p 44-55

Private costs in higher education. *J Higher Education* 8(2) Aut 1982 p 220-27 tabs

Universalisation of elementary education in India : Past experiences, future strategies. *Educational Quarterly* 36(2) Ap 1984 p 1-9

Garg, V.P. and Das, J.R.

Educational wastage : A field study. *Primary Teacher* 9(3) Jl 1984 p 20-23

Gargoti, M.G. Mall

Factors affecting the retention of literacy among neo-literates. Asha Pra. 1979, 200p. Rs.30 *Book Rev, Indian Educational Rev* 15(3) Jl 1980 p 124-25; *J Indian Education* 6(5) Ja 1981 p 53; *Progress of Education* 54(10-11) My-Je 1980 p 214

Garsole, S.G.

Geographic thought as expressed in Marathi text-books in geography, 1841-1941. *Progress of Education* 55(12) Jl 1981 p 325-27

Gaur, J.S. and Mathur, Punima

Effect of personality factors on the level of occupational aspirations of higher secondary school students of Delhi : A study in sex differences. *Asian J Psychology and Education* 3(2) Jl 1978 p 1-14 refs tabs

Gaur, R.S.

Employment to educated masses. *Education Quarterly* 31(3-4) Oc 1979-Ja 1980 p 28-30; *Teacher Education* 13(8-9) Jl-Oc 1979 p 32-38

Personality characteristics of urban and rural adolescent students. *Indian Educational Rev* 15(1) Ja 1980 p 119-22

Value system in the personality of urban and rural adolescents. *J Indian Education* 5(6) Mr 1980 p 11-13 refs

Gautam, R.P.

Family background and military leadership qualities. *J Indian Education* 8(6) Mr 1983 p 27-34 refs tabs

General awareness of military career among rural and urban students. *Indian Educational Rev* 14(1) Ja 1979 p 123-30

Knowledge of military career as a determinant of its choice by higher secondary students. *J Indian Education* 6(1) My 1980 p 8-13 appdx

Gautam, V.K.

Construction of diagonoestic test in physics for class VII. *Indian Education* 11(4) Jl 1981 p 22-23

See also

Deshpande, V.T. *jt. auth.*

Gawade, P.L.
Village school an agent of social change. *Progress of Education* 61(4-5) Nv-De 1986 p 74-76 +

Gaya, Toshan Kanta
See
Verma, Lokesh K. *jt. auth.*

Gaytonde, S.N.
Organisation of the teaching of music in schools. *Progress of Education* 53(4) Nv-De 1978 p 86-91 annex

Gearheart, Bill R. and Weishatin, Mel W.
The handicapped student in the regular classroom. Missouri, Mosby. 1980, 303p. *Book Rev, J Indian Education* 8(1) My 1982 p 80-81

Gedam, K.M.
An approach to vocationalisation of higher secondary education in the state of Maharashta. *Education Quarterly* 38(1) Spr 1986 p 24-27

Geethanath, P.S.
Why do not they go to school. *Experiments in Education* 10(9) Nv 1982 p 169-71 tabs
See also
Dayakera Reddy, V. *jt. auth.*

Gel, Vineeta
See
Jha, J.S. *jt. auth.*

Gelpi, Ettore
Intercultural cooperation in higher education *J Higher Education* 993 Spr. 1984 p. 323-32 refs

George, Mathew
Creative teacher personality and class room teaching behaviour of secondary school teachers. *J Educational Research and Extension* 17(3) Ja 1981 p 150-53 refs tabs
The effect of microteaching and integration of skills on teaching self-concept of student teachers. *J Educational Research and Extension* 18(2) Oc 1981 p 31-39; 19(3) Ja 1983 p 129-37 refs tabs
Institutional plan of the integrated teacher education programme proposed for B.Ed course. *Quest in Education* 18(1) Je 1981 p 53-60

George, Rita and Sudha, B.G.
Aptitude in teaching and job satisfaction among teachers. *J Institute of Educational Research* 10(2) My 1986 p 16-20 refs tabs

George, V.D. and Samsananda Raj, H.
Some adjustment traits of behavioural problem students. *J Institute of Educational Research* 7(3) Se 1983 p 38-42

Gerardi, Robert, J.
Let's have a national retirement programme for mobile educators. *Progress of Education* 55(11) Je 1981 p 303-04
Superintendent : Movers or stayers? *Progress of Education* 55(3) Oc 1980 p 74-76
See also
Benedict, Gary C. *jt. auth.*

Gerardi, Robert J. and Benedict, Gary C.
Stress on the headmasters family. *EPA Quarterly Bulletin* 6(2) Jl 1983 p 41-47 refs

Ghadially, Rehana
See
Khalid Ahmed, Kazi *jt. auth.*

Ghanchi, Dawoodbhai A.
Work ethics for distance education. *University News* 24(42) 8 Nv 1986 p 129-31 refs

Ghonta, Ramesh
Art as unifying principle in education. *Progress of Education* 61(1) Ag 1986 p 17-19+

GHOSE - GHOSH

Ghose, A.M.
Modernisation of our courses and syllabi in the humanities and the social sciences. *J Higher Education* 4(1) Mon 1978 p 75-80

Ghosh, B.
Development of books for professional subjects. *University News* 21(24) De 1983 p 868

Ghosh, B.N.
Lectures on scientific method. New Delhi, Sterling. *Book Rev, J Insititute of Educational Research* 10(2) My 1986 p 25

Ghosh, D.K.
Aspect and modes of external influence in the university administration. *EPA Quarterly Bulletin* 7(3-4) Oc 1984-Ja-1985 p 26-36

Ghosh, Pansy Chaya
Educational pioneers : Episodes from Calcutta history. *New Frontiers in Education* 9(4) Oc-De 1979 p 28-36

Ghose, Papiya and Khurana, Kiran
A study of the effects of socio-economic status (SES) and sex on the levels of self concept, anxiety and adjustment. *J Education and Psychology* 44(3-4) Jl-De 1986 p 141-47

Ghosh, Ratna
See
Kundu, Ramanath *jt. auth.*

Ghosh, S.N.
Key to value orientation. *New Frontiers in Education* 14(1) Ja-Mr 1984 p 38-43

Ghosh, Sailendra Kumar
A new method for the computation of average deviation from a frequency distribution. *Our Education* 1 Jl 1980 p 48-53 refs

Ghosh, Sunanda
An assessment of the relation between teacher-trainees' attitudes and performance in theory and practice of teaching. *Indian Educational Rev* 17(4) Oc 1982 p 20-30 refs tabs

Ghosh, Sunanda and Gordon, Marie
Self concept and vocational aspirations among girls. *J Educational Resarch*

and Extension 18(1) Jl 1981 p 24-27 refs tabs

Ghosh, Sunanda and Sampoornam, K.V.

Effects of TV viewing on achievement. *J Institute of Educational Research* 6(2) My 1982 p 30-46 refs tabs

Gidadhubli, R.G.

Some aspects of higher education in the Soviet Union. *J Higher Education* 2(2) Aut 1976 p 149-65 refs tabs

Gilham, Bill, *ed.*

Problem behaviour in the secondary school. London, Croom Helm. 195p. £5.95 *Book Rev, Education Quarterly* 34(1) Ja 1982 p 46-47

Gill, Surjit Singh

See

Arneja, C.S. *jt. auth.*

Momi, G.S. *et al jt. auth.*

Raghbir Singh *jt. auth.*

Singh, N.P. *jt. auth.*

Gillette, Arthur and Ryan, John

Eleven issues in literacy for the 1990s. *Indian J Adult Education* 45(4) Ap 1985 p 5-19 refs

Girdhari, D.G.

Changing pattern of business education in India. *J Indian Education* 10(6) Mr 1985 p 39-47

Giri, Mehtab

The changing pattern of university academic control over affiliated colleges. *J Higher Education* 6(1-3) 1980-81 p 151-53

Girija, P.R.

See

Bhadra, B.R. *jt. auth.*

Girijesh Kumar

Importance of play for creativity. *Primary Teacher* 10(1) Ja 1985 p 14-15

Girish Bala

A comparative study of adjustment pattern of girls in co-educational colleges and women colleges. *J Higher Education* 3(3) Spr 1978 p 405-08 refs

Girja Kumar and Krishna Kumar

Philosophy of user education. New Delhi, Vikas Pub. 1983, 247p. Rs.125 *Book Rev, J Higher Education* 9(2) Aut 1982 p 289-91

Glasser, William

Schools without failure. New York, Harper. 1969, 266p. *Book Rev, Teacher Today* 23(3) Ja-Mr 1981 p 155-59

Gleazer, Edmund J.

Community colleges. *J Indian Education* 6(1) My 1980 p 30-37

Gnanapragasem, N.S.

Guidelines for continuous assessment. *Educational Rev* 85(12) De 1979 p 231-33

Question bank in chemistry. *Educational Rev* 90(6) Se 1984 p 125-27

Three years of college autonomy. *Educational Rev* 87(9) Se 1981 p 164-65

Godbole, R.D.

A close look at sample 'multiple' - choice questions of ETS. *J Higher Education* 7(3) Spr 1982 p 317-19

Importance of language in answering examination questions. *Progress of Education* 58(5) De 1983 p 112-13+

Merit list on the basis of 2-score is not valid. *J Higher Education* 9(2) Aut 1983 p 269-71

Multiple choice and short answer questions : Effect of study habits of students. *Progress of Education* 55(7) Fe 1981 p 184-95

Objective versus essay examinations. *Progress of Education* 57(1) Ag 1982 p 13-15+

Scaling of examination *Progress of Education* 57(5) De 1982 p 108-10

GOEL - GOYAL

Goel, B.P.

Private cost of postgraduate education. *J Indian Education* 11(2) Jl 1985 p 58-63 refs

Goyal, Bhagat Ram

Educating Harijans. Gurgaon, Academic Press (India). 129p. Rs.50 *Book Rev, Progress of Education* 56(8) Mr 1982 p 200-01

Goel, D.R.

Colleges of education and school broadcasts. *J Indian Education* 5(5) Ja 1980 p 65-72

Foreign students : A study. *Experiments in Education* 8(4) Je 1980 p 74-76; 8(5) Jl 1980 p 93-96; 8(6) Ag 1980 p 108-11

Headmasters and school broadcasts. *Progress of Education* 54(12) Jl 1980 p 221-28

Radio-cum-correspondence in service teacher training courses in India. *Experiments in Education* 10(3) My 1982 p 54-57

Reactions of students towards private tuitions. *Experiments in Education* 8(9) Nv 1980 p 161-66 tabs

School broadcast programme : Some observations. *J Indian Education* 6(3) Se 1980 p 22-26

School broadcasts for primary schools in Andhra Pradesh. *Experiments in Education* 7(8) Oc 1979 p 141-45

Script writers for school broadcasts in India. *J Indian Education* 6(6) Mr 1981 p 28-35

Students and school broadcasts. *Progress of Education* 54(3) Oc 1979 p 50-58

Students and social life : A study. *Experiments in Education* 7(4) Je 1979 p 73-74

A study of school broadcasts in Gujarat. *Educational Rev* 85(11) Nv 1979 p 203-05

A study of school broadcasts in Haryana. *Experiments in Education* 7(5) Jl 1979 p 80-86 refs

Teachers and school broadcasts : *Progress of Education* 54(1) Ag 1979 p 12-20

See also

Shah, M.M. *et al jt. auth.*

Sudama, G.R. *jt. auth.*

Goyal, J.C.

Relationship between teacher attitude and pupil achievement. *J Educational Research and Extension* 20(3) Ja 1984 p 158-66

Goyal, J.C. and Ajit Singh

Experimentation in secondary schools. *Quest in Education* 17(3) Jl 1980 p 228-41 refs

Non-enforcement of conditions of affiliation in colleges of education : A study of reasons. *Indian Educational Rev* 17(3) Jl 1982 p 62-64 refs

Goyal, J.C. and Chopra, R.K.

Teacher education in the context of 10+2 pattern : A case study. *Quest in Education* 19(1) Ja 1982 p 42-57 refs tabs

Goyal, Mahendra Kumar

An estimate of the teachers aggressiveness in schools : A critical approach. *Rajasthan Board J Education* 21(2) Ap-Je 1985 p 15-22

Goyal, R.P.

An analysis of relationships between creativity and academic achievement of eleventh graders. *Educational Rev* 90(5-6) My-Je 1984 p 84-87 refs

Creativity in relation to teaching subjects offered by student teachers. *J Education and Psychology* 41(4) Ja 1984 p 209-14

Personality correlates of creativity in prospective female teachers. *J Educational Research and Extension* 20(3) Ja 1984 p 188-96

Relationships between creativity and intelligence of eleventh grade boys. *Progress of Education* 58(1) Ag 1983 p 13-16 tabs

Goel, S.C.

Issues and options in higher education in India. *New Frontiers in Education* 11(3) Jl-Se 1981 p 26-32

Goyal, S.M.

Systems approach in education. *J Indian Education* 6(3) Se 1980 p 27-30

Goel, Sushil Kumar and Sen, Arun K.

A study of behavioural rigidity among youth adults. *J Education and Psychology* 43(1) 1985 p 34-36

Goel, Sushma

An investigation into the relationship between teachers factual knowledge of teaching practice and their classroom verbal interactions. *J Education and Psychology* 38(3) Oc 1980 p 166-71 refs tabs

Goel, Ved P.

Laboratory instruction in science : Its implications in our schools. *J Indian Education* 5(1) My 1979 p 34-38

Goetha, S.

See

Sudha, B.G. *jt. auth.*

Gogale, S.B.

A study of educational qualifications of teachers of StdX from selected districts of Marathwada. *Progress of Education* 58(10) My 1984 p 231-33 tabs

Goldschmidt, Dietrich

The university as an institution : Present problems and future trends. *J Higher Education* 9(1) Mon 1983 p 65-75 refs tabs

Gomathi, M.

Communication in pedagogy. *Experiments in Education* 8(7) Se 1980 p 124-26

How to teach history? *Educational Rev* 87(5) My 1981 p 84-86

Gomez, R.

Adult education in Tamil Nadu : The Sixth Year Plan : An outline. *Experiments in Education* 10(3) My 1982 p 43-50 refs tabs

Education as a tool for development. *Educational Rev* 98(10) Oc 1982 p 179-81; 88(11) Nv 1982 p 195-98 refs

National Adult Education Programme in Tamil Nadu. *Experiments in Education* 7(9) Nv 1979 p 160-75

Gopala Krishna

Research on counsellor's characteristics : A summary. *Quest in Education* 16(4) Oc 1979 p 335-43

Gopalakrishnan, Chitra

Goals of curriculum in schools. *Education Quarterly* 34(3) Jl 1982 p 20-22

Goals of curriculum in schools. *Indian Education* 11(8-9) Nv-De 1981 p 41-45

Gopalakrishnan, M.

Education and social and moral values : Lessons of history. *Indian Education* 12(3-4) Je-Jl 1982 p 12-16

Gopaliah, G.

A study of moral judgement in children. *Experiments in Education* 8(11) Ja 1981 p 205-10 refs

Gopinatha Rao, C.

Contemporary issues in primary education. *Experiments in Education* 6(6) Ag 1978 p 99-101

Gor, Indravadan M.

New dimensions in the curriculum of teacher education programme. *Progress of Education* 53(8) My 1979 p 159-66

Gordon, Marie

See

Ghosh, Sunanda *jt. auth.*

Gore, M.S.

The education explosion. *University News* 23(28) 23 Jl 1985 p 9-14

Gosain, K.K. and Dwivedi, A.K.

Performance of adolescents on a linear programme in relation to their level of aspiration. *J Institute of Educational Research* 6(1) Ja 1982 p 6-9 refs tabs

Goswami, Pramod Kumar

A study of self concept of adolescents and its relationship to scholastic achievement and adjustment. *Indian Educational Rev* 15(1) Ja 1980 p 95-98

Govinda, R.

Mathematical models in educational research : Issues, problems and prospects. *Perspectives in Education* 1(4) Oc 1985 p 257-66

School education in rural areas : Some ideas and issues. *New Frontiers in Education* 10(4) Oc-De 1980 p 65-72 refs

Govinda, R. and Menon, S.B.
Professional journals in education in India : Some issues. *J Indian Education* 11(3) Se 1985 p 13-20

Govinda, R. *et al*
The scientific method in educational research : Need for rethinking. *New Frontiers in Education* 14(4) Oc-De 1984 p 40-45

Govindarajacharyulu, M.
Unit plan for teacher education in mathematics, 1978-79. *Experiments in Education* 9(1) Mr 1981 p 9-15

Goyal
See
Goel

Graves, Donald H.
Balance the basics : Let them write. New York, Ford Foundation. 1978. 32p. $2 *Book Rev, J Indian Education* 6(4) Nv 1980 p 58-59

Green, Joe L., *ed.*
See
Belok, Michael V. *jt. auth.*

Gregorios, Paulos Mar
Towards some clean and achievable goals for a national educational programme for India. *New Frontiers in Education* 16(3) Jl-Se 1986 p 11-18

Grewal, Avinash
Approaches to and methods of teaching the adults. *Education Quarterly* 32(1) Ja 1980 p 5-7
Relationship between scientific creativity and generalised attitude towards science. *J Education and Psychology* 78(2) Jl 1980 p 399-403

Grewal, Avinash and Gupta, Sarojini
Effect of training the mentally retarded children on certain tasks. *Research Bulletin* 12(1-2) Mr-Je 1982 p 19-26 refs
Information processing and conservation of quantity among the mentally retarded children. *J Institute of Educational Research* 7(3) Se 1983 p 10-14

Grewal, G.S.
In-service education of teachers at the centres of continuing education. *J Indian Education* 8(2) Jl 1982 p 69-73

Grewal, J.S.
Early childhood education : Foundations and practice. Agra, Nat Psychol Corpn. 1984. Rs.120 *Book Rev, Teacher Today* 28(1) Jl-Se 1985 p 107-09
Identification and prevention of potential dropouts at the elementary stage. *Primary Teacher* 9(1) Ja 1984 p 16-19
Special education in Japan. *J Indian Education* 8(3) Se 1982 p 48-51
See also
Jhaj, Didar Singh *jt. auth.*
Rajput, J.S. *jt. auth.*

Grewal, J.S. and Gupta, V.P.
Evaluation in non-formal education. *Education Quarterly* 34(2) Ap 1982 p 29-30

Grewal, J.S. and Subramaniam, K.B.
A correlational study of internal and external test performance. *J Educational Research and Extension* 18(2) Oc 1981 p 55-59 tabs
Grewal, S.S. and Kirpal Kaur
Achievement motivation and anxiety as related to academic success in mathematics. *Experiments in Education* 8(12) Fe 1981 p 221-24; 10(2) Ap 1982 p 34-37 refs
Griggs, Audrey
Teachers centres : The British model. *Rajasthan Board J Education* 15(4) Oc-De 1979 p 1-5
Grover, I.
Understanding processes of universalisation of education. *Primary Teacher* 11(4) Oc 1986 p 15-16
Wastage in primary education : A global perspective. *J Indian Education* 12(3) Se 1986 p 23-29 refs tabs
Gugnani, Hans Raj
Field-work in adult education. *Indian J Adult Education* 41(6-7) 1980 p 19-24
Guha, S.
See
Shah, G.B. *jt. auth.*
Gunasekaran, K.
Case for a merit examination on a national bases. *University News* 22(2) Ja 1984 p 2-3
Vice-chancellor and the statutory bodies of a university. *EPA Quarterly Bulletin* 6(3-4) Oc 1983-Ja 1984 p 22-39 ft-n
Gupta, A.C.
Doctoral theses on educational administration in Indian universities. *EPA Quarterly Bulletin* 7(1-2) Ap-Jl 1984 p 51-59 refs
Gupta, A.K. and Sharma, S.K.
The effects of feedback, supervisor, tape recorder and peer supervisor on a teaching skill : Stimulus variation. *Experiments in Education* 7(4) Je 1979 p 69-72 refs tabs
Gupta, Aneeta and Sharma, Adarsh
Children's aptitudes towards mentally retarded peers. *Indian Educational Rev* 18(4) Oc 1983 p 28-36
Gupta, Arun Kumar
All India seminar on teacher education. *Progress of Education* 55(11) Je 1981 p 282-86
Effective pupil evaluation in distance learning systems : Conspectus and considerations. *University News* 24(42) 8 Nv 1986 p 91-96 refs
Evaluation of SUPW : A model. *J Indian Education* 5(2) Jl 1979 p 8-12
Indian educational system : The role of computers. *J Indian Education* 10(5) Ja 1985 p 1-5
The role of media in education. *Education Quarterly* 35(1) Ja 1983 p 9-11
See also
Sharma, S.K. *jt. auth.*
Gupta, Arun Kumar and Gupta, Pramod Kumar
An experimental study of programmed instruction method of teaching

chemistry on high and low achievers. *J Education and Psychology* 36(4) Ja 1979 p 186-91

An experimental study of programmed instruction method of teaching chemistry in high and low achievers. *J Education and Psychology* 37(3) Oc 1979 p 193-97 refs tabs

Gupta, Arun Kumar and Kapoor, D.R.

A study of professional values among teachers in different organisational climates at 10+2 stage. *EPA Quarterly Bulletin* 6(3-4) Oc 1983-Ja 1984 p 22-31 refs tabs

Gupta, Arun Kumar and Patni, Rajni

Children books : Some evaluation criteria. *Education Quarterly* 33(2) Ap 1981 p 24-26

The impact of juvenile literature. *J Indian Education* 6(6) Mr 1981 p 3-8 refs

Gupta, Arun Kumar and Sharma, Suresh K.

Creativity, intelligence and socio-economic status. *Indian Educational Rev* 17(1) Ja 1982 p 64-70 refs

Pupils creativity in different types of institutional climates. *J Indian Education* 6(3) Ja 1981 p 27-33 refs

Self-concept in relation with locus of control, socio-economic status and intelligence of pupils in private and government schools. *Indian Educational Rev* 15(3) Jl 1980 p 78-80 refs tabs

Gupta, Asha

The religiousity questionnaire. *Indian Educational Rev* 18(4) Oc 1983 p 129-31

Gupta, B.R.

Concern for human values in educational administration. *Indian Education* 10(12) Mr 1981 p 27-39

Gupta, B.S. and Rajput, J.S.

National Adult Education Programme : Strategies of implementation. *Education Quarterly* 32(1) Ja 1980 p 1-3

Gupta, Bishan Swarup

Equality of educational opportunity and Muslims. *Indian Educational Rev* 18(2) Ap 1983 p 84-91

Gupta, Brij Mohan

Some thoughts on general education. *Rajasthan Board J Education* 16(4) Oc-De 1980 p 45-53

Gupta, D.L.

Contemporary educational problems. *Primary Teacher* 6(1) Ja 1981 p 26-27

Gupta, Deepti

See

Sethi, A.S. *jt. auth.*

Gupta, Dhake Lal

The teacher and the inquisitive child. *Primary Teacher* 4(3) Jl 1979 p 25-27

Gupta, Gyan Prakash

Headmaster's key role in changing climate. *Rajasthan Board J Education* 15(2) Ap-Je 1979 p 59-62

Gupta, H.C.

Central Board for Workers education : An introduction. *Indian J Adult Education* 46(5) My 1985 p 16-19+

Gupta, Har Govind
Identifying the changing students. *J Indian Education* 5(4) Nv 1979 p 35-37

Gupta, Indu
See
Gupta, Pushpa *jt. auth.*

Gupta, J.P.
Formation of concepts in children. *Primary Teacher* 11(2) Ap 1986 p 5-12
The gifted and their education. *Primary Teacher* 11(1) Ja 1986 p 17-21

Gupta, K.M.
Planning school time table. *Primary Teacher* 10(2) Ap 1985 p 18-20

Gupta, Kiran and Badarun Nisha
A study of job satisfaction among secondary school teachers. *Asian J Psychology and Education* 4(1) Ja 1979 p 25-30 refs

Gupta, Krishna Kumari
Creativity, intelligence and achievement. *Educational Rev* 85(11) Nv 1979 p 208-11

Gupta, Kusum
Achievement motivation of the most and the least confident students. *Educational Rev* 92(3) Mr 1986 p 55-58 refs tabs
A comparative study of moral values of the children of working and non-working mothers. *Progress of Education* 58(8) Mr 1984 p 193-96+ refs tabs
An experimental study of the effect of different methods of checking the written work. *Educational Rev* 90(11) Nv 1984 p 173-75 refs

Gupta, L.P.
A comparative study of personality syndromes of scheduled castes and non-scheduled castes. *Teacher Education* 13(8-9) Jl-Oc 1979 p 83-84
A comparative study of personality needs and academic achievement of scheduled and non-scheduled caste graduate and post-graduate students. *Quest in Education* 17(1) Ja 1980 p 44-51 refs
A differential study of planning and administration of the co-curricular activities of Meerut University adolescents. *J Educational Research and Extension* 19(4) Ap 1983 p 220-23
A study of personality syndromes and cognitive charactersitics of scheduled castes, backward classes and non-scheduled castes students. *J Higher Education* 4(3) Spr 1979 p 381-87

Gupta, M.B.
See
Mishra, Ajay M. *et al jt. auths.*

Gupta, M.L.
Productivity trends in correspondence education. *J Higher Education* 8(3) Spr 1983 p 349-56 refs tabs

Gupta, M.P.
An analytical study of semester system of education. *J Higher Education* 4(1) Mon 1978 p 41-46 refs tabs
Communication effectiveness of farmers fair, kisan mela. *Indian J Extension Education* 17(3-4) Se-De 1981 p 92-95
A critical study of evaluation under different systems of agricultural education. *J Higher Education* 5(1) Mon 1979 p 89-96

Impact of training media. *Educational Rev* 17(1) Ja 1982 p 22-27 ft-n

Role of educational technology cell in developing countries. *Education Quarterly* 33(2) Ap 1981 p 7-8

Role of media technology in rural education. *J Higher Education* 8(2) Aut 1982 p 239-41

Training needs of farmers in Himachal Pradesh. *Indian J Extension Education* 18(3-4) De 1982 p 70-71

Use of communication media by village level workers. *Indian J Extension Education* 16(3-4) De 1980 p 88-89 tabs

See also

Sangha, G.S. *jt. auth.*

Gupta, M.P. and Sangha, G.S.

Personal traits and viewing behaviour of rural TV owners of Punjab. *Indian J Extension Education* 16(1-2) Je 1980 p 87-89 tabs

Gupta, Madhu and Gupta, Prabha

Delinquent tendencies in the adolescent girls at different age levels and their effect on verbal learning. *Asian J Psychology and Education* 4(3) Nv 1979 p 6-8

The effect of adolescent problems on PA learning : A test of Taylor's drive theory. *J Education and Psychology* 36(4) Ja 1979 p 203-09

Family problems in other areas and delinquent tendencies. *J Education and Psychology* 37(1) Ap 1979 p 67-72 refs

Verbal learning : A study of correlates. *J Education and Psychology* 38(2) Jl 1980 p 111-20; 39(1) Ap 1981 p 42-51

Gupta, Meenu

A study of relationship between the self-concept of student teachers and their supervisors ratings. *Teacher Education* 16(18-19) Ja-Ap 1982 p 38-47 refs tabs

Gupta, P.L.

A comparative study of personality characteristics of over-achievers and underachievers. *Progress of Education* 57(3) Oc 1982 p 53-57 tabs

See also

Kansal, M.R. *jt. auth.*

Gupta, Prabha

See

Gupta, Madhu *jt. auth.*

Khattri, Pradeep Kumar *jt. auth.*

Gupta, Pramod Kumar

See

Gupta, Arun Kumar *jt. auth.*

Gupta, Pushpa

See

Bhatnagar, Suman *jt. auth.*

Gupta, Pushpa and Bansal, Saroj

Impact of training on concept of home science held by home science students. *Education Quarterly* 34(2) Ap 1982 p 14-16

Gupta, Pushpa and Gupta, Indu

Sex knowledge of school girls and their mothers. *Progress of Education* 58(6) Ja 1984 p 138-42 tabs

Gupta, Pushpa and Kavita, Alpana

Non-formal education programme in Udaipur district. *Progress of Education* 60(9) Ap 1986 p 205-08 refs

Gupta, Pushpa and Mathur, S.L.

A critical appraisal of physical facilities in teaching home science in higher secondary schools of Rajasthan. *Rajasthan Board J Education* 16(4) Oc-De 1980 p 25-31

Perception of importance and extent of achievement of the identified objectives of home science programme at school level. *Education Quarterly* 33(2) Ap 1981 p 27-30

Readiness of higher secondary schools in introducting 10+2 system of education in Rajasthan. *Education Quarterly* 32(3) Jl 1980 p 33-36 refs tabs

Usefulness of home science programme at school level. *Progress of Education* 57(10) My 1983 p 224-30 + tabs

Gupta, R.C.

See

Srivastava, S.S. *jt. auth.*

Gupta, R.N.

Programmed instruction : *vs* conventional method of teaching. *J Indian Education* 7(3) Se 1979 p 10-14 refs

A simplified teaching in science. *J Indian Education* 5(1) My 1979 p 11-21 refs

Gupta, R.P.

Directions and degrees of polarisation of value domains. *Bhartiya Shiksha Shodh Patrika* 5(2) Jl-De 1986 p 15-28 refs tabs

A study of prominent trends in value sensitivity profiles of some educated sections of Indian society. *Bhartiya Shiksha Shodh Patrika* 4(1) Ja-Je 1985 p 53-62 refs tabs

A study of some factors considered to be helpful in class teaching. *Bhartiya Shiksha Shodh Patrika* 4(2) Jl-De 1985 p 35-42 refs

See also

Bhardwaj, R.L. *jt. auth.*

Gupta, R.S. *et al*

An analysis of question bank in botany. *Rajasthan Board J Education* 15(4) Oc-De 1979 p 26-37

Gupta, Radhika

See

Saraswathi, T.S. *jt. auth.*

Gupta, Rajendra and Mathur, Rajeswar N.

Individually guided system of instruction in mathematics. *J Indian Education* 10(5) Ja 1985 p 44-48

Gupta, Ram Niwas

Evaluating apperceptive mass in science through word association. *Rajasthan Board J Education* 15(2) Ap-Je 1979 42-50

The uplift of the scholastically backward students in mathematics through sociometric techniques : A study. *J Indian Education* 6(6) Mr 1981 p 20-27 refs

Gupta, Ravi Kant
  See
    Seddey, S.C. *jt. auth.*

Gupta, S.K.
  Distance education : Problems of coordination, cooperation and functional autonomy. *J Higher Education* 7(3) Spr 1982 p 237-42 refs
  Distant study systems in science education. *EPA Quarterly Bulletin* 8(3-4) Oc 1985-Ja 1986 p 39-44
  Integration in physics education. *J Indian Education* 11(2) Jl 1985 p 64-66
  Teaching physical sciences in secondary schools. New Delhi, Sterling. 1981, vi, 184p. *Book Rev, J Indian Education* 8(2) Jl 1982 p 92-93
  Towards a framework for distance education in developing countries. *J Indian Education* 8(2) Jl 1982 p 40-43

Gupta, S.L.
  Factors influencing the growth of girls education at the elementary stage. *Indian Educational Rev* 18(4) Oc 1983 p 77-82
  A study of private costs of schooling girls at the elementary stage. *EPA Quarterly Bulletin* 6(2) Jl 1983 p 31-40 tabs

Gupta, S.M.
  A study of self-concept of high school students at different levels of adjustment and socio-economic status. *J Institute of Educational Research* 10(1) Ja 1986 p 21-24 refs tabs

Gupta, S.P.
  Conceptualising higher education as a system. *Progress of Education* 59(12) Jl 1985 p 260-65 +
  Factorial analysis of achievement of high school students. *National J Education* 3(1) Se 1980 p 50-54 refs tabs
  Motivation development in the classroom. *Educational Rev* 87(4) Ap 1981 p 67-68 refs
  Personality structure of Indian female teenagers. *J Educational Research and Extension* 18(1) Jl 1981 p 12-15 tabs
  A study of job satisfaction at three levels of teaching. *Indian Educational Rev* 18(2) Ap 1983 p 75-78
  A study of leadership style and achieving index of the colleges of education in Punjab. *Progress of Education* 58(2) Se 1983 p 36-42 tabs
  A study of the use of educational technology in colleges of education in Punjab and its effect of their output. *Progress of Education* 57(9) Ap 1983 p 204-07
  See also
    Agarwal, Subhash Chandra *jt. auth.*
    Sharma, Balendu *jt. auth.*

Gupta, S.P. and Bhargava, A.K.
  A study of learning outcomes in mathematics in relation to classroom climate and academic motivation. *Rajasthan Board J Education* 19(4) Oc-De 1983 p 9-15

Gupta, S.P. and Srivastava, J.P.
  Construction and standardisation of teachers job satisfaction scale. *J Education and Psychology* 38(1) Ap 1980 p 43-53 refs tabs
  Construction and standardisation of teachers job satisfaction scale. *J*

Educational Research and Extension 18(3) Ja 1982 p 155-89 refs tabs

A study of relationship between job satisfaction and personality maturity among secondary teachers. *J Education and Psychology* 38(1) Ap 1980 p 29-32 refs tabs

Gupta, Sagar Mal

Second language acquisition : Pidginisations, creolisations hypothesis. *Indian Educational Rev* 15(1) 1980 p 53-61 refs

Gupta, Sandhya

See

Shah, Anupama *jt. auth.*

Gupta, Sarojini

See

Grewal, A. *jt. auth.*

Gupta, Shiv K.

Non-formal education : A new challenge. *Teacher Today* 21(2) Oc-De 1978 p 1-7 refs

Gupta, Solan

See

Srivastava, S.K. *jt. auth.*

Gupta, Sunita

Value structures of higher education and the university teachers. *J Higher Education* 9(2) Aut 1983 p 254-59 refs

Gupta, Surya Bhan

Reflection of the pupils in guided discovery learning method. *Education Quarterly* 33(1) Ja 1981 p 19-21

Teaching of the life sciences through the environment. *Education Quarterly* 32(2) Ap 1980 p 27-29

Gupta, Sushil Prakash

Characteristics of syllabus bond and syllabus free students of class X. *Quest in Education* 19(3) Jl 1982 p 187-93 refs tabs

Persoanlity needs and student teaching competency. *Progress of Education* 58(9) Ap 1984 p 210-12 tabs

Gupta, V.D.

Organising microteaching programme in teacher training institutions. *Indian Education* 11(11-12) Fe-Mr 1982 p 37-41

Gupta, V.K.

See

Sharma, P.K. *jt. auth.*

Gupta, V.P.

Evaluating pupils learning in mathematics. *Primary Teacher* 8(3) Jl 1983 p 12-17

Forest education and environmental awareness. *Education Quarterly* 35(2) Ap 1983 p 20-23 refs

Mathematics teaching at primary levels. *Primary Teacher* 9(2) Ap 1984 p 13-15

Organising microteaching programme in teacher training institutions. *Indian Education* 11(11-12) Fe-Mr 1982 p 37-41

See also

Grewal, J.S. *jt. auth.*

Kathuria, R.P. *jt. auth.*

Gupta, Vijay Kumar

Adult education for socio-economic development in Haryana. *Indian J Adult Education* 41(9) Se 1980 p 26-28 refs

A study of the effect of socio-cultural factors on self-concept of high school students. *Progress of Education* 56(8) Mr 1982 p 188-91 refs tabs

Towards a sound journalism in education. *Progress of Education* 57(4) Nv 1983 p 81-83

Gupta, Y.K.

Prediction of teaching efficiency through teachers' attitude toward professional training. *Educational Rev* 88(3) Mr 1982 p 43-45

See also

Agrawal, Umesh *jt. auth.*

Gupta, Y.K. and Swaroop, M.

A comparative study of personality factors of effective and ineffective teachers in different types of school organisational climate. *Progress of Education* 55(11) Je 1981 p 300-02 tabs

Gupta, Y.K. *et al*

A study of the relationship between teaching efficiency, attitude towards teaching professional and academic achievement of the trainees (E.T.C.). *Educational Rev* 91(11) Nv 1985 p 196-97 refs

Gursharan Kaur

See

Dhatiwal, G.S. *jt. auth.*

Gururaja, Sreelakshmi

Studies on the social maturity of the Indian child. *Indian Educational Rev* 16(2) Ap 1981 p 119-24 refs

Gururani, Bhairav Dutt

Primary education reform and universalisation of elementary education. *Primary Teacher* 4(3) Jl 1979 p 5-6

Whither educational development? *Primary Teacher* 5(3) Jl 1980 p 23-26

Guthrie, Duncan

Child to child programme. *Primary Teacher* 4(1) Ja 1979 13-20

Haag, Daniel

The right to education : What kind of management? Paris, Unesco. 1982, 175p. *Book Rev, Indian Educational Rev* 18(4) Oc 1984 p 143-45

Hacquaert, Armand

The recruitment and training of university teachers. Ghent, I.A. U.P.L. *Book Rev, Teacher Today* 26(4) Ap-Je 1984 p.91-94 tabs

Haecht, Anne Van

Social change and the educational system. *J Higher Education* 6(1-3) 1980-81 p 105-15 refs

Haldar, G.

Mass education under panchayati raj : A proposition. *Indian J Adult Education* 47(7) Jl 1982 p 21-24 +

Hallak, Jacquis

Higher education in France : Recent trends. *J Higher Education* 5(1) Mon

1979 p 1-6

Hallak, Jecquis and Calliods, Francoise

Education, work and employment. Paris, Unesco. 332p. 17 *Book Rev, Teacher Today* 26(1) Jl-Se 1981 p 181-84

Hamida Akhtar Begum and Manfusa, Shams

Experimenter expectancy effect and inter and external locus of control of experimenters and subject. *Asian J Psychology and Education* 7(2) Jl 1981 p 27-33 refs

See also

Akhtar, Hamida

Hanafi, Aziza

In-service teacher education. *Educational Rev* 92(10) Oc 1986 p 161-63

Hans, S.A.B.D.

Tribal culture and educations response : Search for a model of education for the tribal people. *New Frontiers in Education* 16(1) Ja-Mr 1986 p 1-47 refs appdx

Hans Raj

Adult education : Its importance and problems. *Educational Rev* 85(7) Jl 1979 p 133-35

Hanson, Earl D.

Inviting innovation. *Indian Education* 11(5) Ag 1981 p 7-10

Hansra, B.S.

See

Bhardwaj, Neelam *jt. auth.*

Manchanda, Rajinder Kaur *jt. auth.*

Power, S.S. *et al jt. auth.*

Hanumantha Rao, P.

Helping the retarded children to grow. *Primary Teacher* 6(2) Ap 1981 p 8-11

Hanumantha Rao, V.

Educational news and the daily press. *Indian Education* 11(3) Je 1981 p 20-21

Haque

See also

under full name, e.g., Ehsanul Haque

Haque, Adhila

Needs of rural school girls : Implications for non-formal education. *Indian J Adult Education* 39(10) Oc 1978 p 9-13 tabs

Haque, Mohammed A. and Roy, G.L.

Factors related to the adoption of recommended species of fish in composite fish culture. *Indian J Extension Education* 19(1-2) Mr-Je 1983 p 74-83

Fish farmers perception of the problem in comparative fish culture and measures suggested by them for increasing the yield of fish. *Indian J Extension Education* 19(3-4) Se-De 1983 p 56-61 refs tabs

Haragopal, G.

Education as an investment in human resources development. *Indian Education* 11(7) Oc 1981 p 35-38

Students participation in educational administration : A view point. *Indian Education* 11(1-2) Ap-My 1981 p 71-75

Haragopal, G. and Jagannadha Rao, K.

Problems and perceptions of social science teachers in higher education. *J Higher Education* 4(1) Mon 1978 p 67-74 tabs

Haragopal, G. and Ravinder, A.

Perceptions of the key functionaries about NAEP : A critical appraisal. *Indian J Adult Education* 41(5) My 1980 p 36+

Haragopal, G. and Sudershan, G.

Rural adult literacy : An enquiry into the attitudes. *Indian J Adult Education* 39(10) Oc 1978 p 34-42 tabs

Harbans Singh

An investigation into the effect of teachers sex on the students achievement in science. *J Education and Psychology* 41(1-2) Ap-Jl 1983 p 64-66

An investigation into the study habits of adolescents of employed and non-employed mothers. *J Institute of Educational Research* 10(1) Ja 1986 p 5-8 refs tabs

See also

Chauhan, S.S. *jt. auth.*

Hari Narain

Education, science, technology and integrated development. *Indian J Adult Education* 44(1-2) Ja 1983 p 33-50

Harigopal, K.

A study of self ideal disparity and personality factors. *J Institute of Educational Research* 4(1) Ja 1980 p 28-32 refs tabs

Harikesh Singh

Dogmatism and academic achievement. *J Educational Research and Extension* 19(3) Ja 1983 p 138-44

Dogmatism in relation to sex and caste among the teachers trainees. *National J Education* 3(1) Se 1980 p 25-32 refs tabs

Lack of science orientation in rural primary school teachers : A crucial problems. *National J Education* 5(1) Se 1982 p 39-45 refs

Obscurantism among the university students. *J Higher Education* 4(1) Mon 1978 p 91-98 refs tabs

Teacher education in India : Need for radical revitalisation. *J Indian Education* 11(2) Jl 1985 p 35-39

See also

Rai, Markandey *jt. auth.*

Harikesh Singh and Surya Nath Singh

Educational ideas of Karl Marx. *National J Education* 6(1) Se 1983 p 20-28

Harish Chandra

The child labour force. *J Indian Education* 6(5) Ja 1981 p 34-36

Health education programme for primary schools. *Primary Teacher* 6(4) Oc 1981 p 9-14

Harman, S.

Plight of pupils in schools. D.L. Pub. 1978, 177p. £6.60 *Book Rev, Education Quarterly* 31(3-4) Oc 1979-Ja 1980 p 45-46

Harsh, Ram Ratan

Educational journals in India. *Indian Education* 11(3) Je 1981 p 21

Hashiguchi, Kazuko

Problems of education and economy in Japan. *Indian Education* 12(10) Ja

1983 p 5-9

Hashmi, Moneeze

ETV in Pakistan : A glimpse. *Primary Teacher* 11(3) Jl 1986 p 4-5

Hasnain, N.

Encoding as a function of paradigms and types of materials. *Asian J Psychology and Education* 6(3) Nv 1980 p 38-41 refs

Is creative imagination equivalent to usual and auditory imagination. *Asian J Psychology and Education* 6(3) Nv 1980 p 48-52 refs

Proactive inhibition in short-term memory. *Asian J Psychology and Education* 5(1-3) 1979 p 1-8 refs tabs

Hatibaruah, Kathita

Education for community living. *Educational Rev* 88(1) Ja 1982 p 4-6; 88(3) Mr 1982 p 47-50 refs

Educational profile of North-East India. *Educational Rev* 91(12) Fe 1985 p 29-33 refs

Literacy campaign : A world movement. *Educational Rev* 92(1) Ja 1986 p 13-14

Heaton, J.P. and Stocks, J.P.

Overseas students comparison in English studies. London Longman. 1978, 340p. 70d *Book Rev, Education Quarterly* 31(1) Ap 1979 p 38-39

Henderson, Edmund H. and Beers, James W., *eds.*

Developmental and congnitive aspects of learning to spell a reflection of word knowledge. New York, IRA. 148p. *Book Rev, Education Quarterly* 34(1) Ja 1982 p 45-46

Herber, Harbold L., *ed.*

Developing study skills in secondary schools. Int Reading Assn. 169p. *Book Rev, Education Quarterly* 31(2) Jl 1979 p 44-45

Heredia, Rudolf C.

The dilemma of innovative change : An organisational analysis. *New Frontiers in Education* 11(1) Ja-Mr 1981 p 12-28 refs

Examination performance and goal displacement. *New Frontiers in Education* 10(4) Oc-De 1980 p 1-5 refs

Minority rights and reservation policy : Towards coherence and consistence. *New Frontiers in Education* 16(2) Ap-Je 1986 p 60-63

Religious and social behaviour among academics : Some findings of a survey. *New Frontiers in Education* 14(3) Jl-Se 1984 p 39-46 refs

Some dilemmas in college teaching. *New Frontiers in Education* 16(3) Jl-Se 1986 p 30-33

Structure and performance of college education. Bombay, Somaiya Pub. 1981, 192p. Rs.65 *Book Rev, Indian Educational Rev* 17(2) Ap 1982 p 137-38; *J Higher Education* 8(2) Aut 1982 p 254-55

Structure and performance of college education in India : An organisational analysis of arts and science colleges in Bombay. *New Frontiers in Education* 10(2) Ap-Je 1980 p 21-33 refs

Heywood, John, *ed.*

The new technician education. Surev, Soc for Res (Univ. of Surey). 1980, 157p. £8.25 *Book Rev, Teacher Today* 25(2) Oc-De 1982 p 104

Hicks, David and Townley, Charles, *eds.*

Teaching world studies : An introduction to global perspectives in the curriculum. Essex, Longmans. 216p. £6.95 *Book Rev, Education Quarterly* 35(2) Ap 1983 p 71-73

Hira Nand

See

Damyanti *jt. auth.*

Dixit, V.B. *et al jt. auths.*

Hira Nand and Kamlesh Kumar

Folk beliefs associated with dry farming. *Indian J Extension Education* 16(3-4) De 1980 p 36-42 refs tabs

Hiranandani, Devika

Research in education. *Teacher Today* 21(2) Oc-De 1978 p 57-59

Hirevenkanagoudar, L.V. *et al*

Impact of dairy development programme of K.D.D.C. on small, marginal farmers and agricultural labourers of Bangalore district. *Indian J Extension Education* 21(1-2) Ja-Je 1985 p 69-71 tabs

Impact of national demonstration on participant and non-participant farmers. *Indian J Extension Education* 20(1-2) Je 1984 p 76-78

Hobbs, Mary Kay

New patterns in teaching and learning : A look at the People's Republic of China. *Indian J Adult Education* 41(4) Ap 1980 p 25-27

Hola, Ashok K.

Nurturing non-academic talent in the school : A challenge. *J Indian Education* 8(6) Mr 1983 p 35-41 refs

Hommadi, A.H.

The application of modern scientific management principles to the development of the university administration in developing countries. *EPA Quartery Bulletin* 6(2) Jl 1983 p 48-50

Hooda, R.C.

Attainments of students-teachers in education theory : A factorial view. *Indian Educational Rev* 17(4) Oc 1982 p 101-08 refs tabs

See also

Sharma, J.P. *jt. auth.*

Syag, R.N. *jt. auth.*

Hooda, R.C. and Dhaka, Krishna

A study of social cohesion in secondary training institutions and attitude of student teachers. *J Education and Psychology* 42(3) Oc 1984 p 109-14 refs

Hooda, R.C. and Jarial, Gurpal Singh

Development of creativity through the techniques of role playing. *Rajasthan Board J Education* 19(4) Oc-De 1983 p 16-21

Improving students creativity through the application of masterly learning strategy. *J Indian Education* 9(1) My 1983 p 16-19

Is the strategy of masterly learning helpful in improving students creative thinking abilities. *Rajasthan Board J Education* 19(1) Ja-Mr 1983 p 12-16

Hooda, R.C. and Paul, H.R.

Effect of socio-economic status and academics achievement on risk taking behaviour of student teachers. *J Institute of Educational Research* 10(2) My 1986 p 1-3 refs

Hooda, R.C. and Syag, R.N.

Content-cum-methodology : theory and practice. *Experiments in Education* 9(12) Fe 1982 p 221-22 + tabs

Relationship of attainments in theory papers with student teaching in secondary teachers training programme. *J Education and Psychology* 40(4) Ja 1983 p 220-24 refs

Hoods, D.S.

Universal education and social development. *Education Quarterly* 35(3) Jl 1983 p 12-13

Hooja

See also

Ahuja

Hooja, G.B.K.

Education in Canada. *University News* 23(22) 8 Je 1985 p 2-3

Hooja, Meenakshi

Women of Rajasthan : A demographic profile. *Prasar* 8(3-4) Oc 1981-Ja 1982 p 1-17 tabs

Hopper, W.A.F.

Evaluation approach for teaching and testing. *New Frontiers in Education* 13(3) Jl-Se 1983 p 38-41

Modules and modular courses of study. *New Frontiers in Education* 13(1) Ja-Mr 1983 p 53-57 refs

Hopson, Barrie and Scally, Mike

Lifeskills teaching : Maidenhead, McGraw-Hill. 556p. *Book Rev, Education Quarterly* 34(1) Ja 1982 p 50

Horsey, Anita

Conditions of scheduled castes and tribes. *New Frontiers in Education* 11(2) Ap-Je 1981 p 1-36 refs

Hota, Asok K.

Nurturing non-academic talent in the school : A challenge. *J Indian Education* 8(6) Mr 1983 p 35-41 refs

Hua, Z.Y.

Some steps on the reform in higher education. *Teacher Education* 20(30-31) Ja-Ap 1985 p 21-24; *University News* 23(15) 16 Ap 1985 p 4-5

Hubli, S.K. and Jacob, A.S.

Action research; An integrated part of policy and implementation in N.S.S. *Prasar* 9(1-4) Ap-Ag 1983 p 9-19

Hundal, B.S.

Head of the school. *Educational Rev* 88(11) Nv 1982 p 185-88 Politics and education. *Educational Rev* 89(5-6) My-Je 1983 p 99-100

Role of teachers. *Educational Rev* 90(1) Ja 1984 p 3-5

Hurman, John

Oral examination in foreign languages at 16 in the U.K. : A review of test types and assessment principles. *J Indian Education* 11(2) Jl 1985 p 25-34

Husen, Torsten

Present trends in education. *Teacher Education* 17(20-21) Jl-Oc 1982 p 7-22

The teenageer and the school in Europe. *Teacher Today* 26(2) Oc-De 1983 p 1-17 refs diagr

Hussain

See also

under full name/surname, e.g., Asmat Hussain

Hussain, M.A.

Non-formal education : Extension education programme of the universities. *J Indian Education* 6(6) Mr 1981 p 49-52

The role of education in economic development in India. *Indian Educational Rev* 18(4) Oc 1983 p 15-27

Hussain, M.G.

See

Hasnain, N. *jt. auth.*

Ilyina, Lydia

Art schools are accessible to all in the USSR. *Progress of Education* 53(7) Fe 1979 p 138-40

Imtiaz Ali, Sheikh

Problems of students discipline. *Teacher Education* 20(30-31) Ja-Ap 1985 p 25-29; *University News* 23(13) 1 Ap 1985 p 3-4+

Inamdar, Hemant V.

A separate university for women. *Progress of Education* 59(5) De 1984 p 90-94+

Indapurkar, C.D.

The changing nature of language pedagogy. *Progress of Education* 60(6) Ja 1986 p 130-34

A philosophical analysis of methods of teaching at the higher education stage. *J Higher Education* 5(1) Mon 1979 p 7-11

A study of the English pronunication of the teachers of English. *Research Bulletin* 15(3-4) Se-De 1985 p 3-20 tabs

Teaching of structures in English. *Progress of Education* 56(11) Je 1982 p 265-68 + figs

Indira, V.

Attitude of teachers towards small family norm. *Experiments in Education* 11(6) Ag 1983 p 109-10+

A comparative study of attitude of high school teachers belonging to different religious groups towards small family norms. *Progress of Education* 58(3) Oc 1983 p 66-67+

Indiresan, Jayalaskhmi

A comparative study of the attitudes of social and engineering students to certain aspects of higher education. *J Higher Education* 5(2) Aut 1979 p 233-36

The examinee : The neglected factor in the examination system. *J Higher Education* 4(2) Aut 1978 p 268-71

Indiresan, Jayalakshmi and Kamakaraj, K.

Have 'question banks' improved the quality of question papers? *J Higher Education* 8(2) Aut 1982 p 199-209 refs tabs

Indra Deva
See
Deva, Indra
ngle, O.P. *et al*
Evaluation of foundation course organised by Punjabrao Krishi Vidyapeeth, Akola for village development officers under T & V system. *Indian J Extension Education* 19(1-2) My-Je 1983 p 41-45
Ingram, Cregg F.
Fundamentals of educational assessment. New York, Van Nostrans. 1980, 404p. *Book Rev, Teacher Today* 25(3) Ja-Mr 1983 p 106-07
Intodia, S.I. and Shaktawat, G.S.
Role perception and role performance of Sarpancha (Chairman of Gram Panchayats) in Rajasthan. *Indian J Extension Education* 16(1-2) Ja 1980 p 64-68 tabs
Israney, S.M. and Balachander, K.K.
Economics of higher education : Current trends and new priorities *University News* 24(42) 8 Nv 1986 p 111-17 refs
Itnal, C.J.
See
Kunnal, L.B. *et al jt. auths.*
Iyengar
See also
under full surname, e.g., Srinivasa Iyengar, M.A.
Iyengar, T.K.S.
Development of the information sector. *University News* 23(2) 8 Ja 1985 p 3
New dimensions in library science. Bombay, Allied. 1977, 210p. Rs.45 *Book Rev, J Indian Education* 6(4) Nv 1980 p 59-60
Iyer
See
under full name/surname, e.g., Venkata Iyer

Jachuk, Kasturi and Charandas, Jeesur
Free recall of categorised materials : A cross cultural examination of Jensen's theory. *Asian J Psychology and Education* 9(3) 1982 p 1-6
Jacob, A.
Education for women and girls today in cities in India. *Education Quarterly* 34(4) Oc 1982 p 11-13
Jacob, A.S.
See
Hubli, S.K. *jt. auth.*
Jacob, P. Grace
Teaching of English at degree level : Some new directions. *New Frontiers in Education* 11(4) Oc-De 1981 p 31-41 refs
Jacob, Plamthodathil S.
Colleges and community : A case study of Ahmednagar College. *New Frontiers in Education* 13(1) Ja-Mr 1983 p 24-30
New Educational Policy : A view from the grassroots. *New Frontiers in Education* 16(3) Jl-Se 1986 p 19-29

Primery for remedial education. *New Frontiers in Education* 13(4) Oc-De 1983 p 12-16

The remedial approach in college education. *New Frontiers in Education* 11(4) Oc-De 1981 p 15-27

Women students programme in co-educational context : A case study. *New Frontiers in Education* 15(1) Ja-Mr 1985 p 77-81

Jadhao, V.G. *et al*

The efficacy of teaching through environment at primary level. *J Indian Education* 6(4) Nv 1980 p 34-39

Jagan Nath

Discover the power of photography in working with handicapped children. *Our Education* 5 Jl 1984 p 55-56

Jagannadhan, K.

Impact of socio-economic status (Rural) on academic achievement. *J Institute of Educational Research* 9(3) Se 1985 p 27-31 refs

Individualised instruction. *Experiments in Education* 8(1) Mr 1980 p 12-13

Personal and situational variables and academic achievement. *J Institute of Educational Research* 9(1) Ja 1985 p 10-12 refs

Socio-economic status 'urban' and academic achievement. *J Education and Psychology* 44(3-4) Jl-De 1986 p 128-34

Jagannadha Rao, K.

See

Haragopal, G. *jt. auth.*

Jagannath, Hariprasad

Innovations and teachers colleges. *Educational Rev* 87(8) Ag 1981 p 143-47 tabs

Jagannath, V.

Academic motivation and academic achievement. *Experiments in Educaiton* 13(12) Fe 1986 p 208-10 refs

Jagannathan, V.

Equality of educational opportunity. *New Frontiers in Education* 16(2) Ap-Je 1986 p 65-59 tabs

Jagannatha Reddy, D.

The third dimensions of universities. *Experiments in Education* 10(4) Je 1982 p 69-70

Jagdip Kaur

See

Gakhar, Sudesh *jt. auth.*

Jagdish Singh and Singh, A.K.

Satellite technology for primary education. *Primary Teacher* 11(1) Ja 1986 p 22-24

Jagjit Singh, J.

Financial management of colleges : Issues and suggestions. *EPA Quarterly Bulletin* 8(1-2) Ap-Je 1985 p 26-39

Jai Prakash

A comparative study of personal preferences, self-concept and performance of SOS children's village of India and other children of Delhi schools. *Indian Educational Rev* 18(2) Ap 1983 p 125-33 tabs

Jain, Ajit Kumar

Role of universities and colleges in the National Adult Education Programme. *Prasar* 7(1-2) Ap-Jl 1980 p 27-32

Jain, Ambika

Development of primary education under local bodies in Maharashtra, 1892-1984. *Research Bulletin* 16(1-2) Mr-Je 1986 p 3-24 tabs

Jain, D.P.

Indian population situations and population education. *Rajasthan Board J Education* 19(1) Ja-Mr 1983 p 17-21

Progress of elementary education in Andhra Pradesh : Impact of demographic factors. New Delhi, NCERT. 1984, 114p. Rs.15 *Book Rev, Indian Educational Rev* 20(3) Jl 1985 p 113-14

Rural schools and enrolment : A case study of Andhra Pradesh. *J Indian Education* 6(4) Nv 1980 p 40-42

Jain, Dhiraj K.

Effect of sex, academic stream and locality on Hindi vocabulary. *J Education and Psychology* 36(1-2) Ap-Je 1978 p 20-25

Jain, H.C.

Status of science education in India. *J Indian Education* 10(5) Ja 1985 p 12-17

Jain, J.K.

See

Jha, P.N. *jt. auth.*

Jain, K.C.S.

Adult business education : A challenge. *Indian J Adult Education* 43(5) My 1982 p 21-24 refs

Curriculum evaluation : Concept and model. *Rajasthan Board J Education* 15(2) Ap-Je 1979 p 13-19

Jain, Kiran Prabha

Teachers unrest. *Educational Rev* 85(2) Fe 1979 p 29-31; *Progress of Education* 54(1) Ag 1979 p 7-11

Jain, M.L.

Continuing engineering education. *J Higher Education* 5(1) Mon 1979 p 51-56

Jain. M.C.

See

Yadav, K.D. *jt. auth.*

Jain, Nem Kumar

Mendel and laws of hereditary. *J Indian Education* 5(1) My 1979 p 44-49

Jain, P.C.

Research in curriculum for technical education. *Quest in Education* 18(4) Oc 1981 p 307-19

Jain, Pemi and Saxena, Saroj

A comparative study of level of aspiration and modes of frustration reactions among prospective teachers. *National J Education* 7(2) My 1985 p 78-45 refs tabs

Jain, R.P.

Faculty development. *New Frontiers in Education* 13(2) Ap-Je 1983 p 49-54 refs

Failure of an innovation in a university : An investigation. *Experiments in Education* 10(1) Mr 1982 p 15-20; 10(2) Ap 1982 p 32-34 tabs

Failure of an innovation in a university : An investigation. *New Frontiers in Education* 10(4) Oc-De 1979 p 73-79 refs tabs

A study of students expectation of secondary school principals. *Experiments in Education* 7(5) Jl 1979 p 86-91; *J Educational Research and Extension* 18(3) Ja 1982 p 133-41 refs

Jain, Rakesh

Modification of teacher behaviour : Non-verbal dues as a feedback device. *J Indian Education* 12(1) My 1986 p 44-48 refs

A study of correlation between classroom verbal and non-verbal behaviour components. *Educational Rev* 90(3) Mr 1984 p 56-58 refs

See also

Ahluwalia, S.P. *jt. auth.*

Sharma, R.A. *jt. auth.*

Jain, Rashmi

See

Sandhu, N.S. *jt. auth.*

Jain, S.C.

Role of teachers in environmental education. *Indian Education* 12(11-12) Fe-Mr 1983 p 13-15

Jain, S.K.

Trade unions and workers education : International perspective. *Indian J Adult Education* 46(5) My 1985 p 4-9+

Jain, Sunito

See

Singh, M.B. *jt. auth.*

Jain, V.K.

Computer for beginners. Delhi, Pustak Mahal. 1985, 151p. Rs.20 *Book Rev, J Indian Education* 12(3) Se 1986 p 63-64

Jaiswal, Shushuma

See

Singh, B.P. *jt. auth.*

Jaitey, Mamta

NSS : Some issue areas. *Prasar* 9(1-4) Ap 1982-Ja 1983 p 47-50

Jalali, Jayashree

Planning and administration of education in the USSR under the new education policy. *J Educational Planning and Administration* 1(1) Oc 1986 p 76-80

Jaleel Saheb, S.

Assessment and evaluation in adult reading. *Indian J Adult Education* 40(9) Je 1979 p 39-41

A study of the interests of high school students. *Quest in Education* 16(4) Oc 1979 p 307-13

A study of vocational perceptions of high school boys. *Asian J Psychology and Education* 4(2) Jl 1979 p 11-16 refs

See also

Muthiah, M. *jt. auth.*

Pillai, J.K. *jt. auth.*

Jaleel Saheb, S. and Sathiyagirarajan

A study of scientific attitude of college teachers. *J Higher Education* 4(3) Spr 1979 p 387-92

Jalihal, K.A.

See

Channagowda, M.B. *jt. auth.*

Dudhani, C.M. *jt. auth.*

Siddaramaiah, B.S. *jt. auth.*

Veerabhadraiah, V. *jt. auth.*

Jamison, Dean T. and Mcanany, Emile G.

Radio for educational development. London, Sage Pub. 1985, 221p. $14 *Book Rev, J Indian Education* 12(2) Jl 1986 p 62

Jana, B.K.

Behaviour modification : Theory and practice. *Educational Rev* 86(5) My 1980 p 97-99

Developing nuturant effect strategy for environment-oriented primary science education programme. *Experiments in Education* 8(6) Ag 1980 p 102-08; 8(7) Se 1980 p 126-29

Supervision in science education. *Educational Rev* 86(12) De 1980 p 235-39; 87(1) Ja 1981 p 11-13

Janardhana Reddy, D.

College students and adult education. *Educational Rev* 87(9) Se 1981 p 175-76

Evaluation of reading and writing skills of learners. *Educational Rev* 91(10) Oc 1985 p 164-66

Evaluation techniques in adult education. *Indian J Adult Education* 46(4) Ap 1985 p 14-18

See also

Sudhakara Reddy, M.V. *jt. auth.*

Jangira, N.K.

Curriculum transaction for national integration. *J Indian Education* 9(1) My 1983 p 45-51

Improving pupil responses in the classroom. *Primary Teacher* 6(4) Oc 1981 p 15-18

Professional enculturation : Innovative experiments in teaching and training. New Delhi, Book Worth India. 1985, 99p. Rs.70 *Book Rev, Progress of Education* 60(5) De 1985 p 122

Putting questions in the classroom. *Primary Teacher* 6(3) Jl 1981 p 19-21

Structural characteristics of classroom questions, pupils responses and pupil response management behaviour of social studies teachers. *J Indian Education* 8(2) Jl 1982 p 33-39 refs tabs

A study of social cohesion in elementary teachers training institutions and its relationship with their efficiency. *EPA Quarterly Bulletin* 6(1) Ap 1983 p 36-42 refs

Towards a model for integration of teaching skills. *Teacher Education* 15(16-17) Jl-Oc 1981 p 46-56 refs

Towards an achieving classroom. *Rajasthan Board J Education* 19(4) Oc-De 1983 p 30-37

Universal learning strategy for primary schools. *Primary Teacher* 5(1) Ja

1980 p 20-23

Using value-clarifying strategies in the classroom. *Primary Teacher* 8(2) Ap 1983 p 18-21

Value clarifying strategies. *J Indian Education* 11(2) Jl 1985 p 19-24 refs

Jangira, N.K. and Raizada, Madhu

Cognitive behaviour of teachers in the classroom. *J Indian Education* 7(3) Se 1979 p 32-37 refs tabs

Jangira, N.K. and Rath, K.B.

Classroom instruction : Needs of the disabled. *Primary Teacher* 9(3) Jl 1984 p 4-7

Jangira, N.K. *et al*

Effect of training in selected teaching skills using micro-teaching on the teaching competence of social education teachers : A field study. *J Indian Education* 8(4) Nv 1982 p 9-14 tabs

Jarial, Gurpal Singh

Adult education : Problems and techniques. *Experiments in Education* 7(10) De 1979 p 173-76

An appraisal of the standards in education. *Teacher Today* 23(1) Jl-Se 1980 p 26-35 refs

Creativity as a predictor of entrepreneurial success among tribals. *Experiments in Education* 11(12) Fe 1984 p 110-14 ref

Creativity, intelligence and academic achievement : Their relationships and difference with reference to sex and academic subjects. *J Education and Psychology* 39(2) Jl 1981 p 91-96 refs

Development of creativity : A few methods. *Rajasthan Board J Education* 15(2) Ap-Je 1979 p 35-41

Effect of birth order upon creative thinking abilities among adolescents. *J Institute of Educational Research* 6(3) Se 1982 p 9-13 refs tabs

The effect of instructional method upon the creativity of students : A review. *Progress of Education* 55(7) Fe 1981 p 179-80 +

General awareness and creativity. *Experiments in Education* 7(3) My 1979 p 47-49 refs

Is the first born more creative? *Progress of Education* 54(4) Nv 1981 p 91-94 refs tabs

Socially useful productive work. *Experiments in Education* 6(11) Ja 1979 p 187-90

Some misconceptions about creativity. *Experiments in Education* 8(3) My 1980 p 43-46

See also

Hooda, R.C. *jt. auth.*

Katiyar. P.C. *jt. auth.*

Passi, B.K. *jt. auth.*

Sansanswal, D.N. *jt. auth.*

Sharma, Ashwani Kumar *jt. auth.*

Jarial, Gurpal Singh and Sharma, Ashwani Kumar

Creativity and its components as effected by intelligence, personality and their interaction. *Asian J Psychology and Education* 6(2) Jl 1980 p 26-32

A factorial study of the effect of adjustment levels of academic subjects and their interaction upon creativity and its components. *J Institute of*

Education Research 6(2) My 1982 p 1-5 refs

Institutional climate and creativity. *Experiments in Education* 8(8) Oc 1980 p 135-38 refs tabs

An investigation into the effect of increase in some limits on the performance of children on creativity tasks. *Experiments in Education* 11(4) Je 1983 p 63-66

An investigation into the interactional effects of intelligence and grade levels on creativity and its components. *J Institute of Educational Research* 4(3) Se 1980 p 15-19 refs tabs

Jaswal, S.S.

Scrap this examination system. *Educational Rev* 87(11) Nv 1981 p 215-17

Unfair means. *Educational Rev* 89(11) Nv 1983 p 192-93

Jaweed Ashraf

Soviet education : Theory and practice. New Delhi, Sterling. 1978, 280p. Rs.45 *Book Rev, Education Quarterly* 30(3) Oc 1978 p 41-42; *J Higher Education* 4(1) Mon 1978 p 121-24 *National J Education* 20(1) Se 1979 p 62-63; *Teacher Today* 22(3) Ja-Mr 1980 p 100-02

Jayagopal, R.

Adult learning : A psychological analysis in the Indian context. Madras, Univ of Madras. 82p. Rs.40 *Book Rev, Indian J Adult Education* 46(5) My 1986 p 29

Discussion. *Indian J Adult Education* 44(11) Nv 1983 p 10-21

Occupational mobility among a special group of scheduled castes in Tamil Nadu : A survey. *Indian J Adult Education* 47(1) Ja 1986 p 8-12

University and emerging educational technologies for adult and continuing education. *J Higher Education* 4(3) Spr 1979 p 365-71

Jayagopal, R. *et al*

Linking literacy with TRYSEM : An experiment. *Indian J Adult Education* 47(8) Ag 1986 p 15-21 refs

Jayakantham, B.

Relationship between self concept and academic achievement. *Experiments in Education* 7(3) My 1979 p 42-46 refs

Jayalakshmi, S.S.

Life and death : Children's concepts. *Educational Rev* 87(5) My 1981 p 95-98

Jayaprasada Rao, J.T.

Early childhood preschool education : Importance and need. *Indian Education* 12(3-4) Je-Jl 1982 p 31-33

Teaching deaf and hard of hearing children. *Progress of Education* 56(12) Jl 1982 p 289-303+ refs

Jayaraman, Kunthala

Education for women : A five year plan. *J Higher Education* 1(2) Aut 1975 p 255-56

Jayasuriya, J.E.

Curriculum innovation through population education. Colombo, Associated Educ. Pub. 1978, 121p. £3; Rs.45 *Book Rev, Indian Educational Rev* 14(4) Oc 1979 p 145-46

Jayaswal, Rajendra

Challenge of elementary education in India. *Bharatiya Shiksha Shodh*

Patrika 5(2) Jl-De 1986 p 61-67

Jayaswal, S.R.

Education for social, moral and spiritual values. *Bharatiya Shiksha Shodh Patrika* 1(2) Jl 1982 p 5-8 refs

Human factors in evaluation. *University News* 24(35) 16 Oc 1986 p 1-3

Jayaswal, Sita Ram

The integral system of education. *Teacher Education* 13(8-9) Jl-Oc 1979 p 9-15 refs

Jayaweera, S.

Programmes of non-formal education for women. *Indian J Adult Education* 40(12) De 1979 p 33-45

Jena, Shribatsa L.

An anatomy of student teaching. *Education Quarterly* 32(3) Jl 1980 p 10-12

Choosing teaching as a career. *Indian Education* 10(4) Jl 1980 p 24-25

Cost-quality relation in education. *J Indian Education* 6(4) Nv 1980 p 8-12

Economics of non-formal education. *Indian Educational Rev* 17(4) Oc 1982 p 40-47 refs

See also

Shelat, Neela *jt. auth.*

Jenningswray, Zellynne D.

Towards an appropriate strategy for curriculum change in the third world : Experiences from Jamaica. *Perspectives in Education* 1(3) Jl 1985 p 175-94 refs ft-n tabs

Jerardi, Robert J.

Superintendents : Movers or stayers. *J Educational Research and Extension* 18(3) Ja 1982 p 170-74

Jervis, Peter

Adult and continuing education. London, Croom-Helm. 317p. £15.95 *Book Rev, Education Quarterly* 36(2) Ap 1984 p 75-76

Jesdanwalla, Zaibun Y.

The influence of levels of achievement amongst students. *New Frontiers in Education* 11(2) Ap-Je 1981 p 73-80

Jesudasan, Victor

Indian students in the United States. *Indian Educational Rev* 14(1) Ja 1979 p 1-21 appdx refs tabs

Jha, J. and Roy, Vidya Rani

A study of teachers attitude towards teaching as a career and education : A synopsis. *Indian Education* 11(5) Ag 1981 p 27-30

Jha, J.S.

Attitudes of parents towards English medium and non-English medium schools. *J Educational Research and Extension* 16(2) Oc 1979 p 115-24 refs

Jha, J.S. and Gel, Vineeta

The level of activism : A comparative study of male and female college students. *J Educational Research and Extension* 19(3) Ja 1983 p 162-66

Jha, J.S. and Saxena, Bimla

A study of disadvantages associated with different socio-economic groups of girls studying in secondary schools. *J Education and Psychology* 41(1-2) Ap-Jl 1983 p 12-16

Jha, J.S. and Saxena, D.K.

Youth problems, adjustment and scholastic performance : A comparative study. *J Educational Research and Extension* 18(2) Oc 1981 p 49-54 refs tabs

Jha, M.L.

A probe into the problems of educated job Seekers. *J Indian Education* 8(4) Nv 1982 p 20-23

Jha, P.N.

Role of agricultural universities in training of subject-matter specialists and extension personnel of training. *Indian J Extension Education* 19(1-2) Mr-Je 1983 p 36-40

See also

Kher, A.O. *jt. auth.*

Mishra, L.N. *jt. auth.*

Jha, P.N. and Jain, J.K.

Differential interest areas of rural youth and non-school going youth club members. *Indian J Extension Education* 15(1-2) Je 1979 p 39-48 refs tabs

Jha, R.C. and Sinha B.P.

TV broadcast in Delhi : A restropective view. *Indian J Extension Education* 16(3-4) De 1980 p 32-35 tabs

Jha, R.N.

Educational journalism : Possibilities and limitations. *J Indian Education* 11(3) Se 1985 p 31-35

Jha, S.K. and Barde, N.R.

The second change education for the tribals of Vidarbha. *Progress of Education* 58(11) Je 1984 p 270-72

Jha, Sahitya Nand

Education for socialism, secularism, and democracy. Delhi, Amar Pra. 134p. Rs.80 *Book Rev, Educational Rev* 91(11) Nv 1985 p 198

Jhaj, Didar Singh

Constellations of personality traits, intelligence and achievement in relation to scientific creativity. *Asian J Psychology and Education* 11(1) 1983 p 13-20

Jhaj, Didar Singh and Grewal, J.S.

Occupational aspirations of the achievers and underachivers in mathematics. *Asian J Psychology and Education* 11(1) 1983 p 36-39

Jhansi Rani and Bhave, Asha M.

Actual and desired type of participation by rural women in selected areas of decision-making. *Indian J Extension Education* 18(1-2) Je 1982 p 83-89 tabs

Jindal, Asha

Role of computers in education. *Education Quarterly* 38(2) Sum 1986 p 8-12

Jindal, C.R. and Panda, S.K.

Anxiety and achievement : A Rorschach study of high and low-achievers. *Indian Educational Rev* 17(4) Oc 1982 p 118-24 refs

Jindal, S.K. and Pradhan, Netranand

Security, insecurity, adjustment, socio-economic status and family structure as the predictors of academic achievement of intermediate students. *Indian Educational Rev* 18(4) Oc 1983 p 58-65

Jitendra Mohan and Munjal, Nalini
Extraversion and drive as correlates of substitution reminiscence. *Asian J Psychology and Education* 4(3) Nv 1979 p 1-5 refs

Jitendra Mohan and Narender Kumar
A study of social and personal problems of tribal youth. *Asian J Psychology and Education* 6(1) Ja 1980 p 5-8

Jitendra Mohan *et al*
Personality, age and sex as determinants of reminiscence in children. *Asian J Psychology and Education* 7(3) 1981 p 1-7 refs
Study of personality of academic achievement of children. *J Education and Psychology* 39(3) Oc 1981 p 163-68 refs

Joe Prakash, J.
Examination reforms. *Experiments in Education* 11(12) Fe 1984 p 218-19

Jogawar, V.V.
Development of self concept during adolescence. *Asian J Psychology and Education* 9(1) Ja 1982 p 3-7 refs tabs

Johari, Prabha
The role of teacher education in integrating women into development. *Teacher Education* 14(10-11) Ja-Ap 1980 p 50-56

Johl, S.S.
Relevance of agricultural research in India. *New Frontiers in Education* 14(4) Oc-De 1984 p 18-25

John, Pushpitta
New approaches to higher education for women. *Education Quarterly* 34(4) Oc 1982 p 28-30

John, V.V.
54th all Indian Educational Conference, Kurukshetra : Inaugural address 28-12-1980. *Indian Education* 10(11) Fe 1981 p 5-10
India's challenge : Education for social justice. *New Frontiers in Education* 14(2) Ap-Je 1984 p 17-25
Recollections of a reluctant administrator. *Teacher Today* 26(1) Jl-Se 1983 p 133-43
Towards a meaningful first degree. *J Higher Education* 1(1) Mr 1975 p 56-60

Jolly, G.S.
Synthesis of a school magazine. *J Indian Education* 11(2) Se 1985 p 43-54

Jones, Emma L.
See
Peretti, Peter O. *jt. auth.*

Jones, Ralhph H.
Remedial education at Spicer Memorial College. *New Frontiers in Education* 13(3-4) Oc-De 1983 p 27-39

Jose Chander, M.
Approaches to course development in distance education. *University News* 24(42) 8 Nv 1986 p 33-36 refs

Joseph, A.
Educational problems of socially disadvantaged children. *J Indian Education* 11(1) My 1985 p 14-19

Josh, Shabbir Hussain

An investigation into the reading efficiency in English of students of standards XI in Aurangabad city and measures to improve it. *Research Bulletin* 15(1-2) Mr-Je 1985 p 3-9

Measurement of reading efficiency. *Education Quarterly* 32(3) Jl 1980 p 23-24

Politicisation of teachers in India. *Progress of Education* 61(12) Se 1986 p 33-36

Teaching in English : Need to revise objectives. *New Frontiers in Education* 12(4) Oc-De 1982 p 53-58

Joshi, Anant N.

See

Bhalwankar, G. *jt. auth.*

Joshi, Anuradha

See

Sansanwal, D.N. *jt. auth.*

Joshi, C.L.

Education is at grand reduction sale. *Teacher Today* 27(4) Ap-Je 1985 p 59-61

Joshi, D.C.

Management of an innovation : A case of a school for a planned change. *J Indian Education* 5(5) Ja 1980 p 8-16

Researches in higher education. *J Higher Education* 3(3) Spr 1978 p 399-404 refs tabs

Joshi H.R. and Darji, D.R.

A study of the attitude of teacher towards teacher education programme. *Progress of Education* 56(1) Ag 1981 p 22-24

Joshi, Hariprasad O.

Sociometric study of stars and isolates in relation to their adjustment. *Progress of Education* 57(2) Se 1982 p 41-44 tabs

A study of the comparison of socio-metric scroing techniques. *Progress of Education* 61(2) Se 1986 p 43-44 refs

Teacher effectiveness. *J Educational Research and Extension* 20(3) Ja 1984 p 153-57

Joshi, J.N. and Gokher, Subhash

Effect of feedback on the acquisition of algebraic concepts in relation to intelligence and anxiety. *J Education and Psychology* 36(4) Ja 1979 p 180-85

Joshi, J.V.

Moral education : Approach and perspective. *Progress of Education* 57(3) Oc 1982 p 50-52

Problems in moral education. *Progress of Education* 57(2) Se 1982 p 31-34 +

Programme for moral education. *Progress of Education* 57(5) De 1982 p 98-102 +

Techniques of moral education. *Progress of Education* 57(6) Ja 1983 p 122-29+

Joshi, K.L.

Higher education : Historical and other problems. Bombay, Popular. 1981,

143p. Rs.15 *Book Rev, Education Quarterly* 35(4) Oc 1983 p 68-70; *Indian Educational Rev* 18(2) Ap 1983 p 136-37; *Progress of Education* 57(8) Mn 1983 p 189 +

Problems of higher education in India : An approach to structural analysis and reorganisation. Bombay, Popular 1977, 312p. Rs.18 *Book Rev, Indian Educational Rev* 14(1) Ja 1979 p 152-57; *J Higher Education* 4(2) Aut 1978 p 287-90; *New Frontiers in Education* 9(1) Ja-Mr 1979 p 114-15

25 years of UGC : Dilemmas and difficulties. *J Higher Education* 6(1-3) 1980-81 p 63-68 refs

Joshi, Kireet

Reflection on new education. *New Frontiers in Education* 15(1) Ja-Mr 1985 p 13-50

Joshi, M.G.

Twenty Second Headmasters' Conference. *Progress of Education* 56(5) De 1981 p 119+

Joshi, Navin Chandra

Teachers training in higher educaiton. *Rajasthan Board J Educaiton* 15(1) Ja-Mr 1979 p 8-10

Delinking degress from jobs. *Education Quarterly* 33(1) Ja 1981 p 22-23

In higher education : The neglected aspect of good teaching. *Education Quarterly* 32(1) Ja 1980 p 8-10

New direction for higher education. *Teacher Education* 20(30-31) Ja-Ap 1985 p 33-36

Joshi, R.J.

An inquiry into the relation of creativity to academic achievement of the intellectually gifted. *J Educational Research and Extension* 18(3) Ja 1982 p 142-48

Joshi, R.K.

See

Sultan Ahmad *jt. auths.*

Joshi, R.K. and Srivastava, Niti

Discrepancy between high school examination scores and the scores predicted on the basis of intelligence, scientific interest, clerical interest, educational adjustment and family status. *Indian Educational Rev* 18(2) Ap 1982 p 100-06 refs tabs

Joshi, R.N.

Complementary occupational education. *EPA Quarterly Bulletin* 5(3-4) Oc 1982 - Ja 1983 p 14-25 refs

Joshi, R.S.

The revised B.Ed curriculum (Bombay University) as a step toward preparing productive teachers. *Progress of Education* 58(11) Je 1984 p 263-65 +

Joshi, Sneha M.

Effectiveness of skill-based instructional material synchronised with micro-teaching approach in the acquisition of the skill of illustrating with examples. *Indian Educational Rev* 16(3) Jl 1981 p 69-74

Problems of mathematics : A solution. *Progress of Education* 55(1) Ag 1980 p 9-11

Student support services for distance education. *University News* 24(42) 8

Nv 1986 p 59-62 refs

A study of the effect of skill based instructional materials synchronised with micro-teaching technique on the attitudes towards teaching. *Progress of Education* 55(10) My 1981 p 255-60 refs tabs

Joshi, Sneha M. and Ekbote, Eknath

Skill based approach to student teaching. *New Frontiers in Education* 11(2) Ap-Je 1981 p 81-85 refs

Joshi, Uma

Integrated education for disabled children. *Education Quarterly* 33(4) Oc 1981 p 13-14

See also

Talati, Naina *jt. auth.*

Joshi, V.K.

The teaching of grammar through literature. *J Indian Education* 6(4) Nv 1980 p 31-33

Joshi, Vibha

See

Menon, M.B. *jt. auth.*

Joshi, Vibha and Menon, Geeta

Research on women's education in India : A review. *Perspectives in Education* 2(2) Ap 1986 p 77-78

Joyce, Bruce and Weil, Marsha

Models of teaching. New Delhi, Prentice-Hall of India, e2. 1985, 499p. Rs.48 *Book Rev, Perspectives in Education* 1(4) Oc 1985 p 268-70

Julka, Satyapal

Models of education systems : Pitfalls of ignoring socio-economic variables. *J Higher Education* 7(3) Spr 1982 p 319-21

Status of examination reforms. *Education Quarterly* 33(1) Ja 1981 p 24-25

Justa, H.R.

Modernising educational administration at the grassroot level. *Teacher Today* 27(4) Ap-Je 1985 p 45-46

Juyal, P.D.

B.Ed admissions : Non-academic criteria. *Educational Rev* 87(5) My 1981 p 90-93 tabs

Determinants of interpersonal attraction among boys and girls : An empirical study. *J Education and Psychology* 44(3-4) Jl-De 1986 p 148-52

Some demographic variables influencing the attitude of scheduled caste towards the measures adopted for their welfare : An empirical study. *Progress of Education* 61(4-5) Nv-De 1986 p 85-88 refs

Jyan Nath

Discover the power of photography in working with handicapped children. *Our Education* 5 Jl 1984 p 55-58

The use of still photography as learning assistance for the language handicapped in the classroom. *Our Education* 6 Jl 1985-86 p 27-30

Kabra, Lalita

Education in rural area : Socially relevant and integrated strategy. *Teacher Today* 28(4) Ap-Je 1986 p 54-57

Kabra, R.N.
Don't teach : Let them learn? *Teacher Today* 23(3) Ja-Mr 1981 p 137-40

Kadam, Charudatta Parasharam
An experimental study of improvement in the teaching skills under microteaching among the student teachers. *Educational Rev* 91(4) Ap 1985 p 69-72 refs
An experimental study of improvement in the teaching skills under microteaching among the student teachers. *Progress of Education* 58(10) My 1984 p 246-48 refs tabs

Kadiyar, Jagesh Kumar
Science teaching and the nature of science. *Educational Rev* 85(2) Fe 1980 p 28-30

Kaile, Harnek S. and Bajwa, Parminder S.
Intelligence as a correlate of achievement in science across different levels of socio-economic status. *J Institute of Educational Research* 9(1) Ja 1985 p 18-21 refs

Kaikobad, N.F.
Preparing training material from ongoing field experience in NSS. *Prasar* 9(1-4) Ap 1982 - Ja 1983 p 1-8

KAKAR - KAKKAR

Kakar, M.P. and Chandhoke, K.R.
Vocational education programme for schools. *Rajasthan Board J Education* 21(3-4) Jl-De 1985 p 45-50

Kakkar, S.B.
Education for excellence. *Teacher Today* 27(4) Ap-Je 1985 p 37-41
Student attitude towards college *vis-a-vis* university. *J Higher Education* 4(2) Aut 1978 p 258-62
Teacher behaviour and student characteristics. *Indian Educational Rev* 17(1) Ja 1982 p 71-79 refs

Kakar, V.N.
Mass media for civic education. *Indian J Adult Education* 46(9) Se 1985 p 22-26

Kakkad, G.M.
Secondary teacher-education curricula : An analytical study and developing teacher education programme. *Research Bulletin* 14(1-2) Mr-Je 1984 p 20-39 tabs

Kakkar
See
Kakar

Kalathankal, Mathew
Don Bosco and the preventive system of education. *New Frontiers in Education* 11(3) Jl-Se 1981 p 1-25 refs

Kala, Kalyan and Soman, Anjali
Learning Marathi. Pune, Vishakha Pra. 1986, 231p. Rs.150 *Book Rev, Progress of Education* 61(1) Ag 1986 p 24+

Kalia, Ashok K.
Guidance services at primary school level : Some suggestions. *Educational*

Rev 92(1) Ja 1986 p 5-6
The importance of moral education at the high school level. *Educatioal Rev* 90(10) Oc 1984 p 158-60
Personality adjustment problem of adolescents studying in the school with different socio-economic status. *Experiments in Education* 12(10) De 1984 p 169-74 refs tab
Relevance of yoga philosophy in education : A critical evaluation. *Educational Rev* 89(11) Nv 1983 p 195-97
See also
Ahluwalia, S.P. *jt. auth.*
Mathur, S.S. *jt. auth.*

Kalia, Ashok K. and Mathur, S.S.
Effect of incentives on the learning ability of school students. *Progress of Education* 60(2) Se 1985 p 26-30 ref tabs
Social behaviour of teachers and their impact on the social behaviour of students : A socio-econometric study. *Progress of Education* 59(2) Se 1984 p 34-37 refs tabs

Kalia, Narendra Nath
Changing images of males and females : How of feminist sex role liberation in Indian school text books. *Indian Education* 13(10-11) Ja-Fe 1984 p 10-16
What will I be when I grow up : Equalising occupational choices in India's text books. *Educational Rev* 90(9) Se 1984 p 135-38; 90(10) Oc 1984 p 147-49; 90(11) Nv 1984 p 168-69 +

Kalla, Asha
Gandhi Shikshan Bhavan, Colleges of Education : Report of practice teaching, 1978-79. *Quest in Education* 16(2) Ap 1979 p 149-59

Kalpande, V.K.
Application of Getzel's model to the rapport-based programme of school improvement. *Research Bulletin* 12(1-2) Mr-Je 1982 p 3-10 tabs

Kalra, R.M.
Advances in science and technology as a motivational factor for science education. *Education Quarterly* 36(2) Ap 1984 p 24-28
Science curriculum materials for the disadvantaged children. *J Indian Education* 8(1) My 1982 p 3-9 tabs
Science for all. *Teacher Today* 27(2) Oc-De 1984 p 50-55
Some inherent problems in the crucial educational issues in developing countries. *Education Quarterly* 33(4) Oc 1981 p 15-18
Youth and values in developing countries. *Education Quarterly* 35(2) Ap 1983 p 43-47

Kamaljeet Kaur
See
Sodhi, T.S. *jt. auth.*

Kamat, A.R.
Higher education : Kothari Commission and after. *J Higher Education* 8(2) Aut 1982 p 141-43 refs

Kamat, R.V.
A case for autonomy. *J Higher Education* 1(1) Mon 1975 p 91-97 refs

Kamat, Vasudha
See
Deo, Pratibha *jt. auth.*
Kamatkar, M.R.
The school inspection : A plea for evolving new strategies. *Progress of Education* 57(8) Mr 1983 p 184-86
Kamawat, Usha
See
Rai, G.C. *jt. auth.*
Kamawat, Usha and Rai, G.C.
Contact personality factors of science, agricultural science and agricultural engineering undergraduate students. *Indian J Extension Education* 19(3-4) Se-De 1983 p 26-31 refs tabs
Dominant job values and preferences of undergraduate students. *National J Education* 7(1) Se 1984 p 39-50 refs tabs
Kamila, Bana Behari
Creative thinking abilities of blind school children. *J Education and Psychology* 41(4) Ja 1984 p 198-203 refs
Occupational status of parents of Harijans and Tribal Welfare development high school students of Orissa. *National J Education* 6(1) Se 1983 p 56-64 refs tabs
A study of attitude of students towards school of Harijans and Tribal Welfare Department high school of Orissa. *J Education and Psychology* 43(3-4) Oc 1985-Ja 1986 p 187-92 refs
Kamlesh Kumar
See
Hira Nand *jt. auth.*
Kanakaraj, K.
See
Indiesan, Jayalakshmi *jt. auth.*
Kanchan, Ram Singh
Lovable toys : A project on educating the handicapped children. *Primary Teacher* 9(2) Ap 1984 p 31-33
Kane, Michael
See
Lehning, Rolf *jt. auth.*
Kannan, K.P.
The people's science movement in Kerala. *Indian J Adult Education* 40(4) Ap 1979 p 27-35 tabs
Kansal, M.R.
Education in journalism : A proposal. *J Indian Education* 11(3) Se 1985 p 39-42
Kansal, M.R. and Gupta, P.L.
Behavioural characteristics of school principals. *EPA Quarterly Bulletin* 7(1-2) Ap-Jl 1984 p 24-29 refs
Kant
See
under full name, e.g., Shashi Kant

Kanti Prasad *et al*
An experimental study of a 'programme' in set theory. *Bharatiya Shiksha Shodh Patrika* 1(2) Jl 1982 p 10-24 refs tab

Kapadia, S.G.
The headmaster and organiser. *Progress of Education* 53(12) Jl 1979 p 234-36

Kapat, G.B.
See
Senapati, B.B. *jt. auth.*

KAPOOR - KAPUR

Kapoor, D.R.
See
Gupta, Arun K. *jt. auth.*

Kapur, J.N.
Innovations in undergraduate education. *J Higher Education* 1(1) Mon 1975 p 103-09 refs
An operation research approach to educational planning. *Indian Education* 10(1-2) Ap-Je 1980 p 23-28
Some aspects of scientific assessment of learning achievement and creativity. *Indian Education* 10(4) Jl 1980 p 6-10; 10(5) Ag 1980 p 8-12
Some needs of Indian education today. *Indian Education* 9(12) My 1980 p 16-18
Teaching of mathematics in distance education. *University News* 24(42) 8 Nv 1986 p 43

Kapoor, Neena
See
Kaul, Sunita *jt. auth.*

Kapur, Preeti
See
Sen, Anima *jt. auth.*

Kapur, S.D.
See
Kocher, H.C. *jt. auth.*

Kappan, Sebastian
Marxism and Christianity. *New Frontiers in Education* 15(2) Ap-Je 1985 p 22-28

Kaprum, N.S.
Expected performance of pupil teachers and their actual performance during practice teaching. *Quest in Education* 18(2) Ap 1981 p 150-57

Kapur
See
Kapoor

Karim, Samim F.
Conflict between immigrant mother, daughter in United Kingdom. *Asian J Psychological Rev* 7(2) Jl 1981 p 1-11

Karlekar, Malavika
Higher education and the scheduled castes. *J Higher Education* 1(2) Aut

1975 p 179-87 refs tabs

Karnad, Sunanda

See

Khopkar, Asha *jt. auth.*

Karnawat, C.M.

See

Nayyar, S.M. *jt. auth.*

Karunan, J.R. Victor

SEVA credit union : A success story of workers self-reliance. *Indian J Adult Education* 46(5) My 1985 p 37-40 tabs

Kashinath, H.M.

The drop-outs. *Progress of Education* 54(8) Mr 1980 p 163-65

See also

Kasinath, H.M.

Kashyap, Anand

Conceptual basis of the National Adult Education Programme. *Prasar* 7(3-4) Oc 1980-Ja 1981 p 31-37

Kasinath, H.M.

Functions and problems of deputy directors of public instruction in Karnataka state. *EPA Quarterly Bulletin* 8(3-4) Oc 1985-Ja 1986 p 1-6 refs

A study of wastage in teacher training institutions in Karnataka. *Progress of Education* 60(7) Fe 1986 p 156-60 + tabs

See also

Kashinath, H.M.

Kassam, Yusuf O.

The voices of new literates from Tanzania. Tanzania Pub H. *Book Rev, Teacher Today* 22(4) Ap-Je 1980 p 98-99

Kathuria, P.R.

See

Sharma, V.P. *jt. auth.*

Kathuria, R.P.

Aims, objectives and the philosophy of Indian education. *Teacher Today* 24(4) Ap-Je 1982 p 57-64 refs

Elementary education in the People's Republic of China, 1949-1975. *Teacher Today* 21(3) Ja-Mr 1979 p 6-18 refs

Microteaching. New Delhi, Vikas Pub. *Book Rev, Educational Rev* 85(8) Ag 1979 p 158

Primary education in China. *Primary Teacher* 5(4) Oc 1980 p 5-8

Universalisation of education : An experiment. *Primary Teacher* 7(3) Jl 1983 p 12-14

Working with the community as a part of the teacher education programme. *Teacher Education* 13(8-9) Jl-Oc 1979 p 79-82

Kathuria, R.P. and Gupta, V.P.

A study in the evaluation of teacher educators by their students under training in the B.Ed., summer school-cum-correspondence course. *Quest in Education* 18(4) Oc 1981 p 292-301

Katiyar, B.L.
See
Rai, K. *jt. auth.*

Katiyar, P.C. and Jarial, Gurpal Singh
The role of sex in the enhancement of creativity among adolescents through a process-oriented training programme : A study. *Indian Educational Rev* 18(1) Ja 1983 p 40-46 refs tabs

Katiyar, S.N.
Culture and education in Thailand; Historical antecendents. *Teacher Today* 22(3) Ja-Mr 1980 p 71-80
Draft National Policy on Education 1979. *Teacher Today* 22(2) Oc-De 1979 p 79-83
Modernisation and the rural women. *Teacher Today* 24(3) Ja-Mr 1982 p 20-26 refs

KAUL - KOUL

Kaul, Anita
School : A weighted satchel. *Teacher Education* 14(12-13) Jl-Oc 1980 p 63-67
Verbal and non-verbal intelligence as correlates of achievement in mother-tongue and foreign language. *Educational Rev* 9(8) Ap 1985 p 130-33 refs

Kaul, J.N.
Educational planning and administration as a discipline in the universities. *Indian Education* 10(12) Mr 1981 p 30-34
Higher education in India, 1951-71. Simla, IIAS. 1974, 203p. *Book Rev, J Higher Education* 1(2) Aut 1975 p 292-93
The university community and its autonomy. *Indian Education* 11(1-2) Ap-My 1981 p 35-37

Koul, Lokesh and Bhadwal, Satish Chandra
Implication of formative evaluation. *J Indian Education* 12(4) Nv 1986 p 11-16 refs
Institutional magazine : An alternative blueprint. *J Indian Education* 12(3) Se 1986 p 23-29 refs tabs

Kaul, M.K.
Development of personality trait regularity among children. *Primary Teacher* 9(4) Oc 1984 p 26-29

Kaul, M.L.
Development of self-confidence among primary school children. *Primary Teacher* 8(1) Ja 1983 p 25-28 tabs
Gandhian thoughts on basic education : Relevance and development. *J Indian Education* 8(3) Ja 1983 p 11-16 refs

Kaul, P.N.
See
Balasubramaniam, S. *jt. auth.*
Desai, G.R. *jt. auth.*

Kaul, Sheila
National address on objectives of teaching profession. *J Educational*

Research and Extension 20(2) Oc 1983 p 92-102

Kaul, Sunita and Kapoor, Neena

Training personnel for educating young children. *J Indian Education* 12(3) Se 1986 p 53-57; *Progress of Education* 60(3) De 1985 p 103-06 refs

Kaul, Venita *et al*

Dependency and its antecedents : A review. *Indian Educational Rev* 17(2) Ap 1982 p 35-46 refs

Kaur

See also

under full name, e.g., Jagdip Kaur

Kaur, D.K. and Mathur, P.N.

A study of farmers comprehension of illustrations. *Indian J Extension Education* 20(1-2) Je 1984 p 1-6 refs tabs

Kaushal, Joginder

Management of distance education. *University News* 24(42) 8 Nv 1986 p 21-24

Kaushall, S.S.

Glimpses of education in Haryana. Delhi, Rakesh Pra. 1981, 118p. Rs.15 *Book Rev, J Higher Education* 8(2) Jl 1982 p 94

Kaushik, B.N.

The primary teacher and the handicapped child. *Primary Teacher* 4(2) Ap 1979 p 27-29

Kaushik, Shashi Lata and Sharma, Atma Nand

Prediction of success in Bachelor's degree examinations in arts, science and commerce. *Indian Educational Rev* 14(4) Oc 1979 p 128-44 appdx

Kaushik, V. Seth and Desai, Panna

An experiment to study the effect of training in microteaching skills on the teacher competence of primary teachers. *Progress of Education* 53(10-11) My-Je 1979 p 194-200 refs tabs

Kavita, Alpana

See

Gupta, Pushpa, *jt. auth.*

Kawane, S.D.

See

Deshpande, S.W. *jt. auth.*

Kawatra, P.S.

Teachers' college libraries in Orissa : A study. *J Indian Education* 6(2) Jl 1980 p 55-58

Teachers professional attitude to library utilisation. *Educational Rev* 89(9) Se 1983 p 151-52

Kazi

See also

under full name, e.g., Khalid Ahmed, Kazi

Kazi, M.I.

Education in Israel. *Progress of Education* 58(3) Oc 1983 p 64-65

Education today in Saudi Arabia. *Progress of Education* 60(6) Ja 1986 p 143-44

Keeves, J.P.

Educating for literacy and numeracy in Australian schools. ACER. 1978, 60

Book Rev, Education Quarterly 31(1) Ag 1979 p 39

Kelkar, M.G.

Psychology of adult needs and adoption of innovations in the changing rural scene. *Indian J Adult Education* 40(6) Je 1979 p 19-24

Kelkar, S.V.

See

Shivanekar, L.M. *jt. auth.*

Kelu, P.

A socio-econometric study of Peer-grouping patterns among primary school pupils of Kerala. *Experiments in Education* 12(12) Fe 1985 p 209-15 refs tabs

Kent, Frank Spencer

Testing for teaching. London, Hodder 148p. £3.45 *Book Rev, Education Quarterly* 38(2) Sum 1986 p 40-42

Kesawalla, Gulistan J. and Dhakam, Naaz S.

Role of school and coaching class in formal education : A comparative perspective. *Progress of Education* 61(1) Ag 1986 p 5-12 refs

Keshar, Sushama A.

Maintenance of standards with reference to internal assessment. *Progress of Education* 56(10) My 1982 p 246-50

Khadar, M.A. and Singhal, Sushila

Institutional quality, student input and output : Analysis of six Indian universities. *J Higher Education* 9(1) Mon 1983 p 34-35 tabs

Khajapeer, M.

How Vietnam tackled illiteracy? : A report. *Indian J Adult Education* 40(3) Mr 1979 p 39-42 refs ft-n

Pre-service training programme for continuing education instructors in Thailand. *Indian J Adult Education* Se 1979 p 11-16

See also

Kulsum, Umma *jt. auth.*

Khalid Ahmed, Kazi and Ghadially, Rehana

Hopes and concerns of engineering students in India. *J Higher Education* 5(3) Spr 1980 p 401-09 appdx refs tabs

Khamborker, K.R.

Training teaching techniques. Akola, Deshmukh, L.W. 104p. Rs.22.50 *Book Rev, Education Quarterly* 33(1) Ja 1981 p 39-40

Khan, A.G.

Passivisation : To teach or not to teach. *J Indian Education* 8(3) Se 1982 p 44-47

Technical English : American and British usage. *J Indian Education* 5(2) Jl 1979 p 56-58

Teaching of humanities for the computer age. *J Indian Education* 12(4) Nv 1986 p 22-26

Khan, Abdul Haq

Supervision in secondary schools. Delhi, Arya Book Depot. 1980, 61p. Rs.5 *Book Rev, J Indian Education* 6(2) Jl 1980 p 78

Khan, Ansar Ali

Material production for out of school population education. *Indian J Adult Education* 43(7) Jl 1982 p 3-8 refs

Khan, Asudalla *et al*

Scholastic achievement as a function of aspiration, religion and socio-economic status. *J Education and Psychology* 39(4) Ja 1982 p 218-23 refs

Khan, Dildar and Mohammed Ghufran

Visual and auditory effects on recall performance to individual components of the compound stimulus in paired associate learning. *J Institute of Educational Research* 4(1) Ja 1980 p 8-12 refs tabs

Khan, Inayat

Teaching of English through correspondence. *University News* 24(42) 8 Nv 1986 p 45-54 refs

Khan, L. Habib

Educational innovation in Pakistan. *Rajasthan Board J Education* 16(1-2) Ja-Je 1980 p 41-54

Khan, M.A.

Effect of parental deprivation on personality adjustment with special reference to the denotified tribes of U.P. *Indian Educational Rev* 17(1) Ja 1982 p 99-109

Parental deprivation in relations to academic achievement of denotified tribes. *Indian Educational Rev* 14(4) Oc 1979 p 95-98

Khan, M.S.

Commerce education. New Delhi, Sterling. 1982, 126p. Rs.50 *Book Rev, Education Quarterly* 35(3) Jl 1983 p 60-61

Khan, M.W.

Educational and vocational aspirations of Hindu and Muslim school students : A comparative study. *Indian Educational Rev* 20(4) Oc 1985 p 66-67

Khan, M.Z. and Singh, D.R.

College youth, their courses of study and their view of society. *J Higher Education* 4(1) Mon 1978 p 57-66 refs tabs

Khan, Mohammed Ferdouse

Issues and constraints in the introduction of appropriate basic education in Bangladesh. *Perspectives in Education* 1(3) Jl 1985 p 157-66 refs

Khan, Mumtaz Ali

Literate girls : Impact on family. *Educational Rev* 85(4) Ap 1979 p 75-77 tabs

Place of surveying in geography curriculum : A reappraisal. *Teacher Today* 24(2) Oc-De 1981 p 45-53 refs

Khan, Q.U.

Higher education in India : Some issues. *J Higher Education* 5(2) Aut 1979 p 167-82

Khan, Shamsur Rehman

Economic status as a determinant of tension among youths. *Asian J Psychology and Education* 13(1) Ja 1984 p 4-6

Khan, Sharif

Teacher education curriculum. *Educational Rev* 85(6) Je 1979 p 106-11

Khandekar, Prakash and Mathur, P.N.

A measurement of farm magazine effectiveness. *Indian J Extension Education* 16(3-4) De 1980 p 82-87 tabs

Khanijo, M.K.
Diversification of technical education. *Education Quarterly* 37(4) Wint 1985 p 22-27

Khanna, Kailash and Malhotra, G.P.
Reading ability test for elementary school dropouts. *Indian J Adult Education* 44(2) Ap 1983 p 23-30 refs tabs

Khanna, Vinita
See
Roy, Sumita *jt. auth.*

Kharde, R.L.
See
Srivastava, R.M. *jt. auth.*

Khare, Briz B.
Things of the mind : Dialogues with J. Krishnamurti. New York, Philosophical Libi 184p. £14.95 *Book Rev, Education Quarterly* 38(3) Aut 1986 p 47-49

Khattri, Pradeep Kumar and Gupta, Prabha
Reduction of abusive behaviour as a function of types of reinforcement in scheduled and non-scheduled caste children. *J Education and Psychology* 37(4) Ja 1980 p 255-62 refs tabs

Khaund, Aparna H.
See
Chandra, A. *jt. auth.*

Khazan Singh
Increasing the reading speed in English at the higher secondary level. *Rajasthan Board J Education* 19(2-3) Ap-Se 1983 p 15-21

Kher, A.O.
See
Patel, N.C. *jt. auth.*

Kher, A.O. and Jha, P.N.
Factors associated with farmers attitude towards primary agricultural credit society in Gujarat. *Indian J Extension Education* 14(1-2) Ja-Je 1978 p 23-29 refs

Kherde, R.L.
See
Soni, J.S. *jt. auth.*

Kherde, R.L. and Sahay, B.N.
Role performance of village level workers in agriculture production. *Indian J Extension Education* 15(1-2) Je 1979 p 67-69 tabs

Khobre, A.D.
Education in the 21st century. *Educational Rev* 90(10) Oc 1984 p 151-52

Khoi, Le Thang
The future shape of education. *Education Quarterly* 34(1) Ja 1982 p 17-24

Khopkar, Asha and Karnad, Sunanda
Problems of teachers in higher education. *Progress of Education* 60(1) Ag 1985 p 7-9

Khosla, D.N.
Educational journalism : Status, scope and priorities. *Education Quarterly* 37(3) Aut 1985 p 25-31

Status of educational journalism in India : A review. *J Indian Education* 11(3) Se 1985 p 3-12

Whither our single teacher schools? *Teacher Today* 22(4) Ap-Je 1980 p 33-39

Khosla, D.N. and Shukla, Neerja

Educational research by Indian research scholars at foreign universities : A review. *Indian Educational Rev* 16(2) Ap 1980 p 50-58 appdx

Khullar, K.K.

New Education Policy. *Education Quarterly* 38(3) Aut 1986 p 1-3

Khurana, G.

Educational facilities for scheduled castes. *Educational Quarterly* 31(3-4) Oc 1979-Ja 1980 p 31-35

Khurana, Kiran

See

Ghore, Papiya *jt. auth.*

Kidd, J.R.

A China plant and an Indian cane : Adult learning programmes in India and China. *Indian J Adult Education* 40(1) Ja 1979 p 9-36 appdx

Kidd, R. and Byram, M.L.

Encouraging participation in development : Laedza Batanani case studies. *Indian J Adult Education* 40(8) Ag 1979 p 11-29 refs

Kidwai, A.J.

Inaugural address (delivered at the 32nd IAEA Annual Conference). *Indian J Adult Education* 40(10-11) Oc-Nv 1979 p 9-14

Kidwai, Mohsina

Develop unconventional measures of education. *Indian J Adult Education* 45(12) De 1984 p 9-11

King, Kenneth J.

Research on literacy and work among the rural poor. *Indian J Adult Education* 41(1-2) Ja-Fe 1980 p 15-23

Kinkar, Krishna and Prasad Singh

Problem checklist for secondary school teachers. *J Institute of Educational Research* 8(2) My 1984 p 7-11 refs tabs

Kiranmayi, Y.S.

Need for scientific management of universities in India. *University News* 24(43) 16 Nv 1986 p 4-7

Kirillovugryumov, V. and Sumarokov, L.

Raising the efficiency of degree oriented research. *Progress of Education* 56(5) De 1981 p 108-09

Kirpal Kaur

See

Grewal, S.S. *jt. auth.*

Kirpal, Prem

Search for new human values. *Teacher Today* 24(4) Ap-Je 1982 p 13-21

Toward an education for the 21st century. *Teacher Today* 28(2) Oc-De 1985 p 50-61

Kirpal Singh

Bhai Gurdas Library, Guru Nanak Dev University. *University News* 24(40) 23 Oc 1986 p 3-4

Kirsh, Audrey L.
See
Reiter, Henry H. *jt. auth.*
Kishan, R.
See
Shah, M.M. *jt. auth.*
Kishore
See also
under full name/surname, e.g., Lalit Kishore
Kishore Sant
Adult education in Thailand. *Indian J Adult Education* 40(4) Ap 1979 p 17-26 refs
Universities and people's education for development. *J Higher Education* 8(2) Aut 1982 p 185-89 refs
Universities and people's education for development in India. *Teacher Today* 22(3) Ja-Mr 1980 p 64-68
Klausmeier, Herbert J.
Learning and teaching concepts : A strategy for testing applications of theory. New York, Academic Press (N.Y.) 1980, 220p. £22.50 *Book Rev, J Education and Psychology* 39(3) Oc 1981 p 204
Klees, Steven *et al*
Educational evaluation : Trends towards more participating approaches. *Perspectives in Education* 2(3) Jl 1986 p 133-53
Knight, A. John
See
Balasubramaniam, R. *jt. auth.*
Ganeshan, R. *et al jt. auths.*
Knight, A. John and Somasundaram, G.
Small farmers preference for radio programmes and modes of the presentation. *Indian J Extension Education* 16(3-4) De 1980 op 90-93 tabs
Kocher, H.C. and Kapur, S.D.
Construction and standardisation of a group test of general hostility (GTGH) in Indian conditions. *J Education and Psychology* 36(3) Ja 1979 p 437-47 refs
Kochhar, S.K.
Guidance and counselling in colleges and universities. New Delhi, Sterling. 1984, 462p. Rs.26 *Book Rev, J Indian Education* 10(5) Ja 1985 p 53-55
Pivotal issues in Indian education. New Delhi, Sterling. 344p. Rs.80 *Book Rev, Education Quarterly* 33(3) Jl 1981 p 43-44
Teaching of social sciences. New Delhi, Sterling, 1979, 389p. Rs.50 *Book Rev, Education Quarterly* 32(3) Jl 1980 p 47-48
Kochuthresia, V.J.
Pre-school education : An Indian perspective. *J Indian Education* 11(2) Jl 1985 p 3-10 refs
Kogekar, S.V.
Centenary of Deccan Education Society and Fergussan College. *Progress of Education* 59(6) Ja 1985 p 111-18 +
Kohli, Tehal
Classification and comparison of different approaches to identify over and

under achievers. *J Education and Psychology* 38(1) Ap 1980 p 22-27 refs

Kokate, K.D. and Tyagi, K.C.

Differential dairy farming knowledge and perceived training needs of the trained and untrained farmers. *J Educational Research and Extension* 18(4) Ap 1982 p 201-09 refs tabs

Perceptual variability of training needs as viewed by trained and untrained farmers. *Indian J Extension Education* 18(3-4) De 1982 p 65-67

Kolipillai, Victor

Leadership training through non-formal education : The RUHSA experience. *New Frontiers in Education* 13(1) Ja-Mr 1983 p 31-36

Konovatov, Vladimir

The brain, memory and languages. *Progress of Education* 58(1) Ag 1983 p 7-18 +

Kool, V.K. and Agarwal, Rita

A developmental study of short-term recall of numeral sequence. *Asian J Psychology and Education* 5(1-3) 1979 p 44-50 refs tabs

Kool, V.K. and Rana, M.

Tactual short terms memory of blind and sighted chidren. *Asian J Psychology and Education (Special)* 10(1-4) 1982 p 24-32

Korotov, Viktor

Village school in the USSR : Specific features and problems. *Progress of Education* 55(2) Se 1980 p 33-35

KOSHE - KOSHY

Koshe, G.S.

Dr. G.S. Khair : Great educationist. *Progress of Education* 61(2) Se 1986 p 25-26

Status of education journalism. *Progress of Education* 57(7) Fe1983 p 151-53

Koshy, S

See

Bhagat, Rekha *jt. auth.*

Koshy, S. and Bhagat, Rekha

Some aspects of nutrition education associated with feeding infants and toddlers in rural farm families. *Indian J Adult Education* 41(3) Mr 1980 p 15-19

Koshy, T.A.

Group discussion reports. *Indian J Adult Education* 44(1-2) Je-Se 1983 p 25-28

Kothari, Abhay and Kothari, Ramesh Chandra

Health education story through match stick drawings. *Primary Teacher* 4(1) Ja 1979 p 24-25

Kothari, D.S.

Education and human values. *Teacher Today* 28(1) Jl-Se 1985 p 1-10

Kothari, R.G.

Population education. *Educational Rev* 89(9) Se 1983 p 159-61

Kothari, Rajendra

Language laboratory drills and their role in teaching a foreign language

English. *Rajasthan Board J Education* 19(2-3) Ap-Se 1983 p 10-14

Kothari, Ramesh Chandra

Grade system. *Education Rev* 91(10) Oc 1985 p 161-63

See also

Kothari, Abhay *jt. auth.*

Koul

See

Kaul-Kaula

Koura, S.P.

Help books in Punjab schools. *Educational Rev* 85(1) Ja 1979 p 3-8

Krishna

See also

under full name/surname, e.g., Gopala Krishna

Krishna, K.P. and Agarwal, Vijaya Rani

Reading ability and intelligence. *Indian Educational Rev* 18(1) Ja 1983 p 33-39 refs

Krishna Kumar

Breaking away. *Teacher Today* 27(4) Ap-Je 1985 p 1-9

Social context of the school curriculum : Potential and problems of comparative study. *Teacher Today* 22(1) Jl-Se 1979 p 16-19

Waste in Indian higher education. *Educational Rev* 85(11) Nv 1979 p 201-02

See also

Girja Kumar *jt. auth.*

Krishna Kumari, P. *et al*

Study of creative abilities of tribal children in relation to their sex and socio-economic status. *J Institute of Educational Research* 10(1) Ja 1986 p 1-4

KRISHNAMOORTHY - KRISHNAMURTHY

Krishnamurthy, B.H. and Naik, C.

Guidelines in the preparation of an adult education primer. *Indian J Adult Education* 41(1-2) Ja-Fe 1980 p 3-7

Krishnamoorthy, P.V.

Teaching literacy through media. *Indian J Adult Education* 41(10) Oc 1980 p 24-26

Krishnamurthy, S.

Management of teacher education in India. *Indian Education* 11(1-2) Ap-My 1981 p 92-95

Krishnamoorthy, V.

Some glimpses of American higher education. *University News* 23(30) 8 Ag 1985 p 2-4+

Krishan

See also

under full name/surname, e.g., Anantha Krishnan, M.V.

Krishnan, K.

A study of the relationship between the secondary school science and mathematics curricula of Kerala and Tamil Nadu. *J Educational Research and Extension* 18(4) Ap 1982 p 210-19 refs tabs

Krishnan, Prahha

The symbol and the substance : Indian youth in development. New Delhi, Vishwa Yuvak Kendra. 1980, 119p. Rs.15 *Book Rev, J Higher Education* 7(3) Spr 1982 p 332-33

Krishnan, Rita

School achievement of pupils belonging to different levels of socio-economic status. *Asian J Psychology and Education* 9(3) 1982 p 11-17

See also

Samsananda Raj, H. *jt. auth.*

Krishna Raj

See also

under surname 'Raj', e.g., Raj, Mathreyi Krishna

Krishnaraj, K. and Balasubramanian, P.S.

Size and structure of educational organisations. *J Educational Planning and Administration.* 1(1) Oc 1986 p 21-27 refs

Krishna Rao, R.

A comparative study of the relative effectivness of four methods of teaching literacy to adults. *Indian Educational Rev* 17(1) Ja 1982 p 80-85

Needed changes in education. *J Indian Education* 6(2) Jl 1980 p 30-34

Role of educational institutions in the implementation of national policies. *Progress of Education* 54(7) Fe 1980 p 136-40

Krishan Rao, R. and Nageswara Rao, D.

Student welfare services : Problems and prospects. *J Indian Education* 10(6) Mr 1985 p 55-60

Krishna Rao, R. and Papa, R.

Challenging tasks of educational supervisor. *Primary Teacher* 10(1) Ja 1985 p 32-34

Curricula changes at school level in Andhara Pradesh. *Primary Teacher* 8(4) Oc 1983 p 26-29

Krishna Reddy, N.

See

Venkata Rami Reddy, A. *jt. auth.*

Krishnaswami, M.K.

See

Kunnal, L.B. *et al jt. auths.*

Krishnawami, O.R.

An approach to modernisation of commerce courses. *J Higher Education* 2(2) Aut 1976 p 267-72 refs

Kude, U.L.

Anatomy of the crises in education. *University News* 23(11) 16 Mr 1985 p 5+

Kudesia, Sushil

The stage and music in primary schools. *Primary Teacher* 5(2) Ap 1980 p 40-42

Kukushkin, G.T. *ed.*

The system of physical education in the USSR. Moscow, Raduge Pub. 1983, 321p. Rs.6.25 *Book Rev, Progress of Education* 60(10-11) My-Je 1986 p 256

Kulandivel, K.
Inculcating ethical and social values in education. *J Educational Research and Extension* 17(3) Ja 1981 p 191-94

Kuldip Kaur
Attitude of the people towards women literacy in Punjab. *Educational Rev* 91(8) Ag 1985 p 126-29
Education in India, 1781-1985. Chandigarh, Centre for Res in Rural and Industrial Development. 1985, 534p. Rs.280 *Book Rev, Perspective in Education* 2(4) Oc 1986 p 251-53

Kuldip Kumar
Dynamics of children's behaviour. *Primary Teacher* 10(4) Oc 1985 p 9-12
How and why children fear? *Primary Teacher* 10(4) Oc 1985 p 13-16
Inculcating study habits among children. *Primary Teacher* 10(4) Oc 1985 p 24-26
Physical needs of children. *Primary Teacher* 10(4) Oc 1985 p 6-8
Teachers behaviour and its effects on pupils. *Primary Teacher* 10(4) Oc 1985 p 17-23

Kulich, Jindra
Agricultural extension in Romania. *Indian J Adult Educatin* 39(9) Se 1978 p 30-31

Kulkarni, J.G.
The structural approach : Its short comings. *Progress of Education* 55(5) De 1980 p 129-31+

Kulkarni, K.M. and Desai, A.T.
Geography text-books in Gujarat and Maharashtra : A comparative study. *Progress of Education* 59(10-11) My-Je 1985 p 86-98 appdx

Kulkarni, N.B.
Inspection and supervision of primary schools in Maharashtra with special reference to Aurangabad region. *Research Bulletin* 15(3-4) Se-De 1985 p 47-57

Kulkarni, P.A.
See
Bandivedekar, B.S. *jt. auth.*

Kulkarni, V.G. and Gambhir, V.G.
The effect of language barrier on the universalisation of education. *Indian Educational Rev* 16(1) Ja 1981 p 48-59

KULSHRESHTHA - KULSHRESTHA

Kulshrestha, G.P.
Printing for the practising teacher. *Rajasthan Board J Education* 15(2) Ap-Je 1979 p 29-34

Kulshrestha, Gopal Prasad
Exploiting cramming for teaching composition and essay type answers. *Rajasthan Board J Education* 21(2) Ap-Je 1985 p 1-8

Kulshreshtha, Indira
Children's literature in India. *Teacher Today* 24(2) Oc-De 1981 p 10-18 refs
Children literature : Preparation and selection. *Education Quarterly* 35(4) Oc 1983 p 37-40

Un-English expressions in English books. *Primary Teacher* 9(3) Jl 1984 p 8-10

Value education through children's literature. *Education Quarterly* 38(3) Aut 1986 p 18-27

Want to buy children's books? *Teacher Today* 27(4) Ap-Je 1985 p 27-33

Kulshrestha, S.P.

Mini teaching : A new experiment in teacher education. D.A.V. (PG) College, 1979, 24p. Rs.5 *Book Rev, Teacher Today* 22(4) Ap-Je 1980 p 98

Kulshreshtha, Shivendra Kumar

Self-situational deprivations in the school adjustment of tribal children. *J Indian Education* 5(2) Jl 1979 p 41-47

Kulsum, Umma and Khajapeer, M.

Teacher-education effectiveness : A research study. *Indian Educational Rev* 20(2) Ap 1985 p 51-57

Kulwinder Singh

Academic motivation among high school students in relation to academic achievement and sex. *J Education and Psychology* 43(3-4) Oc 1985 - Ja 1986 p 164-68

Creative thinking and culture : A comparative study of tribal and non-tribal high school students of Himachal Pradesh. *Progress of Education* 59(1) Ag 1984 p 11-17 refs tabs

A study of attitude of college and university students towards drug abuse. *J Institute of Educational Research* 7(3) Se 1983 p 1-6

Kumar

See also

under full name, e.g., Kamlesh Kumar

Kumar, A.

Intelligence and originality among science and art students at +2 stage : A comparative study. *Asian J Psychology and Education* 14(1-4) 1984 p 15-18

Programmed and expository instructional treatments effectiveness in relation to neuroticism. *J Education and Psychology* 42(1-2) Ap-Je 1983 p 84-87

Technology in adult education. *Educational Rev* 86(8) Ag 1980 p 157-58

Kumar, A. and Sharma, S.

Effect of anxiety on original thinking of students in different streams at +2 stage. *J Education and Psychology* 40(3) Oc 1983 p 157-61

Kumar, K.L. and Palki, S.D.

Multiple choice items : A framework of educational research. *Indian Education* 13(3-4) Je-Jl 1983 p 15-16

Kumar, Kamla and Khitha, Sadhana

Women in science and technology. *Education Quarterly* 34(4) Oc 1982 p 8-10 refs

Kumar, N.

NAEP : Some suggestions. *Indian J Adult Education* 40(9) Se 1979 p 31

Kumar, Rajni

Secondary education for girls : The what and the new. *Education Quarterly* 34(4) Oc 1982 p 31-33

Kumar, S.

An investigation into the questioning behaviour of science teachers. *Experiments in Education* 6(9) Nv 1978 p 163-66

See also

Menon, M.B. *jt. auth.*

Kumar, S. and Ravindranath, M.J.

Development of creative thinking in the primary school children. *Primary Teacher* 4(1) Ja 1979 p 5-9

Kumaraswamy, T.

Developing curriculum for adult learners. *Educational Rev* 89(3) Mr 1983 p 51-54 refs

See also

Adinarayana Reddy, P. *jt. auth.*

Kundu, Amitabh

See

Moonis Raza *jt. auth.*

Kundu, C.L.

Adult education : Principles, practices and prospects. New Delhi, Sterling. 1984, 107p. *Book Rev, Progress of Education* 69(5) De 1985 p 121-22; *Teacher Today* 27(2) Oc-De 1984 p 95-96

Teacher effectiveness : A resume of research. *National J Education* 3(2) Mr 1981 p 30-52 refs

See also

Wadhwa, B.S. *jt. auth.*

Kundu, C.L. and Wadhwa, B.S.

Attitude and political and protest behaviour. *J Education and Psychology* 42(1-2) Ap-Jl 1984 p 15-22 refs

Kundu, Dibakar

Creative development in school children. *Education Quarterly* 37(3) Aut 1985 p 6-7

Liberal education : A process of man-making. *J Indian Education* 12(4) Nv 1986 p 52-55

The semester system. *J Indian Education* 8(3) Se 1983 p 20-25

Kundu, M.

Concept of 'Raska' implications for tribal education. *New Frontiers in Education* 12(2) Ap-Je 1982 p 42-46

Preparing 'readers' for tribal adult learners : Some viable topics. *Indian J Adult Education* 42(9) Se 1981 p 21-24 refs

Teaching in a poly-cultural context : Lessons from concept, trends and developments in some relevant foundation disciplines. *J Higher Education* 8(2) Aut 1982 p 191-98 refs

Kundu, Manmatha

Tribal education in India : An effective pedagogy. *J Indian Education* 12(4) Nv 1986 p 43-48

Kundu, Nilanjana

See

Bandyopadhyay, Swaraj *jt. auth.*

Kundu, Raj Kala
See
Arvinda Chandra *jt. auth.*

Kundu, Ramanath and Bhaumik, Gita
Social and psychological factors influencing juvenile deliquency. *Our Education* 1 Jl 1980 p 41-47 refs

Kundu, Ramanath and Biswas, Chandidas
Changing pattern of inter personal relationship in adolescent boys and girls. *Indian Educational Rev* 15(1) Ja 1980 p 46-52
Stability of nominee status of adolescent boys and girls. *Our Education* 3-4 Jl 1983 p 13-19 refs

Kundu, Ramanath and Ghosh, Ratna
Status in marital adjustment : Adjusted and maladjusted couples compared. *J Education and Psychology* 38(3) Oc 1980 p 194-202 refs tabs

Kundu, Ramanath and Maite, Basudhara
Isolated children : A need concept. *J Institute of Educational Research* 7(2) My 1983 p 16-19
Isolated children : A psychological study. *Indian Educational Rev* 20(2) Ap 1985 p 28-38

Kundu, Ramanath and Roy Chaudhuri, Jayanthi
A study of the effect of socio-economic status on the frustration reactions on school going children. *J Institute of Educational Research* 9(1) Ja 1985 p 13-17 refs tabs

Kunnal, L.B. *et al*
Adoption of new technologies in dry land sorghum crop production. *Indian J Extension Education* 20(3-4) Se-De 1984 p 60-62

Kunnunkal, T.V.
Reflections on a new National Policy on Education. *New Frontiers in Education* 10(3) Jl-Se 1980 p 25-34
Value based education. *New Frontiers in Education* 14(1) Ja-Mr 1984 p 19-25

Kunwar, N.
Teaching of correct pronunciation in English at primary level. *Primary Teacher* 9(2) Ap 1984 p 24-26

Kunzroo, O.N.
See
Baldev Singh *jt. auth.*

Kuppan, A.
See
Rajmohan, G. *jt. auth.*

Kurashy, Salma
Home work and assignments. *Educational Rev* 89(10) Oc 1983 p 179-81

Kureshi, Afzal
See
Akbar Husain *jt. auth.*

Kureshi, Afzal and Akbar Husain
Evaluator's physique and self evaluation as moderating variables in opposite sex physique attraction. *J Education and Psychology* 43(1) Ap 1985 p 37-43 refs

Kureshi, Afzal *et al*

N-achievement hope of success and fear of failure in relation to level of aspiration. *Asian J Psychology and Education* 3(3) Nv 1978 p 30-34 refs tabs

Kuriakose, J.

Autonomous programme and Loyola College. *New Frontiers in Education* 12(2) Jl-Se 1982 p 26-30

Kurian, C.T.

An open and participatory college administration. *J Higher Education* 2(2) Aut 1976 p 203-11

Kurian, John

Elementary education in India : Myth, reality, alternative. New Delhi, Vikas Pub. 1982, 245p. Rs.125 *Book Rev, Bulletin of Non-formal Education* 3(1) Je 1985 p 16-19; *Progress of Education* 58(4) Nv 1983 p 98+

Salvaging higher education : Limiting the importance of degrees. *J Higher Education* 9(2) Aut 1985 p 207-16

Kurnali, Krishna

See

Sharma, R.A. *jt. auth.*

Labhru, G.L.

See

Wokhlu, O.N. *jt. auth.*

Labs, George

Some issues in moral education. *New Frontiers in Education* 10(2) Ap-Je 1980 p 79-96

Lada, Bestazhev

School in 2000 : The Soviet model. *Progress of Education* 55(9) Ap 1981 p 241-42

Lakshamana Rao

The open book system of examination : An experiment. *Indian Education* 10(9-10) De 1980 Ja 1981 p 33-35

Lakshmi

See also

under full name/surname, e.g., Lakshmi Shankar

Lakshmi, S.

Dear teacher, let the relationship be human. *Experiments in Education* 6(11) Ja 1979 p 197-200

Lakshmi, T.K.S.

See

Yadav, M.S. *et al jt. auths.*

Lakshminaranan, G. and Radhakrishna Menon, K.

Knowledge and attitude of students towards agriculture in secondary school education. *Indian J Extension Education* 18(1-2) Je 1980 p[73-76

Lakshminarayana, M.

Non-formal education of women. *EPA Quarterly Bulletin* 8(1-2) Ap-Jl 1985 p 40-44

Lakshminarayana, U. and Sarma, A. Vizaya Pattatreya
Social, economic and academic awareness and position of collegiate teachers : A study. *J Higher Education* 5(3) Spr 1980 p 395-405 tabs

Lakshmi Reddy, M.V.
See
Niranjan Reddy, B. *jt. auth.*

Lal, Harmesh
Purposeful activities and learning. *Primary Teacher* 8(3) Jl 1983 p 31-33
Understanding counting numbers. *Primary Teacher* 9(3) Jl 1984 p 16-19

Lal, J.N. and Verma, P.C.
Effects of the varying accounts of information on the perception of stimulus person's physical and psychological character. *Asian J Psychology and Education* 7(3) 1981 p 11-16 refs

Lal, Shiv Kumar
Scheduled caste college students in Rajasthan. *J Higher Education* 1(2) Aut 1975 p 244-50 refs

Lal Bahadur Singh
A comparison of academic achievement of Santal and non-Santal undergraduate students of Santal Parganas district of Bihar. *J Educational Research and Extension* 16(3) Ja 1980 p 168-73 refs tabs
A study in anxiety level of Santal (tribal) and non-Santal (non-tribal) undergraduate students of Santal Parganas. *J Institute of Educational Research* 4(1) Ja 1980 p 20-22 refs tabs

Lal Pratap Singh
Effective teaching practice : A microteaching approach. *Teacher Today* 21(3) Ja-Mr 1979 p 71-76 refs
Teacher education and social change : A crucial issue. *Teacher Education* 14(12-13) Jl-Oc 1980 p 57-62

Lal Singh
Effect of socio-economic status on the academic achievement of XI grade students. *J Education and Psychology* 42(4) Ja 1985 p 223-28 refs
See also
Saxena, J.K. *jt. auth.*

Lalit Kishore
Computers in education. *Indian Education* 13(12) Mr 1984 p 8-9
Criterion-referenced testing. *Primary Teacher* 9(3) Jl 1984 p 24-25
Effect of mastering learning procedure and textbook study. *Educational Rev* 91(12) De 1985 p 201-03 refs
Evaluating learning : The need. *Educational Rev* 92(7) Jl 1986 p 110-11 refs
An experiment with individually guided system of instruction in physics. *Experiments in Education* 13(12) Fe 1986 p 211-14 refs
Intent, instruction, individual and inspection in mastery learning model. *Educational Rev* 88(9) Se 1982 p 147-49 refs
Mastery learning : An application of behavioural theory. *Experiments in Education* 11(10) De 1983 p 181-82
A personalised instructional design. *University News* 32(2) Ja 1984 p 9
Rate centred instruction : Feasibility aspect. *Educational Rev* 90(10) Oc 1984 p 161-62
Retenties of subject-matter in physics : Individualised system of instruction

Maqbool Ahmad

Aesthetic education : A concept for behavioural change. *Teacher Today* 23(1) Jl-Se 1980 p 15-19 refs

Art : The case of teacher education. *Teacher Today* 24(2) Oc-De 1981 p 67-73 refs

Maral, J.B.S. and Mansal, Bheema

Intelligence, creativity and indisciplined behaviour in student union activities among the unsecurity students. *Progress of Education* 60(3) Nv 1985 p 83-85 tabs

Marihal, V.G.

The concept of systems approach to educational administration. *Educational Rev* 89(3) Mr 1983 p 41-44 refs

Marish, Savitri

A study of some teacher varibles and teaching methods associated with learning outcomes in biology. *Indian Educational Rev* 15(4) Oc 1980 p 71-75

Markanda, Savita

Adult continuing education : The Indian scene. *Indian J Adult Education* 46(2) Fe 1985 p 21-26 +

See also

Gakhar, Sudesh *jt. auth.*

Marker, N.S.

Survey of teacher education in Maharashtra. *Indian Educational Rev* 15(1) Ja 1980 p 78-84

Marwah, Madhu

See

Bhargava, Mahesh *jt. auth.*

Mascarenhas, M.

Education and secular morality. *Teacher Today* 25(2) Oc-De 1982 p 14-18 refs

Family life education. *New Frontiers in Education* 14(1) Ja-Mr 1984 p 44-50

Population education for quality of life. New Delhi, Oxf-IBH. 362p. Rs.54 *Book Rev, New Frontiers in Education* 12(3) Jl-Se 1982 p 77-79

Reducing test tensions. *Rajasthan Board J Education* 15(4) Oc-De 1979 p 38-42

The relevance of geography as a school subject. *J Indian Education* 6(3) Se 1980 p 31-33

See also

Michael, D. *jt. auth.*

Masiah, S.

Creativity and teacher effectiveness. *Quest in Education* 16(2) Ap 1979 p 165-71

Review of researches on environmental education. *Quest in Education* 19(3) Jl 1982 p 238-45 refs

Mastny, Aleta Yori

Sri Aurobindo's philosophy of spiritual transformation. *J Indian Education* 11(1) My 1985 p 1-8 ft-n

Mathai, Samuel

The aims of education. *New Frontiers in Education* 10(3) Jl-Se 1980 p 35-42

Lehning, Rolf and Kane, Michael

Improving schools : Using what we know? California, Sage Pub. *Book Rev, Teacher Today* 27(4) Ap-Je 1985 p 145-47

Leki, Vanila

Differences in TV viewers and non-viewers in relation to their adjustment and leisure time activities. *Experiments in Education* 12(11) Ja 1985 p 189-92

Leslett, Robert, and Smith, Colin

Effective classroom management : A teachers guide. New York, Nicholas Pub Co. 1984. *Book Rev, Teacher Today* 28(3) Ja-Mr 1986 p 103-04

Levin, Henry M.

Why is'nt educational research more useful? *Indian Educational Rev* 15(1) Ja 1980 p 1-9

Levinger, Beryl and Drahman, Tom

Lets look at our assumptions. *Indian J Adult Education* 41(12) De 1980 p 20-22

Lidhoo, Moti Lal

A comparative study of engineers, doctors, and university teachers in relation to intelligence level of frustration, extraversion intraversion and neuroticism. *Indian Educational Rev* 17(2) Ap 1982 p 108-18 refs

Lidhoo, Moti Lal and Zargar, Abdul Hamid

Degree of neuroticism : Its relation with intelligence and creativity. *Indian Educational Rev* 15(4) Oc 1980 p 86-90

Lindeman, Richard H.

Educational measurement. Bombay, Taraporewala. 1971, 173p. *Book Rev, Teacher Today* 23(2) Oc-De 1980 p 96-97

Linford, A.G.

See

Worlson, R.L. *jt. auth.*

Lingren, Carl E.

Jobs corps : Dreams can come true. *Educational Rev* 87(12) De 1981 p 227

Lodi, P.H.

The verification of Techner's law by method of equal appearing intervals : Some problems. *Asian J Psychology and Education* 4(3) Nv 1979 p 23-30

Lofstedt, Jan Ingvar

Chinese educational policy. New York, Humanities Press; Stockholm, Almquist. 1980, 204p. *Book Rev, J Higher Education* 8(2) Aut 1982 p 251-52

Lokanandha Reddy, G.

Personality characteristics affecting participation in AEP : A study. *Indian J Adult Education* 47(8) Ag 1986 p 11-14 refs

Longford, C.

Education, person and society : A philosophical enquiry. London, Macmillan. 1985. *Book Rev, J Indian Education* 12(4) Nv 1986 p 65-66

Lulla, B.P.

Children and parental role perception. *Progress of Education* 53(4) Nv-De 1978 p 79-85

Education of the socially disadvantaged through non-formal education as an integrated part of formal education. *Indian Education* 10(1-2) Ap-My 1980

p 44-47

Mental health of teacher promotes effective teaching and learning in classroom. *Indian Education* 10(12) Mr 1981 p 4-7; *Progress of Education* 56(2) Se 1981 p 46-48

Non-formal education an integral part of formal education. *Progress of Education* 55(1) Ag 1980 p 24-26

A review of 'Draft National Policy of Education, 1979'. *Progress of Education* 54(9) Ap 1980 p 182-85 +

A review of Draft National Policy of Education, 1979. *Rajasthan Board J Education* 15(4) Oc-De 1979 p 11-14

Streamlining curriculum administration. *Indian Education* 11(1-2) Ap-My 1981 p 76-80

Lutman, Marthe

See

Staple, Cees *jt. auth.*

Luthra, K.L.

Promotion of reading habits among school children : The role of libraries. *J Indian Education* 6(2) Jl 1980 p 66-70

Mcanany, Emile G.

See

Jamison, Dean T. *jt. auth.*

Macaskill, Edwin O. *et al*

A research study about teachers perceptions of job satisfaction. *Indian Educational Rev* 15(3) Jl 1980 p 22-30 refs

Machli, Sada Ram

How to prepare children for examination? *Primary Teacher* 4(3) Jl 1979 p 28-31

Macia, J.

Faculty-administration relations. *New Frontiers in Education* 9(1) Ja-Mr 1979 p 12-26

Mackie, Robert, *ed.*

Literacy and revolution : The pedagogy of Paulo Freire. London, Pluto Press. £3.50 *Book Rev, Teacher Today* 24(1) Jl-Se 1981 p 103-04

Mclachlan, Milla *et al*

Linking formal and non-formal education. *Bulletin of Non-Formal Education* 1(2) 19 Se 1983 p 4-20

Non-formal education : Selected issues. *Bulletin of Non-Formal Education* 1(1) 1 Je 1983 p 5-20

Mcnaria, K.L.

See

Mathur, N.K. *jt. auth.*

McPherson, M. Peter

Expanding third world educational opportunities. *Unversity News* 24(37) 1 Oc 1986 p 1-4 +

Mbaklle, E.P.R.

Motivation in non-formal education : Tanzania experience. *Indian J Adult Education* 40(7) Jl 1979 p 9-18

Madan Singh and Mathur, P.N.

Constraints analysis in adoption of fertilizers and plant protection measures in Bajra cultivation. *Indian J Extension Education* 20(3-4) Se-De 1984 p 53-54

Madan Singh and Singh, R.P.

Cropping pattern in Haryana and Punjab : A temporal analysis. *Indian J Extension Education* 19(1-2) Mr-Je 1983 p 57-61

Fertilizer consumption in Haryana : A determinant of differential agricultural growth. *Indian J Extension Education* 19(3-4) Se-De 1983 p 32-39 refs tabs 20(1-2) Je 1984 p 12-19

Maddison, Alan

Microcomputers in the classroom. London, Hodder. 1982, 189p. £3.95 *Book Rev, Teacher Today* 27(2) Oc-De 1984 p 96-97

Madhumati

See

Sharma, Harish *jt. auth.*

Madhyastha, U.S.

Environmental approach to education. *J Indian Education* 8(2) Jl 1982 p 79-83

Madike, Frank U.

The measuring of teaching : An examination of the theoretical basis of teaching. *Perspectives in Education* 2(4) Oc 1986 p 221-30 refs

Mahajan, Harinder Nanda

Question banks and construction of tests and reporting of results for internal assessment and external examinations. *J Higher Education* 9(2) Aut 1983 p 235-44 refs

Question banks in Indian universities : Potential uses and some psychometric issues. *J Higher Education* 7(3) Spr 1982 p 310-15 refs

Mahajan, Neelam and Bajaj, S.

Impact of nutrition education imparted to rural house wives under the applied nutrition programme. *Indian J Extension Education* 19(3-4) Se-De 1983 p 90-93 refs tabs

Mahalingam

See under

full name/surname, e.g., Sundaramahalingam, A.

Mahanta, D.

An investigation into the results of the new higher secondary examination in West Bengal. *Our Education* 1 Jl 1980 p 9-22 refs tabs

MAHAPATRA - MOHAPATRA

Mohapatra, Damodar

A programmed text on operant conditioning. *J Educational Research and Extension* 20(3) Ja 1984 p 164-71

Mohapatra, J.K.

Congnition of learning or definitions of physical concepts. *J Education and Psychology* 44(3-4) Jl-De 1986 p 118-23

Mohapatra, Mahesh P.
See
Puhan, Biranchi N. *jt. auth.*
Mahapatra, S.K.
See
Patel, S. *jt. auth.*
Mahapatra, Sitakant
Bakhen : Ritual invocation songs of a primitive community. New Delhi, Prachi Pra. 1979, 71p. Rs.20 *Book Rev, J Indian Education* 7(3) Se 1979 p 59
Mohapatra, Subash Chandra
Blue print in designing test. *Experiments in Education* 8(7) Se 1980 p 119-23 refs tabs
Maharana, Sadasiba
See
Mohanty, Jagannath *jt. auth.*
Mahesh, Vimla
See
Sharma, R.A. *jt. auth.*
Mahesh, Vimla and Saxena, Alka
Effect of practice on teaching efficiency and teaching attitude of B.Ed students. *Indian Educational Rev* 18(1) Ja 1983 p 109-15 tabs
Mahesh, Vimla and Srivastava, J.P.
Effect of varying sources of feedback upon the general teaching competence of student teacher under micro teaching situation. *Indian Educational Rev* 16(3) Jl 1981 p 51-58
Maheshwar Dayal
Strategies for development of appropriate rural technologies and their extension. *New Frontiers in Education* 14(4) Oc-De 1984 p 10-17
Maheshwri, S.B.
Commerce-based socially useful and productive work. *Rajasthan Board J Education* 20(4)-21(1) Oc 1984-Mr 1985 p 43-51
Mahipal and Rai, G.C.
Relationship of role performance with some selected socio-psychological characteristics of the leaders of multipurpose cooperative societies. *Indian J Extension Education* 16(3-4) De 1980 p 46-51 refs tabs
Mahtab Singh
Systems in school administration. *Educational Rev* 87(3) Mr 1981 p 47-50 refs
Mair, Nirmal S.
Programmed learning : An empirical approach. Kurukshetra, Vishal 1984, 117p. Rs.50 *Book Rev, Indian Educational Rev* 20(4) Oc 1985 p 173-74
Maite, Basudhara
See
Kundu, Ramanath *jt. auth.*
Maitra, Krishna
Primary school children in Switzerland : Their achievement in multi-lingual environment. *Primary Teacher* 8(2) Ap 1983 p 28-30
Role of language in the development of concepts in science. *Progress of*

Education 60(4) Nv 1985 p 86-90 refs

Maitra, S.N.

A report of the seminar on the role of voluntary agencies in the National Adult Education Programme. *Indian J Adult Education* 40(1) Ja 1979 p 37-43

Maitra, Satyen

Adult and non-formal education : A few observation. Calcutta, BSSL. Rs.10 *Book Rev, Indian J Adult Education* 44(10) Oc 1983 p 32

Majumdar

See

Mazumdar

Makhija, V.K.

See

Dixit, V.B. *et al jt. auth.*

Makhija, V.K. and Singh, Y.P.

What constitutes a practical agricultural graduate. *Indian J Extension Education* 21(3-4) Jl-De 1985 p 62-67

Makkar, S.L.

Development of the educand : The role of the teacher. *J Indian Education* 12(4) Nv 1986 p 56-58

Evaluation of interests. *Primary Teacher* 10(3) Jl 1985 p 27-28

Forming good habits. *Primary Teacher* 10(2) Ap 1985 p 21-22

Importance of non-verbal communication. *Primary Teacher* 11(2) Ap 1986 p 4-6

Some personal traits of a good teacher. *Primary Teacher* 8(3) Jl 1983 p 37-38

Teachers' role in education. *Primary Teacher* 11(3) Jl 1986 p 16-17

See also

Pawar, S.S. *et al jt. auths.*

Malancherwvill, George

Shift system in Kerala colleges. *New Frontiers in Education* 9(4) Oc-De 1979 p 46-57

Malaviya, A. *et al*

Teachers concept of rural orientation in home science education. *Indian J Extension Education* 21(3-4) Jl-De 1985 p 95-98 tabs

Malaviya, V.V.

Improving teacher education. *Indian Education* 12(11-12) Fe-Mr 1982 p 32-34

Malhan, P.K.

See

Natarajan, V. *jt. auth.*

Malhara, S.B.

Developing creativity : The essential human trait. *J Indian Education* 10(6) Mr 1985 p 9-14

Malhotra, Asok

See

Banerjee, Sushanta *jt. auth.*

Malhotra, G.P.
See
Khanna, Kailash *jt. auth.*
Malhotra, R.N.
See
Seth, M. *et al jt. auths.*
Malhotra, R.V.R. and Jitendra Mohan
Personality, noise and performance. *Asian J Psychology and Education* 4(2) Jl 1979 p 27-37 refs
Malhotra, S.P.
Contribution of teachers in the development of creativity among students : A review of researches. *Quest in Education* 18(2) Ap 1981 p 158-64
Dimensions of teacher classroom behaviour and their relationship with demographic and professional factors : A review of researches. *Progress of Education* 54(2) Se 1979 p 26-28
A factorial study of process variables of teacher classroom behaviour and product variables of pupils reaction. *Quest in Education* 18(1) Ja 1981 p 4-12 refs
Jurisprudential way of teaching social sciences. *Progress of Education* 60(7) Fe 1986 p 161-66
Relationship of sex and age of the teacher with liking of boys and girls for their teachers at different grade levels. *J Education and Psychology* 38(3) Oc 1980 p 172-80 refs tab
Teacher adjustment as related to his classroom behaviour. *Asian J Psychology and Education* 9(4) 1982 p 36-41
Teacher classroom behaviour in the classes of boys and girls at different grade levels in relation to teachers sex and age. *J Educational Research and Extension* 16(2) Oc 1979 p 100-14 refs tabs
Teacher student mutual linking at different grade levels. *Indian Educational Rev* 18(3) Jl 1983 p 95-101 refs
Teaching values in the class : Jurisprudential technique. *Education Quarterly* 36(4) Wint 1984 p 9-11
Malhotra, S.P. and Dhamija, Neelam
Effect of tape recorder as a medium of instruction upon the memorising ability and pronounciation of the nursery students. *Progress of Education* 56(5) De 1981 p 114-16 refs tabs
Malhotra, S.P. and Panda, S.K.
Systems approach to educational planning in higher education in India. *Quest in Education* 19(3) Jl 1982 p 246-54 refs
Malhotra, S.P. and Syag, R.N.
Carry over effect of micro-teaching on student-teachers from college of education to regular school teaching. *Progress of Education* 55(8) Mr 1981 p 208-10 tabs
Mali, A.I.
See
Deshpande, K.N. *jt. auth.*
Mali, M.G.
Factors affecting the retention of literacy among neoliterates. Asha Pra. 1979, 220p. Rs.30 *Book Rev, Progress of Education* 54(10-11) My-Je

1980 p 214; *Teacher Education* 14(10-11) Ja-Ap 1980 p 77
Social benefits and economics of single teachers schools. *J Educational Research and Extension* 16(3) Ja 1980 p 183-84
Social benefits and economics of single teacher's schools. Kolhapur, Gargoti. 1979, 66p. *Book Rev, J Indian Education* 6(3) Se 1980 p 58-59

Malik
See also
Mullick

Malik, J.P.S.
Effective use of community resources in the teaching of science. *Progress of Education* 54(6) Ja 1980 p 116-18
Personality traits of successful science teachers. *Progress of Education* 59(10-11) My-Je 1985 p 235-39
Teachers perception of their classroom learning climate : A study. *Progress of Education* 57(8) Mr 1983 p 173-76

Malik, Rashila
The decision making by farm women regarding improved agricultural practices. *Indian J Extension Education* 15(3-4) De 1979 p 64-69 tabs

Malik, Suman Bala
Creative approach and teaching of chemistry. *Teacher Today* 21(3) Ja-Mr 1979 p 53-59
Education and modern society. *Primary Teacher* 10(2) Ap 1985 p 9-10
Plants help teaching learning process. *Primary Teacher* 10(1) Ja 1985 p 25-27

Malik, Suman Bala and Saxena, A.B.
Noise pollutant : Need for proper education *Primary Teacher* 6(4) Oc 1981 p 39-41

Malkova, Zoya
Soviety school looks into the future. *Progress of Education* 57(12) Jl 1983 p 285-87

Mall, N.N.
Preventive, therapeutic and rehabilitative aspects of exercise and sports. *New Frontiers in Education* 13(2) Ap-Je 1983 p 58-66 refs

Mall, Thankamma
Physiological response to exercise. *New Frontiers in Education* 13(3) Ap-Je 1983 p 67-77 refs

Malla Reddy, M.
Education and manpower development. *Indian Education* 10(1-2) Ap-My 1980 p 29-34
The relative impact of micro-teaching and conventional teaching. *Indian Education* 10(5) Ag 1980 p 31-41

Malla Reddy, M. and Muddu, Viswanath
A scientific view of creativity. *Indian Education* 10(6) Se 1980 p 19-23

Malla Reddy, M. and Philip, Rhoda
Issues in teacher education. *Indian Education* 10(3) Je 1980 p 40-50

Malla Reddy, M. and Ravishankar, S.
Curriculum development and educational technology. New Delhi, Sterling. *Book Rev, J Institute of Educational Research* 12(2) My 1986 p 26
Programme instruction (PI) : Significance and implications. *Indian Education*

10(4) Jl 1980 p 27-32
Systems approach to curriculum improvement. *Indian Education* 11(1-2) Ap-My 1981 p 84-88
Systems approach to educational management. *Indian Education* 11(6) Se 1981 p 15-19

Mallikarjun, B.
Role of the radio and newspaper in NAEP. *Indian J Adult Education* 40(3) Mr 1979 p 43-45
Text-book teaching and adult education. *Indian J Adult Education* 41(5) My 1980 p 19-21 +

Mallikarlunaiah, M.C.
Education in past-present-future. *Educational Rev* 87(10) Oc 1981 p 191

Malnahan, S.K.
Popularity of Hindi in the USSR. *Progress of Education* 58(4) Nv 1983 p 93-95

Mamel, Mehtab Singh
A study of the supervisory tasks. *Educational Rev* 85(10) Oc 1979 p 189-95

Mamtora, K.T.
Educational technology. *Educational Rev* 86(1) Ja 1980 p 1-4
A golden means to internal assessment, external examination. *Progress of Education* 54(3) Oc 1979 p 63-66
Internal vs external assessment. *Educational Rev* 85(8) Ag 1979 p 153-55
Population education and school curriculum. *Educational Rev* 84(11) Nv 1978 p 207-09
Sex education. *Educational Rev* 88(2) Fe 1982 p 30-33

Manavalan, R.
Practice school programme at BITS : A new concept in higher education. *J Higher Education* 8(2) Aut 1982 p 235-38 tabs

Manchanda, Rajinder Kaur and Hansra, B.S.
Gain and retention of nutritional knowledge by the members of ladies Charcha Mandals by the use of selected extension teaching methods. *Indian J Extension Education* 19(3-4) Se-De 1983 p 94-96 tabs

Mane, M.G.
Discussion. *Indian J Adult Education* 44(11) Nv 1983 p 10-21
Educate women to reduce inequalities. *Indian J Adult Education* 45(12) De 1984 p 7-8

Mangat, S.K.
Dimensions of teacher adjustment. Kurukshetra, Vishal Pub. 1985. Rs.60 *Book Rev, Research Bulletin* 15(1-2) Mr-Je 1985 p 53-56
Measuring adjustment of the teacher. *J Education and Psychology* 42(3) Oc 1984 p 134-39 refs

Mangat, Shavinder K. and Roy, Sunita
Participation and interest of rural school going girls in household and farm activities. *Indian J Extension Education* 19(1-2) Mr-Je 1983 p 69-73

Mangla, Sheela
Scaling of some important classroom behaviour attributes of colleges teachers. *J Educational Research and Extension* 20(2) Oc 1983 p 139-52

Mani, Gomathi
Attitude of rural adult learners : towards adult education. *Indian J Adult*

Education 41(5) My 1980 p 11-14

A comparative study of the education of student teaching by teacher educators and the supervising school teachers at the secondary level. *Experiments in Education* 8(12) Fe 1981 p 213-17 appdx tabs

Impact of motivational aspects of attendance in adult education centres : A case discussion. *Indian J Adult Education* 43(5) My 1982 p 25-28 tabs

Language errors in a mathematics class. *Experiments in Education* 7(8) Oc 1979 p 139-41

Motivation through mathematical games. *Experiments in Education* 11(3) My 1983 p 39-41; *Teacher Today* 27(1) Jl-Se 1984 p 44-47

Prep index : Proficiency in educational practice. *Experiments in Education* 7(11) Ja 1980 p 207-08+

A sample study of evaluation of teacher by students. *J Higher Education* 5(2) Aut 1979 p 228-32

Value of open ended evaluation. *Experiments in Education* 9(7) Se 1981 p 125-27

Mani, R.S.

Inquiry training model of teaching : An overview. *Indian Educational Rev* 20(4) Oc 1985 p 50-65

Pattern of teacher class-room behaviour and their relation to students liking in the science classes of secondary schools. *Educational Rev* 92(9) Se 1986 p 145-48 refs

Manjusha, M.

Text book production in the Indian context. *Progress of Education* 60(6) Ja 1986 p 135-38

Mann, Rajinder Singh

Discrimination learning among illiterate rural adults as function of their intelligence. *Progress of Education* 55(7) Fe 1981 p 189-91 +

Mann, S.S.

Teaching practice in training course : An evaluation. *Experiments in Education* 6(4) Je 1978 p 57-60

Maniche, Peter

On the development of fellowship and personality in education. *Indian J Adult Education* 44(8-9) Ag-Se 1983 p 25-28

Mansingh, R. Israel

See

Sivamohan, V.S. *jt. auth.*

Manvikas, Sharada

The climate of research in colleges of education. *Progress of Education* 56(6) Ja 1982 p 140-42

Creating creative atmosphere in our educational institutions. *Progress of Education* 56(3) Oc 1981 p 69-70

Manzoor Ahmed

Income generation projects : The link between adult education and the satisfaction of basic needs. *Indian J Adult Education* 39(10)Oc 1978 p 21-26

Myths and realities of literacy efforts. *Indian J Adult Education* 41(8) Ag 1980 p 3-6

and lecture model. *J Indian Education* 10(5) Ja 1985 p 40-43 refs
Self paced learning for primary school. *Primary Teacher* 11(1) Ja 1986 p 11-12
Towards a performance based classroom. *Primary Teacher* 8(4) Oc 1983 p 23-25
See also
Pangotra, N.N. *jt. auth.*

Lalitha, M.S.
A strategy for the professional self-improvement of teachers : Paper presented at the SITU Council of Educational Research, Madras on 11-3-1978. *Experiments in Education* 6(2) Ap 1978 p 21-26 refs
See also
Krishnakumari, P. *et al jt. auths.*

Landsheer, Gilbert De
Teacher selection. *J Indian Education* 8(2) Jl 1982 p 52-58 refs ftn

Latif
See also
under full name/surname, e.g., Abu Hamid Latif

Latif, I.H.
A note on school education and text books. *Progress of Education* 58(8) Mr 1984 p 178-80 +

Lauby, Paul T.
Asian higher education : A new challenges. *New Frontiers in Education* 14(4) Oc-De 1984 p 46-53

Lavingia, K.U.
Students image of satisfied and dissatisfied teachers. *Quest in Education* 16(3) Jl 1979 p 209-16 refs
A study of job satisfaction among clerks of Saurashtra University. *J Education and Psychology* 39(4) Ja 1982 p 259-61

Lawn, Martin
See
Ozga, Jennifer *jt. auth.*

Laxmi Devi, A.
Time utilisation pattern of rural farm women. *Indian J Adult Education* 47(1) Ja 1986 p 13-16 tabs

Laxmi Devi, A. and Venku Reddy, S.
Role expectation and role performance of rural women in farm activities. *Indian J Extension Education* 20(3-4) Se-De 1984 p 27-34 refs tabs

Laxminarayan, G. and Menon, Radha Krishna
Factors responsible for the selection of agricultural courses and the career aspirations of secondary school boys. *Indian J Extension Education* 15(3-4) De 1979 p 33-36 tabs

Lebra, Joyce *et al*
Women and work in India : Continuity and change. New Delhi, Promilla. 310p. Rs.250 *Book Rev, New Frontiers in Education* 16(2) Ap-Je 1986 p 106-08

Leelavathy, T.K.
Wastage and stagnation : A case for lower primary school. *EPA Quarterly Bulletin* 6(3-4) Oc 1983 Ja 1984 p 15-21 refs

The Indian renaissance. *New Frontiers in Education* 11(4) Oc-De 1981 p 1-7

Patterns and problems of higher education. *New Frontiers in Education* 11(2) Ap-Je 1981 p 37-72; 11(3) Jl-Se 1981 p 33-72

The University Grants Commission : A personal view. *J Higher Education* 6(1-3) 1980-81 p 55-61

Mathew, A.

The role of the University Grants Commission in framing the policy of higher education. *J Higher Education* 9(2) Aut 1983 p 177-93 refs

Mathew, E.T.

University finance in India : A case study of the University of Kerala. New Delhi, Sterling. 1980, 120p. Rs.32 *Book Rev, Education Quarterly* 33(1) Ja 1981 p 40-41

Mathias, T.A.

The financial aspect of college autonomy. *New Frontiers in Education* 10(1) Ja-Mr 1980 p 40-43

Private agencies in Indian education. *New Frontiers in Education* 10(3) Jl-Se 1980 p 59-66

World culture and global values. *New Frontiers in Education* 15(4) Oc-De 1985 p 1-27 refs

Mathur, Ashok

Vocabulary : Its importance and techniques of teaching. *Rajasthan Board J Education* 15(1) Ja-Mr 1979 p 17-20

Mathur, Jayshree

A case for social philosophy of education. *J Indian Education* 8(5) Ja 1983 p 17-20

Mathur N.

Effecting teaching in primary schools : A strategy. *Primary Teacher* 6(3) Jl 1981 p 4-10

Mathur, N.K. and Mcnaria, K.L.

What can we contribute to school chemistry curriculum? *Teacher Today* 25(2) Oc-De 1982 p 62-65

What can we contribute to schools : A strategy. *Primary Teacher* 6(3) Jl 1981 p 4-10

Mathur, P. and Satapathy, A.

An opinion survey of high school teachers in Delhi regarding 10+2 systems of education. *Asian J Psychology and Education* 4(1) Ja 1979 p 21-24

Sex differences in self-actualisation. *J Institute of Educational Research* 4(2) My 1980 p 13-17 refs tabs

Mathur, P.N.

Dynamics of autonomy in education and Banasthali experiment. *Rajasthan Board J Education* 16(4) Oc-De 1980 p 1-9

Education *vis-a-vis* life values. *National J Education* 7(2) My 1985 p 1-8

See also

Bhagat, R. *jt. auth.*

Kaur, D.K. *jt. auth.*

Madan Singh *jt. auth.*

Pandey, S.N. *jt. auth.*

Mathur, P.N. *et al*

Readership pattern, nature of content and sources of information of farm periodicals in India. *Indian J Extension Education* 14(1-2) Ja-Je 1978 p 39-44

Mathur, Punima

See

Gaur, J.S. *jt. auth.*

Mathur, Rajeshwar N.

A new strategy for primary education. *Indian Education* 12(1-2) Ap-My 1982 p 30-31

See also

Gupta, Rajendra *jt. auth.*

Mathur, R.S.

Utilisation of feedback from evaluation studies of adult education programme. *Indian J Adult Education* 45(3) Mr 1984 p 17-22

Mathur, S.

Valedictory address. *Indian J Adult Education* 40(10-11) Oc-Nv 1979 p 64-68

Mathur, S.C.

National integration : A view point. *University News* 23(34) 8 Se 1985 p 3+

Mathur, S.G. and Saxena, A.B.

Institutional planning : An approach to effective learning environment. *Education Quarterly* 33(1) Ja 1981 p 10-11

Mathur, S.L.

Trends in work educatior. *Rajasthan Board J Education* 20(4) 21(1) Oc 1984-Mr 1985 p 16-20

See also

Gupta, Pushpa *jt. auth.*

Kalia, Ashok K. *jt. auth.*

Mathur, S.S.

Autonomy in university administration. *J Educational Planning and Administration* 1(1) Oc 1986 p 13-20 refs

A sociological approach to Indian education. Agra, Vinod Pustak Mandir. 1985, 452p. Rs.30 *Book Rev, Education Quarterly* 37(3) Aut 1985 p 57-59; *Perspective in Education* 2(3) Jl 1986 p 187-88

See *also*

Kalia, Ashok K. *jt. auth.*

Mathur, S.S. and Kalia, Ashok K.

Effect of different types of treatment environment on the cheating pattern of school students. *J Institute of Educational Research* 7(3) Se 1983 p 7-9

Values as a function of caste. *J Education and Psychology* 42(1-2) Ap-Jl 1984 p 36-40 refs

Mathur, S.S. and Vasudeva, Parminder

The perception of adolescent problems by the parents. *J Education and Psychology* 36(3) Oc 1978 p 99-106

Mathur, Satish G.

Creativity and mental health. *J Educational and Psychology* 39(2) Jl 1981 p 106-10

Place of educational technology in non-formal education. *Education*

Quarterly 31(1) Ap 1979 p 7-8

Mathur, Sunderlal

See

Bhargava, S.S. *jt. auth.*

Mathur, T.B.

Basic characteristic of a researcher. *J Indian Education* 8(6) Mr 1983 p 55-57

Mathur, V.S.

Adult education in India : Retrospect and prospect. *Education Quarterly* 30(3) Oc 1978 p 8-10

Adult education : Need to expand dimensions. *Education Quarterly* 32(3) Jl 1980 p 30-32

Adult education : Some more vital dimensions. *Teacher Today* 25(2) Oc-De 1982 p 8-13

The challenge of examination reform. *J Indian Education* 6(2) Jl 1980 p 52-54

Examinations : Some new dimensions. *Rajasthan Board J Education* 15(4) Oc-De 1979 p 22-25

Improving primary education. *Primary Teacher* 9(3) Jl 1984 p 1-3

IAEA General Secretary's report (1978-1979). *Indian J Adult Education* 40(10-11) Oc-Nv 1979 p 39-44

Indian women's right to education. *Education Quarterly* 31(1) Ap 1979 p 18-20

Level integration in the educational process. *Education Quarterly* 36(4) Wint 1984 p 1-3

National integration : Role of colleges. *Education Quarterly* 34(2) Ap 1982 p 27-28+

Need to humanise education. *J Indian Education* 6(4) Nv 1980 p 23-25

Need to revitatise teacher education. *Education Quarterly* 35(4) Oc 1983 p 8-13

Population education and the new secondary school. *J Indian Education* 12(3) Se 1986 p 3-5

Population education : The problem of teacher orientation. *Education Quarterly* 34(3) Jl 1982 p 4-8

Population growth : Role of education. *Rajasthan Board J Education* 16(4) Oc-De 1980 p 14-20

Renewed relevance of population education. *J Indian Education* 5(2) Jl 1979 p 52-55

Report of the General Secretary, Mr. V.S. Mathur for 1979-80. *Indian J Adult Education* 41(11) Nv 1980 p 23-30

Towards a national system of education : Valedictory address, 30-12-1980. *Indian Education* 10(11) Fe 1981 p 19-20

Training of teachers for adult education. *Teacher Today* 21(2) Oc-De 1978 p 8-11

Worker's education today. *Indian J Adult Education* 44(3) Mr 1983 p 3-12

Mattai, Ravi J.

The rural university : The Jawaja experiment in educational innovation. Bombay, Popular. xvi, 360p. Rs.150 *Book Rev, Education Quarterly* 38(3) Aut 1986 p 52-54

Mattoo, B.K.

Home adjustment patterns of adolescent boys and girls at various levels of socio-economic status and general intelligence. *J Education and Psychology* 40(3) Oc 1982 p 136-42

Social and emotional adjustment patterns of adolescents boys and girls at various levels of socio-economic status and general intelligence. *Indian Educational Rev* 15(1) Ja 1980 p 110-14 tabs

Maunikar, Sharda

The teacher pupil relationship during upanishadic period and its relevance to modern education. *Progress of Education* 55(11) Je 1981 p 287-92 refs

Mayuri, K.

Effect of schooling on learning abilities and academic achievement of primary school children. *Asian J Psychology and Education* 11(3) 1983 p 32-37 refs tabs

See also

Moses, S. *jt. auth.*

Mayuri, K. and Reddy, S.V.

A comparative study of the learning abilities, academic achievement and disposition towards school, of the primary school children from progressive and less progressive schools. *J Educatioanl Research and Extension* 19(3) Ja 1,983 p 180-86

Mazel, Michelle

36 years of education in Israel. *Progress of Education* 58(8) Mr 1984 p 181-82

MAZUMDAR - MAJUMDAR

Mazumdar, A.K.

See

Pathak, S. *jt. auth.*

Mazumdar, Aurobindo

Education through the press. *J Indian Education* 11(3) Se 1985 p 24-30

Majumdar, Gunada

National programme for adult education. *Indian J Adult Education* 39(11-12) Nv-De 1978 p 60-64

Mazumder, H.B.

Primary education in rural West Bengal : A survey. *Primary Teacher* 10(3) Jl 1985 p 16-19

A quest for values in education. *J Indian Education* 8(5) Ja 1983 p 25-29

Majumdar, Suresh

A child with learning difficulties : Importance of play in remedial works. *Indian Educational Rev* 17(3) Jl 1982 p 23-27

Mazumdar, Vina

Higher education of women in India. *J Higher Education* 1(2) Aut 1975 p 156-65 tabs

Mehare, K.T. and Patil, Geeta Devi

A study of attitude of B.Ed pupil teachers towards teaching profession. *J Institute of Educational Research* 10(2) My 1986 p 8-11 refs

Mehrotra, G.P.
See
Khanna, Kailash *jt. auth.*
Mehrotra, R.C.
New educational technology and the teaching of chemistry. *J Higher Education* 1(1) Mon 1975 p 31-42 refs tabs
Science, technology development and the universities. *J Higher Education* 6(1-3) 1980-81 p 25-39 tabs
Mehrotra, R.N.
Recommendations of the UGC panel on teacher education. *J Higher Education* 1(1) Mon 1975 p 127-30 ft-n
Mehrotra, S.N.
Quick appraisal of projects under NAEP. *Indian J Adult Education* 30(10) Oc 1978 p 27-33
Mehta, B.N.
See
Digvijai Singh, *jt. auth.*
Mehta, G.L.
Clinical supervision : A new technique. *Educational Rev* 87(8) Ag 1981 p 154-55 refs
Mehta, H.K.
A peep into the remedies of adolescents (High school and college level). *Progress of Education* 55(1) Ag 1980 p 2-5
Mehta, H.K. and Patel, N.H.
How to accelerate the programme of socal education. *Progress of Education* 53(4) Nv-De 1978 p 74-78
Mahatma Gandhi's philosophy of education : Its salient features recalled. *Progress of Education* 54(3) Oc 1979 p 59-62+ figs
Mehta, J.S.
SUPW and CS as compulsory subject at secondary stage. *Rajasthan Board J Education* 20(4)-21(1) Oc 1984-Mr 1985 p 1-7
Socially useful productive work and community services : Concepted status in Rajasthan. *Rajasthan Board J Education* 19(4) Oc-De 1983 p 1-8
Mehta, M.L.
NAEP and the University Grants Commission. *Prasar* 7(1-2) Ap-Jl 1980 p 11-26
Mehta, Mangala
Problems faced by departments of commerce. *Educational Rev* 90(10) Oc 1984 p 153-54
Mehta, P. and Sharma, R.C.
A study of internal assessment. *J Education and Psychology* 37(3) Oc 1979 p 167-72 refs
Mehta, Perin H.
Guidance services in India towards the end of 1981 : Report of a status survey. *Indian Educational Rev* 18(2) Ap 1983 p 1-16 refs tabs
Interests of boys with superior scholastic ability : *Indian Educational Rev* 19(2) Ap 1984 p 1-8
Problems in the dissemination of educational and occupational information to secondary school pupils. *J Indian Education* 5(6) Mr 1980 p 50-57

Strengthening guidance services and programmes for career development. *J Indian Education* 8(2) Jl 1982 p 12-25 refs

Mehta, Pradeep Kumar

Education and assistance : A case study of Government College, Sawai Madhopur, Rajasthan. *J Higher Education* 3(3) Spr 1978 p 390-99 refs tabs

Mehta, Prayag

Evolving new extension and training strategies for rural development. *Indian J Extension Education* 19(1-2) Mr-Je 1983 p 1-11 refs tabs

Mehta, R.C.

Organisational structure of adult education programmes in Rajasthan. *Prasar* 5(3-4) Oc 1977-Ja 1978 p 5-10

Mehta, S.J.

Creativity in language teaching. *Quest in Education* 18(1) Ja 1981 p 19-26

Mehta, S.J. and Charles, D.L.

An experiment on releasing creativity of adults through language arts. *Experiments in Education* 8(3) My 1980 p 49-53

Mehta, S.M.

The concept of educational technology. *Teacher Today* 22(4) Ap-Je 1980 p 48-51

Radio and school education. *Teacher Today* 21(3) Ja-Mr 1979 p 39-43

Mehta, Suresh Chandra

Can creativity be fostered in students? *Educational Rev* 89(8) Ag 1983 p 135-38 refs

Mehta, V.B.

Admission in colleges of education. *Teacher Education* 16(18-19) Ja-Ap 1982 p 61-63

Mehta, Vimla

Disciplinary education in the present social setup. *Teacher Education* 13(8-9) Jl-Oc 1979 p 58-61

Problems of literacy and the remedial measures. *J Indian Education* 5(6) Mr 1980 p 14-19 tabs

Social education of the child. *Teacher Education* 14(10-11) Ja-Ap 1980 p 65-68

Mellor, Warren L.

Risk reduction and the management of change. *Indian Education* 11(1-2) Ap-Mr 1981 p 5-12

Menaria, K.L.

See

Mathur, N.K. *jt. auth.*

Mendi, G.B.

See

Palted, G.M. *jt. auth.*

Mendis, George

Curriculum development in Sri Lanka. *Rajasthan Board J Education* 16(1-2) Ja-Je 1980 p 72-81

Menon

See also

under full name/surname, Radhakrishna Menon, K.

Menon, A.G.G.
See
Abdul Rehman, O. *jt. auth.*

Menon, B. Syamdass and Bhat, Vasant D.
Systematic observation in understanding instruction : A review and some rethinking. *New Frontiers in Education* 14(3) Jl-Se 1985 p 36-46 refs

Menon, Geeta
See
Joshi, Vibha *jt. auth.*

Menon, I.C.
In the mind of men : Psychological foundations of educational planning. *New Frontiers in Education* 9(4) Oc-De 1979 p 46-57

Menon, K.P.A.
Management of agriculture and rural development programme : Problems and prospects. *Indian J Extension Education* 21(1-2) Ja-Je 1985 p 10-19

Menon, K.R. *et al*
Job content and context factors in job satisfaction of deputy agricultural officers. *Indian J Extension Education* 14(1-2) Ja-Je 1978 p 1-5 refs

Menon, M.B.
See
Yadav, M.S. *jt. auth.*

Menon, M.B. and Bhat, Vasant
Group-based learning experiences. *New Frontiers in Education* 13(1) Ja-Mr 1983 p 58-61

Menon, M.B. and Joshi, Vibha
Designing the instructional system for the open university : A perspective. *University News* 24(42) 8 Nv 1986 p 37-41 refs tabs

Menon, M.B. and Kumar, S.
System of evaluation in student teaching programme. *National J Education* 6(1) Se 1983 p 7-19

Menon, M.B. and Sahoo, P.K.
Case study method in research on instructional process. *New Frontiers in Education* 14(4) Oc-De 1984 p 26-33 refs

Menon, M.B. *et al*
Instructional skills : A new perspective. *Teacher Education* 18(22-23) Ja-Ap 1983 p 6-19 refs

Menon, P.S.K.
Post-matric scholarship for scheduled castes and scheduled tribes students. *J Higher Education* 1(2) Aut 1975 p 263-66

Menon, S.B.
See
Govinda, R. *jt. auth.*
Yadav, M.S. *jt. auth.*

Menon, S.M.
Piaget : A reappraisal in an educational perspective. *New Frontiers in Education* 13(4) Oc-De 1983 p 1-6 refs

Merh, Sushma
Education for environment : The Indian perspective. *Indian Education* 12(11-12) Fe-Mr 1983 p 16-25

Mhaiki, Paul J.
Adult education in other countries. *Indian J Adult Education* 41(6-7) Ja-Jl 1980 p 37-39

Michael, D. and Mascarenhas, M.
Literature as moral education in schools. *Teacher Today* 23(1) Jl-Se 1980 p 8-13

Minz, Nirmal
Higher education in the tribal context. *New Frontiers in Education* 12(1) Ja-Mr 1982 p 50-53

MISHRA - MISRA

Mishra, A.K.
See
Panda, S.K. *jt. auth.*

Mishra, A.N.
An investigation into the pattern of leadership behaviour of the headmasters, headmistresses of Puri district. *Experiments in Education* 6(2) Ap 1978 p 31-35 refs
The teaching of English in India. *Educational Rev* 16(3) Mr 1980 p 43-44
Why is our education ineffective? *Educational Rev* 85(11) Nv 1979 p 213-15

Misra, Ajay Mohan *et al*
Intercaste differences in frustration among girls of scheduled and non-scheduled castes. *J Institute of Educational Research* 4(1) Ja 1980 p 13-15 refs
A study of attitude towards learning of science among scheduled castes students. *J Education and Psychology* 41(3) Oc 1983 p 112-16 refs tabs
Study of specific global measures of self-concept and adjustment among adolescent. *J Institute of Educational Research* 9(3) Se 1985 p 4-7 refs tabs

Mishra, Arun K.
Vocationalisation of education : Experiences and imperatives. *New Frontiers in Education* 15(3) Jl-Se 1985 p 48-60

Misra, Atmanand
Address to XXII Conference of Indian Association of Teacher Educators : An objective of teacher education. *Teacher Education* 15(14-15) Ja-Ap 1981 p 21-29

Mishra, B.C.
Communalism and the role of the teachers. *Experiments in Education* 12(11) Ja 1985 p 202-06
Creativity in students of two types of schools. *Experiments in Education* 13(11) Ja 1986 p 201-04 refs
A correlational study of intelligence and various components of creativity. *Progress of Education* 60(2) Se 1985 p 36-39 refs tabs

Misra, C.B.
An investigation into the causes of backwardness in children in higher secondary schools of Pilibhit city. *J Education and Psychology* 37(3) Oc 1979 p 187-92 refs

Misra, C.H.K.

Trends of research on educational technology in India. *J Institute of Educational Research* 7(3) Se 1983 p 19-25

Misra, C.K.

SUPW : Need, concept and objectives. *Rajasthan Board J Education* 20(4)-21(1) Oc-Mr 1984 p 8-15

Mishra, Chintamani

Difference of locus of control and educational achievement and sub-cultures. *Indian Educational Rev* 19(1) Ja 1984 p 18-26

Misra, Girishwar

Current status of studies on approval motive : A critical appraisal. *J Education and Psychology* 37(3) Oc 1979 p 203-12

Deprivation and development. *Indian Educational Rev* 18(1) Ja 1983 p 12-32 refs

Misra, Girishwar and Tiwari, B.N.

Current status of studies on approval motive : A critical appraisal. *J Education and Psychology* 42(3) Oc 1984 p 154-62 refs

Misra, Govindanand

States endeavour for primary education. *Teacher Education* 18(22-23) Ja-Ap 1983 p 75-76

The status of the teacher. *Teacher Education* 18(24-25) Jl-Oc 1983 p 53-60

Misra, Karuna Shankar

Adult education : A challenge to teachers. *Education Quarterly* 30(3) Oc 1978 p 11-12 refs

Credibility of internal assessment of practice teaching. *Quest in Education* 19(2) Ap 1982 p 146-59 refs

Evaluating students learning in science : A challenge to science educators. *Quest in Education* 18(2) Ap 1981 p 139-49

Incidence of anxiety among teachers. *Asian J Psychology and Education* 4(1) Ja 1979 p 44-47

Influence of anxiety on effectiveness of biology teachers. *J Indian Education* 5(1) My 1979 p 50-53

Personality traits of creative science. *J Indian Education* 5(5) Ja 1980 p 27-30 refs tabs

Personality traits of flexible science teachers. *Quest in Education* 17(3) Jl 1980 p 269-75

Piaget's views on learning : *J Indian Education* 6(3) Se 1980 p 3-8 refs

Relationship of home and school environments to intellectual performance. *J Indian Education* 20(3) Ag 1983 p 174-86

Selection of media for instruction. *Education Quarterly* 32(2) Ap 1980 p 25-26

Should India neglect her creative potential? *Quest in Education* 16(3) Jl 1979 p 217-21

Stability of divisions over the college career. *Progress of Education* 54(2) Se 1979 p 29-36 + tabs

A study of scientific creativity of boys in two institutional settings. *Experiments in Education* 7(12) Fe 1980 p 223-24 tabs

A study of student disciplinary practices and teacher effectiveness in relation to classroom anxiety among student teachers. *Experiments in*

Education 8(8) Oc 1980 p 142-45 refs tabs

Misra, Lakshmi

Adult education programme and women. *Educational Rev* 86(2) My 1980 p 41-43

Continuing education and the role of universities. *Indian Education* 9(12) Mr 1980 p 19-22

Educational policy : A few suggestions. *Primary Teacher* 4(3) Jl 1979 p 31-32

The role of universities in the eradication of illiteracy. *Educational Rev* 91(8) Ag 1985 p 134-36

Mishra, Malti

See

Rao, V.K. *jt. auth.*

Misra, Monica

Burnout : Implications for teacher motivation. *New Frontiers in Education* 13(3) Jl-Se 1983 p 48-55 refs

Education and cultural deprivation. *New Frontiers in Education* 10(2) Ap-Je 1980 p 1-13 refs

Mishra, N.L.

Central evaluation : A time saving device. *J Educational Planning and Administration* 1(1) Oc 1986 p 43-53

Evaluation methodology in distance education system : A practical approach. *University News* 24(42) 8 Nv 1986 p 97-103

Monitoring : Its role and mechanics in examination management. *University News* 24(47) 16 De 1986 p 5-9

Mishra, Nilakantha

The school of future. *Educational Rev* 86(8) Ag 1980 p 140-43

Misra, R.C.

Delinking of degrees from jobs : Getting jobs without degrees. *Education Quarterly* 32(1) Ja 1980 p 30-31

Innovations in examinations in India. *Rajasthan Board J Education* 16(1-2) Ja-Je 1980 p 4-15

Misra, R.G.

The credibility of external examination marks. *J Indian Education* 5(5) Ja 1980 p 21-26 tabs

Educational relevance of external examinations. *Education Quarterly* 31(2) Jl 1979 p 27-29

Mishra, R.N. and Jha, P.N.

Impact of lab to land programme in increasing, adoption, productivity and income of farmers in North Bihar. *Indian J Extension Education* 21(1-2) Ja-Je 1985 p 77-79 tabs

Mishra, R.S.

Limits in higher education. *University News* 23(35) 16 Se 1985 p 11-13 refs

Mishra, Rajeshwar

Literacy and development. *Indian J Adult Education* 42(9) Se 1981 p 11-16; 42(10) Oc 1981 p 3-7 refs tabs

Mishra, Rama

A study of teaching behaviour of teachers in relation to their personality adjustment. *Progress of Education* 59(8) Mr 1985 p 186-89

Mishra, S.P. and Sinha, B.P.

An analysis of motivational dispositions of farm entrepreneurs. *Indian J Extension Education* 19(1-2) Mr-Je 1983 p 47-50 refs tabs

Credit orientation of farm entrepreneur. *Indian J Extension Education* 17(3-4) Se-De 1981 p 44-53 refs tabs

Socio-economic and human resources of farm entrepreneurs : A relation and analysis. *Indian J Extension Education* 16(1-2) Je 1980 p 25-33 refs tabs

Misra, V.D.

Anxiety in criminals and non-criminals : A comparison. *J Education and Psychology* 37(3) Oc 1979 p 184-86 refs

Mistry, S.P.

Changing concepts and functions of educational management. *Progress of Education* 61(3) Oc 1986 p 54-57 refs

Political calculus and educational designs. *Progress of Education* 59(2) Se 1984 p 31-33

Mistry, Veena R.

Teaching encounter of a third kind. *J Indian Education* 6(4) Nv 1980 p 26-30

See also

Fozdar, Ameeta *jt. auth.*

Mitra, Indrani

See

Basu, A.K. *et al jt. auth.*

Mitra, Shib K.

Education for non-violence. *J Indian Education* 5(2) Jl 1979 p 31-40

Research and practice in education. *J Indian Education* 8(2) Jl 1982 p 59-64

What is a progressive school? *Indian Education* 11(4) Jl 1981 p 15-18

Mlekwe, Victor M.

The use of qualitative research in workers education. *Perspectives in Education* 2(2) Ap 1986 p 99-108 refs

Modh, N.A.

The role of rural primary school teacher. *Primary Teacher* 5(4) Oc 1980 p 22-23

Mohammed

See also

under full name/surname, e.g., Omar Bin Mohammed Hasim

Modi, B.M.

Income pattern and education, Ahmedabad, Sonal Pub. 1984, 156p. Rs.121 *Book Rev, Education Quarterly* 37(2) Sum 1985 p 71

Mohammed, Zaki M. and Ranjit Singh

Farmers information sources at different stages of innovation decision process. *Indian J Extension Education* 14(1-2) Ja-Je 1978 p 78-82 refs

Mohammed Ghufran

See

Khan, Dildar *jt. auth.*

Mohammed Muzammil

Education in the scheme of plan priorities in Uttar Pradesh. *Education Quarterly* 33(2) Ap 1981 p 16-20

Progress of education in Uttar Pradesh. *Education Quarterly* 32(4) Oc 1980 p 17-21 tabs

Mohammed Nurul Anwar

See

Akhtar, Hamida *jt. auth.*

Mohan

See

under full name/surname, e.g., Jitendra Mohan

Mohan, Asha

Psychology of adult learning. *Indian J Adult Education* 45(10) Oc 1983 p 26-30

Mohan, S.

Teacher human relation management. *Experiments in Education* 11(8) Oc 1983 p 145-46

Mohan Kumar, V.

Frustrations and suggestions of an adult education trainer. *Indian J Adult Education* 46(3) Mr 1985 p 14-18

Games and simulations in adult education. *Educational Rev* 91(10) Oc 1985 p 177-79

Mohan Singh, R.

The role of communication media in effective teaching. *J Indian Education* 5(5) Ja 1980 p 31-34

Mohanraj, V.M.

Impact of pictorials on children. *Primary Teacher* 10(1) Ja 1985 p 28-31

Mohan Raju, P.

Student : Environmental awareness. *Indian Education* 10(5) Ag 1980 p 19-22

Mohanty, B. and Satapatty, O

Socio-economic profile of technical graduates in Orissa University of Agriculture and Technology. *J Higher Education* 8(3) Spr 1983 p 363-73 refs

Mohanty, B.B.

Adult education and mass media for civic education : A critical approach. *Indian J Adult Education* 46(9) Se 1985 p 10-16 refs

Communication support to the National Adult Education Programme. *Indian J Adult Education* 40(8) Ag 1979 p 30-34

Mohanty, B.S.

Discussion. *Indian J Adult Education* 44(11) Nv 1983 p 10-21

Mohanty, Banamali and Pani, Bijayashree

Emotional and social development of pupils of class X. *Asian J Psychology and Education* 4(1) Ja 1979 p 1-4 refs

Mohanty, Jagannath

Adult education programmes in Britain. *Indian J Adult Education* 41(1-2) Ja-Fe 1980 p 35-39

Art education in the new system of education. *Progress of Education* 60(8) Mr 1986 p 179-82 refs

Children's media laboratory as a learning resource centre. *Primary Teacher* 5(2) Ap 1980 p 22-24

Development of skills through art education. *Primary teacher* 10(1) Ja 1985 p 7-9

Distance learning : A democratic approach to non-formal education. *Education Quarterly* 37(4) Wint 1985 p 11-14

Education as investment in human resources development. *Indian Education* 11(10) Ja 1982 p 6-15

Educational broadcasting for adults in the United Kingdom and the lessons for India. *Education Quarterly* 30(2) Ap 1980 p 18-20

Educational broadcasting : Radio and television in education. New Delhi, Sterling. 168p. Rs.75 *Book Rev, Education Quarterly* 37(2) Sum 1985 p 78-79; *J Education and Psychology* 42(3) Oc 1981 p 171-72

Educational technology and communciation media. Cuttack, Nalanda Pub. 188p. Rs.14 *Book Rev, Education Quarterly* 33(3) Jl 1981 p 46-47

Educational technology for primary schools. *Primary Teacher* 11(4) Oc 1986 p 5-7

Educational television programmes under INSAT. *Education Quarterly* 35(1) Ja 1983 p 16-18

Evaluation in adult education. *Indian J Adult Education* 47(6) Je 1986 p 27-30 refs

Identifying and encouraging children's creativity. *Primary Teacher* 11(3) Jl 1986 p 6-8

Indian education in the emerging society. New Delhi, Sterling. 1982, 205p. Rs.60 *Book Rev, Education Quarterly* 34(2) Ap 1982 p 55-57; *J Indian Education* 8(2) Jl 1982 p 94

An investigation into the problems and prospects of school community cooperation for demonstration and improvement of education. *Experiments in Education* 8(1) Mr 1980 p 16-22 refs

Language development of children. *Primary Teacher* 11(1) Ja 1986 p 13-16

Let our children play and learn. *Primary Teacher* 9(2) Ap 1984 p 19-20

Life-long education : A way of life. *Indian Education* 11(4) Jl 1984 p 19-21

Literature for children. *Primary Teacher* 8(4) Oc 1983 p 14-17 refs

The open university in achievement in educational technology. *Education Quarterly* 31(3-4) Oc 1979-Ja 1980 p 21-23

Reorganisation in practice teaching. *Rajasthan Board J Education* 15(1) Ja-Mr 1979 p 11-16

Reschooling not deschooling. *J Indian Education* 6(3) Se 1980 p 44-47

Society and education. *Educational Rev* 86(4) Ap 1980 p 65-67

Speech development of young children. *Primary Teacher* 9(3) Jl 1984 p 26-28

Television programmes through INSAT : A national innovation. *Indian Education* 12(1-2) Ap-My 1982 p 33-35

Writing for educational television. *Indian Education* 11(6) Se 1981 p 26-28

Mohanty, Jagannath and Behera, S.C.

Teacher education programmes under INSAT. *EPA Quarterly Bulletin* 8(1-2) Ap-Je 1985 p 59-66 refs

Mohanty, Jagannath and Maharana, Sadasiba

ETV programme for the children in the age group 9-11 under INSAT. *J Educational Planning and Administration* 1(1) Oc 1986 p 54-62 tabs

Mohanty, Jagannath and Naik, Prafulla Kumar

An evaluative study of ETV programme under INSAT. *Our Education* 6 Jl 1985-86 p 1-11 tabs

Mohanty, Sunil Behari

Adapting educational models : India and Britain. *Educational Rev* 87(10) Oc 1981 p 196-98

Adult education and teacher education. *Educational Rev* 87(5) My 1981 p 94-95 refs

Communication and the NAEP. *Indian J Adult Education* 40(12) De 1979 p 47-48

The community school. *Educational Rev* 85(2) De 1979 p 238-39 refs

The concept of secularism in education. *Educational Rev* 88(8) Ag 1982 p 140-41 refs

A day in a single-teacher school at Carrington. *Primary Teacher* 5(4) Oc 1980 p 9-11

A day in German classrooms. *Teacher Today* 23(2) Oc-De 1980 p 44-47

Education of secondary school teachers in Orissa. *Teacher Education* 14(10-11) Ja-Ap 1980 p 8-15 refs

Educational journalism. *Educational Rev* 91(9) Se 1985 p 145-46

Educational provisions for slow learners. *Experiments in Education* 11(5) Ja 1983 p 79-82 refs

Effective school broadcast. *Primary Teacher* 10(3) Jl 1985 p 10-12

Innovation in student teaching through NSS in Orissa State. *Educational Rev* 90(2) FE 1984 p 21-24 refs

Life long education, in service education programme for primary school teachers. *Experiments in Education* 9(9) Nv 1981 p 61-64 refs

Masterly learning. *Experiments in Education* 11(1) Mr 1983 p 15-18

Non-formal approach in education. *Progress of Education* 55(5) De 1980 p 120-21+

Non-formal education for universalisation of education : A study in Orissa State. *Pirmary Teacher* 11(4) Oc 1986 p 17-22

School inspection in Scotland (U.K.) and Orissa (India). *EPA Quarterly Bulletin* 7(1-2) Ap-Jl 1984 p 34-40 refs

Strategies for adult and non-formal education programme. *Indian J Adult Education* 39(11-12) Nv-De 1978 p 23-26

The student teaching programme : A review of researches. *Progress of Education* 56(10) My 1982 p 228-35 refs

Teacher effectiveness. *Research Bulletin* 14(3-4) Se-De 1984 p 3-9

Training of primary school teachers in Scotland and its implications for Indian situation. *Primary Teacher* 8(4) Oc 1983 p 1-5

Universalisation of elementary education. *Education Quarterly* 35(2) Ap 1983 p 24-32 refs

A visit to a British single teacher school. *Indian Education* 10(4) Jl 1980 p 39-40

See also

Shelat, N.A. *jt. auth.*

Mohapatra

See

Mahapatra

Mohinder Singh

Service and maintenance of sophisticated scientific instruments in universities. *J Higher Education* 4(2) Aut 1978 p 279-80

Mohini, Chandra
See
Desai, K.G. *jt. auth.*
Mohini, Tejinder
See
Sodhi, G.S. *jt. auth.*
Mohite, Prasana
Language performance of pre-school children with special reference to their socio-economic status. *Quest in Education* 16(2) Ap 1979 p 97-102 refs
Readiness programmes for schools : A search for a viable model *Quest in Education* 16(4) Oc 1979 p 314-26 refs
Mohite, Prasana and Mukul, Neena
Teahcer education for early childhood. *Educational Rev* 92(9) Se 1986 p 141-44
Mohsini, S.R.
Authentic development : The role of adult education. *Indian J Adult Education* 44(1-2) Ja-Fe 1983 p 6-16
Awareness in adult education programme : Meaning and scope. *Indian J Adult Education* 44(11) Nv 1983 p 3-7
Momi, G.S. *et al*
Farmers opinion about the rural broadcast of AIR Jullundar, Punjab. *Indian J Extension Educaiton* 19(1-2) Mr-Je 1983 p 87-91 tabs
Mookerjee
See
Mukerji
Moon, Stephen
Theology and education. *New Frontiers in Education* 12(4) Oc-De 1982 p 14-24
Moonis Raza and Aggarwal, Y.P.
Inequalities in the levels of literacy in India. New Delhi, NIEPA. 1983. *Book Rev, Education Quarterly* 36(4) Wint 1984 p 53-54
Mooniz Raza and Kundu, Amitabh
Evaluation in higher education. *J Higher Education* 5(3) Spr 1980 p 359-69 refs
Moore, T.W.
Philosophy of education : An introduction. London, Routledge. 1982, 142p. $3.95 *Book Rev, Education Quarterly* 35(3) Jl 1983 p 65-66
Moorjani, Janki D.
See
Dixit, Ramesh C. *jt. auth.*
Morren, Paul
Education for international understanding. *Education Quarterly* 34(1) Ja 1982 p 25-27
Morris, Lee A. *et al*
The open elementary school : Cognitive and the nomenological correlates. *Education Quarterly* 32(4) Oc 1980 p 30-34
Mosavi, S.M.
An investigation into the attitude of later adolescent of the KAVAL towns of U.P. towards family and marriage. *Teacher Education* 13(8-9) Jl-Oc 1979

p 39-44 appdx refs tabs

Study and practice of engineering in Iran. *J Higher Education* 4(1) Mon 1978 p 114-18 refs

Moses, Damyanti S.

Developing scientific aptitude in students : The role of science teachers. *Primary Teacher* 9(2) Ap 1984 p 27-30

Moses, S. and Mayuri, K.

Effect of schooling on learning abilities and academic achievement of primary school children. *Indian Educational Rev* 19(1) Ja 1984 p 120-25

Moyle, Colin

Perspective leadership. *EPA Quarterly Bulletin* 8(1-2) Ap-Je 1985 p 17-25 refs

Msimuko, Arthur K.

Programme planning in university continuing education. *Indian J Adult Education* 41(4) Ap 1980 p 13-18 + ft-n

Muazzam, Mohmmed Raziduddin

Who is responsible for criminal mentality in children? *Primary Teacher* 4(1) Ja 1979 p 21-22

Mudaliar

See

under full name/surname, e.g., Murgesa Mudaliar, N.

Muddu, Vishwanath

Behavioural objectives in science instruction. *Indian Education* 11(7) Oc 1981 p 30-32

Environmental education : Conceptual framework. *Indian Education* 11(7) Oc 1981 p 30-32

Environmental education : Conceptual framework. *Indian Education* 12(8-9) Nv-De 1982 p 15-17

Instructional technology. *Indian Education* 10(9-10) De 1980-Ja 1981 p 13-15

Relationship between creative abilities, dimension creativity and intelligence. *Experiments in Education* 9(11) Ja 1982 p 189-91 tabs refs

Science education in India. *Indian Education* 12(1-2) Ap-My 1982 p 31-33

A study of some personality correlates of intelligence and creative abilities among high school students in Andhra Padesh. *Indian Education* 10(4) Jl 1980 p 19-23

A study of the effectiveness of the use of motion pictures as aids in the teaching of biological sciences as compared to the usual methods. *Experiments in Education* 8(8) Oc 1980 p 138-41 refs tabs

See also

Malla Reddy, M. *jt. auth.*

Mujoo, H.N.

See

Srivastava, Kumkum *et al jt. auths.*

MUKERJI - MUKHERJEE - MUKHERJI - MOOKERJEE

Mukherji, Benimadhab

Formation of mathematical signs by fingers. *Primary Teacher* 11(4) Oc 1986 p 36-39

Quiz to create lively interest. *Primary Teacher* 11(3) Jl 1986 p 18-19
Teaching English alphabets : A play-way method. *Primary Teacher* 8(2) Ap 1983 p 31-38
Writing alphabet and numerals. *Primary Teacher* 10(2) Ap 1985 p 23-27

Mukherjee, Bira
The disabled children of our country. *Primary Teacher* 6(1) Ja 1981 p 11-14

Mukherjee, D.P.
The 'language' of language. *Progress of Education* 56(6) Ja 1982 p 126-31 +

Mukherji, Daleep
The teacher and the society. *New Frontier in Education* 9(1) Ja-Mr 1979 p 1-11

Mukerji, K.A.
Financial crisis of the University of Calcutta. *J Higher Education* 1(1) Mon 1975 p 121-24 tabs

Mukerji, Kemal and Basu, Moitrayee
Assessment of delinquency. New Delhi, Wiley East. 1980, 134p. *Book Rev, Asian J Psychological Rev* 7(2) Jl 1981 p 64

Mukherjee, M.
See
Chatterji, S. *jt. auth.*

Mukherjee, Ranjit
Mothers in nursery and kindergarten. *Primary Teacher* 11(2) Ap 1986 p 21-23

Mookerjee, Ratna
Self-disclosure and occupational person. *J Educational Research and Extension* 20(2) Oc 1983 p 113-17
A study of Rorschach's indices of intelligence. *Asian J Psychology and Education* 9(1) Ja 1982 p 8-14 refs

Mookerjee, Ratna *et al*
Relationship between anxiety and academic achievement. *J Institute of Educational Research* 6(1) Ja 1982 p 10-12 refs tabs

Mukerji, S.K.
Developing colleges of basic sciences and humanities in agricultural universities. *J Higher Education* 5(2) Aut 1979 p 195-201

Mukerjee, S.N.
56th All India Educational Conference : Presidential address. *Indian Education* 12(11-12) Fe-Mr 1983 p 31-32

Mukherjee, S.P.
See
Bose, P. *jt. auth.*

Mukhopadhyay, B.
Comparative adult education. *Educational Rev* 85(3) Mr 1979 p 53-55
See also
Sharma, I.S. *jt. auth.*

Mukhopadhyay, B. and Datta, I.
Emerging needs and problems of pre-school education in India. *Educational Rev* 87(12) De 1981 p 231-33; 88(1) Ja 1982 p 11-14

Mukhopadhyay, Ban Behari

Class tests are language testing. *Indian Education* 11(5) Ag 1981 p 16-19

Improving the essay test. *Educational Rev* 87(3) Mr 1981 p 55-58

Text book : Does it require a periodic change? *Progress of Education* 56(1) Ag 1981 p 14-16 refs

Transcendental meditation in school curriculum. *Indian Education* 10(7) Oc 1980 p 21-25

Under one roof. *Indian Education* 10(4) Jl 1980 p 11-14

Vocational guidance at plus-two stage. *Educational Rev* 92(1) Ja 1986 p 9-11 refs

Mukhopadhyay, M.

Educational innovations : Towards better schooling. *Indian Education* 12(1-2) Ap-My 1982 p 5-10

Management of educational technology : New challenge in education. *Education Quarterly* 37(2) Sum 1985 p 10-18 refs

Mukhopadhyay, M. and Balaguruswamy, Sushila

Earning competences through CBTC : A study of some correlates. *Indian Education* 11(7) Oc 1981 p 13-15

Mukhopadhyay, M. and Rao, K.S.

Educational management : Challenges for professionalisation. *Perspectives in Education* 1(2) Ap 1985 p 91-98 refs

Mukhopadhyay, M. *et al*

Development of teaching competence. *Indian Educational Rev* 17(1) Ja 1982 p 12-21 refs

Mukhopadhyay, S.

Know visually impaired child in your class. *Primary Teacher* 11(3) Jl 1986 p 23-25

Mukhopadhyay, S. and Saxena, S.

The correlates of change-proneness of secondary school teachers. *Indian Educational Rev* 17(2) Ap 1982 p 123-28 refs

Mukhopadhyay, Sudesh

Must we punish children? *Primary Teacher* 5(2) Ap 1980 p 15-17

Mukul, Neena

See

Mohite, Prasana *jt. auth.*

Mulay, Sumati

See

Singh, K.M.P. *jt. auth.*

Mulay, Sumati and Sabarathana, V.E.

Research methods in extension education : Techniques of rural research. New Delhi, Manasayan. 1980, xii, 339p. Rs.40 *Book Rev, Indian J Extension Education* 16(3-4) De 1980 p 98

Mulji, Rosaleen

Multilingualism : The bright side of the coin. *Education Quarterly* 38(2) Sum 1986 p 19-21

Mullick

See also

Malik

Mullick, S.P.
Objective based learning materials : Why and how? *Primary Teacher* 8(1) Ja 1983 p 31-33

Mulusa, T.
Non-formal education for school drop-outs. *Indian J Adult Education* 48(1-2) Ap-My 1980 p 41-47

Munck, M.E. Ingrid
Model building in comparative education. Stockholm Almquist. 1979, 199p. *Book Rev, Indian Education Rev* 15(1) Ja 1980 p 122-24

Munjal, Nalini
See
Jitendra Mohan *jt. auth.*

Munni Reddy, D.
See
Venkata Rammi Reddy, A. *jt. auth.*

Mura, M.B.
Research for human central development. *J Indian Education* 10(6) Mr 1985 p 15-23 refs

Muralidharan, R.
NBT's gift to preschoolers. *Primary Teacher* 11(2) Ap 1986 p 31-32

Muralidharan, R. *et al*
A pre-school intervention study in two municipal corporation schools of Delhi. *Experiments in Education* 10(4) Je 1982 p 61-68; 10(5) Jl 1982 p 90-93 refs tabs

Murari, Pushpa and Sinha, V.
Age and sex distribution in institutionalised mentally deficient children. *Asian J Psychology and Education* 3(3) Nc 1978 p 9-11 refs tabs
See also
Pushpa, Murari

Murgesa Mudaliar, N.
Higher secondary scheme in Tamil Nadu : An evaluation after the first year. *Educational Rev* 85(7) Jl 1979 p 121-22

Murickan, Jose
Indian family facing inner contradictions. *New Frontiers in Education* 16(1) Ja-Mr 1986 p 49-66 ft-n

Murphy, H.N.
See
Raghava, G. *et al jt. auths.*

Murthy
See
under full name/surname, e.g., Sundaramurthy

Murugan, Usha
Gandhi Shikshan Bhavan's Smt. Surajaba College of Education : Report on content enrichment through projects during, 1981-82. Quest in Education 19(3) Jl 1982 p 179-86

Murugkar, Lata
Developmental goals and woman's higher education. *J Higher Education* 8(3) Spr 1983 p 321-26 refs

Muse, Ivan D. and Sharma, Motilal

Towards improving education for the rural youth : The working of two universities in India and America. *J Indian Education* 8(6) Mr 1983 p 20-26

Mutha, Dinesh Narain

See

Pramod Kumar *jt. auth.*

Muthiah, M.

Influence of periapatetic training programme on the adoption of recommended farm practices. *Indian J Extension Education* 14(3-4) Jl-De 1978 p 62-64

Muthiah, N.

Decision-making. *J Educational Planning and Administration* 1(1) Oc 1986 p 67-75

Job satisfaction of college teachers relationship with age and experience and sex differences. *Experiments in Education* 8(12) Fe 1981 p 218-20 tabs

Personality patterns of officers of correctional administration and faculty members. *Experiments in Education* 10(6) Ag 1982 p 99-101 refs

Muthiah, N. and Jaleel Saheb, S.

Science and non-science college teachers : An analysis of persoanlity traits. *National J Education* 2(2) Mr 1980 p 1-5 refs

Muthu, S.

Valedictory address. *Indian J Adult Education* 40(10-11) Oc-Nv 1979 p 64-48

Muttagi, Iqbal Aziz and Roy, Sumirmal

Changes in knowledge and attitude of students attending an environment-oriented biology courses. *Experiments in Education* 12(6) Ag 1984 p 104-10 refs tabs

Myers, Robert G.

Connecting worlds : A survey of developments in educational research in Latin America. Ottawa, IDRC. 1980, 88p. *Book Rev, Education Quarterly* 34(3) Jl 1982 p 51-52

Nagappa, T.R.

Adult education for women. *Indian J Adult Education* 41(8) Ag 1980 p 23-25 refs

NAEP : A strategy. *Indian J Adult Education* 40(7) Jl 1979 p 44-46

Rural library movement in India. *Indian J Adult Education* 40(9) Se 1979 p 17-21

The unsolved problem. *Indian J Adult Education* 39(11-12) Nv-De 1978 p 35-40

Nagar, Janarda

Bhartiya Rashtriya Shikshan Aayojana. Rajasthan, R.V.L.T.S.M. (Hindi). 1983, 82p. Rs.20 *Book Rev, Progress of Education* 58(6) Ja 1984 p 147

Nagaraj, N. and Byra Reddy, H.N.

Relative effectiveness of lecture, tape recorder lecture and their combinations with selected visuals. *Indian J Extension Education* 21(3-4) Jl-De 1985 p 43-52 refs tabs

Nagaraja, C.S. and Ram Kumar, Usha
School broadcasting. *J Indian Education* 9(1) My 1983 p 20-24
Nagarajan, V. and Selvam, S.
A perspective survey on television viewing and community learning needs. *Indian J Adult Education* 40(4) Ap 1979 p 37-42 refs tabs
Nagarath, M. Pla and Waples, Maria E.
To live or not to live with values. New Delhi, AIACS. 1980, 143p. Rs.28 *Book Rev, Education Quarterly* 23(2) Ap 1981 p 41-42
Nagasekharan Reddi, N.
Mrs. Gandhi and the Indian Left. *Student Action* 2(8) Ja 1984 p 12-13+
Nagda, Bhanwar Lal
Creative education in primary schools. *Primary Teacher* 4(4) Oc 1979 p 31-34
Making primary education creative. *Primary Teacher* 8(1) Ja 1983 p 18-19
Teaching through activities. *Primary Teacher* 5(2) Ap 1980 p 42-46
Nagendra, *ed.*
Premchand. Delhi, Bansal and Co. 221p. Rs.80 *Book Rev, Education Quarterly* 35(2) Ap 1983 p 77-79
Nagendra Singh
Classroom verbal interaction of teachers trained through integrated and conventional approaches : A comparison. *Indian Educational Rev* 18(1) Ja 1983 p 129-32 refs tabs
A comparative study of relationship of attitudes towards teaching, teaching competence and role performance among teachers trained through integrated and traditional methods. *Progress of Education* 60(5) De 1985 p 111-15+ tabs
Education : A medium of transmitting values. *Primary Teacher* 9(4) Oc 1984 p 17-20
Nageswara Rao, D.
See
Krishna Rao, R. *jt. auth.*
Nagla, Bhupendra Kumar
Youth unrest in contemporary Indian university. *J Higher Education* 8(3) Spr 1983 p 289-98 refs
Nagpal, G.L.
Internal assessment and dropouts. *Progress of Education* 53(10-11) My-Je 1979 p 201-02 +
Nagpal, R.N.
Academic promise and fulfilment. New Delhi, New Soc Pub. 1981, 139p. Rs.48 *Book Rev, Education Quarterly* 34(2) Ap 1982 p 53-54; *J Higher Education* 8(3) Spr 1983 p 403-04
Nahta, Asha
A study of perceived need satisfaction at middle and bottom levels. *Asian J Psychology and Education* 6(2) Jl 1980 p 8-11 refs
Naidu, K. Dayachandrama
See
Venkataiah, M. *jt. auth.*

Naidu, M.V.

Rotation of leadership and deanship in universities. *Indian Education* 11(5) Ag 1981 p 42-44

Naidu, Muthyalayya

From English to regional languages. *Educational Rev* 89(10) Oc 1983 p 175-77

The pros and cons of semester system. *Educational Rev* 85(3) Mr 1979 p 41-42

Revamping Indian doctorates. *Educational Rev* 87(1) Ja 1981 p 13-14

Talent drain inside universities. *Educational Rev* 86(2) Fe 1980 p 31-33

Naidu, R.V.

Student aspirations for their future position in life. *Indian Education* 10(6) Se 1980 p 34-39

Students rating of teaching efficiency. *Experiments in Education* 7(9) Nv 1979 p 153-56 refs tabs

Teacher education. *Experiments in Education* 11(10) De 1983 p 167-71

Naidu, T.R.V.

See

Singte, M.B. *jt. auth.*

Naidu, Usha S. and Parasuraman, S.

Health education of youth in India. Bombay, TISS, 1982, 67p. *Book Rev, Education Quarterly* 35(3) Jl 1983 p 59-60

NAIK - NAYAK

Naik, Chitra

Teacher education for the future. *Progress of Education* 59(8) Mr 1985 p 162-67 +

Naik, J.P.

The Education Commission and after. New Delhi, Allied. 1982. 258p. Rs.120 *Book Rev, New Frontiers in Education* 13(3) Jl-Se 1983 p 85-96; *Progress of Education* 57(9) Ap 1983 p 213-14

A quick appraisal of the National Adult Education Programme in Gujarat. *Indian J Adult Education* 40(2) Fe 1979 p 1-4

Three channels of education in developing countries : Some needed reforms. *Indian J Adult Education* 40(5) My 1979 p 1-6

Nayak, Jeevan

Adult education : A reminiscence. *Indian J Adult Education* 43(1) Ja 1982 p 3-5 +

Naik, Prafulla

See

Mohanty, Jagannath *jt. auth.*

Naik, R.B.

Folow up of students into passed SSC/HSC examinations up to 50% marks. *Research Bulletin* 15(3-4) Se-De 1985 p 42-56 tab

Nair

See

Nayar

Nanda, S.K.
This problem of standards in education. *Educational Rev* 86(9) Se 1980 p 178-79

Nanda-Mahajan
See also
under Mahajan

Nandapurkar, G.G. and Sirdeshpande, K.H.
Imparting mass training to farmers. *Indian J Adult Education* 41(12) De 1980 p 28-30 tabs

Nandi, Proshanta K.
Disruption in communication at social occasions : An essay in social psychology. *Indian Educational Rev* 18(1) Ja 1983 p 120-28 refs
Educational leadership for the third world. *J Indian Education* 10(6) Mr 1985 p 1-8 refs

Nandwani, S.C.
Education and social values in developing countries. *J Indian Education* 8(3) Se 1982 p 3-8

Nanjundappa, D.M.
Working of university finances. New Delhi, Sterling. 1976, 363p. Rs.70 *Book Rev, J Higher Education* 3(3) Spr 1978 p 424-25

Nankar, P.L.
A survey on vocational expectations of junior college students. *Research Bulletin* 12(3-4) Se-De 1982 p 44-48

Naqvi, H.J.
Role of libraries in adult education. *J Indian Education* 6(1) My 1980 p 48-52

Narang, Chamanlal
A few facts and safeguards about learning. *Progress of Education* 53(7) Fe 1979 p 133-37 refs ft-n

Narasimhan, C.V.
A peep in the child's behaviour. *Educational Rev* 89(12) De 1983 p 213-15

Narasimhan, N.
Teaching well : How they do it in Japan. *Primary Teacher* 11(1) Ja 1986 p 1-3

Narasimha Raju, A.P.S.V.V.S.N.L.
Distance education with special reference to Andhra Univerisity, Waltair. *Educational Rev* 92(12) De 1986 p 205-09 refs

Narayana
See also
under full name/surname, e.g., Anantha Narayana, H.S.

Narayana, K.P.
Universalisation of primary education — A far cry. *Student Action* 2(9) Mr 1984 p 6

Narayana, R.
Higher education in an authoritarian sociey : A case study of Bengal. *J Higher Education* 7(3) Spr 1982 p 219-26 refs

Narayana Pillai, A.S.
My problems : A mentally retarded child speaks. *Teacher Today* 23(3) Ja-Mr 1981 p 23-26

Narayana Rao, S.

Concept development in children. Triputi, Sri Venkateswara Univ. 1977, *Book Rev, J Indian Education* 6(2) Jl 1980 p 77-78

Narayanareddy, C.

Andhra Pradesh Open University : Some reflections. *University News* 24(42) 8 Nv 1986 p 17-20

Narender Kumar

See

Jitendra Mohan *jt. auth.*

Narendra Prasad

Economics of education. *Indian Education* 11(6) Se 1981 p 33-35

Narendra Pratap Singh

A comparative study of moral judgement in children. *Educational Rev* 90(4) Ap 1984 p 61-65; *Experiments in Education* 12(6) Ag 1984 p 99-103 refs tabs

Naresh Kumar

Use of puppets as audio-visual aids. *Primary Teacher* 8(3) Jl 1983 p 29-30

Wither primary education? *Primary Teacher* 7(3) Jl 1982 p 24-25

Natarajan, K.V.

Evaluation system in Indian conditions. *J Indian Education* 9(1) My 1983 p 42-44

Gaps in technical education and training. *J Indian Education* 6(6) Mr 1981 p 9-11

Innovation in student evaluation. *J Indian Education* 5(6) Mr 1980 p 3-5

Innovation in student evaluation. *Quest in Education* 17(1) Ja 1980 p 81-85

The making of a successful teacher. *J Indian Education* 12(1) My 1986 p 22-25

Pragmatisation of student evaluation. *J Educational Research and Extension* 20(3) Ja 1984 p 172-77

Natarjan, T.R.

The case for and against English as medium of instruction in higher secondary schools. *Experiments in Education* 8(1) Mr 1980 p 10-12

Natarajan, V.

Introduction of examination reform. *New Frontiers in Education* 13(3) Jl-Se 1983 p 24-37

On the reliability of ratings in interviews. *J Educational Research and Extension* 16(3) Ja 1980 p 125-34

Oral examinations. *New Frontiers in Education* 9(1) Ja-Mr 1979 p 63-69

See also

Davies, J. *jt. auth.*

Natarajan, V. and Arora, Asha

Evaluating the AIU correspondence course on evaluation methodology and examination. *New Frontiers in Education* 10(4) Oc-De 1980 p 15-21

Natarajan, V. and Malhan, P.K.

Conventional methods of teaching in universities. *New Frontiers in Education* 14(1) Ja-Mr 1984 p 62-70

Natarjan, V. and Ved Prakash

Evaluating teacher aptitudes. *New Frontiers in Education* 12(3) Jl-Se 1982 p 50-52

Facility value and discrimination index of supply type question. *Indian Educational Rev* 15(2) Ap 1980 p 102-08

Moderation of examination results. *J Higher Education* 4(3) Spr 1979 p 407-10

Natarajan, V. and Veena

Computer storage and retrieval of MBA admission test items. *New Frontiers in Education* 13(1) Ja-Mr 1983 p 20-23

Nataraju, M.S. and Channegowda, M.B.

Differential adoption of improved dairy practices by small farmers, marginal farmers and agricultural labourers. *Indian J Extension Education* 20(3-4) Se-De 1984 p 63-66

Sources of information utilised for adoption of improved dairy mangement practices by small farmers, marginal farmers and agricultural labourers. *Indian J Extension Education* 21(3-4) Jl-De 1985 p 99-100 refs tabs

Nathalang, Ekevidya

Some aspects of educational innovations in Thailand. *Rajasthan Board J Education* 16(1-2) Ja-Je 1980 p 82-85

Nathawat, S.S.

Profiles of Jaipur students : Their expectation of education and institution. *Prasar* 9(1-4) Ap 1982-Ja 1983 p 51-58

Nautiyal, K.C.

Directive principles of state policy and education in the concurrent list : Some policy implications. *Teacher Education* 17(20-21) Jl-Oc 1982 p 30-39 refs tabs

Education as a concurrent subject : A new tool for educational reform. *J Indian Education* 8(2) Jl 1982 p 27-32 ft-n tabs

Educational structure, administration and planning in France. *Teacher Education* 17(20-21) Jl-Oc 1982 p 69-80

Investment shyness in elementary school buildings. *J Indian Education* 7(3) Se 1979 p 43-49 refs

Primary education in France. *Primary Teacher* 6(4) Oc 1981 p 35-38

Nautiyal, K.C. and Sharma, Y.D.

Equalisation of educational opportunities for scheduled castes and scheduled tribes. New Delhi, NCERT. 1979. *Book Rev, J Indian Education* 6(1) My 1980 p 78-79

Nayak

See

Naik

NAYAR - NAYYER - NAIR

Nair, A. Sukumaran

Effect of general and test anxiety on cognitive performance in mathematics. *Quest in Education* 17(3) Jl 1980 p 242-49 ref

Some social-familial variables causing under achievement in secondary school mathematics. *J Educational Research and Extension* 18(2) Oc 1981 p 10-14 refs tabs

Nayar, D.P.

Managing education for rural development : Overall problems and

strategies. *Education Quarterly* 30(3) Oc 1978 p 15-18
Planning for the handicapped. *Education Quarterly* 33(4) Oc 1981 p 10-11+

Nair, G.S.K.
See
Pillai, K.S. *jt. auth.*

Nair, P. Thankappan
Tribes of Arunachal Pradesh. Guwahati, Spectrum Pub. 1985. 319p. Rs.165 *Book Rev, Teacher Today* 28(2) Oc-De 1985 p 124-25

Nair, R. Sukumaran
The Calicut University adjustment inventory. *J Educational Research and Extension* 18(1) Jl 1981 p 22-42 tabs
An investigation into the diagnostic study of the remedial programme with a view to identifying the conceptual errors and gaps in standard IX, physics. *Experiments in Education* 11(5) Jl 1983 p 75-79 refs tabs
An investigation into the relationship between socio-economic status, intelligence, science aptitude and science interest of secondary school pupils. *Experiments in Education* 11(4) Je 1983 p 57-62
An investigation into the relative effectiveness of inductively and deductively sequenced modes of teacher-centred presentation in secondary school physics. *Experiments in Education* 12(7) Se 1984 p 113-23; 12(8) Oc 1984 p 138-39 tabs
A study of certain personality variables related to high and low achievers in biology in secondary schools. *J Educational Research and Extension* 19(4) Ap 1983 p 207-19 refs tabs

Nair, Rajasekharan
A statistical analysis of performance in the secondary school leaving certificate examination : Communitywise. *J Institute of Educational Research* 6(3) Se 1982 p 14-19 tabs
Turning point in sex differentials in higher education. *J Higher Education* 6(1-3) 1980-81 p 122-28 tabs

Nayyer, S.M. and Karnawat, C.M.
Restructuring teacher education in Rajasthan. *Teacher Today* 25(2) Oc -De 1982 p 54-61

Nair, T.K.D.
Classroom composition : What is the objective? *Primary Teacher* 6(4) Oc 1981 p 29-31
Decision-making : A framework for educational institutions. *Indian Education* 13(10-11) Ja-Fe 1984 p 17-19
Inspection and supervision of the future. *New Frontiers in Education* 16(1) Ja-Mr 1986 p 79-84
Teaching of science and mathematics in primary classes of Kerala. *J Indian Education* 7(3) Se 1979 p 3-9 annex
Training of educational administrators. *Indian Education* 11(1-2) Ap-My 1981 p 49-52

Nayar, Usha
Women, education and work : A review. *J Higher Education* 1(2) Aut 1975 p 283-92 refs

Nayudamma, Y.
Impact of emerging sciences and technologies on society : Excerpts from

Shanti Swarup Bhatnagar Memorial oration. *New Frontiers in Education* 13(3) Jl-Se 1983 p 72-78

Nayyar
See
Nayar

Neerada Reddy, P.
Rates of return occupational pattern of non-professional graduates. *Indian Education* 10(1-2) Ap-My 1980 p 48-52

Neeru Bala and Roy, Sumita
Utilisation of household knowledge by farm women. *Indian J Extension Education* 15(3-4) De 1979 p 22-26 tabs

Nenty, H. Johnson
The effect of performance attribution on attitude to study, achievement motivation and tendency to cheat in examination. *Progress of Education* 59(10-11) My-Je 1985 p 224-34

Neuman, Yoram
Grouping effect in rating scales : The case of faculty attitudes. *J Education and Psychology* 38(2) Jl 1980 p 76-87 refs tabs

Nicholls, John
See
Wells, Gordon *jt. auth.*

Nickandrov, Nicholas
Active learning in the context of adult education. *Teacher Today* 22(3) Ja-Mr 1980 p 1-5

Nigam, Raghuvir Sahay
Adult education for women. *Educational Rev* 86(3) Mr 1980 p 49
Environment and education. *Educational Rev* 87(6) Je 1981 p 110-13
Environmental education. *Progress of Education* 53(6) Ja 1979 p 111-14
Findings by UPSC Chairman. *Educational Rev* 86(11) Nv 1980 p 214-15
Kothari Commission's warning. *Educational Rev* 87(1) Ja 1981 p 18-19
Media of education. *Educational Rev* 85(7) Jl 1979 p 127-28
New components of education. *Educational Rev* 85(2) Fe 1979 p 23-24
New education scheme. *Educational Rev* 84(12) De 1978 p 221-23
Subjects for school and college curriculum. *Educational Rev* 85(10) Oc 1979 p 181-83
Unemployment and education. *Educational Rev* 86(8) Ag 1980 p 143-44

Nihalain, Paroo *et al*
Indian and British English. New Delhi, OUP. 1979, 260p. Rs.40 *Book Rev, J Indian Education* 7(3) Se 1979 p 58

Nimbalkar, M.R.
Adult education in Goa : Retrospect and prospects. *Indian J Adult Education* 47(1) Ja 1986 p 17-22 tabs
An evaluation of the adult education programme in Goa during the period, 1978-82. *EPA Quarterly Bulletin* 8(3-4) Oc 1985-Ja 1986 p 45-54

Ninan, K.N.
Reforming our educational system : Some perspectives. *Progress of Education* 58(11) Je 1984 p 273-75 +

Niranjan Reddy, B.
Training in workers education. *Indian J Adult Education* 45(4) Ap 1984

p 20-22

Niranjan Reddy, B. and Lakshmi Reddy, M.V.

Teacher training : The role of micro-teaching. *J Indian Education* 12(4) Nv 1986 p 17-21

Nirmal Singh

A perspective on higher education in India : The case of private control. *J Higher Education* 5(1) Mon 1979 p 21-31

Nischal, K.

The influence of sexist bias on female role in rural areas. *J Indian Education* 8(3) Se 1982 p 29-32

Northcott, Paul

Off campus MBA programme : Deakin University. *Indian Education* 12(5-6) Ag-Se 1982 14-18

Nurul

See also

under full name/surname, e.g., Mohammed Nurul Anwar

Nurual Hasan, S.

Challenges in education culture and social welfare. New Delhi, Allied. Vol. 1. 1977, 358p. Rs.60 *Book Rev, Teacher Today* 21(3) Ja-Mr 1979 p 103-04

Nyoni, Nazar Gerves

Mass education in Tanzania. *Indian Education* 10(9-10) De 1980-Ja 1981 p 20-22

Oad, L.K.

Impact of Indian thought in developing a value-pattern in education. *J Indian Education* 6(8) Ja 1981 p 8-12

Research in examination : A sociological perspective. *Quest in Education* 17(1) Ja 1980 p 66-73

Shiksha Ke Nutan Ayam. Jaipur, Rajasthan Hindi Academi.1978. 293p. *Book Rev, J Indian Education* 6(1) My 1980 p 77-78

Socially useful productive work. *J Indian Education* 5(2) Jl 1979 p 3-7

Oak, A.W.

Life styles of home science graduates. *Research Bulletin* 14(3-4) Se-De 1984 p 10-32 tabs

Oak, A.W. *et al*

A study of family and social etiquettes of adolescents. *Research Bulletin* 12(1-2) Mr-Je 1982 p 35-42

Oberai, Neena

Radiovision for non-formal education. *Progress of Education* 55(2) Jl 1981 p 335-37 +

See also

Sharma, Motilal *jt. auth.*

Odunusi, T.O.

Science educators perception of readiness for learning science in Nigerian secondary schools. *Perspectives in Education* 2(3) Jl 1986 p 171-77 refs

O'Hara, Michael

The myth of staff development at the tertiary level of education. *J Higher Education* 7(3) Spr 1982 p 297-302 refs

Ojha, Shailendra Kumar
See
Rajiv Ranjan Singh *jt. auth.*

Okedara, J.T.
Concepts and measurement of literacy, semi literacy and illiteracy : A literature review. *Indian Educational Rev* 17(3) Jl 1982 p 42-61 refs
Orginal diffusion of external examiner system in the conduct of univerisity examination. *Indian Educational Rev* 16(2) Ap 1981 p 29-45 refs

Ologe, S.A.
Training of adult literacy instructors : Some observations. *Indian J Adult Education* 47(8) Ag 1986 p 22-30 refs

Om Prakash
Educational attainment of children in the sweeper community of AIIMS campus : An exploratory study. *Indian Educational Rev* 15(4) Oc 1980 p 97-103

Omar Bin Mohammed Hasim
The Malaysian examinations syndicate. *Rajasthan Board J Education* 16(1-2) Ja-Je 1980 p 36-40

Omerbin Sayeed and Varma, Ravi Kumar
University system : Organisational context, structure and performance. *J Higher Education* 5(3) Spr 1980 p 409-15 refs tabs

Omolewa, Michael
Mass literacy campaigns in Nigeria, 1940-60. *Indian J Adult Education* 41(9) Se 1980 p 15-23

Oommen, Chinna
How to come over reading disability. *Primary Teacher* 11(1) Ja 1986 p 29-33

Oomonen, M.A.
Hidden curricula in social sciences : An introductory note based on the economics courses in Indian universities. *New Frontiers in Education* 11(1) Ja-Mr 1981 p 44-65 refs appdx tabs

Oranu, Raph N.
Vocational education and technological development of a nation. *Indian Education* 12(3-4) Je-Jl 1982 p 5-11

Orpen, Christopher
How much role conflict is there in the job of university lecturer : An international comparison. *J Higher Education* 7(3) Spr 1982 p 260-66 refs
Student evaluation of instructions as a function of expected and obtained performance. *J Higher Education* 9(1) Mon 1983 p 89-94 refs

Osuala, Esogwa C.
Androgogy versus pedagogy in adult business education programme. *Indian Education* 10(9-10) De 1980-Ja 1981 p 23-27
Androgogy versus pedagogy in adult business education programme. *Teacher Today* 24(3) Ja-Mr 1982 p 14-19 refs
Career development of Nigerian students : Implications for guidance counsellors. *Quest in Education* 18(2) Ap 1981 p 165-76
Parental influence on academic achievement of students. *Asian J Psychology and Education* 7(1) Ja 1981 p 1-7

Parental influences on academic achievement of students. *Indian Education* 10(6) Se 1980 p 4-9

The management of business education in Nigeria. *Indian Education* 11(1-2) Ap-My 1981 p 89-91

Teacher education in Nigeria : A historical perspective. *Indian Education* 13(3-4) Je-Jl 1983 p 21-23; 13(5-6) Ap-Se 1983 p 26-28

Oswal, M.G.

The role of social sciences in health education. *J Indian Education* 5(2) Jl 1979 p 23-26

Owen, John E.

Indian children in English schools : A study in cultural contact. *Educational Rev* 92(8) Ag 1986 p 121-25

The Inner London Education Authority : A record of achievement. *Educational Rev* 91(9) Se 1985 p 141-45

Sociology in U.S. teacher training. *Educational Rev* 88(9) Se 1982 p 153-55

The U.S. school system : Some recent trends. *Educational Rev* 87(11) Nv 1981 p 209-11

Owie, Ikponmwosa

Teacher perception of their principals P.C.I. and rating of the principals. *J Education and Psychology* 41(1-2) Ap-Jl 1983 p 26-29

Oza, A.P.

Class room interaction sequence of categories. *Progress of Education* 58(3) Oc 1983 p 61-63

Ozga, Jennifer and Lawn, Martin

Teachers, professionals and class : A study of organised teachers. London, Falmer Press. 1981, 153p. *Book Rev, Education Quarterly* 35(1) Ja 1983 p 44-45

PACHAURY - PACHORI

Pachaury, A.C.

Creative pupil perception of Angami Nagas serving in elementary schools of Nagaland. *J Educational Research and Extension* 18(4) Ap 1982 p 224-28 refs tabs

Creative pupil perception by the Gujarati teachers. *J Education and Psychology* 43(3-4) Oc 1985-Ja 1986 p 153-57 refs

Creativity but isn't there in the classroom. *Progress of Education* 54(12) Jl 1980 p 229-30

Logico-mathematical reasoning of mathematics teachers. *J Educational Research and Extension* 16(2) Oc 1979 p 80-88 tabs

Pachori, R.S. and Tripathi, S.G.

Impact of intensive agriculture extension and research programme on the farmers knowledge of technology. *Indian J Extension Education* 19(3-4) Se-De 1983 p 72-73

Padma, K.

Attitude of literate women of Hyderabad slums. *Experiments in Education* 11(8) Oc 1983 p 138-40

Padma, M.S.

History of vocationalisation : A review. *Teacher Today* 21(4) Ap-Je 1979 p 39-44 refs

Science teaching observation : A need for tools. *Progress of Education* 55(5) De 1980 p 122-23 + tabs

Padmanabhaiah, S.

Attitudes of teachers toward non-detention system of examinations. *Experiments in Education* 7(5) Jl 1979 p 77-80 refs tabs

Padmanabhan, C.B.

Alternatives in financing Indian education. *New Frontiers in Education* 13(1) Ja-Mr 1983 p 42-48

An approach to financial management in education with special reference to colleges in India. *J Higher Education* 7(3) Spr 1982 p 293-97

Financial management in education. New Delhi, Select Books. 1984, 236p. Rs.60 *Book Rev, Education Quarterly* 37(2) Sum 1985 p 80-81

Financial management in Indian education : Its functional approach. *Indian Educational Rev* 20(4) Oc 1985 p 121-32

Financial management of universities and colleges in India. *Indian Education* 11(1-2) Ap-My 1981 p 43-48

Financial management of universities and colleges in India. *New Frontiers in Education* 10(4) Oc-De 1980 p 59-64

Financial management of universities in India. *J Higher Education* 9(2) Aut 1983 p 282-85

Financing of education and equality of opportunity in Indian education. *Perspectives in Education* 1(3) Jl 1985 p 167-73 refs ft-n

Financing of education in the Sixth Five-Year Plan. *New Frontiers in Education* 13(2) Ap-Je 1983 p 17-29 refs tabs

Integration of education with economic needs. *New Frontiers in Education* 12(1) Ja-Mr 1982 p 37-49

Is financing Indian higher education equitable? *University News* 23(8) 23 Fe 1985 p 25-27

Principles and techniques of Indian education and finance. *New Frontiers in Education* 12(2) Ap-Je 1982 p 36-41

Towards rational financial policy for Indian education. *Education Quarterly* 37(3) Aut 1985 p 1-5

University budgetary reforms for sound financial management. *New Frontiers in Education* 15(3) Jl-Se 1985 p 65-72

Padmanabhan, N.S.

Education and social justice. *Educational Rev* 86(5) My 1980 p 85-87

'Higher secondary' : In what sense? *Educational Rev* 86(10) Oc 1980 p 198-99

Padmavathy, D.

Effectiveness of field-trips in teaching biological sciences. *Educational Rev* 91(10) Oc 1985 p 171-76

Padmavati, S.

Higher medical education for women. *J Higher Education* 1(3) Aut 1975 p 256-58 refs

Pal
See
Paul

Palaniyandi, R.
See
Subramania Pillai, G. *jt. auth.*

Paliwal, M.P.
Social change and education : Present and future. New Delhi, Uppal Pub H. 1984, 354p. Rs.175 *Book Rev, Teacher Today* 28(2) Oc-De 1985 p 123-24

Paliwal, M.R.
A policy frame for the development in education in Rajasthan. *Teacher Today* 27(2) Oc-De 1984 p 34-36

Palki, S.D.
See
Kumar, K.L. *jt. auth.*

Palsane, M.N.
Continuing and non-formal education. *J Higher Education* 4(3) Spr 1979 p 343-48
See also
Ram, Usha *jt. auth.*

Palted, G.M.
Pursuit of quality in postgraduate studies and research in educaiton. *Quest in Education* 18(2) Ap 1981 p 108-16

Palted, G.M. and Mench, G.B.
Professional preparation of college teachers. *Quest in Education* 16(2) Ap 1979 p 114-29

Palted, G.M. and Suryavanshi, V.R.
Improving college instruction through self-instructional micro-teaching. *Indian Educational Rev* 18(4) Oc 1981 p 66-71

Pan, Tarak Nath
Classification of learners according to their learning styles : A new approach. *Indian Educational Rev* 20(2) Ap 1985 p 88-95; *Progress of Education* 57(9) Ap 1983 p 194-99 refs
Need of Piagetian testing for intellectual assessment. *J Indian Education* 8(1) My 1982 p 37-39 ft-n

Panchal, B.R.
See
Darji, D.R. *jt. auth.*

Panchal, B.R. and Darji, D.R.
Innovating proneness in the secondary teachers' training colleges. *Indian Educational Rev* 16(3) Jl 1981 p 14-20
Innovative proneness of teacher education. *J Education and Psychology* 39(1) Ap 1981 p 66-72 refs
A study of innovative proneness of teacher educators. *J Institute of Educational Research* 4(1) Ja 1980 p 23-27; 4(2) My 1980 p 24-29 refs tabs

Panchamukhi, P.R.
Devaluation of education : A quantitative analysis. *J Higher Education* 1(1)

Mon 1975 p 15-30 tabs

Economics of univerisities finances : Basic principles and practice. Dharwar, Karnata Hist Res Soc. 1977, 238p. Rs.22 *Book Rev, Indian Educational Rev* 15(4) Oc 1980 p 117-19; *J Higher Education* 4(1) Mon 1978 p 125-26

PANDA - PANDAY - PANDE - PANDEY - PANDEYA - PANDIA

Pandey, Anirudh

A comparative study in the areas of adjustment between intellectually bright and average higher secondary adolescents. *Indian Educational Rev* 15(2) Ap 1980 p 120-24 refs tabs

Panda, Anita

See

Panda, K.C. *jt. auth.*

Pandey, Asha

Teacher education : Goal identification and strategies. *J Indian Education* 12(3) Se 1986 p 58-62 refs

Pandey, B.B.

A study of relationship between adjustment level of aspiration and achievement. *J Institute of Educational Research* 10(3) Se 1986 p 18-20 refs

Pandey, Davesh Dutt

Uses and abuses at periodical test system in evaluation of classroom learning. *Indian Educational Rev* 18(4) O 1983 p 135-42

Pandey, I.C.

Reorientation of geological education. *J Higher Education* 4(2) Spr 1979 p 327-32

Panda, K.C.

See

Patnaik, S.P. *jt. auth.*

Panda, K.C. and Dash, P.C.

Effect of simulated information on assessment of congnitive competence : A test of expectancy hypothesis. *Indian Educational Rev* 15(2) Ap 1980 p 22-35 refs

Panda, K.C. and Panda, Anita

Education of disabled : Integration and mainstreaming : A sociological perspective. *National J Education* 6(1) Se 1983 p 1-6 refs

Special education : An interdisciplinary approach for education of the young disabled. *National J Education* 6(2) My 1984 p 48-58

Pande, K.D.

Role of science institute in promoting environmental education. *Indian Education* 12(11-12) Fe-Mr 1983 p 26-30

Pandey, K.N.

Who will teach the teacher? *Teacher Education* 20(30-31) Ja-Ap 1985 p 40-42

Pandey, M.D.

Essay writings in primary schools. *Primary Teacher* 5(1) Ja 1980 p 33-34

The teacher and the society. *Primary Teacher* 4(3) Jl 1979 p 32-33

Panda, M.L.
Use of semi-programmed learning material for teaching demonstrated method in science to B.Ed students. *Progress of Education* 59(12) Jl 1985 p 256-59 tabs

Pande, M.P. and Patil, Geeta Devi G.
A study of the relationship between study habits and scholastic achievement of students of secondary schools. *J Educational Research and Extension* 20(3) Ja 1984 p 197-202

Pandia, Mahendra N.
What should our children read. *Progress of Education* 57(12) Jl 1983 p 266-68

Pandey, N.N.
Co-curricular interests of secondary school students. *J Institute of Educational Research* 6(3) Se 1982 p 1-8 refs tabs

Panda, Namita
Relationship between sociometric index N-Ach and rated pupil characteristics. *J Educational Research and Extension* 19(4) Ap 1983 p 224-32 refs tabs

Pandeya, Pratibha
See
Ahluwalia, S.P. *jt. auth.*

Pandey, R.C. *et al*
A study of creativity in relation to socio-economic status of high school students. *J Institute of Educational Research* 10(1) Jl 1986 p 9-12 refs

Pandey, R.N.
See
Pandey, R.C. *et al jt. auths.*

Pandey, R.P. and Singh, R.A.
A correlationship study of school examination mark, intelligence and achievement scores. *Asian J Psychology and Education* 3(3) Nv 1978 p 6-8 refs tabs

Pandey, Rajendra
Sociology of youth. New Delhi, Sterling. 1984, 187p. Rs.100 *Book Rev, Perspectives in Education* 1(4) Oc 1985 p 272-73

Pandey, Ram Shakal
Can education ignore metaphysics, epistemology and ethics. *Progress of Education* 53(7) Fe 1979 p 122-25 refs

Education : Viewpoints of religion and philosophy. *Educational Rev* 85(5) My 1979 p 81-82 refs

Educational aims and philosophy. *Educational Rev* 85(1) Ja 1979 p 16-18 refs

Philosophical models of teaching. *Teacher Today* 21(3) Ja-Mr 1979 p 19-24 refs

Panda, S.K. and Mishra, A.K.
Effects of sex, training and experience on the personality development of teachers. *Indian Educational Rev* 18(4) Oc 1983 p 106-10

Pandey, S.N. and Mathur, P.N.
Differential information gaps under the training and visit extension system. *Indian J Extension Education* 19(3-4) Se-De 1983 p 18-25 refs tabs

Pandey, S.N. and Roy, N.K.

Factors associated with effectiveness of farm broadcast. *Indian J Extension Education* 14(1-2) Ja-Je 1978 p 54-56

Panda, Santosh K.

International perspectives in distance learning : A plea for India. *Education Quarterly* 34(1) Ja 1982 p 7-11 refs ft-n tabs

Systems approach to planning new educational media in the developing countries. *Education Quarterly* 35(1) Ja 1983 p 12-15 refs

See also

Jindal, C.R. *jt. auth.*

Malhotra, S.P. *jt. auth.*

Sahoo, S.C. *jt. auth.*

Shankar, Laxmi *jt. auth.*

Singh, Harindra M. *jt. auth.*

Panda, Santosh K. and Swain, Nihar R.

Environmental education for adult learners. *Education Quarterly* 38(3) Aut 1986 p 4-7

Pandey, Sarla Kumari

Some psychological correlates in the sense of responsibility. *Progress of Education* 60(1) Ag 1985 p 2-6 refs

Pandey, Sarla Kumari and Upadhyay, Rajeshwar

Degree of the sense of responsibility in relation to some socio-eocnomic variables. *Progress of Education* 59(7) Fe 1985 p 150-56 refs tabs

Pandey, Saroj

School climate and teachers attitude. *Teacher Education* 14(12-13) Jl-Oc 1980 p 41-47 refs tabs

Pandit, Avinash S.

Teaching geography to the blind. *Progress of Education* 56(10) My 1982 p 241-45

Pandit, B.B.

An analytical study of the motives of primary school teacher trainees for choosing teaching as a career. *Progress of Education* 55(9) Ap 1981 p 227-31 tabs

Quality control in educaiton through 'control chart' technique. *Progress of Education* 56(6) Ja 1982 p 132-35 + tabs

A study of teacher trainees motives for the choice of teaching career and achievement in teaching skills. *J Education and Psychology* 40(3) Oc 1982 p 152-56

A study of the achievement in theory and teaching competence of teacher trainees. *Progress of Education* 56(11) Je 1982 p 275-77 tabs

Pandit, Indu

Education of the pre-school child. *Progress of Education* 54(10-11) My-Je 1980 p 194-98

Non-formal education : A perspective. *Indian J Adult Education* 41(12) De 1980 p 13-19 refs

Pandit, V.K.

See

Waghmare, S.K. *jt. auth.*

Pandurangam, K.

Education in Andhra Pradesh. *Indian Education* 11(8-9) Nv-De 1981 p 34-36

Pangotra, N.N.

Fundamentals of educational technology. Chandigarh, Int. Pub. 103p. Rs.22 *Book Rev, Progress of Education* 56(8) Mr 1982 p 200

Role structure of teachers in relation to modernisation : A study of college teachers in Chandigarh. *National J Education* 5(1) Se 1982 p 5-14

The school and moral education. *Progress of Education* 54(8) Mr 1980 p 154-59

School dropouts : A crucial problems. *J Indian Education* 12(2) Jl 1986 p 42-45

Typical patterns of verbal behaviour of succesful secondary school English teachers. *Indian Educational Rev* 16(3) Jl 1981 p 59-68

Vitalising teacher education. *Educational Rev* 89(2) Mr 1983 p 55-57 refs

Pangotra, N.N. and Lalit Kishore

On mastery learning instructional plan. *Educational Rev* 92(4) Ap 1986 p 66-69 refs

Pani, Bijayashree

See

Mohanty, Banamali *jt. auth.*

Pani, P.

See

Sansanwal, D.N. *et al jt. auths.*

Pani, R.N.

See

Pani, S.P. *jt. auth.*

Pani, S.P. and Pani, R.N.

A new outlook on education *J Indian Education* 11(1) My 1985 p 62-70 refs

Panigrahi, Sudarsan C.

Differential personality traits of tribal and non-tribal adolescents at different levels of intelligence and socio-economic status. *J Education and Psychology* 44(1) Ap 1986 p 51-57 refs

See also

Raina, B.L. *jt. auth.*

Panital, Iris

An adaptation of effective questioning for preservice and in-service teachers in India. *Indian Educational Rev* 17(4) Oc 1982 p 1-19

Microteaching : A handbook for teachers. Delhi, OUP. 1980, x, 147p. Rs.12 *Book Rev, Education Quarterly* 33(2) AP 1981 p 38-39; *Progress of Education* 56(7) Fe 1982 p 177

Pankajam, C.

Vocational education. *Educational Rev* 87(3) Mr 1981 p 41-46 refs

Pant, Daya

The need for guidance services at primary stage. *Primary Teacher* 9(4) Oc 1984 p 5-7

Pant, K.C.

Union Education Minister addresses convocation of Annamalai Univeristy. *University News* 23(26) 8 Jl 1985 p 6-7

Papa, R.
See
Krishna Rao, R. *jt. auth.*

Papali, A.B.A.
Teaching of words through cards. *Primary Teacher* 5(2) AP 1980 p 37-40

Pappachan, P.O.
Intelligence in relation to different levels of socio-economic status. *J Institute of Educational Research* 7(3) Se 1983 p 15-18

Parameswaran, E.G.
The child, the family and the school. *Indian Education* 10(3) Je 180 p 11-18
A psychological view of the child and child education. *Indian Education* 9(10-11) Ja-Fe 1980 p 16-18

Parasher, S.V.
Indian English : Model, identity and use. *J Indian Education* 5(1) My 1979 p 68-75 refs

Parasuraman, S.
See
Naidu, Usha S. *jt. auth.*

PAREEK - PARIKH

Parikh, B.A.
The effect of the medium of instruction on the achievement of the students. *J Educational Research and Extension* 17(3) Ja 1981 p 137-41 refs
A study of certain personality variables of the divorcee and the happily married males. *Asian J Psychology and Education* 3(3) Nv 1978 p 35-41 refs tabs

Parikh, B.S.
Population and population education in India. *Teacher Education* 18(22-23) Ja-Ap 1983 p 20-30

Parikh, J.C.
An investigation into the controversial issue on continuity and non-continuity in learning. *J Education and Psychology* 40(4) Ja 1983 p 229-33 refs
A study of attitude of the teachers towards the postgraduate course in education. *Progress of Education* 53(10-11) My-Je 1979 p 208-13 refs tabs
See also
Patel, M.M. *jt. auth.*

Parikh, Jyoti and Yadav, R.
Handicapped children : A programme for the parents. *Primary Teacher* 6(1) Ja 1981 p 5-10

Pareek, M.
A survey of the primary schools of Tonk Phatak (Jaipur) areas. *Educational Rev* 91(7) Jl 1985 p 116-19 tabs
See also
Sharma, C.M. *jt. auth.*

Parikh, P.
Gandhi Shikshan Bhavan's Smt. Surajaba College of Education : A report *Quest in Education* 19(2) Ap 1982 p 110-17

Parikh, Pratibha

A study of community education in Gandhi Shikshan Bhavan, 1979-80. *Quest in Education* 17(2) Ap 1980 p 127-40

Parikh, Ramlal

Education for rural development. *University News* 23(1) 1 Ja 1985 p 3-4

Imperative need for value based higher education. *University News* 23(2) 8 Ja 1985 p 5-6

Mass movement for adult literacy : Formidable tasks. *Indian J Adult Educaiton* 47(5) My 1986 p 6-8

New Education Policy : Some urgent tasks. *Teacher Education* 20(30-31) Ja-Ap 1985 p 15-18; *University News* 23(18) 8 My 1985 p 7-8

Renewing the adult education movement. *Indian J Adult Education* 45(4) Ap 1984 p 3-4

Pareek, Udai

Education and rural development in Asia. New Delhi, Oxf-IBH. 232p. *Book Rev, New Frontiers in Education* 13(1) Ja-Mr 1983 p 73-74

The pedagogy of behaviour simulation. *Indian Educational Rev* 16(1) Ja 1981 p 1-24 refs

Parihar, D.S.

On improving the programmes of classes I and II. *Primary Teacher* 6(1) Ja 1981 p 22-25

Universalisation of primary education. *Primary Teacher* 8(1) Ja 1983 p 23-24

Parikh

See

Pareek

Parisudharao, N.

See

Bhaskara Rao, D. *et al jt. auths.*

Parmaji, S.

Caste levels and performance during medical training. *Indian Education* 12(5-6) Ag-Se 1982 p 10-13

Educational jobs. Delhi, Leeladevi Pub. 1979, 118p. Rs.45 *Book Rev, Education Quarterly* 32(4) Oc 1980 p 48; *Indian Educational Rev* 10(5) Ag 1980 p 44-45; *Indian J Extension Education* 16(3-4) De 1980 p 96-97; *J Education and Psychology* 39(1) Ap 1981 p 73-74; *New Frontiers in Education* 12(1) Ja-Mr 1982 p 80-81

Teacher education : The drift and its reversal. *Indian Education* 10(1-2) Ap-My 1980 p 53-58

Parmaji, S. and Sudhakar, V.

The philosophy of inter-disciplinary approach in science education. *Indian Education* 12(1-2) Ap-My 1982 p 23-26

Parmaji, S. and Suryaprakash Rao, A.

Ability of estimation by approximation : A study. *New Frontiers in Education* 13(4) Oc-De 1983 p 69-72

Parmaji, S. *et al*

An investigation into the relative performance levels of English literature students of Kakatiya University in relation to their caste background. *Progress of Education* 60(2) Se 1985 p 34-35

Parrott, Elizabeth

Microteaching in higher education : Research, development and practice. Guildford, Soc Res Higher Education. 1977, 107p. *Book Rev, Indian Educational Rev* 15(4) Oc 1980 p 113-16; *J Higher Education* 5(2) Aut 1979 p 266-68

Parshad, R.

Comparison of the multiple regression and the configurational approach to predictory correlates of the communication effectiveness of village level workers. *Indian J Extension Education* 18(3-4) De 1982 p 16-22 refs

Parthasarathy, K.

See

Jayagopal, R. *et al jt. auths.*

Parthasarathy, R.

See

Rao, V.N. *jt. auth.*

Parvathamma, C.

Employment problems of university graduates. New Delhi, Ashish Pub H. 159p. Rs.100 *Book Rev, Education Quarterly* 37(3) Aut 1985 p 60-61

New horizons and scheduled castes. New Delhi, Ashish Pub H. 184p. Rs.100. *Book Rev, Education Quarterly* 38(2) Sum 1986 p 51-52

Pasricha, Prem

Guidance and counselling. *New Frontiers in Education* 11(4) Oc-De 1981 p 46-47; 12(1) Ja-Mr 1982 p 1-36

Passi, B.K.

A case for analysis and development of learning and administrative skills in education. *J Education and Psychology* 38(4) Ja 1981 p 207-10

Passi, B.K. and Ajit Singh

Microanalysis of teaching skills : An illustration of prompting. *J Indian Education* 5(5) Ja 1980 p 17-20 refs

Passi, B.K. *et al*

Problem oriented curriculum and its procedural arrangement in a college of education. *Progress of Education* 59(8) Mr 1985 p 171-76

Should implications be incorporated in research reports. *Teacher Education* 16(18-19) Ja-Ap 1982 p 9-16 refs

Some salient issues in teacher education. *National J Education* 6(2) My 1984 p 7-20 refs

Passi, Subhashini

Cognitive development and the communicative mothers. *Progress of Education* 60(6) Jl 1986 p 128-29 +

A plea for utilisation of vacations. *Experiments in Education* 10(3) My 1982 p 57-58

Patankar, K.

Report of the practice teaching programme at Gandhi Shikshan Bhavan, 1979-80. *Quest in Education* 17(2) Ap 1980 p 113-26

Patankar, Kamal A.

Report of the practice teaching programme at Gandhi Shikshan Bhavan's Smt. Surajaba College of Education, 1981-82. *Quest in Education* 19(2) Ap 1982 p 98-105

Patel, A.D.
A comparative study of the opinions of teachers of different faculties of the Sardar Patel University with regard to internal assessment. *J Education and Psychology* 39(4) Ja 1982 p 248-53

Patel, A.U.
Communication channels and its impact on knowledge of the farmers of the South Western Nigeria. *Indian J Extension Education* 14(3-4) Jl-De 1978 p 1-7

Patel, Ashok A.
See
Prajapati, M.R. *jt. auth.*

Patel, B.V.
Can listening skills be modified? *J Education and Psychology* 37(4) Ja 1980 p 239-46; *Rajasthan Board J Education* 15(9) Oc-De 1979 p 15-21
An experiment in the teaching of listening comprehension in Gujarat pupils of class VIII. *J Education and Psychology* 36(3) Oc 1978 p 91-98
An experiment in the teaching of listening comprehension in Gujarati to pupils class IX. *J Education and Psychology* 39(4) Ja 1982 p 224-31 refs
Reading comprehension as a function of self-concept. *J Education and Psychology* 44(2-3) Jl-De 1986 p 92-95

Patel, B.V. and Vora, I.A.
Teacher efficiency as a function of class obtained at professional degree and social maturity. *J Education and Psychology* 42(3) Oc 1984 p 163-70 refs

Patel, Bhasker and Bhaumik, Gita
Impact of some personality variables on academic achievement : A replication study. *J Education and Psychology* 40(4) Je 1983 p 207-13 refs

Patel, C.B.
Improvement of teachers professional competency in the use of classroom techniques. *J Education and Psychology* 41(4) Ja 1984 p 246-53 appdx
Improvement of teachers professional competency in the use of classroom techniques. *Progress of Education* 58(4) Nv 1983 p 81-84 appdx tabs
A study of micro-teaching in the context of methods, subjects, sex and I.Q. *J Education and Psychology* 44(1) Ap 1986 p 21-28 refs

Patel, D.N.
Impact of readability levels, writing styles, grade and reading ability upon pupils comprehension. *J Education and Psychology* 41(1-2) Ap-Jl 1983 p 49-54
The impact of study habits of intellectually backward pupils upon their academic achievement. *Progress of Education* 56(2) Se 1981 p 33-37; *Quest in Education* 18(4) Oc 1981 p 335-43 refs tabs
An inquiry into the efficacy of close procedure as a measure of readability of reading materials and reading abilities of pupils. *Progress of Education* 55(2) Se 1980 p 36-41
An inquiry into the reading ability of the bright students. *Progress of Education* 56(4) Nv 1981 p 89-90 + tabs
Listening comprehension in relation to different catagories of readers. *J Education and Psychology* 40(1-2) Ap-Jl 1982 p 66-73; *Progress of*

Education 56(12) Jl 1982 p 292-98 ref

School achievement of BC and non-BC pupils in the context of reading ability and reading speed. *Progress of Education* 58(11) Je 1984 p 258-62 refs tabs

Patel, H.N.

See

Mehta, H.K. *jt. auth.*

Patel, J.B.

See

Qurashi, Z.M. *jt. auth.*

Patel, Jashbhri M.

Preparation of tryout of assignments and to study their effect on the achievements of pupils of class V in the subject of geography. *J Education and Psychology* 38(2) Jl 1980 p 129-34 refs ft-n

Patel, K.J. and Dasa, P.A.

A study of the teacher effectiveness as a function of age, sex, area and qualification. *J Education and Psychology* 42(1-2) Ap-Jl 1984 p 91-98 refs

Patel, K.R.

See

Sheth, K.V. *jt. auth.*

Patel, Leela K.

A study of correlations between performance of academic degree and B.Ed degree examinations. *J Education and Psychology* 39(3) Oc 1981 p 177-83

Patel, M.M. and Parikh, J.C.

Comparative study of attitudes of boys and girls towards education. *J Education and Psychology* 42(1-2) Ap-Jl 1984 p 85-90 refs

Patel, M.P.

A correlaitonal study of the student ratings of instruction with examination performance. *J Education and Psychology* 40(3) Oc 1982 p 117-26

Patel, N.C. and Kher, A.O.

An evaluation of training programme for extension personnel. *Indian J Extension Education* 32(9) Se 1978 p 42-43

Patel, N.C. *et al*

Occupational choice of agricultural students. *Prasar* 7(3-4) Oc 1980-Ja 1981 p 18-25 refs

Patel, N.H.

See

Mehta, H.K. *jt. auth.*

Patel, P.G.

Impaired language mechanisms involved in specific reading disability. *Indian Educational Rev* 16(2) Ap 1981 p 46-49

Patel, R.J.

New dimensions for agricultural higher education. *J Education and Psychology* 36(4) Ja 1979 p 228-33

Patel, S. and Mahapatra, S.K.

Relation between physique and intelligence among socio-culturally advantaged and deprived children of class VII. *J Educational Research and Extension* 19(3) Ja 1983 p 150-54

Patel, S.K.
Education, employment and income inequality : A Marxian perspective. *Indian Educational Rev* 14(4) Oc 1979 p 13-23 refs
Patel, Sumitra L.
An experimental inquiry into the dynamics of behaviour in a group setting. *Experiments in Education* 8(5) Jl 1980 p 79-84 refs
Influence of counselling on self-esteem. *J Education and Psychology* 37(1) Ap 1979 p 35-41 refs
Students attitude towards study. *J Education and Psychology* 36(3) Oc 1980 p 181-88 refs tabs
Superstitions among school children. *Educational Rev* 90(4) Ap 1984 p 74-76; 90(5-6) My-Je 1984 p 88-90 tabs
Patel, Sushil Kumar
See
Sharma, Inder Prabha
Patel, T.M.
Development of battery of diagnostic tests in arithmetic for the students of standards V, VI and VII in Gujarati medium schools in Greater Bombay. *Indian Educational Rev* 15(4) Oc 1980 p 81-85
Patel, Tara
See
Sah, Vimal P. *jt. auth.*
Patel, V.B.
Role of mass media in distance education. *Quest in Education* 18(4) Oc 1981 p 320-27 refs
Patel, V.T. and Patil, B.C.
Problems in Indian education. New Delhi, Oxf-IBH. 1982, vii, 168p. Rs.36 *Book Rev, Indian Educational Rev* 17(4) Oc 1982 p 152-54
Patel, Vajubhai
Contemporary issues in elementary education. *Experiments in Education* 6(5) Jl 1978 p 88-89
Patel, Vinod B.
Status and scope of correspondence education in India. *Progress of Education* 57(7) Fe 1983 p 146-48+ refs
Patel, Yashomati
Academic achievement of the pupils of class X in the background of their previously attended school. *J Education and Psychology* 36(1) Oc 1978 p 154-59

PATHAK - PHATAK

Pathak, A.B. and Shukla, Rajesh Prasad
The study of aspirations and achievement motivation of scheduled castes student teachers. *J Education and Psychology* 42(4) Ja 1985 p 196-201 refs
Pathak, A.B. and Singh, R.R.
Achievement motivation and aspirations of tribal adolescent : A comparative study. *Rajasthan Board J Education* 19(1) Ja-Mr 1983 p 6-11
Television and students. *J Indian Education* 12(3) Se 1986 p 39-43

Pathak, Anil

Media in distance education : Need for an integrated approach. *University News* 24(42) 8 Nv 1986 p 73-77 refs

Pathak, K.N.

Role of AEP in development : Some observation from Bihar. *Indian J Adult Education* 46(4) Ap 1985 p 19-22

Phatak, Pramila

Social maturity of children in India. *Indian Educational Rev* 18(1) Ja 1983 p 1-11 tabs

Pathak, R.D.

A study of job involvement and job performance among bank employees. *J Psychology and Education* 9(4) 1982 p 28-35

Pathak, R.S.

Problems in the analysis and teaching of the structure of the English nominal group. *J Indian Education* 5(4) Nv 1979 p 42-55 refs

Pathak, S.

A multiple regression analysis of factors related with attitude of farmers. *Indian J Extension Education* 17(3-4) Se-De 1981 p 73-80 refs tabs

Pathak, S. and Mazumdar, A.K.

Multivariate regression analysis of adoption behaviour of jute farmers. *Indian J Extension Education* 14(3-4) Jl-De 1978 p 45-50

Perceived attributes of message and communication fidelity. *Indian J Extension Education* 21(3-4) Jl-De 1985 p 23-32 refs tabs

Pathak, S. *et al*

Impact of national demonstration on knowledge, attitude and adoption levels of farmers of West Bengal. *Indian J Extension Education* 15(1-2) Je 1979 p 49-54 refs tabs

Pathak, V.B.

Effective teacher education in the eighties : A new suggestions. *Teacher Education* 20(30-31) Ja-Ap 1985 p 19-20

Quality of the output of the teacher education programme. *Teacher Education* 15(14-15) Ja-Ap 1981 p 100-05 tabs

Who go for teacher education in Eastern U.P. *National J Education* 2(2) Mr 1980 p 26-37 tabs

Pathak, Yogini and Dave, Aruna

An evaluation of effect of participation programme on overall development of children of a municipal nursery school in Baroda. *Quest in Education* 18(4) Oc 1981 p 278-91

Pathani, R.S.

See

Bisht, A.R. *jt. auth.*

Pathusha, K.M.

College development wing : An appraisal. *University News* 23(1) 1 Ja 1985 p 5-6+

Pathy, Jagannath

Progressive students in community education : An appraisal. *J Higher Education* 7(3) Spr 1982 p 315-17

Pathy, M.K.

A programme of curriculum and methodology for the deprived class.

Experiments in Education 10(1) Mr 1982 p 7-13 ref

A sample study of the high school dropouts in rural Western Orissa. *Indian Educational Rev* 17(3) Jl 1982 p 134-39 refs

Pati, Sura Prasad

Adult education in Orissa before independence. *Educational Rev* 92(12) De 1986 p 209-11 refs

New 10+2+3 pattern of education : Its problems with special references to Orissa. *Educational Rev* 92(5-6) My-Je 1986 p 84-86

Patil, B.C.

See

Patel, U.T. *jt. auth.*

Patil, Geeta Devi G.

A study of the relationship between attitude of teacher trainees of private and government B.Ed colleges towards profession and their teaching competence. *Research Bulletin* 16(1-2) Mr-Je 1986 p 27-34 refs tabs

See also

Mehare, K.T. *jt. auth.*

Pande, M.P. *jt. auth.*

Patil, P.A.

See

Buch, M.B. *jt. auth.*

Patil, R.N.

Adult education : Retrospect and prospect. *Progress of Education* 54(4-5) Nv-De 1979 p 74-77

National Adult Education Programme and teacher educators : The strategy for implementation. *Progress of Education* 54(6) Ja 1980 p 98-100

Patil, S. Subhashchandra and Channegowda, M.B.

Information input pattern of agriculture researchers at regional research station, Dharwad, Karnataka state. *Indian J Extension Education* 21(1-2) Ja-Je 1985 p 72-73

Patil, V.S.

See

Sethurao, M.K. *et al jt. auths.*

Patil, V.T.

Studies on Gandhi. New Delhi, Sterling. 1983, 296p. Rs.13. *Book Rev, Education Quarterly* 36(2) Ap 1984 p 73-74

Patil, Vinod

Adult education : An article of faith. *Progress of Education* 55(7) Fe 1981 p 172-76 refs

Patki, S.M.

Teaching of history, method and techniques. Milind Pub. 337p. Rs.30. *Book Rev, Progress of Education* 54(12) Jl 1980 p 239-40

PATNAIK - PATTANAYAK

Patnaik, B.N.

A note in supports of the grammar-translation method. *Indian Educational Rev* 18(3) Jl 1983 p 106-11 refs

Pattanayak, D.P.

Crisis in higher education in India. *J Higher Education* 6(1-3) 1980-81 p 51-54 refs

Multilingualism and mother tongue education. New Delhi, OUP. 1981, 185p. Rs.80 *Book Rev, Progress of Education* 56(11) Je 1982 p 280

Non-formal education for development : A critique. *Indian J Adult Education* 40(2) Fe 1979 p 22-26

Oral component in literacy. *Indian J Adult Education* 40(12) De 1979 p 1-6

Relevance, renovation and processes of change. *J Higher Education* 1(1) Mon 1975 p 43-48

Patnaik, P.K.

A mass movement for functional literacy. *Indian J Adult Education* 47(2-3) Fe-Mr 1986 p 24-41+

Patnaik, S.P.

Teacher competence and pupil performances : The effect of self craft, anxiety and motivation. *J Indian Education* 12(1) My 1986 p 16-21 refs

Patnaik, S.P. and Panda, K.C.

Personality and attitude patterns of good and poor teachers working in secondary school. *J Education and Psychology* 39(4) Ja 1982 p 232-40 refs tabs

Patnaik, Surrendra Kumar

An exploratory study of role conception of teachers. *Asian J Psychology and Education* 6(2) Jl 1980 p 12-16

Patnekar, Vijayakumar

A searchlight on community need based curriculum. *Progress of Education* 55(1) Ag 1980 p 6-8

Patni, Rajni

See

Gupta, Arun Kumar *jt. auth.*

Patra, A.N.

The deaf and their education in India. *Education Quarterly* 33(1) Ja 1981 p 1-2

Origin and development of pre-school education in India. *Education Quarterly* 31(1) Ap 1979 p 13-14

Patra, Santosh K.

See

Puhan, Biranchi N. *jt. auth.*

Patranabis, James

See

Bhattacharya, Buddadeva *jt. auth.*

Patrick, G.A.

Education and welfare state. *Education Rev* 87(12) De 1981 p 237-39

Pattanayak

See

Patnaik

Pattanshethi, C.C.

An introduction to research methods in social sciences. Coimbatore, Rainbow Pub. 1981 166p. Rs.36. *Book Rev, Progress of Education* 56(4) Nv 1981 p 98+

Paturkar, V.V.
See
Supe, S.V. *et al jt. auths.*

PAUL - PAL

Pal, Anasuya
See
Rungla, I.U. *jt. auth.*

Paul, Debasish
School magazine : Problems and remedies. *J Indian Education* 11(3) Se 1985 p 58-60

Paul, H.R.
See
Hooda, R.C. *jt. auth.*

Pal, Hans Raj
Developing communication skills in teachers. *Education Quarterly* 32(3) Jl 1980 p 27-29 refs
Developing social skills of teachers. *Experiments in Education* 7(2) Ap 1979 p 26-28 refs
Students perception of the micro teaching programme. *Progress of Education* 55(8) Mr 1981 p 204-07 tabs

Pal, Manabendra Nath
Management information systems in university administration *J Higher Education* 2(2) Aut 1976 p 213-21 refs tabs

Pal, Rama
See
Tiwari, Govind *jt. auth.*

Pal, Rama and Dixit, Ashok K.
Social class and marital status as correlates of modernisation. *Asian J Psychology and Education* 14(1-4) 1984 p 25-33 refs

Pal, S.K. and Saxena, P.C.
Quality control in educational research. New Delhi, Metropolitan. 1985, 660p. Rs.250. *Book Rev, Perspectives in Education* 1(4) Oc 1985 p 270-71

Pal, Suraksha
Management of learning systems. *Indian Education* 13(7) Oc 1983 p 16-18

Patyal, C.B.
Socially useful productive work : Some thoughts on its implementation in our schools. *Asian J Psychology and Education* 6(1) Ja 1980 p 32-34; *Progress of Education* 59(9) Ap 1980 p 186-89
Some basic understandings of socially useful productive work, S.U.P.W. *Progress of Education* 53(9) Ap 1979 p 187-90
A study of the effect of low and high readability materials in geography on reading comprehension in the context of I.W. *Asian J Psychology and Education* 3(3) Nv 1978 p 17-21 ref tabs
A study of the effect of low and high readability materials in geography on the reading comprehension of students in the context of reading abilities. *J Educational Research and Extension* 18(4) Ap 1982 p 193-200 refs tabs

A study of the effect of low and high readability materials on the reading comprehension of students in the context of reading abilities. *J Institute of Educational Research* 4(2) My 1980 p 35-38 refs tabs

Pavate, T.V.

Role of satellites in the promotion of distance education. *University News* 24(42) 8 Nv 1986 p 83-84

Pawar, S.S.

See

Saini, G.S. *jt. auth.*

Talukdar, R.K. *jt. auth.*

Pawar, S.S. *et al*

Role perception of farm youth leaders in diffusion and adoption of agricultural technology in Punjab. *Indian J Extension Education* 20(1-2) Je 1984 p 58-61 tabs

Pawate, C.I.

The Panchatantra and Aesop's fables : A study in genre. Delhi, Amar Pra. 1986, viii, 122p. Rs.75. *Book Rev, Education Quarterly* 38(3) Aut 1986 p 49-50

Penzel, Fred

See

Relte, Henry H. *jt. auth.*

Pereira, L.S.

Some trends in the development of examinations in Sri Lanka. *New Frontiers in Education* 10(4) Oc-De 1980 p 6-14 refs

Peretti, Peter O. and Jones, Emma L.

Crucial issues in deschooling society. *Education Quarterly* 33(4) Oc 1981 p 19-21 refs

Perrott, Elizabeth

Micro-teaching in higher education : Research, development and practice. University of Surrey. 107p. *Book Rev, J Higher Education* 5(2) Aut 1979 p 266-68

Perumal, G.

See

Ganeshan, R. *et al jt. auths.*

Perumal, G. and Rai, G.C.

Job satisfaction and job performance of agricultural extension officers of Tamil Nadu. *Indian J Extension Education* 14(1-2) Ja-Je 1978 p 73-75

Perumal, N.

Training of extension personnel in India : A brief review. *Indian J Extension Education* 19(1-2) Mr-Je 1983 p 23-32

Pestonjee, D. and Usmani, S.M.

Creativity in relation to alienation, egostrength and intelligence. *J Education and Psychology* 40(1-2) AP-Jl 1982 p 39-44

Peter, K.C.

Communication : Concepts and skills. *New Frontiers in Education* 12(1) Ja-Mr 1982 p 54-79 refs

Faculty improvement programmes. *New Frontiers in Education* 13(3) Jl-Se 1983 p 56-67

Teaching methods that ensure the learning situation. *New Frontiers in*

Education 10(1) Ja-Mr 1980 p 44-49

Peters, R.S.

Moral development and moral education. London, Allen and Unwin. 1981, 187p. £4.50 *Book Rev, Progress of Education* 57(2) Se 1982 p 46

Peterson, Steven A. and Somit, Albert

Student protest : A biomedical perspective. *J Higher Education* 3(3) Spr 1978 p 333-34 refs ft-n tabs

Pethy, Abhay

Some reflections on value education. *New Frontiers in Education* 14(1) Ja-Mr 1984 p 51-54

Petters, Dorthy E.

Staff and student supervision. London, Allen and Unwin. 1979, 157p. £2.95. *Book Rev, Education Quarterly* 32(1) Ja 1980 p 42

Phalachandra, B.

See

Sherdombo Rao, *jt. auth.*

Phatak

See

Pathak

Philip, Rhoda

See

Malla Reddy, M. *jt. auth.*

Phutela, Rakesh

See

Gakhar, Sudesh *et al jt. auths.*

Philkhane, S.V.

Education : An input for dairy industry in India. *J Higher Education* 8(3) Spr 1983 p 385-90

Pillai

See also

under full name/surname, e.g., Narayana Pillai, A.S.

Pillai, J.K.

Affective tone in the primary classroom. *Indian Education* 16(3) Jl 1981 p 35-43

The dual role of women. *New Frontiers in Education* 12(4) Oc-De 1982 p 39-42

Gandhiji on adult education. *Indian J Adult Education* 39(10) Oc 1978 p 19-20

Motivational profile of college teachers. *Indian Educational Rev* 15(1) Ja 1980 p 115-18

Trends and alternative models in adult education. *New Frontiers in Education* 13(3) Jl-Se 1983 p 68-71

See also

Gabrial, P.J. *jt. auth.*

Pillai, J.K. and Gabrial, P.J.

Abilities and subject specialisation. *J Higher Education* 9(1) Mon 1983 p 108-14

Pillai, J.K. and Jaleel Saheb, S.

A study of anxiety : Summer Institute of Gandhian Thought. *Indian*

Education 10(8) Nv 1980 p 10-19

Pillai, K.S.

Adult education in Kerala : Some innovative experiments. *Indian J Adult Education* 45(3) Mr 1984 p 7-12

Pillai, K.S. and Nair, G.S.K.

Interests and involvement in continuing education programmes among primary school teachers. *Prasar* 5(1-2) Ap-Jl 1977 p 36-44

Pillai, Kamala S.

Effect of certain sociological factors on achievement in language. *Experiments in Education* 11(5) Jl 1983 p 85-89

A study of sex difference in science achievement of secondary school pupils. *J Educational Research and Extension* 19(4) Ap 1983 p 249-57 refs

Pinto, Marina

Federalism and higher education : The Indian experience. Bombay Orient Longman. 1984, 250p. Rs.85. *Book Rev, Perspectives in Education* 1(4) Oc 1985 p 267-68

Pinto, S.

Education and industrial productivity : A case study of workers and supervisors employed in the engineering industry in Pune metropolitan region. *Research Bulletin* 16(1-2) Mr-Je 1986 p 43-57

Pirozzola, Francis J. and Wittcock, Merlin C., eds.

Neuropsychological and congnitive processes in reading. New York, Academic Press. 1981. *Book Rev, J Education and Psychology* 40(4) Ja 1983 p 242-44

Pluckrose, Henry

Children in their primary schools. Middlesex. Penguin Books. 1979, 175p. £1.25. *Book Rev, Education Quarterly* 32(3) Jl 1980 p 45-46

Ponkshe, A.R.

A guide book for competitive examination. Pune, Vidyarthi Griha Pra. 148p. Rs.20. *Book Rev, Progress of Education* 54(10-11) My-Je 1980 p 214+

Popkewiz, Thomas S.

Paradigm and ideology in educational research : The social functions and the intellectual. Sussex, Falmer Press. 1984, 208p. £7.25. *Book Rev, Education Quarterly* 36(4) Wint 1984 p 56-57; *Progress of Education* 60(7) Fe 1986 p 169-70

Portia, D.R.

Curriculum development for the Indian schools. Kakananda, Satyavani Pub. vi, 112p. *Book Rev, J Indian Education* 8(2) Jl 1982 p 93

Is 10+2+3 a failure. *Educational Rev* 85(3) Mr 1979 p 50-51

See also

Vijayabharath, M. *jt. auth.*

Posmowski, Pierreite

Breaking inter-science barriers. *Educational Rev* 84(12) De 1978 p 231-35

Postiglione, Gevard A.

Educational expansion and the pedagogical encounter : What can we learn from history. *Indian Education* 12(5-6) Ag-Se 1982 p 5-10; 12(7) Oc 1982 p 4-9

Postman, Neil
    Teaching as a conserving activity. London, Melbourne House. £6.50. *Book Rev, Teacher Today* 23(3) Ja-Mr 1981 p 153-55
Prabhakar Singh
    Cybernatic approach to teaching. *Progress of Education* 58(10) My 1984 p 238-40+
    Functioning of feedback. *J Indian Education* 12(1) My 1986 p 52-54
    Self-expression of blind students. *Primary Teacher* 11(4) Oc 1986 p 12-14
    Teacher education at crossroads. *Teacher Education* 15(14-15) Ja-Ap 1981 p 30-36 refs
    The Western shadow over Indian education. *J Indian Education* 8(1) My 1982 p 25-31
Prabhakara Rao, D.
    Advancement in higher education teaching method : A review. *Educational Rev* 90(2) Fe 1984 p 28-29
Prabhu, Hemalata
    Motivation of the faculty. *New Frontiers in Education* 9(1) Ja-Mr 1979 p 27-30
Prabhu, Swayam
    See
    Gakhar, S. *jt. auth.*
Prabhu-Mirashi, L.S.
    A simple method of determining the refractive indexes of a liquid. *Progress of Education* 53(9) Ap 1979 p 170-75 refs
Pradhan, N.
    University education : Access and success. *Education Quarterly* 38(3) Aut 1986 p 13-17
Pradhan, Netranand
    See
    Jindal, S.K. *jt. auth.*
Prahallada, N.K.
    Learning through dramatics. *Primary Teacher* 9(3) Jl 1984 p 14-15
Prahallada, N.N.
    The concept of working with the community. *J Indian Education* 12(4) Nv 1986 p 27-31
    Contemporary significance of value education. *J Indian Education* 8(6) Mr 1983 p 56-60
    Homework : Some suggestions. *Primary Teacher* 9(1) Ja 1984 p 1-3
    Making classroom instruction interesting. *Primary Teacher* 10(2) Ap 1985 p 4-5
    Need for national policy on moral education. *J Indian Education* 10(5) Ja 1985 p 25-28
    Significance of parent teacher associations. *Primary Teacher* 11(4) Oc 1986 p 27-28
    Toning up primary school health programme. *Primary Teacher* 11(3) Jl 1986 p 13-15
Prajapati, M.R. and Patel, Ashok A.
    Attitude of extension workers towards some selected components of TV programme. *Indian J Extension Education* 20(3-4) Se-De 1984 p 55-56

Prakash

See also

under full name/surname, e.g., Ved Prakash, J.

Prakash, G.N.

Planning educational research. *Indian Educational Rev* 18(3) Jl 1983 p 91-94

See also

Shrivastava, G.N.

Prakash, G.N. and Srivastava, S.S.

Personality trait differences : First, second, and third division high school students. *National J Education* 2(1) Se 1979 p 41-49 refs

Prakash, Jyothi

See

Adinarayana, K. *jt. auth.*

Prakofler, M.A.

Soviet schools : Today and tomorrow. *Student Action* 2(4) Ag 1983 p 24

Pramod Kumar and Mutha, Dinesh Narain

Certain psychological correlates of teacher effectivenes. *J Education and Psychology* 41(3) Oc 1983 p 106-11 refs ft-n

Teachers effectiveness related with value orientation at secondary level teaching. *J Education and Psychology* 43(1) Ap 1985 p 22-26 refs

Pramod Reddy, M.

Education human resources development. *Indian Education* 11(11-12) Fe-Mr 1982 p 7-11

Prasad

See also

under full name/surname, e.g., Kanti Prasad

Prasad, Bindu

Relationship of constitutional factors to learning difficulties among primary school children. *Indian Educational Rev* 17(2) Ap 1982 p 1-19 refs-ft-n tabs

Prasad, C.

Agricultural extension curriculum and change agents : Some new guidelines. *J Higher Education* 5(1) Mon 1979 p 75-88

Training for agricultural development. *Indian J Extension Education* 19(1-2) Mr-Je 1983 p 12-22 refs

See also

Amar Singh *jt. auth.*

Prasad, Hemlata

Motivating adult learners in rural areas : An analytical study. *Indian J Adult Education* 46(2) Mr 1985 p 19-24

Prasad, M.S.

See

Amalraj, V.A. *jt. auth.*

Prasad, S.C.

Sex differences in expression of aggression. *Asian J Psychology and Education* 6(2) Jl 1980 p 33-35

Prasad, S.N.

Paulo Freire's criticism of educational system. *J Indian Education* 11(2) Jl

1985 p 11-18 refs

Teaching peace : A challenge to teacher education. *J Indian Education* 12(4) Nv 1986 p 32-37

University as a sanctuary for international awakening and peace. *Progress of Education* 60(6) Ja 1986 p 139-42+

Prasad, U.S.

Vocationalisation of commerce education and the role of University. *J Higher Education* 9(2) Aut 1983 p 271-77

Prasad, Vandana

Promotion of creativity and achievement of discovery method. *Indian Educational Rev* 14(4) Oc 1979 p 86-94

Prasada Rao, C.R.

See

Ramana, V.V. *jt. auth.*

Prasad Singh

See

Kinkar, Krisna *jt. auth.*

Prasada Rao, D.L. and Venkata Rao, P.

Problems of teachers working in tribal areas. *Educational Rev* 89(8) Ag 1983 p 139-41

Prasada Rao, Y.F.W.

See

Vidyasagar, G. *jt. auth.*

Prasanna, K.C.

See

Abraham, Mercy *jt. auth.*

Praveen, C.

See

Baskaran, K. *jt. auth.*

Prema, P.

Evaluation of instruction and materials. *New Frontiers in Education* 13(2) Ap-Je 1983 p 55-57

Premchand

Magnitude of illiteracy in India-1981. *Indian J Adult Education* 43(1) Ja 1982 p 11-14 annex tabs

Premchand, Vibha

Fostering creativity in class rooms. *Indian Education* 11(4) Jl 1981 p 26-28

Proactive inhibition; A case for forgetting. *Experiments in Education* 9(6) Ag 1981 p 107-09 refs

Reasons for decreasing importance of values in education. *Educational Rev* 87(11) Nv 1981 p 203-05

Premi, Kusum K.

Educational equality and economic opportunities : A comparative study of scheduled castes and non-scheduled castes. *J Higher Education* 9(3) Spr 1984 p 363-72 refs

Price, R.F.

China's immediate future : Renewed cultural borrowing. *J Higher Education* 8(3) Spr 1983 p 299-310

Pritam Singh

Comprehensive evaluation of curriculum : A model. *J Indian Education* 11(1) My 1985 p 52-61

Evaluating a curriculum : The quantity central approach. *J Indian Education* 12(1) My 1986 p 9-15

Micro-evaluation in elementary science. *J Indian Education* 5(5) Ja 1980 p 47-54

Prohit, D.K. Sharma

See

Sharma, D.K.

Psacharopoulos, George

Earning and education in OECD countries. Paris, OECD. 194p. £5 : 2; f 20. *Book Rev, Indian Educational Rev* 18(1) Ja 1983 p 133-35

Puhan, Biranchi N.

Relationship between difficulty level and internal consistency of item. *Education Quarterly* 32(2) Ap 1980 p 21-22

Puhan, Biranchi N. and Das, Suresh C.

Contributions of memory and speed to psychology honours examination scores. *Asian J Psychology and Education* 5(1-3) 1979 p 26-33

Puhan, Biranchi N. and Mohapatra, Mahesh P.

Effects of memory and speed on history honour examination scores. *J Education and Psychology* 39(2) Jl 1981 p 83-90

Puhan, Biranchi N. and Patra, Santosh K.

Teacher student interaction and class room performance of high school students. *Asian J Psychology and Education* 3(2) Jl 1978 p 42-51 refs

Puhan, Biranchi N. and Rath, Pratap K.

Projective inventory : A new approach to personality assessment. *Asian J Psychology and Education* 7(1) Ja 1981 p 16-24

Punalekar, Devyani S.

Obstacles ot evaluation : Teachers' views. *Progress of Education* 57(10) My 1983 p 231-34+

Pundlik, S.S.

The question papers for std. XII. *Progress of Education* 56(1) Ag 1981 p 8-9

Puranik, P.D.

National integration through education. Pune, Vidyarthi Griha Pra. 96p. Rs.15 *Book Rev, Progress of Education* 53(6) Ja 1979 p 119

Purkait, B.R.

See

Samadhar, Sunanda *jt. auth.*

Purohit, D.K. Sharma

See

Sharma, D.K.

Purushothama Rao, T.

Content analysis : An emerging paradigm in educational research. *Progress of Education* 61(3) Oc 1986 p 58-61

Pushpa

See also

under name/surname, e.g., Murari, Pushpa

Pushpa, M.

Factors of social deprivation affecting the primary school children. *Indian Educational Rev* 16(2) Ap 1981 p 1-14 refs

Primary school children : Development of their cognitive abilities. *Primary Teacher* 6(4) Oc 1981 p 5-8

Qamar Jahan

See

Siddiqui, W.H. *jt. auth.*

Qamar Jahan and Siddiqui, W.H.

Educational philosophy of Zakir Husain. *Educational Rev* 88(8) Ag 1982 p 135-37; 88(9) Se 1982 p 157-58

Qamaruddin

Essay type questions : Their significance and use. *J Indian Education* 9(1) My 1983 p 25-30

How to make pre-primary education more effective. *Primary Teacher* 6(2) Ap 1981 p 18-23

Improving elementary education in rural areas. *Primary Teacher* 9(4) Oc 1984 p 8-10

Improving evaluation at the elementary stage. *Primary Teacher* 9(2) Ap 1984 p 11-12

Inservice training of teachers. *Primary Teacher* 8(2) Ap 1983 p 26-27

The Mahdawi movement in India. *Indian Educational Rev* 18(4) Oc 1984 p 88-94

The primary school teachers : An instrument of social change. *Primary Teacher* 4(2) Ap 1979 p 5-9

Qayum, M.A.

Organisation of education in remote rural areas of Afghanistan. *Indian J Adult Education* 40(5) My 1979 p 33-35

Quarmby, A.

See

Fussell, D. *jt. auth.*

Quraishi, Z.M.

Nature and concepts of regression analysis and prediction. *Quest in Education* 16(3) Jl 1979 p 195-201 refs

Quraishi, Z.M. and Patel, J.B.

Achievement motivation of college students and its relation to socio-economic factors. *J Education and Psychology* 41(1-2) Ap-Jl 1983 p 55-58

Rabindranathan, M.R.

Development of women's education at the university stage. *J Higher Education* 1(2) Aut 1975 p 258-62 refs tabs

Regional imbalance in the growth of higher education in India. *J Higher Education* 4(1) Mon 1978 p 33-40

Radha, K.V.

Social and personal adjustment in relation to teaching success in science.

National J Education 7(2) My 1985 p 31-37 refs

Radhakrishna Menon, K.
See
Lakshminaranan, G. *jt. auth.*
Subramaniam, R. *et al jt. auths.*

Radha Krishna Moorthy, S.
The need for autonomous boards of under-graduate courses. *J Higher Education* 6(1-3) 1980-81 p 154-55

Radhakrishnamurthy, I.V.
Pedagogical training for college teachers in Andhra Pradesh. *J Educational Research and Extension* 20(2) Oc 1983 p 123-38

Radhakrishnan, N.
Higher education and training in non-violence : The Shanti Sena of Gandhigram Rural Institute. *University News* 23(32) 23 Ag 1985 p 5-7

Raghav, Mukesh
National foundation : Better school health. *Teacher Today* 25(2) Oc-De 1982 p 66-71

Raghava, G. *et al*
School as a socialising agent : A preliminary study. *J Indian Education* 6(6) Mr 1981 p 16-19

Raghavachari, V.P.
The socialist education system of GDR. *Indian Education* 11(8-9) Nv-De 1981 p 29-33; 11(10) Ja 1982 p 16-20
Unification of teachers movement in India. *Indian Education* 11(7) Oc 1981 p 18-24

Raghvacharyulu, S.V.V.
Work experience in teacher education. *Indian Education* 10(3) Ag 1981 p 11-13

Raghavakumari, A.S.
Affective dimension of classroom instruction in relation to a few teacher variables. *Quest in Education* 17(4) Oc 1980 p 327-37 refs

Raghavan, G.N.S.
Concepts of civic education. *Indian J Adult Education* 46(9) Se 1985 p 5-9

Raghavendra
See
Siddaramaiah, B.S. *jt. auth.*

Raghavendra Rao, P.
Motivating the teacher for inservice education. *Progress of Education* 58(12) Jl 1984 p 301-05

Raghaviah, Y.
The changing character of university : Government relations in India. *Indian Education* 11(1-2) Ap-My 1981 p 38-43
The amidget bureaucratic phenomenon : Reflections on system transformations in universities. *J Higher Education* 9(2) Aut 1983 p 157-76 refs

Raghubir Singh and Gill, Surjit Singh
A study of time utilisation by rural school and college students during summer vacation. *J Higher Education* 4(1) Mon 1978 p 81-86 refs tabs

Raghunathananda, Swami

The need for ethical and social values in education. *J Educational Research and Extension* 20(1) Jl 1983 p 37-84

Raghuram Singh, M.

Awareness and knowledge of recent developments in education among B.Ed students and their correlates. *Experiments in Education* 6(8) Oc 1978 p 131-41 tabs figs

Case studies in the teaching of economics. *Experiments in Education* 10(7) Se 1982 p 119-23

Coaching and counselling. *Experiments in Education* 12(1) Mr 1984 p 3-7

Education in 2001 : The emerging scene : a conceptual approach. *Experiments in Education* 11(7) Se 1983 p 113-20

The educationally disadvantaged in the U.S.A. and the U.K. *Experiments in Education* 10(5) Jl 1982 p 79-89 refs

Effective teaching and learning of science in higher secondary schools. *Experiments in Education* 6(11) Ja 1979 p 191-96

Organisation of guidance services in schools. *Experiments in Education* 9(5) Jl 1981 p 77-82

Raghuveer Singh

Involvement of teachers and students in the National Adult Education Programme. *Prasar* 7(1-2) Ap-Jl 1980 p 33-38

Raghuveeran, B.

Demand patterns for the courses in plus two : A case study. *Experiments in Education* 9(6) Ag 1981 p 95-99 tabs

Rahman, Z.

See

Ansari, G. *jt. auth.*

Rahudkar, W.D.

See

Chole, R.R. *jt. auth.*

Rai, G.C.

See

Chouhan, V.L. *jt. auth.*
Kamwat, Usha *jt. auth.*
Mahipal *jt. auth.*
Perumal, G. *jt. auth.*
Ram Kumar *jt. auth.*

Rai, K.

Adoption behaviour of secondary school teachers in relation to their socio-economic status and the organisational climate of the school. *National J Education* 2(2) Mr 1980 p 38-45 refs tabs

Rai, K. and Katiyar, B.L.

Impact of different feedback sources on acquisition of teaching skills in microteaching situation. *National J Education* 2(1) Se 1979 p 24-31 refs tabs

Rai, Kamala

Adjustment of secondary school girls studying in co-education and segregated institutions in relation to their socio-economic status. *National J Education* 7(2) My 1985 p 46-55

Problems of girls in co-educational institutions. *National J Education* 7(1) Se 1984 p 29-38 refs tabs

Rai, Kamala and Gandhi, Pritty

Differential personality factors of high and low feedback acceptance groups in micro-teaching. *J Institute of Educational Research* 4(1) Ja 1980 p 33-36 refs tabs

Rai, Markandey and Harikesh Singh

Elites resistance to NAEP. *Indian J Adult Education* 42(10) Oc 1981 p 9-10+

Rai, P.N.

Achievement motive in low and high achievers : A comparative study. *Indian Educational Rev* 15(3) Jl 1980 p 117-23 refs

Adjustment and scholastic achievement of low and high achievers : A comparative study. *Quest in Education* 16(2) Ap 1979 p 106-13

See also

Pandey, R.C. *et al jt. auths.*

Rai, V.K.

Causes of scholastic dishonesty among the examinees. *Our Education* 5 Jl 1984 p 39-45 refs

Clinical approach to student teaching. *Educational Rev* 88(2) Fe 1982 p 28-29

A comparative study of alienation from the school among the first generation learners and *vice versa. Educational Rev* 89(8) Ag 1983 p 132-34; *Experiments in Education* 11(3) My 1983 p 50-52 refs

Criterion vs norm-referenced tests. *Educational Rev* 91(1) Ja 1985 p 3-6 refs

Culture and curriculum : Should there be a common curriculum for universal education. *Educational Rev* 92(10) Oc 1986 p 166-69

Philosophy of education and the teacher. *Educational Rev* 85(6) Je 1979 p 101-03 refs

What is the philosophy of education? *Educational Rev* 89(11) Nv 1983 p 193-95

Rai, V.K. and Srivastava, Asha

An investigation into students motivity for joining B.Ed course. *Educational Rev* 88(7) Jl 1982 p 119-21 refs tabs

Rai, Vikram

Rural primary school. *Primary Teacher* 4(2) Ap 1979 p 31-33

Raina, B.L. and Panigrahi, S.C.

Education and development. *Education Quarterly* 37(2) Sum 1985 p 1-6 refs

Raina, M.K.

Biochemical consequences of examination stress. *Indian Educational Rev* 18(2) Ap 1983 p 17-39 refs tabs

Raina, M.K., ed.

Creativity research : International perspective. New Delhi, NCERT. 1980, 332p. Rs.20 *Book Rev, Teacher Today* 25(3) Ja-Mr 1983 p 109

Raina, M.K. and Sengupta, M.

Indian Educational Review through ten year. *Indian Educational Rev* 14(1) Ja 1979 p 56-68 refs

Raina, M.K. and Vats, Arunima

Effect of training on attitude towards creative teaching and learning. *Indian*

Educational Rev 18(1) Ja 1983 p 104-09 refs

An exploratory study of quality of school life, relationship with sex, socio-economic status and the type of school. *Perspectives in Education* 2(3) Jl 1986 p 161-69 refs

Socio-economic status, anthropometric measures and biochemical variables. *Indian Educational Rev* 19(1) Ja 1984 p 52-59

Raina, T.N.

Comparison of Hindu and Muslim student teachers responses to a measure of authoritarianism in India. *Indian Educational Rev* 15(4) Oc 1980 p 15-23 refs tabs

Generation gap : A comparative study of parent and children on a measure of authoritarianism. *Indian Educational Rev* 19(2) Ap 1984 p 37-50

Sex differences in creativity in India : A second look. *Indian Educational Rev* 17(3) Jl 1982 p 122-28 refs tabs

Raina, V.K.

Behavioural objectives and teaching of history. *J Indian Education* 5(4) Nv 1979 p 23-27 refs

Environmental education. *J Indian Education* 6(2) Jl 1980 p 19-24

Examinations in history : A content analysis of secondary level question papers. *J Indian Education* 8(6) Mr 1983 p 50-54 refs tabs

Inservice teachers and student-teacehers : A compartive study attitude towards teaching. *J Education and Psychology* 41(3) Oc 1983 p 138-45

Piagetian theory and teaching of history. *J Indian Education* 5(1) My 1979 p 54-58

Prepartion of history teachers for new curriculum. *Education Quarterly* 35(3) Jl 1983 p 17-20 refs

Theory into practice : An analysis of B.Ed theory and practice marks. *Indian Educational Rev* 17(4) Oc 1982 p 134-40 refs tabs

Rais Ahmed

INSAT-1B and higher educaiton. *J Higher Education* 9(3) Spr 1984 p 301-03

Reorientation in teaching, learning and evaluation. *J Higher Education* 5(3) Spr 1980 p 331-33

Universities : Perspectives and problems. *J Higher Education* 7(3) Spr 1982 p 177-87

Raisz, R.P.

Implementation of college autonomy. *New Frontiers of Education* 10(1) Ja-Mr 1980 p 28-34

Raizada, B.S.

See

Thadani, Beena *jt. auth.*

Raizada, B.S. and Thadani, Beena

Sex differences in achievement motivation. *Rajasthan Board J Education* 20(1-2) Ja-Je 1984 p 38-42

Raizada, Madhu

See

Jangira, N.K. *jt. auth.*

Raizada, P.

Commerce at the secondary stage in India. *Education Quarterly* 31(3-4) Oc 1979-Ja 1980 p 25-27

Post-secondary vocational education in England and Wales. *J Indian Education* 5(2) Jl 1979 p 18-22

Raizada, Prabhakar

Creativity in typing. *Primary Teacher* 10(3) Jl 1985 p 29-32

Training and employment of educated youth : The twentieth point of the 20-point programme. *J Indian Education* 10(6) Mr 1985 p 24-29

Typewriter draws designs and maps. *Primary Teacher* 10(2) Ap 1985 p 15-17

Rai

See also

under full name/surname Samsananda Rai, H.

Raj, B. Asul and Knight, A. John

Differential perception of farm practices : Attitudes by progressive and non-progressive farmers. *Indian J Extension Education* 14(1-2) Ja-Je 1978 p 64-65

Raj, Mathreyi Krishna

The status of women in science in India. *J Higher Education* 5(3) Spr 1980 p 381-93 tabs

Raj, N. Casimir

Our experience as an autonomous college. *Educational Rev* 91(4) Ap 1985 p 61-65 refs

Raj, N. Casimir and Raman, A.

Research as a tool in the undergraduate teaching learning process : The experience of an autonomous college. *Progress of Education* 61(12) Se 1986 p 29-32

Raj Singh and Sharma, M.L.

Impact of compulsory primary education legislation on the rural society of Haryana. *Education Quarterly* 31(2) Jl 1979 p 23-25

Raja Ganesan, D.

Aptitudes of vocationalisation of education. *Experiments in Education* 7(1) Mr 1979 p 16-18 refs

Education about death. *Experiments in Education* 6(9) Nv 1978 p 151-59 refs

Orientation of teachers and heads of schools to the basic concepts of management : A preliminary excercise in management education. *Experiments in Education* 7(4) Ja 1979 p 64-69

A short training programme in question writing for college teachers. *J Higher Education* 5(2) Aut 1979 p 255-60

Raja Ganeshan

See

Ganeshan, Raja

Rajagopal, M.V.

Planning education for the eighties. *Indian Education* 10(1-2) Ap-My 1980 p 5-9

Rajagopal, Visalaksh

Parents and homework for children. *Educational Rev* 85(5) My 1979 p 83-85

Rajagopalan, K.

Authority and freedom in play. *Primary Teacher* 8(3) Jl 1983 p 9-11

Rajagopalan, S.

Improvement of reading skills. *Experiments in Education* 8(10) De 1980 p 175-80

A study of the pupils knowledge of English grammar and its relationship to their proficiency in English in standard IX. *Experiments in Education* 7(2) Ap 1979 p 21-25

Teachers and social change. *Experiments in Education* 7(8) Oc 1979 p 131-36;7(9) Nv 1979 p 166-70+; 7(10) De 1979 p 176-79; 7(12) Fe 1980 p 220-22 refs

Rajagopalan, Shantha

The residential system. *Experiments in Education* 10(8) Oc 1982 p 137-41

Rajagura, G. *et al*

Trimester system of education : As perceived by students. *J Higher Education* 3(3) Spr 1978 p 386-89 tabs

Rajaiah, B.

Creativity and innovation in education. *Educational Rev* 92(8) Ag 1986 p 127-29 refs

Higher education in India. *Educational Rev* 91(8) Ap 1985 p 124-25 tabs

Relevance of National Educational Policy. *Educational Rev* 89(3) Mr 1983 p 48-50

Reservations in Higher education and jobs. *Educational Rev* 88(3) Mr 1982 p 55-58

Reservations in Higher education and jobs. *Experiments in Education* 10(9) Nv 1982 p 159-63

School organisation and teachers. *Educational Rev* 86(4) Ap 1980 p 63-64

School organisation : Teachers participation : Some problems. *Progress of Education* 55(5) De 1980 p 140-42

Student participation in college administration. *Experiments in Education* 12(3) My 1984 p 46-49

Whither National Educational Policy? *Educational Rev* 86(6) Je 1980 p 114-15

Rajamani, N.C.

Media education. *Experiments in Education* 8(11) Ja 1981 p 203-04

An investigation into the problem of job satisfaction among secondary school teachers. *Indian Education* 12(8-9) Nv-De 1982 p 40-41

Rajamohan, G.

Locus of control and level of anxiety among college students. *J Educational Research and Extension* 17(3) Ja 1981 p 178-84 refs tabs

Rajan

See also

under full name/surname, e.g., Sundararajan

Rajan, R.

Materials and curriculum for community educaiton. *Educational Rev* 92(8) Ag 1986 p 137-38

State Resource Centre for Non-Formal Education in Tamil Nadu. *Educational Rev* 90(2) Fe 19984 p 25-27 refs

Rajanna, B.

See

Siddaramaiah, B.S. *jt. auth.*

Raja Reddy, M.T.
Helping child in reading. *Educational Rev* 87(6) Je 1981 p 113-15
Rajasekharan, V.
A case and programme for pre-primary education. *Experiments in Education* 6(4) Je 1978 p 64-65 refs
Correlation between attitude to and attainment in mathematics. *Experiments in Education* 6(8) Oc 1978 p 143-48 refs
An evaluative study of science syllabus in secondary schools of Tamil Nadu. *Experiments in Education* 6(10) De 1978 p 169-77 refs tabs
Investment in education. *Experiments in Education* 6(5) Jl 1978 p 82-84
Reforming primary education. *Experiments in Education* 7(1) Mr 1979 p 9-13
Relationship between socio-economic status and academic achievement. *Experiments in Education* 6(1) Mr 1978 p 233-36 refs tabs
A study on the technique of programmed instruction. *Experiments in Education* 7(7) Se 1979 p 117-21 refs tabs
Vocationalisation of secondary education. *Experiments in Education* 6(3) My 1978 p 51-54
Rajendra
See
Sirohi, Seema *jt. auth.*
Rajendran, K.K.S.
Education for human excellence. *Educational Rev* 84(11) Nv 1978 p 210-14
Rajiv Ranjan Singh and Ojha, Shailendra Kumar
Effect of school environment on the attitudes of Santal students. *J Institute of Educational Research* 10(3) Se 1986 p 28-31 refs
Rajmohan, G. and Kuppan, A.
Locus of control and level of anxiety among college student. *Asian J Psychology and Education* 6(3) Nv 1980 p 12-16 refs
Rajput, J.S.
Community work in teacher education programmes. *Teacher Today* 24(2) Oc-De 1981 p 40-43
Community work in teacher education programme. *University News* 21(21) Nv 1983 p 711-12
Elementary education and science. *Primary Teacher* 4(3) Jl 1979 p 11-14
Management of non-formal and adult education. *Indian Education* 11(1-2) Ap-My 1981 p 59-63
See also
Gupta, B.S. *jt. auth.*
Jadhoo, V.G. *et al jt. auths.*
Upreti, D.C. *jt. auth.*
Rajput, J.S. and Grewal, J.S.
Role of environmental studies in motivating children's learning. *Progress of Education* 53(12) Jl 1979 p 228-33 ref
Rajput, Sarla
Non-formal education and social transformation. *Progress of Education* 54(1) Ag 1979 p 2-6+
Providing suitable environment for children's development. *Primary Teacher* 5(1) Ja 1980 p 14-19

The role of parents in moulding the child's behaviour. *Primary Teacher* 5(3) Jl 1980 p 31-35

Teacher : A practical context. *Primary Teacher* 6(1) Ja 1981 p 19-21

Universalisation of elementary education : The alternative strategies. *Indian Education* 10(3) Je 1980 p 24-28

Raju

See also

under full surname, e.g., Narasimha Raju, A.P.S.U.V.S.N.L.

Raju, Santhamma

Nuffied science teaching project. *Progress of Education* 55(6) Ja 1981 p 155-56 refs

Rajyalakshmi, C.

Motivational problems in functional literacy programmes. *Indian J Adult Education* 42(1-2) Ja-Fe 1981 p 7-12

Problems in evaluating adult literacy programmes. *Indian J Adult Education* 41(6-7) Je-Jl 1980 p 25-29

Raling, M.G.

The logic of extension. *Indian J Extension Education* 15(3-4) De 1979 p 1-8 refs

Rallia Ram, Mayawanti

Muslim educated women in North India. *J Higher Education* 1(2) Aut 1975 p 250

Ram, R.B. and Singh, S.K.

Child literacy in Bihar, 1961-71. *J Indian Education* 8(2) Jl 1982 p 74-78 tabs

Ram, Usha and Palsane, M.N.

Diagonsis of mental retardation. *J Education and Psychology* 38(2) Jl 1980 p 94-98 refs

Rama, G.W.

Education and democracy. *J Higher Education* 9(1) Mon 1983 p 1-19 refs

Ramachandra, B.

A study of verbal classroom patterns of high school science teachers. *Indian Education* 10(8) Nv 1980 p 12-15

Ramachandrachar, K.

A cluster analysis of some operational measure of pupil-teachers performance at the B.Ed level. *Indian Educational Rev* 14(1) Ja 1979 p 140-47

Restructuring education for a learning society. *J Indian Education* 11(1) My 1985 p 9-13 refs

A study of relative effectiveness of hand synchronised OHP-tape, isolated tape and isolated OHP : Presentation of a science programme to non-science teachers at two levels of protest performance. *Quest in Education* 19(3) Jl 1982 p 194-205 refs figs tabs

Ramachandran, V.

The principal. *Indian Education* 11(1-2) Ap-My 1981 p 56-58

Ramachandra Pillai, P.

General and technical education in Andhra Pradesh. Hyderabad, Educ Telugu Akad. 1981, viii, 181p. Rs.7.50 *Book Rev, Indian Educational Rev* 17(2) Ap 1982 p 133-35

Ramachandrareddy, B.
Verbal classroom behaviour of high school science teachers : Social extraverts vs social introverts. *J Education and Psychology* 40(1-2) Ap-Jl 1982 p 18-28 refs

Ramachary, Akaram
Correlation between scientific attitude and achievement in science. *Experiments in Education* 10(7) Se 1982 p 123-27 refs tabs

Ramagopal, Bhagat
The child and the teacher. *Primary Teacher* 6(4) Oc 1981 p 19-21

Ramamohana Rao, M. and Sastry, D.S.N.
Impact of training on the educational beliefs of secondary teacher trainees. *Experiments in Education* 10(10) De 1982 p 179-83 refs tabs

RAMAMURTHI - RAMAMURTHY

Ramamurthy, M.S.
Stress experience of higher education students. *J Higher Education* 9(2) Aut 1983 p 245-49 tabs

Ramamurthi, P.V.
See
Bharathi, V. *jt. auth.*

Ramamurthy, Sree
A study into the role diffusion experienced by junior lecturers. *Quest in Education* 16(4) Oc 1979 p 275-98

Ramamurhty, T.
Training in educational journalism. *J Indian Education* 11(3) Se 1985 p 21-23

Raman
See also
under full name/surname, e.g., Anantha Raman, M.

Raman, A.
See
Raj, N. Casimir *jt. auth.*

Raman, Vasanthi
Some notes on the intelligentsia. *J Higher Education* 1(2) Aut 1975 p 211-22 refs

Ramana, V.V. and Prasad Rao, C.R.
Variations in economic position of college teachers by college management, sex and caste. *J Higher Education* 9(2) Aut 1983 p 259-68 refs

Ramana Reddy, I.V.
Rationalisation of educational system in the scientific and technological age. *Experiments in Education* 10(2) Ap 1982 p 23-25
Relative effect of co-educational and single sex schooling on academic adjustment of secondary school pupils. *J Education and Psychology* 44(1) Ap 1986 p 5-10 refs tabs

Ramanathan, G.
Commentaries on the human frontier. *Quest in Education* 16(3) Jl 1979 p 175-94

Perspectives on teacher education. *Quest in Education* 19(2) Ap 1982 p 118-36

Rama Sarma, A.

The role of a headmaster. *Indian Education* 11(5) Ag 1981 p 37-38

Ramasubban, Radhika

Economic education and educational policy reflections of an amateur. *J Higher Education* 8(2) Aut 1982 p 179-83 refs

The teaching of sociology. *J Higher Education* 1(1) Mon 1975 p 77-86

Ramasubban, T.A. *et al*

Interconversion of awards in trimester and traditional systems of education for the P.G. programmes. *J Higher Education* 4(2) Aut 1978 p 273-77

Ramaswamy, E.A.

What education workers need? *Indian J Adult Education* 46(5) My 1985 p 20-33 ft-n

Ramaswamy, R.

Modern approaches to management of education and the way of Mahatma Gandhi. *Experiments in Education* 12(3) My 1984 p 50-56

Rambalak, Guswami

Modern evaluation technique. *Primary Teacher* 5(4) Oc 1980 p 40-44

New education pattern. *Primary Teacher* 5(1) Ja 1980 p 27-30

Ramchand and Sohal, T.S.

A comparison of techniques for measuring aspiration of dairy farmers. *Indian J Extension Education* 19(1-2) Mr-Je 1983 p 95-98

Ram Chander

A comparative study of academic achievement of active and regular participants in co-curricular activities and that of non-participants. *J Educational Research and Extension* 16(3) Ja 1980 p 135-41 ref

Ramchandran, P.K. *et al*

Utilisation and credibility of the sources of information at various stages of adoption of farm innovations. *Indian J Extension Education* 15(3-4) De 1979 p 46-51 refs tabs

Ram Dutt

A comparative study of reliability of the true-false items and multiple choice items. *Rajasthan Board of Journal Education* 19(2-3) Ap-Je 1983 p 1-5

Ramesh, G.

Aesthetic education : Historical perspective. *National J Education* 5(1) Se 1982 p 46-52 refs

Ramesh Babu, A.

See

Singh, Y.P. *jt. auth.*

Ramesh Babu, A. and Singh, Y.P.

Pusarank sheet for Q-sort technique. *Indian J Extension Education* 20(1-2) Je 1984 p 52-57 refs tabs

Ramesh Babu, A. and Sinha, B.P.

Communication behaviour of extension personnel with regard to modern rice technology. *Indian J Extension Education* 21(3-4) Jl-De 1985 p 11-15 tabs

Ramesh Babu, M. and Chalam, K.S.

Expenditure on education as a social investment. *Educational Rev* 90(12)

De 1984 p 193-95

Ramesh Chandra

Developing population education programme for teacher training colleges. *Teacher Education* 13(8-9) Jl-Oc 1979 p 62-69 ft-n

Educational planning for economic development. *J Education and Psychology* 36(1-2) Ap-Je 1978 p 26-33 ref

Searching links between population, family size and quality of life. *Teacher Today* 27(1) Jl-Se 1984 p 49-58

Ram Kumar and Dubey, V.K.

Role performance of veterinary assistant surgeons working in veterinary hospitals of Punjab. *Indian J Extension Education* 20(1-2) Je 1984 p 69-70 tabs

Ram Kumar and Rai, G.C.

A socio-psychological study of the leaders of village panchayats. *Indian J Extension Education* 15(3-4) De 1979 p 39-45 refs tabs

Ram Kumar, Usha

See

Nagaraja, C.S. *jt. auth.*

Ramkumar, Vasantha

Self-concept and achievement. *J Higher Education* 1(1) Mon 1975 p 124-26 refs

A structural framework for multi-disciplinary studies. *Indian Educational Rev* 14(1) Ja 1979 p 85-91 refs

Ramkumar, Vasantha and Thomas, Achamma

Role expectations role performance and training needs of biology teachers of secondary schools. *J Educational Research and Extension* 16(3) Ja 1980 p 153-61 refs tabs

Ram Reddy, G.

University administration in India : Some critical issues. *Indian Education* 11(1-2) Ap-My 1981 p 24-34

Rana, Kamala

Effective participation of voluntary agencies in the national programme for eradication of illiteracy. *Prasar* 5(3-4) Oc 1977-Ja 1978 p 11-19

NAEP and the involvement of educational women. *Prasar* 7(1-2) Ap-Jl 1980 p 39-47

Rana, M.

See

Kool, V.K. *jt. auth.*

Rana, R.P.S.

Post-graduate education and research : cost analysis. *J Higher Education* 6(1-3) 1980-81 p 155-60 tabs

Randhava, Ajit *et al*

Imparting nutrition education to rural school children : Impact of the dramatisation method. *Indian Educational Rev* 20(2) Ap 1985 p 1-8

Randhava, T.S.

See

Dhillon, D.S. *et al jt. auths.*

Randhava, Tarlochan Singh

Adoption of NPK and 2n nutrients in rice crop in Punjab. *Indian J Extension*

Education 21(1-2) Ja-Je 1985 p 91-93

Ranganna, B.

See

Channegowde, M.B. *jt. auth.*

Rangarajan, M.R.

Role of research in higher education. *Educational Rev* 92(5-6) My-Je 1986 p 81-83 refs

Rangpal, D.L.

A blueprint for establishing community colleges in India. *New Frontiers in Education* 11(1) Ja-Mr 1981 p 66-68

Ranjan, R.

See

Sinha, H.S.P. *jt. auth.*

Ranjit Singh

Linking literacy with development : Some suggestions. *Indian J Adult Education* 42(10) Oc 1981 p 11-13

Nationalise primary education to eradicate illiteracy. *Indian J Adult Education* 46(4) Ap 1985 p 23-25

Selected characteristics of farmers in relation to their adoption of farm mechaniztion. *Indian J Extension Education* 19(3-4) Se-De 1983 p 11-17 refs tabs

Value orientation in relation to adoption of farm mechanisation by the farmers of Ludhiana, Punjab. *Indian J Extension Education* 18(3-4) De 1982 p 10-15 refs

See also

Mohammed, Zaki M. *jt. auth.*

Ranjit Singh and Saini, R.K.

Socio-personal correlates and gain in the knowledge of correspondence course trainers. *Indian J Adult Educaiton* 45(4) Ap 1984 p 30-33 tabs

Rao

See also

under full name/surname, e.g., Jayaprasada Rao, J.T.

Rao, Asha

A tool for undergraduate in selecting a specialisation. *Progress of Education* 58(1) Ag 1983 p 19-24

Rao, C.K.M.

Unit cost of teacher training for primary schools. *Progress of Education* 55(10) My 1981 p 264-66

Wastage in primary education in Raipur district, M.P. *Indian Education* 10(8) Nv 1980 p 37-40

Rao, C.N.R.

Scientific research in educational institutions : Problems and challenges. *University News* 23(27) 16 Jl 1985 p 9-11

Rao, C.S.S.

Agricultural extension management system in India : Past, present and modalities in future. *Indian J Extension Education* 21(1-2) Jl-Je 1985 p 32-35

Role of monitoring and evaluation in making training programme more effective. *Indian J Extension Education* 19(1-2) Mr-Je 1983 p 33-35

State boards of teacher education : Some urgent tasks ahead. *Education Quarterly* 31(2) Jl 1979 p 15-16

Rao, D.S.

Farmers functional literacy project : Bhimili study. *Indian J Adult Education* 40(5) My 1979 p 36-40 tabs

Rao, G.S.

Literacy for tribals. *Indian J Adult Education* 40(4) Ap 1979 p 1-4 refs

Rao, K.S.

In-service education of science teachers. *Educational Rev* 85(11) Nv 1979 p 216-19

See also

Mukhopadhyay, M. *jt. auth.*

Rao, M.K.S.

See

Desai, G.R. *jt. auth.*

Rao, S.V.N. and Sohal, T.S.

Job satisfaction of veterinary assistant surgeons. *Indian J Extension Education* 16(3-4) De 1980 p 74-77 tabs

Performance appraisal of extension workers. *Indian J Extension Education* 15(3-4) De 1982 p 57-61 refs

Rao, Sudha V.

Education and rural development. New Delhi, Sage Pub. 334p. Rs.150 *Book Rev, Education Quarterly* 38(3) Aut 1986 p 55-58; *Perspectives in Education* 2(3) Jl 1986 p 188-90

Rao, T.S.

Stability of divisions : A study of B.Eds. *National J Education* 3(1) Se 1980 p 40-48 tabs

Towards task-oriented teacher education. *Teacher Education* 16(18-19) Ja-Ap 1982 p 30-32

Rao, Usha

Problems of overcrowded classes : A pilot study. *Indian Educational Rev* 15(4) Oc 1980 p 107-12

Rao, V.K. and Mishra, Malti

Attitude of primary school teachers towards religious education. *Experiment in Education* 11(5) Jl 1983 p 89-2 refs

Rao, V.K.R.V.

Some thoughts on higher education. *J Higher Education* 6(1-3) 1980-81 p 1-7

Rao, V.N.

Mental health problems of school children. *Educational Rev* 91(12) De 1986 p 201-03 refs

Rao, V.N. and Parthasarathy, R.

Teacher as a counsellor. *Educational Rev* 90(12) De 1984 p 185-87 refs tabs

Rao, V.N. and Sohal, T.S.

Factor effecting job satisfaction of veterinary assistant surgeons of Vijayawada and Hyderabad areas, A.P. *Indian J Extension Education* 14(1-2) Ja-Je 1978 p 6-8 refs

Rao, V.N. *et al*

Behavioural problems in school children : Implication for teacher training programe. *Experiments in Education* 12(3) My 1984 p 41-46 refs tabs

Rashid Ahmad, A. and othes

Students life at the Bangladesh Agricultural University. *Indian J Extension Education* 17(3-4) Se-De 1981 p 96-100 tabs

Rasool, G.

Leadership among youth. *J Education and Psychology* 38(2) Jl 1980 p 88-93 refs

Priorities in National Policy of Education. *EPA Quarterly Bulletin* 7(1-2) Ap-Jl 1984 p 1-5 refs

Rastogi, K.G.

Education and society. *Primary Teacher* 6(2) Ap 1981 p 24-27

Evaluation of National Adult Education Programme. *Indian J Adult Education* 39(11-12) Nv-De 1978 p 53-59 tabs

Homework and its correction. *Primary Teacher* 6(4) Oc 1981 p 32-34

A model for developing language curriculum of school stage. *Teacher Today* 23(1) Jl-Se 1980 p 36-40 tabs

Moral education in schools. *Primary Teacher* 5(2) Ap 1980 p 33-36

Non-formal education : Concept, nature and scope. *Bulletin of Non-formal Education* 1(3) De 1983 p 15-33

Non-formal education. *Experiments in Education* 9(2) Ap 1981 p 33-36; 9(3) My 1981 p 39-43 refs

Non-formal education. *J Indian Education* 6(3) Se 1980 p 34-39

Objective and modes of non-formal education. *Teacher Today* 22(3) Ja-Mr 1980 p 42-48

Role of teachers organisations in Non-Formal Education Programme. *Primary Teacher* 9(4) Oc 1984 p 1-4

Rastogi, S.P.

Attitudes and beliefs of Harijan students. *J Higher Education* 4(2) Aut 1978 p 251-58

The impact of constitutional provision upon the uplift of Harijans. *Indian Educational Rev* 15(4) Oc 1980 p 76-80

See also

Rudra, K.K. *jt. auth.*

Ratan, R.P. Singh

See

Roy, N.K. *et al jt. auths.*

Rath, K.B.

Teaching of concepts in early years. *Primary Teacher* 8(2) Ap 1983 p 22-25

See also

Jangira, N.K. *jt. auth.*

Rath, Pratap K.

See

Puhan, Biranchi N. *jt. auth.*

Rath, Sudhakar

Some personality correlates along anxiety, extraversion and neuroticism dimensions. *Asian J Psychology and Education* 3(3) Nv 1978 p 46-51 refs tabs

Rather, A.R.

New dimensions in teacher education. *Teacher Education* 18(24-25) Jl-Oc 1983 p 44-48 refs

New directions in teacher education. *Progress of Education* 59(8) Mr 1985 p 177-80 refs

Rathnaiah, E.V.

Education for equality. *Indian Education* 10(1-2) Ap-My 1980 p 35-39

Teachers participation in educational administration. *Indian Education* 11(1-2) Ap-My 1981 p 67-70

Ratzlaf, Harold C.

Teaching evaluation : Are students comments redundant? *Progress of Education* 58(3) Oc 1983 p 68-70 tabs

Raval, H.H.

The situational approach in teaching English. *Progress of Education* 56(1) Ag 1981 p 17-18+

The teaching of composition in English. *Progress of Education* 55(8) Mr 1981 p 214-16

Ravi, V.K.

Problems of student teaching : An opinion survey. *Experiments in Education* 11(8) Oc 1983 p 134-37

Ravindran, D.J.

See

Saraswathi, L.S. *jt. auth.*

Ravindranath, M.J.

Towards development of attitudes : A paradigm. *Education Quarterly* 35(2) Ap 1983 p 8-11 refs

See also

Bhatt, Vasant D. *jt. auth.*

Kumar, S. *jt. auth.*

Ravindranath, M.J. and Bhatt, V.D.

Inquiry based science teaching : A few approaches. *Education Quarterly* 33(3) Jl 1981 p 21-23

Ravindranathan, M.N.

Educational problems in scheduled castes. *Educational Rev* 87(4) Ap 1981 p 69-74

An examination of the role of the part time education in Indian educatinal system. *Experiments in Education* 9(11) Ja 1982 p 194-201

Pathology in Indian education. *Education Quarterly* 35(3) Jl 1983 p 1-6

Perspectives of research in tribal education. *Experiments in Education* 9(1) Mr 1981 p 15-18; 9(2) Ap 1981 p 21-26

Pre-primary education in India from 1949-61 and its related problems. *Experiments in Education* 8(5) Jl 1980 p 84-83 ref

Problems in adult education. *Experiments in Education* 11(1) Mr 1983 p 5-11

The problem of cultural integration of the tribal education as the chief instrument of change. *Education Quarterly* 35(4) Oc 1983 p 20-24

Problems of rural and tribal schools. *Educational Rev* 88(8) Ag 1982 p 131-32; 88(9) Se 1982 p 149-50

The role of part-time education in our educational system. *J Indian*

Education 6(5) Ja 1981 p 37-40

Rural teachers and their problems. *Educational Rev* 87(10) Oc 1981 p 184-90

Teacher school and community variables coming in the way of value inculations process among the children. *Experiments in Education* 11(9) Nv 1983 p 159-62

See also

Roy, R. *jt. auth.*

Ravishanker, S.

Computer guided instructional systems. *Indian Education* 10(11) Fe 1981 p 44-45

Education in the Sixth Plan. *Indian Education* 11(7) Oc 1981 p 33-34; 11(8-9) Nv-De 1981 p 45-47; 11(10) Ja 1982 p 46-47; 11(11-12) Fe-Mr 1982 p 41-42

Education in the VI Five Year Plan : Science and technology and education. *Indian Education* 12(3-4) Je-Jl 1982 p 37-38

Educational technolgy in historical perspective. *Indian Education* 10(8) Nv 1980 p 31-32

A study of the role of audio visual aids in secondary school teaching. *Indian Education* 10(6) Se 1980 p 24-28

Technological aids in teaching-learning process. *Educational Rev* 87(8) Ag 1981 p 156-58

Television as an educational medium. *Teacher Today* 24(4) Ap-Je 1982 p 50-56 refs

See also

Malla Reddy, M. *jt. auth.*

Rawat, B.

See

Srivastava, R.K. *jt. auth.*

Ray

See

Roy

See also

under full name/surname, e.g., Samanta Ray, Chintamani

Raza

See

under full name/surname, e.g., Moonis Raza

Razdan, M.N.

A reassessment of home examination. *Rajasthan Board J Education* 15(2) Ap-Je 1979 p 20-28

REDDI - REDDY

See also

under full name/surname, e.g., Nagesekhara Reddi, Adinarayana Reddy, P.

Reddy, B.L.

See

Walson, M.J. *jt. auth.*

Reddy, Ch. S.
See
Saini, G.S. *jt. auth.*

Reddy, Janardhana
Extension service in universities. *Indian Education* 11(7) Oc 1981 p 16-18

Reddy, N.Y.
The place of the mentally retarded in Indian society. *Indian Education* 9(10-11) Ja-Fe 1980 p 12-24 refs

Reddy, Ramachandra
Development of concepts in mathematics. *Experiments in Education* 10(6) Ag 1982 p 108-09 refs

Reddy, S.V.
See
Mayuri, K. *jt. auth.*

Reddy, V.E.
Dynamics of rural learning system. *Indian J Adult Education* 40(7) Jl 1979 p 19-23

Reddy, V.E. and Bhat, K.S.
The out of school youth. Sterling. 299p. *Book Rev, J Higher Education* 4(2) Aut 1978 p 290-91

Reddi, Y.R. and Nagaraj Rao, M.
Child health and nutrition. *Indian Education* 9(10-11) Ja-Fe 1980 p 40-42

Rehman
See also
under full name/surname, e.g., Abdul Rehman, O.

Rehman, S.
Communication technology for adult education. *Indian J Adult Education* 40(12) De 1979 p 13-18

Reiter, Henry H. and Kirsch, Audrey L.
Preference and tolerance of disability groups as a function of age and educational level. *Our Education* 5 Jl 1984 p 1-3 refs

Relte, Henry H. and Penzel, Fred
Psychological aspects of systematic lupus erythematosus. *Asian J Psychology and Education* 11(3) 1983 p 5-18

Rensburg, Patrickvan
Education and culture for liberation. *Indian J Adult Education* 44(10) Oc 1983 p 6-15

Renu Debi
Long age, education and national integration. *Teacher Education* 16(18-19) Ja-AP 1982 p 72-76 refs

Rice, Marion J.
Harijan wasti. *Progress of Education* 55(2) Se 1980 p 51-57

Richards, J.C.
Conversation in action. Bombay, OUP. 1982, 110p. Rs.77.50. *Book Rev Progress of Education* 57(6) Ja 1983 p 143

Richter, Derek, ed.
Women scientists : The road to liberation. New York, Macmillan. £10. *Book Rev, Teahcer Today* 24(4) Ap-Je 1982 p 135-36

Richter, Maurice N.

Technological and social complexity. Albany, State Univ of N.Y. Press. 1982, 120p. $34.50. *Book Rev, J Higher Education* 9(1) Mon 1983 p 148-49

Ricker, Charles T.

Communication methods between AEOS, VLW's and farmers in Rajasthan's IAAP district. *Prasar* 5(1-2) Ap-Jl 1977 p 15-24 refs tabs

Ritzen, J.M.M.

Education, economic growth and income distribution : Contributions to economic analysis. Amsterdam, North-Holland Pub. xx, 257p. *Book Rev, Indian Educational Rev* 18(2) Ap 1983 p 134-35

Rizvi, Entramul Hassan

Importance of technical education at primary levels. *Primary Teacher* 5(1) Ja 1980 p 30-31

Robbins, Lord

Higher education revisited. London, Macmillan. 1980, 117p. £12 *Book Rev, Education Quarterly* 32(4) Oc 1980 p 47-48

Robinson, S.E.

Non-formal education in Rajasthan. *Bulletin of Non-Formal Education* 1(4) Mr 1984 p 27-36

Rogers, A.

Second thoughts on adult education and development. *Indian J Adult Education* 40(7) Jl 1979 p 1-8

Rogers, Everett M.

See

Apparao, G. *et al jt. auths.*

Rohatgi, P.K.

Activities of the technological forecasting and research management call of Indian Institute of Science, Bangalore. *J Higher Education* 4(1) Mon 1978 p 109-11

Rokade, V.S. and Anarasa, S.A.

Review of the existing arrangements of pre-service and in-service training for teachers and suggestions for improvement. *Education Quarterly* 35(4) Oc 1983 p 17-19

Roling, Niels

See

Chamala, Shankariah *et al jt. auths.*

Rosser, John H.

A peace movement that was lost. *Teacher Education* 14(10-11) Ja-Ap 1980 p 57-59

Rout, Pravakar

Education for rural people. *J Indian Education* 12(2) Jl 1986 p 20-23 refs

Need for instructional material. *Teacher Education* 13(8-9) Jl-Oc 1979 p 26-31

Rout, Upendra Nath

A comparative study of two item type parallel objective achievement test in general science. *Experiments in Education* 6(7) Se 1978 p 117-21; *J Educational Research and Extension* 16(3) Ja 1980 p 176-80 refs

A new approach to State Non-Formal Education Centre in tribal areas for all age groups. *Experiments in Education* 6(4) Je 1978 p 60-63

ROY - RAY

Roy, B.
See
Seth, M. *et al jt. auths.*

Roy, Biswanath
Effective education through needs, constraints and teacher motivation. *Education Quarterly* 31(1) Ap 1979 p 11-12
Ivan Illich : De-schooling society and non-formal education. *Bulletin of Non-Formal Education* 3(1) Je 1985 p 11-15
Teacher : laboratory-cum-clinic. *J Indian Education* 6(4) Nv 1980 p 43-52

Ray, G.L.
See
Haque, Mohammed A *jt. auth.*
Sagar, R.L. *jt. auth.*
Singh A.K. *jt. auth.*

Ray, G.L. and Samanta, R.K.
Who shall repay agricultural loan? Calcutta, Bikshan. xiv, 193p. Rs.40 *Book Rev, Indian J Extension Education* 18(3-4) De 1982 p 74-75

Ray, Jasobonta
Teachers' role as a member of classroom structure. *Our Education* 5 Jl 1984 p 69-72 refs

Roy, N.K.
See
Pandey, S.N. *jt. auth.*

Roy, N.K. *et al*
Adoption behaviour of leaders and their followers. *Indian J Extension Education* 20(3-4) Se-De 1984 p 19-26 refs tabs

Ray, P.K.S.
Effect of strategies developed through micro teaching with integration of teaching skills using summative model upon student teachers teaching competence. *Teacher Education* 14(12-13) Jl-Oc 1980 p 27-33 refs tabs

Roy, R. and Ravindranath, M.N.
Education in a rural community : An indepth study of a village in Karnataka. *Quest in Education* 18(4) Oc 1981 p 265-77

Roy, S.
See
Sudama, G.R. *et al jt. auths.*
Yadav, M.S. *jt. auth.*

Ray, S.K. *et al*
Impact of training and visit system of extension on tribal farms in Hoogly district : A case study. *Indian J Extension Education* 18(1-2) Je 1982 p 59-65 refs tabs

Roy, Sumirmal
See
Muttagi, Iqbal Aziz *jt. auth.*

Roy, Sunita
See
Mangat, Shavinder K. *jt. auth.*
Neeru Bala *jt. auth.*

Roy, Sumita and Khanna, Vinita
Effectiveness of three modes of communication for presenting information on household sanitation to the rural women. *Indian J Extension Education* 21(3-4) Jl-De 1985 p 33-36 refs tabs

Roychoudhury, Namita
See
Deo, Pratibha *jt. auth.*

Rozario, A.J.
Parallel colleges in Kerala. *New Frontiers in Education* 13(1) Ja-Mr 1983 p 37-47

Ruddar Dutt
Planning and development of distance education. *J Higher Education* 9(3) Spr 1984 p 205-14 tabs

Rudduck, Jean
Learning through small group discussion : A study of seminar work in higher education. Univ. of Surrey. 1978, *Book Rev, J Higher Education* 5(2) Aut 1979 p 269-72

Rudenka, Inna
Interview with Vsevolod Stoletov, President of the USSR Academy of Educational Sciences. *Teacher Education* 14(12-13) Jl-Oc 1980 p 68-70

Rudra, K.K. and Rastogi, S.P.
Regional distribution of selected technical educational facilities in India. *J Higher Education* 4(1) Mon 1978 p 23-31 refs tabs

Ruhela, Satya Pal
Making of our New Education Policy. *University News* 23(16) 23 Ap 1985 p 2-3

Rukma Rao, V.
See
Basu, Bharati *jt. auth.*

Rumble, Greville
Open correspondence institute, India. *Indian Education* 12(1-2) Ap-My 1982 p 36-40

Rungla, I.U. and Pal, Anasuya
An applied psycholinguistics experiment in remedial teaching of English grammar. *Indian Educational Rev* 14(1) Ja 1979 p 136-40 refs

Rusia, P.N.
Non-formal education in Madhya Pradesh. *Bulletin of Non-Formal Education* 1(2) 19 Se 1983 p 21-30

Rusk, Robert R. and Scotland, James
Doctrines of great educators. London, Macmillan. 1979. *Book Rev, National J Education* 3(1) Se 1980 p 75

Russell, Donovan
Education and the survival turning point. *Experiments in Education* 11(1) Mr

1983 p 3-5; *Teacher Education* 13(8-9) Jl-Oc 1979 p 5-8

Ryan, John
See
Gillette, Arthur *jt. auth.*

Sabaratham, V.E. .
See
Mulay, Sumati *jt. auth.*

Saberwal, Satish
Education, in quality and industrialisation. *J Higher Education* 1(2) Aut 1975 p 189-97 refs

Sabjan, Shaikh
Educational innovations : Role of educational administration. *Progress of Education* 60(7) Fe 1986 p 150-55 +

Sachdeva, J.L.
A brief report of the Ahmedabad conference. *Indian J Adult Educaiton* 41(11) Nv 1980 p 7-8
A brief report of the Patna conference. *Indian J Adult Education* 42(1) Nv 1981 p 8-10
32nd Annual Conference of IAEA (A brief report). *Indian J Adult Education* 40(10-11) Oc-Nv 1979 p 56-58

Sachdeva, P.D.
Strengthening teacher organisations. *Indian Education* 11(6) Se 1981 p 29-33

Sadagopal, Anil
Unscientific approach and irrational thinking of our educational elite. *Indian Education* 12(1-2) Ap-My 1982 p 11-13

Sadhana
See
Kumar, Kamla *jt. auth.*

Safaya, Raghunath
Attitude development for moral judgement. *Educational Rev* 92(10) Oc 1986 p 163-65
Education and socialistic pattern of society. *Educational Rev* 87(11) Nv 1981 p 813-14
Mass media in education. *Educational Rev* 86(6) Je 1980 p 116-17
Microteaching. *Educational Rev* 86(12) De 1980 p 227-34 refs
Moral and religious education. *Educational Rev* 88(10) Oc 1982 p 173-75; 88(11) Nv 1982 p 190-92; 88(12) De 1982 p 209-13
Moral education. *Educational Rev* 87(12) De 1981 p 229
The new education policy in India. *Educational Rev* 92(2) Fe 1986 p 26-27
A new look for education. *Educational Rev* 91(3) Mr 1985 p 41-43
Restructuring of courses. *Educational Rev* 88(2) Fe 1982 p 37-38
System analysis in educational planning. *Educational Rev* 85(5) My 1979 p 88-93 figs
World literacy. *Educational Rev* 86(10) Oc 1980 p 187-88

Safi, S.A.
Mental and physical health through education. *Indian Education* 10(7) Oc

1980 p 26-28
Sagar, R.L. and Ray, G.L.
Factors contributing to the farmers productivity of crops. *Indian J Extension Education* 20(1-2) Je 1984 p 20-28 refs tabs
Sah, Beena
See
Uniyal, M.P. *jt. auth.*
Sahab Singh
Teacher effects and perceived behaviour changes in students. *National J Education* 5(1) Se 1982 p 53-61 refs tabs
Values of successful teachers. *National J Education* 3(1) Se 1980 p 17-24 refs tabs

SAHAI - SAHAY

Sahay, B.N.
See
Kherde, R.L. *jt. auth.*
Sahai, Sobhana
See
Saraswati, R.M. *et al jt. auths.*
Sahay, U.K.
Literacy and world population. *J Indian Education* 5(1) My 1979 p 59-63 tabs
Saharia, K.K.
Problems in professional socialisation as faced by agriculture and veterinary graduates in Assam. *J Education and Psychology* 44(2-3) Jl-Oc 1986 p 135-40
Sahay
See
Sahai
Sahdev Kumar
Consciousness : Raising education. *Bharatiya Shiksha Shodh Patrika* 4(2) Jl-De 1985 p 21-25 refs
The lotus in the stone : An allegory for explorations in dreams and consciousness. Delhi, Motilal. 211p. Rs. 195 *Book Rev, Bharatiya Shiksha Shodh Patrika* 4(2) Jl-De 1985 p 45-47
Sahi, P.N.
Student unrest : A psychoanalysis. *Teacher Today* 24(1) Jl-Se 1981 p 61-68
Sahoo, P.K.
Case study as a method of research. *J Institute of Educational Research* 7(2) My 1983 p 37-42
Distance education : A world wide perspective. *J Indian Education* 12(2) Jl 1986 p 46-53 refs
Distance education in Indian universities : Some concerns for further development. *Education Quarterly* 37(4) Wint 1985 p 1-10 refs
Evaluation of National Adult Education Programme. *Indian Education* 13(8-9) Nv-De 1983 p 8-11
Finance of distance education at university level. *University News* 24(42) 8

Nv 1986 p 119-28 refs
Higher education in India : Certain issues. *New Frontiers in Education* 13(3) Oc-De 1983 p 62-68
Non-formal adult education : Perspectives of research. *Education Quarterly* 31(3-4) Oc 1979-Ja 1980 p 6-8
Programme evaluation : A conceptual analysis. *J Educational Planning and Administration* 1(1) Oc 1986 p 34-42 refs
Vocational education : Needs and scope at +2 stage. *Experiments in Education* 6(12) Fe 1979 p 207-12; 8(9) Nv 1980 p 155-60
Vocational preferences of tenth grade boys and girls. *Experiments in Education* p 32-36 tabs refs
See also
Menon, M.B. *jt. auth.*
Yadav, M.S. *et al jt. auths.*

Sahoo, P.K. and Dwivedi, T.N.
Adult education in a slum of Baroda city. *Indian J Adult Education* 40(8) Ag 1979 p 35-41 refs

Sahoo, S.C. and Panda, S.K.
A study of n-achievement and anxiety of school adolescents with respect to their sex and socio-economic status. *Progress of Education* 56(7) Fe 1982 p 165-69 + refs tabs

Saini, B.K.
10+2+3 pattern : Its history. *Educational Rev* 87(1) Je 1981 p 3-6+; 87(2) Fe 1981 p 31-35

Saini, G.S.
Information needs of the small and marginal farmers of Punjab state. *Indian J Extension Education* 17(3-4) Se-De 1981 p 101-02

Saini, G.S. and Pawar, S.S.
A study of the profile of Yuv Dal's (Youth Clubs) members. *Indian J Extension Education* 18(1-2) Je 1982 p 99-101

Saini, G.S. and Reddy, Ch. S.
Communication of information through Rural Youth Club leaders. *Indian J Extension Education* 21(1-2) Ja-Je 1985 p 80-82
Information source contact of Rural Youth Club leaders. *Indian J Extension Education* 20(3-4) Se-De 1984 p 57-59

Saini, R.K.
See
Ranjit Singh *jt. auth.*

Sakkar, S.B.
Attitude of teacher trainees and their parents towards academy. *Asian J Psychology and Education* 13(3-4) 1984 p 49-51

Saksena
See
Saxena

SALAMA - SALMA

Salma Begum, A.K.
A study of fears in adolescents. *J Institute of Educational Research* 9(3) Se 1985 p 14-16 refs tabs

Salama, I.A.
  Physical education and sport in the developing countries. *Students Action* 2(2) Je 1983 p 10-11+
Salamatullah
  In search of panacea for educational ills. *J Indian Education* 8(4) Nv 1982 p 3-8
Sales-Pontes, A. Hilda
  A book week in a school. *Progress of Education* 55(11) Je 1981 p 295-99
Sarma
  See
    Salama
Saluja, Chunnilal
  Science teaching through local environment. *Primary Teacher* 5(4) Oc 1980 p 35-37
Saluja, P.R.
  Learning spellings meaningfully. *Primary Teacher* 5(1) Ja 1980 p 31-32
  Teaching reading through dramatisation in primary classes. *Primary Teacher* 4(3) Jl 1979 p 22-24
Salunkhe, V.G.
  Beneficiaries of Small Farmers Development Agency. *Indian J Extension Education* 16(1-2) Je 1980 p 61-63
  Multivariate regression analysis of involvement of small farmers in SFDA. *Indian J Extension Education* 16(3-4) De 1980 p 70-73
Samaddar, Sunanda and Purkait, B.R.
  Materialism and scientism in the educational philosophy of Pandit Iswar Chandra Vidyasagar. *Perspectives in Education* 2(4) Oc 1986 p 213-20 refs

SAMANT - SAMANTA

Samant, D.G.
  Implications of grades for university teachers. *J Higher Education* 4(2) Aut 1978 p 271-73
  Laws of teaching. *Progress of Education* 56(1) Ap 1981 p 10-13
  Work load of teacher educators. *Progress of Education* 53(6) Ja 1979 p 96-101
Samant, D.G. and Bhimasankaran, C.V.
  Anatomy of teaching. *Progress of Education* 57(5) De 1982 p 103-07
  Transformation analysis. *Progress of Education* 50(3) Oc 1981 p 62-65
Samanta, R.K.
  Agricultural research service scientists : Their value orientation and overall modernity. *J Higher Education* 9(1) Mon 1983 p 114-17 refs
  Perception of work environment by agricultural research service scientists of ICAR institutes. *Indian J Extension Education* 21(3-4) Jl-Se 1985 p 53-61 refs tabs
  See also
    Ray, G.L. *jt. auth.*
Samanta Ray, Chintamani
  A study of the temperament of secondary school teachers of Orissa.

Experiments in Education 6(10) De 1978 p 182-84

Samar, M.S.

Promoting abilities in the disabled : A case study. *J Indian Education* 12(1) My 1986 p 58-61

Teaching of mathematics : A point of view. Ajmer, Regional College of Education. 118p. *Book Rev, Education Quarterly* 33(4) Oc 1981 p 36

Sambasiva Rao, Avula

57th All India Conference, Visakhapatnam : Address by Sri Avula Sambasiva Rao. *Indian Education* 13(5-6) Ag-Se 1983 p 3-4

Sampath, K. *et al*

Introduction to educational technology. New Delhi, Sterling. viii, 292p. Rs.25 *Book Rev, Education Quarterly* 34(1) Ja 1982 p 47-48

Sampoornam, K.V.

See

Ghosh, Sunanda *jt. auth.*

Samsananda Raj, H.

See

George, V.D. *jt. auth.*

Thomas, Immanuel *jt. auth.*

Samsananda Raj, H. and Krishana, Rita

Intelligence, socio-economic status and family size as correlates of achievement. *J Institute of Educational Research* 4(3) Se 1980 p 1-6 refs tabs

Sancheti, D.C.

Coordination between universities and professional bodies. *University News* 23(26) 8 Jl 1985 p 2-3

Sancheti, Neelu

The Ford Foundation and Indian education : Some issues of motives and power. *New Frontiers in Education* 14(3) Jl-Se 1984 p 1-13 refs

Sandeep, P.

Classroom interaction and cognitive development in primary school children. *Indian Educational Rev* 15(4) Oc 1980 p 62-65

Sandhu, D.K. and Shukla, A.N.

Content analysis of Tiranjan programme of AIR, Jullunder. *Indian J Extension Education* 17(3-4) Se-De 1981 p 7-16 refs

Sandhu, N.S.

See

Sangha, G.S. *jt. auth.*

Sandhu, N.S. and Adarsh Bala

Relative use of non-projected visual aids at the school level. *J Indian Education* 6(1) My 1980 p 44-47

Sandhu, N.S. and Jain, Rashmi

Attitude of university college teachers towards teaching as a career. *Teacher Education* 17(20-21) Jl-Oc 1982 p 40-45 tabs

Sandhu, Tara Singh

AIR's historic vistories in Punjab. *Student Action* 2(6) Oc 1983 p 7-8

Cognito-affecto development of high school students : Piagetian perspective. *Indian Educational Rev* 20(3) Jl 1985 p 32-36

Sandya, P.N. and Singh, Y.P.
Journal communication of IARI theses. *Indian J Extension Education* 18(1-2) Je 1982 p 34-44 tabs

Sane, K.V.
Low cost equipment for chemistry teaching. *New Frontiers in Education* 13(1) Ja-Mr 1983 p 49-52

Sanganeswara Rao, D.
Private agencies and management of education. *Indian Education* 11(1-2) Ap-My 1981 p 95-98

Sangha, G.S.
An educational game for children. *Primary Teacher* 5(1) Ja 1980 p 11-13
See also
Dhillon, D.S. *et al jt. auths.*
Gupta, M.P. *jt. auth.*

Sangha, G.S. and Gupta, M.P.
Credibility of television as a source of information. *Indian J Extension Education* 21(1-2) Ja-Je 1985 p 74-76 tabs

Sangha, G.S. and Sandhu, N.S.
Competencies of the agricultural extension officers regarding selection and use of extension methods. *Indian J Extension Education* 16(3-4) De 1980 p 43-45 refs tabs

Sangram Singh
Correspondence education : Problems and prospects. *University New* 21(21) Nv 1983 p 700-702

Sankaram, V. and Dorasami, K.
Some comments on the moderation of question papers in mathematics education. *J Higher Education* 8(2) Aut 1982 p 246-47 refs
See also
Shankaram, V.

Sankara Narayan, D.
Computer science and technology : Facility, requirements and certification of academic programmes. *J Higher Education* 7(3) Spr 1982 p 324-26
University computer centre : Structure, functions and management, *J Higher Education* 5(1) Mon 1979, p 108-12

Sanoria, Y.C. and Sharma, D.K.
Comparative analysis of adoption behaviour of benficiaries of farm development programme. *Indian J Extension Education* 19(1-2) Mr-Je 1983 p 84-86

Sanoria, Y.C. and Singh, K.N.
Communication patterns of agricultural scientists : A path analysis. *Indian J Extension Education* 16(1-2) Je 1980 p 39-45 refs tabs
Communication patterns of agricultural scientists : A system analysis. *Indian J Extension Education* 14(1-2) Ja-Je 1978 p 17-22 refs
Communication patterns of extension personnel : A path analysis. *Indian J Extension Education* 15(1-2) Je 1979 p 19-25 refs tabs

Sansanwal, D.N.
An experimental study in programmed learning for teaching research methodology course at M.Ed level. *Indian Educational Rev* 14(4) Oc 1979 p 72-79

An experimentation in the use of programmed learning material for revision purpose. *Experiments in Education* 7(6) Ag 1979 p 109-10+

See also

Buch, P.M. *et al jt. auths.*

Passi, B.K.and others *jt. auths.*

Sansanwal, D.N. and Buddhisagar, Meena

Different styles of writing instructional strategy with traditional teaching. *Experiments in Education* 7(12) Fe 1982 p 158-62 refs

Sansanwal, D.N. and Jarial, Gurpal Singh

Creativity and its components in relation to different levels of intelligence and academic subjects among high school students. *Asian J Psychology and Education* 11(2) 1983 p 9-13

Sansanwal, D.N. and Joshi, Anuradha

Comparison of instructional strategy with traditional teaching. *Experiments in Education* 7(12) Fe 1980 p 225-26 tabs

Effect of personality intelligence and their interaction on achievement through instructional strategy. *Indian Education* 10(5) Ag 1980 p 23-26

Evolvement of an instructional strategy at B.Ed level for teaching-learning. *J Educational Research and Extension* 18(2) Oc 1981 p 1-9

Sansanwal, D.N. *et al*

Comparison of reception and selection strategies of concept attainment. *J Institute of Educational Research* 10(2) My 1986 p 12-15 refs

An experimental study of the effect of dependency and adjustment on the achievement of students studying through programmed learning material using different response modes. *Indian Educational Rev* 17(4) Oc 1982 p 140-46

Facilitation of creative thinking abilities through transcendent mediation. *J Indian Education* 6(3) Se 1980 p 9-13 tabs

Sant

See also

under full name/surname, e.g. Kishore Sant

Sant Prakash

Accelerating correspondence education in our country. *Education Quarterly* 32(1) Ja 1980 p 19-20

An effective approach for the success of adult education programme. *Education Quarterly* 35(2) Ap 1983 p 12-15

Taking science and technology to the rural sector. *Education Quarterly* 30(3) Oc 1978 p 21-23

Santhanam, M.R.

Degree-job delink. *Education Quarterly* 38(1) Spr 1986 p 9-14

Some recent studies on teaching and teaching behaviour. *Experiments in Education* 6(3) My 1978 p 39-50; 6(4) Je 1978 p 66-71 refs

Teacher preparation in non-conventional areas : Especially in technical and vocational fields. *Experiments in Education* 9(8) Oc 1981 p 133-38 refs

Santhanam, S.

Functions of colleges of education. *J Educational Research and Extension* 16(2) Oc 1979 p 77-79

Santos, Felex P.

Educational reforms and innovations in the Philippines. *Rajasthan Board J*

Education 16(1-2) Ja-Je 1980 p 55-64

Sanyal, Bikas C.

Higher education and the labour market in Asia. *J Higher Education* 8(2) Aut 1983 p 166-67 refs tabs

Higher education and the labour market in the Philippines. Paris, Unesco; New Delhi, Wiley Eastern 1981, 316p. *Book Rev, J Higher Education* 8(2) Aut 1982 p 255-57

Saraf, S.N.

Education for all : Dimensions and dilemmas. *University News* 27(21) Je 1985 p 2-5

Financial resources : Dimensions and dilemmas. *University News* 23(19) 16 My 1985 p 2-6 annex

Higher education and Five Year Plans : Policies, plans and perspectives. *University News* 23(3) 16 Ja 1985 p 2-5; 23(4) 23 Ja 1985 p 2-6; 23(5) 1 Fe 1985 p 2-4

Saraswat, R.K.

Teacher of handicapped children. *Primary Teacher* 10(4) Oc 1985 p 33-26

Saraswat, R.M.

See

Agrawal Umesh *jt. auth.*

Saraswat, R.M. *et al*

A study of retention course. *Experiments in Education* 9(6) Ag 1981 p 102-07

Saraswathi, L.S.

A profile of the clientele in the NFE centres for 6-14 years in Tamil Nadu. *Experiments in Education* 6(6) Ag 1978 p 106-08; 6(7) Se 1978 p 111-16; *Indian J Adult Education* 40(9) Se 1979 p 22-30

Saraswathi, L.S. and Ravindran, D.J.

The hidden dreams : The neo-literates speak. *Indian J Adult Education* 41(12) De 1980 p 23-27

Problem-oriented literacy method in practice in Thirukkazhukun- dram block of Tamil Nadu. *Indian J Adult Education* 41(3) Mr 1980 p 7-13

Saraswathi, T.S.

See

Verma, Amita *jt. auth.*

Saraswathi, T.S. and Gupta, Radhika

Educate a woman and you educate a family. *Perspectives in Education* 1(1) Ja 1985 p 49-54 refs tabs

Sarkar, A.K.

Correlates of children's attitudes towards their parents. *Quest in Education* 19(1) Ja 1982 p 21-34 refs tabs

Introversion, neuroticism and achievement in mathematics in school going adolescent girls. *Quest in Education* 18(1) Ja 1981 p 13-18

Sarkar, K.R.

Population education for developing countries. New Delhi, Sterling. 1986, 224p. Rs.125 *Book Rev, Education Quarterly* 39(3) Aut 1986 p 51-52

Sarkar, S.

See

Basu, A.K. *et al jt. auths.*

Sarma
See
under full name/surname, e.g., Chandrasekhara Sarma, A.
See also
Sharma

Saroj Bala
Adult literacy work through National Service Scheme. *Experiment in Education* 12(12) Fe 1985 p 222-24

Sartain, Harry W., *ed.*
Mobilising family forces for worldwise reading success. New York, IRA. vi, 86p. *Book Rev, Education Quarterly* 34(1) Ja 1982 p 48-49

Sastry, D.S.N.
See
Ramamohana Rao, M. *jt. auth.*

Sataiger, Ralph C.
Roads to reading. Unesco. 1979, 141p. $ 5 *Book Rev, J Indian Education* 6(5) Ja 1981 p 51-53

Satapathy, A.
See
Mathur P. *jt. auth.*

Satapathy, C. *et al*
Stimulating effect of mass media as perceived by adopters discontinuants and rejectors. *Prasar* 7(3-4) Oc 1980-Ja 1981 p 16-17 refs

Satapatty, C.
See
Mohanty, B. *jt. auth.*

Sathappan, S.
The relationship between economic status and value patterns of adolescents. *Asian J Psychology and Education* 4(2) Jl 1979 p 46-50 refs

Sathe, Dipake D.
SSA : A new theorem in geometry. *Progress of Education* 57(4) Nv 1982 p 91-92

Sathe, Subasini P.
Methods of teaching in relation to English textbooks for std. XII. *Progress of Education* 56(1) Ag 1981 p 5-7

Sathiaraj, P. Joseph
Student perception of leadership characteristics. *J Indian Education* 8(1) My 1982 p 15-18 refs tabs
Student perception of the purposes of higher education. *J Higher Education* 9(3) Spr 1984 p 395-97 refs

Sathiyagimirajan, S.
Relationship between profession perception and levels of knowledge competence of the college teachers. *J Educational Research and Extension* 18(4) Ap 1982 p 220-23 refs tabs
See also
Amaladass, G. *jt. auth.*
Stephen, J. *jt. auth.*

Sathyavathi, K.
See
Raghava, G. *et al jt. auths.*
Satish Chandra
Higher education in India : Plans and prospects. *J Higher Education* 1(1) Mon 1975 p 5-18 refs tabs
Satvir Singh
Coaching institutions in India : A survey. *J Indian Education* 8(4) Nv 1982 p 33-40 refs tabs
See also
Srivastava, A.B.L. *jt. auth.*
Sativir Singh and Sehgal, Meena
Factor structure of psychoticism in relation to hostility, anxiety neuroticism and ability measures. *Asian J Psychology and Education* 4(3) Nv 1981 p 18-21 refs
Sativir Singh and Vanvira, Kiran
Structure of interrelations among fear of success, motivation and personality measures. *Asian J Psychology and Education* 6(2) Jl 1980 p 17-20 refs tabs
Satvir Singh *et al*
Factor structure of correlates of graphic expression measure of N-achievement among rural children. *Asian J Psychology and Education* 7(2) Jl 1981 p 55-59
Satya Prakash Singh
Educo-ecology : A concept for understanding educational milieu. *J Indian Education* 8(1) My 1982 p 10-14 figs
Satyanarayana, B.S.
Educational problems of scheduled caste college, students in Karnataka. *J Higher Education* 7(3) Spr 1982 p 253-60 refs-ft-n tabs
See also
Akhtar Bano *jt. auth.*
Shashikala Devi, U. *jt. auth.*
Sudha, B.G. *et al jt. auths.*
Satyanarayana Rao, P.P.
Adult education in India. *Educational Rev* 91(5-6) My-Je 1985 p 84-85 refs
Satya Raju, R.
Commerce curriculum in India : Need for reforms. *J Higher Education* 9(2) Aut 1983 p 277-79
Management education in India : Some reflections. *Educational Rev* 90(1) Ja 1984 p 14-15
Satyarthi, M.K.
Anxious attitude of students in relations to some backward variables. *Asian J Psychology and Education* 4(1) Ja 1979 p 35-39 refs
A study of the effect of economic status on students attitude towards school experience. *Asian J Psychology and Education* 9(3) 1982 p 7-10
Satyasundaram, I.
Anatomy of school drop-outs. *Education Quarterly* 36(1) Ja 1984 p 31-35
Developing self-study habits. *Primary Teacher* 10(3) Ja 1985 p 13-15
Dimensions of population education. *Education Quaterly* 35(2) AP 1983

Encouraging self-study habits. *Rajasthan Board J Education* 20(1-2) Ja-Je 1984 p 43-46
Is notes dictation bad? *Educational Rev* 85(4) Ap 1979 p 64-65
Semester system : A critical appraisal. *Education Quarterly* 32(1) Ja 1980 p 12-15
Vocationalisation of education : Some issues. *J Indian Education* 5(6) Mr 1980 p 25-31

Saunders, Fay E.
Discrimination and inequalities between the sexes at school. *J Indian Education* 5(5) Ja 1980 p 35-42

Saunders, Ruth and Bingham-Newan, Ann M.
Piagetian perspective for preschools : A thinking book for teachers. New Jersey, Prentice-Hall. 1984. *Book Rev, Teacher Today* 27(4) Ap-Je 1985 p 147-48

Savinder Kaur and Dhaliwal, Amar Jit Singh
Reading comprehension of correspondence trainees. *Indian J Extension Education* 20(1-2) Je 1984 p 73-75 tabs

Savur, Shaila
Socially useful productive work in Gandhi Shikshan Bhavan, 1979-80. *Quest in Education* 17(2) AP 1980 p 106-11

Sawant, G.K.and Bhoite, H.S.
Rural development in Ralegan Siddhi : A case study. *Indian J Extension Education* 21(1-2) Ja-Je 1985 p 61-64

SAXENA - SAKSENA

Saxena, A.B.
The appropriate educational technology. *Education Quarterly* 33(2) Ap 1981 p 4-6
Creativity and teaching of science at the primary level. *Primary Teacher* 8(3) Jl 1983 p 23-26
Environmental studies in the national curriculum. *Education Quarterly* 38(3) Aut 1986 p 8-12
Evaluation and environmental studies. *Primary Teacher* 6(1) Ja 1981 p 28-34
Noise pollutant : Need for proper education. *Primary Teacher* 6(4) Oc 1981 p 39-41
Piaget in the context of primary education. *Primary Teacher* 5(3) Jl 1980 p 10-17 tabs
Science teachers and educational reconstruction. *J Indian Education* 8(2) Jl 1982 p 65-68
See also
Jadhoo, V.G. *et al jt. auths.*
Mathur, S.G. *jt. auth.*

Saxena, A.B. *et al*
Development of an environmental awareness test. *Indian Educational Rev* 16(3) Jl 1981 p 21-26

Saxena, A.K. and Sharma, P.
Some testable suggestions for the study of creativity in rural children. *J*

Education and Psychology 39(3) Oc 1981 p 183-88

Saxena, A.P.

Environmental education : A total perspective. *Education Quarterly* 35(4) Oc 1983 p 29-36

Saxena, Alka

See

Mahesh, Vimla *jt. auth.*

Saxena, Anil K.

An investigation into existing and expected personal characteristic image patterns of secondary school going children. *Quest in Education* 17(1) Ja 1980 p 59-65 refs

Needed research in science education in India. *Teacher Today* 22(4) Ap-Je 1980 p 61-66

The role of science learning centres for primary school children. *Primary Teacher* 6(2) Ap 1981 p 5-7

Saxena, Bimla

See

Jha, J. *jt. auth.*

Saxena, D.K.

See

Jha, J.S. *jt. auth.*

Saxena, Daya and Bhatnagar, Suma Rani

A comparative study of time utilisation pattern of tribal and non-tribal women in Rajasthan. *Indian J Extension Education* 21(1-2) Ja-Je 1985 p 83-85 tabs

Saksena, Gopal

Educational TV programme. *Education Quarterly* 38(1) Spr 1986 p 21-23

Saxena, J.C.

Annual report : 1983-84. *Indian J Adult Education* 45(12) De 1984 p 39-47

Saxena, J.K. and Lal Singh

Power motive in relation to sex and value orientation. *Asian J Psychology and Education* 9(1) Ja 1982 p 29-33 refs

Saxena, Mukul

Socio-ecological and linguistic factors of illiteracy. *Indian J Adult Education* 45(10) Oc 1984 p 9-15 tabs

Saxena, P.C.

Problems of academic over-and underachievers in different curricula. *National J Education* 3(2) Mr 1981 p 53-71 tabs

See also

Pal, S.K. *jt. auth.*

Saxena, P.C. and Upadhyaya, Usha

Maternal deprivation : A review of literature. *National J Education* 2(2) Mr 1980 p 15-25 refs

Saxena, Ramesh P.

Inactivity : The bane of schools for the visually handicapped. *Teacher Today* 23(1) Jl-Se 1980 p 49-53

The productment of the parents of pre-school blind children. *J Indian Education* 6(5) Jl 1981 p 3-7

Sensory training : A basic subject to the personality development of the visually handicapped child. *Teacher Today* 23(3) Ja-Mr 1981 p 16-21

Saxena, Saroj

See

Jain, Pemi *jt. auth.*

Mukhopadhyay, S. *jt. auth.*

Saxena, Saleshwara

Educational planning in India. New Delhi, Sterling. 1979, 202p. Rs.45 *Book Rev, Education Quarterly* 31(2) Jl 1979 p 38

Scally, Mike

See

Hopson, Barrie, *jt. auth.*

Scotland, James

See

Rusk, Robert R. *jt. auth.*

Scott, Denis H.

Helping the maladjusted child. Milton Kegney, Open Univ. Press. 126p. *Book Rev, Education Quarterly* 35(3) Jl 1983 p 54-57

Scrimshow, Peter

Community service, social education and curriculum. London, Hodder. 85p. £3.95 *Book Rev, Education Quarterly* 34(4) Oc 1982 p 58-59

Seddey, S.C.

Trends in professional education among women. *J Higher Education* 8(3) Spr 1983 p 327-34

Seddey, S.C. and Gupta, Ravi Kant

Determinants of levels of higher education in states. *J Higher Education* 9(1) Mon 1983 p 133-34 refs tabs

Sedere, Mohottige U.

Criterion referenced measurement. *New Frontiers in Education* 9(1) Ja-Mr 1979 p 52-62 refs

Formal non-formal and informal education : A classification. *New Frontiers in Education* 11(1) Ja-Mr 1981 p 73-78 refs

Seetharam, R.

Guidance and counselling programmes in schools. *Asian J Psychology and Education* 4(2) Jl 1979 p 17-21

Seetharamu, A.S.

Choices for research in education : A note of criteria. *Indian Educational Rev* 18(1) Ja 1983 p 116-20

Seetharamu, A.S. and Usha Devi, M.D.

Education in rural areas : Constraints and prospects. New Delhi, Ashish Pub H. 1985, 220p. Rs.100 *Book Rev, Education Quarterly* 37(4) Wint 1985 p 60-62

School facilities and dropouts in Karnataka : A case study. *Primary Teacher* 10(2) Ap 1985 p 11-14

Sehgal, Krishna

The impact of sex and academic discipline on the level knowledge of current affairs. *Progress of Education* 53(12) Jl 1979 p 223-27+ tabs

Systems analysis : Its application to teacher education. *Quest in Education* 18(3) Jl 1981 p 197-204 refs

Sehgal, Meena
See
Satvir Singh *jt. auth.*
Sekhar, S.
Brain drain and drain of brain. *Experiments in Education* 11(12) Fe 1984 p 214-15
Teacher education : A futurology : The new dimensions of teacher education. *J Educational Research and Extension* 16(2) Oc 1979 p 72-76
Selvam, S.
See
Nagarajan, V. *jt. auth.*
Sen, A.K.
Primary school teachers as community health workers. *Teacher Today* 28(2) Oc-De 1985 p 67-70 tabs
Sen, Anima
Education and care of the mentally retarded. *Indian Education* 11(8-9) Nv-De 1981 p 18-20
Sen, Anima and Kapur, Preeti
Attitude towards work environment and its relation with personality traits and choice of leisure time activities among a group of executives. *Our Education* 3-4 Jl 1983 p 1-8 refs tabs
Sen, Arun K.
See
Chadha, N.K. *jt. auth.*
Goel, Sushil Kumar *jt. auth.*
Sen, Asoke
Child's year and tomorrows world. *Education Quarterly* 31(3-4) Oc 1979-Ja 1980 p 13-15
Economy in education. *Education Quarterly* 32(2) Ap 1980 p 6-7
International Year for the Handicapped : Education for the disabled. *Education Quarterly* 33(3) Jl 1981 p 5-7
Role of books in adult education. *Education Quarterly* 32(4) Oc 1980 p 1-3
Thoughts on adult education. *Education Quarterly* 3(2) Jl 1979 p 5-7
Thoughts on adult education. *Indian J Adult Education* 43(6) Je 1982 p 11-14+
Sen, Bimen
Education for one world : A long term perspective. *University News* 23(7) 16 Fe 1985 p 3-6
Sen, Indra
Education and traditional values in India. *Education Quarterly* 35(1) Ja 1983 p 1-4
Indian education thought in recent times. *Education Quarterly* 34(2) Ap 1982
The role of the teacher in the free progress method of integral education. *Education Quarterly* 36(1) Ja 1984 p 1-5
Senapati, B.B. and Kapat, G.B.
A study of interest and ability of the secondary school students in science. *Our Education* 2 Jl 1981 p 39-44 refs

Sengupta, D.
    Patterns of education. *Education Quarterly* 31(2) Jl 1979 p 1-4

Sengupta, M.
    Intellective and non-intellective factors associated with engineering creativity. *Indian Educational Rev* 17(1) Ja 1982 p 93-98
    Technology invades education. *Education Quarterly* 37(2) Sum 1985 p 7-9
    Training of teachers for engineering based vocations. *Teacher Today* 21(4) Ap-Je 1979 p 25-31 refs
    See also
        Raina, M.K. *jt. auth.*

Sengupta, Manjaree and Kapat, G.B.
    A study of some determinants of personality characteristics of preadolescent children. *Our Education* 1 Jl 1980 p 2-8 refs tabs

Sengupta, Manjit
    Teaching young minds. *Indian Educaiton* 10(7) Oc 1980 p 3-6

Sengupta, Pallab
    Oppose Jha Commission report. *Student Action* 2(2) Jl 1983 p 7-8
    All unite to fight at todays challenges. *Student Action* 2(1) My 1983 p 2-3

Seshadri, C.
    Educaiton, quality and culture : An analysis. *J Higher Education* 3(3) Spr 1978 p 315-19 refs
    Educational theory : A logical analysis. *Perspectives in Education* 1(1) Ja 1985 p 21-24 tabs
    Moral education : Some points to ponder. *Education Quarterly* 34(3) Jl 1982 p 1-4
    Non-detention in schools : An academic exploration. *Education Quarterly* 36(2) Ap 1984 p 10-23
    Research in philosophy of education. *Indian Educational Rev* 18(4) Oc 1983 p 99-105
    Teacher education : The continuing debate. *J Indian Education* 12(4) Nv 1986 p 3-10
    Teachers and value education. *New Frontiers in Education* 14(1) Ja-Mr 1984 p 31-37
    Teaching of geometry : How can it be modernised? *Rajasthan Board J Education* 15(1) Ja-Mr 1979 p 21-23
    See also
        Anand, R.D. *jt. auth.*

Seshadri, Malathi
    See
        Yadav, M.S. *jt. auth.*

Seshagiri Rao, C.
    See
        Bajpai, J.N. *jt. auth.*

Seshagiri Rao, D.
    Teaching the slow-learners in mathematics. *Indian Education* 11(4) Jl 1981 p 29-31

SETH - SHETH

Sheth, Ansuya T.

Systems approach to community development : An empirical analysis. *Indian J Adult Education* 45(4) Ap 1984 p 26-29

Sheth, D.L.

The problem of reservations : Economic backwardness or social injustice. *Indian J Adult Education* 47(5) My 1986 p 9-15+; 47(6) Je 1986 p 4-7+; 47(7) Jl 1986 p 14-21

Sheth, K.V. and Patel, K.R.

An exploration into occupational choices of higher secondary students. *Progress of Education* 56(6) Ja 1982 p 147-50+ tabs

Seth, M. *et al*

Behaviour pattern of educators : A study. *Indian J Adult Education* 44(3) Mr 1983 p 24-30+

Group interaction among adult women participating in the functional literacy programme in Delhi. *Indian J Extension Education* 19(1-2) Mr-Je 1983 p 62-68

Group interaction among women participants of a functional literacy programme in Delhi : A study. *Indian J Adult Education* 44(10) Oc 1983 p 24-28; *Indian J Extension Education* 19(1-2) Mr-Je 1983 p 62-68

Seth, Mridula

Experience of adult education teachers : An interview. *Indian J Adult Education* 43(7) Jl 1982 p 17-20

Mass education involving college students as instructors : A case study. *Indian J Adult Education* 47(1) Ja 1986 p 3-7

Seth, S.C.

Implications of future and the emerging educational personnel profile. *Teacher Education* 18(22-23) Ja-Ap 1983 p 33-54 tabs

Setharao, M.K. *et al*

An evaluation of the Summer Institute on Water Management in Black Soils. *Indian J Extension Education* 16(1-2) Je 1980 p 69-72 tabs refs

Sethi, A.S. and Gupta, Deepti

Development of moral judgement in boys and girls at two age levels. *J Education and Psychology* 42(1-2) Ap-Jl 1984 p 41-44 refs

Sethi, K.K.

Some thoughts on 10+2 system. *Education Quarterly* 32(2) Ap 1980 p 30-35

Sethi, B. *et al*

Some entrepreneurial characteristics in adoptionn of an improved farm technology. *Indian J Extension Education* 20(1-2) Je 1984 p 29-37 refs tabs

Shafi, Rafat S.

Preparing teaching learning materials for adult education. *Indian J Adult Education* 41(5) My 1980 p 15-18

Training kit for instructors. *Indian J Adult Education* 41(9) Se 1980 p 11-14

Shah, A.B. and Bhan, Susheela, *eds.*

Non-formal education and the NAEP. New Delhi, OUP. 1980, viii, 245p. Rs.65 *Book Rev, Education Quarterly* 33(2) Ap 1981 p 39-40; *J Education and Psychology* 39(3) Oc 1981 p 204; *Progress of Education* 56(5) De 1981 p 122

Shah, Anupama

Conventional and modern media in distance education. *University News* 24(42) 8 Nv 1986 p 69-72 refs

Opinions of college home science students regarding home science education in Assam. *Progress of Education* 56(11) Je 1982 p 269-74 refs tabs

Shah, Anupama and Chetenlal, Neera

Relative effectiveness of graphic aids and projected aids enriched with museum experiences in teaching food and digestion to VIII standard students of Navredna Higher Secondary School, Baroda, 1982-83. *Experiments in Education* 11(9) Nv 1983 p 151-59 refs tabs

Shah, Anupama and Gupta, Sandhya

Effectiveness of visual aids : A comparative study. *Indian J Adult Education* 47(6) Je 1986 p 21-26 refs

Shah, Anupama, and Shah, Rita

Level of satisfaction of teachers and students regarding the traditional and modern systems of education as practised in the two selected home science institutions. *J Education and Psychology* 41(3) Oc 1983 p 117-25 tabs

Shah, Beena

A study of job satisfaction of secondary school teachers in relation to their grade, organisation and sex. *Progress of Education* 60(3) Oc 1985 p 64-67 tabs

See also

Uniyal, M.P. *jt. auth.*

Shah, Beena and Sharma, Anshu

A study of the effect of family climate on students academic achievement. *Progress of Education* 59(5) De 1984 p 103-06 tabs

Shah, C.K.

Authoritarianism and some personality traits of school children. *J Education and Psychology* 40(1-2) Ap-Jl 1982 p 85-89

Shah, C.S.

Colleges in the Eastern region. *New Frontiers in Education* 10(2) Ap-Je 1980 p 52-56

Shah, C.Z.

An experiment in the subjective assessment of essays. *Progress of Education* 55(6) Ja 1981 p 150-54 tabs

Shah, G.B.

University goes to masses. *Indian J Adult Education* 40(5) My 1979 p 28-32

Shah, G.B. and Guha, S.

A study of adjustment and insecurity feeling among the adolesents of two types of family. *J Education and Psychology* 43(1) Ap 1985 p 54-58 refs

Shah, Ghanashyam

Economic differentiation and tribal identity : A case study of Chaudhris. Delhi, Ajanta. 1984, 152p. Rs.80 *Book Rev, Perspectives in Education* 1(2) Ap 1985 p 128-31

Shah, Gunvant, B.

Distance education : An overview. *University News* 24(42) 8 Nv 1986 p 10-12

Distance education for dark ghettos. *Teacher Today* 28(4) Ap-Je 1986 p 6-11

Distance education. *Teacher Today* 24(1) Jl-Se 1981 p 16-20

Doctoral research in India. *Teacher Today* 25(3) Ja-Mr 1983 p 1-5

Peace education through yoga. *Teacher Today* 27(2) Oc-De 1984 p 38-41

Shah, J.N.

A comparative study of some personal and psychological variables and reading comprehension. *J Education and Psychology* 39(2) Jl 1981 p 97-105

Shah, K.M.

Impact of parents vocations and education upon the interest of pupils. *J Education and Psychology* 44(3-4) Jl-De 1986 p 153-57

Shah, K.R.

Adult education in Gujarat : An evaluation study. *Indian J Adult Education* 44(11) Nv 1983 p 22-27 +

Demand and financing of higher education in Canada. *J Higher Education* 5(2) Aut 1979 p 251-52

Shah, L.R.

Involvement of universities and colleges in the National Adult Education Programme : An appraisal. *Prasar* 7(1-2) Ap-Jl 1980 p 1-10

Role of universites in the National Adult Education Programme. *Indian J Adult Education* 40(7) Jl 1979 p 31-35

Universities and national development : Linkage with environment. *Education Quarterly* 31(2) Jl 1979 p 17-19

Shah, M.M.

A study of socio-economic status of the first year college students of M.S. University, Baroda in relation to the academic achieve- ment. *Experiments in Education* 11(3) My 1983 p 44-47

Shah, M.M. and Kishan, R.

Contribution of intelligence, adjustment, dependency and class- room trust to academic achievement. *J Institute of Educational Research* 6(1) Ja 1982 p 13-16 refs

Effect of intelligence, adjustment, achievement. *J Education and Psychology* 39(4) Ja 1982 p 241-47 refs

Shah, M.M. *et al*

Science education : Objectives. *Experiements in Education* 7(7) Se 1979 p 121-28

Shah, Madhu *et al*

Adoption in student teaching : A tryout. *Experiments in Education* 9(9) Nv 1981 p 156-59; 10(2) Ap 1982 p 38-40

Shah, Madhuri R.

Zakir Husain Memorial Lecture : Role of continuing education. *Indian J Adult Education* 42(12) De 1981 p 19-33

Shah, Maya

Economic factors explaining variations in literacy rates in rural areas : A case study of Gujarat. Baroda, M.S. Univ of Baroda (Economics Services

No. 7). 1981, 58p. Rs.10 *Book Rev, Indian J Adult Education* 44(4) Ap 1983 p 40

Shah, Rita

See

Shah, Anupama *jt. auth.*

Shah, S.G.

Development and tryout of multi media package an effective questioning in the context of microteaching. *Indian Education* 10(9-10) De 1980-Ja 1981 p 16-19

An investigation into teachers reactions to self instruction multi- media package course. *Quest in Education* 17(4) Oc 1980 p 360-66 refs

Shah, S. Shamim

Educational survey report on Muslim managed schools and colleges in India with special emphasis on science education. New Delhi, Hamdard Educ Soc. 226p. *Book Rev, Education Quarterly* 37(2) Sum 1985 p 69-71

Shah, V.

See

Chatterjee, T.K. *jt. auth.*

Shah, Varasha M.

See Deb, Subimal *jt. auth.*

Shah, Vimal P. and Patel, Tara

Social context of tribal education. New Delhi, Concept. 212p. Rs.150 *Book Rev, Education Quarterly* 38(2) Sum 1986 p 49-51

Who goes to college? Rachna Pra. 1977, 219p. *Book Rev, J Higher Education* 4(3) Spr 1979 p 427-30

Shahare, M.L.

Eradicating women's illiteracy : A challenge. *Indian J Adult Educaiton* 45(12) De 1984 p 32-38

Shaheen Saeed

Pupils and teachers' perception of the aims of education : A comparative study. *Indian Educational Rev* 17(3) Jl 1982 p 1-9

Shahi, Suresh Prasad

See

Sinha, Awadesh Kumar *jt. auth.*

Shahoo, Shankar

See

Tripathi, A. *et al jt. auths.*

Shaktawat, G.S.

See

Intodia, S.I. *jt. auth.*

Shakuntala, S.N.

See

Sudha, B.G. *jt. auth.*

Shamim Akhtar

See

Siddiqui, Zakia A. *jt. auth.*

Shamsuddin

Causes of general backwardness among school children. *Indian Education* 10(8) Nv 1980 p 33-36

Causes of general backwardness among school children. *Primary Teacher* 11(3) Jl 1986 p 9-12
Education under Moslem rule. *Indian Education* 9(12) Mr 1980 p 27-30
Human relationships and modern high schools administration. *Indian Education* 11(1-2) Ap-My 1981 p 64-66
The influence of socio-economic factors on teachers career. *Indian Education* 10(3) Je 1980 p 33-39
Maintaining school records. *Primary Teacher* 11(4) Oc 1986 p 23-26
Marks of leadership among children. *Education Quarterly* 32(1) Ja 1980 p 28-29
Methods of moral education. *Progress of Education* 56(12) Jl 1982 p 289-91
Modern education and training in yoga. *Progress of Education* 60(8) Mr 1986 p 188-90 +
A new look on nation builders. *Primary Teacher* 10(3) Jl 1985 p 1-4
Noble callig but poor returns. *J Indian Education* 10(5) Ja 1985 p 29-33
Practice teaching : Its supervision. *Asian J Psychology and Education* 4(1) Ja 1979 p 31-34
Pursuit of excellence through education : A few issues. *Primary Teacher* 11(2) Ap 1986 p 1-3
The role of teachers in a changing society. *Education Quarterly* 36(2) Ap 1984 p 38-39
The role of teachers in changing society. *Indian Education* 10(7) Oc 1980 p 17-20
The role of teachers in a changing society. *J Indian Education* 12(4) Nv 1986 p 49-51
Suggestions for maintaining school records. *Progress of Education* 53(6) Ja 1981 p 157-60
Teachers as builders of a new nation. *Education Quarterly* 35(4) Oc 1983 p 14-16+ refs
Teachers as builders of a new nation. *Progress of Education* 59(8) Mr 1985 p 168-70+
Teachers, students and parents. *Indian Education* 10(12) Mr 1981 p 8-12
University education today. *Progress of Education* 59(5) De 1984 p 95-98 +

Shankar
See also
under full name/surname, e.g., Udai Shankar

Shankar, Lakshmi
Sex education. New Delhi, Sterling. 1978, 168p. Rs.50 *Book Rev, Education Quarterly* 31(2) Jl 1979 p 42

Shankar, Laxmi and Panda, Santosh K.
Achievement of regular and correspondence students : A comparative study. *Progress of Education* 56(10) My 1982 p 236-40+ tabs

Shankar, R.
Literacy and adoption of improved agricultural practices, Deoria study. *Indian J Adult Education* 40(3) Mr 1979 p 31-38

Shankaram, V.
See
Anand, Rishi *jt. auth.*
Dorasami, K. *jt. auth.*

Shanmuga Sundaram, R.
A study of academic achievement in relation to motivation and self-concept. *J Educational Research and Extension* 18(2) Oc 1981 p 40-48 refs tabs
Shanmugasundaram, V.
Human values in higher education. *University News* 22(48) 23 De 1984 p 5-7 refs
Shanmugham M. and Sivagamsundari, M.K.
Effectiveness of coaching and self-study in schools. *Experiments in Education* 8(8) Oc 1980 p 145-48 refs tabs
Shanmugham, N.
Inplant experience programme. *Experiments in Education* 6(5) Jl 1978 p 75-78
Shanthamani, V.S.
A comparative study of R&D units with special reference to motivation, involvement and level of aspiration. *Asian J Psychology and Education* 9(4) 1982 p 1-12
Shao-xi-Shi
Higher education in China. *University News* 23(14) 8 Ap 1985 p 2-3
Sharanjit Kaur and Gakhar, Sudesh
Academic achievement among children of working and non-working mothers in relation to socio-economic status and mothers attitude towards education. *Quest in Education* 18(3) Jl 1981 p 228-34 refs
Shardamba Rao and Phalachandha, B.
Towards a programme for educational health. *J Indian Education* 7(3) Se 1979 p 38-42

SHARMA - SARMA

Sharma, A.D.
See
Bhardwaj, R. *jt. auth.*
Sharma, A.K.
Formation and role of peace value concepts of the number system at the elementary stage of education. *Quest in Education* 17(2) Ap 1980 p 181-87
Sarma, A.L.N. *et al*
Need for equatic ecosystem education in the context of environmental science education in the formal school system. *Education Quarterly* 37(3) Aut 1985 p 8-12 refs
Sharma, A.P. and Chaturvedi, Kanak
Verbal interaction patterns of pre-school teachers through observation technique of equivalent talk categories. (E.T.C.) *J Education and Psychology* 30(3) Oc 1978 p 148-53
Sharma, Adarsh
What ails our school and college magazine. *J Indian Education* 11(3) Se 1985 p 61-62
See also
Gupta, Aneeta *jt. auth.*

Sharma, Anshu
See
Shah, Beena *jt. auth.*

Sharma, Arun Kumar
Educational goals and drop-out factors in a rural population. *Indian Educational Rev* 18(3) Jl 1983 p 1-7 tabs

Sharma, Arvind
Do all students in departments of studies in religion constitute a single population? *J Higher Education* 4(1) Mon 1978 p 86-91 appdx refs
A new method of student evaluation. *Educational Rev* 87(5) My 1981 p 83-84
Reflection of the current controversy on the teaching of comparative religion in Queensland schools. *Progress of Education* 56(9) Ap 1982 p 204-09

Sharma, Aryendra Kumar
See
Sharma, K.G. *jt. auth.*

Sharma, Ashwani Kumar
Creativity and its components as effected by socio-economic status and personality. *Experiments in Education* 8(7) Se 1980 p 129-32 refs tabs
Creativity in relation to socio-economic status and academic achievement. *Experiments in Education* 9(9) Nv 1981 p 153-56 refs
See also
Jarial, Gurpal Singh *jt. auth.*

Sharma, Ashwani Kumar and Jarial, Gurpal Singh
A factorial study of the effect of socio-economic status (SES) adjustment and their interaction upon the creativity of high school students. *Experiments in Education* 9(9) Nv 1981 p 151-53 refs tabs

Sharma, Atmananda
Education for a productive and rewarding life. *J Indian Education* 6(3) Se 1980 p 14-21
See also
Kaushik, Shashilata *jt. auth.*

Sharma, B.D.
Tribal development : The concept and the frame. New Delhi, Prachi Prakashan, 1978. 220p. Rs. 36 *Book Rev, J Indian Education* 7(2) Jl 1979 p 70; *Teacher Today* 25(2) Oc-De 1982 p 102-03

Sharma, B.K.
See
Das, P. *jt. auth.*

Sharma, Balender and Gupta, S.P.
A study of the relationship between organisation climate and teachers job satisfaction. *Educational Rev* 88(10) Oc 1982 p 177-79 refs
A study of the relationship between organisational climate and teachers job satisfaction. *J Educational Research and Extension* 19(3) Ja 1983 p 143-49

Sharma, Bharat Bhusan
Experimental verification of various methods of examination in history at the lower and higher stages. *Indian Educational Rev* 14(4) Oc 1979 p 47-53

Sharma, C.D.

Organisation of libraries in schools and their effective use. *Teacher Today* 25(2) Oc-De 1982 p 44-50 refs

Sharma, C. Ganesh

Life style and aging. *Asian J Psychology and Education* 7(1) Ja 1981 p 25-26

Sharma, C.M. and Pareek, M.

A study of motives of secondary school teachers. *Progress of Education* 58(1) My 1984 p 241-45 refs tabs

Sharma, D.K.

Decision-making and organisational health in a technical education system. *Experiments in Education* 12(8) Oc 1984 p 133-37 refs tabs

Distance education systems of the future. *University News* 24(42) 8 Nv 1986 p 55-57 refs

Organisational health and decision-making in higher education : A comparative study. *University News* 24(38) 8 Nv 1986 p 3-5

To study the effectiveness of Peers managed micro teaching programme under simulated conditions. *Experiments in Education* 10(8) Oc 1982 p 150-54 + tabs

See also

Darji, D.R. *jt. auth.*

Sanoria, Y.C. *jt. auth.*

Sharma, D.K. and Darji, D.R.

Effective management of universities and research *J Higher Education* 5(1) Mon 1979 p 112-16

Management of a university. *Educational Rev* 92(10) Oc 1986 p 169-71

Sharma, D.K. and Garg, Chandra

Computer assisted instruction. *J Indian Education* 5(4) Nv 1979 p 17-22 refs tabs

Sharma, D.K. and Sharma, R.K.

Educational technology for teacher education : An experimental study. *J Indian Education* 6(6) Mr 1981 p 36-41 refs

Sharma, D.K. and Tyagi, M.P.

Effect of yoga asana on learning : An experiment on primary students. *J Institute of Educational Research* 4(2) My 1980 p 30-34 refs tabs

Sharma, D.K. and Yash Pal Singh

Hardware educational technology : An experiment with television instruction. *Experiments in Education* 9(10) De 1981 p 176-82 refs

A study on television instruction. *J Institute of Educational Research* 6(1) Ja 1982 p 17-22 refs tabs

Sharma, D.L.

Teachers teaching skills and the teacher education programme. *Progress of Education* 55(8) Mr 1981 p 202-03 refs

Sharma, D.R. and Surendra Singh

A study of the effectiveness of programmed learning method to teach modern mathematics to high, normal and low creative students. *Experiments in Education* 9(3) My 1981 p 49-54 refs

Sharma, D.V.

Environmental education for adult education functionaries. *Indian J Adult*

Education 41(3) Mr 1980 p 3-5

Investment in adult education instructors. *Indian J Adult Education* 41(12) De 1980 p 9-12 +

Sharma, Dinesh

Issues in educational journalism. *J Indian Education* 11(3) Se 1985 p 36-38

See also

Pachaury, A.C. *jt. auth.*

Sharma, Dinesh and Pachaury, A.C.

Creative child : Sikkimese teachers perception. *J Indian Education* 11(1) My 1985 p 34-41 refs tabs

Sharma, G.D.

Institutional costs of university education. New Delhi, Assn of Indian University. 1980, 165p. Rs.40 *Book Rev, Indian Educational Rev* 15(3) Jl 1980 p 125-26; *J Higher Education* 6(1-3) 1980-81 p 163-64

Resource allocation on education : An inter, intra-country and inter-temporal pattern analysis. Assn Indian Univ. 1978, 139p. Rs.20 *Book Rev, J Higher Education* 4(3) SPr 1979 p 426-27

Teaching language through environment. *Primary Teacher* 5(3) Jl 1980 p 36-40

Sharma, G.D., *eds.*

See

Amrik Singh *jt. auth.*

Sharma, G.R.

Adjustment problems of college students preparing for four selected professions : A comparative study. *Indian Educational Rev* 17(4) Oc 1982 p 68-78 refs tabs

Adjustment problems of non-professional college students. *J Higher Education* 4(2) Aut 1978 p 262-66

A comparative study of adjustment problems of professional and non-professional college students. *J Education and Psychology* 37(2) Jl 1979 p 130-38 refs tabs

A peep into Glaser's model of instructional system. *Teacher Today* 22(1) Jl-Se 1979 p 36-39

Research on family as a determinant of child's personality development. *J Educational Research and Extension* 17(3) Ja 1981 p 185-90 refs

Seeking a model of good teaching. *J Indian Education* 7(2) Se 1979 p 15-19

Sharma, Gaya Prasad

Children's curiosity and teaching. *Primary Teacher* 5(3) Jl 1980 p 41-42

Sharma, Geeta

See

Sharma, R.A. *jt. auth.*

Sharma, Gopal

The art of story-telling. *Primary Teacher* 10(3) Jl 1985 p 35-36

Sharma, H.L.

Orientation of teachers for non-formal education centres. *Primary Teacher* 11(3) Jl 1986 p 26-28

Sharma, H.S.

Influence of socio-economic status on the nature of the problems of adolescent boys. *J Educational Research and Extension* 18(4) Ap 1982 p 230-35 refs tabs

Sharma, Hari Datt

Development schedule for first standard primary students. *Primary Teacher* 6(4) Oc 1981 p 26-28

How to teach perception - deviant children? *Primary Teacher* 7(3) Jl 1982 p 9-11

Sharma, Hari Shankar

Inter-relations between a teacher and a child. *Primary Teacher* 4(4) Oc 1979 p 28-30

Why do children forget? *Primary Teacher* 8(3) Jl 1983 p 34-36

Sharma, Harish and Aggarwal, Veena

A study of congnitive tasks in relation to intelligence and school achievement. *J Institute of Educational Research* 4(3) Se 1980 p 36-41 refs

Sharma, Harish and Madhumati

A study of performance of the entrants of adult education centres of Chandigarh in relation to their intelligence and socio-economic status. *Quest in Education* 19(1) Ja 1982 p 58-63 + refs tabs

Sharma, Harish and Sushma

A study of intelligence achievement, motivation and adjustment of the juvenile delinquents. *J Institute of Educational Research* 9(3) Se 1985 p 21-26 refs tabs

Sharma, Harish Chandra and Ahuja, Malvinder

Anxiety and step-size as correlates of performance through programmed instruction. *J Education and Psychology* 36(4) Ja 1979 p 173-79

Performance as a function of anxiety and feed back in a self- instruction situation. *Quest in Education* 18(1) Ja 1981 p 39-45 refs

Sharma, Harswarup

Academeic grades and verbal behaviour. *J Educational Research and Extension* 18(1) Jl 1981 p 16-20 tabs

Sharma, I.S.

The language centre of Birmingham. *Primary Teacher* 9(2) Ap 1984 p 21-23

Policy for the periodic change of text books in India. *J Indian Education* 8(6) Mr 1983 p 42-45 tabs

Teaching language through games. *Primary Teacher* 8(3) Jl 1983 p 27-28

Written expression : Different aspects. *Primary Teacher* 8(1) Ja 1983 p 14-17

Writing school text-books : Pedagogical dimensions. *J Indian Education* 10(6) Mr 1985 p 33-38 refs

Sharma, I.S. and Mukhopadhyay, B.

Language comprehensibility : A problem in primary school text books. *Primary Teacher* 7(3) Jl 1982 p 5-8

Sharma, Inder Prabha

Adult education and communal harmony : Role and relevance. *Indian J Adult Education* 45(10) Oc 1984 p 48+

Sharma, Inder Prabha and Patel, Sushil Kumar

Adult education programme in Chandigarh : An empirical study *Indian J Adult Education* 47(5) My 1986 p 24-28

Sharma, J.D.

Implementation of NAEP : A look back. *Indian J Adult Education* 40(10-11) Oc-Nv 1979 p 59-63

Implementation of the NAEP : A short review. *Indian J Adult Education* 40(10-11) Oc-Nv 1979 p 52-54

National Adult Education Programme and the role of voluntary organisations. *Indian J Adult Education* 39(9) Se 1978 p 38-41

Sharma, J.P.

Comparative study of modular teaching and traditional teaching methods at B.Ed level in subject of civic. *Progress of Education* 57(9) Ap 1983 p 202-03 +

See also

Banga, Shakuntla *jt. auth.*

Sharma, J.P. and Hooda, R.C.

Content-based methodology and method-based content strategies for pre-service teachers training. *Experiments in Education* 9(4) Ja 1981 p 59-63 refs

Content-cum-methodology strategy. *Progress of Education* 56(2) Se 1981 p 45+

Sharma, J.P. and Syag, R.N.

Hoshangabad science teaching experiment for improving teachers training. *Progress of Education* 55(10) My 1981 p 261-63

Sharma, Jagdish C.

Linkages among research, extension, farmers and input and credit organisations at various levels. *Indian J Extension Education* 18(1-2) Je 1982 p 16-24 refs

Sharma, Jai Kishan

Education for third world countries. Delhi, B.R. Pub. 1986, *Book Rev, J Educational Planning and Administration* 1(1) Oc 1986 p 91-92

Sharma, Jai Prakash

Are we interested in sending our children to primary schools? *Teacher Today* 24(4) Ap-Je 1982 p 65-71 refs

A comparative study of reliability of true-false items and multiple choice items. *Rajasthan Board J Education* 19(2-3) Ap-Se 1983 p 1-5

A comparative study of three teaching strategies at B. Ed level. *Experiments in Education* 11(3) My 1983 p 41-44

Sharma, Janak Raj

School library in the modern concept of education. *Teacher Today* 29(1) Jl-Se 1986 p 64-71 refs

Sharma, K.G. and Sharma, Aryendra Kumar

Personality traits of democratic and *laissez faire* type of teachers. *Indian Educational Rev* 15(2) Ap 1980 p 109-13 refs tabs

Sharma, K.K.

The art of teaching : An analysis. *Educational Rev* Se 1983 p 145-47 refs

Microteaching at pre-service level. *J Indian Education* 7(3) Se 1979 p 24-28

See also

Srivastava, A.B.L. *jt. auth.*

Sharma, K.K. and Abraham, Mary

Exploration of local resources for science teaching. *Experiments in*

Education 7(2) Ap 1979 p 31-34

Sharma, K.K. and Walia, S.

Perceptual change in teacher trainees : A personal perspective. *Progress of Education* 53(9) Ap 1979 p 176-86 refs

Sharma, K.K. *et al*

A case for Indian philosophy of education : Some issues. *Progress of Education* 51(4) Nv 1982 p 74-76

Sharma, K.N.

Semantic retrievals in creative products. *Asian J Psychology and Education* 5(1-3) 1979 p 9-20 refs

Sharma, K.R.

Scheduled tribes and equality of educational opportunity. *Indian Education* 12(10) Ja 1983 p 10-13

A study of educational backwardness of tribal students. *Educational Quarterly* 35(2) Ap 1983 p 33-38

A study of language development, scholastic achievement and tribal students. *Research Bulletin* 14(1-2) Mr-Je 1984 p 3-21 tabs

Teaching the tribal children. *Education Quarterly* 35(4) Oc 1983 p 26-28

Tribal students and role of schools. *Primary Teacher* 9(4) Oc 1984 p 11-13

Sharma, Kamala Kant

See

Bhargava, S.C. *jt. auth.*

Srivastava, A.B.L. *jt. auth.*

Sharma, Khemraj

Improving the quality of tribal education. *Education Quarterly* 32(4) Oc 1980 p 22-26

Sharma, Krishan Dev

Education of a national minority : A case of the Indian Muslims. New Delhi, Kalamkar Pra. 263p. Rs.50 *Book Rev, J Indian Education* 5(5) Ja 1980 p 86

Sharma, Krishnan Kumar

Effect of different techniques of feedback upon the attainment of teaching skills related to stimulus variation among teachers. *Indian Educational Rev* 14(4) Oc 1979 p 54-60

Sharma, Kumud

Women and the media : A case for critical correction. *Indian J Adult Education* 46(9) Se 1985 p 27-30

Sharma, M.D.

Attitudes in vital areas. *J Indian Education* 8(3) Se 1982 p 9-13 refs tabs

The attitudes of convent and general school boys : A comparative study. *J Indian Education* 6(3) Se 1980 p 40-43

Sharma, M.K.

Education in Arunachal Pradesh : Contribution by Vivekanand Kendra. *EPA Quarterly Bulletin* 7(1-2) Ap-Jl 1984 p 6-14 refs

A plea for health educational pyramid in Assam. *EPA Quarterly Bulletin* 6(2) Jl 1983 p 13-21 refs

Social isolates in classrooms. *Educational Rev* 87(1) Ja 1981 p 15-17

Sharma, M.L.
See
Raj Singh *jt. auth.*
Sharma, Mali Ram
An apology for new education. *Teacher Today* 27(4) Ap-Je 1985 p 63-69
Dear teacher, do you really teach? *Teacher Today* 24(3) Ja-Mr 1982 p 75-80
Dizzying disorientation. *Rajasthan Board J Education* 21(3-4) Jl-De 1985 p 1-9
Is there anything like teachers will? *Teacher Today* 24(1) Jl-Se 1981 p 50-57
Who fails, student or the system? *Rajasthan Board J Education* 20(3) Jl-Se 1984 p 1-7
Sharma, Mohindera
A study of conflict in a university. *J Higher Education* 4(1) Mon 1978 p 1-10 refs ft-n
Sharma, Motilal
Dimensions of school climate. *Indian Educational Rev* 15(1) Ja 1980 p 35-45 refs tabs
Distance education. *Teacher Today* 27(2) Oc-De 1984 p 44-48
Educational technology in adult continuing education. *National J Education* 2(1) Se 1979 p 50-56 refs
Non-formal education for rural development. *Teacher Today* 21(2) Oc-De 1978 p 19-27 refs
Radio vision as an educational medium. *Indian Education* 12(10) Ja 1983 p 17-20
School climate and its relationship with headmasters leadership behaviour. *Teacher Today* 24(3) Ja-Mr 1982 p 42-49 refs
See also
Muse, Ivan D. *jt. auth.*
Sharma, Motilal and Oberai, Meena
Instruction through radio vision : A comparative study. *Indian Educational Rev* 18(4) Oc 1983 p 37-46
Radio vision in and out of the classroom. *Education Quarterly* 34(2) Ap 1982 p 17-21
Sharma, Motilal and Tripathi, C.K.
Radio vision and biology class : An exploratory study. *Progress of Education* 55(2) Se 1980 p 45-50
Teaching history through radio vision. *J Indian Education* 6(3) Se 1980 p 48-50
Sharma, Mukul Kumar
Effect strategy for college students assessment. *Educational Rev* 90(9) Se 1984 p 128-32 refs
Sharma, N.R.
Locus of control among high and low achievers at different levels of socio-economic status. *J Institute of Educational Research* 9(1) Jl 1985 p 1-5 refs
Sharma, Nandita
Methods and contents in teacher preparation for adult education. *Teacher*

Education 16(18-19) Ja-Ap 1982 p 48-52

Preparation of adult education teachers : Methods and contents. *Indian J Adult Education* 43(5) My 1982 p 18-20 +

Sharma, O.P.

Academic freedom in India. *Teacher Today* 24(3) Ja-Mr 1982 p 27-32

Education for national development. Meerut, Anu Pra. 162p. Rs.50 *Book Rev, Teacher Today* 24(4) Ap-Je 1982 p 136-37

Sharma, P.

See

Saxena, A.K. *jt. auth.*

Sharma, P.C.

Concept and objectives of National Adult Education Programme. *Progress of Education* 53(1-2) Jl 1979 p 218-22

Intake criteria for teacher trainees : A study. *Indian Education* 10(3) Je 1980 p 29-32

NAEP : The national and regional objectives. *Indian J Adult Education* 40(6) Je 1979 p 42-44

Some psycho-social attributes of student leaders : A differential study. *J Higher Education* 6(1-3) 1980-81 p 136-48 refs tabs

Sharma, P.C. and Sharma, Ram Dev

Teaching skills : Identification and developing instructional material for it : An analytical view. *Educational Rev* 91(5-6) My-Je 1985 p 94-95

Sharma, P.D.

Mass media for promotion of sports and physical education. *Primary Teacher* 11(2) Ap 1986 p 28-30

Posture education in Indian schools. *J Indian Education* 7(2) Jl 1979 p 48-51

The role of mass media in the promotion of sports and physical education in the country. *Progress of Education* 61(4-5) Nv-De 1986 p 89-91

Sharma, P.K. and Gupta, V.K.

An attitudinal study of experienced and non-experienced B.Ed. teachers towards their profession. *Progress of Education* 55(12) Jl 1981 p 321-24 tabs

Sharma, Prema

Development of social competence : Schools obligation to children and adolescents. *Quest in Education* 17(3) Jl 1980 p 217-27 refs

Sharma, Premlata

Adaptation in instructional material : A prime need for hearing impaired children in IED. *J Indian Education* 12(2) Jl 1986 p 54-59

Learning disability : Challenge to primary school teachers. *Primary Teacher* 11(3) Jl 1986 p 20-22

Study habits and underachievement among rural girls. *J Education and Psychology* 42(3) Oc 1984 p 115-18 refs

Sharma, Purnima

Population education in education institutes. *Rajasthan Board J Education* 22(1) Ja-Mr 1986 p 8-17

Sharma, R.A.

Factor analysis of language learning abilities in Hindi achievement with special reference to delta class. *J Education and Psychology* 39(1) Ap

1981 p 22-27 refs tabs

Sharma, R.A. and Jain, Rakesh

Non-verbal : A challenge to verbals teacher behaviour studies. *Progress of Education* 60(3) Oc 1985 p 54-58 refs tabs

Sharma, R.A. and Kurnali, Krishna

Relationship between creative structures of high school science students. *J Education and Psychology* 41(3) Oc 1983 p 133-37

Sharma, R.A. and Mahesh, Vimla

The classroom verbal interaction patterns of effective and ineffective teachers. *J Education and Psychology* 37(2) Jl 1979 p 90-96 refs

Sharma, R.A. and Sharma, Geeta

Factor analysis of language learning abilities in Hindi achievement with speical reference to delta class. *J Education and Psychology* 39(1) Ap 1981 p 12-21 refs tabs

Sharma, R.C.

Environmental education. Delhi, Metropolitan. 1981, 144p. *Book Rev, Indian Educational Rev* 19(1) Ja 1984 p 157-59

Teacher association : Management relationship. *EPA Quarterly Bulletin* 6(1) AP 1983 p 1-13

See also

Mehta, P. *jt. auth.*

Sharma, R.D.

Emergence of primary school psychology. *Primary Teacher* 9(2) Ap 1984 p 16-18

Emerging of early childhood education in India. *J Indian Education* 12(1) My 1986 p 31-40 refs

Nutrition education in adult education programme. *Indian J Adult Education* 47(7) Jl 1986 p 22-28 refs

Student teachers and the teaching profession. *Experiments in Education* 12(8) Oc 1984 p 145-49; 12(11) Ja 1985 p 199-201 refs tabs

Sharma, R.K.

See

Sharma, D.K. *jt. auth.*

Sharma, R.P. and Verma, M.N.

The effect of schedules of reinforcement and extroversion on programmed instruction achievement. *Indian Educational Rev* 14(4) Oc 1979 p 33-42 refs tabs

Sharma, R.R.

A study of the preference of a school subject. *J Institute of Educational Research* 6(3) Se 1982 p 29-32 refs

See also

Uniyal, M.P. *jt. auth.*

Sharma, R.S.

Curriculum for population education. *Rajasthan Board J Education* 15(2) Ap-Je 1979 p 1-12 refs

Developing educational technology for deprived sections of the Indian society. *Bulletin of Non-Formal Education* 3(3) De 1985 p 1-17

Developing reading habits among children. *Primary Teacher* 4(2) Ap 1979 p 23-26

Non-formal education in search of a direction. *Bulletin of Non-Formal Education* 2(2) Oc 1984 p 20-26 refs
Supervision of schools for visually handicapped. *Education Quarterly* 36(1) Ja 1984 p 36-45
Sharma, Radha Rani
Education of the gifted. *Teacher Today* 23(2) Oc-De 1980 p 37-43 refs
Education of women in India : Inequalities and bottlenecks. *Education Quarterly* 34(4) Oc 1982 p 20-27 refs tabs
Self-concept and adjustment as factors in academic achievement. *Indian Educational Rev* 18(2) Ap 1983 p 46-59 refs tabs
Sessional evaluation in colleges : A research study. *J Higher Education* 7(3) Spr 1982 p 280-86 tabs
Sharma, Ram Dev
See
Sharma, P.C. *jt. auth.*
Sharma, Ram Nath
Sri Aurobindo's philosophy of education. Agra, Vinod Pustak Mandir. 1985. 244p. Rs.30 *Book Rev, Education Quarterly* 37(3) Aut 1985 p 62-63
Sharma, Ramesh Chandra
Impact of non-detention on scholastic achievement at school stage. *EPA Quarterly Bulletin* 6(1) Ap 1983 p 23-28
School characteristics and incidence of stagnation in rural primary schools. *Primary Teacher* 8(4) Oc 1983 p 18-22 refs
Sharma, Ravindranath
University reforms in India : Problems and solutions. *Education Rev* 90(1) Ja 1984 p 10-13; 90(2) Fe 1984 p 30-33; 90(3) Mr 1984 p 50-53; 90(4) Ap 1984 p 65-67 refs
Sharma, S.
See
Kumar, A. *jt. auth.*
Sharma, S. and Singh, T.R.
Rural women's level of knowledge and persuation for the acceptance of solar cooker device. *Indian J Extension Education* 20(1-2) Je 1984 p 47-51 tabs
Sharma, S.K.
Effect of megha teaching approach in acquisition of teaching skills *J Education and Psychology* Ap-Jl 1982 p 48-52 refs
See also
Gupta, A.K. *jt. auth.*
Syag, R.N. *et al jt. auths.*
Sharma, S.K. and Gupta, A.K.
A comparative study of the effect of different types of feedbacks in microteaching. *Asian J Psychology and Education* 9(1) Ja 1982 p 41-44 refs tabs
Sharma, S.L.
Modernising effect of university education. New Delhi, Allied. 1979, 236p. Rs.45 *Book Rev, J Higher Education* 6(1-3) 1980-81 p 161-63
Sharma, S.N.
Effect of academic motivation on cognitive and effective behaviours. *Indian*

Educational Rev 16(2) Ap 1981 p 108-12 refs

Systems approach to education and training. *Teacher Education* 16(18-19) Ja-Ap 1982 p 3-8 refs

Sharma, S.R.

American influence on Indian education. New Delhi, Raaj Pra. 1979, 175p. Rs.70 *Book Rev, Education Quarterly* 32(2) Ap 1980 p 50-51

Sharma, Sachidanand

Teaching arithmetic in primary schools. *Primary Teacher* 8(1) Ja 1983 p 29-30

Sharma, Sadhana

See

Sharma, Sagar *jt. auth.*

Sharma, Sagar and Sharma, Sadhna

Interrelationship among measures of job involvement, job satisfaction and general anxiety. *Asian J Psychology and Education* 3(2) Jl 1978 p 35-39 refs

Sharma, Santosh

Evaluation in professional courses. *J Indian Education* 12(1) My 1986 p 49-51

Sharma, Savitri

Women students in India : Status and personality. New Delhi, Concept Pub. 171p. Rs.50 *Book Rev, Education Quarterly* 32(2) Jl 1980 p 46-47 : *Indian Education* 9(12) Mr 1980 p 45-47; *Teacher Education* 14(10-11) Ja-Ap 1980 p 76-77; *Teacher Today* 23(1) Jl-Se 1980 p 103; *Indian Educational Rev* 15(2) Ap 1980 p 128-29

Sharma, Sita Ram

American influence on teacher education in post independence India. *J Education and Psychology* 37(3) Oc 1979 p 158-66 ref

Sharma, Suresh K.

See

Gupta, Arun Kumar *jt. auth.*

Sharma, Sushma

Prevention of disruptive behaviour. *Primary Teacher* 10(4) Oc 1985 p 37-39

Role of classroom management behaviour in teaching effectiveness. *Primary Teacher* 10(1) Ja 1985 p 16-18

Sharma, Swadesh

Lets draw figures from doodling. *Primary Teacher* 5(4) Oc 1980 p 24-30 figs

Sharma, T.R.

Toppers in the post-graduate examinations of Punjabi University : A study *Educational Rev* 19(1) Ja 1984 p 1-17

Sharma, Usha

See

Anand Bhushan *jt. auth.*

Sharma, V.N.

Kusiarie : A mysterious butter-fly. *Primary Teacher* 4(1) Ja 1979 p 23

Sharma, V.P.

Effectiveness of test-types on high and low achievers. *Indian Educational Rev* 20(4) Oc 1985 p 78-89

Scaling of examination scores. *Indian Educational Rev* 20(4) Oc 1985 p 40-49

Sharma, V.P. and Bhargava, Mahesh

Academic attainment and prolonged deprivation in relation to some personal variables. *J Education and Psychology* 37(4) Ja 1980 p 247-54 refs

Sharma, V.P. and Kathuria, P.R.

Scholastic achievements and vocational interests as correlated to prolonged deprivation. *J Education and Psychology* 41(1-2) Ap-Jl 1983 p 69-76

Sharma, V.R.

Functional education and integrated rural development. *Our Education* 5 Jl 1984 p 17-22

Sharma, Veer Narayan

Teaching of languages at primary levels. *Primary Teacher* 4(4) Oc 1979 p 24-26

Sharma, Vibha

See

Sansanwal, D.N. *et al jt. auths.*

Sharma, Y.D.

See

Nautiyal, K.C. *jt. auth.*

Sharma, Purohit, D.K.

See

Sharma, D.K.

Sharraja, Jagmohan

Importance of music in elementary education. *Primary Teacher* 6(3) Jl 1981 p 16-18

Shashikala Devi, U. and Satyanarayana, B.S.

High school students and teachers interest in yoga as a part of school curriculum. *Quest in Education* 17(4) Oc 1980 p 352-59 refs

Shashi Kant

Attitude of teaching trainees towards teaching during pre and post student teaching period : A differential study. *Asian J Psychology and Education* 3(3) Nv 1978 p 1-5 refs tabs

Shawn, D.G.

Planning a new school for visually handicapped children in Nigeria. *National J Education* 7(1) Se 1984 p 51-56

Shejwalkar, P.C.

Effective reorganisation for higher education. *Progress of Education* 56(3) Oc 1981 p 71-73

Shelat, N.A. and Mohanty, S.B.

Innovation in student teaching. *Educational Rev* 89(4-6) My-Je 1983 p 94-95

Shelat, Neela and Jena, Shribatsa

Pricing of higher education. *New Frontiers in Education* 11(3) Jl-Se 1981 p 73-79 refs

Sheldon, Neil A.

Fundamental of computing. London, Hutchinson. 128p. *Book Rev, Education Quarterly* 38(3) Aut 1986 p 46

Shelly, Shabri

Economic dimensions of inequality in India. *New Frontiers in Education* 16(2) Ap-Je 1986 p 41-45

Shen, Philip

Modernisation and the autocratic tradition in China. *New Frontiers in Education* 14(2) Ap-Je 1984 p 10-16 ft-n

Shete, N.B.

Agricultural training needs of tribal farmers in Maharashtra. *Indian J Extension Education* 14(3-4) Jl-De 1978 p 65-67

Characteristics of extension personnel of Maharashtra extension system in relation to communication behaviour. *Indian J Extension Education* 14(1-2) Ja-Je 1978 p 57-61

Shethu Rao, M.K.

See

Bhaskaran, C. *jt. auth.*

Shibata, Shingo

Peace education versus mass media in Japan. *Indian Education* 13(8-9) Nv-De 1983 p 19-22

Shinde, G.B.

A profile in background determinants of education in Panchmahal district. *Quest in Education* 17(1) Ja 1980 p 35-43

Shinde, Y.K.

Constructional administration of scientific attitude scale. *Research Bulletin* 15(1-2) Mr-Je 1985 p 26-31

Shirur, Rajani R.

Performance appraisal of faculty in higher education in institutions. *EPA Quarterly Bulletin* 5(3-4) Oc 1982-Ja 1983 p 36-41

Planning adult education programme for peasants. *Indian J Adult Education* 40(8) Ag 1979 p 42-44

Socio-psychological implications in population education. *Experiments in Education* 8(1) Mr 1980 p 14-15

Teaching-learning in higher education M.B. style. *J Higher Education* 7(3) Spr 1982 p 302-06 refs

Shirur, Rajani R. and Thetagraj, R.

A dialogue with the rural youth : Chingleput study. *Indian J Adult Education* 40(7) Jl 1979 p 24-27

Shivananda, D.S.

See

Sudha, B.G. *et al jt. auths.*

Shivananda, D.S. and Usha, G.P.

Reading ability of over and under achievers. *Indian Educational Rev* 20(2) Ag 1985 p 95-100

Shivanekar, L.M.

Modifying and extending basic skills programme : Encounters with micro-teaching. *Research Bulletin* 15(3-4) Se-De 1985 p 30-41 refs

Reinforcement programme package to reduce orthographical errors : A dilemma. *Research Bulletin* 15(1-2) Mr-Je 1985 p 41-52 refs tabs

Shivanekar, L.M. and Kelkar, S.V.

A group experiment in teaching reading to beginners. *Research Bulletin*

12(3-4) Se-De 1982 p 10-20 tabs

Shreedhara Swamy, S.

Open University : Problems and prospects. *Progress of Education* 57(8) Mr 1983 p 170-72+

Shrimali, K.L.

In search of a philosophy of education. *National J Education* 5(1) Se 1982 p 1-4

Shrivastava

See

Srivastava

Shukla, A.N.

See

Momi, G.S. *et al jt. auths.*

Sandhu, D.K. *jt. auth.*

Shukla, Anita

The concept of alientation : Views of Marx and Durkham. *Indian Educational Rev* 12(5-6) Ag-Se 1982 p 19-22

Meaning of alienation : Current status. *Progress of Education* 57(12) Jl 1983 p 269-78 refs

Measurement of alienation : A review of tools. *J Educational Research and Extension* 20(3) Ja 1984 p 203-10

Research on alienation in a few fields : A review. *Educational Rev* 92(10) Oc 1986 p 171-75 refs

Shukla, C.S.

Some issues in microteaching. *Teacher Education* 15(14-15) Ja-Ap 1981 p 83-89

See also

Bhattacharyya, G.C. *jt. auth.*

Shukla, N.K.

See

Tripathi, S.N. *jt. auth.*

Shukla, Neerja

Physical education in primary schools. *Primary Teacher* 5(1) Ja 1980 p 8-10

A possible model for non-formal education. *Education Quarterly* 31(1) Ap 1979 p 4-6

See also

Khosla, D.N. *jt. auth.*

Singh, R.P. *jt. auth.*

Shukla, P.C.

Administrative styles as related to headmasters sex. *Educational Rev* 92(7) Jl 1986 p 107-08 refs

Construction and standardisation of the educational leadership behaviour description questionnaire. *J Education and Psychology* 42(1-2) Ap-Jl 1984 p 51-54 refs

Development of a scale in Hindi to measure teachers attitude towards teaching profession. *Educational Rev* 91(3) Mr 1985 p 53-54 refs

The magical formula of education 10+2+3 or 8+4+3 or 7+5+3. *Education Quarterly* 30(3) Oc 1978 p 19-20

Management of B.Ed admission in Uttar Pradesh. *Educational Rev* 91(9) Se 1985 p 147-49

A study of educational leadership in relation to location of the schools. *Progress of Education* 57(7) Fe 1983 p 161-63 tabs

A study of educational leadership in relation to sex of the students. *Indian Education* 12(8-9) Nv-De 1982 p 20-24 tabs

A study of educational leadership in relation to teachers attitudes. *EPA Quarterly Bulletin* 7(1-2) Ap-Jl 1984 p 15-23

A study of job satisfaction in relation to leadership style. *J Education and Psychology* 41(1-2) Ap-Jl 1983 p 59-63

University administration in Uttar Pradesh. *Indian Education* 12(3-4) Je-Jl 1982 p 20-24

Shukla, P.C. and Nasreen Ara

Socio-economic status : As related to the students attitude towards teaching profession. *Educational Rev* 90(7-8) Jl-Ag 1984 p 111-14 refs tabs

Shukla, P.D.

Administration of education in India. New Delhi, Vikas Pub. 1983, 216p. Rs.95 *Book Rev, New Frontiers in Education* 13(1) Ja-Mr 1983 p 74-75

Towards new pattern of education in India. New Delhi, Sterling. 1984. *Book Rev, J Indian Education* 10(6) Mr 1985 p 61-62; *J Institute of Educational Research* 9(1) Ja 1985 p 32-34

Shukla, P.K.

See

Chowdhry, S.K. *jt. auth.*

Shukla, P.R.

An analysis of classroom transaction of science teachers. *Experiments in Education* 12(11) Ja 1985 p 192-98 refs

Shukla, Prakash Chandra

Adjustment problem at plus two. *Educational Rev* 87(2) Fe 1981 p 36-37 refs tabs

Changing trends in teacher education. *Progress of Education* 55(10) My 1981 p 246-48

Needs and significance of leadership study at primary level. *Educational Rev* 87(12) De 1981 p 235

The problems of sub-deputy inspectors of schools. *Progress of Education* 53(8) Mr 1981 p 217-18

A study of adjustment problem of the students of plus two levels. *Progress of Education* 55(9) Ap 1981 p 232-33 tabs

A study of creativity in relation to sex, locality and school subjects. *Indian Educational Rev* 17(2) Ag 1982 p 128-32; *J Educational Research and Extension* 18(4) Ap 1982 p 255-58

Shukla, R.P.

Teaching function of teaching and teaching competence. *Educational Rev* 90(11) Nv 1984 p 177-79 refs

Shukla, R.S.

An illusion about educational growth. *Teacher Today* 21(2) Oc-De 1978 p 44-47

Shukla, Rajesh Prasad
See
Pathak, A.B. *jt. auth.*

Shukla, S.K.
Sociometric approach to personality. *J Institute of Educational Research* 7(2) My 1983 p 24-30

Shukla, S.R.
Adoption behaviour of small farmers. *Indian J Extension Education* 16(1-2) Je 1980 p 55-58 tabs

Shukla, Sureshchandra
Indian educational thought and experiments : A review. *Teacher Today* 22(2) Oc-De 1979 p 1-21
Innovations in education : The colonial historical context. *Our Education* 2 Jl 1981 p 15-21; *Teacher Today* 24(2) Oc-De 1981 p 1-19
Moral education : Some comparative considerations. *National J Education* 3(1) Se 1980 p 9-16
Perspectives on women's education. *National J Education* 3(2) Mr 1981 p 7-16 refs ft-n
"Public" educational system in a colonial context. *Teacher Today* 26(4) Ap-Je 1984 p 41-50 refs
Social aspects of non-formal education. *Bulletin of Non-Formal Education* 2(2) Oc 1984 p 1-19 refs

Shukla, U.
On university mathematics. *J Higher Education* 2(2) Aut 1976 p 261-64

Siddaramaiah, B.S. and Jalihal, K.A.
An experimental study of one-sided and two sided presentation of messages with advance organizers. *Indian J Extension Education* 18(1-2) Je 1982 p 45-50 refs tabs
A scale to measure extension participation of farmers. *Indian J Extension Education* 19(3-4) Se-De 1983 p 74-76

Siddaramaiah, B.S. and Raghavendra
Content analysis of Indian Journal of Extension Education. *Indian J Extension Education* 19(1-2) Mr-Je 1983 p 92-94 refs tabs

Siddaramaiah, B.S. and Rajanna, B.
Relative effectiveness of combinations of radio, slide show and film show : An experimental evidence. *Indian J Extension Education* 20(1-2) Je 1984 p 7-11 refs tabs

Siddaramaiah, B.S. *et al*
A scale to measure the attitude of college students towards strike. *J Education and Psychology* 36(4) Ja 1979 p 200-02

Sidda Reddy, K.
See
Venkata Rami Reddy, A. *jt. auth.*

Siddiqui, A.Q. *et al*
Factors affecting academic achievement of school children. *J Education and Psychology* 41(3) Oc 1983 p 126-32 refs tabs

Siddiqui, Shahejehan
Concept in the teaching of life sciences. *Indian Education* 11(11-12) Fe-Mr 1982 p 29-30

Environmental factors related to underachievement in science. *Educational Rev* 89(11) Nv 1983 p 185-89 tabs

Piaget's developmental psychology and its implication in the teaching of science. *Educational Rev* 92(7) Jl 1986 p 113-14 refs

The role of concepts in the teaching of life sciences. *Educational Rev* 88(2) Fe 1982 p 21-23

Siddiqui, W.H.

Development of education in Nepal. *Educational Rev* 85(9) Se 1979 p 166-69 refs tabs

Formulating Marxist theory of education. *Progress of Education* 58(1) Ag 1983 p 2-5 refs

Indianisation of education and philosophy : A critique. *J Indian Education* 8(5) Ja 1983 p 3-10 ft-n

Primary education in Nepal. *Educational Rev* 87(7) Jl 1981 p 127-30

A study of truancy in relation to security-insecurity, parental acceptance and peer acceptance. *J Institute of Educational Research* 4(2) My 1980 p 9-12 refs

See also

Ansari, Ghazala *jt. auth.*

Qamar Jahan *jt. auth.*

Siddiqui, W.H. and Qamar Jahan

Gandhiji an educational philosopher. *Educational Rev* 87(12) De 1981 p 223-25; 88(1) Ja 1982 p 7-9

Siddiqui, W.H. and Wizarat Husain

Higher education in Nepal : At a glance. *Educational Rev* 88(11) Nv 1982 p 199-201; 89(1) Ja 1983 p 3-4; 89(2) Fe 1983 p 24-25

National development service : A scheme of study service in Nepal. *Education Quarterly* 32(2) Ap 1980 p 36-38

Secondary education in Nepal : A profile. *Educational Rev* 86(10) Oc 1980 p 194-97

Siddiqui, Zakia A. and Bilgrami, R. Fatima

Relationship of disciplined and indisciplined behaviour with academic achievement of adolescent students. *J Education and Psychology* 42(3) Oc 1984 p 119-22

Siddiqui, Zakia A. and Khatoon, Z.

Comparison of students performance under the semester and non-semester system of education in Aligarh Muslim University. *J Higher Education* 3(3) Spr 1978 p 369-79 refs tabs

Siddiqui, Zakia A. and Shamim Akhtar

Anxiety in relation to academic achievement of high school students. *Indian Educational Rev* 18(4) Oc 1983 p 106-10

Sidhanta, T.N.

Workers education : A trade union reprensentative view point. *Indian J Adult Education* 46(5) My 1985 p 14-15+

Sidhu, P.S.

Unending task of teacher education. *Educational Rev* 87(2) Fe 1981 p 27-30 refs

Sidur, Mikhail

Prolonged-day school plus aesthetic education : Experiment in a Soviet

Singh, H.R. and Chatia, C.K.
On relative efficiency of examiners. *Indian Educational Rev* 15(4) Oc 1980 p 35-38

Singh, Harindra M. and Panda, Santosh K.
The philosophy of correspondence education. *Education Quarterly* 32(4) Oc 1980 p 28-29

Singh, I.S. and Dash, A.S.
A cross-sectional development study of belief in honesty. *J Education and Psychology* 39(2) Jl 1981 p 117-20

Singh, Ida
Continuing education for women in slums. *Experiments in Education* 9(6) Ag 1981 p 99-102

Singh, Indrasen
The role of sex on perceiver in perception of male and female stimulers person. *J Education and Psychology* 41(4) Ja 1984 p 193-97 refs

Singh, Inder B.
Current perspectives in mass communication theory and research. *Indian J Extension Education* 16(3-4) De 1980 p 52-66 refs

Singh, J.N. *et al*
Training needs of dairy farmers. *Indian J Extension Education* 15(3-4) De 1979 p 77-82 tabs

Singh, K.M.P. and Mulay, S.
Job satisfaction of developmental personnel : A catalytic force for rural development. *Indian J Adult Education* 43(5) My 1982 p 6-12 refs

Singh, K.N.
Challenges of extension in the eighties. *Indian J Extension Education* 18(1-2) Je 1982 p 1-9
Management of agriculture and rural development. *Indian J Extension Education* 21(1-2) Ja-Je 1985 p 1-9
See also
Ambastha, C.K. *jt. auth.*
Sanoria, Y.C. *jt. auth.*
Tripathi, A. *et al jt. auths.*

Singh, K.R.P.
Educational thought of Dr. Zakri Husain : A critique. *Indian Educational Rev* 20(4) Oc 1985 p 109-15
Integrated education for children with speech and hearing impairment : A plan of action. *Primary Teacher* 9(1) Ap 1984 p 4-7
Preparing better teachers. *J Indian Education* 12(2) Jl 1986 p 3-7
Values in Soviet education. *Primary Teacher* 11(3) Jl 1986 p 1-3

Singh, L.B. *et al*
Intelligence, anxiety, extraversion and achievement motivation as a function of sex-difference in Santal. *J Institute of Educational Research* 7(3) Se 198? p 26-31

Singh, L.P.
Effective change in secondary school administration. *J Indian Education* 6(2) Jl 1980 p 14-18; 6(4) Nv 1980 p 3-7
Life-long education and teacher preparation. *Teacher Today* 22(3) Ja-Mr 1980 p 29-33

Research on classroom climate. *Indian Educational Rev* 16(3) Jl 1981 p 27-34

Retrospect and prospect of research on educational planning in India. *National J Education* 2(2) Mr 1980 p 52-58 refs

See also

Singh, H.M. *jt. auth.*

Singh, L.P. and Dwivedi, Jagdesdwar

Effectiveness of microteaching on the development of psychomotor skills. *Teacher Education* 16(18-19) Ja-Ap 1982 p 21-29 tabs

Singh, L.P. and Singh, T.

A study of the comparative effects of microteaching under simulated and mixed conditions upon general teaching competence and attitude towards teaching. *J Educational Research and Extension* 16(3) Ja 1980 p 142-52 refs tabs

Singh, M.B. and Jain, Sunita

Nature of characteristics of the children enrolled in laboratory nursury school from 1965-1978. *Asian J Psychology and Education* 10(1-4) 1982 p 33-39

Singh, M.K.

Autonomy in education. *Educational Rev* 87(6) Je 1981 p 101-02

Singh, N.P. and Gill, S.S.

Relationship of training needs fulfilment with personal characteristics of the farmers. *Indian J Extension Education* 21(3-4) Jl-De 1985 p 8-94 refs tabs

Training needs of farmers. *Indian J Extension Education* 18(1-2) Je 1982 p 66-72 tabs

Singh, N.P. and Singh, P.M.

Occupational socialisation of rural youth. *Indian J Extension Education* 14(1-2) Ja-Je 1978 p 35-42 tabs

Singh, N.P. and Singh, R.P.

First line extension projects of ICAR : A comparative analysis. *J Indian Education* 12(2) Jl 1986 p 24-34

Singh, P.M.

See

Singh, N.P. *jt. auth.*

Singh, Pushpa *et al*

Contextual effects on achievement motivation among lecturers. *J Education and Psychology* 43(1) Ap 1985 p 50-53 refs

Singh, R.

NAEP and universal literacy : Some suggestions. *Indian J Adult Education* 40(5) My 1979 p 41-43

Singh, R. *et al*

Childhood parental loss and subsequent adult depression. *Indian J Adult Education* 7(2) Jl 1981 p 50-54

Singh, R.A.

See

Pandey, R.P. *jt. auth.*

Singh, R.J.

Creativity : A socio-psychological interpretation. *National J Education* 7(2) My 1985 p 17-24 refs

Creativity across cultures : The Indian scence. *Bhartiya Shiksha Shodh*

Patrika 4(1) Ja-Je 1985 p 37-50 refs
On the conflicting claims about the history of creativity research. *J Educational Research and Extension* 17(3) Ja 1981 p 129-36 refs
Personality adjustment of creative and non-creative student teachers in India. *Indian Educational Rev* 15(4) Oc 1980 p 49-55
Relating creative thinking abilities with academic achievement and teaching skills of student teachers. *J Indian Educaion* 10(5) Ja 1985 p 49-51
Teacher creativity and family background : A study of relationship. *Asian J Psychology and Education* 6(3) Nv 1980 p 42-48 refs
Value orientations of creative and non-creative student-teachers in India. *Quest in Education* 17(4) Oc 1980 p 318-26 refs

Singh, R.P.
The changing teachers. *Teacher Today* 27(2) Oc-De 1984 p 21-25
Classroom practices in the past twenty five-years. *Teacher Today* 26(1) Jl-Se 1983 p 101-06
Creativity in relation to adjustment. *Quest in Education* 19(3) Jl 1982 p 227-33 tabs
Developing primary school science curriculum based on Piaget's theory. *Primary Teacher* 6(2) Ap 1981 p 12-15
Documentation and dissemination of educational research. *Teacher Today* 24(2) Oc-De 1981 p 26-31
Education in imperial colony. New Delhi, Nat Pub H. 1979, Rs.50 *Book Rev, Indian Educational Rev* 16(1) Ja 1981 p 125-26; *J Indian Education* 5(6) Mr 1980 p 64
Education of the disabled child. *Primary Teacher* 8(2) Ap 1983 p 10-12
Educational journalism : Concept and practice. *Education Quarterly* 35(3) Jl 1983 p 26-28
Educational research in South East Asia. *Indian Educational Rev* 14(4) Oc 1979 p 43-46
Higher education in the USA. *J Indian Education* 6(1) My 1980 p 38-41
Modernity of tradition in Indian education : The revival of Indian languages and indigenous systems of education. *Perspectives in Education* 1(4) Oc 1985 p 231-36 refs
Moral education : A unique experiment. *Primary Teacher* 8(1) Ja 1983 p 5-6
National Teachers Commission, I and II. *Teacher Today* 27(4) Ap-Je 1985 p 18-20
Non-formal education : Concept, definition and scope. *Educational Quarterly* 31(3-4) Oc 1979-Ja 1980 p 1-5
The prediction of creativity : A study. *Indian Educational Rev* 17(2) Ap 1982 p 20-26 refs
Quality in education and its relevance. *Education Quarterly* 35(1) Ja 1983 p 5-8
Research in history of education in India. *Teacher Today* 25(3) Ja-Mr 1983 p 16-23 refs
The role of sex in creative potential among adolescents. *Teacher Education* 17(20-21) Jl-Oc 1982 p 46-50 refs tabs
Studies in teacher education : An overview. New Delhi, Bahri Pub. 1980, 104p. Rs.40 *Book Rev, Education Quarterly* 32(4) Oc 1980 p 40-47; *J Indian Education* 6(3) Se 1980 p 59-60

Teachers in higher education : A review of their problems and status. *Educational Quarterly* 37(1) Spr 1985 p 4-11

Teachers role in promotion of creative talent. *Teacher Education* 18(24-25) Jl-Oc 1983 p 49-52 refs

See also

Madan Singh *jt. auth.*

Roy, N.K. *et al jt. auths.*

Singh, N.P. *jt. auth.*

Singh, R.P., and Shukla, Neerja

Non-formal education : An alternative to formal system. New Delhi, Bahri Pub. 1979, 90p. Rs.36 *Book Rev, Bulletin of Non-Formal Education* 1(1) 1 Je 1983 p 32-33; *Education Quarterly* 32(4) Oc 1980 p 48-49; *National J Education* 3(1) Se 1980 p 76

Test and testing in teacher education in India. *Indian Educational Rev* 14(1) Ja 1979 p 30-55 appdx refs

Singh, R.R.

See

Phatak, A.B. *jt. auth.*

Singh, S.K.

See

Ram, R.B. *jt. auth.*

Singh, S.N.

Educational philosophy of Bertrand Russell. Varanasi, BHU. 1979, 125p. Rs.35 *Book Rev, J Indian Education* 7(3) Se 1979 p 60

See also

Apparao, G. *et al jt. auths.*

Somasundaram, D. *jt. auth.*

Singh, T.R. *jt. auth.*

Vasantha Kumar, J. *jt. auth.*

Singh, S.N., *ed.*

Health and population education. Varanasi, BHU. 1979, 187p. Rs.35 *Book Rev, J Indian Education* 7(3) Se 1979 p 60

Singh, S.N. and Tandon, O.P.

University autonomy in the contemporary context. *National J Education* 2(1) Se 1979 p 7-14 refs

Singh, S.P.

Objectives of teacher education : A feedback. *Teacher Education* 15(14-15) Ja-Ap 1981 p 45-47

Singh, T.

Diffusion of innovation among training colleges of India. Jaunpur, Bharat Bharati Pra. 1978, 139p. Rs.30 *Book Rev, J Indian Education* 7(2) Jl 1979 p 70

Innovated practice teaching programme at the faculty of education, Banaras Hindu University, Varanasi. *Teacher Education* 15(14-15) Ja-Ap 1981 p 106-11

See also

Singh, L.P. *jt. auth.*

Singh, T.R.
See
Agarwal, S. *jt. auth.*
Sharma, S. *jt. auth.*
Singh, T.R. and Singh, S.N.
Differential perception of the characteristics of innovations of farming couples for high yielding varieties of wheat and family planning practices. *Indian J Extension Education* 16(3-4) De 1980 p 16-21 refs tabs
A study on interplay of belief values and attitude, of farming couples on rational and adoption behaviour under different innovation situation. *Indian J Extension Education* 18(1-2) Je 1982 p 73-82 refs tabs
Singh, V.B.
Indian English : Search for an independent standard. *Teacher Today* 23(3) Ja-Mr 1981 p 73-80 refs
Singh, V.D.
Resource development for adult literacy. *J Indian Education* 5(2) Jl 1979 p 13-17
The software for the NAEP. *Indian J Adult Education* 41(1-2) Ja-Fe 1980 p 9-13
Singh, V.K., *ed.*
See
Daulat Singh *jt. auth.*
Singh, V.P.
See
Chadha, M.D. *jt. auth.*
Singh, V.V.
See
Phatak, A.B. *jt. auth.*
Singh, Y.P.
See
Makhija, V.K. *jt. auth.*
Ramesh Babu, A. *jt. auth.*
Sandhya, P.N. *jt. auth.*
Singh, Y.P. and Ramesh Babu, A.
Basic management issues in extension. *Indian J Extension Education* 21(1-2) Ja-Je 1985 p 20-31
Singhal, Asha
See
Bhatnagar, Suman *jt. auth.*
Singhal, R.P.
Attacking adult illiteracy in India : Problems and strategies. *EPA Quarterly Bulletin* 6(3-4) Oc 1983-Ja 1984 p 1-14 ft-n tabs
Horizontal and vertical linkages in education. *Education Quarterly* 35(2) Ap 1983 p 1-7 figs
Reformulating educational policy in India : Issues to ponder. *University News* 23(28) 23 Jl 1985 p 19-24
West Germany's occupational education. *J Indian Education* 5(1) My 1979 p 64-67

What schools can do to promote national integration. *Education Quarterly* 33(2) Ap 1981 p 1-3

Singhal, Sushila

Educational development in rural-urban sectors in India. *New Frontiers in Education* 11(1) Ja-Mr 1981 p 19-29 tabs

Organisation and functioning of universities in India. *J Higher Education* 1(2) Aut 1975 p 223-40 refs tabs

See also

Khadar, M.A. *jt. auth.*

Srivastava, Chitra *jt. auth.*

Singte, M.B. and Naidu, T.R.V.

Teacher's time as a resource for quality improvement in agricultural university education in Maharashtra. *Progress of Education* 61(3) Oc 1986 p 62-67 refs

Sinha, A.K.

See

Sinha, H.S.P. *et al jt. auths.*

Sinha, A.K. and Sinha, P.C.

Estimation of average proportion of failures at a university examination : A numerical approach. *Indian Educational Rev* 15(4) Oc 1980 p 104-05

Sinha, Arvind K.

Dimensions of organisational climate. *Indian Educational Rev* 18(4) Oc 1983 p 1-14

Quality education : Review of the concept and empirical dimensions. *Indian Educational Rev* 20(4) Oc 1985 p 1-19 refs ft-n

Sinha, Awadesh Kumar and Shahi, Suresh Prasad

A study of courses of indiscipline among students as viewed by teachers and students. *J Education and Psychology* 38(3) Oc 1980 p 159-65

Sinha, B.P.

See

Anuradha, G. *jt. auth.*

Chauhan, N.K. *jt. auth.*

Jha, R.C. *jt. auth.*

Mishra, S.P. *jt. auth.*

Ramesh Babu. A. *jt. auth.*

Sehty, B. *et al jt. auths.*

Sinha, B.P. *et al*

Some correlates of farm telecast viewing by Delhi farmers. *Indian J Extension Education* 14(3-4) Jl-De 1978 p 51-57

Sinha, Balanand

See

Mookerjee, Ratna *et al jt. auths.*

Sinha, Binod K.

Adult education for tribal population. *Indian J Adult Education* 43(6) Je 1982 p 7-10

Sihha, H.S.P. and Ranjan R.

An analysis of tribal loanees in repayment of loans. *Indian J Extension Education* 17(3-4) Se-De 1981 p 54-65 refs tabs

Sinha, H.S.P. and Sinha, S.K.

Adoption of the high yielding varieties of maize by the farmers of Sikkim. *Indian J Extension Education* 16(1-2) Je 1980 p 46-50 tabs

Sinha, H.S.P. *et al*

A study of attitude of farmers of Chhota Nagpur towards soil conservation programme. *Indian J Extension Education* 20(3-4) Se-De 1984 p 9-18 refs tabs

Sinha, Jitendra Kumar

Progress of literacy during 1951-80. *Indian Educational Rev* 17(1) Ja 1982 p 109-19 appdx

Sinha, K.

See

Sinha, H.S.P. *et al jt. auths.*

Sinha, L.S.

Teacher absenteeism in primary schools. *Primary Teacher* 11(2) Ap 1986 p 24-27

Sinha, M.N. *et al*

A study of the job activities of the milk procurement personnel. *Indian J Extension Education* 16(1-2) Je 1980 p 82-83

Sinha, N.K. and Bimal, B.K.

Farm leadership in relation to age. *Indian J Extension Education* 14(1-2) Ja-Je 1978 p 76-78

Sinha, P.C.

See

Sinha, A.K. *jt. auth.*

Sinha, Pramila

Social maturity of children in India. *Indian Educational Rev* 18(1) Jl 1983 p 1-11 tabs

Sinha, R.R.

Factors affecting use of audio-visual aids. *Indian J Extension Education* 18(3-4) De 1982 p 62-64

Suspense box : A new visual aid. *Indian J Extension Education* 17(3-4) Se-De 1981 p 89-91

Sinha, Rita

Attitude of creative persons towards conflicting situations. *J Education and Psychology* 41(1-2) Ap-Jl 1983 p 23-25

The secure and insecure children. *J Indian Education* 8(1) My 1982 p 19-22 refs

Sinha, S.K.

See

Sinha, H.S.P. *jt. auth.*

Sinha, S.P.

A study of interest and personality patterns of succesful men in different occupations. *Indian Educational Rev* 15(4) Oc 1980 p 66-70

Sinha, Sidheshwar Dhari

Pedagogical linguistics. *J Indian Education* 7(3) Se 1979 p 29-31

Sinha, Suddha R.

Effect of school system on the competence of secondary school students. *Indian Education Rev* 15(1) Ja 1980 p 62-77 refs tabs

Sinha, Uma *et al*
Development of an interest inventory. *Indian Educational Rev* 18(3) Jl 1983 p 47-62 refs tabs

Sinha, V.
See
Murari, Pushpa *jt. auth.*

Sinha, Vijay Laxmi
Development of reading ability among the students of class VI to X. *Rajasthan Board J Education* 21(2) Ap-Je 1985 p 9-14

Sirdeshpande, K.H.
See
Nandapurkar, G.G. *jt. auth.*

Sirohi, Seema
Involvement of rural woman in farming. *Indian J Extension Education* 21(3-4) Jl-De 1985 p 110-11

Sirohi, Seema and Rajendra
Sex consciousness among rural women. *Indian J Extension Education* 17(3-4) Se-De 1981 p 108-11 tabs

Sisodia, M.L. and Agrawal, B.M.
Making undergraduate education more relevant : A model developed at the University of Rajasthan, Jaipur. *J Higher Education* 8(2) Aut 1982 p 241-45 appdx

Sisodia, M.L. *et al*
An analysis of question bank in mathematics. *J Higher Education* 4(3) Spr 1979 p 392-400

Sivadasan Pillai, K.
Adult/Non-formal education programmes in India : Legislative, conceptual and evaluative analysis. *Indian J Adult Education* 41(5) My 1980 p 7-10
Crucial issues in teacher education. *Teacher Education* 15(14-15) Ja-Ap 1981 p 48-50
Demylifying educational research. *Teacher Today* 26(4) Ap-Je 1984 p 66-68
Emerging frontiers in education. *Indian Education* 11(4) Jl 1981 p 24-25
Fighting illiteracy in Kerala. *Indian J Adult Education* 42(1-2) Ja-Fe 1981 p 3-6
Non-formal education in Britain. Trivandrum, Kalamketan. 124p. Rs.50 *Book Rev, Indian J Adult Education* 46(4) Ap 1985 p 26-28
Training field functionaries : Teachers and supervisors. *Experiments in Education* 9(2) Ap 1981 p 31-33
Yet another experiment with adult education. *Indian Education* 12(8-9) Nv-De 1982 p 13-14

Sivagamsundari, M.K.
See
Shanmugham, M. *jt. auth.*

Sivamohan, V.S. and Mansingh, R. Israel
A probe into the study of English language. *J Educational Research and Extension* 16(3) Ja 1980 p 174-75

Sivasankara Reddy, K.
Attitude towards God : A study of the generation gap. *Experiments in Education* 11(9) Nv 1983 p 162-64 +

Attitude towards education of students, parents and teachers. *Experiments in Education* 12(4) Je 1984 p 64-68; 12(6) Ag 1984 p 95-99 refs

Attitude towards education of students, parents and teachers. *J Education and Psychology* 42(4) Ja 1985 p 229-33

Smith, Colin

See

Leslett, Robert *jt. auth.*

Smith, Donald K.

Planning university adult education programmes for the 1980's : Prospects and problems. *Indian J Adult Education* 40(3) Mr 1979 p 15-29

Sneldass, P. and Wringe, C., *eds.*

Can we teach children to be good? London, Allen and Unwin. 1982. 115p. *Book Rev, Teacher Today* 27(11) Jl-Se 1984 p 93-94

Sodhi, G.S. and Mohini, Tejinder

Development of Piagetion operational comprehension among school adolescents. *J Institute of Educational Research* 10(3) Se 1986 p 21-23 refs

Sodhi, T.S.

Education in Kenya and the Punjab State of India : A comparative study. *J Indian Education* 12(3) Se 1986 p 44-52 refs

A study of the attitudes of high school students towards discipline. *Quest in Education* 16(4) Oc 1979 p 236-44 refs

Sodhi, T.S and Kamaljeet Kaur

Educational concepts of Guru Nanak in Japji Sahib. Ludhiana, Mukand Pub. 1980, 40p. Rs.5 *Book Rev, J Indian Education* 8(6) Mon 1983 p 76-77

Sodhi, T.S. and Surya Bala

Student's problems of economic and material facilities : A study. *Indian Educational Rev* 17(3) 1982 p 10-22 refs tabs

A study of physical health and fitness problems of students. *Quest in Education* 17(4) Oc 1980 p 338-51 refs

Soedjatmoko

Development as learning. *Perspectives in Education* 1(4) Oc 1985 p 211-29 refs

Sohal, T.S.

See

Anand, Usha *jt. auth.*

Ram Chand *jt. auth.*

Rao, S.V.N. *jt. auth.*

Sohal, T.S. and Tyagi, K.C.

Role of knowledge in adoption of dairy innovations. *Indian J Extension Education* 14(3-4) Jl-De 1978 p 16-25 refs

Sohi, Baghel Singh

A comparative study of awareness across illiterate and literate rural adults. *Prasar* 7(3-4) Oc 1980-Ja 1981 p 38-45

Sohi, J.S. and Kherde, R.L.

Multi-rater approaches for performance appraisal of cattle development extension workers. *Indian J Extension Education* 21(3-4) Jl-De 1985 p 112-15 ft-n

A study of dairy adoption behaviour of small and marginal farmers in

Punjab. *Indian J Extension Education* 16(1-2) Je 1980 p 84-86 tabs

Sohani, G.P.

The ideal teachers. Pune, Nutan Pra. 160p. Rs.10 *Book Rev, Progress of Education* 56(9) Ap 1982 p 224

Soljam, Nikse Nikola

Recurrent education in Yugoslavia. Zegrab, Progled Jugsolovenhi. 1983, 116p. *Book Rev, J Higher Education* 9(3) Spr 1984 p 418-19

Soloman, Gerald *et al*

Anxiety among visually handicapped children. *J Education and Psychology* 38(4) Ja 1981 p 219-26 refs tabs

Som, P.

Examining the attitude of teachers towards classroom teaching in relation to some socio-personal variables. *Our Education* 3-4 Jl 1983 p 138-45 refs

Somaiya, S.K.

See

Ayyar, Parvathy S. *jt. auth.*

Soman, Anjali

See

Kala, Kalyan *jt. auth.*

Somantarey, Shree Chinamani

An emerging concept of teacher education. *Experiments in Education* 6(6) Ag 1978 p 102-03 refs

Somasundaram, D. and Singh, S.N.

Communication gap between extension workers and paddy growing small farmers. *Indian J Extension Education* 14(3-4) Jl-De 1978 p 26-33

Factors affecting the knowledge of adopter and non-adopter small farmers. *Indian J Extension Education* 14(1-2) Ja-Je 1978 p 30-34 refs

Somasundaram, G.

See

Knight, A. John *jt. auth.*

Somit, Albert

See

Peterson, Steven A. *jt. auth.*

Sood, J.K.

Curriculum innovation and implementation : Bridging the gap. *Education Quarterly* 33(3) Jl 1981 p 17-20 refs

The dynamics of science teacher education. *Education Quarterly* 36(2) Ap 1984 p 29-33

Science, society and trends in science education : A search for relevance in the developing countries. *Teacher Today* 24(2) Oc-De 1981 p 19-25 refs

A study of attitudes towards science and scientists among certain groups of students and teachers in India. *Indian Educational Rev* 14(4) Oc 1979 p 61-66

Sood, Renu

Role of achievement, anxiety, alienation and value discrepancy in academic achievement of scheduled caste students. *J Higher Education* 6(1-3) 1980-81 p 117-22 refs tabs

Sopani, I.N.

Indira Gandhi on education. *Teacher Today* 27(3) Ja-Mr 1985 p 1-10

Sowaid, M. *et al*

A study of parent child interaction and achievement motivation among tribal high school students. *J Institute of Educational Research* 10(3) Se 1986 p 24-27 refs

Spagnoli, Cathy

The world of sound. *Primary Teacher* 5(2) Ap 1980 p 18-21

Sreedhara Swamy, S.

Education and human resource development. *Progress of Education* 57(11) Je 1983 p 246-49

Education of the deaf. *Indian Education* 11(8-9) Nv-De 1981 p 7-11

Educational planning. *Indian Education* 10(3) Je 1980 p 19-23

54th All India Educational Conference, Kurukshetra, Haryana, December 27 to 31, 1980 : A review. *Indian Education* 10(9-10) De 1980-Ja 1981 p 39-54

Indian education scene in 1981. *Indian Education* 11(10) Ja 1982 p 42-45; *Progress of Education* 56(8) Mr 1982 p 196-97+

Indian education scence, 1982. *Indian Education* 12(10) Ja 1983 p 26-29

Teachers organisations in India. Hyderabad, AIFEA. 1980, 241p. Rs.35 *Book Rev, Indian Education* 11(6) Se 1981 p 38-40

Population growth : Ecology and environmental pollution. *Indian Education* 13(12) Mr 1984 p 16-18

Sreedhara Swamy, S. and Thayaru, R.M.

Programmed instruction in mathematics. *Experiments in Education* 10(9) Nv 1982 p 167-69

Sree Lakshmi Devi, S.

See

Srinivasa Rao, R. *jt. auth.*

Sreeramamurthy, M.

Adult as a learner : Pedagogical perspective. *Quest in Education* 18(2) Ap 1981 p 117-29 refs

Are the educational standards deteriorating? *Indian Educational Rev* 18(2) Ap 1980 p 37-49 refs tabs

Educational alternatives. *Experiments in Education* 9(7) Se 1981 p 115-20 refs

Expectations of teaching in individuals of lower socio-economic class. *Indian J Adult Education* 39(11-12) Nv-De 1978 p 27-34 tabs

Parental influences over course relation. *Experiments in Education* 7(10) De 1979 p 179-90+ appdx refs tabs

Psycho-social aspects of population education. *Progress of Education* 59(5) De 1984 p 99-102+

Role of teacher organisations in promoting national integration, 30-12-1980 : Presidential address. *Indian Education* 10(11) Fe 1981 p 16-18

A study into the effect of impulsiveness and controlledness over the academic achievement. *Indian Educational Rev* 15(3) Jl 1980 p 103-16 appdx refs

Tasks for schools. *Education Quarterly* 32(4) Oc 1980 p 8-9

Teaching styles of city teachers. *Teacher Education* 13(8-9) Jl-Oc 1979 p 70-78 tabs

Srinagar, G.U.
See
Aswal, G.S. *jt. auth.*
Srinivasacharyulu, G.
Development of adult education. *Educational Rev* 86(1) Ja 1980 p 14-16
An investigation into the attitude of teacher trainees towards practical aspects of B.Ed programme. *Experiments in Education* 7(7) Se 1979 p 145-48 tabs
Srinivasa Iyengar, M.A.
Text books must instill patriotism in school children. *Educational Rev* 89(12) De 1983 p 217
Srinivasa Murti, K.
A gifted child : A national asset. *Primary Teacher* 10(3) Jl 1985 p 33-34
Srinivasan, K.J.
A case for education as a discipline. *Experiments in Education* 11(12) Fe 1984 p 208-09
Learning mathematics through Cube games. *Experiments in Education* 11(6) Ag 1983 p 98-100
Statistics in physical education. *Experiments in Education* 8(4) Je 1980 p 71-74
Srinivasan, Seetha
Bridging the gap : An experiment in remedial education. *New Frontiers in Education* 15(1) Ja-Mr 1980 p 86-90
Srinivasan, V.
Innovative educational programmes : Some hurdles. *J Indian Education* 10(6) Mr 1985 p 30-32
Srinivasaraghavan, T.
Evaluation of performance of candidates at post graduate examinations. *J Higher Education* 4(3) Spr 1979 p 410-13
Srinivasa Rao, R.
The differential effects of using projected and non-projected visual media in the teaching of social studies. *Experiments in Education* 6(10) De 1978 p 178-81 refs tabs
Education of handicapped children. *Education Quarterly* 32(1) Ja 1981 p 24-27
Educational progress in Andhra Pradesh : A trend report. *Education Quarterly* 31(1) Ap 1979 p 21-23 refs
Management of educational resources : A system approach. *Experiments in Education* 7(1) Mr 1979 p 13-15 refs
Management of research in universities. *Experiments in Education* 8(2) Ap 1980 p 25-26 refs
Role of mass media in rural development. *Experiments in Education* 6(12) Fe 1979 p 205-06
A study of the effect of pre-school education on primary and secondary school education. *Experiments in Education* 8(11) Ja 1981 p 193-97 tabs
Srinivasa Rao, R. and Sree Lakshmi Devi, S.
Sex role stereotyping in language texts. *Experiments in Education* 7(3) My 1979 p 50-53 refs

Srinvasa Rao, R. and Suguma, V.

Differential effects of using a projected and non-projected visual media in teaching science. *Experiments in Education* 7(9) Nv 1979 p 157-59 refs tabs

SRIVASTAVA - SHRIVASTAVA

Srivastava, A.B.L. and Satvir Singh

The use of computers in education. *J Indian Education* 8(2) Jl 1982 p 3-11 refs

Srivastava, A.B.L. and Sharma, K.K.

Elementary statistics in psychology and education. New Delhi, Sterling. 1985. *Book Rev, J Institute of Educational Research* 10(1) Jl 1986 p 31

Srivastava, A.K.

A study of motivational aspects of occupational choice of the Indian students of graduate studies. *National J Education* 6(1) Se 1983 p 40-47 refs tabs

Srivastava, A.L.

Demands of modernisation and educational process : Two systems. *Teacher Today* 23(1) Jl-Se 1981 p 55-81 refs

Srivastava, A.P.

The education and development of your child — A guide. New Delhi, Learning Systems. 1982, 110p. *Book Rev, Education Quarterly* 36(2) Ap 1981 p 74-75

Linkages between teaching and learning in higher education. *National J Education* 7(1) Se 1984 p 1-18 refs

Srivastava, Anand P.

Emergency ward at colleges. *University News* 24(43) 16 Nv 1986 p 1-3

Teaching learning process : The desired apporach. *University News* 24(39) 16 Oc 1986 p 4

Srivastava, Asha

See

Rai, V.K. *jt. auth.*

Srivastava, B.K.

See

Verma, P.C. *jt. auth.*

Srivastava, Chitra and Singhal, Sushila

Faculty leadership styles and intellectual commitment among college students. *J Higher Education* 6(1-3) 1980-81 p 131-36 tabs

Srivastava, Devendra

Operant learning classroom applications. *Teacher Education* 14(12-13) Jl-Oc 1980 p 48-56 refs

Srivastav, G.N. Prakash

Action research in practice. *Progress of Education* 54(10-11) My-Je 1980 p 199-201

Computer technology and the future of education. *Education Quarterly* 37(3) Aut 1985 p 13-16

Development of norms for Hindi adaptation of junior-senior HSPQ. *Asian J Psychology and Education* 9(3) 1982 p 43-47

Jean Piaget on congnitive development of child. *Asian J Psychology and Education (Special)* 10(1-4) 1982 p 40-48 refs
Piaget on play. *Primary Teacher* 10(3) Jl 1985 p 5-9
See also
Prakash, G.N.

Srivastava, G.N. Prakash and Dubey, Rajeswari
A study of personality trait differences of low and high achiever students of higher secondary. *J Education and Psychology* 40(3) Oc 1982 p 149-51

Srivastava, G.N. Prakash and Srivastava, S.S.
A study of prediction of academic achievement through personality tests. *J Institute of Educational Research* 4(3) Se 1980 p 20-27 refs tabs

Srivastava, G.N. Prakash and Wafadar, A.J.
A study of factors in the choice of teaching profession in Afghanistan and India : A comparative study. *National J Education* 6(1) Se 1983 p 48-55 refs tabs

Srivastava, Ghanshyam Saran
A new technique for teaching arithmetic. *Primary Teacher* 5(4) Oc 1984 p 27-28

Shrivastava, Ginny
Material preparation and curriculum development : A note for consideration. *Prasar* 5(3-4) Oc 1977-Ja 1978 p 24-27

Shrivastava, Gyandendra P.
A study of national integratedness in NSS and non-NSS students. *J Education and Psychology* 36(4) Ja 1979 p 192-99

Srivastava, H.S.
Towards a successful adult education programme. *Education Quarterly* 30(3) Oc 1978 p 4-7

Srivastava, J.P.
See
Gupta, S.P. *jt. auth.*
Mahesh, Vimala *jt. auth.*

Srivastava, Kumkum *et al*
Attitude of high school boys and girls towards mathematics. *J Institute of Educational Research* 9(1) Ja 1985 p 25-31 refs tabs

Srivastava, Neelam and Tewari, Devki
A scale to measure teachers attitude towards population education in secondary schools. *J Education and Psychology* 41(1-2) Ap-Jl 1983 p 30-36
A study of the attitude of secondary school teachers during and after emergency period towards the need of population education. *J Education and Psychology* 37(2) Jl 1979 p 115-20 refs tabs

Srivastava, Neelu
Achievement motivation and self concept in the settings. *Asian J Psychology and Education* 4(1) Ja 1979 p 5-9

Srivastava, Niti
See
Joshi, R.K. *jt. auth.*

Shrivastava, Om
A critical look at a micro-level adult education project. *Indian J Adult*

Education 44(3) Mr 1983 p 21-23

Languages issues in adult education. *Indian J Adult Educaiton* 41(6-7) Je-Jl 1980 p 33-36

Srivastava, P.K.

A comparative study of internal and external assessment of post- graduate level. *Progress of Education* 55(12) Jl 1981 p 231-34 tabs

See also

Agarwal, S. *jt. auth.*

Srivastava, Pradeep Kumar

Open university at door step. *University News* 23(25) 1 Jl 1985 p 5-7

Probing mechanics of open university. *Educational Rev* 91(8) Ag 1985 p 121-23

A study of internal assessment. *Quest in Education* 16(4) Oc 1979 p 327-34 refs

See also

Srivastava, J.P. *jt. auth.*

Srivastava, R.C.

College administration : The study of faculty and student participation in college administration. New Delhi, Metropolitan Book Co. 1980, p 308 Rs. 75. *Book Rev, Indian Educational Rev* 15(3) Jl 1980 p 126-27; *J Higher Education* 6(1-3) 1980-81 p 166-67

Educational journalism : In defence of writing in newspaper. *J Indian Education* 11(3) Se 1985 p 45-47

Participation, faculty satisfaction and perceived institutional climate. *J Higher Education* 9(1) Mon 1983 p 94-107

Study of educational administration in India. *EPA Quarterly Bulletin* 8(1-2) Ap-Je 1985 p 67-79 refs

Srivastava, R.K. and Rawat, B.

Attitudes of Harijan women towards education : A comparative study of a city and surrounding villages. *Indian J Adult Education* 43(7) Jl 1982 p 27-31 refs tabs

Srivastava, R.M. and Kharde, R.L.

Traditional beliefs of tribal Mundas associated with cattle husbandry. *Indian J Extension Education* 19(3-4) Se-De 1983 p 77-82 refs tabs

Srivastava, R.N.

Literacy as a communication skill. *Indian J Adult Education* 40(3) Mr 1979 p 1-14 refs tabs

Srivastava, R.P.

The teaching of reading. New Delhi, Bahari Pub. 1979, 144p. Rs.45 *Book Rev, J Indian Education* 5(6) Mr 1980 p 65; *National J Education* 3(1) Se 1986 p 77

Srivastava, R.S. and Bose, K.

Theory and practice of teacher education in India. Allahabad, Chugh Pub. 1978, 344p. Rs.65 *Book Rev, J Higher Education* 7(3) Spr 1982 p 327-30

Srivastava, Rajni

Sociological problems in tribal education : A case study. *Indian Educational Rev* 17(3) Jl 1982 p 110-13

Some psychological problems of tribals of Mirzapur : A case study. *Indian Educational Rev* 18(2) Ap 1983 p 106-10 tabs

Srivastava, Rakesh K.
See
Misra, Ajay Mohan *et al jt. auths.*
Srivastava, Ramji
Anxiety, personality types and sex as the determine of the influence of the noise distractibility in reversal and non-reversal shifts. *Asian J Psychology and Education* 4(3) Nv 1979 p 9-13 refs
Creativity as a function of birth order socio-economic status and personality types. *J Education and Psychology* 36(3) Oc 1978 p 113-17
Srivastava, Ramji and Alam, Q.G.
World mindedness as related to personal values and religion of collegeates. *J Education and Psychology* 38(1) Ap 1980 p 33-35 refs tabs
Srivastava, Ranjana
Economics of educational planning in India. *Education Quarterly* 32(2) Ap 1980 p 1-5 ft-n
Role of education in development of science and technology in India. *Education Quarterly* 31(3-4) Oc 1979-Ja 1980 p 16-20
Srivastava, S.K.
Job satisfaction and organisational climate among university teachers. *J Higher Education* 9(2) Aut 1983 p 251-54 refs
Srivastava, S.K. and Gupta, Solan
Achievement motivation and job satisfaction in primary school teachers. *J Education and Psychology* 43(3-4) Oc 1985-Ja 1986 p 193-96 refs
Srivastava, S.N. and Verma, S.C.
University libraries in India : Their organisation and administration. New Delhi, Sterling. 1980, 351p. Rs.75 *Book Rev, Education Quarterly* 33(2) Ag 1981 p 40-41; *Teacher Today* 24(4) Ap-Je 1982 p 138-39
Srivastava, S.S.
See
Prakash, G.N. *jt. auth.*
Srivastava, G.N. Prakash *jt. auth.*
Srivastava, S.S. and Gupta, R.C.
Sixteen personality factor qualification grid for teacher effectiveness. *National J Education* 5(1) Se 1982 p 15-28 refs
Shrivastava, Sudha
See
Singh, A.P. *jt. auth.*
Srivastava, Sumita
College going girls : Their occupational choices, goals and problems. *J Indian Education* 11(2) Jl 1985 p 40-44
Srivastava, Surya Kumar
Achievement motivation and anxiety among school students. *J Institute of Educational Research* 10(3) Se 1986 p 9-11 refs tabs
See also
Swarn Pratap *jt. auth.*
Srivasudrappa, G.
Impact of ancient Indian philosophical thought on educational theory and practice. *National J Education* 7(2) My 1985 p 9-16

Staple, Cees and Lutman, Martha

Folk high schools in Netherland. *Indian J Adult Education* 44(8-9) Ag-Se 1983 p 34-40 refs

Steele, Ian

Development in history teaching. London, Open Books. 125p. £1.50 *Book Rev, Indian Educational Rev* 16(2) Ap 1981 p 129-32; *Teacher Today* 22(2) Oc-De 1979 p 92-94

Stephen, J. and Sathiagirirajan, S.

College teachers compared with engineers, doctors and lawyers in personality factors. *J Educational Research and Extension* 18(3) Ja 1982 p 187-90 refs tabs

Stockes, J.P.

See

Heaton, J.P. *jt. auth.*

Stones, Edgar

Supervision in teacher education : A counselling and pedagogical approach. London, Metheun 1984, 163p. £4.95 *Book Rev, Progress of Education* 61(2) Se 1986 p 46+

Stolyarov, Yuri

Creative technology for school children. *Primary Teacher* 8(2) Ap 1983 p 4-9

Styler, W.E.

Adult education and political systems. Nottingham, Univ of Nottingham. 227p. £12.95 *Book Rev, Indian J Adult Education* 47(1) Ja 1986 p 30-32 +

Subba Rao, C.S.

Community work in teacher education. *Teacher Education* 13(8-9) Jl-Oc 1979 p 16-20

The curse of correspondence courses in teaching education. *Quest in Education* 19(3) Jl 1982 p 234-37

Subbarao, D.

See

Vasudeva Rao, B.S. *jt. auth.*

Subbarao, D. and Vasudeva Rao, B.S.

The dynamics of instruction in adult education : A perspective plan. *Educational Rev* 88(8) Ag 1982 p 133-34

Subbarayan, Peri

Unutilised manpower of educated unemployed. *Educational Rev* 85(1) Ja 1979 p 11-15

Subba Reddy, B.V.

See

Sudarsen, V. *jt. auth.*

Subba Reddy, H.N. and Channagowda, M.B.

Information sources consulted by dairy farmers in the cultivation of green fodders in Tumkur district. *Indian J Extension Education* 18(1-2) Je 1982 p 92-94

Subhalakchumi, A.

The communication behaviour of school heads : Self-perceptions versus faculty perceptions. *Experiments in Education* 11(8) Oc 1983 p 134-47

Subhash, C.
See
Syag, R.N. *et al jt. auths.*
Subodh Kumar
See
Srivastava, Kumkum *et al jt. auths.*

SUBRAMANYA - SUBRAHMANIAN - SUBRAHMANYAM - SUBRAMANIAM - SUBRAMANIYAM - SUBRAMANYAM - SUBRAHMONIA
See also
under full name/surname, e.g., Bala Subramaniam
Subramaniam, G.
Towards building up a question bank. *Experiments in Education* 7(7) Se 1979 p 113-17 tabs
Validated programmed materials. *Experiments in Education* 9(4) Je 1981 p 71-74 tabs
Subramaniam, Jeyam
Education and its purpose. *New Frontiers in Education* 14(2) Ap-Je 1984 p 52-54
Subramaniam, K.B.
See
Grewal, J.S. *jt. auth.*
Subhramanya, N.
Inculcating discovery attitude in pupils through arithmetical secreations. *Primary Teacher* 4(2) Ap 1979 p 19-22
Triangular numbers. *Primary Teacher* 6(2) Ap 1981 p 16-17
When the teachers become a student. *Primary Teacher* 4(4) Oc 1979 p 15-17
Subramaniyam, P. and Sudha, B.G.
Moral education at the primary level : An attitudinal study, *Quest in Education* 18(1) Ja 1981 p 27-38 refs
Subramaniam, R. *et al*
Time lag in adoption of poultry farming. *Indian J Extension Education* 16(1-2) Je 1980 p 59-60
Subrahmonia, Ranjani
Problems faced by the women engineers of today. *Progress of Education* 59(9) Ja 1985 p 124-31 figs
Subrahmanyam, S.
Adjustment problems of primary school children : A survey in Andhra Pradesh. *Education Quarterly* 37(7) Spr 1985 p 32-37
Differential characteristics of good and poor readers in the range of 9-14. *Experiments in Education* 11(6) Ag 1983 p 95-97
The effectiveness of two different methods of teaching reading in primary school children. *Experiments in Education* 8(10) De 1980 p 185-87 refs tabs
The effectiveness of two different methods of teaching reading in primary schools. *J Educational Research and Extension* 18(3) Ja 1982 p 129-32 tabs
Home environment and reading achievement in primary school children.

Experiments in Education 7(3) My 1979 p 39-42 ref
Problems of school dropouts : A study with a special reference to scheduled castes and scheduled tribes in Andhra Pradesh. *Education Quarterly* 38(3) Aut 1986 p 28-32
Reading problems of children in the age range of 9-14. *Experiments in Education* 12(8) Oc 1984 p 140-44 tabs
Reading, writing and arithmetic scores as predictors of academic success in primary school children. *Experiments in Education* 13(11) Ja 1986 p 195-200 tabs
The relative importance of some selected factors on reading achievement of primary school children. *J Institute of Educational Research* 7(2) My 1983 p 31-36
A study of some intellectual correlates of scholastic attainment of VII class children. *J Education and Psychology* 44(3-4) Jl-De 1986 p 112-17

Subramanian, V.
Rationalising communication strategy in college classes. *J Higher Education* 5(3) Spr 1980 p 35-42

Subramanyam, V.S.
See
Anatharaman, M. *jt. auth.*

Subramonia Pillai, G.
Effects of creative teaching method upon eighth graders. *J Indian Education* 5(4) Nv 1979 p 12-16 refs
Gaps in teacher education. *Experiments in Education* 11(12) Fe 1984 p 213-18
Linkage of higher education with environment. *J Higher Education* 4(3) Spr 1979 p 373-80
The need for an educational technology. *Quest in Education* 17(1) Ja 1980 p 74-80
Programmed learning in Madurai University. *Experiments in Education* 6(9) Nv 1978 p 159-63
Refining the question. *J Higher Education* 5(3) Spr 1980 p 422-24
Reliability and usability of measuring instruments. *Experiments in Education* 10(10) De 1982 p 175-79 refs
Linkage of higher education with environment. *J Higher Education* 4(3) Spr 1979 p 373-80 refs

Subramonia Pillai, G. and Palaniyandi, R.
A factor analysis of creative thinking of the standard students. *Experiments in Education* 10(6) Ag 1982 p 101-05 tabs

Sudame, G.R.
See
Bostia, K.C. *jt. auth.*

Sudame, G.R. and Goel, D.R.
Educational television in India : Organisation and utilisation. *EPA Quarterly Bulletin* 8(1-2) Ap-Je 1985 p 45-58 refs
Students and the STV programme. *Experiments in Education* 12(10) De 1984 p 174-80
A study of school broadcasts in India. *Indian Education* 12(3-4) Je-Jl 1982 p 25-30

Sudame, G.R. and Thiagarajan, A.P.
Academic difficulties of college youth : A case study of the scheduled castes. *Indian Education* 12(5-6) Ag-Se 1982 p 23-29
Enrolment of the scheduled castes in general colleges : A case study of Tamil Nadu. *Experiments in Education* 9(4) Je 1981 p 63-69 tabs
Sudame, G.R. *et al*
School broadcastes in India. *Perspectives in Education* 1(2) Ap 1985 p 123-27
Sudarsana Rao, R.
See
Chalam, K.S. *jt. auth.*
Sudarsen, V. and Subba Reddy, B.V.
Equality for tribals : The role of education. *Experiments in Education* 9(12) Fe 1982 p 213-15
Sudershan, G.
See
Haragopal, G. *jt. auth.*
Sudha, B.G.
See
George, Rita *jt. auth.*
Subramaniyam, P. *jt. auth.*
Sudha, B.G. and Goetha, S.
Problems of girls as a function of material employment and anxiety. *J Institute of Educational Research* 6(1) Ja 1982 p 29-37 refs tabs
Sudha, B.G. and Shakuntala, S.N.
Internal and external examination marks of B.Ed. students : A critical analysis. *Indian Educational Rev* 20(2) Ap 1985 p 39-50
Sudha, B.G. and Tirath, Lalitha V.
The effect of personality trait variation on the intensity of problems of girls. *J Education and Psychology* 37(2) Jl 1979 p 103-14 refs
Sudha, B.G. *et al*
A study of the problems of school teachers. *J Institute of Educational Research* 4(1) Ja 1980 p 37-40 refs tabs
Sudhakar, V.
See
Parmaji, S. *jt. auth.*
Sudhakara Reddy, M.V.
Mode of priority of researches in adult education. *Experiments in Education* 10(1) Mr 1982 p 14-15
Research in adult education. *Educational Rev* 87(9) Se 1981 p 174-
Sudhakara Reddy, M.V. and Janardhana Reddy, D.
The literacy scence in India. *Indian Education* 12(7) Oc 1982 p 23-26
Sudha Rao, K.
An investigation of the relationship between the effective entry characteristics and comments and letter grades on classroom performance. *Indian Educational Rev* 15(2) Ap 1980 p 11-21
Vocationalisation of education and higher secondary stage in India : Psychological impediments, consequences and implications. *Perspectives in Education* 2(3) Jl 1986 p 153-66 tabs

Sudhir Kumar, M.A.
See
Anand, C.L. *jt. auth.*

Sudhir Kumar, M.A. and Lalrinkini
Non-formal education programmes in Mizoram : Retrospect and prospects. *Indian J Adult Education* 44(11) Nv 1983 p 28-33 tabs

Sugathan, M.
Studies on creative artists : A survey. *J Institute of Educational Research* 4(3) Se 1980 p 28-35 refs

Suguna, V.
See
Srinivasa Rao, R. *jt. auth.*

Sujatha, B.N.
Development of teacher education in Mysore district from 1956 to 1976. *Experiments in Education* 12(7) Se 1984 p 123-31
School adjustment and its relation to academic achievement of socially dis-advantaged children. *Education and Psychology Rev* 43(3-4) Oc 1985-Ja 1986 p 197-205 tabs

Sujeevan Rao, V.
Strengthening the link between AIFEA and its affilates. *Indian Education* 10(7) Oc 1980 p 38-43

Sukamyogi, Aimi
Guidance in choosing one's career. *Progress of Education* 56(8) Mr 1982 p 198

Sukha, S.P.
Educational administration. Agra, Vinod Pustak Mandir. 1982, 397p. Rs.22 *Book Rev, J Indian Education* 12(1) My 1986 p 62-63

Sukhbir Singh and Dubey, V.K.
Adoption of scientific feeding practices by cattle owners of the ICDP, Karnal. *Indian J Extension Education* 14(1-2) Ja-Je 1978 p 70-72

Sukhwal, B.L.
Designing maps for school children : Implications of the research on children's congnitive processing and visual perception. *J Indian Education* 12(3) Se 1986 p 15-22 ref

Sultan Ahmad and Joshi, R.K.
Effect of socio-cultural disadvantage on verbal creative thinking ability among school going children. *J Education and Psychology* 37(4) Ja 1980 p 231-38 refs tabs
Effect of socio-cultural disadvantage on verbal originality, fluency and flexibility of creativity. *J Institute of Educational Research* 8(2) My 1984 p 16-24 refs tabs

Sumarokov, L.
See
Kirillovygryumov, V. *jt. auth.*

Sumayao, Blanda R.
In search of alternatives to the schooling model : The case of the NEFRY Project. *Bulletin of Non-Formal Education* 1(4) Mr 1984 p 1-26 refs-ft-n

Sundarajan, R. *et al*
A study of the farm school on the air. *Indian J Extension Education* 14(1-2)

Ja-Je 1978 p 48-49

Sundaram

See

under full name/surname, e.g., Shanmuga Sundaram, R.

Sundaramahalingam, A.

Character building : The basic structure of education. *Experiments in Education* 10(7) Se 1982 p 127-28 refs

Sundaramurthy, S.

Teacher training : A re-education process. *Education Quarterly* 34(1) Ja 1982 p 12-14

Whither vocation. *Education Quarterly* 35(3) Jl 1983 p 26-28

Sundararajan, S.

An experimental study to compare the effectiveness of lecture and lecture-cum-film strip in teaching one unit in general science for std. VII pupils. *Experiments in Education* 6(5) Jl 1978 p 78-81 refs

Problems of teaching general science for standard VI in Tamil Nadu and their impact on pupil achievement in general science. *Experiments in Education* 7(11) Ja 1980 p 193-201; 7(12) Fe 1980 p 211-19; 8(1) Mr 1980 p 6-9 tabs

Sundararao, G.

See

Bhaskara Rao, D. *et al jt. auths.*

Sundaresh, Aruna

Constitution law and reservations. *New Frontiers in Education* 16(2) Ap-Je 1986 p 33-40

Supe, S.V.

An introduction to extension education. New Delhi, Oxf-IBH. 1983, viii, 166p. Rs.12.50 *Book Rev, Indian J Extension Education* 19(3-4) Se-De 1983 p 98

See also

Ingle, O.P. *et al jt. auths.*

Supe, S.V. *et al*

Technological gap in adoption of H4 cotton practices. *Indian J Extension Education* 19(3-4) Se-De 1983 p 69-71

Suraj Kaur

See

Verma, T. *jt. auth.*

Suraj Singh

See

Amar Singh *jt. auth.*

Surana, Bhanwar

Newspaper reporting on education. *J Indian Education* 11(3) Se 1985 p 43-44

Surana, D.C.

Educational television and higher education. *University News* 24(36) 21 Se 1986 p 1-5

Surana, M.L.

Girl dropouts in rural Haryana : A socio-economic analysis. *Indian Educational Rev* 20(2) Ap 1985 p 109-16

Surendra
Geoscience in our educational system. *J Indian Education* 5(5) Ja 1980 p 55-57

Surendra Pratap Singh
Microteaching as an innovation in teacher education. *Teacher Education* 15(14-15) Ja-Ap 1981 p 73-79

Surendra Singh
See
Sharma, D.R. *jt. auth.*

Suri, Aruna and Suri, S.P.
Musical preference in relation to discrimination between notes and certain personality variables. *J Education and Psychology* 36(3) Oc 1978 p 123-32 refs

Suri, M. Shahnaz
American influence on higher education in India. New Delhi, Sterling. 88p. Rs.30 *Book Rev, Education Quarterly* 32(1) Ja 1980 p 42-43

Suri, S.P.
See
Suri, Aruna *jt. auth.*

Suri, Surinder
Fundamental questions. *J Higher Education* 1(1) Mon 1975 p 111-19
Teaching of history in Indian colleges : Need for a new approach. *New Frontiers in Education* 10(4) Oc-De 1980 p 43-58
Teaching of social sciences. *New Frontiers in Education* 10(4) Oc-De 1980 p 27-42

Suriakanthi, A.
An analysis of the development of self-concepts among children belonging to an orphanage. *J Educational Research and Extension* 18(3) Ja 1982 p 149-54 refs tabs

Surjeet Singh
Stratification in the educational system. *J Indian Education* 11(1) My 1985 p 25-33
See also
Arneja, C.S. *jt. auth.*

Surya Bala
See
Sodhi, T.S. *jt. auth.*

Surya Nath Singh
National integration and the role of Indian academics. *National J Education* 3(2) Mr 1981 p 1-6
Research in history of education : Methodological issues and problems. *National J Education* 5(1) Se 1982 p 33-38 refs
See also
Harikesh Singh *jt. auth.*

Suryaprakasa Rao, A.
Ability of estimation by approximatics. *Experiments in Education* 12(4) Je 1984 p 71-74
See also
Parmajit, S. *jt. auth.*

Suryavanshi, V.R.
See
Palted, G.M. *jt. auth.*
Sushma
See
Sharma, Harish *jt. auth.*
Sushma and Upamanyu, V.V.
Psychological factors associated with the socio-economic status. *Asian J Psychology and Education* 4(2) Jl 1979 p 1-10 refs
Sushila Kumari
See
Agarwal, Saroj *jt. auth.*
Sutradhar, Samir Kumar
Higher education in Assam 1866-1979. *Educational Rev* 86(9) Se 1980 p 165-71
Swadeshi, Satya
Education for parenthood in the 80s. *Educational Rev* 86(5) My 1980 p 90-91
Swain, Nihar R.
See
Panda, Santosh K. *jt. auth.*
Swami, Banshi Lal
Children's is problems. *Educational Rev* 84(11) Nv 1978 p 205-06
Sociology of psychological weaning. *Educational Rev* 86(11) Nv 1980 p 207-09
Swaminathan, M.
Communicating with adults through drama in mobile creches. *Indian J Adult Education* 40(12) De 1979 p 7-12
Swaminathan, M.S.
Educational development of the scheduled castes. *J Indian Education* 8(1) My 1982 p 40-55 tabs
Women and rural development. *New Frontiers in Education* 12(3) Jl-Se 1982 p 56-63
Swaminathan, Mina
Needed two revolutions in one non-formal education for women and girls. *Education Quarterly* 34(4) Oc 1982 p 5-7
Swamy
See also
under full name/surname, e.g., Sreedhara Swami, S.
Swamy, C.K.
Implementation of autonomy at St. Joseph's College. *New Frontiers in Education* 12(2) Ap-Je 1982 p 61-67
Swant, G.K. *et al*
Information sources of the adopters of cross-breeding in cattle in Pune district of Maharashtra. *Indian J Extension Education* 15(1-2) Je 1979 p 75-76
Swarn Pratap and Srivastava, Surya Kumar
A study of achievement motivation among graduate, post graduate and Ph.D. students. *J Education and Psychology* 41(1-2) Ap-Jl 1983 p 88-91

A study of sex differences among university students towards different types of values. *J Education and Psychology* 42(4) Ja 1985 p 219-22 refs

Swaroop, M.

See

Gupta, Y.K. *jt. auth.*

Swetharanyam, S.

Teaching physics at the higher secondary stage : A study. *Experiments in Education* 9(10) De 1981 p 169-72

Syag, R.N.

See

Hooda, R.C. *jt. auth.*

Malhotra, S.P. *jt. auth.*

Passi, B.K. *et al jt. auths.*

Sharma, R.C. *jt. auth.*

Syag, R.N. and Hooda, R.C.

Non-formal education : A strategy for educating rural masses. *Progress of Education* 56(3) Oc 1981 p 66-68 refs

A study of academic achievement, interests and psychological integration of orthopaedically handicapped adolescents. *J Institute of Educational Research* 6(1) Ja 1982 p 1-5 refs tabs

Working with the community and teacher education. *Experiments in Education* 10(8) Oc 1982 p 144-46

Syag, R.N. *et al*

A comparative study of the effect of micro teaching and Diod model to improve teaching competency of pre-service teachers. *J Institute of Educational Research* 6(1) Ja 1982 p 38-41 refs tabs

Syrovalkin, Sergal, *Tr.*

Einstein and the philosophical problems of 20th century physics. Moscow, Progress Pub. 1983, 508p. Rs.11.25 *Book Rev, Teacher Today* 27(4) Ap-Je 1985 p 148-49

Tahir, Gidado

Adult education and the new national policy on education in Nigeria : Problems and prospects. *J Indian Education* 12(2) Jl 1986 p 8-14 refs

Tahira Khatoon

Relationship between teachers' classroom verbal behaviour and their attitudes towards teaching. *J Institute of Educational Research* 10(3) Se 1986 p 5-8 refs tabs

Tahira Khatoon and Verma, M.R.

A study of the influence of personal factors on teachers attitude towards their job. *J Institute of Educational Research* 6(2) My 1982 p 6-11 refs tabs

A study of the influence of personal factors on teachers attitude towards their job. *J Education and Psychology* 41(3) Oc 1983 p 159-67

Takawale, Ram

Progress of higher education in Maharashtra. *Progress of Education* 59(10-11) My-Je 1985 p 218-23 +

Talati, Naina and Joshi, Uma

A comparative study of vocational interest of home science students in relation to the selected variables. *Progress of Education* 61(4-5) Nv-De 1986 p 92-95 tabs

Talesra, Hem Lata

Distance education, backward classes and the new social order. *University News* 24(42) 8 Nv 1986 p 29-31

Higher education among women : An analysis of the situation in a district of India. *Perspectives in Education* 2(2) Ap 1986 p 121-24

Talukdar, R.K. and Pawar, S.S.

Listening behaviour of the radio owning farmers in Assam. *Indian J Extension Education* 18(1-2) Je 1982 p 90-91

Tamboli, M.A.

Curriculum load and stress at primary level : A study. *Primary Teacher* 11(1) Ja 1986 p 25-28

Tandon, O.P.

See

Singh, S.N. *jt. auth.*

Tandon, Rajesh

Issues and experiences in participatory research in Asia. *Teacher Today* 22(3) Ja-Mr 1980 p 55-60

Tanwar, R.S.

Creativity and education. *J Indian Education* 5(5) Ja 1980 p 58-64

Need for qualitative analysis of creative responses. *Progress of Education* 55(7) Fe 1981 p 170-71 refs

Tarang, J.S.

Developing instructional strategies. *Indian Educational Rev* 17(1) Ja 1982 p 28-42 refs

Tarlok Singh

Educational values of illiterate and literate adults belonging to scheduled and non-scheduled castes. *J Educational Research and Extension* 19(3) Ja 1983 p 173-79

Humanising literacy campaign. *Indian J Adult Education* 45(4) Ap 1984 p 23-25 +

Is caste a stigma for acquistion of literacy skills? *Quest in Education* 19(2) Ap 1982 p 171-77 refs tabs

Marks and marking behaviour of examiners : A observation. *Rajasthan Board J Education* 16(4) Oc-De 1980 p 32-34

Relationship between academic achievement, extraversion and neuroticism. *J Education and Psychology* 40(4) Ja 1983 p 202-06 refs

Universities role in poverty eradication. *Teacher Education* 20(30-31) Ja-Ap 1985 p 6-10

See also

Amrit Kaur *jt. auth.*

Taskar, N.T.

Primary education in rural India. *Teacher Education* 20(30-31) Ja-Ap 1985 p 37-39

Taylor, H.J.

Runs of identical marks in marksheets and their bearing on the reliability of marking. *Indian Educational Rev* 15(3) Jl 1980 p 51-60 appdx

Taylor, James C. and White, Vernon J.

Why distance education? *Indian J Adult Education* 47(8) Ag 1986 p 2-10 +

Teather, David

Change in universities of the European tradition. *New Frontiers in Education* 14(1) Ja-Mr 1984 p 71-80 ft-n

Teg Bahadur

See

Veerasamy, S. *jt. auth.*

Terry, P.M.

See

Abercromble, M.L.J. *jt. auth.*

Tewari

See

Tiwari

Thadani, Beena

To investigate the relationship between achievement motivation and academic achievement of socially deprived students. *Rajasthan Board J Education* 20(3) Jl-Se 1984 p 13-16

See also

Raizada, B.S. *jt. auth.*

Thadani, Beena and Raizada, B.S.

Level of aspiration and locality. *Educational Rev* 91(8) Ag 1985 p 137-38 refs

Personality characteristics of first-born children of Rajasthan. *Educational Rev* 92(4) Ap 1986 p 75-77 refs tabs

Relationship between achievement motivation and level of aspiration of socially deprived students. *Educational Rev* 90(7-8) Jl-Ag 1984 p 119-21 tabs

Thaker, G.S. and Malhan, I.V.

Renovating school libraries. *J Indian Education* 11(1) My 1985 p 71-75

Thakkar, Aruna

Perspectives in preschool education. Bombay, Popular. 1980, 84p. Rs.30 *Book Rev, Education Quarterly* 33(3) Jl 1981 p 50-51

Thakore, Rashmini

Vitalising practice teaching. *Progress of Education* 55(5) De 1980 p 133-39 refs

Thakur, J.S.

Teaching of imperatives : When and where. *Primary Teacher* 8(1) Ja 1983 p 11-13

Thangaraj, M.A.

Preparing a college for autonomy. *New Frontiers in Education* 10(2) Ap-Je 1980 p 34-43

The teacher and his profession. *New Frontiers in Education* 9(1) Ja-Mr 1979 p 31-38

Thangaswamy, Kokila S.

Instructional strategies for creativity. *Indian Education* 11(6) Se 1981 p 23-25

Politicisation of education. *Indian Education* 12(3-4) Je-Jl 1982 p 17-19

Thangavelu, G.
Introduction of population education as a subject in secondary schools. *Experiments in Education* 8(9) Nv 1980 p 166-72 tabs
Need and scope of population study. *Experiments in Education* 8(8) Oc 1980 p 148-52 refs tabs
Thanvi, Ramesh
Declarations and recommendations of thirty-second IAEA conference. *Teacher Today* 22(2) Oc-De 1979 p 87-90
Thanvi, Shiv Ratan
Teaching through dramatisation. *Primary Teacher* 5(2) Ap 1980 p 25-26
Tharu, Jacob
Examinations reforms : Towards an integrated perspective. *New Frontiers in Education* 14(2) Ap-Je 1984 p 30-35
Thatte, Yadunath
Sane Guruji Kathamala : An organisation trying to make children emotionally literate. *Progress of Education* 57(9) Ap 1983 p 200-01+
Thayaru, P.M.
See
Sreedhara Swamy, S. *jt. auth.*
Thetaraj, R.
See
Sheru, R.R. *jt. auth.*
Thiagarajan, A.P.
A study of the scheduled caste students in some secondary schools of Tamil Nadu. *Indian Education* 11(5) Ag 1981 p 22-26 tabs
See also
Sudame, G.R. *jt. auth.*
Thimmappa, M.S.
See
Ameerjan, M.S. *jt. auth.*
Thom; Douglas J.
Using basic psychology in school administration. *Indian Education* 13(12) Mr 1984 p 1-2
Thomas, Achamma
See
Ram Kumar, Vasantha *jt. auth.*
Thomas, Anita S. and Arvindra Chandra
Reactions of students towards the course : Mass communication in home science. *Educational Rev* 92(9) 1986 p 153-57 refs
Relationship between knowledge and ability gain in the course : Mass communication in home science. *Experiments in Education* 13(11) Ja 1986 p 189-94 refs
Thomas, Anita S. and Tewari, Namrata
TV viewing behaviour of urban women : A study. *Indian J Adult Education* 47(5) My 1986 p 19-23 +
Thomas, Immanuel and Sam Sananda Raj, H.
Self-esteem and academic achievement : A study of ninth grade students. *J Institute of Educational Research* 6(3) Se 1982 p 24-28 refs tabs

Thomas, J.B. *et al*

International dictionary of education. London, ELBS. 1979, 381p. £1.50 *Book Rev, Education Quarterly* 32(1) Ja 1981 p 51-52

Thomson, John M.

Education and development. *Indian Education* 10(5) Ag 1980 p 5-7

Thota, Ananda Rao

The paradoxical situation of English in India. *Indian Education* 10(8) Nv 1980 p 23-25

Some issues in the pedagogies of the general English studies. *Indian Education* 10(11) Fe 1981 p 40-43

Thrimurthy, Syama

Creative thinking ability as a function of sex and achievement. *J Education and Psychology* 44(1) Ap 1986 p 36-40 refs

Thripuri Sundari, R. Bala

Continuing education. *Education Quarterly* 32(4) Oc 1980 p 5-7

Tickoo, Champa

Indian universities. New Delhi, Orient Longman. 1980, 197p. Rs.50 *Book Rev, J Higher Education* 6(1-3) 1980-81 p 164-666

Tikkiwal, B.D. and Tikkiwal, G.C.

A comparative study of direct and indirect methods of absolute grading systems. *Indian Educational Rev* 16(2) Ap 1981 p 113-18 tabs

Tikkiwal, G.C.

See

Tikkiwal, B.D. *jt. auth.*

Tiku, M.N.

Education and economics. *Educational Rev* 85(9) Se 1979 p 161-65

Tilak, Jandhyala B.G.

Planning education for economic development. *Perspectives in Education* 1(1) Ja 1985 p 35-47 refs tabs

Unit cost analysis of higher education in India. *J Higher Education* 5(2) Aut 1979 p 183-93

Wastage in education in India : A case study in Andhra Pradesh. *Indian Educational Rev* 17(2) Ap 1982 p 58-85 refs tabs

Tilak, Jandhyala B.G. and Bhatt, G.K.

Costs of supply of education at micro level : A case study of two education clusters in the district Gurgaon Haryana. *EPA Quarterly Bulletin* 8(3-4) Oc 1985-Ja 1986 p 55-59

Tirth, Lalitha V.

See

Deshpande, Shashikala *jt. auth.*

Sudha, B.G. *jt. auth.*

Tirupati Rao, U.

Toning up of higher education in India. *Educational Rev* 91(12) De 1985 p 211-14

TIWARI - TEWARI

Tewari, B.C.

Adult education : How far real : How far commercial. *Teacher Today* 27(2) Oc-De 1984 p 17-20

Tewari, B.G.

Failures : Pillars of success or breeders of despondency and criminality. *Rajasthan Board J Education* 20(3) Jl-Se 1984 p 8-12

A search for alternatives in education. *Rajasthan Board J Education* 21(3-4) Jl-De 1985 p 51-62

Tiwari, B.N.

See

Misra, Girishwar *jt. auth.*

Tewari, D.D.

Education for a just social and economic order : The Gandhian approach. *Teacher Education* 18(24-25) Jl-Oc 1983 p 1-2 refs

The Gandhian alternatives in education. *Teacher Education* 18(22-23) Ja-Ap 1983 p 55-68

Lifelong learning : Some problems and the wayout. *Teacher Education* 14(10-11) Ja-Ap 1980 p 69-74

National integration and education. *Teacher Education* 20(30-31) Ja-Ap 1985 p 1-5

Presidential address. *Teacher Education* 15(14-15) Ja-Ap 1981 p 1-9

Tewari, Devki

See

Srivastava, Neelam *jt. auth.*

Tiwari, Govind and Pal, Rama

A study of family background : Intellectual abilities of educationally advantaged and disadvantaged group. *Asian J Psychology and Education* 7(1) Ja 1981 p 40-43

Tiwari, Govind *et al*

The effect of anxiety and aspiration on academic of adolescents boys and girls. *Asian J Psychology and Education* 6(1) Ja 1980 p 35-38 refs

Family background, intellectual ability and academic achievement. *Asian J Psychology and Education* 7(2) Ja 1981 p 12-15

Religiousity as function of age and sex. *Asian J Psychology and Education* 6(2) Jl 1980 p 36-40 refs

Tewari, Namrata

See

Thomas, Anita S. *jt. auth.*

Tewari, Narayan Datt

Inaugrural address. *Indian J Adult Education* 41(11) Nv 1980 p 17-21

Tewari, Neelam

See

Misra, Ajay Mohan *et al jt. auths.*

Tiwari, P.L.

Educational administration in Rajasthan. *Teacher Today* 24(3) Ja-Mr 1982 p 66-68

Tewari, R.P.

Critique of education for our people. Delhi, South Asian Pub. 210p. Rs.50 *Book Rev, Education Quarterly* 32(4) Oc 1980 p 44-45

Tiwari, R.S.

Adult education programme : Some apprehensions. *Indian J Adult Education* 39(10) Oc 1978 p 14-18

Tobin, Patty
Sophia : Wisdom is her name. *New Frontiers in Education* 14(2) Ap-Je 1984 p 85-96
Tollo, Donald J.
The community junior college. *J Indian Education* 6(1) My 1980 p 42-43
Tomory, Edith
A history of fine arts in India and the West. New Delhi, Orient Longman. 532p. Rs.40 *Book Rev, New Frontiers in Education* 12(3) Jl-Se 1982 p 79-80
Townley, Charles, ed.
See
Hicks, David *jt. auth.*

TRIPATHI - TRIPATHY

Tripathi, A. *et al*
Constranits in adoption of H.4 rice technology in coastal Orissa. *Indian J Extension Education* 18(1-2) Je 1982 p 51-58 refs tabs
Tripathi, Abha
See
Gakhar, S. *jt. auth.*
Tripathi, B.K.
A study of social acceptance, class room behaviour and academic achievement. *Teacher Education* 13(8-9) Jl-Oc 1979 p 85-88
Tripathi, C.K.
See
Sharma, Motilal *jt. auth.*
Tripathi, Devendra K.M.
See
Tripathi, Narendra K.M. *jt. auth.*
Tripathi, H.B.
See
Deo, Pratibha *jt. auth.*
Tripathi, Kailash Nath
Effects of extrinsic rewards on performance : A review. *J Education and Psychology* 38(4) Ja 1981 p 242-52 refs
Tripathi, Lalji
Development of an extrinsic programme in English grammar and studying its relative effectivness in relation to the conventional method of teaching. *Asian J Psychology and Education* 11(3) 1983 p 25-31 tabs
Tripathi, M.K.
A correlational study of organisational climate and teacher attitudes. *National J Education* 6(2) My 1984 p 21-32 refs tabs
Cultural determinants of motivation. *National J Education* 3(2) Mr 1981 p 24-32 refs
Organisational climate and teacher attitude : A study of relationship. *Indian Educational Rev* 15(1) Ja 1980 p 85-94 tabs
Women's struggle for the new roles. *National J Education* 7(2) My 1985 p 56-60 appdx refs

Tripathi, Narendra K.M.

Approval motive and perceived locus of control. *J Institute of Educational Research* 4(2) My 1980 p 18-23 refs tabs

Congnitive complexity and approval motivation. *J Education and Psychology* 36(1-2) Ap-Je 1978 p 71-77; 37(4) Ja 1980 p 225-30 refs

Tripathi, Narendra K.M. and Tripathi, Devendra K.M.

Personality correlates of approval motive. *J Education and Psychology* 40(3) Oc 1982 p 143-46

Tripathy, Prabina K.

Identification of learning needs of non-formal learners in the age-group 6-14. *Primary Teacher* 8(4) 1983 p 6-8

Role of non-formal education in the context of universalisation of elementary education. *Progress of Education* 60(5) De 1985 p 107-10 refs

See also

Dalal, K.C. *jt. auth.*

Tripathi, S.B.K. *et al*

Socio-personal factors in the job satisfaction of higher secondary school teachers. *J Education and Psychology* 39(1) Ap 1981 p 57-65 refs

Tripathi, S.C.

See

Pachori, R.S. *jt. auth.*

Tripathi, S.N. and Shukla, N.K.

The national integration camp. *J Indian Education* 6(1) My 1980 p 26-29

Tripathi, V.

The story of Literacy House. *Indian J Adult Education* 40(9) Se 1979 p 37-40

Tripathi, V.K.

A study of the personality profiles of teachers and pupil-teachers. *J Education and Psychology* 36(1-2) Ap-Je 1978 p 63-70 refs

Trivedi, M.D.

Self-concept of student-teachers of Colleges of Education. *J Education and Psychology* 39(3) Oc 1981 p 169-75; *Teacher Education* 15(14-15) Ja-Ap 1981 p 37-44 refs

Trivedi, Narmad H.

Education for neoliterates. *Progress of Education* 54(1) Ag 1979 p 21-22

Reconstruction and adult education. *Educational Rev* 87(5) My 1981 p 81-83

Social reconstruction through adult education. *Progress of Education* 55(7) Fe 1981 p 177-78+

Trivedi, R.S.

Can education strengthen the cohesive bonds of the nation. *J Education and Psychology* 41(3) Oc 1983 p 168-71

Our universities are not super markets. *Quest in Education* 17(1) Ja 1980 p 27-34

Tsesarsky, Lev

New programmes of Soviet schools. *Progress of Education* 56(9) Ap 1982 p 221-22

Tuli, Malkh Raj

The campus unrest : Students perception. *J Education and Psychology*

43(1) Ap 1985 p 59-64 refs

Mathematical creativity and personality. *J Education and Psychology* 44(1) Ap 1986 p 16-20 refs

Sex and regional differences in mathematical creativity. *Indian Educational Rev* 17(3) Jl 1982 p 128-34; *J Education and Psychology* 39(4) Ja 1982 p 211-47

Tuli, N.R.

Study habits as correlates of achievement in mathematics. *J Education and Psychology* 38(3) Oc 1980 p 141-48 tabs

Tukeja, S.K.

Universal primary education and literacy programmes in China : Some reflections. *Indian J Adult Education* 46(2) Fe 1985 p 4-9+

Tyagi, K.C.

See

Kokate, K.D. *jt. auth.*

Sohal, T.S. *jt. auth.*

Tyagi, K.C. and Sohal, T.S.

Antecedents of communication of dairy innovations. *Indian J Extension Education* 17(3-4) Se-De 1981 p 1-6 refs

Antecedents of dairy farmers empathy. *Indian J Extension Education* 19(1-2) Mr-Je 1983 p 51-56

Factors associated with adoption of dairy innovations. *Indian J Extension Education* 20(3-4) Se-De 1984 p 1-8 refs

Tyagi, K.G., *ed.*

Indian education index (1948-78). S.P. Agrawal, Gen ed. New Delhi, Manasayan. 1200p. Rs.450 : $100 *Book Rev, Progress of Education* 56(5) De 1981 p 123

Tyagi, M.P.

See

Sharma, D.K. *jt. auth.*

Tyagi, Sushil Kumar

What is mathematics? *Indian Educational Rev* 20(3) Jl 1985 p 102-10

Ubaidullah, M.

In-school population education programme in India. *Educational Rev* 92(7) Jl 1986 p 103-04

Training methodology of population education for NAEP functionaries. *Educational Rev* 89(10) Oc 1983 p 165-68

Uchat, D.A.

See

Desai, Haribhai G. *jt. auth.*

Uchat, D.A. and Desai, Haribhai G.

Self-concept of female students of single sex colleges and co-education colleges : A comparative study. *J Institute of Educational Research* 6(2) My 1982 p 33-36 refs tabs

Uday Shankar

Education of Indian teachers. New Delhi, Sterling. 1984, 332p. Rs.125 *Book Rev, National J Education* 6(1) Se 1983 p 65-66

Exceptional children. New Delhi, Sterling. 1984. 220p. Rs.75 *Book Rev, Education Quarterly* 37(1) Spr 1985 p 69-70; *Teacher Today* 28(1) Jl-Se 1985 p 109-10

Udgaonkar, B.M.

New directions for international scientific cooperation. *J Higher Education* 2(2) Aut 1976 p 167-83 refs

Some comments on the Draft National Policy on Education, 1979. *New Frontiers in Education* 10(3) Jl-Se 1980 p 83-91

Ujagar Singh

Determinants of choice of studies at university level. *J Higher Education* 2(2) Aut 1976 p 253-59 refs tabs

Umar, Zafar

See

Zafar Umar

Umar, S.

Educational technology : An approach to systematic learning. *Asian J Psychology and Education* 11(2) 1983 p 23-27

Uniyal, M.P. and Bisht, A.R.

Neurosis : Developing a measuring scale. *J Educational Research and Extension* 16(3) Ja 1980 p 162-67 refs tabs

School climate and reactions to frustration. *Indian Educational Rev* 15(2) Ap 1980 p 95-101 appdx refs

Uniyal, M.P. and Shah, Beena

Dynamics of motivation for adult learners. *Indian J Adult Education* 44(10) Oc 1983 p 3-5 + refs figs

The level of aspiration of teacher trainees of rural and urban areas in relation to their achievement. *Indian Educational Rev* 16(1) Ja 1981 p 60-65

Uniyal, M.P. and Sharma, R.R.

Societal and institutional magnitudes of activism. *Indian Educational Rev* 20(4) Oc 1985 p 123-36

UPADHYAY - UPADHYAYA

Upadhyay, G.C.

Attitude towards working women : A depth study in rural Kumaon. *Experiments in Education* 9(10) De 1981 p 172-76 refs

Textbooks and national integration. *Experiments in Education* 11(7) Se 1983 p 126-28

Upadhyaya, M.L.

New pattern of legal education. *University News* 22(2) Ja 1981 p 8-9

Upadhyaya, Rajeshwar

Student participation in university administration. *National J Education* 2(2) Mr 1980 p 45-51 refs tabs

See also

Pandey, Sarla Kumari *jt. auth.*

Upadhyaya, S.N.

See

Verma, O.P. *jt. auth.*

Upadhyaya, Usha

Sense of deprivation among high school students. Varanasi, Yojana Pra. 1985, 136p. Rs.75 *Book Rev, J Indian Education* 12(2) Jl 1986 p 60-62

Sense of deprivation and intelligence. *J Institute of Educational Research* 10(3) Se 1986 p 1-4 refs tabs

See also

Saxena, P.C. *jt. auth.*

Upasani, N.K.

Critical factors in human assessment : A plea for evaluating non-scholastic aspects of students growth. *Progress of Education* 56(3) Oc 1981 p 54-61 refs

Curricular reform in higher education. *Quest in Education* 19(2) Ap 1982 p 137-45

Educational research in India : The need for quality control. *Progress of Education* 56(4) Nv 1981 p 78-81+

Effective college teaching. Bombay, SNDT Women's Univ. 1980, 100p. *Book Rev, Progress of Education* 55(12) Jl 1981 p 238

Evaluation of teaching performance. *Quest in Education* 17(4) Oc 1980 p 283-97; 18(1) Ja 1981 p 67-80

Management of learning in higher education. *Quest in Education* 16(4) Oc 1979 p 264-74; 17(1) Ja 1980 p 13-20

The modes approach to teaching. *Quest in Education* 17(2) Ap 1980 p 141-51

Teacher-education for schools in transition. *Quest in Education* 16(3) Jl 1979 p 222-35

Upmanyu, Sushma and Upmanyu, V.V.

Structure of socio-matric status in relation to personality characteristics and intelligence. *J Institute of Educational Research* 6(1) Ja 1982 p 23-28 refs tabs

Upmanyu, V.V.

See

Upmanyu, Sushma *jt. auth.*

Uppal, R.S.

Education on the Sixth Plan. *Teacher Education* 15(16-17) Jl-Oc 1981 p 1-29 annex tabs

Uppal, S.C.

Staff structure for university libraries : A proposal. *University News* 24(37) 1 Oc 1986 p 5-8

Upreti, D.C.

Attitude of teachers towards contemporary socio-economic political issues in India. *Teacher Today* 25(2) Oc-De 1982 p 19-43 tabs

School reform in USSR. *Rajasthan Board J Education* 20(4) 21(1) Oc 1984-Mr 1985 p 21-29

Upreti, D.C. and Rajput, J.S.

Review of 10+2 pattern of education in some states : Implementation stage. *Teacher Today* 24(1) Jl-Se 1981 p 30-36

Usha, G.P.

See

Shivananda, D.S. *jt. auth.*

Usha Devi, M.D.
Integrated child development in the non-formal system of education. *Progress of Education* 56(6) Ja 1982 p 143-46
See also
Seetharamu, A.S. *jt. auth.*
Ushasree, S.
The self-concept and scholastic achievement of the socially disadvantaged. *J Institute of Educational Research* 10(1) Ja 1986 p 17-20 refs
Usmani, S.M.
See
Pestonjee, D. *jt. auth.*

Vaidya, N.
The growth of logical thinking in science during adolescence. New Delhi, Oxf-IBH Pub. 1979, 215p. Rs.15 *Book Rev, J Indian Education* 5(1) My 1979 p 90
The Piagetian journey from Molluska through Moppets to Methappor, 1896-1980. *Indian Educational Rev* 15(4) Oc 1980 p 1-14 refs ft-n
Vallamattam, John
The aims of education. *New Frontiers in Education* 10(3) Jl-Se 1980 p 42-46
Private agencies and minority institutions. *New Frontiers in Education* 10(3) Jl-Se 1980 p 67-70
Vaman Rao
An overview of India's educational system. *Indian Education* 10(1-2) Ap-My 1980 p 40-43
Van Den Ban, A.W.
The challenge of agricultural extensions in the 1980s. *Indian J Extension Education* 18(3-4) De 1982 p 1-9
See also
Chamola, Shankuriah *et al jt. auths.*
Vandenberg, Lela
See
Melachlan, Milla *et al jt. auths.*
Vanjari, S.S.
See
Adhaoo, S.H. *jt. auth.*
Vanvaria, Kiron
See
Satvir Singh *jt. auth.*
Varghese, B.G.
Putting the clock back. *Teacher Education* 14(12-13) Jl-Oc 1980 p 23-30

VARMA - VERMA

Verma, Amita
Experiments in community development through early childhood : Intervention experiences of the department of child development. *Quest in Education* 19(1) Ja 1982 p 7-20 refs

Verma, Amita and Saraswathi, T.S.

The child development curriculum and its relevance to job competencies expected in the field. *J Higher Education* 9(1) Mon 1983 p 119-24

Verma, B.D.

Effects of achievement motivation on learning outcomes following programmed instructional material. *Indian Educational Rev* 20(3) Jl 1985 p 37-46

Verma, B.P.

Construction and validation of criterion referenced test : An empirical study. *J Education and Psychology* 41(4) Ja 1984 p 184-92 refs

Effects of immediate and delays feedback on performance in programmed instruction. *J Institute of Educational Research* 7(2) My 1983 p 20-23

Verma, D.P.

Organisation and management of distance education : The delivery system. *University News* 24(42) 8 Nv 1986 p 25-28

University research. *University News* 24(41) 1 Nv 1986 p 1-4

Verma, Dhirendra

Adult education in Canada : The changing scenario. *Indian J Adult Education* 40(5) My 19979 p 7-12 refs

An efficient approach to the use of audio-visual aids in the classrooms. *Education Quarterly* 30(3) Oc 1978 p 24-27

Health education programme for adults : Some guidelines. *Indian J Adult Education* 43(6) Je 1982 p 3-6 refs

A new approach to curriculum design in technical education. *J Indian Education* 5(4) Nv 1979 p 28-34 refs

Technical-vocational education. *J Indian Education* 6(5) Ja 1981 p 23-26

Verma, Dinesh Kumar

Instructional media for distance education. *Indian Educational Rev* 20(3) Jl 1985 p 72-78

Verma, Gajendra K. *et al*

Illusion and reality in Indian secondary education. Teackfield, Ltd. 1980, 1-xvii, 146p. Rs.120 *Book Rev, J Indian Education* 6(6) Mr 1981 p 62-63

Varma, Janak

Diagnosing mentally retarded children. *Primary Teacher* 10(4) Oc 1985 p 30-32

Verma, Jyoti

Social responsiblity in college students. *Indian Educational Rev* 18(2) Ap 1983 p 69-74

Verma, Lokesh K.

Analysis of re-evaluation cases in Northern universities. *J Higher Education* 5(2) Aut 1979 p 213-20

Appraisal of internal assessment. *Teacher Education* 14(10-11) Ja-Ap 1980 p 28-33 refs

Attitude of university examiners in arts and science subjects towards spot evaluation. *J Higher Education* 7(3) Spr 1982 p 286-88 refs tabs

Internal vs external choices in question papers. *J Indian Education* 6(1) My 1980 p 21-25

Open book examination. *National J Education* 2(1) Se 1979 p 57-64 refs

Opinions of university examiners towards spot evaluation. *Progress of*

Education 56(4) Nv 1981 p 95-97

Some innovations for the improvement of examinations. *Indian Educational Rev* 16(3) Jl 1981 p 1-13

A study of locus of control of high and low creative high school students of different levels of socio-economic status. *J Education and Psychology* 38(2) Jl 1980 p 99-104 refs

Variability in evaluation and re-evaluation of answer scripts. *Experiments in Education* 8(3) My 1980 p 56-58 refs

Verma, Lokesh K. and Gaya, Toshar Kanta

Internal assessment in relation to external marks of B.A. (Hons) students of Utkal University : A statistical study. *Indian Educational Rev* 17(2) Ap 1982 p 27-34 tabs

Verma, M.N.

See

Sharma, R.P. *jt. auth.*

Verma, M.R.

See

Tahira Khatoon *jt. auth.*

Verma, M.S.

Construction of an achievement test in chemistry. *Experiments in Education* 11(2) Ap 1983 p 29-32

A diagnostic test in chemistry. *Educational Rev* 87(7) Jl 1981 p 131-37 refs

Relationship between the scores of projects, assignments, unit tests, half-yearly examinations and annual examinations. *Experiments in Education* 8(11) Ja 1981 p 197-201 refs tab

Verma, Margaret

Building young children's self-concepts through a non-sex approach to early childhood education curriculum materials. *Indian Educational Rev* 20(4) Oc 1985 p 20-33

Helping the child to become human. *Primary Teacher* 4(4) Oc 1979 p 10-14

Humanising experiences for young children through literature. *Primary Teacher* 5(3) Jl 1980 p 5-9

Sex stereotyping in block play of preschool children. *Indian Educational Rev* 15(3) Jl 1980 p 31-37 refs

Varma, Meera

Implementation of nutrition education in the adult education curriculum. *Prasar* 5(3-4) Oc 1977-Ja 1978 p 35-40

Verma, O.P. and Upadhyay, S.N.

Adjustment, anxiety and conflict. *Asian J Psychology and Education* 7(3) 1981 p 28-32 refs tabs

Verma, P.C.

See

Lal, J.N. *jt. auth.*

Verma, P.C. and Srivastava, B.K.

A study of attitudes of teachers trainees towards women's participation in social activities and professions. *Asian J Psychology and Education* 11(1) 1983 p 21-27

Verma, P.L.

Language based SUPW activities. *Rajasthan Board J Education* 20(4)-21(1)

Oc 1984-Mr 1985 p 36-42
Twenty five years of educational research in Rajasthan. *Teacher Today* 26(1) Jl-Se 1983 p 87-100 refs
Verma, P.S.
Internal and external examination scores in science and mathematics : A study. *J Indian Education* 5(6) Mr 1980 p 6-10
Varma, R.P.
Educating the disadvantaged : A few suggestions. *National J Education* 6(2) My 1984 p 1-6 refs
Verma, R.P. *et al*
Assessment of gain in knowledge of sugarcane development workers after a 4 month training course. *Indian J Extension Education* 2(1-2) Je 1984 p 66-68
Verma, Ram Swarup
Socio-psychological makeup of Tharu and Boksa adolescents. *Bhartiya Shiksha Shodh Patrika* 4(2) Jl-De 1985 p 27-33
Verma, Ramesh
Education under Dogra rule 1846-1947. *Educational Rev* 91(5-6) My-Je 1985 p 86-87
Meeting the challenges in education. *Educational Rev* 92(3) Mr 1986 p 46-49
Pathology of Indian education. *Educational Rev* 86(11) Nv 1980 p 201-03
Varma, Ravi Kumar
See
Omerbin Sayeed *jt. auth.*
Verma, S.
See
Verma, T. *jt. auth.*
Verma, S.C.
Integrated Rural Development Programme : Current status. *Indian J Extension Education* 18(1-2) Je 1982 p 10-15
See also
Srivastava, S.N. *jt. auth.*
Varma, S.K.
Clinical psychology and leisure. *Asian J Psychology and Education (Special Number)* 8 1981 p 1-24 refs tabs
See also
Dwarka Prasad *jt. auth.*
Verma, S.K. *et al*
A study of response bases through a questionnaire without questions. *J Education and Psychology* 40(1-2) Ap-Jl 1982 p 74-84
Verma, Shivendra K.
Linguistics in literacy programmes. *J Indian Education* 5(6) Mr 1980 p 43-49
Verma, T. and Suraj Kaur
Existing linkages among various agencies for self-employment activities for rural women of Haryana. *Indian J Extension Education* 21(1-2) Ja-Je 1985 p 65-68 refs tabs
Verma, T. and Verma, S.
Training needs of rural women : An action research. *Indian J Extension*

Education 21(3-4) Jl-De 1985 p 104-07 tabs

Vasantha, A.

Scientific research in universities : Need for a policy. *Progress of Education* 53(3) Mr 1979 p 149-55 +

Vasanthakumar, J. and Singh, S.N.

A study of block level administration for small and marginal farmers agricultural development. *Indian J Extension Education* 21(1-2) Ja-Je 1985 p 53-60 tabs

VASHISHT - VASHISHTHA

Vashistha, K.C.

An investigation into personality correlates of high and low achievers in bio-sciences. *Progress of Education* 58(5) De 1983 p 118-20 tabs

Vashishtha, K.K.

Teachers education in India. New Delhi, Concept. 1979, 159p. Rs.54 *Book Rev, Education Quarterly* 32(2) Ap 1980 p 53; *J Higher Education* 7(3) Spr 1982 p 327-30; *Teacher Education* 14(10-11) Ja-Ap 1980; p 75-76; *Teacher Today* 22(3) Ja-Mr 1980 p 96-98

Vashistha, Kailash Chandra

Responsibility feelings of teachers and its relationship with their students adjustment and achievement. *Experiments in Education* 9(5) Jl 1981 p 89-92

Vashistha, Kamla

Search for a skilled friend, philosopher and guide. *Teacher Today* 24(4) Ap-Je 1982 p 44-49 refs

Vashishtha, Umesh C.

Importance and role of gifted in society. *Indian Education* 10(5) Ag 1980 p 16-18

See also

Passi, B.K. *et al jt. auths.*

Vasudeva, Parminder

See

Mathur, S.S. *jt. auth.*

Vasudeva Rao, B.S.

Adult education in India : A historical review. *Educational Rev* 92(8) Ag 1986 p 130-34 refs

Adult education programme : A study on women's performance. *Indian J Adult Education* 47(6) Je 1986 p 8-12 refs tabs

See also

Subba Rao, D. *jt. auth.*

Vasudeva Rao, B.S. and Ganeswara Rao, K.

Farmers' functional literacy centres : A case study. *Indian J Adult Education* 43(6) Je 1982 p 15-18

Vasudeva Rao, B.S. and Subba Rao

Adult and continuing education and national development. *Educational Rev* 90(1) Ja 1984 p 7-9 refs

Vats, Arunima

Visual thinking and education. *Primary Teacher* 11(2) Ap 1986 p 13-16

Visual thinking : Its physiological bases and educational significance. *Indian Educational Rev* 18(2) Ap 1983 p 60-68 refs

See also

Raina, M.K. *jt. auth.*

Vatsayayan, Kapila

Education and national integration. *Teacher Today* 27(1) Jl-Se 1984 p 63-67

Ved Prakash

Construction of a locus of control questionnaire. *J Indian Education* 6(1) My 1980 p 53-57 tabs

A critical study of an objective type test. *J Indian Educational Rev* 8(3) Se 1982 p 14-19 tabs

Scoring objective type items : A new method. *Indian Educational Rev* 20(4) Oc 1985 p 143-50

See also

Natrajan, V. *jt. auth.*

Vedanayagam, E.G.

Guideline in the elementary school. *Experiments in Education* 6(6) Ag 1978 p 93-98 refs

An opinion survey on selected aspects relating to the restructuring of the school education system as 10+2 in Tamil Nadu. *Experiments in Education* 6(1) Mr 1978 p 223-30 tabs

Remedial education with reference to reading. *New Frontiers in Education* 13(4) Oc-De 1983 p 17-26

See also

Balachandran, E.S. *jt. auth.*

Vedantam, Vatsala

Distance teaching. *University News* 23(1) 16 Mr 1985 p 2-3

Veena

See

Natarajan, V. *jt. auth.*

Veerabhadraiah, V. and Jalihal, K.A.

Job involvement of extension supervisors : A factor analysis. *Indian J Extension Education* 19(3-4) Se-De 1983 p 1-10 refs tabs

Veeraamy, S.

See

Subramaniam, R. *et al jt. auths.*

Veerasamy, S. and Tej Bahadur

Some psychological correlates of adoption of improved rice technology by small farmers of South Arcot district. *Indian J Extension Education* 15(3-4) De 1979 p 87-89 tabs

Veerkar, Pratibha

A study of the effect of integrated approach to teaching social studies in the primary schools. *Research Bulletin* 12(1-2) Mr-Je 1982 p 11-18

Venkata Iyer

Dynamic reading skills. New Delhi, Sterling, vi, 175p. Rs.70 *Book Rev, Education Quarterly* 38(3) Aut 1986 p 61-62

VENKATAIAH - VENKATIAH

Venkatiah, M.
- Centralisation of libraries : Merits and demerits. *J Indian Education* 8(5) Ja 1983 p 52-54
- University library and documentation service. *J Indian Education* 6(1) My 1980 p 19-20

Venkataiah, N.
- Are the secondary school teachers satisfied with the environmental factors. *Experiments in Education* 10(4) Je 1982 p 71-74 refs
- Attitudes of the professional and non-professional students towards entrance examinations. *J Education and Psychology* 40(4) Ja 1983 p 195-201 refs tabs
- Construction of attitude scales : Attitude towards improved agricultural practices; attitude towards adult literacy. *Indian J Adult Education* 40(2) Fe 1979 p 27-40 appdx
- Improving professional status of teachers. *Educational Rev* 85(7) Jl 1979 p 136-38
- International Literacy Day. *Experiments in Education* 7(6) Ag 1979 p 103-05
- Non-formal education for adult tribes. *Experiments in Education* 8(3) My 1980 p 54-56
- Problems in practice teaching, *Indian Education* 10(9-10) De 1980-Ja 1981 p 7-12
- Reading materials for neo-literates. *Experiments in Education* 7(8) Oc 1979 p 136-39; *Indian J Adult Education* 40(9) Se 1979 p 8-10
- Role of teachers. *Educational Rev* 85(1) Ja 1979 p 9-10
- A study of achievement of students of different socio-economic status. *J Institute of Educational Research* 4(3) Se 1980 p 42-45 refs tabs
- Two image of the personality profile of college teachers. *Experiments in Education* 11(4) Je 1983 p 66-68

Venkataiah, N. and Adinarayan Reddy, P.
- Expenditure on education with special reference to adult education. *Educational Rev* 89(5-6) My-Je 1983 p 81-84 tabs
- Learning choices of adults. *Experiments in Education* 9(5) Jl 1981 p 85-87 tabs
- National Adult Education Programme and the disabled. *Educational Rev* 88(7) Jl 1982 p 109-10
- Qualities of an ideal researchers as perceived by the research supervisors. *Experiments in Education* 11(10) De 1983 p 177-80
- Significance of adult continuing education and extension programmes in universities. *University News* 22(1) Ja 1984 p 17-19

Venkataiah, N. and Naidu, K. Dayachandrama
- A study of the relationship of certain selected variables of the teachers to their teaching success. *J Education and Psychology* 43(3-4) Oc 1985-Ja 1986 p 174-82 refs

Venkataiah, R.N. and Subba Reddy, B.V.
- Non-formal adult education for tribes. *Educational Rev* 86(6) Je 1980 p 111-14

Venkataraman, R.

Teaching : Promise and performance. *Experiments in Education* 7(6) Ag 1979 p 106-07

Venkata Rami Reddy, A.

Attitude of students towards English and regional media. *Quest in Education* 18(2) Jl 1981 p 205-19

A comparative study of the attitude of post graduate students of two institutions towards internal assessment. *J Education and Psychology* 38(1) Ap 1980 p 4-16 refs tabs

Do students achieve better in regional medium than in English medium? *Indian Educational Rev* 19(2) Ap 1984 p 79-90

How do engineering students look at internal assessment? *Asian J Psychology and Education* 7(1) Ja 1981 p 31-39

Internal assessment : Expectations and experiences. *Asian J Psychology and Education* 4(2) Jl 1979 p 22-26 refs

Job satisfaction of teachers working under different managements. *Education Quarterly* 30(3) Oc 1978 p 28-29

Students reactions towards English and regional media : A comparative study. *J Higher Education* 5(1) Mon 1979 p 101-08 refs tabs

A two-year follow up study on internal assessment. *J Higher Education* 4(1) Mon 1978 p 47-56 refs tabs figs

Venkata Rami Reddy, A. and Babjan, A.O.

Are married teachers more satisfied with their jobs than the unmarried? *Indian Educational Rev* 16(2) Ap 1981 p 15-18 refs

Effect of type of management and sex on job satisfaction of teachers, *Quest in Education* 17(4) Oc 1980 p 309-17 ref

Venkata Rami Reddy, A. and Balakrishna Reddy, P.

Creativity of adolescent boys and girls in relation to some variables. *Indian Educational Rev* 19(1) Ja 1984 p 60-72

Venkata Rami Reddy, A. and Chandra Reddy, T.

Attitude of students towards introduction of regional medium at the post graduate level. *Education Quarterly* 32(1) Ja 1980 p 16-18

Venkata Rami Reddy, A. and Krishna Reddy, N.

Art teachers satisfied with their jobs : A study. *J Indian Education* 6(2) Jl 1980 p 59-65 refs

Job satisfaction of teachers working under different managements. *Education Quarterly* 30(3) Oc 1978 p 28-29

Venkata Rammi Reddy, A. and Muni Reddy, D.

The regional languages and English as media of instruction. *J Indian Education* 6(4) Nv 1980 p 13-16

Venkata Rami Reddy, A. and Pratapa Simha, G.

Which do they want, IA or TS : A comparative study. *J Higher Education* 4(3) Spr 1979 p 400-06

Venkata Rami Reddy, A. and Sidda Reddy, K.

They want the new system of evaluation. *Education Quarterly* 32(3) Jl 1980 p 104 refs

Venkata Rami Reddy, V.

PG's want a change over to internal assessment. *Asian J Psychology and Education* 13(1) Ja 1984 p 11-19 refs

Venkataramu, K.S.

Linguistic development of pre-school children. *Educational Rev* 90(10) Oc 1984 p 155-57

Motivation in education. *Educational Rev* 88(3) Mr 1982 p 41-42

Teachers role in pupils mental development : A psychoanalytic approach. *Educational Rev* 88(9) Se 1982 p 145-47

Venkatarangachar, H.K. and Ravindranatha, M.N.

Non-formal education and development. *J Indian Education* 8(1) My 1982 p 68-70

Venkata Rao, D.

The teaching of history. *Indian Education* 12(8-9) Nv-De 1982 p 38-39

Venkata Rao, P.

See

Prasada Rao, D.L. *jt. auth.*

Venkatsubramanian, K.

Education and economic development in India : Tamil Nadu : A case study. Delhi, Frank Bros & Co. 1980, xxiii, 243p. Rs.95 *Book Rev, Indian Educational Rev* 16(1) Ja 1981 p 126-28

Nutritious meal programme of Tamil Nadu. *EPA Quarterly Bulletin* 5(3-4) Oc 1982-Ja 1983 p 1-13 refs tabs

Wastage in primary education. New Delhi, Orient Longman. 1978, 86p. Rs. 15 *Book Rev, Progress of Education* 53(12) Jl 1979 p 238

Venkateshwara Rao, V.

Democratisation and decentralisation of university administration. *Indian Education* 13(7) Oc 1983 p 19-22

Management of universities in India : Need for structural reforms. *Indian Education* 12(8-9) Nv-De 1982 p 9-12

Restructuring the academic courses : Its significance and implications. *Progress of Education* 57(6) Ja 1983

Venkatramreddy, B.

54th All India Educational Conference, Kurukshetra; Presidential address 28-12-1980. *Indian Education* 10(11) Fe 1981 p 11-15

Vocationalisation at +2 stage. *Indian Education* 10(4) Jl 1980 p 3-5

Venkitaraman, A.R.

Four years of autonomy at American college. *New Frontiers in Education* 12(2) Ap-Je 1982 p 47-51

Implimentation of college autonomy. *New Frontiers in Education* 10(1) Ja-Mr 1980 p 28-34

Venku Reddy, S.

See

Laxmi Devi, A. *jt. auth.*

Venugopal, K.C.

Developing listening skill in school pupils with the help of audio-tape recorder. *J Indian Education* 12(1) My 1986 p 55-57

Microteaching : A novel teacher training technique. *J Indian Education* 7(3) Se 1979 p 20-23

Verghese, Alexander V.

Education, earning and occupation of weaker castes. *J Higher Education* 9(3) Spr 1984 p 373-81 refs tabs

Verghese, C. Paul
Higher education in Kerala. *New Frontiers in Education*12(2) Ap-Je 1982 p 21-24

Verghese, M.V.
Education, technology and development : A perspective. New Delhi, NIEPA. 29p. *Book Rev, Education Quarterly* 36(4) Wint 1984 p 53-54

Verma
See
Varma

Verman, O.P. and Yadav, K.
A study of some personality of talented students in science. *J Educational Research and Extension* 16(2) Oc 1979 p 89-93 refs tabs

Vernal, Louis
Students attitudes towards school. *Indian Educational Rev* 14(4) Oc 1979 p 1-12 refs ft-n

Verry, Donald and Davies, Bleddyn Pryce
Universities costs and output : Studies on education. Elsevier Scientific Pub vol. 6. 1978, 244p. *Book Rev, J Higher Education* 4(1) Mon 1978 p 124-25

Verstraeten, A.
Draft National Policy on Education, 1979 : Some comments. *New Frontiers in Education* 10(3) Jl-Se 1980 p 47-58

Vidart, Daniel
Environmental education : Theory and practice. *J Indian Education* 6(2) Jl 1980 p 35-51 ft-n

Vidhu Mohan
Counselling of the socially disadvantaged child. *Asian J Psychology and Education* 11(2) 1983 p 1-8

Vidyasagar, G. and Prasada Rao, Y.F.W.
A strategy for child centred approach. *Primary Teacher* 11(4) Oc 1986 p 1-4

Vij, D.R.
NCTE : An introduction. *Educational Rev* 88(1) Ja 1982 p 14-17

Vijayabharathy, M. and Portia, D.R.
Adult education : Its impact upon democracy. *Educational Rev* 90(3) Mr 1984 p 53-55

Vijayalakshmi, G.
An investigation into the problem of research scholars. *Experiments in Education* 12(4) Je 1984 p 69-71

Vijayaragavan, K. and Subramanyan, V.S.
Communication behaviour of gardenland and dry land farmers. *Indian J Extension Education* 16(1-2) Je 1980 p 77-81 tabs
Socio-psychological factors associated with communication behaviour of farmers. *Indian J Extension Education* 17(3-4) Se-De 1981 p 22-30 refs tabs

Vijaya Ratnam, S.
Some crucial problems in education. *Educational Rev* 86(4) Ap 1980 p 61-63

Vijaylakshmi, C.H.
Application of action research in teaching mathematics. *Indian Education*

12(1-2) Ap-My 1982 p 52-55
Programmed instruction in mathematics. *Indian Education* 11(11-12) Fe-Mr 1982 p 15-21

Vikram Sinha Rao, K.
Crises in higher education. *Progress of Education* 57(8) Mr 1983 p 181-83

Virendra Singh
The students bodies in the universities. *J Higher Education* 8(2) Aut 1982 p 228-33 tabs

Virk, J.
Personality characteristics of academically talented students. *J Education and Psychology* 44(1) Ap 1986 p 41-46 refs

Visvesvaran, H.
Population education : Concepts and aims. *Experiments in Education* 7(6) Ag 1979 p 95-102
Training of teachers. *Experiments in Education* 7(4) Je 1979 p 59-63 refs

Viswanathan, T.V.
Teaching economics through case study method : An experiment learning efficiency. *Experiments in Education* 9(10) De 1981 p 182-86; *J Educational Research and Extension* 18(2) Oc 1981 p 60-64 tabs

Vora, I.A.
An investigation into social maturity as a function of area and modernisation. *J Education and Psychology* 40(1-2) Ap-Jl 1982 p 53-61 refs
A study of creative thinking ability as a function of intelligence, parential behaviour and radicalism. *J Education and Psychology* 41(3) Oc 1983 p 146-52 refs
A study of effects of anxiety and attitude in reading achievement. *J Education and Psychology* 38(1) Ap 1980 p 36-42 tabs
A study of reading achievement in relation to sex attitude and anxiety. *J Education and Psychology* 36(1-2) Ap-Je 1978 p 41-53 refs
See also
Patel, B.V. *jt. auth.*

Vora, Maya K.
The role of school libraries in primary and secondary schools. *Indian Educational Rev* 14(1) Ja 1979 p 92-99

Vrtilkova, Miluse
New law on Czechoslovak education. *Student Action* 3(2) Se 1984 p 25

Vyas, Bhawani Shankar
Challenge of education : Face to face with realities. *Teacher Today* 28(2) Oc-De 1985 p 23-26

Vyas, Premila
A study of international students perceptions of selected factors from the urban university environment. *Indian Education Rev* 15(3) Jl 1980 p 97-102 tabs

Vyas, R.N.
Education for political leadership. Ambika Pub. 1970, 92p. Rs.30 *Book Rev, Teacher Today* 22(2) Oc-De 1979 p 91-92

Vyasulu Reddy, Usha
Scope and content of educational journalism. *Indian Education* 11(3) Je 1981 p 17-19

Wadhera, R.C.
Educational facets : Fair and unfair. *J Indian Education* 12(1) My 1986 p 26-30
Sainik schools : Perceptions and reflections. *J Indian Education* 8(4) Nv 1982 p 43-47
Scenario of Sainik Schools. *J Indian Education* 12(2) Jl 1986 p 15-19

Wadhwa, B.S.
See also
Kundu, C.L. *jt. auth.*

Wadhwa, B.S. and Kundu, C.L.
Neuroticism and extraversion of university student dissidents and nondissidents. *Asian J Psychology and Education* 14(1-4) 1984 p 52-56 refs

Wadhwa, Surender
A study of graduate teachers adjustment and its relationship with students academic achievement. *J Education and Psychology* 36(3) Oc 1978 p 118-22 refs

Wadia, Khorshed A.
Guiding creative talent : The role of the counsellor. *J Indian Education* 8(4) Nv 1982 p 15-19 refs

Wafadar, A.J.
See
Srivastava, G.N. *jt. auth.*

Wagh, K.C.
How to draw a cat? *Primary Teacher* 4(3) Jl 1979 p 18-27

Waghmare, K.W.
See
Supe, S.V. *et al jt. auths.*

Waghmare, S.K. and Pandit, V.K.
Constraints in adoption of wheat technology by the tribal farmers of Madhya Pradesh. *Indian J Extension Education* 18(1-2) Je 1982 p 95-98

Wahid, Abdur Rahman
Peasantrian, Islamic education and community development. *New Frontiers in Education* 14(2) Ap-Je 1984 p 26-29

Wahle, Roy P.
A study of educational leadership in India. *J Education and Psychology* 44(2-3) Jl-De 1986 p 77.91

Wain, C.T., *ed.*
Mathematical education. Van Nostrant Reinhold Co. 197p. £8.50 *Book Rev, Education Quarterly* 3(3-4) Oc 1979-Ja 1980 p 48

Walatara, Douglas
Education and attention : A basis for the humanities. Delhi, Macmillan 1980, xii, 125p. Rs.50 *Book Rev, Education Quarterly* 33(3) Jl 198 p 45-46

Walia, S.
See
Sharma, K.K. *jt. auth.*
Walkar, Stephen, *ed.*
See
Boston, Len *jt. auth.*
Wanchoo, V.N., *ed.*
World views of science education. New Delhi, Oxf-IBH. p 414 Rs. 90 *Book Rev, Education Quarterly* 34(4) Oc 1982 p 57-58
Wangu, Ravi
Establishing cross-cultural validity of disciplined-indisciplined scale (D-I scale). *Indian Educational Rev* 20(4) Oc 1985 p 34-39
Wani, S.P.
A comparative study of attainments in the algebraic concept formations of standard VIII students. *Research Bulletin* 12(1-2) Mr-Je 1982 p 27-34
A study of effectiveness of non-traditional methods for teaching mathematics to class X. *Research Bulletin* 12(3-4) Se-De 1982 p 30-43
A study of fulfilment of minimum needs of the schools coming under the school complex centre. *Research Bulletin* 15(1-2) Mr-Je 1985 p 10-18 tabs
Wannashoti, C.
See
Buch, P.M. *et al jt. auths.*
Waples, Maria E.
See
Nagarath, M. Pla *jt. auth.*
Warren, Keith
Primary science education with local resources in Asia. *Primary Teacher* 5(2) Ap 1980 p 4-10
Warthein, Jorge
Seeking an adequate approach for relating the education of adults with their work. *Indian J Adult Education* 39(9) Se 1978 p 23-27
Warty, K.G.
A study of Gandhian education. Bombay, Somaiya Pub. 1981, 138p. Rs. 10 *Book Rev, Progress of Education* 56(7) Fe 1982 p 177
Wasaser, Frederich
The functions and problems of the urban university in the West : A comparative perspective. *J Higher Education* 8(3) Spr 1987 p 375-81
Washikar, S.S.
Micro-teaching. Pune. Nutan Phra. (H) 74p. Rs.7 *Book Rev, Progress of Education* 56(6) Ja 1982 p 153
Wasi, Muriel
Educating women in India : Ends and means. *Education Quarterly* 34(4) Oc 1982 p 1-4
Living and learning. Dalta Book Centre. 1978, 107p. Rs.20 *Book Rev, Education Quarterly* 31(1) Ap 1979 p 35-36; *Teacher Today* 21(3) Ja-Mr 1979 p 101-02
The voluntary agency and adult education. *Education Quarterly* 30(3) Oc 1978 p 1-3

Weil, Marsha
See
Joyce, Bruce *jt. auth.*
Weishahn, Mel W.
See
Gearheart, bill R. *jt. auth.*
Wells, Gordon and Nicholls, John
Language and learning : An international perspective. Sussex, Falmer Press. 1985, vii, 171p. *Book Rev, Education Quarterly* 38(3) Aut 1986 p 60-61
Wen Jiao
Education in China. *Indian Education* 10(8) Nv 1980 p 20-22
Werthein, Jorge
The political economy of adult education in Cuba. *Perspectives in Education* 1(3) Jl 1985 p 135-56 refs
Weston, Keith and Wilson, Raymond
Contemporary issues in comparative education. Kent, Croom Helm. 227p. £15.95 *Book Rev, Education Quarterly* 38(3) Aut 1986 p 51
White, Patricia
The aims of education restated. London, Routledge. 1982, 177p. £8.95 *Book Rev, Teacher Today* 26(1) Jl-Se 1983 p 186
Beyond domination : An essay in the political philosophy of education. London, Routledge. 1983, 183 p £11.95 *Book Rev, Education Quarterly* 36(4) Wint 1984 p 54-55
White, Vernon J.
See
Taylor, James C. *jt. auth.*
Whiting, Norman
School self-evaluation : Some initial considerations. *J Education and Psychology* 40(3) Oc 1982 p 107-16 refs
Widdowson, H.G.
Teaching language as communication. London, OUP. 1978, 168p. £3.50 *Book Rev, Progress of Education* 56(1) Ag 1981 p 25
Wijetunga, W.M.K.
Promotion and co-ordination of non-formal education in Sri Lanka. *Indian J Adult Education* 39(11-12) Nv-De 1978 p 50-52
Williams, Elaine
Electronic link for distant teachers and pupils. *Progress of Education* 56(4) Nv 1981 p 82-83
Williams, Sarah S.
Attitude of high school pupils towards their teachers and its relationship with achievement in science. *J Educational Research and Extension* 18(1) Jl 1981 p 21-23
Wills, W. David
Spare the child. Penguin Educ. (Repr.) 1973, 153p. 40d. *Book Rev Teacher Today* 22(3) Ja-Mr 1980 p 98-100
Wilson, Bryon, *ed.*
Education, equality and society. London, Allen and Unwin. 1975, 200p. *Book Rev, J Indian Education* 5(5) Ja 1980 p 84-86

Wilson, M.J. and Chaturvedi, J.
Adoption of improved technology of flue-cured Virginia (FCV) tobacco in Andhra Pradesh. *Indian J Extension Education* 21(3-4) Jl-De 1985 p 108-09
Wilson, M.J. and Reddy, B.L.
Attitude of teacher volunteers towards farmers functional literacy programme : Guntur study. *Indian J Adult Education* 40(6) Je 1979 p 29-33 refs
Windler, Gerhard
Art education : The aesthetic relationship between mother and child. *Indian Education* 11(7) Oc 1981 p 5-7
Wittcock, Merlin C., *ed.*
See
Pirozzolo, Francis J. *jt. auths.*
Wizarat Husain
See
Siddiqui, W.H. *jt. auth.*
Woghalikar, G.A.
The role of vocational guidance. *J Indian Education* 9(1) My 1983 p 7-11
Wokhlu, O.N. and Labhru, G.L.
Leadership in technical education institutions. *Indian Educational Rev* 19(1) Ja 1984 p 159-60
Woodhall, Maurean
The use of student loans in the finance of higher education : A summary of Western experience. *J Higher Education* 5(3) Spr 1980 p 417-21 refs tabs
Woods, Ronald
See
Garrow, Robin *jt. auth.*
Worison, R.L. and Linford, A.G.
An investigation of sex differences in general intellectual ability in rural and urban children. *J Education and Psychology* 37(1) Ap 1979 p 10-18 refs
Wringe, C., *ed.*
See
Snelders, P. *jt. auth.*
Wydiffe, Nirmala
Autonomy at Lady Doak College. *New Frontiers in Education* 12(2) Ap-Je 1982 p 55+

YADAV - YADAVA

Yadava, J.S.
Communication and management of Integrated Rural Development Programme. *Indian J Extension Education* 21(1-2) Ja-Je 1985 p 42-47
Mass media for civic education : The challenges of research. *Indian J Adult Education* 46(9) Se 1985 p 17-21 refs
Yadav, K.
See
Verman, O.P. *jt. auth.*

Yadav, K.D. and Jain. N.C.

Socio-economic factors influencing the adoption and non-adoption of hybrid cattle in Western M.P. *Indian J Extension Education* 20(1-2) Je 1984 p 71-72

Yadav, M.S. and Menon, M.B.

Development of a question bank for a course on educational evaluation at B.Ed level. *J Higher Education* 3(3) Spr 1978 p 357-67 refs tabs

Development research in the context of instruction : Significance and design. *National J Education* 6(2) My 1984 p 59-67 refs

Research needs in technical education. *J Indian Education* 6(4) Nv 1980 p 17-22

Yadav, M.S. and Roy, S.

University and national development : Linkage with the environment. *New Frontiers in Education* 10(3) Oc-De 1980 p 22-26 refs

Yadav, M.S. and Seshadri, Malathi

Modernisation of mathematics instruction at secondary school : A development of project. *Indian Educational Rev* 19(1) Ja 1984 p 36-51

Yadav, M.S. *et al*

Educational research as an interdisciplinary endeavour. *New Frontiers in Education* 12(3) Jl-Se 1982 p 14-22

Higher education in India : Survival and revival. *Indian Educational Rev* 20(3) Jl 1985 p 1-11

Integrating education with development in the community : Role of university teachers. *New Frontiers in Education* 14(2) Ap-Je 1984 p 43-51

Quantitative and qualitative approaches in educational research. *J Education and Psychology* 43(1) Ap 1985 p 5-13

Yadav, R.

See

Parikh, Jyoti *jt. auth.*

Yadav, R.C. and Singh, H.P.

Wastage at the Ph.D. level. *New Frontiers in Education* 12(4) Oc-De 1982 p 43-48

Yadav, R.D.

Universalisation of elementary education : Non-formal education programme and the instructor : A study in Uttar Pradesh. *Bulletin of Non-Formal Education* 3(1) Je 1985 p 1-10 refs

Yadav, R.K.

Far from the main campus. *J Higher Education* 1(1) Mon 1975 p 99-102

Indian education and national culture. *National J Education* 3(2) Mr 1981 p 17-23 refs

Social demands on the university. *National J Education* 3(1) Se 1980 p 1-8 refs

University and national development. *Perspectives in Education* 1(2) Ap 1985 p 71-74

Yadav, R.S.

An advanced cognitive theory of learning for a curriculum model. *Progress of Education* 58(7) Fe 1984 p 155-66 refs

A comparative study of lecture method, guided discovery approach and discovery approach in the teaching of science. *J Education and*

Psychology 44(1) Ap 1986 p 58-65 refs

Correlating among I.Q., age, academic achievement and parental income of high school science students. *J Institute of Educational Research* 10(3) Se 1986 p 12-17 refs tabs

Examination reform and future prospects. *Quest in Education* 18(3) Jl 1981 p 243-62

An experimental study for the validation of guided-discovery method over lecture method at different academic levels on VII grade students. *Progress of Education* 57(4) Nv 1982 p 84-90 tabs

An experimental study of contribution of learning objective to achievement scares through lecture and guided discovery methods. *Asian J Psychology and Education* 14(1-4) 1984 p 1-14 refs

An experimental study of effectiveness of demonstration methods over lecture method in terms of learning objectives of VI grade students. *Asian J Psychology and Education* 9(3) 1982 p 30-42

Role of mass media in distance education. *EPA Quarterly Bulletin* 7(3-4) Oc 1984-Ja 1985 p 37-52 refs

A study of correlation among intelligence, academic acheivement and creativity. *Progress of Education* 61(3) Oc 1986 p 50-53 refs tabs

Yadav, Raj Kumar

A study of relationship between values and vocational preferences of adolescents. *Quest in Education* 17(2) Ap 1980 p 165-72 refs

Yadav, S.K.

Intelligence, motivational tendencies of scheduled castes and non-scheduled caste secondary students. *J Education and Psychology* 37(2) Jl 1979 p 83-89 refs tabs

Research review on implementation of the educational schemes of scheduled castes. *Indian Educational Rev* 18(3) Jl 1983 p 112-22 refs

A study of relaal educp between vocational anxiety and attitude towards teaching profession among teacher trainees. *Progress of Education* 57(8) Mr 1983 p 177-80 tabs

A study of the scheduled castes awareness about the schemes for their educational progress. *Indian Educational Rev* 17(1) Ja 1982 p 85-93

Yadav, Saroj

Population education corner : A promising innovation. *Primary Teacher* 190(2) Ap 1985 p 1-3

Yadav, Satish Kumar

Case study of a gifted child. *J Education and Psychology* 38(1) Ap 1980 p 61-66 refs tabs

Development of creative thinking abilities at the primary stage. *Primary Teacher* 6(3) Jl 1981 p 11-15

Physical education and primary school curriculum. *Primary Teacher* 5(1) Ja 1980 p 4-7

A study of attitude towards teaching profession among teacher trainees. *Progress of Education* 55(10) My 1981 p 251-54 tabs

Yanwen, Zheng

Education in China. *Indian Education* 13(5-6) Ag-Se 1983 p 29+

Yash Pal Singh

See

Sharma, D.K. *jt. auth.*

Young, B.L.

Teaching primary science. London, Orient Longman. 1984, 217p. *Book Rev, Teacher Today* 28(2) Oc-De 1985 p 121-23

Yung Chung Kim

Modernisation and the Korean experience. *New Frontiers in Education* 14(2) Ap-Je 1984 p 1-9 refs

Zachariah, Mathew

A note on the private sector in education. Indian *Educational Rev* 15(1) Ja 1980 p 104-09

Zafar Umar

Acquisition of general information : Role of sex and general intelligence. *Educational Rev* 85(2) Fe 1979 p 25-28 refs tabs

Zahirul Haque, A.B.M.

Incentive in industry. *Asian J Psychology and Education* 4(2) Jl 1979 p 51-53

Zakir, K.L.

Environment education : Need for attitudinal change. *Indian J Adult Education* 45(3) Mr 1984 p 23-25+

Role of adult education in active aging. *Indian J Adult Education* 45(10) Oc 1984 p 23-25

Zargar, Abdul Hamid

Creativity and neuroticism : A correlational analysis. *Educational Rev* 89(5-6) My-Je 1983 p 91-93 refs tabs

See also

Liddoo, Motilal *jt. auth.*

Zechariah, Mathew

Fair access to higher education : Reflections on India's and China's experience of the past thirty years. *J Higher Education* 8(3) Spr 1983 p 311-20

Zettersten, Arne

New technologies in language learning. London, Pergamon Press. 1980, 189p. £9.95 *Book Rev, Teacher Today* 29(1) Jl-Se 1986 p 107-08

Zoseph, K.S.

Towards the making of a better teacher. *Teacher Education* 16(18-19) Ja-Ap 1982 p 53-60

Zuberi, Anwar Jahan

A comparative study of majority and minority communities in India on feeling of security, self-acceptance and level of aspiration. *Teacher Education* 14(12-13) Jl-Oc 1980 34-40 refs

CICIL LIST

CONCEPTS IN COMMUNICATION, INFORMATICS & LIBRARIANSHIP

(CICIL)

General Editor: **S.P. AGRAWAL**

CICIL-1 Development of Library Services in India: Social Science Information
S.P. Agrawal Rs. 150

CICIL-2 Development of Documentation in India: Social Science Information
S.P. Agrawal Rs. 250

CICIL-3 UNESCO and Social Sciences: Retrospect and Prospect
S.P. Agrawal and **J.C. Aggarwal** Rs. 250

CICIL-4 INDIANA : A Bibliography of Bibliographical Sources
M.K. Jain Rs. 200

CICIL-5 Dimensions of Library and Information Science: Kaula Festschrift
V. Venkatappaiah (Eds.) Rs. 600

CICIL-6 Book Numbers: Some Indian Methods
M.P. Satija and **S.P. Agrawal** Rs. 100

CICIL-7 National Policy for University Libraries in India: Problems and Perspectives
N.B. Inamdar and **L.S. Ramaiah** (Ed.) Rs. 250

CICIL-8 Media Utilisation for the Development of Women and Children
B.S. Thakur and **Binod C. Agrawal** Rs. 150

CICIL-9 Terrorism: An Annotated Bibliography
Susheela Bhan (Ed.) Rs. 275

CICIL-10 Transnational Library Relations: The Indo-American Experience
M.B. Konnur Rs. 175

CICIL-11 Geography of Marketing and Commercial Activities in India (Documentation on Research Information)
R.S. Dixit Rs. 130

CICIL-12 Information India 1988: Global View
S.P. Agrawal and **J.C. Aggarwal** Rs. 200

CICIL-13 Women's Education in India: Historical Review, Present Status and Perspective Plan
S.P. Agrawal and **J.C. Aggarwal** Rs. 360

CICIL-14 Cultural Communication in India: Role and Impact of Phonograms
J.M. Ojha (in press)

CICIL-15	Second Historical Survey of Educational Development in India: Select Documents 1985-1989 **S.P. Agrawal** and **J.C. Aggarwal** (in press)
CICIL-16	Documentation Encyclopaedia of UNESCO and Education **J.C. Aggarwal** and **S.P. Agrawal** Rs. 800 (set of 2 parts)
CICIL-17	Attitude Towards Information: A Study of Post-Graduate Teachers and Researchers in Social Sciences **N.G. Satish** (in press)
CICIL-18	Librarianship and Bureaucratic Organisation: A Study in the Sociology of Library Profession in India **P.K. Jayaswal** Rs. 175
CICIL-19	Literature Search **K.A. Isaac** Rs. 150
CICIL-20	Child Education in India: Index to Scholarly Writings in Indian Educational Journals and Newspapers since independence **S.P. Agrawal** and **Naresh Kanta** Rs. 100
CICIL-21	Lok Sabha and Vidhan Sabha Elections in India 1989 & 1990: Process and Results with Comparative Study of Manifestos **S.P. Agrawal** and **J.C. Aggarwal** Rs. 250
CICIL-22	Islamic Studies in India: A Survey of Human, Institutional and Documentary Sources **Mohamed Taher** Rs. 180
CICIL-23	Panchayati Raj: An Annotated Bibliography **N.B. Inamdar, N.G. Satish** and **Anil Takalkar** (in press)
CICIL-24	Information India 1989-90: Global View **S.P. Agrawal** and **J.C. Aggarwal** Rs. 500
CICIL-25	First Handbook of Psychological and Social Instruments **Udai Pareek** and **T. Venkateswara Rao** (in press)
CICIL-26	Educational and Social Uplift of Backward Classes: At What Cost and How? Mandal Commission and After **S.P. Agrawal** and **J.C. Aggarwal** Rs. 275
CICIL-27	Mass Media and New Horizons: Impact of TV & Video an Urban Milieu **H.R. Trivedi** Rs. 180
CICIL-28	Indian Writings on Education : An Indicator to Indian Educational Journals Grouped by Subject Deseriptors 1979 to 1986 (in two parts) **S.P. Agarwal** Rs. 900 (per set)
CICIL-29	Nation in Crisis **S.P. Agrawal** and **J.C. Aggarwal** Rs. 200